UNDERSTANDING
GLOBAL
CULTURES

FIFTH EDITION

Martin Gannon dedicates this book, with fond memories, to the late Mr. Francis X. Long, distinguished faculty member at the Scranton Preparatory School, Scranton, Pennsylvania.

Rajnandini Pillai dedicates this book to her family and friends. Thank you all for your support.

UNDERSTANDING
GLOBAL
CULTURES

Metaphorical Journeys Through 31 Nations,
Clusters of Nations, Continents, and Diversity

FIFTH EDITION

MARTIN J. GANNON
California State University, San Marcos;
Professor Emeritus, University of Maryland

RAJNANDINI PILLAI
California State University, San Marcos

Los Angeles | London | New Delhi
Singapore | Washington DC

Los Angeles | London | New Delhi
Singapore | Washington DC

FOR INFORMATION:

SAGE Publications, Inc.
2455 Teller Road
Thousand Oaks, California 91320
E-mail: order@sagepub.com

SAGE Publications Ltd.
1 Oliver's Yard
55 City Road
London EC1Y 1SP
United Kingdom

SAGE Publications India Pvt. Ltd.
B 1/I 1 Mohan Cooperative Industrial Area
Mathura Road, New Delhi 110 044
India

SAGE Publications Asia-Pacific Pte. Ltd.
3 Church Street
#10-04 Samsung Hub
Singapore 049483

Senior Acquisitions Editor: Patricia Quinlin
Associate Editor: MaryAnn Vail
Assistant Editor: Theresa Accomazzo
Editorial Assistant: Katie Guarino
Production Editor: Libby Larson
Copy Editor: Paula L. Fleming
Typesetter: C&M Digitals (P) Ltd.
Proofreader: Theresa Kay
Indexer: Sheila Bodell
Cover Designer: Gail Buschman
Marketing Manager: Kelley McAllister
Permissions Editor: Karen Ehrmann

Printed in the United States of America

Library of Congress Cataloging-in-Publication Data

Gannon, Martin J.

Understanding global cultures : metaphorical journeys through 31 nations, clusters of nations, continents, and diversity / Martin J Gannon, Rajnandini

Pillai. — 5th ed.

p. cm.
Includes bibliographical references and index.

ISBN 978-1-4129-9593-1 (pbk.)

1. Cross-cultural studies. 2. Cross-cultural orientation. 3. National characteristics. I. Pillai, Rajnandini. II. Title.

GN345.7.G36 2013
305.8—dc23   2012002813

This book is printed on acid-free paper.

13 14 15 10 9 8 7 6 5 4 3 2

Brief Contents

Detailed Contents

Preface

Understanding Cultures in Depth

> *If we are right in suggesting that our conceptual system is largely meta-phorical, then the way we think, what we experience, and what we do every day is very much a matter of metaphor.*
>
> —Lakoff and Johnson (1980, p. 1)

The major emphasis in this book is on an in-depth understanding of a culture through the use of the cultural metaphor, which is any activity, phenomenon, or institution that members of a given culture consider important and with which they identify emotionally and/or cognitively (e.g., the Turkish coffeehouse and the Chinese family altar). As such, the metaphor represents all or most of the underlying values expressive of the culture itself.

Frequently outsiders have a difficult time relating to and/or understanding a specific cultural metaphor, such as American football, and the underlying values of a culture that it expresses. This book is designed to address this difficulty. Culture allows us to "fill in the blanks," often either semiconsciously or unconsciously, when action is required, and cultural metaphors help us to see the values leading to action. This is probably the most interesting feature of culture (see Brislin, 1993; Triandis, 2002). Cultural metaphors, the basis of this book, represent an effective way to profile and to learn about ethnic cultures, national cultures, the diffusion of a base culture such as the Chinese culture and the English culture across nations, continental cultures, and even diversity within a nation, as the description of kaleidoscopic diversity in India in Chapter 29 demonstrates.

In Chapter 1 we describe how cultural metaphors are developed and how we integrate other approaches to cultures. For example, many national cultures have prominent bipolar or dimensional profiles that allow a researcher to rank order them on various scales, such as power distance or the degree to which there is an unequal distribution of power and rewards (see, for example, Hofstede, 2001). In every chapter, we use these other approaches to gain additional knowledge and perspectives and integrate them within our discussion. Cultural anthropologists such as Florence Rockwood Kluckholn, Fred L. Strodtbeck, and Edward T. Hall developed some of the approaches described in Chapter 1. The bipolar or dimensional approach comes from cross-cultural psychology and cross-cultural management.

The first edition of this book in 1994 had 17 chapters describing 17 cultural metaphors, but the chapters were not logically fitted into parts. This fifth edition includes 12 major parts and 35 chapters; one new part, "Popular Music as Cultural Metaphors," was added for this edition. This part includes two chapters about the Brazilian samba and the Argentine tango. As such, the book has evolved and become richer over time in terms of both new perspectives and depth of material.

We have focused on Scandinavian egalitarian cultures separately from other egalitarian cultures such as Canada, for they are unique in several ways. For example, they tend to base fines for traffic violations not only on the severity of the action but also on violators' income levels, which results in wide variances. Hence two parts are devoted to egalitarian cultures rather than only one part. Similarly, as in the fourth edition, a new, separate part of the book focuses on India. As such, there are three chapters on Chinese culture, as in the third edition—covering China at home, Chinese around the world, and Singapore—and two chapters devoted to India in the fifth edition.

We have also updated all chapters and have significantly rewritten several of them. There are two new chapters in this edition, Chapter 6 focusing on Vietnam and Chapter 33 emphasizing Argentina.

When Martin Gannon began work on cultural metaphors in 1987, there was a concern that there would be an automatic negative reaction to the concept, because cultural metaphors are related to stereotypes. From the 1950s until about 1990, the typical reaction to any generalization about groups was "That is a stereotype," and the clear meaning was that such a generalization was biased to the point of being unuseful. As explained in Chapter 1, however, humans use such generalizations automatically, and some stereotypes are legitimate whereas others are not. Clearly, one illegitimate stereotype is a generalization that allows no exceptions. Cultural metaphors, on the other hand, are probabilistic statements that apply to a group but not to every individual within it. And, as the introductory quote from Lakoff and Johnson points out, humans tend to learn through the use of metaphors.

We would also like to add a short explanation about the many statistics presented in this book and their relationships to the cultural metaphors and the numerous examples used to illustrate them. Frequently the statistics are presented in a comparative fashion, for example, the number of citizens per square kilometer in the United States (32.9) and Singapore (7,042.2). These and similar statistics are taken primarily from The Economist's *Pocket World in Figures* (2011). We have also used many other sources and have duly noted them. In some instances the statistics are presented without a citation simply to facilitate the ease of reading. When doing so, we have checked with at least two sources. In most if not all such instances, the statistics are generally well known. As suggested, we have used statistics not only to enrich understanding but also to facilitate ease of reading.

Certain work in cultural anthropology bears directly on the concept of cultural metaphors, particularly Clifford Geertz's (1973) well-known description of male Balinese society in terms of the cockfight. Each of the metaphors in this book uses three to eight characteristics of each metaphor to describe the culture of the nation being assessed. Through the use of each metaphor and its characteristics, we can begin to see the society in a new and different way and, we hope, in the same manner as its members do. We can also compare societies through the use of these metaphors and their characteristics. There is empirical evidence that (1) cultural metaphors do exist; (2) individuals, both within their own national culture and from other national cultures, tend to think of national cultures in this fashion; and (3) they are important for understanding cross-cultural differences (Gannon, Locke, Gupta, Audia, & Kristof-Brown, 2005).

Although each metaphor is a guide or map, it is only a starting point against which we can compare our own experiences and through which we can start to understand the seeming contradictions pervasive in most, if not all, societies. Thus a cultural metaphor provides an in-depth understanding but one that should be enriched periodically, if not constantly, by new information and experiences.

Also, while we are describing a dominant, and perhaps the dominant, metaphor for each society, other metaphors may also be suitable. Each metaphor provides an in-depth perspective on a culture but only a partial perspective. In this book we do not address the issue of suitable alternatives or supplementary metaphors. Furthermore, our descriptions explicitly recognize and focus on the regional, racial, and ethnic differences within each nation.

Still, the unit of analysis for most of the chapters in this book is the nation, as a good amount of evidence suggests that commonalities exist across regional, racial, and ethnic groups within each nation that can be effectively captured by cultural metaphors. As pointed out in "The Malaysian *Balik Kampung*" (Chapter 18), if citizens in a nation cannot identify at least one activity, phenomenon, or institution expressive of their values, the probability is high that the nation will experience conflict and may even be rent asunder. Furthermore, as indicated above, we can employ cultural metaphors to profile a major base culture, such as that of China and its evolution across borders; culture across a continent; and even diversity within one nation.

This book contains 31 cultural metaphors for specific nations. There are 220 nations in the world. Realistically, then, the approach could be used for all or most nations, thus providing a starting point for understanding commonalities across nations and differences between them. We are currently working on several additional cultural metaphors, but they are not ready to see the light of day.

Chapter 1 contains a section describing how to read and use this book. Also, faculty who adopt the fifth edition will have access to an *Instructor's Manual* containing sample tests, discussion questions, new exercises, short case studies, descriptions of innovative methods that current users of the previous editions of the book have employed, and PowerPoint slides that can be shown in class. This manual is accessible through the Sage website: www.sagepub.com.

Acknowledgments and Coauthors

Work on this book began in 1988 when Martin Gannon conducted a seminar for MBA and doctoral students at the University of Maryland. The task proved to be very difficult, and only a small number of papers reached a stage where they could be included in the first edition in 1994. As indicated above, only 17 chapters describing cultural metaphors for specific nations were in that edition.

Clearly this book could not have been written without the help of individuals who are intimately familiar with the specific cultures for which we sought to construct metaphors. They served as coauthors of the various chapters. Our basic approach was for each coauthor to use the methods for constructing metaphors as outlined in Chapter 1 when writing his or her chapter, preceded and followed by intensive discussions both among the coauthors and with other knowledgeable individuals. Each chapter was rewritten in light of the suggestions offered by these individuals.

For the first edition, Martin Gannon wrote the Preface, Chapter 1, and several other chapters and was responsible for restructuring and editing the remaining chapters. The coauthors of the remaining chapters in this and previous editions were Diana Liebscher and Eileen Fagen, Britain; Stefania Amodio and Lynne Levy, Italy; Douglas O'Bannon and Julie Kromkoski, Germany; Peter Brown and Sharon Ribas, France; Ana Hedin and Michelle Allison, Sweden; Paul Forward, Canada; Amy Levitt, Russia; Stacey Hostetler and Sydney Swainston, Belgium; Katherine Feffer Noonan and Manuel Bacerra, Spain; Daniel Cronin and Cormac MacFhionnlaoich, Ireland; Michele Lopez, Mexico; Amy Levitt, Turkey; Efrat Elron, Israel; Isaac Agboola, Nigeria; Diane Terry, Japan; Amit Gupta and Jeffrey Thomas, India; Hakam Kanafani, the United States; Pino Audia, Chinese family altar; Takako Sugiyama, Singapore; Jennnifer Lynn Roney, Poland; Christin Cooper and Maria Masatroianni, Brazil; Rozhan Othman, Malaysia; Louise Warberg, Saudi Arabia; Carlos Cantarilho, Portugal; and Paul Dowling, Africa.

Several of the doctoral students who were both participants in this cross-cultural management seminar and eventual coauthors of individual chapters have now become faculty members at major universities. They include Pino Audia, Dartmouth; Amit Gupta, Indian Institute of Management, Bangalore; Douglas O'Bannon, Webster University; Cormac MacFhionnlaoich, University College–Dublin; and Manuel Bacerra, Instituto de Empresa, Spain. Others with university affiliations are Jennifer Lynn Roney, Southern Methodist University; and Roshan Othman, Universiti Kebangsaan Malaysia.

Typically, after a chapter evolved over a semester's time, we added the names of the students who wrote the initial papers as coauthors. Martin Gannon and Rajnandini

Pillai completed the task of revising the fourth and fifth editions of this book and its chapters after students graduated.

In addition to the authors, many others contributed to the editions of the book. Most if not all coauthors interviewed several people, and each chapter was read and critiqued by several citizens or residents of the countries being described. Martin Gannon would like to thank his former colleagues at the Robert H. Smith School of Business, University of Maryland at College Park, for their advice and suggestions, including Michael Agar, Mercy Coogan, Stephen Carroll, Edwin Locke, Sabrina Salam, Allyson Downs, and Guenther Weinrach. He also wants to thank the following for providing a supportive environment: Rudolph Lamone and Howard Frank, former deans of the Robert H. Smith School of Business; Maryann Waikart, former director of the MBA Program; and Mark Wellman, former director of the MBA Program. Both Rajnandini Pillai and Martin Gannon want to thank Interim Dean Regina Eisenbach, former dean Dennis Guseman, and Professors Kathleen Watson and Gary Oddou of the California State University, San Marcos, for helping to facilitate the final stages of writing.

Furthermore, given both the scope and depth of this project, we were almost overwhelmed not only by its complexity but also by its details. We have painstakingly attempted to eliminate any errors, however small, that would serve to detract from the general focus of the book. We accept responsibility for any inadvertent errors that might have occurred. If you encounter even a minor error, we hope that you will bring it and any suggestions for improving the book to our attention. Our email addresses are listed at the end of the Preface.

Rajnandini would like to thank Prashant Valanju, Shama Gamkhar, and Shakuntala Desai for their suggestions on Chapter 28, "India: The Dance of Shiva." She would also like to thank Arisa Isayama for her suggestions on Chapter 3, "The Japanese Garden," and Durgesh Rajsingh for his suggestions on Chapter 17, "The Traditional British House." Martin Gannon would like to thank his son, Reid, who provided invaluable input to Chapter 16 on American football; Reid is much more knowledgeable than his father about the intricacies of this game, and the extended discussions they had while watching televised football games over the years led to many new insights that have been incorporated into this chapter. Professor June Poon of the Universiti Kebangsaan Malaysia provided suggestions for Chapter 18, "The Malaysian *Balik Kampung*," as did her graduate students: Kok Wai, Chow Sook Woon, Syamala Nairand, and Kalaimar Vadivel.

We are very pleased that Michael Berry, a U.S. American who went to Finland as a Fulbright scholar and remained as Senior Lecturer at the Turku School of Economics and Adjunct Professor of Intercultural Relations and History in three Finnish universities, wrote Chapter 10, "The Finnish Sauna," for both the fourth and fifth edition. Michael, who is married to a Finnish Senior Lecturer of English and Communication, was a Visiting Scholar at the University of Maryland in 1990–1991 and a very involved member of the seminar in which the original ideas for this book evolved. His contributions to the area of cross-cultural understanding are well recognized, and they include a well-received approach for facilitating communication across cultures and several insightful articles on the differences between Finnish and U.S.-American communication styles. One of his courses, Culture and International Management, was designated the exceptional Finnish intercultural business course for 2007 (by the Finnish Association of Graduates in Economics and Business Administration).

Similarly, it was our good fortune to have Christine Nielsen, Professor of International Business and Strategy, University of Baltimore, write the new chapter on the Argentine tango. She is a recipient of the University System of Maryland Board of Regents' Faculty Award for Teaching, the highest honor awarded in recognition of exemplary faculty achievement. Also, she was the 2007 Fulbright-SyCip Distinguished Lecturer in the Philippines, the first woman to receive this award. Nielsen's teaching and research interests are multicultural leadership and strategy, cross-cultural management, and entrepreneurship in developing countries. Chris is a recipient of a Governor's Citation from the State of Maryland for "outstanding service as Director of International Programs" and for "contributions to further the economic development agenda of Maryland's businesses." Over the past 30 years, Chris has served as the director of numerous international business programs for managers, including 9 years as Academic Director of the University of Baltimore's International Management and Compliance Training Program for Northrop Grumman Electronic Systems. Between 1999 and 2001, she served as the Academic Director of an MBA program in Argentina, hosted at the Universidad Nacional de Lomas de Zamora in the outskirts of Buenos Aires. Her love for Argentina and its people has deepened over the past 10 years and has inspired her in-depth research into Argentine culture as expressed through the tango. In 2006 Nielsen and Juan Gabriel Mariotto, Deputy Secretary of Communication, Office of the Argentine President, co-authored "The Tango Metaphor: Essence of Argentina's National Identity."

We also were fortunate to have three longtime observers of Vietnam from Australia write a new chapter on Vietnam for this edition. Dr. Paul R. Cerotti is a Senior Lecturer in the College of Business at RMIT University, Melbourne. Paul is currently the Program Director for the Master of Commerce and the Global Business Study Tours. Paul has won Australian National Teaching Awards and various Vice Chancellor awards for excellence in teaching. His work has taken him to Italy (his birthplace and where he spent his youth), the United States, and many parts of Asia. Claire Davison is an Associate Lecturer in the College of Business at RMIT University. Her PhD research is in the area of social media and virtual identity with wider interests in the use of social media as a cross-cultural tool, social value creation, globalization, and social democracy. In 2010 Claire was awarded the Vice Chancellor's Award for teaching excellence. Melanie Gardiner is an Australian journalist with a master's degree in communication. Melanie is a Lecturer in the College of Business at RMIT University and has travelled extensively throughout Asia, including Vietnam. With a background in marketing and communication, her research interests include cross-cultural marketing, innovation, and small and family businesses.

We would also like to thank Moritz Botts, Department of International Management at the European University Viadrina Frankfurt (Oder) campus, and Zoran Cirjakovic, Faculty of Media and Communications, Serbia, for providing helpful feedback on the fourth edition, which we incorporated into the fifth edition. Moritz, in particular, provided a detailed analysis of the chapters in the fourth edition.

As usual, the staff at SAGE Publications performed its work admirably, and we are especially appreciative of the help that our editors, Lisa Shaw and Patricia Quinlin, provided. We would also like to thank the following at SAGE Publications: MaryAnn Vail, editorial assistant; Libby Larson, production editor; and Paula L. Fleming, copy editor.

—Martin J. Gannon
California State University, San Marcos
E-mail: mgannon@csusm.edu

—Rajnandini Pillai
California State University, San Marcos
E-mail: rpillai@csusm.edu

PART I

Introduction

Chapter 1 provides a description of a cultural metaphor, that is, any major phenomenon, activity, or institution with which all or most of its members closely identify cognitively and/or emotionally. This book primarily focuses on cultural metaphors for nations, but it also discusses cultural metaphors for ethnic groups crossing into and settling permanently in other national cultures (e.g., the Chinese) and cultural metaphors for entire continents. Likewise, the book highlights how nations close to each other tend to have similar cultural metaphors and features, as in the case of the Scandinavian nations. It also describes how a nation can have two or more cultural metaphors offering different but complementary insights (e.g., the Indian dance of Shiva [traditional India] and the kaleidoscope of Indian diversity [modern India]). The final section of this chapter describes when culture does and does not matter.

CHAPTER 1

Understanding Cultural Metaphors

The great pedagogic value of figurative uses of language is to be found in their potential to transfer learning and understanding from what is known to what is less well-known and to do so in a very vivid manner. . . . Metaphors are necessary because they allow the transfer of coherent chunks of characteristics—perceptual, cognitive, emotional, and experiential—from a vehicle which is known to a topic which is less so.

—Andrew Ortony (1975, p. 53)

There are many good and obvious reasons for studying cross-cultural differences, including a conservative estimate that <u>somewhere between 25% and 50% of our basic values stem from culture</u> (for such estimates, see Haire, Ghiselli, & Porter, 1966; Hofstede, 2001). Other aspects of workforce diversity, such as age and socioeconomic status, also account for significant variances in our values and attitudes, but clearly culture is critical.

Failures in cross-cultural communication and negotiation have very tangible bottom-line results. To cite one simple example, one U.S. American female CEO of a medium-size company was having great difficulty establishing business partnerships in China until she by chance wore a dignified red dress to a meeting. There, her first partnership was established. Red is a favorite color of the Chinese, as it signifies good luck. She continued to wear the red dress and continued to establish successful partnerships.

For a more complex example, we can look at the experience of Disney, which negotiated a contract with the French government to establish Euro-Disney outside of Paris in the 1980s. The contract was heavily loaded in Disney's favor, but the company suffered near disaster because of issues such as its ban on the sale of wine, which usually accompanies meals in France. The French stayed home or went elsewhere rather than endure such inconveniences.

More recently, Daimler-Chrysler Corporation was dissolved in 2004 at least in part because of cultural conflicts between German and U.S. executives, including the latter's lack of understanding of the German system of corporate governance. Large German corporations with more than 2,000 employees are required to have two boards of directors. The first German board—composed of representatives of trade unions, employees, large-scale investors such as banks, and government—appoints the second board and has some jurisdiction over it. A U.S. board, because there is only one, can unilaterally authorize such actions as large-scale employee layoffs and changes in reward systems. In Germany, the second board must receive authorization from the first board before proceeding with such major changes. Because of the U.S. penchant for disregarding the importance of the two boards and the German penchant for having many formal meetings before decisions could be enacted, change was extremely difficult to implement. David Ricks (2006) provides numerous additional examples demonstrating how cross-cultural differences create major and sometimes fatal difficulties in many areas of business, including accounting, finance, and supply-chain management.

An even more fundamental reason for studying culture is that our globalized world demands cross-cultural expertise if we are to survive. Amy Chua (2003) clearly supports this point of view:

> After the fall of the Berlin Wall a common political and economic consensus emerged, not only in the West but to a considerable extent around the world. Markets and democracy, working hand in hand, would transform the world into a community of modernized, peace-loving nations. In the process, ethnic hatred, extremist fundamentalism, and other "backward" aspects of underdevelopment would be swept away. The consensus could not have been more mistaken. Since 1989, the world has seen the proliferation of ethnic conflict, the rise of militant Islam, the intensification of group hatred and nationalism, expulsions, massacres, confiscations, calls for renationalization, and two genocides unprecedented since the Nazi Holocaust. (p. 123)

Chua's pertinent comment appeared in her 2003 book. Since that time, the incidence of such problems has only increased, and the worldwide Great Recession that started in 2008 has exacerbated them. As this book goes to press, the European Union is facing a crisis that may lead to its dissolution, and representatives from the more prosperous nations, such as Germany and France, have verbally attacked some of the less prosperous member nations, such as Greece and Italy, for not planning in a fiscally prudent manner. Terrorist attacks in major cities across the world are now commonplace, and they reflect deep cross-cultural and religious conflicts that have been simmering for years. These and many other examples make Chua's comment even more relevant today than in 2003, and efforts to increase cross-cultural understanding are not only desirable but necessary. As argued elsewhere, many reasons support the view that global disintegration rather than global integration may be our fate (see S. J. Carroll & Gannon, 1997). We are just as likely to become a global battlefield as to become a global village or a global community.

To highlight how difficult but critical it is to understand the importance of culture, it is useful to examine a short case study developed by Martin Gannon. By way of background, he attended a 10-day cross-cultural training program led by Professor Richard Brislin at the East-West Center, University of Hawaii at Manoa. The 35 attendees, all professionals involved in cultural studies in some way, included professors from a diverse range of disciplines and immigration officials from several nations. During the course of the program, a well-known cross-cultural training exercise, The Albatross (Gochenour, 1977), was conducted, which produced a number of insights. Gannon has since used this case study more than 250 times in a variety of settings involving students and managers. The reactions of students and managers to this case study tend to be very consistent. Readers are invited to read Case Study 1.1 and to answer the questions after it before we provide any additional details.

CASE STUDY 1.1

I recently participated in a cross-cultural training session at the East-West Center, Hawaii. There were six male volunteers (including me) and six female volunteers. We walked into a room where a man was dressed in Eastern or Asian garb but in a somewhat indistinguishable manner; he could have been a king or a Buddhist monk. A woman sat beside him, and she was dressed in a similarly indistinguishable fashion.

There was no talking whatsoever in this training session, which lasted for about 10 minutes. The "king" beckoned the males to sit on chairs, after which he indicated that the females should sit at the males' feet. He then greeted each male silently and in standing position; he clasped each male by the arms and then gently rubbed his hands on the male's sides. The males did as the king instructed, but there was some nervousness and laughter, although no talking. The king then bowed to each female. Next, the king presented a large vase of water to each male and invited him to drink from it. He then did the same thing with each female.

The king and queen then walked before the volunteers, peering intently at the females. After a minute or two, the king put on a satisfied look and made a noise as if contented. He then looked at the queen, who nodded in agreement. The queen took the hand of one female to lead her to a sitting position on the ground between the king and queen. Next, the king and queen tried to push the female's head toward the ground as she sat on the ground between them (they were on chairs), but she resisted. They tried once again, but she still resisted. The training session then ended.

Instructions. Each small group should appoint a recorder/secretary to report back to the larger group. Time limit is 10 minutes. Please answer the following questions:

1. What kind of a culture is this? Please describe.

2. How would you interpret the differential treatment of males and females in this culture?

In each of the 250 sessions Gannon has held on this case study, there have been about 6 subgroups, each of which reported back to the entire class, so he has received about 1,500 interpretations of the story. In 9 of 10 instances, the subgroup describes the culture in the following manner: a male-dominated traditional culture, probably Asian or African or Mideastern, ritualistic, and conservative. Sometimes a subgroup tries to identify the religion involved, and frequently Buddhism or Islam is cited. And, although almost all subgroups feel that females are in a subordinate role, a few believe that females have high status, albeit clearly separate from that of the dominant males.

In fact, this is an Earth-worshipping culture in which males are clearly subordinate to females, and the only way to integrate all of the information provided is to use this framework. For example, the male leader was not being friendly when he patted the males; rather, he was checking for weapons, as males tend to have too much testosterone and too strong a tendency to engage in immature fighting. Similarly the females were seated in the place of honor (nearest to the ground), and the males were relegated to the bleachers. The males drank first to test for poison, thus ensuring the safety of the females. Even the "king," whose ambiguous position is highlighted by the quotation marks, must ask permission of the female leader before selecting a favored female to engage in a ritual; she was placed nearest the ground in an honored position between the two leaders. Frequently Gannon asks why a particular female was chosen, and rarely does anyone guess the reason: A visual inspection indicated that she had the largest feet, an obvious sign of importance in an Earth-worshipping culture. In many cultures the number 3 is used, and it was being used in this ritual until the favored female resisted.

This exercise is usually sufficient to make the point that having a framework is very useful in understanding any culture. If the trainees had been told that the culture was Earth worshipping, they could have successfully integrated the various stimuli that were confusing them. Furthermore, the feedback session after the original training provided insight, as the young woman selected for the ritual was asked why she resisted. This young woman was a very accomplished cultural anthropologist who has devoted her career to the study of village life around the world. She was in her mid-30s, well published, and tenured at a good university; she was also attractive, divorced, and without children. Her response focused on the maltreatment that she had experienced at the hands of various men in her life and on her resolve never to allow such maltreatment to occur again. For example, her father ran off with a younger woman when she was a baby, and she never saw him again. She worked to provide the funds necessary for her husband to attend college, but immediately after graduation he divorced her. Her male dissertation advisor proposed a sexual relationship with her and, after she rejected the idea, made her life so miserable that she changed advisors. Similarly, while the faculty in her university department unanimously recommended her for promotion and tenure, a male dean delayed the promotion for a year and wanted to reject her application but could not do so given her outstanding record. Having experienced such negative incidents, she had decided to live alone with her dog, was in therapy, and had decided with some finality that no man would have such control over her life and work in the future.

Thus, she had interpreted the ritual as a form of subservience to men, as the "king" was pushing her head toward the ground; so was the "queen," but she did not mention this fact. The pedagogical point is that this young woman, given her educational training and work experiences in different villages, was as knowledgeable as or more knowledgeable than any of the other 35 professionals in the room, but her perspective—warped by unpleasant experiences with men—had led her to react emotionally, even to the extent that she was not able to think about an alternative framework such as an Earth-worshipping culture. Gannon, one of the six male participants, points out that he, too, felt overwhelmed and had no idea what was going on.

The case study highlights other critical aspects of culture that operate subtly, often on the unconscious or semiconscious level. Culture has been aptly compared to a computer program, which once activated by a few commands or stimuli begins to operate automatically and seemingly in an independent manner (Fisher, 1988; Hall, 1966; Hofstede, 1991, 2001). Clearly such automaticity occurred, but unfortunately the stimuli were not properly matched to the cultural framework in play because of the negative relationships with males that this young woman had experienced.

Frequently, when foreigners violate a key cultural value, they are not even aware of the violation, and no one brings the matter to their attention. The foreigners are then isolated and begin to experience negative feelings. As one U.S. businessperson in Asia aptly pointed out, one of the central problems doing business cross-culturally is that once a visitor makes a major cultural mistake, it is frequently impossible to rectify it. In fact, several months may pass before one realizes that polite rejections signify isolation and banishment. Sometimes foreigners make such a mistake and eventually leave the country without even realizing or identifying what they have done.

Even small cultural mistakes can have enormous consequences. Many older and even some younger Germans, for instance, do not like to converse too much during meals. They will ordinarily begin the meal by taking a sip of beer or soda, then pick up the knife and fork and hold them throughout the meal, putting them down only when they have finished eating. For many Germans, eating is a serious business, not to be disturbed by trivial comments and animated conversation. Many Italians, on the other hand, tend to talk constantly during meals and wave their hands repeatedly. As a result, a German and an Italian dining with one another may feel aggrieved, consciously or unconsciously, by each other's behavior, and much time is wasted negotiating acceptable rules of behavior that could otherwise be spent on substantive issues, including the development of trust.

Furthermore, while technological and societal changes have been rapid in recent decades, many key aspects of culture tend to change only slowly, frequently at a snail's pace, and the influence of culture persists for centuries even after mass immigrations take place. Irish Americans have the "gift of the gab," befitting a cultural heritage that has a strong oral tradition, and they are disproportionately represented in fields such as trial law and politics, where this gift is an asset. English and French residents of Canada think and feel differently in large part because of their respective cultural heritages, and these differences have threatened the very existence of that country.

Language Barriers

Individuals from English-speaking countries are at a particular disadvantage culturally because the people of many non-English-speaking countries use both English and their own native languages. It is common for English-speaking visitors to a non-English-speaking country to assume cultural similarity accompanies a common language, when dissimilarity is really the norm. English has become the language favored in international business, and mixtures of languages such as Chinglish and Spanglish have become prominent, thus creating both opportunities and pitfalls for natives of English-speaking countries.

It should be noted that knowing a country's language, while clearly helpful, is no guarantee of understanding its cultural mind-set. Some of the most difficult problems have been created by individuals who had a high level of fluency but a low level of cultural understanding. Glen Fisher (1988), a former foreign service officer, describes a situation in Latin America in which a U.S. team's efforts were seriously hampered because of the condescending attitude of one member, whose fluency in Spanish was, ironically, excellent. Fortunately another member of the team saved the day because she showed a genuine interest in the culture and its people, even though she was just beginning to learn how to speak Spanish. Moreover, members of a culture tend to assume that highly fluent visitors know the customs and rules of behavior, and they judge those visitors severely when violations occur.

Americans are at a particular disadvantage in trying to understand the mind-sets of other cultures. U.S. businesspeople and travelers tend to follow frantic schedules, sometimes visiting Hong Kong, Thailand, Japan, and Taiwan within the space of 2 weeks. To expect these U.S. travelers to understand these cultures in such a short period of time is unrealistic. Few U.S. Americans reside in foreign countries for any period of time, and, even when doing so, they tend to isolate themselves from the natives in "golden ghettoes." By contrast, most Europeans speak two or more languages, including

English, and they experience great cultural diversity simply by traveling a few hundred miles from one country to another. Many Asians, because of their knowledge of the English language and education in Europe and the United States, are similar to these Europeans in terms of cultural sophistication.

Using Cultural Metaphors

This book describes an innovative method, the cultural metaphor, for understanding easily and quickly the cultural mind-set of a nation and comparing it to those of other nations. In essence, the method involves identifying some phenomenon, activity, or institution of a nation's culture that all or most of its members consider to be very important and with which they identify cognitively and/or emotionally. The characteristics of the metaphor then become the basis for describing and understanding the essential features of the society.

For example, the Italians invented the opera and love it passionately. Five key characteristics of the opera are the overture, spectacle and pageantry, voice, externalization, and the interaction between the lead singers and the chorus (see Chapter 21). We use these features to describe Italy and its cultural mind-set. Thus, the metaphor is a guide, map, or beacon that helps foreigners understand quickly what members of a society consider to be very important. This knowledge should help them to be comfortable in the society and to avoid making cultural mistakes. The cultural metaphor is, however, only a starting point and subject to change as the individual's first-hand knowledge increases.

Cultural metaphors can be used to profile ethnic groups, nations, clusters of nations, diversity within one nation, and even continents. We have taken this approach in this book for nations, the base culture and its evolution across national borders, and for two continents. We have also extended the use of cultural metaphors to explore the role of diversity in a nation (see Chapter 29).

Constructing Cultural Metaphors

Countless social scientists, particularly cross-cultural psychologists and cultural anthropologists, have devoted their lives to the study of culture. Our cultural metaphors are based partially on the work of cross-cultural psychologists and cultural anthropologists, who emphasize a small number of factors or dimensions, such as time and space, when comparing one society to another.

Dimensional Approaches

Six Age-Old Dimensions

The first of these dimensional approaches was described by two anthropologists, Florence Kluckhohn and Fred Strodtbeck (1961). They compare cultures across six dimensions, pointing out that philosophers, social scientists, and commentators interested in understanding cultural differences have focused attention on these dimensions for hundreds of years. These six dimensions are as follows:

1. What do members of a society assume about the nature of people? Are people good, bad, or a mixture?

2. What do members of a society assume about the relationship between a person and nature? Should humans live in harmony with nature or subjugate it?

3. What do members of a society assume about the relationship between people? Should a person act in a self-serving manner or consider the group before taking action? What are the relative strengths of individualism versus groupism or collectivism in influencing decision making, conformity, and so forth?

4. What is the primary mode of activity in a given society? Is it *being*—accepting the status quo, enjoying the current situation, and going with the flow of things? Or is it *doing*—changing things to make them better, setting specific goals, and accomplishing them within specific schedules?

5. What is the conception of space in a given society? Is it considered *private* in that meetings are held in private, people do not get too close to one another physically, and so on? Or is it deemed *public*, such that everyone participates in meetings and decision making, emotions may be expressed publicly, and people stand in close proximity to one another?

6. What is the society's dominant temporal orientation: past, present, or future?

Kluckhohn and Strodtbeck note that while each society has a dominant cultural orientation that can be described in terms of these six dimensions, other weaker orientations may exist simultaneously in different geographical regions and among different racial and ethnic groups.

Hall on Communication Patterns

Another well-known anthropologist, Edward T. Hall, has spent more than 40 years developing and writing about a similar dimensional classification system (for a good summary, see Hall & Hall, 1990). He focuses on the communication patterns found within cultures, and he emphasizes four dimensions along which societies can be compared:

1. Context, or the amount of information that must be explicitly stated if a message or communication is to be successful

2. Space, or the ways of communicating through specific handling of personal space; for example, North Americans tend to keep more space between them while communicating than do South Americans.

3. Time, which is either *monochronic* (scheduling and completing one activity at a time) or *polychronic* (not distinguishing between activities and completing them simultaneously). However, this distinction encompasses far more than simply this basic dichotomy. Other distinguishing features along the continua of low-context and high-context behavior include the following: meeting commitments and deadlines versus considering time commitments to be flexible and of low priority; being committed to the job versus committed to people and relationships; concentrating on the job versus being easily distracted; emphasizing promptness versus basing promptness on relationships; being accustomed to short-term relationships versus tending to form life-long relationships; and adhering to plans versus changing plans often (Hall & Hall, 1990).

4. Information flow, which is the structure and speed of messages between individuals and/or organizations

Hall then arrays societies along an overarching high-context/low-context dimension. In a high-context society, time tends to be polychronic, and there is a heavy investment in socializing members so that information does not need to be explicitly stated for it to be understood. Members of such a culture have known one another for long periods of time, and there is strong agreement as to what is expected and not expected. In the high-context Japanese society, there is even an aphorism that expressly addresses this issue: He who knows does not speak; he who speaks does not know (see Chapter 3). Hence, verbal communication is frequently not necessary and may well even impede transmission of the message. Also, members of high-context societies tend to have less physical space between them when communicating than those in low-context societies.

As Hall notes, high-context societies tend to require a strong leader to whom everyone else expresses submission or at least great respect. In the Arabic countries, such a leader will sit in his office surrounded by people seeking his help and advice. He will not address the issues and people sequentially, as would tend to happen in monochronic countries such as the United States and Germany. Rather, he will deal with several issues and people as conditions seem to warrant, going from one group to the other in a seemingly haphazard fashion that takes into consideration their sensitivities and need to save face or avoid embarrassment.

Hall tends to array the societies he has studied in the following way, going from high-context to low-context: Japan, the Arab countries, France (approximately in the middle of the continuum), the United States, and Germany. Hall has a bias against low-context societies, even though he recognizes that it is much easier to interface with a low-context society because information about rules and permissible behaviors is explicitly stated. To him, such societies tend to be too mechanical and lack sensitivity to the needs of individuals. He does not critically analyze some of the problems found in high-context societies, particularly the overwhelming power of the leader, which can be used indiscriminately, or the in-group bias that hinders relations with anyone outside of the culture.

Hall's system begins to break down when he talks about the low-context way in which the Japanese interact with foreigners but the high-context way in which they interact among themselves. Here he seems to be describing the classic in-group/out-group phenomenon rather than an overarching dimension along which societies can be arrayed. Triandis, Brislin, and Hui (1988) have argued that the major dimension separating societies is individualism-collectivism, in which the in-group and out-group distinction is critical, and this seems to be the dimension that Hall is describing. Furthermore, as described in the various chapters of this book, there are many specific kinds of individualism and collectivism.

Still, Hall's work has been significant and insightful, particularly his treatment of time and space and his discussion of the belief that low-context communication is always superior to high-context communication. Rather, the effectiveness of the message is related to the degree of context that exists in an interaction. If everyone shares the same values and has been socialized in depth to operate in terms of them, high-context communication is preferred. If there is less sharing of the same values and disagreements as to what is acceptable behavior, low-context communication is preferred. Throughout this book we will use some of Hall's basic concepts, especially the monochronic-polychronic distinction and that between high-context and low-context communication.

Establishing Country Profiles

A third major dimensional approach, developed by Geert Hofstede (1991, 2001), has been independently confirmed and in some instances refined by other researchers such as the Chinese Culture Connection (1987). This group consists of Michael Bond, a long-time professor of cross-cultural psychology at the University of Hong Kong, and 25 Chinese associates. (For examples of frameworks similar to Hofstede's, see S. H. Schwartz, 1994, and Trompenaars & Hampden-Turner, 1998.) Hofstede is a prominent organizational psychologist whose research is based primarily on a large questionnaire survey of IBM employees and managers working in 53 countries, completed 1967–1973. Hofstede's work is especially significant because the type of organization is held constant; his is the only large-scale cross-cultural study in which the respondents all worked for a multinational corporation that had uniform personnel policies. He develops empirical profiles of these 53 countries across 5 dimensions of basic cultural values:

1. Power distance, or the degree to which members of a society automatically accept a hierarchical or unequal distribution of power in organizations and society at large

2. Uncertainty avoidance (acceptance of risk), or the degree to which members of a given society deal with the uncertainty and risk of everyday life and prefer to work with long-term acquaintances and friends rather than with strangers

3. Individualism, or the degree to which individuals perceive themselves to be separate from a group and to be free from group pressure to conform

4. Masculinity-femininity, or the degree to which a society looks favorably on aggressive and materialistic behavior and clearly separates male from female roles. It should be noted that many experts do not like the term *masculinity-femininity* and prefer the term *assertiveness*.

5. Time horizon (short-term to long-term), or the degree to which members of a culture are willing to defer present gratification to achieve long-term goals

The GLOBE Study

A fourth dimensional approach was developed by Robert House and a team of 162 researchers in 62 national societies in the landmark Global Leadership and Organizational Effectiveness (GLOBE) study published in 2004. We will refer to this study throughout the book as the *GLOBE study*. GLOBE used the terms *societies* and *societal culture* instead of *country* or *nation* to indicate the complexity of the culture concept; in a few instances the researchers sampled two subcultures from a single nation, for example, black and white citizens of South Africa. Based on previous work and their own findings, the GLOBE researchers (House, Hanges, Javidan, Dorfman, & Gupta, 2004) identified nine cultural dimensions: uncertainty avoidance, power distance, institutional collectivism, in-group collectivism, gender egalitarianism, assertiveness, future orientation, humane orientation, and performance orientation. They also developed separate measures for the value or importance and the actual practice of each of these nine dimensions, for example, valuing equal treatment for all and actually instituting practices that reinforce this value. Thus they moved beyond the Hofstede framework by emphasizing not only values but actual practices to see if there are discrepancies between them.

Uncertainty avoidance/acceptance of risk and power distance are similar to their counterparts in Hofstede's framework. With regard to collectivism, they distinguish between institutional and in-group collectivism. In-group collectivism represents the extent to which people are loyal to their organizations and/or families. In many cultures organizations tend to hire only those with whom they are very familiar, that is, family members, members of the larger family or kinship group, and individuals trusted by family members. Employees are typically guaranteed employment, even during difficult economic times, and in return they are expected to work hard for the company, sometimes even putting the company's needs ahead of their own. In many instances non-family members will work loyally for a family business for several years, and in return the family provides the capital that allows them to establish their own businesses. Another classic example of in-group collectivism is Toyota, which retrains workers during economic recessions rather than terminating them.

Institutional collectivism describes the extent to which members of a culture identify with broader societal interests. As a culture increasingly values its institutional collectivism, the emphasis on both the value and practice of in-group collectivism also rises significantly, as we might expect, according to the GLOBE study (House et al., 2004).

Gender egalitarianism refers to the degree to which male and female roles are distinct from one another, while assertiveness refers to the extent to which a culture encourages individuals to be tough, forceful, and aggressive as opposed to being timid and submissive in social relationships. Thus the GLOBE researchers have separated Hofstede's masculinity-femininity dimension into two dimensions: gender egalitarianism and assertiveness.

Future orientation refers to the extent to which people of a culture engage in planning and investing in the future. It is very similar to the short-term/long-term time horizon dimension in Hofstede's framework. Humane orientation describes the extent to which a culture rewards people for being fair, altruistic, generous, caring, and kind to others. Finally, performance orientation describes the extent to which an organization or society rewards people for setting and meeting challenging goals and improving performance.

The GLOBE researchers divided data from the 62 societies into regional clusters based on prior research, common language, geography, religion, and historical accounts. They arrived at 10 clusters, which are very similar to those derived by other researchers: Anglo, Latin Europe, Nordic Europe, Germanic Europe, Eastern Europe, Latin America, Middle East, Sub-Saharan Africa, Southern Asia, and Confucian Asia. The GLOBE analysis indicated that scores of respondents correlated within a cluster but were unrelated to the scores of respondents in different clusters.

- Societies in the Anglo cluster (Canada, the United States, Australia, Ireland, England, South Africa [white sample], and New Zealand) were high in performance orientation and low in in-group collectivism.
- The Latin Europe cluster (France, Portugal, Spain, French-speaking Switzerland, Italy, and Israel) had fewer high scores on any of the cultural dimensions and the scores were quite moderate, but the cluster scored low on humane orientation and institutional collectivism.
- The Nordic European cluster of countries, which include Denmark, Sweden, and Finland, scored high on future orientation, gender egalitarianism, institutional collectivism, and uncertainty avoidance/acceptance of risk and low on assertiveness, in-group collectivism, and power distance.
- The Germanic Europe cluster of countries (Austria, the Netherlands, Switzerland, and Germany) scored high in performance orientation, assertiveness, and future orientation and low in humane orientation and both forms of collectivism.

- The Eastern Europe cluster included Greece, Hungary, Albania, Slovenia, Poland, Russia, Georgia, and Kazakhstan. These countries scored high on in-group collectivism, assertiveness, and gender egalitarianism. They scored low on performance orientation, future orientation, and uncertainty avoidance/acceptance of risk.
- The Latin America cluster of countries (Ecuador, El Salvador, Colombia, Bolivia, Brazil, Guatemala, Argentina, Costa Rica, Venezuela, and Mexico) scored high on in-group collectivism and low on performance orientation, future orientation, and uncertainty avoidance/risk acceptance.
- The Middle East cluster, which included Qatar, Morocco, Egypt, Kuwait, and Turkey, had high scores for in-group collectivism and low scores on gender egalitarianism, future orientation, and uncertainty avoidance/acceptance of risk.
- Sub-Saharan Africa included Zimbabwe, Namibia, Zambia, Nigeria, and South Africa (black sample); these countries had high scores on humane orientation and had average scores on most other dimensions.
- The Southern Asia cluster (Philippines, Indonesia, Malaysia, India, Thailand, and Iran) had high scores on in-group collectivism and humane orientation and average scores on most other dimensions.
- Finally, the Confucian Asian cluster, which includes Singapore, Hong Kong, Taiwan, China, South Korea, and Japan, had high scores for performance orientation and high scores for both forms of collectivism (institutional and in-group). These countries, too, had average scores on most other dimensions.

The various dimensional approaches developed by Kluckhohn and Strodtbeck, Hall, Hofstede, and the GLOBE researchers, along with similar works of others, have become enormously influential. Nonetheless, because they rely on a small number of dimensions so as to construct profiles of various societies, they by necessity leave out many features of the cultural mind-sets that are activated in daily cultural activities, and they neglect the institutions that mold these mind-sets. Dimensional approaches are helpful for understanding cultures and providing an overall perspective on cultural differences, but one will experience great difficulty in applying these approaches to daily interactions. In effect, these dimensions are instructive but somewhat lifeless and narrow in that they leave out many facets of behavior.

Using Metaphor

The metaphoric method highlighted in this book supplements and enriches the four major dimensional approaches described above so that a visitor can understand and, most important, begin to deal effectively with the flesh and blood of a culture. While the metaphor itself cannot encompass all of the reality that is found within each society, it is a good starting point for understanding and interacting effectively with it. At the same time, the various chapters of the book are linked through the use of the four dimensional approaches, which retain significance.

Throughout this book, we have attempted to identify metaphors that members of given societies view as very important, if not critical. However, we needed to identify metaphors that would be relatively complex so that we could make several direct comparisons between the metaphor and the nation being represented by it. Also, we wanted to have a metaphor for each society that would have several features useful for describing that society. In addition, we sought to include numerous factors or variables such as religion and small-group behavior when using the metaphor to describe the society, recognizing that these factors are important in some societies but not others. For each society, we used the dimensions of the four dimensional approaches described above. In addition, we focused on all of the following:

- Religion
- Early socialization and family structure
- Small-group behavior
- Public behavior
- Leisure pursuits and interests
- Total lifestyle: Work/leisure/home and time allocations to each
- Aural space: The degree to which members of a society react negatively to high noise levels
- Roles and status of different members of a society
- Holidays and ceremonies
- Greeting behavior
- Humor
- Language: Oral and written communication
- Non-oral communication such as body language
- Sports as a reflection of cultural values
- Political structure
- Educational system
- Traditions and the degree to which the established order is emphasized
- History, but only as it reflects cultural mind-sets or the manner in which its members think, feel, and act (not as a detailed chronology of events)
- Food and eating behavior
- Class structure
- Rate of technological and cultural change
- Organization of and perspective on work, such as a society's commitment to the work ethic, superior-subordinate relationships, and so on
- Any other categories that are appropriate

Using all of these categories initially, we studied each national culture in depth and interviewed several of its natives. After writing an initial draft of a chapter, we presented it at seminars where it was reviewed by natives and long-term residents of the society being described. The chapter was then rewritten in light of the suggestions offered, and additional comments were solicited. This iterative process typically led to rewriting a chapter 5 or 6 times and sometimes 9 or 10 times.

Reading and Using This Book

To understand the book thoroughly and use it most effectively, readers should understand the rationale behind each of its 12 major parts. Many nations could fit into more than one part of the book. We have placed chapters in various parts because they fit comfortably there and are representative of the themes for the parts themselves, as our discussion suggests. The book itself can be used flexibly and selectively, as it is not necessary to read the chapters sequentially or to read all of them. Ideally the reader should understand thoroughly the material here in Chapter 1; as indicated above, the four dimensional frameworks are used to integrate the material and to link the chapters to one another.

Cultural metaphors can be employed to profile an ethnic group, a specific nation, a base nation from which a cluster of nations sharing similar values and attitudes emerges, the cluster of nations itself, a continent, and even diversity within a nation such as India. In this book, the unit of analysis for most chapters is the nation and its national culture. However, three chapters on the Chinese in Part VIII illustrate the importance of each root culture, not only of the spread of this culture but also its transformation as its members move permanently to other nations, and the implications for one specific nation, Singapore. We have also developed cultural metaphors for two continents, Australia and Africa, particularly Sub-Saharan Africa, in Part XII. Furthermore, there are two chapters on India in Part IX of the book. One explains how the dance of Shiva helps to illuminate why the dominant religion of India, Hinduism, must be understood before trying to interact with members of this culture. The second chapter then looks at the amazing diversity in India and describes various non-Hindu religious and ethnic groups and their importance in understanding not only India but almost all nations, if not every nation. Fewer than 10% of the approximately 220 nations in the world are monocultural, and these two chapters on India are reflected in the numerous comparable multiethnic situations found elsewhere.

Two parts of the book (Parts VI and VII) are based on the distinction that Samuel Huntington (1996) proposed: torn national cultures, that is, cultures such as Russia and Mexico that have experienced dramatic changes in values at one or a few periods in history; and cleft cultures, or those in which it is difficult to integrate the national culture due to the existence of sharply different subcultures. We have expanded on Huntington's concept of cleft cultures to include those that experience difficulty integrating into a national culture because of geographic differences, such as the north and south of Italy.

Four parts of the book highlight a framework linking culture and economics more closely (Parts II through V). This framework was independently developed by Harry Triandis (2002) and Alan Fiske (1991b). There are minor differences between the two frameworks, and sometimes Fiske does not clearly demarcate the cultural level from the individual level. For our purposes, however, the two frameworks can be treated as identical. From this framework we can identify why we have chosen these four major parts or topics of the book. It should be noted that we explore two major types of egalitarianism in Parts III and IV, that found in the Scandinavian nations (Part III) and that found in other nations (Part IV).

Part X focuses on bullfighting as a cultural metaphor but shows how the meanings associated with various types of bullfighting (the Portuguese and Spanish versions) differ significantly. Finally, we introduce a new part in this edition, Part XI: Popular Music as Cultural Metaphor. We focus on the wildly popular music of the Brazilian samba and the Argentine tango, both of which originated in the slums of Brazil and Argentina. Today these musical genres have achieved international prominence and recognition, in large part because of the manner in which they express the cultural values of Brazil and Argentina.

A Two-Dimensional Typology of Cultures

Both Harry Triandis and Alan Fiske, who have explored the linkage between culture and economics, seek to identify four generic types of cultures. They begin their analyses with the cultural dimension of individualism-collectivism, which has been the dimension of most interest to researchers because of its obvious importance. Also, they emphasize the extent to which there is a large degree of inequality or power distance in the culture. Thus a four-cell typology of cultures emphasizes either individualism or collectivism and either low power distance or high power distance (see Figure 1.1). There are two generic types of collectivism (horizontal/low–power distance and vertical/high–power distance) and two generic types of individualism (horizontal/low–power distance and vertical/high–power distance).

Low–Power Distance Collectivism

Horizontal/low–power distance collectivism reflects community sharing, in which members of the in-group share all of their goods, as in a small village, even to the extent that there is no such phenomenon as theft. There is not much differentiation

Figure 1.1 Four Generic Types of Cultures

		Individualism	Collectivism
POWER DISTANCE	Low (horizontal)	Equality Matching	Community Sharing
	High (vertical)	Market Pricing	Authority Ranking

between individuals, and ethics are based on group membership: in-group or out-group. In essence, members of out-groups are viewed as nonpersons.

High–Power Distance Collectivism

Vertical/high–power distance collectivism or authority ranking, found in large parts of Asia, Africa, and Latin America, involves a psychological relationship between the leader or leaders and all others in the culture. Frequently such a culture is symbolized not by the handshake, which reflects equality, but by different forms of bowing. Only a relatively few U.S. Americans and Europeans have experienced such a culture in depth because the relationship between superior and subordinate in most U.S. firms is instrumental and focuses only on work-related goals. In contrast, a dynamic two-way relationship exists between subordinates and leaders in authority-ranking cultures: While the leaders receive more rewards, they are responsible for safeguarding the livelihoods of subordinates, even to the extent of finding them new positions when bankruptcy occurs. In turn, the subordinates are expected to be committed to the leader and the organization. Terminating employees to save money is anathema. Ethics is still determined in large part by group membership (in-group and out-group), and status as signified by family background, position at work, and so on is also critical.

It is important to realize, however, that there are at least two major types of authority-ranking cultures. One type is paternalistic, and the image of the leader is that of a kind father. The second is authoritarian, and the image of the leader is that of a harsh father. It is sometimes difficult to separate paternalistic and authoritarian authority-ranking cultures, but we attempt to do so.

Low–Power Distance Individualism

Horizontal/low–power distance individualism or egalitarianism/equality matching is dominant in Scandinavian nations such as Sweden and Norway. All individuals are considered equal, even when some are taxed heavily, and it is expected that those who cannot make individual contributions to the common good will do so at a later time if possible.

High–Power Distance Individualism

Finally, vertical/high–power distance individualism or market pricing is found in the United States and other market-dominated nations. Although individualism is emphasized, so too is the free market, and inequality resulting from its operation is deemed not only as acceptable but expected. There is, in principle, equality of opportunity and a level playing field, but not equality of outcomes. Ethics revolves around the operation of such a market. The fact that the Organisation for Economic Co-operation and Development (OECD) has found that, among the 20 most developed economies in the world, inequality is greatest in the United States should come as no surprise, given our cultural perspective (OECD, 2008).

A Scaling Perspective

Fiske, in particular, relates these concepts to the four types of statistical scales: nominal, ordinal, interval, and ratio. His argument is that individuals have difficulty making decisions and use these scales to approximate roughly how to interact with others.

1. Community sharing represents nominal scaling, as names are given only to entities (e.g., in-group vs. out-group).

2. In an authority-ranking culture, individual A may be more important than individual B, and individual C may be more important than individual B, but there is no common unit of measurement. The scale is ordinal in nature. Hence we cannot say C is twice as important as A.

3. In equality matching, the culture has a common unit of measurement, but it does not make value judgments about individual worth, as there individuals can be measured along too many dimensions. In this sense the scaling is interval.

4. In market pricing, there is a common unit of measurement and a true zero point (zero money), which allows members of the culture to transform every other dimension and compare it monetarily. In this case the scaling is ratio.

Fiske provides an insightful example of these four types of culture in his discussion of a small town's decision about the purchase of an expensive fire truck. The issue becomes, Who should receive the new fire protection? The reader may want to stop at this point to consider the matter. The answers are (a) community sharing—only members of the in-group; (b) authority ranking—all members of the in-group, but the leaders receive more attention and monitoring of their homes; (c) equality matching—everyone is protected; and (d) market pricing—only those who can pay the taxes are protected. This example is not far-fetched. In the United States there have been several recorded instances when fire trucks did not respond, sometimes because a home was just outside the fire department's district and sometimes because the owners of the homes did not contribute monetarily to the fire department's upkeep.

In Hofstede's (1980b) original analysis of 40 nations, he divided them at the median score both on individualism-collectivism and power distance. No nation is in the community-sharing quadrant, probably because this form of collectivism is not appropriate for such large entities as nations. Interested readers can view the dispersion of the 40 nations into the other three quadrants by consulting the original work. As the table of contents of this book indicates, we have devoted separate parts of the book to authority-ranking cultures, equality-matching cultures, and market-pricing cultures.

When Culture Does, and Does Not, Matter

When does culture matter? There are times when culture is not important and other times when it is critically important. In this book we emphasize culture, but we do caution the reader to consider other factors.

Limitations on Culture

Frequently occupational similarities neutralize culture. For instance, when two medical doctors are working jointly on a problem, their medical backgrounds can help them to work together smoothly regardless of cultural backgrounds. Also, similarity of social class can diminish the importance of culture. For example, throughout the world middle-class families tend to use positive reinforcement in raising their children and provide them with opportunities to develop skills and self-esteem. These families may provide their children with music lessons and ask them to perform in front of guests, who respond enthusiastically. Conversely, blue-collar families throughout the world tend to emphasize negative reinforcement and punishment, which negatively influence skill development, opportunities to function in a public or leadership role, and feelings of self-esteem (see Kâgitçibaşi, 1990).

However, sometimes powerful groups will exclude others from opportunities and then stereotype them negatively, thus consigning them to permanent inferior status. This clearly happened in Ireland and India when the English ruled those nations for centuries. Apartheid, now outlawed in South Africa, began as a reaction to scarcity of jobs and led to the stigmatization of native Africans for nearly a century (see Olson, 1982). If the playing field is level, as is more probable when markets are genuinely competitive, this outcome is mitigated.

At times social class or occupational similarity and culture become confused in the minds of visitors. Some U.S. Americans, for example, complain about the rudeness of Parisian shopkeepers, whereas other U.S. Americans describe wonderful relationships with their occupational peers in France. Presumably the different experiences reflect social class or occupational similarities as much as if not more than culture.

Sometimes the nature of the problem minimizes the importance of cultural differences. For example, when companies from two or more nations are working together on a joint project that their top managements strongly support, organizational members are more likely to forget cultural differences, especially when ample rewards for goal attainment along with punishments for failure are at stake.

When trust is present, culture decreases in importance. Jarvenpaa, Knoll, and Leidner (1998) studied 75 virtual work teams throughout the world, which were integrated via the Internet. The major finding was that, if "quick trust" can be established, culture is not a major issue. However, developing trust is frequently neither easy nor quick. For example, a virtual Internet team with members from several nations must adjust to differences in time zones and the lack of commitment that may accompany not actually knowing the other team members on a firsthand basis. Similarly, interactions are facilitated much more easily if the teams have worked together for a few days face-to-face, which frequently does not occur because of cost or other considerations.

The Impact of Technology

One of the most controversial issues is the degree to which technological changes, such as the Internet, influence culture. As Patricia Wallace (1999) points out, the Internet has not resulted in a global village, as is so often stated. Rather, individuals with similar interests—including crime and terrorists—seek one another out on the Internet. As such, the Internet has led to as much differentiation as integration and possibly more differentiation, as Amy Chua's 2003 book, *World on Fire,* persuasively demonstrates. Still, the world is becoming more flat as globalization has spread and individuals from different cultures are learning more about one another due to increased travel, the Internet, more business contact with people of other cultures, and so on (Friedman, 2005).

Whether the world will become more integrated is still an open question, and we may well have a future in which war is ongoing throughout the world rather than a global community arising with shared interests and values. In fact, Alan Rugman (2005) has argued that globalization is a fiction and that nations prefer regional agreements among groups of nations that are similar in language, culture, and proximity. Pankaj Ghemawat (2011) argues similarly, describing the situation as one of semiglobalization because of the many differences in values and religious beliefs found today.

These viewpoints echo the GLOBE study discussed above, which argues that there are 10 clusters of nations. Ghemawat (2011) shows that the degree of internationalization achieved in a variety of areas, such as university students studying outside their nations (approximately 2%), venture capital investment outside of one's nation (20%), and international Internet traffic (20%), is very low. He believes that, at best, genuine global integration of economies is at least 200 to 300 years away.

Further, any indirect form of communication across cultures such as email presents special difficulties. For example, a high-context and high-level manager in Indonesia became angry when he received a terse message from his U.S. counterpart, not because of the content but because of the manner in which the message was phrased. That is, instead of starting the email with "Dear Mr. XXX," the writer just started putting forth his ideas concisely and succinctly, without following the protocol associated with authority-ranking cultures. There is some evidence that younger, more technologically accepting managers are much less bothered by low-context communication than older managers, although data are mixed on this point. As a general rule, technological and economic changes do matter, especially when they are disruptive of cultural patterns. Still, problems are minimized when changes are introduced gradually and are not directly injurious to deep-seated values. On the other hand, as the comparison of northern and southern Italy indicates, cultural patterns found in the 11th century have persisted into the present, leading to concrete economic differences between these two regions (Chapter 21).

When Culture Matters

As suggested in the preface, perhaps the most interesting feature of culture is that it triggers unconscious values, which in turn lead to action. Thus it is not surprising that culture is important when individuals must communicate directly. If individuals expect that outsiders will follow their cultural rules and are unwilling to facilitate the relationship by developing new rules acceptable to all, communication is likely to break down.

As shown in numerous research studies, culture is particularly important in cross-cultural negotiations. Understanding both the similarities and differences of the cultures represented by the negotiators is a good way to facilitate interaction and goal attainment. U.S. Americans, for example, have a reputation for being direct and low-context when communicating information, and this becomes a problem when the communication is phrased in terms of "take it or leave it." Billion-dollar deals have died on the table because of such behavior.

Culture is also important when individuals move to another nation or culture for an extended period of time. The well-known phenomenon of culture shock does occur and, if not handled properly, can lead to major problems. Many managers from a company's headquarters who are sent to work in a subsidiary for an extended period cling to the values and ways of behaving found in their base culture, even to the extent of isolating themselves in "golden ghettoes."

The Impact of Stereotypes

Culture is also relevant if distorted stereotypes are present. There is some confusion surrounding the definition of *stereotype*, but at a minimum it is a distorted view or mental picture of groups and their supposed characteristics on the basis of which one tends to evaluate individuals from each group. Stereotypes can be erroneous and lead to unwarranted conclusions, particularly if no exceptions are allowed; for example, we might assume that all Italians are emotional and talk constantly while moving their hands and arms. In such a situation allowing no exceptions to a stereotype is a universal syllogism. In the case of Italians, the stereotype is clearly erroneous in many instances, as anyone who has transacted business in northern Italy will confirm; there, the level of formality is frequently high in business relationships, especially in terms of dressing properly, showing up for meetings on time, being prepared, and so on. Ironically, in-group members frequently use universal stereotyping as a form of humor but react negatively if out-group members employ it.

Note, however, that all human beings use stereotypes, as they are a shorthand and easy way to classify the multitude of stimuli to which we are exposed. The issue is not stereotyping itself but whether stereotypes are accurate.

Most of us take an extremely negative position on stereotyping. It can be very embarrassing to be accused of stereotyping, especially since refuting the charge is frequently difficult. In today's world the accusation is frequently raised, and as a result, it has become difficult to discuss genuine differences. However, many social psychologists now take the position that there are real differences between groups and societies and that the negative connotations associated with stereotyping have led us to deemphasize these legitimate differences. From this perspective a stereotype represents only a starting point, one that must be rigorously evaluated and changed as experience with groups warrants. Adler with Gunderson (2007) argues persuasively that using stereotypes is legitimate and helpful if they are descriptive rather than evaluative, the first best guess, based on data and observation, and subject to change when new information merits it.

Metaphors are *not* stereotypes. Rather, they rely on the features of one critical phenomenon in a society to describe the entire society. There is, however, a danger that metaphors will include some inaccurate stereotyping, and we have attempted to guard against this possibility by having the various chapters of this book reviewed by natives or long-term residents of the societies being described. In some instances we were unable to construct a metaphor that satisfied natives, residents, or ourselves. Hence this book includes only metaphors about which there is consensus.

Admittedly, it is very difficult to test the validity of these metaphors empirically, at least at this time. However, we have completed one six-nation study of cultural metaphors and confirmed that they are critical (Gannon, Locke, Gupta, Audia, & Kristof-Brown, 2005). In addition, we employ two tests in deciding whether a particular phenomenon can be considered a valid cultural metaphor: whether there is consensus and whether a metaphor other than the one we have selected increases our understanding of a particular society. Also, we have noted in many instances that not all members of a society adhere to the behavioral patterns suggested by the metaphor by using such phrases as "Some Germans," "Many Italians," and "The Irish tend to." In effect, we are highlighting patterns of thought, emotion, and behavior that a society manifests and that are clearly and concisely portrayed by means of a simple and easily remembered metaphor. In this way visitors can use the metaphor as an initial guide, map, or beacon to avoid cultural mistakes and to enrich cross-cultural communications and interactions. In addition, instructors using the previous editions of this book have received very positive reactions from students and experienced international managers to the descriptions of each national culture in the book. Also, numerous book reviews have been uniformly very positive. In sum, as experience accumulates, the visitor can modify and enlarge the frame of reference, but each metaphor provides an initial starting point and basis for discussion.

Culture: "Fuzzy" but Vital

Culture frequently does not matter, but at other times, it is very influential. We have described only some of the instances when culture does and does not matter. Culture probably counts the most when there are feelings of inequity (perceived or real) and a scarcity of resources and opportunities. It is comforting to cluster with others similar to ourselves, especially when we are rejected by dominant groups. As Huntington (1996) persuasively argues, a major threat to world security is the increase in ethnic wars that has accompanied globalization and privatization, and this tension has remained strong since the publication of his thesis (N. Ferguson, 2006). Cultural differences are especially exacerbated when accompanied by extreme religious and ideological viewpoints. Many cultural problems are solved in the long run through intermarriages and increased social and business contacts, all of which are hindered by religious and ideological differences.

All of the factors described above, and some others not described because of space limitations, are important for evaluating when culture does or does not matter. The position taken in this book is that culture is important and is of critical significance in many situations, though not in all of them. Culture also interacts with political, social, and economic forces and is, in that sense, a fuzzy concept. But clearly it is possible to understand cultures and use this understanding to enhance relationships between individuals and groups. Throughout the remainder of the book, we will be employing the methodology described in this chapter to demonstrate how cultural metaphors can strengthen understanding and to show how those metaphors are related to the core values, attitudes, and behaviors of various nations.

PART II

Authority-Ranking Cultures

I n this part of the book, we focus on authority-ranking cultures, in which there is a high degree of collectivism but also a high degree of power distance. Unlike market-pricing cultures, in which the relationship between the superior and subordinate is primarily one-way, these cultures emphasize that superiors and subordinates have obligations toward one another that transcend job descriptions. This is particularly true of nations such as Japan and Thailand and, to a lesser extent, nations such as Poland and Brazil. Ordinal statistical scaling dominates relationships; that is, person A is more important than person B, and person C is more important than person B, but there is no common unit of measurement. Thus, it is impossible to say, for example, that C is twice as important as A.

There are at least two major types of authority-ranking cultures: paternalistic and autocratic. Some cultures are a more or less pure form of one type or the other, but in other cases, the two types may overlap or the culture may transition from paternalistic to autocratic. Such transitions occur when a leader is initially viewed as helpful but paternalistic but later demands not only allegiance but complete subjection of subordinates. In this book the focus is primarily, although not exclusively, on paternalistic authority-ranking cultures.

Since 1970, 85 nations have moved away from an authority-ranking culture in terms of governmental structure, but only about 40 of them could be considered democratic in any sense of the term. An outstanding example of an unrealized democracy is Russia, which has experienced a reversion of democratic reforms made during the 1990s, especially since 2000 (see Chapter 24) . Still, the movement away from authority-ranking structures continues, as we witnessed in the Arab Spring of

2011 during which Tunisia, Yemen, Egypt, Bahrain, Syria, and Libya had mass demonstrations. In some of these nations, major transitions to democratic forms of government appear to be occurring, for example, in Tunisia and Egypt. Frequently such authority-ranking nations are ruled by large clans or families or have ethnic and religious groups around which such clans form. Movement away from an authority-ranking mentality threatens the rulers, who frequently attack with a vengeance, as we have recently seen in Syria and Libya. As attested by the global movement toward democratic forms of governments since 1970, the trend is away from authority-ranking governments. However, it may take years for underlying cultures to change significantly even after some democratic reforms are instituted.

CHAPTER 2

The Thai Kingdom

Bhumibol, the world's longest-serving monarch, enjoys a reverence seldom seen in modern times. Regarded by some as semi-divine, he is known for his lifelong dedication to helping the country's needy. Bhumibol is a constitutional king with no formal political role, but has repeatedly brought calm in times of turbulence and is considered the country's moral authority.

—"Thais Tickled Pink" (2007)

Deep rifts such as these are enough to paralyze any country, but in Thailand, the monarchy has historically acted as a bridging institution. It is revered not only by the elite but also in the countryside, where the king enjoys an almost divine status. Most Thais think of the monarchy as a sacred institution and Thailand has some of the world's most stringent lèse majesté laws (which criminalize offenses against the monarch). . . . But Abhisit's justice minister has gone a step further and suggested that the current maximum penalty for lèse majesté convictions, 15 years of imprisonment, should be extended to 25 years. This does not tally well with Abhisit's stated commitment to liberal democracy.

Note to reader: Abhisit was the prime minister.

—Lintner, 2009, pp. 114–115

Thailand, with its population of 64 million and a land mass about equal to that of France or the states of New York and California combined, is at the crossroads of Southeast Asia. Various peoples from China and India and the bordering nations of Laos, Burma, Malaysia, and Cambodia originally populated it. All of these peoples have influenced the development of Thai culture in one way or another.

The nation itself is divided into several distinct regions. Low-lying Bangkok, one of the largest cities in the world, is one such region. Built on a delta, Bangkok is sinking at the rate of 2 inches a year and may be completely inundated within the next 100 years. Southern Thailand borders Malaysia, whereas northern Thailand borders Laos and Burma. Northern Thailand includes the city of Chiang Mai, Thailand's second-largest city, and is home to the hill tribes, some of which move periodically from one mountainous area to another. The Thai government is trying to stop this practice, as these tribes frequently cut down trees that are hundreds of years old for firewood, and is trying to curb the logging companies in the northeast for the same reason. Excessive cutting of trees has led to erosion and sometimes mudslides, which kill the villagers living below the mountains.

About 45% of the Thai workforce is still involved in agriculture, and Thailand is one of only seven or eight food-exporting nations in the world. While food is abundant and Thai cuisine world famous, agriculture contributes only 9.9% to Thailand's gross national product, while industry contributes 44% and services 46%. There are wide disparities in income, both within and between regions (such as Bangkok and the northeast). Thailand's economic growth rate was extremely high for about 20 years, averaging 7% until 1997, when it was negatively affected by the Southeast Asian financial crisis of 1997. The economy has recovered, but some deep philosophical and economic divisons between groups, as described below, threaten the democratic fabric of the national government.

U.S. Americans and Thais share many similarities, but they also are quite different from one another. When Americans visit Thailand, they are frequently entranced by the friendliness of the people; the many Buddhist temples or *wats*; and the contrast between rural and urban life, particularly the urban life found in Bangkok, the nation's capital. Thailand's parliamentary, democratic system of government was heavily influenced by Britain, for until recently Thais were often educated in England rather than the United States.

In 1932 Thailand abolished the absolute monarchy. Under its rules, citizens could not touch members of the royal family. This resulted in some bizarre situations; one royal, who could not swim, drowned because numerous onlookers felt they were barred from offering a helping hand. Since 1932 the country has experienced 17 coups, 56 governments, and 16 constitutions, with the most progressive constitution taking effect in 1997. Given so many changes, it is little wonder that the most distinctive symbol in Thailand is King Bhumibol, who has been in power since 1947. The Thai kingdom was in decline until he became king upon the assassination of his older brother, King Mahidol, in 1946.

Since 1947 the king has created what is arguably the most powerful and workable kingdom in a world that increasingly views kings as anachronistic. He is a talented and sophisticated man known for his love of the arts and is himself a noted jazz composer. Most important, he symbolizes critical features of Thai culture and, it can be reasonably argued, is the glue that is holds the nation together. Bhumibol is the world's longest-reigning monarch and, as Lintner (2009) notes, the trauma that his succession will inevitably entail will be immense.

However, deep philosophical and economic divisions constitute a major menace to Thailand. Many citizens would like the nation to become more democratic and less influenced by its military, many of whose leaders go into business after retirement and supposedly benefit because of their favored status and contacts. Others, on the other hand, feel that the Thai military have helped the nation enormously in dealing with border conflicts and internal security. In 2012 Bangkok experienced its greatest flooding in the past 50 years, and the army helped citizens by providing transportation, evacuations, and related activities, thereby building upon its reputation. Thailand also has one of the highest levels of economic inequality in Asia, and the gross domestic product (GDP) per citizen is only US$3,840 (for comparison, U.S. GDP is $45,592). Since 2000 the deep divisions have crystallized into two opposing groups: the yellow shirts, supportive of the establishment (the king's color is yellow); and the red shirts, representing the more radical and more disenfranchised elements in Thai society, including the rural poor in the north and northeast and other interests. In 2011 major clashes occurred between the yellow and red shirts in Thai cities, particularly Bangkok. There were deaths on both sides but especially among the red shirts, who torched major parts of downtown Bangkok as they retreated from a military attack. Overt tension has receded, but underlying issues and problems remain.

In this chapter we will not speculate on the issue of succession to the rule of King Bhumibol. Rather, our focus is on the Thai kingdom and why it is consonant with the underlying core values of all or most Thais. The characteristics of this cultural metaphor are loose vertical hierarchy, freedom and equality, and the Thai smile.

Loose Vertical Hierarchy

Thailand is an authority-ranking culture in which vertical collectivism is emphasized. However, probably because it is at the crossroads of many competing cultures, the Thais follow far fewer rules than most authority-ranking cultures. As Harry Triandis and Michele Gelfand (1998) have shown empirically, on the cultural dimension of looseness-tightness of rules, the Thais are at the extreme end of looseness. Thus Thai culture probably holds many more contradictions and tensions than most other cultures.

Visitors to Thailand are immediately confronted with some of these contradictions. About 95% of the population is Buddhist, and there are numerous Buddhist *wats* in Thailand, but most Thais do not frequent them except for scattered ceremonial days. Still, Buddhist values are ingrained in the Thais, as discussed below, and are taught both in the culture at large and in the schools. Also, belief in spirits is widespread; throughout the nation are spirit houses in which residents leave food for the spirits to whom they pray. This belief in spirits is a legacy from the nation's rural past and present.

Today hotels and other organizations are modernizing the construction of spirit houses through the use of ceramic tile instead of wood. However, this is controversial, as traditionalists believe that the spirits will visit only wood houses. As might be expected in such an environment, Thais tend to believe in fortune-telling, and each year they spend about US$63 million on visits to traditional fortune-tellers. There are even call centers devoted only to fortune-telling (Fuller, 2011b).

During the Vietnam War, U.S. Americans used Thailand as a recreational area for military personnel on leave, which helped to promote the well-known and widespread prostitution found in Thailand. This has had some very unfortunate consequences, including the fact that Thailand experienced an abnormally high rate of HIV infection. The spread of HIV has decreased significantly in recent years. However, upper-middle-class Thai women can be Victorian in their attitudes. It is not unusual for a young man to visit a girlfriend's home on dates for many months and, when they are outside the home, for them to be escorted by an older sister or aunt.

The King's Role

The king has been particularly effective in using vertical hierarchical rules to manage the nation. While the king does not involve himself in daily governmental affairs, he becomes active during times of crisis and in the past has requested that prime ministers and generals voluntarily vacate their positions of power. Nothing more needs to be said to accomplish their removal, and there is no additional discussion about it.

Similarly, until recent years, the king or members of his family handed out individual diplomas at all university graduations. Each proud graduate wanted to have his or her picture taken with the king, so two cameras were used for each photo in the event that one of them failed to record this moment. The king also appears at prominent *wats* for Buddhist ceremonies.

As these activities suggest, the king is very involved in the lives of Thais, and they revere him. Thais can become infuriated when the king is insulted in any way. One unfortunate visitor to Thailand became angry with a waiter in a restaurant, threw his cash payment for the meal on the floor, and stomped on it. He failed to realize that the king's picture is found on Thai money, and an enraged Thai attacked him mercilessly because of the perceived desecration. Another unfortunate visitor ripped up his Thai money as a sign of dissatisfaction at the airport, only to be arrested and jailed for 6 months. At movie theaters, every film is preceded by a special royal anthem during which all are expected to stand. The government banned YouTube in 2007 because of a 44-second video that satirized the king, and Paul Handley's (2006) critical biography of the king received similar treatment. Although Handley is an Australian, he went to jail and was released only when the king pardoned him.

The use of such laws has increased markedly in recent years, while some elements within the red-shirt faction are pushing for the abolition of such laws. Although members of this faction respect the king for all that he has accomplished over his long tenure, they feel he should not be treated as a demigod, and they are particularly worried about the continuation of such laws after King Bhumibol retires. Given his advanced age, such a retirement is inevitable in the near future (Fuller, 2011a).

The essence of a paternalistic authority-ranking culture is a dynamic, two-way relationship between a superior and others. *Kreng cai,* or taking the other person's feelings into account, is a key concept in Thailand. All of the actions of the king reflect this orientation, and both feelings and obligations are two-way or circular in nature. *Kreng cai* is similar to the Japanese concept of *amae* or looking to others for security and assurance. Thais are very sensitive to feelings and clearly recognize nuances of behaviors that the typical U.S. American does not recognize. Similarly, Thais are adept at sorting themselves out in a reception line by status, even though they may not have met previously. In one instance, a male and a female doctoral student were invited to dinner at a U.S. American professor's home, and one of them—in this case, the female—kept emphasizing that her family was of a much higher social status in Thailand than the other student's. Such behavior is low in egalitarian cultures, but in authority-ranking cultures its frequency is much higher. Ironically, the female Thai student had confided to the professor that she would like to meet other Thais, and the dinner was arranged specifically to facilitate the introduction.

As might be expected in an authority-ranking culture, members of the military are also important players. Many generals have business interests. There is a good amount of corruption in Thailand, at least in part because of the extremely complex social class structure involving competing interests of different groups. As suggested above, these include businesspeople, the military, the politicians, the king, the rural poor, trade unions, and others. On the 2011 Index of Economic Freedom, developed by the Heritage Foundation and published yearly in the *Wall Street Journal*, Thailand ranks 62nd of 179 nations (T. Miller, 2011). The Index includes 10 separate measures, including fiscal soundness, openness to trade and investment, government size, business and labor regulation, property rights, corruption, monetary stability, and financial competition.

Personal and Family Interactions

Rather than shake hands, although the handshake is becoming more common, particularly in international business, Thais tend to *wai* to one another: They hold both hands together as if in prayer and bow their heads to greet each another. Bowing lower than the other person signifies lower social status, and bowing at the same level signifies equality in social class ranking. Sometimes a superior will just nod the head, and at other times he will complete an attenuated *wai* that is scarcely noticeable. Supposedly, this pattern of the *wai* and its relation to social class structure emerged when someone conquered in battle would show the victor that he was totally subservient; his bow to the victor exposed his head to any blow that the victor wanted to administer. If a blow was not administered, the victor was signalling that a two-way relationship of fealty had been born, but one in which there was a clear superior and a clear inferior. Thus it is not surprising that at public ceremonies, such as university graduations, anyone who wants to leave before the king must do so in an unobtrusive manner, making sure that he or she is lower than the king at all times.

In relationships within families, this vertical ranking also prevails. Many Chinese Thai families live in a compound comprised of several homes, one for the father and mother and one each for married family members. They meet at night and at other times in a common area in the center. Typically, at least one night per week, there is a large family gathering and dinner. The oldest son usually is the major decision maker in the family business if the father has retired, and the younger sons serve as vice presidents. If one of the sons is not very effective, he will retain the title but be assisted by either an in-law or outsider who will be the real decision maker in that part of the business. The family frequently rewards such important outsiders after several years by subsidizing the creation of their own businesses, thus strengthening the family's business network. This Chinese-Thai approach to business is based on the traditional Chinese practice of *guanxi*, which can be translated as having relationships. An invisible web of obligations is established through such practices. To be without *guanxi* is problematic in a person's life, as it signifies that the individual has no relations and, implicitly, cannot be fully trusted.

Furthermore, each family emphasizes this hierarchical ranking. One young woman who received her MBA in the United States did not want to return to Thailand and marry a man she had known since childhood, but she did so when her mother said, "If you don't return and marry him, I never want to see you again." However, the young woman and her mother did follow the dictates of loose authority ranking, agreeing that she would not have children for 5 years; if the marriage did not live up to expectations, she could divorce her husband and remarry, which in fact she did. In another situation, a Chinese Thai family met to discuss an emergency problem: A younger female member of the family was very unhappy in the United States at a university in which she had just enrolled. In this instance, a family member was immediately dispatched to bring her home.

An Educational Tradition

This form of vertical ranking is exemplified in the flower ceremony held in universities once a year. For decades Buddhist monks were the educators in Thailand, and the ceremony originated in their schools. A U.S. Fulbright professor was so startled by this ceremony that he wrote the following description:

> Today, students paid homage to their professors—a symbolic celebration of rather common significance to them. I found it an astonishing phenomenon.
>
> In a large auditorium, representatives from each department within the Faculty crawled up, in the manner of Asian supplication, and gave beautiful floral

offerings to their "Aacaan" (professors). Their choral chants asked for blessing and showed gratitude. Their speeches asked for forgiveness for any disrespect or non-fulfillment of expectation. They promised to work diligently.

In a moment of paradox, I remembered I must not forget to pay the premium on my professional liability insurance this year. (George, 1987, p. 5)

Still, Thais implicitly recognize both the humor in this ceremony and the loose nature of authority ranking practiced in their nation. While many students make such declarations, they have difficulty honoring them.

Education in Thailand, as in other authority-ranking cultures such as Japan, has historically stressed memorization and the taking of copious notes in lectures. Discussion is not emphasized. If a student asks a professor a question and the professor does not know the answer, the professor may well give an incorrect answer that the student will dutifully record, even though the student is aware that the answer is incorrect. In this way face is saved for both people. One U.S. business professor could not get his Thai students to respond to a direct question, so he assigned teams in class in which one member per team reported to the class the group's answers to the questions posed by the professor. Interactions began to become more informal and tension-free once this format was employed. This is consistent with an authority-ranking culture that stresses collectivism. A similar pattern of authority-ranking behavior involving managers and employees can be found in some traditional Thai firms, but it is less common in the multinationals and larger firms now operating in Thailand. Similarly, many MBA programs in Thailand tend to stress Western-style case discussion and interaction, which does involve individual student responses to a professor's direct questions.

Ethnic Relations

The looseness of rules is reflected in generally positive relationships between the two main ethnic groups in Thailand, the Chinese and the ethnic Thais. About 80% of the population is composed of ethnic Thais, and they are powerful in politics and the military. Another 10% of the population is composed of the ethnic Chinese, who generally believe in Confucianism and, to some extent, Taoism (for an explanation of Confucianism and Taoism, see Chapter 25). The ethnic Chinese tend to own prosperous family-run firms, most of which are relatively small in size. A good amount of intermarriage takes place between these two groups, and some Thais argue that they are more liberal and accepting than their counterparts in other nations, even those in Southeast Asia.

One reason for the high rate of intermarriage is that these two groups are compatible in terms of the overlapping religious and ethical perspectives of Buddhism, Confucianism, and Taoism. This is not always the case; discrimination and hostility to some ethnic groups exist, but seemingly to a much smaller extent than in most nations.

In short, the king's actions are consistent with the core values of the authority-ranking Thais. He does, however, respect the loose nature of the rules, as evidenced by his hands-off policy on daily governmental affairs and related issues.

Freedom and Equality

Thailand means "land of freedom," and the name is apt, as it is the only nation in Southeast Asia—and one of the very few in the world—that has never been conquered. In the 1700s the Thai army was in grave danger during a war with Burma, but its leader, Taksin, reorganized the remaining 500 soldiers and led a brilliant counterattack. Taksin became king and established the capital in Bangkok. Later, he went insane and was replaced by a king from whom the current king traces his lineage directly.

A Military Tradition

With Thailand bordering several nations, the Thais have always been concerned about their military strength, and Thai soldiers are well trained, many of them in the United States and Australia. The military is involved in governmental affairs, even to the extent of overthrowing elected governments. However, the king's word is followed by all, including the military, so much so that leaders will relinquish power to citizens when the king requests it. It would be difficult for Thailand if the military were weak, given the complex region in which Thailand resides, and the issue is the balance between civilian and military rule.

The king has always been physically fit and exercises regularly, and some of the rapport he enjoys with the military may stem from this fact. However, he has experienced some major medical issues in recent years. His son served in the military for many years, but the Thais are not fond of him, probably because of the carefree lifestyle he has chosen rather than the ideal lifestyle exemplified by his father.

Westerners are frequently perplexed by the contradictions of Thai behavior. On the one hand it reflects authority ranking. But it also reflects pride stemming from the tradition of freedom from foreign domination. Even during World War II, Japan did not invade Thailand because of a diplomatic agreement motivated in large part by the Japanese fear of a drawn-out and costly confrontation with the fabled Thai military. However, the Thais did allow the Japanese military to use captured soldiers in the construction of the railroad linking Burma (now Myannar) and Thailand, as immortalized in the classic film *Bridge on the River Kwai*.

Also, Thais see themselves as equal to Westerners because of this tradition and expect to be treated accordingly. Thus both freedom and equality are key components of Thai culture. As indicated previously, in the relationship between superiors and subordinates, there are obligations on both sides, and even Thai subordinates expect to be treated with respect.

Thai Boxing

Thai fighting, particularly Thai boxing, is a unique manifestation and expression of freedom, equality, military prowess, and, interestingly, the relationships between males and females. The roots of Thai boxing can be found in the experiences of the Chinese, who immigrated to Thailand 800 years ago and were forced to fight marauding tribes with a formless style of combat using head, teeth, fists, knees, ankles, and elbows (*muay Thai*). This hand-to-hand combat is still part of the military training.

Modern Thai boxing, as practiced in the two major stadiums in Bangkok, is something to behold. Light gloves are worn, and kicking is permitted. There are typically 10 fights per night, each of which lasts 5 rounds of 3 minutes each. Each stadium is small, holding only about 1,000 customers, almost all of whom are males, but many other Thais stand outside and follow the action intently by radio and, in some cases, television. Before a fight, each fighter performs a small ritual indicating the school or philosophy of fighting in which he has been trained. An Asian band plays throughout each round, but slowly in the first two rounds. In the third round, the band increases its sound and speed, thus exciting the crowd, and many fans rise excitedly and begin to place bets through the use of hand movements. In some ways, this behavior is similar to that surrounding the Balinese cockfight (see Geertz, 1973).

About 50% or more of the fights do not go the full five rounds, as the fighting is bone chilling; knockouts are common. While some people are repelled by Thai boxing, the Thais have excelled at it and have produced many famous champions. As an expression of military prowess, Thai boxing is outstanding. It also symbolizes how far Thais are willing to go to preserve freedom and equality. Separation of sexes, which can be Victorian at times, also occurs during Thai boxing matches.

The Thai Smile

Anyone who has visited Thailand for even a few days can be dazzled by the friendliness of the Thais, and the Thai smile is legendary. Some of this demeanor comes directly from the Thai practice of Buddhism. There are two general streams of Buddhism, one of which, Theravada Buddhism, emphasizes an internal focus and meditation more than the other (see H. Smith, 1991). Theravada Buddhism is widely practiced in Thailand.

The Impact of Buddhism

Thai Buddhism, given its inward focus, stresses the key concept of the "middle way," which emphasizes keeping emotions and even body movements under control. The Thais believe that anger and emotionality lead to more anger and more emotionality, which restricts freedom due to the fact that individuals engage in activities that they would otherwise avoid. Thais tend to be sophisticated diplomats and negotiators because of these beliefs. Similarly, the king is reserved during his public appearances. He does not use emotional approaches and arguments, as do many of his counterparts throughout the world.

The Thais, as Buddhists, believe in karma or the concept that one's behavior leads to consequences. Thus Thais believe that behavior in this life determines the life form an individual will assume in the next life and that one lives many life cycles. Behaving inappropriately toward others, including subordinates or superiors, helps to determine the next life form. For example, Buddhist monks frequently rescue dogs, as many Buddhists believe that dogs were formerly humans who were assigned to a lower life form due to misbehavior in a past life. However, if a person has a disability such as being one-legged, some Thais may avoid that person because of the bad karma that supposedly led to this manner of punishment. In one instance, Thai workers in an open-group setting arranged their chairs and desks so as to exclude such an individual from having any contact with them.

Furthermore, as might be expected in a face-saving culture, Thais hate to say no directly. They use statements such as "We'll need to think it over," and "That may be a problem," as a proxy for no. Many Westerners spend months negotiating a particular issue only to realize belatedly that a slight movement of the shoulder is the equivalent of saying no. When negotiating with Westerners, Thais prefer to emphasize personal relationships and to make the contract of secondary importance, even to the extent of not using a contract at all. In one instance, negotiators from Northrop Grumman negotiated effectively with their Thai counterparts until they indicated that company lawyers would be joining the discussions, at which time the Thais—both politicians and businesspeople—became unavailable through any form of communication.

Smiles in Context

No matter what happens, however, the Thai will keep smiling. Thus a smile should not be interpreted as conveying deep friendship; rather, it is a mechanism for making life pleasant and avoiding difficulties that might lead to the dreaded expression of negative emotions. Thais, in fact, genuinely dislike complainers, including demanding Western tourists, and will avoid them. In contrast, Israelis complain about many things at parties that have come to be called "griping parties," but they still have a good time (see Chapter 20).

However, the Thai smile can be genuine and, as is common in collectivistic cultures, must be evaluated in terms of the context or situation. For example, Thais love to have *sanuk* or fun, and they punctuate the workday with periods of fun group activity. If work is boring and monotonous, Thais may quit, especially if periods of *sanuk* are denied. Japanese firms sometimes pay Thai workers less than do U.S. firms and work them longer hours, but they ensure that the workday is broken up by such periods of respite.

As this discussion suggests, Thais have a different conception of time than Westerners. Being Buddhist, they do not make sharp distinctions between the past, present, and future. In Buddhism time is only one circle, not three. In his first MBA class at Thammasat University, Martin Gannon arrived at 5:50 P.M., one half hour before the class period, to make sure everything was prepared, but the first Thai student did not appear until 7:00 P.M. and the last student to arrive did so at 8:00 P.M. Given his U.S. orientation, Gannon complained about this behavior, but one smiling Thai student confided, "We love to start class on Thai time and quit on American time." It was difficult to respond to this comment.

Accepting Things as They Are

Another, related Thai belief is captured in the virtually untranslatable phrase *mai pen rai*. Essentially, this means that humans have little if any control over nature, technology, and many other forces. Carol Hollinger (1967/1977), a U.S. high school teacher in Thailand, fell in love with Thai culture, particularly this aspect of it, and titled her book Mai Pen Rai *Means Never Mind*. This phrase does not signify a acceptance of a fatalistic view of life, sometimes found among conservative Muslims or Christians. Rather, it is an acceptance of things as they are and the willingness to make life as pleasant as possible regardless of life's circumstances. When Thais use this phrase, they tend to flash their distinctive smiles, and even that small action immediately lessens the magnitude of the problem, whatever it is.

The royal family, and particularly the king, follows a similar pattern of behavior. Although serious, the king enjoys parties and performs his own jazz compositions at them. He clearly is happy interacting with all types of people and will smile through boring ceremonies that other international leaders would not even think of attending. As indicated previously, throughout his life he has maintained excellent physical conditioning, although his health has been declining in recent years. Given the many onerous duties that he must perform while smiling, such conditioning has probably been critical.

John Fieg (Fieg & Mortlock, 1976/1989) has captured the essence of Thai culture and the three characteristics highlighted in this chapter (loose authority ranking, freedom and equality, and the Thai smile) in his classic study comparing Thais and U.S. Americans. In both cultures there is a love of freedom, a dislike of pomposity, and a pragmatic outlook. But the differences are significant, and Fieg uses the image of a rubber band to highlight Thai values, attitudes, and behaviors. When the rubber band is held loosely between the fingers, its looseness is comparable to the manner in which most Thais interact with one another during the day. However, as suggested previously, Thais also have a complex status system in which relationships are vertical and hierarchical. Once this status system is activated in any way—for example, a superior giving a direct order to a subordinate—Thais tend to respond immediately to its dictates, and so the rubber band tightens. As soon as the demands of the status system have been met, Thais can return to looser and more liberated behavioral patterns.

To describe U.S. Americans, in contrast, Fieg uses a string held tightly between the fingers for most of the day. Periodically the string is loosened, but U.S. Americans do not enjoy the same degree of behavioral freedom that Thais experience; that is, the string can never be as loose as the rubber band. In the achievement-oriented society of the United States, many internal and external controls motivate individuals. Examples of external control include the numerous legal, accounting, and governmental forms that U.S. Americans routinely fill out. Imbuing children with the desire to work hard and to respond enthusiastically to the demands of the Protestant work ethic reflects internal control. Such internal and external control is present in Thailand to a much lower degree than in the United States.

As indicated previously, Thailand experienced severe economic difficulties starting in 1997 when the value of its currency was halved. The new constitution in 1997 addressed the need for change, focusing on such issues as democratic election reforms and the elimination of bribes. There are frequently more than 1,000 protests against the government each year, prompting the *Economist* to portray Thailand as a "land of frowns" (E. McBride, 2002). Such activity is to be expected as a nation's educational level and wealth increase and the nation's citizens express a desire for popular elections rather than military-influenced dominance. Still, at the personal level, the Thai smile is one cultural characteristic that remains unchanged.

In sum, Thailand is a fascinating nation, and its core values overlap with those of the United States. But it is clearly different from the United States, and the Thai kingdom is an apt metaphor for capturing the essential features of this land of freedom.

CHAPTER 3

The Japanese Garden

Lacking wide-open spaces, and living close together as they do, the Japanese learned to make the most of small spaces. They were particularly ingenious in stretching visual space by exaggerating kinesthetic involvement. Not only are their gardens designed to be viewed with the eyes, but more than the usual number of muscular sensations are built into the experience of walking through a Japanese garden. The visitor is periodically forced to watch his step as he picks his way along irregularly spaced stepstones set in a pool. . . . Even the neck muscles are brought into play.

—Edward T. Hall, 1966, pp. 52–53

The worst earthquake in Japan's recorded history left a trail of blazing buildings, inundated coastal communities, wrecked roadways and potentially unstable nuclear power plants. But it barely made a dent in the implacably Japanese trait of exhibiting concern for others even in the worst of circumstances.

— Laura King, *Los Angeles Times*, March 13, 2011

Japan is an island nation of 1,279 million citizens. There are 339.2 people per square kilometer, making Japan one of the most densely populated nations in the world. Compared to the United States, it is relatively small in size: 377,727 square kilometers versus 9,372,610. Japan ranks first among nations in terms of its population's median age, 44.7 years, with 30.5% over 60. Its economy is the third largest, behind that of the United States and China. It is also the land of "disappearing children," with the number of children having declined for over 27 consecutive years;

it is on track to lose 70% of its workforce by 2050, according to a report by the non-profit Japan Center for Economic Research in 2008 (Harden, 2008). In comparison, children in India today exceed the population of the entire United States.

Japan was hit by a massive 9.0 earthquake on March 11, 2011. This was followed by an unprecedented tsunami, which wiped out whole towns in northeastern Japan and caused its Fukushima Dai-ichi nuclear power plants to fail catastrophically. According to Japanese leaders, this was the worst disaster to hit the country since World War II. However, despite recriminations against the government and despair with weak leadership from Tokyo, the Japanese people have a renewed sense of pride in their country and belief in its ability to recover from the disaster. The rest of the world has been supporting the Japanese and watching in admiration as they build themselves back up.

Corporate Cultures

In the early 1980s, almost all U.S. writing on Japan praised this country wholeheartedly and tended to highlight only its positive features. Best-selling examples include William Ouchi's *Theory Z: How American Business Can Meet the Japanese Challenge* (1981) and Ezra Vogel's ambitiously titled *Japan as Number One: Lessons for America* (1979). By 1990 many U.S. writers and citizens had radically altered their view of Japan from one of uncritical admiration to one of "fear and loathing," as a *Fortune* article so aptly expressed the viewpoint (L. Smith, 1990). Some reasons for this shift in perspective were the economic successes of Japan at the time and the difficulty U.S. firms had in penetrating Japan's markets. Japan ranks number 20 on the 2011 Index of Economic Freedom, below countries such as Bahrain, Chile, Estonia, Cyprus, and Macau (T. Miller, 2011).

In the 1990s, the economic bubble burst, and Japan experienced a period of stagnation, commonly known as the "lost decade." Its economy started to revive after 2002, only to be hit by the global financial crisis of 2007–2009 and then by the earthquake and tsunami in 2011, which have already surpassed Hurricane Katrina (in the United States in 2005) as the world's costliest natural disaster. The government has proposed a very aggressive recovery plan to pull the country out of recession caused by crippled global supply chains, destroyed factories, and reduced consumer spending in the wake of the earthquake and tsunami (Tabuchi, 2011).

Japanese companies declaring bankruptcy frequently attempt to place their employees with other companies, and the shame associated with failure has led to many suicides among managers. It is hard to imagine comparable action by managers in the United States, who supposedly are more motivated by guilt than shame. Suicide is very much a part of the Japanese cultural tradition, going back to the days of the samurais, who viewed it as noble and possibly preferable to being captured and tortured. Nobuo Shibata, the 48-year-old president of a small sheet metal company, and his brother took their own lives and left this plaintive note: "We apologize to all our employees for the slump in our business" (Sugawara, 1998). According to the World Health Organization, Japan's suicide rate remains one of the highest among developed countries. In May 2011, the number of suicides hit a 2-year high at 3,281, a 20% increase over the same month in the previous year. In recent years, there has also been an alarming increase in the number of suicides among elderly people, largely because of health and economic troubles. Another alarming trend is the use of Internet suicide pacts by strangers. The government has earmarked millions of dollars to help with mental health problems and combat the stubbornly high suicide rate.

Japanese companies have now begun to accept some Western-style management practices, including a direct link between individual performance and compensation, vast differences in individual compensation, and downsizing of the workforce. Carlos Ghosn became CEO of the embattled Nissan and turned the company around by introducing drastic changes, such as downsizing and plant relocations, while being sensitive to cultural norms (referred to sometimes as the "Carlos Ghosn effect"). For example, he downsized the workforce by offering a generous buyout to current employees; he opened new factories that were typically 50 miles from the old factory; and although he helped workers to relocate, the buyouts simultaneously averted involuntary layoffs. Ghosn has become a symbol of enlightened management in Japan, among both managers and employees. He soon became a hero to ordinary Japanese, and salarymen (the commonly used Japanese term for white-collar business workers) mimicked his business wardrobe. At one time, he popped up on short lists for the post of prime minister, even though he was ineligible. Sony's Welsh-born CEO, Howard Stringer, is another example of a foreign CEO of an iconic Japanese company, signifying a more globalized Japan.

However, the reality of the Japanese situation and culture is more complex than most U.S. Americans imagine. The concept that Japan is a collectivistic nation needs to be qualified. In Geert Hofstede's (2001) classic study of 53 nations, Japan ranked 22 to 23 on individualism, which indicates that many nations are more collectivistic. Still, Japan is a classic authority-ranking nation, and to expect it to become a market-pricing or vertically individualistic nation overnight is unrealistic. The interesting balance between individualism and collectivism in Japanese culture is illustrated by the more recent GLOBE study (House et al., 2004) in which the Japanese were found to score high on societal collectivism practices but in the medium range on in-group collectivism. Apparently, large Japanese multinational corporations such as Mitsui and Mitsubishi have noticed this gap, as they have returned to the practice of having dormitories for single men and single women (separated by gender) so that they can get to know one another outside of work, thus facilitating their in-group collectivism and effectiveness at work.

To gain some perspective on Japanese culture, it is useful to compare the basic metaphors or mind-sets through which U.S. Americans and the Japanese see the world. Whereas football reflects the U.S. perspective, most if not all Japanese would immediately identify the Japanese landscape or wet garden as an appropriate metaphor for understanding the Japanese culture. In fact, the *Sakuteiki* or "Records of Garden Making," written almost 1,000 years ago by a Japanese court noble, is considered to be possibly the oldest book on gardening ever written.

Garden as Metaphor

Wet and Dry Gardens

There are two general types of Japanese gardens: the wet or landscape garden (*Tsukiyama*) and the dry Zen Buddhist or religious garden (*Karesansui*). The major difference between them is that the dry garden does not have water or a pond but, rather, raked pebbles to simulate water. Hence the wet and dry Japanese gardens are functionally equivalent to one another, and both are designed to create both a sense of integration between the observer and nature and an atmosphere in which meditation can take place. A third style of garden, called *Chaniwa,* is built for the Japanese tea ceremony. In this chapter the focus is on a wet Japanese garden.

Like the water flowing through a Japanese garden, Japanese society is fluid, changing yet retaining its essential character. Alone, each droplet has little force, yet when combined with many others, enough force is produced to form a waterfall, which cascades into a small pond filled with carp. The pond appears calm, yet beneath the surface a pump constantly recirculates water back to the top of the waterfall. A rock tossed into the pond causes a ripple, then sinks to the bottom, ever to remain separate. Undoubtedly the scene is designed to replicate nature and to capture its true essence, and the sound of the gently flowing water amid this small creation of beauty evokes a feeling of harmony, oneness with nature, and perhaps even timelessness.

The garden itself serves as a reminder of the centrality of nature to the development of Japanese society, religion, art, and aesthetics—and not just nature itself but the way in which the Japanese perceive nature. As the garden is part of nature, the Japanese tend to view themselves as also integral with it. In contrast to the Western view of nature as something to be confronted and subdued, the Japanese generally see it as something to be accepted.

A Love of Nature

The Japanese, an agricultural people, developed a passionate love of nature and a keen awareness of the beauties inherent in it. Japan's temperate climate, abundant rainfall, and proximity to the sea on all sides contribute to a view of nature as a friendly blessing and source of growth and fertility. Thus it is not surprising that the earliest Japanese literature manifests a deep appreciation of the beauties of the sea, mountains, and wooded glens.

The three basic elements of the Japanese garden include stone, plants, and water. Usually these are combined to form larger elements common to Japanese landscape gardens, such as flowing water and ponds and groupings of stone, trees, and shrubs, each as natural looking as possible to evoke the feeling of artlessness.

Japan, like the water in a Japanese garden, is seldom still. This complex, dynamic society has undergone enormous change in the past 150 years, transforming itself from a feudal state into a modern industrialized nation that has fought two world wars, the latter of which resulted in utter defeat. Since then the country has risen to become a major economic power. In the process, the Japanese have absorbed Western technology, science, education, and politics while retaining their unique cultural identity.

Still, underlying this profound change is the perspective that is mirrored in the Japanese garden. To see how the elements of such a garden are manifested in Japanese society, we focus on four topics:

1. *Wa* (harmony) and *shikata* (the proper way of doing things), with emphasis on the form and order of the process

2. *Seishin* or "spirit" training

3. The combination of droplets in a waterfall or the energies of individuals in group activities

4. Aesthetics

Wa and *Shikata*

To understand Japan it is important to know its history, which can be viewed as a continual search for *wa* or harmony in interpersonal relations. In the Japanese garden, this is reflected in harmonious relations among elements that create a sense of the effective interaction between human beings and nature. The Japanese are a homogeneous people who have lived in relative isolation for centuries, although the geographical features of the country do make for diversity in the population with regard to dress, food, customs, language, and so on. Prior to the end of the last ice age about 11,000 years ago, Japan was connected by land to the rest of Asia. Because those people who wandered into it could go no further, they remained and mixed with those who came later. Historical records show that a considerable number of people flowed into Japan from the Korean peninsula until the 8th century CE. By that time the mixing was nearly complete, and for the past 1,000 years, immigration has been infinitesimal.

Borrowing From the Chinese

Virtually devoid of natural resources such as iron and oil, the Japanese borrowed the technique of rice farming from the Chinese sometime around the year 1000 BCE. Each village became self-sufficient, but the complexity and interrelatedness of the tasks associated with rice farming led the Japanese to emphasize the importance of group activities and group harmony, without which there would be starvation.

In the 7th century BCE, this emphasis on harmony was expressed in the country's first "constitution," written by Prince Shotoku. The first of the 17 articles made harmony the foundation for all of the others. This is in marked contrast to the Western conception of the importance of life, liberty, and the pursuit of individual happiness.

Furthermore, the Japanese have always had a distinct awareness of the difference between things foreign and native, and early on, they recognized the value of borrowing from others while maintaining their Japanese-ness. After 552 CE, when Buddhism was formally introduced to the Yamato court from China, the Japanese increasingly became conscious of the superior continental civilization of the Chinese. From the 7th to the 9th century, they made a conscious and vigorous effort to borrow Chinese technology and institutions; they studied the philosophy, science, literature, arts, and music of China in depth, and these, in turn, deeply influenced Japanese thought, culture, and habits. The Japanese even adopted the Chinese writing system, which had a unique character for each of the thousands of Chinese words. However, even though the Japanese wrote in Chinese, they spoke only Japanese, which is as different from Chinese as it is from English. Japan's island location was far enough from China to escape invasion but close enough to benefit from interacting with this nation, which at that time was the most technologically advanced and powerful in the world. From the 9th to the 12th centuries, the Japanese blended these new elements with their own culture to form a new synthesis. In 2010 China officially overtook Japan to become the world's second-largest economy, although its GDP per person remains far less than that of Japan (US$3,270 vs. US$38,460). On the one hand, Japan has benefited from the expansion of the Chinese economy, but on the other, it fears China's growing military and economic prowess in the region.

The Shogun Era

In the 12th century, Yoritomo Minamoto first used the title of *shogun* or generalissimo of Japan and established his headquarters in Kamakura, which is 1 hour's drive from Tokyo, or Edo as it was called at that time. Although the imperial family living in Kyoto was still allowed to perform ceremonial activities, real power rested with the shogun, and clan lords reported directly to him. This shogun era lasted until 1868, at which time the imperial family's power was restored (Meiji Restoration). In 1868 the shogun was deposed, the shogunate ended, and the country's capital and imperial residence were moved from Kyoto to Tokyo.

During the shogun era, the emphasis on harmony continued but in a distinctly different manner. Interestingly, the shogun system was similar to European feudalism. About 10% of the population consisted of samurai or warriors, who pledged absolute loyalty to the shogun. Thus this system is quite different from the Chinese Confucian system, in which loyalty to family is the overriding value. The subjugation of the samurai to the shogun paved the way for the transference of loyalty to the ultimate family, the nation. In addition, the samurai were also men of learning, and they prided themselves on their fine calligraphy and poetic skills.

However, most of the population had only limited rights, and a samurai could kill commoners on the spot if they failed to abide by the many rules and practices pervasive throughout society. Under such conditions, it is little wonder that the Japanese sought to achieve harmony and to protect face, which is an unwritten set of rules by which people in a society cooperate to avoid unduly damaging each other's prestige and self-respect. While all cultures emphasize the protection of face, the Asian concept includes "giving face." For example, something is always left on the table for the defeated adversary in business negotiations, and baseball games may end in ties rather than wins. Even today the Japanese tend to apologize in advance before making a critical comment on another person's project so as to avoid the loss of face for either party; many of them begin a formal speech in a comparable manner. The Japanese language is filled with ritual apologies, which sometimes seem like mere formalities, but at a time of great national crisis, the language is the glue that holds the country together (King, 2011).

Japan's sense of isolation was heightened during the reign of Shogun Ieyasu in the 16th century when he banished Jesuit missionaries, cut off the ears of Christians, and mandated that only coastal vessels not fit for ocean travel could be built. With the exception of a small Dutch trading area in the Kyushu port of Nagasaki, relations with the outside world were cut off.

Out of Seclusion

In 1853 Japan was forced to end its self-imposed seclusion when Commodore Perry and a quarter of the U.S. Navy arrived off the shores of Edo. The Japanese government had no choice but to sign unequal trade treaties with the United States and principal European powers. These developments led to a weakening of the shogun system and its replacement by the imperial family in 1868.

Furthermore, it is extremely difficult for a foreigner or *gaijin* (or *gaikokujin*, which has become the more acceptable term in recent years) to be fully accepted in Japan, as this would upset harmonious relations between and among groups that have taken years to develop. A foreigner is like the rock tossed into the garden's pond; it momentarily disturbs the harmony but quickly disappears from sight. Many visiting U.S. Americans misperceive the extreme care and attention given to them as genuine friendship or at least genuine acceptance. The reason for this leads us naturally to a discussion of *shikata*, which is necessary if *wa* is to be maintained.

Because of the subsistence-level economy that developed in rice-growing villages and the emphasis on nature, the Japanese came to believe that there is an inner order (the individual heart) and a natural order (the cosmos) and that these two are linked by form (see De Mente, 1990). *Shikata* is the way of doing things, with special emphasis on the form and order of the process; in compound forms, the term is *kata*. Thus there is a *kata* or several *kata* for eating properly, for using the telephone, for treating foreigners, and so on. To the Japanese, the process or form for completing an activity is just as important as completing the activity successfully, whereas U.S. Americans have historically been concerned with the final result rather than the process of achieving it. In business, the Japanese emphasis on total quality management (TQM) and *kaizen* (continual improvement) is consistent with *shikata*, as the Japanese tend to feel that doing something in the proper manner will ultimately lead to doing it in the most successful manner.

The Proper Way

Kata were developed within this hierarchical society because it was assumed that everyone has specifically categorized and defined life roles (*bun*) in which obligations are spelled out in detail. Edwin Reischauer (1988) has termed the Japanese the most punctilious people on Earth because of such explication, if not the most polite. A person's outward conduct, as manifested in obedience to rules, is a reflection of inner character. There are even *kata* associated with Japanese baseball, and visiting U.S. baseball players frequently find it difficult to adjust because they must hold the bat in a particular way and observe other rules that they consider irrelevant.

The importance of *kata* cannot be overemphasized, and there are specific *kata* for activities that U.S. Americans tend to handle in many different ways, such as greeting visitors and exchanging business cards. When a *kata* for a new activity does not exist, the Japanese may have difficulty completing the task. Thus some Japanese officers who wanted to discontinue fighting in World War II bemoaned the fact that no *kata* for surrender had been developed simply because it was so unthinkable. As they stated, "We don't know how to surrender" (De Mente, 1990, p. 68).

Seishin Training

To live comfortably in such a rule-ordered society, people need a great deal of self-control, and they are socialized from birth to acquire it. In the Japanese garden, the carp symbolize masculinity, valor, endurance, and tenacity. Analogously the concept of *seishin* or spirit, which is an integral part of the Japanese philosophy of life, stresses the importance of self-discipline and devotion to duty. Through discipline and adversity, people achieve self-development and, most important, self-mastery. *Seishin* training has been most commonly applied to the study of martial arts, flower arrangements, and the tea ceremony. In the case of the martial arts, physical training is seen as a means to the spiritual end of attaining inner balance and harmony. Mastery of skills requires self-control and self-discipline; this leads to the development of inner strength. In the past, a number of Japanese companies also offered *seishin* training to new recruits, although in some quarters this was considered to be a relic of Japan's prewar educational system and thus considered to be nationalistic and militaristic.

Buddhist Influence

Seishin training tends to be associated with Zen Buddhism, a form of Buddhism that has enjoyed a resurgence of interest in Japan since the 1970s. While Hinduism incorporates a belief in many personal gods, Buddhism rejects them. It does, however, accept the Hindu emphasis on meditation as a major vehicle for achieving nirvana or salvation. Buddha emphasized four Noble Truths: Suffering is inevitable; it occurs because of selfish or self-centered desires; such desires can be overcome; and the method of overcoming them is to follow the Eightfold Path. It is approximately comparable to the Ten Commandments.

Zen Buddhism proposed that people can free themselves from their self-centered world by perceiving the timelessness and oneness of the universe. Likewise, in a Japanese garden, the whole of nature can be seen as well as the individual parts. Also, each part of the garden can capture the essence of nature in its own way. The garden depicts a freed world, which has been physically reduced and spiritually enlarged to suggest the size and grandeur of nature. Japanese, who recognize that they are part of nature and hence mortal, essentially stop time by allowing it to have its own way. In the same manner, although the seasons may change, the appearance of the Japanese garden, the stones, trees, and water in it, is always unchanged.

Another aspect of the Buddhist influence is the natural stoicism, orderliness, and perseverance of the Japanese people, qualities that were very much in evidence as the Japanese dealt with the multiple disasters caused by the earthquake of 2011. This is captured by the common Japanese word *gaman*, which loosely translates to something like "toughing it out." Stoicism is also built into the Japanese language in the term "*shikata ga nai*" or "it can't be helped" (Kristof, 2011). Even the traditional rituals of death, which are deeply influenced by Buddhism, were swept aside by the tsunami, as the Japanese had to abandon the practice of cremation and bury thousands of their dead in mass graves, partitioned by pieces of plywood. In the midst of chaos, soldiers were on hand to imbue the ceremony with dignity, and family members, who had lost everything themselves, tried to ease the journey of the departed into the afterlife with rice balls, cans of coffee, favorite artifacts, or simple bouquets of flowers (Wines, 2011).

Perhaps the best way to understand Japanese behavior is to take part in such martial arts as karate and sword play. Karate (literally, "the way of the empty hand") originated in Okinawa, Japan, and is a combination of preexisting Okinawan martial arts called *te* and Chinese martial arts. It is both a form of self-defense against marauders and a form of spiritual training. Once again, forms or *kata* constitute much of the training that karate students receive, and they practice these forms by themselves for hours before engaging in any kind of combat. Eventually karate students are taught to "think through" an obstacle, and one of the most difficult challenges facing a parent is to see a 9-year-old son or daughter trying to "think through" or break a 1-inch-thick plywood board with an open-handed blow. Sometimes the karate instructor will have unsuccessful students repeat the exercise three or four times so as to exhibit self-control and learn to handle adversity, and some young students have broken their hands while engaged in this activity.

Going to "Hell Camp"

Although theoretically the ultimate result of *seishin* is an improved state of personal spiritual growth and freedom, many Japanese use it to attain practical ends, such as better performance in school or work. Some large Japanese firms appeal to this element of Japanese thought in their training programs, which have been called "hell camp" because the trainees are allowed to sleep only a few hours per day and undertake physically demanding activities designed to instill a sense of self-discipline and devotion to the company; the trainees are given several "badges of shame," which they can remove from their clothing only when they successfully complete the various examinations and other hurdles. In many modern transformations of the philosophy, the central emphasis is on the development of a positive inner attitude by means of which external constraints can be overcome and difficulties resolved. Japanese tend to believe that any obstacle can be overcome provided one tries hard enough. Conversely, U.S. Americans emphasize ability as much as or more than effort.

Like the Chinese, the Japanese believe strongly in the principles that Sun Tzu, the ancient Chinese general, put forth in *The Art of War* (see McNeilly, 1996, whose book also includes a 1963 translation of Sun Tsu). They see the marketplace as a battlefield but accept Sun Tzu's first principle, namely to avoid war or confrontation if at all possible simply because both sides deplete critical resources. Still, the Japanese revere Miyamoto Musashi, a legendary samurai who combined kendo and Zen while killing 37 opponents; then he retired to a cave, where he died. Musashi's 1974 book, *A Book of Five Rings*, describes the set of rules that many Japanese managers follow when doing business. This paradoxical and simultaneous acceptance of inner reflection and merciless activity against business opponents is similar to the Chinese paradox of being both sincere and deceptive (see Chapter 25). A popular 14-hour film was made of Musashi's life and book.

Combining Droplets or Energies

Achieving harmony through *kata* and *seishen* training leads naturally to the topic of combining energies of individuals in groups or, analogously, combining droplets of water in the garden to form a waterfall. This emphasis on the group begins at birth, for mothers tend to shower a great deal of love and attention on their children, especially boys. In Japan infants and children are constantly in contact with their mothers, are treated permissively, are seldom left alone, and often sleep with their parents until the age of 7 or 8. For the first 2 years of life, children are swaddled and carried by their mother in a special device attached to her body. All of these practices result in a high degree of dependence on the mother and encourage an attitude termed *amae* in Japanese, which means to look to others for affection. As children grow up, this dependence on their mothers as the source of gratification is transferred to the group, particularly the mentor or *senpai*. The system of *senpai* and *kohai* is a complex relationship with obligations on both sides. The Japanese often meet their first *senpai* in school when they join a club or organization, and this relationship can last for a long time. The closest Western concept is the mentor-apprentice relationship, but the Japanese tie is much more formalized. The *kohai* are trained like soldiers or athletes and are expected to respect and obey their *senpai*. They also use formal and polite language, which is very different from the language used with their friends or peers. The *senpai* has to earn the respect of the *kohai* and vice versa (Hogg, 2006).

An Elder Advisor

During the first few years at a business firm, employees may be assigned to an older individual or *senpai*, who will show them how to perform their job and help them adjust to their new environment. More commonly, *senpai-kohai* relationships develop informally. The *senpai* offers advice and encouragement and may play an important role in the socialization of the youngest employees. This relationship allows the *kohai* to express views informally without fear of censure from a larger group.

The Japanese emphasis on the group permeates practically every aspect of Japanese life. Some people argue that Japan's low crime rate can be attributed to the importance of the group in Japanese society and a strong desire not to bring shame on the group. It can be seen in the educational system, the structure of business organization and work, and the political system, among other social institutions.

At school, children are identified by their class. Japanese children enter the first grade of elementary school in the April after their 6th birthday and spend about 6 years in elementary school, 3 years in middle school, 3 years in high school, and 4 years at university. There are 30 to 40 students in a typical elementary class, and they are divided into teams for several activities. They learn the traditional subjects that children all over the world learn in elementary school, but they also learn traditional Japanese arts such as haiku (a form of poetry that was developed in Japan more than 400 years ago). Many schools offer English classes and use information technology extensively.

There is intense competition to get into certain schools. If attending public school, children will go to an elementary school and middle school located in the same district in which they live. They will then take an exam to determine which high school they will attend, because public high schools are rank ordered based on test results. If attending a private school, students must pass an entrance exam for the appropriate level (elementary, middle, high), but once admitted, they normally have access to a university, because most private schools are affiliated with universities.

Student Attitudes

A well-known Japanese proverb, "The protruding nail will be hammered," aptly explains the behavior of individual students. Adhering to this proverb does not pose a problem for most students, who have learned that security, acceptance, and love flow from the group. In fact, most students display a sense of belonging that would be envied by many of their counterparts in the West, who often feel alienated and alone.

On the other hand, life can be intolerable for the rare student who does not fit comfortably in a group. Fellow students relentlessly bully, pick on, tease, and persecute such individuals. This phenomenon, *ijime*, usually translated as bullying, leads to several deaths every year, and the number of reported incidents has been increasing recently. If such a student has any friends, they quickly desert him or her for fear of being excluded from the group, which is the worst fate that can befall a Japanese child or adult. Sadaharu Oh, the Japanese baseball hero, had a Chinese father and was subject to various forms of discrimination in the schoolyard because of his ancestry, although his long-standing home run record is hailed today as a display of Japanese fortitude (Beech, 2011).

Students achieve group identification not only with their class but also with their school, particularly at the college level. The university they attend frequently determines their future career prospects, as the top businesses hire primarily, if not exclusively, from the top universities. Ties made in college days are important in Japanese life, and throughout their lives Japanese will identify themselves with the university they attended.

Managers and Workers

In Japan a job means identification with a larger entity through which people gain pride and the feeling of being part of something significant. An individual's prestige is tied directly to the prestige of his or her employer. The company is typically viewed, not as an entity trying to take advantage of its employees to make profits, but as a provider of individual security and welfare. When the Japanese are asked what they do, they usually respond with the name of the company for which they work and not the job they perform. In contrast, U.S. Americans will normally respond to the question of "what they do" by mentioning the occupation or job first, and they may not even divulge the name of the company.

Japanese workers or managers usually perceive their company and other institutions with a strong sense of *us* versus *them*. According to Akira Saito of Chuo University, as quoted in the *Economist*, this is a vestige of the feudal system of Bushido, which governed a samurai warrior's allegiance to his shogun or overlord and a master's duty to take care of his subjects. However, the 1990s were characterized by a slumping Japanese economy, and this brought about a number of changes in the workforce, including a rise in the temporary workforce from 20% to 35%. An interesting outcome of this was the institution of a law to protect whistleblowers in 2006, after a rise in tip-offs about improper practices.

In recent years, there has been much discussion about the future of lifetime employment in Japan. Matsushita's decision to cut 8,000 jobs in 2002 was widely seen as a turning point in industrial relations in Japan. In the 2000s, the practice of layoffs and downsizings has continued, but according to labor experts, Japanese lifetime employment is too deeply embedded in its institutions and human resources practices to be completely abolished (Moriguchi & Ono, 2006). However, most young Japanese are already abandoning the ethic of the salaryman (Beech, 2011). A new class, the "precarious proletariat" or "precariat" (workers without job security), has emerged in recent years. About 20 million workers do not enjoy the security, wages, or benefits usually associated with full-time jobs, and the precariat constitutes 34% of the labor force, up from 20% in 1990. Poverty, often seen as a problem suffered in other countries, has been revealed to be a problem in Japan, with 14% of children and 21% of the elderly living below the poverty line (Osawa & Kingston, 2010).

Another distinctive structure of the business firm in Japan is supposedly that it fosters group identification. Prior to World War II, much of Japanese industry was organized into six huge *zaibatsu* or family-owned companies, each of which consisted of about 300 smaller companies and their suppliers. Each *zaibatsu* combined the activities of many subcontractors with whom it had long-term contracts, a manufacturing organization, a major financial institution, and an export-import organization. Such a form of organization is outlawed in the United States and other developed countries and was actually forbidden by law in Japan after World War II. However, a nonfamily variant of the *zaibatsu*, the *keiretsu*, has emerged and become prominent.

U.S. and European managers frequently complain bitterly about the operations of the *keiretsu*, as these organizations have great power over many activities in the marketplace and can persuade Japanese distributors not to carry the products of foreign companies. Ironically, however, the most dynamic and prosperous companies in the Japanese economy tend to be those that are not members of a *keiretsu* (Tasker, 1987).

Since 1990 there has been an increase in entrepreneurial activities among younger managers, some of whom have started their own firms rather than accepting employment in established firms. Such entrepreneurial efforts will increase as the world economy becomes more global, but identification with the company will probably remain much stronger in Japan than in the United States.

Importance of the Group

Organizational structure and work allocation in Japanese firms also emphasize the group. Work is often assigned to various office groups and is viewed essentially a group effort. Frequently there are no formal job descriptions existing separate work groups. A company will sometimes reward the office group and not the individual for work well done. Even the physical arrangement of the office emphasizes the group mentality: The manager sits in front of the workers in a classroom-style setting, and they work in subgroups with their own supervisors. If the work group is small, everyone will sit around a table, with the most senior members closer to the manager. As a general rule, the Japanese do not allow managers to have their own offices, and, even if the work requires that they be given one, managers tend not to prefer this arrangement. This sometimes frustrates U.S. employees of Japanese companies that set up shop in the United States. The U.S. TV show *The Office*, which parodies bureaucratic office culture and dimwit bosses and is based on the popular British show of the same name, is considered to be an unlikely candidate for a Japanese version because the office culture in Japan is so sacrosanct. Still, this did not prevent the show's creator, Ricky Gervais, from creating a short Japanese satirical version on *Saturday Night Live*.

Japanese groups abound in society—women's associations, youth groups, parent-teacher associations, and hobby groups, to name just a few. Political parties and ministerial bureaucracies often divide into opposing factions. When sightseeing, the Japanese tendency to perform activities in a group is particularly evident, as they tend to wear the same type of clothes and behave as if they were one person. As the recent earthquake and tsunami revealed, the Japanese have a tremendous sense of community and tend to cooperate rather than turn on each other during a crisis. Even during the Kobe earthquake of 1995, stories were told about how people left their belongings on the street rather than in their houses, which might be swallowed by the earthquake. They trusted their neighbors to look out for them. In 2011, the global media were astounded that there was barely any looting in the aftermath of the earthquake and the tsunami, which rendered thousands homeless and destitute.

Decision making in Japan also reflects this emphasis on the group. For example, in a Japanese company, a business proposal is usually initiated at the middle or lower levels of management. The written proposal, called *ringisho*, is distributed laterally and then upward. Each person who reviews it must provide a personal seal of approval. Making decisions requires a great deal of time, largely because a good amount of informal discussion has preceded the drawing up of the *ringisho*. In spite of its time-consuming nature, the consensus approach to decision making has important merits. Once a decision is made, it can be implemented quickly and with force because it has the backing of everyone in the department. By contrast, U.S. managers frequently make decisions quickly, but a great amount of time and effort is required for implementation, often because only a few key people were involved in the decision-making process.

A particularly telling contrast occurred when Travelers Group and Nikko Securities were contemplating a joint venture. After Sandy Weill of Travelers and his Japanese counterparts agreed on the basic issues, Weill placed a conference call to New York to obtain board approval, which he secured in 30 minutes. Conversely, the Nikko board required 12 days of briefings and discussion to approve a decision that had been resolved in its favor. However, decision-making practices on both sides of the Pacific have evolved over the years as Japanese and U.S. companies have borrowed best practices from each other.

Responsibility to the Group

Just like the water droplet, the individual is significant only insofar as he or she represents the group. If individuals disagree with one another, the overall interest of the group comes before their needs. Cooperativeness, reasonableness, and understanding of others are the virtues most admired in an individual. Harmony is sought, and conflict is avoided if at all possible.

The extent to which the individual is responsible to the group, and the group responsible for the actions of the individual, is illustrated by the following incident. A U.S. teacher was accompanying an eighth-grade Japanese class on its annual field trip to Kyoto when one of the Japanese teachers kindly informed her that the students would be required to sit in the school auditorium for an hour on returning from Kyoto. When the U.S. teacher inquired why, he responded that one of the students had been 10 minutes late to the school meeting earlier that morning; therefore, all would be punished.

Another example is the Toyota recall crisis, which began in 2009 when Toyota had to recall millions of cars worldwide because of a gas pedal malfunction. The company president, Akio Toyoda, a grandson of the founder, was initially criticized for being slow to react. However, Jeffrey Liker and Timothy Ogden, writing in *Toyota Under Fire: Lessons for Turning Crisis Into Opportunity* (2011), highlight how Japanese culture and especially the Toyota Way helped the company weather the crisis. They point out that the company did not lay off people in a panic, even during the recession. Instead, the company focused on training its people to fix the problems. Top leaders also took responsibility for their mistakes and profusely apologized to their various constituents. Mr. Toyoda even testified before the U.S. Congress. Dealers serviced customers with an unprecedented level of speed and excellence. As a result, Toyota ended 2010 as the largest auto company in the world, and sales were back to pre-recall levels.

Like the water that flows in the garden, the Japanese people prefer to flow with the tide. Observers have noted the relative absence among the Japanese of abstract principles, moral absolutes, and definitive judgments based on universal standards, in contrast to the West. The Japanese think more in terms of concrete situations and complex human relations; therefore, while to Westerners the Japanese may seem to lack principles, to the Japanese, Westerners may seem harsh and self-righteous in their judgments and lacking in human feeling.

Comparisons and Contrasts With the West

As Ellen Frost (1987) points out, many Japanese refer to this difference by saying that the Japanese are "wet" people whereas Westerners are "dry." She elaborates:

By "dry" they mean that Westerners attach more importance to abstract principles, logic and rationality than to human feeling. Thus, Westerners are said to
view all social relations, including marriage, as formal contracts which, once
they no longer satisfy individual needs, can be terminated. Their ideas of
morality are generalized and absolute, with little regard for the particular
human context. . . . By contrast, the "wet" Japanese are said to attach great importance to the emotional realities of the particular human circumstances. They
avoid absolutes, rely on subtlety and intuition, and consider sensitivity to human
feelings all-important. They notice small signs of insult or disfavor and take
them deeply to heart. They harbor feelings of loyalty for years, perhaps for life,
and for that reason are believed to be more trustworthy. (p. 85)

Some see the Japanese identification with nature as the explanation for the origin
of the relativism of Japanese attitudes. Others point to the influence of Chinese
thought, with its situational approach to applying principles (see Chapter 25).
Whereas in the West the division is between good and evil, in China the division is
between yin and yang, two complementary life forces. Thus the Japanese tend to see
situations more in terms of tones of the color gray, whereas U.S. Americans see them
as black and white. However, others suggest that this relativism stems from the child-
rearing techniques discussed previously. Most probably all of these explanations are
interrelated and have some validity.

The emphasis on situational ethics is illustrated in the Japanese legal system. If
people who are convicted show genuine remorse, then it is highly likely that they will
receive a more lenient sentence. Furthermore, the laws passed by the Japanese Diet or
central government are loosely structured so that the courts can interpret them in
ways that different situations demand. By contrast, the U.S. Congress attempts to write
laws in such a way that all possible issues are spelled out carefully, and as a result,
judges must operate within relatively strict limits. Furthermore, the Japanese orientation toward harmony and group loyalty means that conflict resolution is valued, not
the individualistic assertion of legal rights. Consequently, the legal system and
Japanese values reinforce the emphasis on group consensus or solutions prior to coming to court. There is also a strong cultural aversion to litigation. The opposite situation exists in the United States, where individuals involved in legal disputes are aware
that judges must interpret laws that are already finely delineated.

This practice does not mean that the Japanese do not have a sense of right and
wrong. It is simply that they place greater emphasis on the particular situation and
human intentions than Westerners do. The major issue is whether an action harms
others and has a disruptive effect on the group and community. Many experts assert
that the Japanese are motivated primarily by a sense of shame to correct a problem
when such disruption occurs, whereas individualistic Westerners are motivated
mostly by a sense of guilt at their failure to fulfill responsibilities. Such an orientation
is particularly evident in attitudes toward sex and drinking.

Private Lives

Traditionally marriages in Japan were arranged, and even today both families and companies act as intermediaries, although this practice is becoming outdated. Women are increasingly passing up marriage for their careers. Japanese government figures indicate that the percentage of women ages 25 to 39 who have never married has surged from 40% to 54%. This is comparable to 40% in this age group for U.S. women according to U.S. census data. A book about single career women by Junko Saka, *Howl of the Loser Dogs,* sold more than 300,000 copies. The typical Japanese male expects the wife either to give up her job or to manage both the career and the children while he works long hours, and modern Japanese women are rebelling against these expectations. They are increasingly looking for a partner who will give them a lot of autonomy and freedom in the relationship. All of this makes for a low birthrate of 1.29 per woman (compared to 2.13 for the United States) and has grave implications for labor policy.

Drinking and even drunkenness are good-naturedly tolerated and even encouraged. In fact, almost anything people do while drunk, except driving, is considered forgivable. Intoxication allows the Japanese to express themselves freely without fear of repercussions, and it is normal for members of a Japanese work group to spend several hours after work drinking and eating as a group before catching a late bus home. However, Western women sometimes find this behavior difficult to accept, even when a Japanese man is very polite when not drinking. In one celebrated instance, a British female high school teacher finally lost patience with a Japanese coworker who had repeatedly harassed her while he was drinking, and she "decked him" at an office party. However, while Japanese may indulge in unruly behavior while drinking, they rarely engage in displays of hostility and violence. Indeed, with the Japanese emphasis on politeness, it is quite common to see tipsy "salarymen" bowing to each other as they bid goodbye after a get-together!

Like the natural order of the Japanese garden, the Japanese believe in a natural order in society. Therefore, as reflected in the history of hereditary power and aristocratic rule in feudal Japan and in modern Japanese organizations, different ranks and status are considered natural. Within an organization, a person's rank is usually more important than his or her name. For example, the principal of a school is often addressed simply by the Japanese word for principal, *kocho sensei.* This emphasis on title establishes an individual's rank within an organization while serving to reinforce group identity.

Establishing Status

The Japanese are great believers in establishing a person's status as quickly as possible so that the proper interaction and communication can take place. When meeting for the first time, Japanese businessmen follow the *kata* or form of immediately exchanging business cards, *meishi,* largely to establish each person's specific position and group affiliation. This exchange is not to be taken lightly, and the recipient of such a card is expected to read the card carefully and even repeat the person's name and title before putting the card away. To put the card away immediately, as many U.S. Americans do, would be insulting to the giver.

Language is also used to reinforce the natural order of rank and status. Various endings are added to words of introduction that subtly indicate the status of a person, particularly in the case of a foreigner or *gaikokujin*. The Japanese language is famous for such subtlety. Even at work, honorifics are used to address higher-status managers, but they are frequently dropped during the later stages of a working day, as these managers indicate by their language and behavior that everything is going smoothly.

Even slight differences in age or in length of time at a company establish rigid differences in status and seniority that employees must acknowledge. Historically, junior employees were expected to use an honorific term when addressing a senior employee. However, this practice is declining; today, more than 59% of companies with more than 3,000 employees have a policy of not using such honorifics, compared to only 34% in 1995. Hierarchy thrives, however, inside the sumo wrestling stable where all wrestlers must live and train for the duration of their careers. Lunch is eaten in order of rank, and junior stable mates serve as glorified servants to their seniors. Finally, low-ranked wrestlers are not allowed to give out autographs and are expected to live on a small stipend instead of a regular salary (Beech, 2011).

A good part of personal self-identification derives from status. Furthermore, people are expected to act according to their status. To do otherwise would be unbecoming. As they serve as role models and are addressed by the honorable title *sensei*, teachers in Japan must pay particular attention to their behavior outside of school. For example, if caught driving while under the influence of alcohol, a teacher would lose face and probably have to resign his or her position.

A hierarchy exists not just within the group but between different groups. Most Japanese have a clear idea of the informal rank among universities, business firms, and even countries. This latter ranking helps to explain Japanese attitudes toward people from different countries. For example, those from developed countries, such as the United States, England, France, and Canada, are considered to possess higher status than those from developing Asian or African countries. Despite labor shortages, Japanese immigration policies and social practices discourage the hiring of foreigners. Even immigrants of Japanese descent find it extremely difficult to integrate with local communities because the government does not facilitate such integration (Tabuchi, 2011). Within Japan, certain groups, particularly the 600,000 Koreans, suffer discrimination. At one time in history, the Japanese had a caste system similar to that of India. Although this system is outlawed, the outcasts or *burakumin* are still considered inferior by many Japanese.

Because of their long historical isolation from foreign influences, the Japanese have a complex relationship with outsiders. Foreigners in Japan report experiencing indignities like being passed by a taxi driver who chooses to pick up a Japanese passenger instead or being denied admittance to some restaurants and night clubs. National Public Radio's correspondent in Japan, Eric Weiner (2001), reported that even a U.S. American who went through the convoluted process of becoming a Japanese citizen was considered to be a "*gaikokujin* who carries a Japanese passport" and was barred from "Japanese-only" establishments. In 2008, many Japanese chefs looked down their noses at the new Michelin guide to Tokyo's restaurants because they could not imagine how a "bunch of foreigners" could rate Japanese food (Fackler, 2008b). At the same time, the Japanese love French luxury goods, and Japan is the single largest market for Louis Vuitton products (JETRO, 2006). Even in that most hallowed of sports, sumo wrestling, which is often considered to embody the soul of Japan, the Japanese have been forced to recruit international talent from countries such as Mongolia, Estonia, Georgia, and Bulgaria because of dwindling interest from Japanese recruits. Today, more than half the high-ranked wrestlers are *gaijin* (Beech, 2011). They must adhere to the strict hierarchy of the sumo stable described earlier, however. Thus, the essence of Japanese culture is preserved and carefully guarded even within a sport that is dominated today by non-Japanese.

Room for Competition

Like the pond, from the outside, the Japanese appear to be an extremely harmonious people. However, this appearance does not take into account the intense competition that exists in Japanese society. Firms compete fiercely for market share, rival political parties compete for power, and individuals compete ferociously to enter the top universities. On the personal level, conflict occurs between family members, between friends, and between coworkers. However, individuals often suppress their true feelings, and, if open conflict erupts, it is kept within the confines of the group.

In general, Japanese usually express the group opinion, *tatemae*, although it may differ from what they really think, *honne*. They associate this duality with the legitimate needs of the group and the reinforcing role of each person within it. Frost (1987) explains this dichotomy as follows:

> *Tatemae* . . . is used in connection with a view made from an accepted or objective standpoint. *Honne* has the meaning of one's true feelings or intentions. . . . This doesn't mean anyone is lying. There is a delicate but important difference between *tatemae* and *honne* which comes up in any situation where a person must consider more than one's own feelings on the matter. (p. 92)

To Westerners, this lack of frankness smacks of insincerity. However, to many Japanese, the failure to observe *honne* and *tatemae* shows insensitivity and selfishness. Japanese tend to appreciate foreigners who outwardly conform to certain rules of behavior. Whether they actually respect these rules is not relevant; observance of them is a sign of appropriate and hence sincere conduct on their part.

Contrary to expectation, the emphasis on status and rank coincides with a lack of class consciousness. About 90% of the Japanese consider themselves to belong to the middle class. In Japanese society ties are vertical; loyalties overwhelmingly tend to lie with the immediate group. For example, a Japanese factory worker for Toyota identifies himself as a Toyota man and has little solidarity or identification with a factory worker for Honda.

Promotion is based significantly on seniority in Japan, although this is not the only consideration, and today firms emphasize individual performance. People may not jump a rank and must serve a prerequisite number of years in the previous rank to be eligible for promotion. However, only a limited number of positions are available for a much larger number of eligible employees. Therefore, the company promotes a certain percentage of eligible employees from each group until people reach a specific age, at which time it is unlikely they will be promoted further.

It is important to note that hierarchy in Japan is not directly associated with clear authority and clearly delineated roles, as it is in the West. For example, senior but less competent employees may be given relatively high titles that entail minimal responsibility, and extremely able young people may have more responsibility than their titles indicate. Also, while the Japanese emphasize group consensus and harmony, in fact Japanese managers tend to share information with their subordinates and delegate decision-making authority to them less than U.S. managers. As these examples suggest, appearance does not always reflect reality in Japan. The water in the garden's pond appears to be quite calm, even still, yet the architect of this garden knows that beneath the surface, the water is continually being sucked into a horizontal pipe and pumped back to the top of the waterfall.

Aesthetics

The Japanese aesthetic sense is well developed and distinctive, and in fact, it may be this culture's most important contribution to the world. As with most if not all of the activities discussed previously, this aesthetic sense is heavily based on the interaction between human beings and nature.

Nature-Based Religion

Japan has only one indigenous religion, Shintoism, which is nature based and animistic; even the word for God is translated as "up the mountain" in Japanese. Joseph Campbell (1962) captures the aesthetic sense of this religion in the following passage:

> Such a place of worship is without images, simple in form, wonderfully roofed, and often painted a nice clear red. The priests, immaculate in white vesture, black headdress, and large black wooden shoes, move about in files with stately mien. An eerie music rises, reedy, curiously spirit-like, punctuated by controlled heavy and light drumbeats and great gongs; threaded with the plucked, harp-like

sounds of a spirit-summoning *kot*. And then noble, imposing, heavily garbed dancers silently appear, either masked or unmasked, male or female. These move in slow, somewhat dreamlike or trancelike, shamanizing measure; stay for a time before the eyes, and retire, while utterances are intoned. One is thrown back two thousand years. The pines, rocks, forests, mountains, air and sea of Japan awake and send out spirits on those sounds. They can be heard and felt all about. And when the dancers have retired and the music has stopped the ritual is done. One turns and looks again at the rocks, the pines, the air and the sea, and they are as silent as before. Only now they are inhabited, and one is aware anew of the wonder of the universe. (p. 475)

The importance of nature can be seen not only in Shintoism but also in Japanese painting, literature, and language. Long before it was considered acceptable in the West, landscape painting was a major theme of the *sansuiga* painting introduced from China at the end of the Kamakura period (1185–1333). Nature is often the subject of the seasonal references in *waka* and haiku poetry and in the seasonal introductions that the Japanese customarily use in correspondence. The Japanese language is full of references to nature; it even has a word to describe the sound of cherry blossoms falling. Sadly, the Japanese are also aware that nature can wreck havoc. Natural disasters are seen as part of Japan's *unmei* or destiny, a term that is written by combining the characters for *movement* and *life* (Kristof, 2011).

Aesthetic Theory

Aesthetically, the water in the Japanese garden and the garden itself try to represent nature as it is, not to order and impose a visible form on it as a Western garden may but to capture its intrinsic being. Gardeners do not create the beauty but merely allow it to express itself in louder and plainer terms. In doing so, they not only consider the placement of the rocks and trees but the effect that time, namely the change of the seasons, will have on the garden. They observe the laws of *mujo* or mutability and *sisei ruten* or perpetual change of the universe. For example, the garden may be designed in such a way that in winter the bare branches have their own particular appeal. Given this emphasis on the natural impermanence of things, it is not surprising that the three great nature-watching rituals in Japan are snow gazing in February or thereabouts, cherry blossom viewing, and viewing the ninth moon of the year or the harvest moon, all of which preferably occur in a Japanese garden.

Gardeners also observe another Japanese aesthetic theory that developed from the Japanese acceptance of nature: uniqueness. No two trees are alike. Therefore gardeners do not search for the perfect rock, for such a rock cannot exist in a world characterized by uniqueness, but rather look for a tree or rock that expresses its own individuality. Gardeners also do not seek to perfectly order a garden, which is made of imperfect and unique objects. To insist on a harmony other than the underlying, naturally revealed one would be unnatural.

Zen Buddhism's influence on the development of Japan and the Japanese garden, not just the religious garden but the landscape garden, has been enormous, as suggested previously. In Japan, the Buddhist concept of transience has been integrated into the indigenous concept of nature as an extension of oneself. This integration can be seen in the emphasis on oneness with nature and the Buddhist feeling that worldly display counts for nothing. For example, Zen teachings gave rise to the principles of *wabi* and *sabi* inherent in the tea ceremony, the Japanese garden, and flower arrangements. *Wabi* is the aesthetic feeling of discovering richness and serenity in simplicity; it is an emotional appreciation of the essence of things, including the ephemeral quality of life. *Sabi* refers to a feeling of quiet grandeur enjoyed in solitude, and it normally involves the beauty that comes from the natural aging of things. To the Japanese, something old, even its imperfections, is to be respected. Clearly, the Japanese garden is an ideal setting for experiencing *wabi* and *sabi*.

Tranquility and Impermanence

In *The Global Business*, Ronnie Lessem (1987) discusses two principles that explain the Japanese aesthetic, *shibui* and *mononoaware*. *Shibui* refers to a quality of beauty that has a tranquil effect on the viewer; the object, whether natural or man-made, clearly reveals its essence through perfection of form, naturalness, simplicity, and subdued tone. *Mononoaware* refers to the merging of one's identity with that of an object or mood, especially one tinged with recognition of the impermanence of things. Lessem suggests that this aesthetic awareness leads to a sensitivity to humanity and nature that is rare in Europe or the United States.

The Japanese may stroll in the garden, or perhaps just sit on its edge, listening to the water and soaking in its beauty. The garden provides a place of escape from society, both physically and spiritually, just as many Japanese seek refuge through their hobbies.

This refuge usually takes the form of some kind of identification with nature, as in the case of cultivating one's own tiny landscape garden or arranging flowers. Millions of Japanese express themselves through the traditional arts, dancing, music, and literature. In developing their individual skills, they practice self-control and self-discipline. Pursuit of a hobby, called *shumi,* which means tastes, is important to self-identity and even self-respect in Japan.

Except for the sound of the flowing water, all is quiet near the Japanese garden. Likewise, silence is an important value to the Japanese. As mentioned previously, a common Japanese proverb is "Those who know do not speak; those who speak do not know." Conversation is often punctuated by long stretches of silence. The Japanese say that it is during these silent intervals that real communication takes place and that they can sense others' feelings and thoughts. Westerners should not feel compelled to fill in the gaps with conversation, which may only annoy the Japanese, who already perceive Westerners as talking too much.

Similarities and Contrasts

In Hofstede's (2001) research on the five dimensions of culture, the Japanese were portrayed as tending to avoid uncertainty and seeking comfort in familiar situations. The more recent GLOBE study (House et al., 2004) finds the Japanese not much different from U.S. Americans in this regard, being somewhere in the middle range.

In addition, Japan ranked first on masculinity in the Hofstede study, thus indicating that its people are aggressive in the pursuit of worldly success and material possessions. As indicated previously, the carp in the Japanese garden symbolically represent masculinity. However, on the comparable dimension in the GLOBE study, gender egalitarianism, Japan ranked somewhere in the middle.

According to the World Economic Forum gender gap report for 2010, Japan ranked 94 out of 134 nations on the Global Gender Gap Index, about the most unequal of the world's richest countries. In 2010, the Bank of Japan made history by appointing its first female branch manager in its 128-year existence. Japanese work culture makes it practically impossible for a woman to have a career and a family. As former cabinet minister in charge of gender equality, Kuniko Inoguchi, put it, "Japan is losing half of its brainpower as it faces a labor shortage" (Fackler, 2007). The Equal Employment Opportunity Law (1986) and the Childcare Leave Law (1992) are on the books, but enforcement is weak. Still, the country is making slow but sure progress, with companies like Shiseido, Japan's leading cosmetics company, promising to increase the ratio of female leaders from 19% to 30% in 2013. Both Shiseido and the Bank of Japan have female-friendly policies with regard to child care facilities and maternity leave (Sanchanta, 2010).

Unlike the Chinese, who are sometimes hampered by an excessive devotion to the past and ancestor worship, the Japanese have historically been great borrowers from other cultures and are quick to change when conditions warrant such action. In this sense, the Japanese are similar to the individualistic U.S. Americans. But the Japanese are clearly different from U.S. Americans, as our metaphor of the Japanese garden indicates. Still, worried Japanese elders are concerned that the water in the garden will not continue to flow smoothly because the "new humans" may have lost their appreciation of things Japanese. Iwao (1990) argues that there have been three major changes in the Japanese character since 1980: a tendency toward diversity and individuality, a need for swift results and instant gratification, and a desire for stability and maintenance of the status quo. It is true that young Japanese seek more leisure time and are more likely to devote themselves to personal goals than their elders did. As Iwao suggests, consumer behavior reflects a movement toward diversity and individuality. Female roles, as well as attitudes toward marriage and work, are also changing, as indicated earlier.

In 2008, concerned by a rapidly aging society's burgeoning health care costs, the government enacted a law that required companies and local governments to measure the waistlines of Japanese people between the ages of 40 and 74 as part of their annual checkups, setting limits of 33.5 inches for men and 35.4 inches for women (Onishi, 2008). There is a campaign against becoming a *metabo* (a more acceptable term than *obesity* that is shorthand for metabolic syndrome, which is a condition characterized by high blood pressure, abdominal obesity, etc.).

As this chapter indicates, Japan has suffered economically since 1990 and has been buffeted by many winds of change, including the imposition of Western-style individualistic management practices. However, the past few years have also witnessed the emergence of the *hodo-hodo zoku* or "so-so folks," a generation of young people who are not very interested in promotions and advancement. They would much rather have less money and prestige in exchange for more time for their families and other pursuits.

The recent natural disasters could change all that. Professor Hiroki Azuma, author of *Otaku: Japan's Database Animals*, suggests that the Japanese people seem to have completely transformed their *kyara* (character) and are proud to be Japanese again after the prolonged stagnation and despair of the last two decades (Azuma, 2011). The Japanese spirit was very much in evidence during the penalty shootout, come-from-behind victory of the Japanese women's soccer team against the United States in the 2011 World Cup final, a feat that was cheered by the entire world. On the business front, Iwatani, Orr, and Salsberg (2011) suggest that the sleeping giant that is Japan Inc. has begun to stir with increased merger-and-acquisition activity, a greater sense of urgency in corporate boardrooms, some bold moves by some Japanese companies to use English as a global corporate language, and attempts to recruit very talented non-Japanese executives.

A lone pine in Rikuzentakata city was all that was left of the 70,000 trees that had lined the beach before the tsunami. It became the national symbol of Japan's tenacity and will to emerge stronger after the destruction of March 11, 2011. Similarly, the water in the Japanese garden is flowing quickly and with force. It may even alter the shape of the pond somewhat. The change of the seasons will also bring changes to the garden. Yet the basic design and elements of the Japanese garden will always remain, for this island nation of relatively homogeneous people relies heavily on groups to maintain stability and ensure that change and progress occur within the framework of a high-context culture that emphasizes the natural ordering of individuals, groups, and activities.

CHAPTER 4

Bedouin Jewelry and Saudi Arabia

This is a very, very conservative society. They have moved in about 50 years from, frankly, living in the desert in mud huts to now skyscrapers and superhighways and luxury cars. But the roots of this society go back centuries and centuries as a very insular, inward-looking, family-oriented and tribal-oriented society.

—Ambassador Robert W. Jordan, speaking to *Frontline* in 2004

The concert is a sign that things are changing rapidly here. Evidently the government has decided that a minimum of openness in our new world economy and in our information-based world is necessary for us and also for good understanding among cultures

—Jürgen Krieghoff, German ambassador to Saudi Arabia,
speaking about the first public concert for a
mixed-gender audience in Riyadh, 2008

I n 2011, the so-called Arab Spring saw the overthrow of tyrannical regimes in Egypt and Tunisia and resistance to dictatorial governments across the Middle East. The world nervously watched Saudi Arabia, the most powerful oil-producing nation in the region, for signs of instability and caught its collective breath when the revolution did not spread there. As the quotes above indicate, Saudi Arabia is engaged in a fascinating struggle between the forces of tradition and modernity, embodied respectively by the wandering Bedouin in desert camps and glittering skyscrapers in the cities. Speaking at the grand reopening of London's Savoy hotel, Prince Alwaleed bin-Talal (aka the Warren Buffet of the Middle East) summarized it: "I am for modernisation, not total Westernisation. Like this hotel, we need to upgrade Saudi Arabia but we will never lose all our traditional beliefs" (Thomson, 2010b).

Like many nations, Saudi Arabia is confronting the tension between traditional and modern beliefs, values, and lifestyles. The Saudi royal family is the official guardian of the Muslim holy shrines of Mecca and Medina, but it is supporting modernization, at least partially because the economy is too dependent on oil and there is only a limited supply of it. Saudi Arabia emcompasses both a fundamentalist brand of Islam that looks to the 7th century for inspiration and an efficient and forward-looking energy corporation, Saudi Aramco, that is firmly anchored in the 21st century (Coy, 2011). The Saudi family erected a modern concert hall completed in 1989, but no symphonies or operas were performed for many years because of the conservative opposition's insistence on strict Islamic standards. In a groundbreaking first, a German-based group, Artis Piano Quartet, played European classical music for a mixed-gender audience in 2008. The public concert included works by Mozart and Brahms.

Mutaween, or the religious police, routinely punish women they deem immodestly dressed or merchants who do not close their shops during the five daily prayer periods. No religion other than Islam may be practiced in public, churches and synagogues are illegal, and proselytizing for any non-Muslim faith is illegal. Similarly the government executes prisoners by ritual decapitation with a sword. Even foreign workers, constituting over 6 million of the 25.3 million population, are not exempt, and some have been seized without formal legal process and subjected to harsh treatment. The Saudi Labor Ministry estimates that 90% of private sector jobs are held by foreigners, who send almost US$27 billion home by way of remittances per year. Many of these individuals are attracted by the promise of plentiful jobs and largesse but end up feeling dehumanized and exploited. They complain of labor laws being nothing more than "ink on paper." With unemployment at 10.5% and restlessness growing among young people across the Middle East, the Saudi government has spent almost US$100 billion to improve opportunities for the country's citizens. In 2011, the government announced that there would be a cap on the number of years that foreign workers could spend in the country. This measure was aimed at increasing the Saudi-ization of the workforce. King Abdullah, widely regarded as a gradualist reformer, is trying to diversify the economy with the help of Saudi Aramco through projects such as the King Abdullah University of Science and Technology, at which women can study with men and don't have to wear veils (Coy, 2011). Saudi Arabia ranks number 54 out of 179 nations on the 2011 Index of Economic Freedom, as compared to neighbors Bahrain at number 10, Qatar at 27, and Oman at 34 (T. Miller, 2011).

This tension between modernization and conservatism is likely to increase in all the Gulf States. More than half of their population is under age 20. In Saudi Arabia, 31.9% of the 25.3 million residents are under 15. The tension was acute in Saudi Arabia during the early to mid-1990s because of the 1990 Gulf War with Iraq, in which

Saudi Arabia and other Arab nations were allies of the Western powers. After September 11, 2001, tensions between the West and Saudi Arabia again increased. More recently, Islamic traditionalists have muted their criticisms and seem to accept the need for modernization or at least some aspects of it. The gross domestic product per capita is about US$19,020, and the rise in oil prices over the last few years, except during the immediate aftermath of the global downturn in 2008, has generated a sizable petrodollar economy. According to the Institute of International Finance, the Arab region is the world's largest producer of crude oil, accounting for 30% of global exports. High global demand for oil, especially by the emerging economies, and high oil prices drive the GDP of these countries. Saudi Arabia has a production level of 8.9 million barrels per day (mbd), its capacity of 12.5 mbd accounts for more than one half of the world's spare production capacity, and it possesses 24% of the world's oil reserves. However, the country has one of the world's highest birth rates, and the population is expected to reach 40 million by 2025. Due to this demographic trend, it is easy to imagine a return to tradition and a rejection of modernization. Given this tension between tradition and modernization, Bedouin jewelry is an appropriate cultural metaphor for Saudi Arabia.

History and Geography

Saudi Arabia became a nation in 1932, when Ibn Saud united disparate tribes into one nation and named himself king. Oil was discovered 10 years later, but the country remained fairly isolated until the 1970s. Then, suddenly, Saudi Arabia was slaking the world's thirst for oil, and the country was yanked into the 20th century. This nation is still stumbling, struggling to reconcile deeply held traditional values with disconcerting new realities. By examining the ancient art form of Bedouin jewelry, we can address the values and beliefs of Saudi culture. Who the Saudis are today began with the Bedouin of the Arabian desert.

Saudi Arabia stretches across three fourths of the hot, dry, rugged Arabian peninsula. Its land mass is about 24% of that of the United States. The country's borders are the Red Sea on the west; Jordan, Iraq, and Kuwait on the north; the Arabian (Persian) Gulf, Qatar, and the United Arab Emirates on the east; and Oman and Yemen on the south. Small, jagged mountains rise in western Saudi Arabia near the Red Sea. From there, the land gradually slopes down to the Arabian Gulf in the east. Three major deserts lie in between. The largest is the Rub al-Khali, the Empty Quarter. It is the greatest continuous sand desert area on Earth and extends over 250,000 square miles in southern Saudi Arabia. Although several oases spring out of this harsh landscape, the country has no natural rivers or lakes. But Saudi Arabia does have one enormous consolation. Beneath this austere terrain are the largest reserves of oil in the world.

Several million years ago, this area was covered by shallow seas filled with mollusks, brachiopods, and plankton. When these creatures died, they sank to the seabed. Eventually the waters receded, and the sea floor was compressed at high temperatures under layers of sedimentary rock. The organisms were transformed into oil and natural gas.

Much later, the Arabian Peninsula was a grassy savannah. Until about 18,000 years ago, ample rainfall supported vegetation and wildlife. But the last Ice Age ended in a prolonged drought. Rivers evaporated, leaving dry valleys called *wadis*. The fertile land turned into desert. Now, rainfall averages 0 to 4 inches per year. When a rare downpour does occur, the wadis are briefly filled with water once again before it soaks into the ground or evaporates away. During much of the year, temperatures are 90°F to 120°F. However, strong winds and cooler temperatures can make winter days quite cold. These raging winds also generate the stinging sandstorms common to the Arabian desert. Surviving in this environment takes skill, courage, and fortitude.

The Desert Bedouins

For centuries, the Bedouins of Saudi Arabia have made the desert their home. Their way of life is a sophisticated adaptation to a harsh environment. The fact that they have been successful at it for so long is a source of fierce pride. Many Bedouins feel far superior to townspeople, and they display a certain arrogance for having braved the deserts and won. Surely theirs is a purer, worthier life, as they see it.

The word *Bedouin* comes from the Arabic *badawi,* which means desert dweller. Bedouins live in extended family groups, moving when they need new pasture or water. The only animals that can comfortably live in the desert are goats, sheep, and— most of all—camels. Goats supply milk and hair for tents. Sheep give meat and wool for carpets and blankets. Camels provide milk, meat, hair for tents, dung for fuel, urine for shiny hair, and transportation, all of which almost makes up for their nasty tempers. In addition, camels can go many days without food or water. Raising and selling camels to townspeople has always been a source of income for these desert dwellers. According to Gardner (2003), the truck, which has become the foundation of contemporary Bedouin livelihoods, is increasingly changing the communication networks of Bedouins by moving them from tents to the marketplaces of towns and villages. Trucks enable Bedouins to scout for distant pastures, visit friends and family, carry animals to the market, and transport crops back to camp (Gardner, 2003).

Because the desert provides scant food for livestock, Bedouin camps must move often, usually every couple of weeks. Camps consist of 2 to 30 tents, with most camps having fewer than 10. Each tent houses a nuclear family plus perhaps an unmarried uncle, mother, sister, or brother. A Bedouin tent is a long, low, black structure made of camel and goat hair and has a wide front opening. The shape is ideal for protection against wind and sandstorms. Each tent is divided into two sections: one side is for the mother and daughters, the other for the father and sons. The tents and all possessions can be packed up and the family get on its way within 2 hours.

Bedouins pay little attention to national borders. Saudi Arabian borders are poorly defined, but the Bedouin need for pasture and water takes precedence over arbitrary lines, anyway. Families camp on the edge of the desert, occasionally visiting towns for supplies. Their habit is to live in the higher areas during the hottest part of the year so they can escape the worst heat and sandstorms. Later they move back to the lowlands to avoid cold temperatures and winds. Bedouins are continuously on the alert for chance thunderstorms, which mean lush pastures are sprouting, flowers are blooming, and wadis are filling.

Camel raiding has been a traditional pursuit of Bedouin men. Although it is now outlawed, the raiding rules are still important for illustrating the strict code of Bedouin honor. First, the hostility must be explicitly declared; using the element of surprise is shameful. Therefore raiding is not done at night. Second, no women or children may be harmed. Third, sunrise raids are fairer, so that victims have more chance to track and retrieve their camels before nightfall. Breaking these rules brings shame to the perpetrators, severely tarnishing their honor.

Personal Characteristics

Bedouins are known throughout the world for their generosity. A guest, even an unexpected stranger, will be fed and housed for 3 days. In fact, if those raiders arrived at the opposing camp, they would receive the same welcome, and they would not be harmed during their stay. While an ordinary meal consists of milk and milk products, dates, flat bread, and perhaps rice, the guest's feast also includes fresh meat and pine nuts. Pale green coffee with cardamom, as well as tea, is served. Afterward, poets and dancers (always male) provide entertainment. Poets, or storytellers, are important and valued in Bedouin culture. Because few Bedouins can read or write, poets function as historians and educators as well as entertainers.

Bedouin loyalty goes first to the extended family. No one can survive the hard desert life alone. Other people are essential for shared chores and protection. But the meager desert offerings cannot support whole clans, let alone tribes, in the same spot at once. The family unit is large enough, yet small enough, for safety and survival in the desert. Intense feelings of loyalty and dependence are fostered and preserved in this unique family group setting. Home is viewed as people, not place.

One way the Bedouin extended family is strengthened is through consanguineous marriage (marriage to a close relative). A Bedouin girl marries young, at about 14 years of age. For several reasons, her ideal spouse is a first cousin: She is already familiar with her cousins, having grown up in the same camps; a husband cannot mistreat her with fathers and brothers nearby; she can remain near her mother and sisters; her future children will enhance and perpetuate the group; and the dowry she brings to the marriage will remain within the family. For centuries, intermarriage has bound Bedouin families to one another and to their culture. (In fact, the very conservative Wahhabi sect and the Saudi royal family intermarried generations ago, and some writers have suggested that the religious conservatism of this theocratic nation was strengthened by this union.) Thus it is not surprising that Saudis are much more collectivistic and more likely than U.S. Americans to denigrate out-group members (Al-Zahrani & Kaplowitz, 1993).

The Forces of Progress

Bedouin life remained constant for many hundreds of years. Until oil. The discovery of the treasure trove beneath the desert has affected every Saudi citizen, and that includes even these inscrutable, self-sufficient nomads. The wandering Bedouin lifestyle, which withstood the severity of the desert, is succumbing to the forces of progress.

What are these forces? First, camels were once the main source of Bedouin income. But Saudi preferences have changed as beef has become more available through international trade, modern domestic transportation systems, and improved refrigeration methods. Camels are now an expensive hobby rather than a primary source of food. Second, more Bedouins are taking permanent jobs in towns for a steady income, requiring them to settle nearby. Third, they like the conveniences that make life easier: canned tomato paste for rice, flashlights, portable radios, insulated coolers, sewing machines, and trucks. These possessions are cumbersome to haul to a new camp every few weeks. Fourth, some of their locales have been breached by oil pipelines, highways, storage tanks, and industrial sites. Fifth, the Saudi government wants them settled.

The government considers the Bedouin a disruptive element. They do not pay taxes, their trucks are unlicensed, their women do not always wear veils and often drive, they can disappear at will into the desert, and their loyalties are to the tribe rather than to the government. Basically the Bedouin refuse to be controlled, which is threatening for an absolute monarchy like the House of Saud.

Along these lines, it is interesting to note that many Egyptians and Kuwaitis, when discussing Saudi Arabia, frequently employ a mild form of put-down by saying: "Oh, those Bedouins!" Once again, such statements, while stereotypic, suggest that Saudi Arabia does indeed have a distinctive national culture.

Some governmental efforts to settle the Bedouin have not been very successful. Housing for the Bedouin has been built in major population centers, but most of it does not meet their needs and remains empty. The desert dwellers feel cramped in the stationary rooms, and they are baffled by appliances. They prefer carpets spread on sand rather than on hard concrete floors. Most of the housing units are small and designed for nuclear families, with high privacy walls between houses. Because there is no place for their animals, sometimes Bedouin families will camp outside their new walls and keep the animals inside the house.

A more appropriate governmental attempt to encourage settlement is to bring necessities to the desert. Water trucks and nurses visit the more permanent camps. Sometimes cash grants are distributed. Special hospitals that have campsites right outside the rooms treat Bedouin patients. The government recruits young men for Bedouin National Guard units, where their strength, agility, and desert skills are highly valued. These transitional measures are somewhat successful, and increasing numbers of Bedouin are settling permanently. Only a small number of Bedouin wander Saudi Arabia today.

Most Saudis feel ambivalent about the Bedouin. The nomads are envisioned as simplistic, dirty, and crafty—in general, uncivilized. They are both ridiculed and feared. Yet they are admired for their virtues of generosity, boldness, and courage. Bedouin are idealized, much as knights and cowboys are in other places. But no matter how far Saudis are removed from the desert, the Bedouin ethos is the bedrock of their culture. Prince Alwaleed, one of the richest men in the world, frequently holds meetings with international business leaders in luxurious desert camps near Riyadh.

Jewelry as Wealth

Silver Bedouin jewelry is one of the few art forms of the desert dwellers, made all the more beautiful by their spartan surroundings. But it is more than adornment; it is also a woman's personal wealth. Usually a woman acquires her first jewelry as part of her dowry. Later on, family savings are invested in either jewelry or livestock. The designs are similar from one woman to the next, although the cost varies depending on the silver content. It is impossible for an amateur to determine the amount of silver in a particular piece. In this way, all women can own similar types and amounts of jewelry, regardless of financial status. A woman will choose to wear certain pieces every day and then add other pieces for special occasions.

Traditional Bedouin jewelry is purchased from either settled artisans or itinerant silversmiths, the vast majority being men. Sometimes a craftsman will live among a tribe, if it is a large one. His workmanship ranges from exquisite to crude, but all of it is eye-catching. Necklaces, bracelets, rings, belts, earrings, nose rings—the kinds of jewelry worn by women everywhere are worn by Bedouins, too. The artisan incorporates multiple silver beads, chains, bells, and cylindrical pendants into his basic designs. Then he adds filigree, heavy granulation, and gemstones. The stones can be amber, coral, carnelian, garnet, or turquoise; sometimes they are only colored glass or plastic. The stones are often associated with specific beliefs and values, with red being the most popular: Coral is associated with wisdom, and garnet is associated with the alleviation of some illnesses. Turquoise, which is said to glow when the wearer is happy, along with coral and amber, has been among the most common stones used in Bedouin silver jewelry. Many pieces have tiny objects placed inside of bells and pendants that rattle melodiously with movement. Others have Koranic verses permanently sealed within cylindrical charm cases. Craftsmen add one item that is unique to Bedouin jewelry: coins.

Progress now threatens the popularity of Bedouin silver jewelry, just as it does the Bedouin lifestyle itself. Townspeople prefer gold jewelry, and as the Bedouin people leave the desert, they are also beginning to choose to work in gold. In addition, many of the silversmiths are retiring, and younger people are not interested in pursuing the trade. Westerners living in Saudi Arabia who are interested in handcrafted items are largely credited with keeping the craft alive. Still, traditional silver jewelry can be studied as a metaphor for Saudi culture. Salient features of Bedouin jewelry are its bold form, handcrafted appearance, traditional design, and female ownership.

Bold Form

To an outsider, Bedouin silver jewelry is overwhelmingly ostentatious. Westerners would feel garish and conspicuous wearing the favorite Bedouin styles: multiple chains, pendants, bells, and coins, decorated with knobs of thick granulation and strands of filigree, inlaid with colored stones—all in the same piece. One, called a *kaff* (glove), has a ring for each finger, a section for the back of the hand, and a bracelet, all connected with chains and bells. Sometimes a piece will have only one type of decoration, such as a ring with filigree, but the decoration will be used very liberally for an exotic effect.

Likewise the Saudi personality is lavish, too. Saudis' generosity is legendary. When entertaining, they overwhelm their guests with abundance. Saudis are proud to serve two or three times the required amount of food, and they insist that guests consume more than their fill. The host typically does not eat along with his guests. He walks around checking on everyone's intake, urging them on and plying them with additional courses.

Good personal relationships are valued professionally and individually. Saudis will do almost anything for even a casual friend. They like to be helpful and endeavor to fulfill expectations. But an oral promise has its own value as a generous response, even if action does not follow. Results can be a separate thing altogether. For themselves, Saudis do not hesitate to ask for special favors, for rules to be bent, or for special treatment (Nydell, 1987).

Opulent Language

Just as the silver jewelry of the Bedouin gives the owner an aura of opulence, the Arabic language surrounds Saudis with a mystique of extravagance and vitality. Saudi Arabia is the birthplace of Arabic, and Saudis are secure in the belief that their language is superior to all others (Khalid, 1979). Arabic has phonetic beauty, rich synonyms, rhythmic cadences, and majesty. The structure of the language encourages repetition and exaggeration. But thoughts themselves are often vague, and sometimes only general meanings are implied. The language overemphasizes the significance of words in themselves and underemphasizes their meaning. This unbounded medium has far-reaching effects.

In the first place, eloquence and verbosity are equated with knowledge. Like silver jewelry that appears expensive but has low silver content, an effective speaker can appear prudent and rational by using his verbal skills. Poets are held in high esteem, and they frequently mesmerize and motivate audiences to action. Advanced education and sophistication do not reduce an Arab's susceptibility to a good sermon or a political harangue. The grace and fluency of the words count more than the logic and veracity of the argument (Khalid, 1979). Therefore oral testimony is considered superior to circumstantial evidence, businessmen often get bogged down in language as they trail off from the main point, and students are better at memorizing course work than using it.

Bedouin jewelry is bold in design, but the individual components of each piece are often flamboyant as well. Perhaps this is related to the Saudi's characteristic generosity and feeling of superiority. More must be better. Or possibly it is *proxemics*, which Edward T. Hall (1966) describes as "man's use of space as a specialized elaboration of culture" (p. 1). Certainly Saudis love to have ample space in their homes. Ideally ceilings should be high and views unobstructed. A sitting room may have 25 chairs arranged around the edges, with what seems like a cavernous speaking distance between them. But in public, Saudis do not mind being crowded.

Privacy in Public

In fact, Hall (1966) concludes that Saudis do not have any sense of privacy at all in a public place. They find it difficult to understand that privacy can exist while being surrounded by other people. No zone of privacy surrounds Saudi bodies in public. Consequently, they are not bothered by the jostling and noise of public places in the Middle East. Lack of public privacy zones explains their aggressive behavior at accidents, where Saudis surround the scene, yell advice, and shake their fists—even if they did not witness the incident. It is not unusual for them to join haggling sessions they happen to come across. They nonchalantly cut off other drivers, perhaps because they believe no one has a right to claim the public space into which they are about to travel.

Rarely do these situations lead to physical confrontation. Actual violence is almost unheard of here. Likewise, as a country, Saudi Arabia does not invade enemy territory, although it often engages in strong rhetoric. In fact, Saudis are premier mediators. They aim for consensus, although their initial position may be extreme. They willingly make concessions and expect others to reciprocate (Adler, 2007).

There is not much concept of personal privacy, either. The Arabic word closest to *privacy* means loneliness. Saudis feel that friends should see each other often, and there is no compunction about dropping in unannounced. Greetings are effusive and extensive: "Praise be to Allah," "Welcome to you," "Hello, friend." Common inquiries center on the state of a person's health or the cost of a recent purchase but never refer to female family members. Saudis are quick and generous with praise for others and like to highlight their own accomplishments as well (Samovar & Porter, 1994).

Geert Hofstede (2001) concludes that Arab countries score 53 out of 100 on the masculinity scale, giving them a rank of 23 out of 53 nations. This average score might seem surprising, but feminine societies stress solidarity, emotional displays, relationships among people, and resolution of conflicts by compromise. Masculine cultures stress achievement, competition, and resolution of conflicts by violence. Arab culture incorporates several of Hofstede's feminine characteristics. In the more recent GLOBE study (House et al., 2004), gender egalitarianism was defined as the way in which societies divide roles between men and women. Although Saudi Arabia was not included in the study, the Middle Eastern cluster, which included countries such as Egypt, Qatar, and Kuwait, scored low on gender egalitarianism; this could be an indicator of Arab societal culture.

Handcrafted Appearance

The second feature of Bedouin jewelry is its handcrafted appearance. While some of the jewelry shows intricate and precise workmanship, other pieces are crude and casually made. This does not diminish or detract from their desirability, however. Both kinds are considered legitimate, just as the Saudi considers the Bedouin to be both desert riffraff and the embodiment of deep cultural values. According to Gardner (2003), the Bedouin occupy a distinct and complex position in the Saudi cultural milieu: Although they are often disdained as uneducated, provincial, and irreverent, they fascinate their compatriots with their perceived resilience and fierce independence, thus inspiring pride and admiration. Cursory examination of the jewelry leaves no doubt that both types are handmade: Bells are often mismatched, pendants have irregular shapes, stones are slightly jagged, granulation is lumpy and uneven, fasteners are often simple hemp strings, and cheap cloth backings are attached to prevent the wearer from burning her skin. These raw aspects of the jewelry mirror the harshness of desert life.

Saudis believe in fate: that people have little control over their lives. Bedouin jewelry reflects this acceptance in several ways. The jewelry itself represents an adaptation to life in the desert. The cloth protects from the hot sun, the gemstones are found locally, and the coins are acquired from trade caravans and pilgrimage routes—all demonstrating improvisation, using what is at hand.

Saudis have traditionally felt "subjugated to nature," as defined by Florence Kluckholn and Fred Strodtbeck (1961, p. 13), living at the whims of their natural environment (and Allah). Fate decreed that they accept these natural forces, but economic advancement has meant leaping to "mastery over nature." Today desalinization plants process drinking water, irrigation systems water crops, and drilling equipment extracts oil and natural gas. Creeping sand dunes are still a problem. Saudis are becoming expert at mastering nature, but their mind-set is still fatalistic.

"Being" is more important than "doing" in Saudi culture. Adler (2007) defines a being orientation as a condition in which people, events, and ideas flow spontaneously within the moment. The future is not nearly as important as the past and the present; present gratification is not delayed for future gain. You could say people with a being orientation live for today. Fate and Allah are in charge of the future.

Edward T. Hall (1983) suggests that time is not fixed or segmented for polychronic people. Time is considered loose and fluid rather than compartmentalized. Therefore occasions do not have definite beginnings and endings, and schedules are not as important as people. Saudis are polychronic and irreverent about time boundaries. Consequently, guests may be kept waiting, deadlines are often missed, and appointments are broken. Polychronic people are able to carry on many activities simultaneously. For example, several customers may be helped at the same time, or different business negotiations may be managed simultaneously in the same office. This behavior exemplifies the being orientation.

Traditional Design

The Bedouin favor traditional styles of jewelry that are decorate and valuable. Styles worn today are the same as the ancients wore, and they are always silver. New and unusual designs are seldom crafted. Individualism and creativity are discouraged in both Bedouin silversmithing and in Saudi culture. This country ranks 26th of 53 nations on Hofstede's (2001) scale for individualism, which places it on the collectivist side of the spectrum. Collectivism is having a "we" consciousness, belonging to a cohesive in-group beginning at birth, and taking the group's opinions as one's own. Private opinions and individual achievement are not highly valued in this setting. The more recent GLOBE study (House et al., 2004) places the Middle East cluster of countries (Turkey, Egypt, Kuwait, Qatar, and Morocco) at the high end of the collectivism scale.

One of the strongest manifestations of Saudi collectivism is the family. The extended family is the norm, although with new prosperity, more nuclear families are living alone. Even then, other members are either close by or in the same walled compound, the Bedouin camp replicated in modern times. These families collectively form clans, tribes, and the nation of Saudi Arabia. Like a piece of Bedouin jewelry that has several components, which are assembled by silversmiths through the process of soldering, the country has distinct segments also.

For Saudis, family is paramount. It determines how they think, whom they marry, and where they work. Familial involvement is not viewed as interference but is welcomed as support. Loyalty to family takes precedence over work or friends, and it is rewarded with protection by the group. In the workplace, relatives receive preferential consideration in hiring and promotion opportunities. Families never leave a member in need. There are no daycare centers or nursing homes. The oldest male member is honored as head of the family. Children are reared not only by their own parents but by all adults in the family. In fact, friends will feed, care for, and discipline others' children. This results in a remarkably homogeneous upbringing for the country's young. Like the desert nomads, people with this background cannot comfortably live alone. To be separated from the family is the ultimate punishment.

Honor and Shame

Honor and shame are major features of modern Saudi culture, just as they were in camel-raiding days. When people's honor is tarnished, they feel shame and lose face. So does their family, which by association is also shamed. Members of collectivist cultures place importance on fitting in harmoniously and saving face. Honor can be lost through being stingy, treating the old and weak poorly, fathering only daughters, being passed over for special favors, and through the immoral sexual conduct of female family members.

Understanding the importance of honor and shame in Saudi culture provides insight into certain behaviors. Mackey (2002) maintains that shame is a factor in Saudi generosity. She even argues that hospitality is provided to add to the giver's reputation, not necessarily to benefit the recipient. Fear of making a mistake and suffering the resulting shame may explain substantial delays in the business world. Many Saudis drink or gamble when outside of their country, even though these acts are forbidden by Islam. In fact, Westerners flying into Saudi Arabia are often surprised by the Clark Kent–Superman behavior of returning Saudis, who quickly take off their Western attire and don traditional Arab clothes before departing the airplane. Perhaps Saudis feel honor is not lost if no one is there to bestow shame.

Another cohesive force, besides family and honor, is marriage. The marriage model is the same for modern Saudis as it was for the nomads. Partners are chosen by elder family members. Marriage is such a momentous undertaking that young people welcome the group's opinion. Although it is rarely invoked, both the man and the woman have the right of refusal and can ask for another choice when selecting a mate. Marriage to first or second cousins is common. The benefits of keeping money and people in the family supersede any genetic concerns. Most marriages take place before age 20, and the new couple usually lives with the husband's family (Mackey, 2002). However, larger dowries and college educations are pushing this age higher. New marriages are based not on romantic expectations but on a desire for companionship, children, and, later, love. Although Muslims may have up to four wives, most men have only one at a time. Prince Alwaleed is married to his fourth wife, Princess Ammeerah, having divorced three others. They have a modern marriage that is more like a partnership, and she works for his company and travels the world with him. She believes that "Islam is something you carry within" and does not wear a *burkha*. At the wedding of Britain's Prince William and Kate Middleton in 2011, the Saudi prince was in traditional attire, and his young wife was in a tan lace dress with a very stylish hat and no veil. An old proverb states, "A man between two women is like a lamb between two wolves" (Peters, 1980, 24).

The Role of Religion

Religion is like the hemp that draws all the parts of a Bedouin necklace together. All Saudis are Muslim. The king is not only their political leader but their religious leader as well, and the Koran is the framework for running the country. Piety is honorable for a Saudi, and religion is not separated from daily life. Fatalism is expressed by the frequent use of the qualifier *inshallah,* or God willing. A Muslim's greatest joy comes from performing the *haj* or pilgrimage to Mecca. The charm cases incorporated into silver jewelry contain verses that praise Allah and ask for daily protection. Permeating the cohesion of family, honor, and marriage are the inviolate religious beliefs of Saudi Muslims.

Saudi Arabia ranks 7th out of 53 nations on power distance (Hofstede, 2001), which is the extent to which less powerful citizens accept that power is distributed unequally. The culture is also high context, which means that only a small amount of information must be explicitly stated for understanding to occur because so much information is implicit. In short, Saudi Arabs adhere to many written and unwritten rules, tolerate hierarchies, follow formalities, practice obedience, and encourage conformity. However, the construction of the Royal Mecca Clocktower just south of the grand Mosque in Mecca and the division of the holy city along class lines, with the rich inside air-conditioned high-rises and the poor pushed to the periphery, is generating a lot of criticism from those who feel that all these grand makeovers should stop at the gates of Mecca, which they see as an embodiment of an Islamic ideal of egalitarianism (Ouroussoff, 2010).

Female Ownership

Custom and tradition play prime roles in the acquiring and wearing of Bedouin jewelry. What is striking is that it is wholly female. Not many other joys of Saudi culture belong entirely to women. Their reasons for wearing adornment are universal: vanity, superstition, sentiment, and pleasure. Ownership bestows honor on the wearer as a woman of property and guarantees her the security of having negotiable assets. Her wealth also adds beauty to an austere desert life. Bedouin jewelry is rarely old. Unlike Western jewelry, often handed down through generations, a Bedouin woman's jewelry is generally melted down upon her death. It would be unacceptable to a new bride (Ross, 1979). Sometimes, in times of dire need, it is sold to augment the family's finances.

Like the serendipitous nature of Bedouin jewelry, the role of Saudi women contains surprises, too. The world disdains the limitations under which Saudi women live, but perhaps outsiders are not qualified to pass judgment. What do Saudi women themselves think?

Saudi females do not necessarily see themselves as repressed. Many think of themselves as protected and are frequently shocked at the crimes such as rape and physical beatings that their Western counterparts suffer. Neither men nor women want to subject females to the stress, temptations, and indignities of the outside world. Most women feel satisfied that the present system provides them with security and respect, and they pity the rest of the world's women. Besides, even though males head the family, women have enormous influence inside their own homes. Through their extended family they have wonderful support systems. Women do not defer to their husbands in private as they do in public. As elsewhere in Saudi life, there is much discussion between a husband and wife when they have a difference of opinion. This, then, has been the world of Saudi females for centuries.

The long black *abaya* and veil, the separate entrances for men and women, and the prohibitions against their driving may seem less protective today and more restrictive today than they once did. The barriers to change are daunting, although change has occurred in other Arab countries. Some Saudi women have already started pressing for greater personal and social freedom, while at the same time realizing what they will be losing. Like the flamboyant desert jewelry that has adorned Bedouin women for centuries, the traditional life of Saudi women will slowly lose its luster. In February 2009, King Abdullah reshuffled his cabinet and chose the first ever woman minister, Norah al-Faiz. In 2011, a group of Saudi women used Facebook, Twitter, and YouTube to organize a mass mobile protest against the ban on driving. Manal al-Sharif, one of the campaign organizers and an information technology specialist, was detained on charges of disturbing public order and inciting public opinion. Some women felt that the topic of women drivers was such a lightning rod that raising the issue might set back efforts to gain more important freedoms, such as the right to vote or an end to the legal guardianship that allows men to control every aspect of a Saudi woman's life (MacFarquhar, 2011).

Saudi Arabian culture is rooted deep in the desert, where the Bedouin people developed an incredible ability to survive under extreme conditions. Most Saudis feel they are of this desert, even if they have no Bedouin ancestry. For hundreds of years, Saudi values and beliefs were safe, sheltered from the outside world. For hundreds of years, Bedouin women proudly wore their distinctive jewelry, with its bold form, handcrafted appearance, traditional design, and female ownership. With Bedouin jewelry, we can create a metaphor for modern Saudi Arabian culture.

The perception of the jewelry has undergone radical change in recent years. There may soon come a time when the country's values and culture are challenged at their core as well. The vision for the future is to turn the country into a major industrial power by 2020, and this is to be accomplished partly by building six new cities throughout the country with industrial centers, which will double as housing and commercial hubs (Mouawad, 2008). Saudi Arabia has one of the largest economies in the Middle East and is an important political power in the region. The Saudis are well aware of the democratic movements surrounding them. In 2011, more than 100 Saudi activists, writers, and academics warned King Abdullah about corruption, nepotism, and "the widening gap between state and society" (Coy, 2011). Saudi Arabia's future is inextricably intertwined with that of the world, and it behooves us to understand the forces that shaped its rich past and those at play in the present that will shape its future.

CHAPTER 5

The Turkish Coffeehouse

Coffee should be black as hell, strong as death, and sweet as love.

—Turkish Proverb

What came through was not a country divided, but a glimpse at a rapidly growing nation together in common cause. If Turkey's national character can be conveyed in sport, it showed up on Sunday and fought until the end.

—Charles McDermid, reporting in *Time* magazine on the World Championship International basketball final game Turkey lost to the United States, September 13, 2010

Turkey is a remarkable land of contrasts. Joining the continents of Asia and Europe, it has elements of old and new, Islam and Christianity, mountains and plains, and modern cities and rural villages. Often referred to as the cradle of civilization, Turkey is filled with archeological remnants of the ancient Greeks and Romans along with treasures of the sultans and caliphs of the Ottoman dynasty, which began in the 12th century and officially ended in the early 20th century. Perhaps most interesting of all are the people of Turkey, rich in emotions, traditions, and hospitality. Turkish origins can be traced to the Mongols, Slavs, Greeks, Kurds, Armenians, and Arabs. Like the Thais, the Turks have never been conquered or colonized by other peoples in the modern era. This distinction, along with a geographic boundary straddling two continents, makes Turkey unique. Turkish culture today is a marriage of Turkish traditions and Western ideologies.

Turkey is a mountainous peninsula slightly larger than Texas, and it shares borders with Azerbaijan, Georgia, Armenia, Bulgaria, Greece, Iran, Iraq, and Syria. Considered a strategic location due to its control of the straits linking the Black and Aegean Seas,

Turkey was the only NATO country other than Norway to border the states of the former Soviet Union until 1999, when Poland joined NATO. The western portion of Turkey, Thrace, is located in Eastern Europe, while the larger eastern section, Anatolia, is part of Asia. Of 75.8 million people, 80% are Turkish and 20% Kurdish, and about 26.4% are less than 15 years of age. Armenians, Greeks, and Jews also make up a small proportion of the population. Adult literacy estimates are at 88.7%, and the average life expectancy is about 70.3 years for men and 75.2 years for women. Turkey ranks number 67 out of 179 nations on the 2011 Index of Economic Freedom (T. Miller, 2011). This suggests that Turkey is a relatively good nation in which to do business in terms of such measures as corruption and bureaucracy. It has a GDP of US$735 billion and a GDP per head of US$9,940. Unlike almost all other Islamic societies, the Republic of Turkey was established in 1923 as a secular democratic nation. However, a small but growing minority would like to see Turkey become once again a theocratic nation. The Turks are proud of both their achievements as a modern state and their rich heritage.

An appropriate metaphor for understanding Turkish culture is the coffeehouse, a part of everyday life in Turkey. In the oft-cited famous words of the great Turkish 20th-century poet, Yahya Kemal, coffee has created its own "culture" in Turkey. What the Turkish coffeehouse represents is quite different from its counterparts in other countries. An emphasis on both Islam and secularity is the first of four characteristics of the coffeehouse that mirror Turkish culture. Coffeehouses also provide an important forum for recreation, communication, and community integration. Moreover, the customers who frequent coffeehouses reflect a male-dominated culture. Finally, the Turkish coffeehouse found in villages and towns is modest in comparison to the exotic taverns, distinguished pubs, and chic cafes that are found in the larger cities.

A Unique History

Before we can understand how these four characteristics of the coffeehouse reflect Turkish culture, we need to know something about the unique history of Turkey. Ancient Anatolian civilization dates back to 6500 BCE. As early as 1900 BCE, the Hittites occupied Turkey. About 700 years later, the Phrygians and Lydians invaded the land. These early Anatolian groups ruled until the Persian Empire took hold in the 6th century BCE. Then the Greek-Hellenistic rule emerged, followed by the Romans in 100 BCE. Each succeeding group left its mark on the people by contributing customs, language, and trade practices.

In the year 330 CE, Constantine the Great named Constantinople (today's Istanbul) the capital of the Byzantine Empire. Arabs relocated westward, and by 700 CE the empire included Anatolia, Greece, Syria, Egypt, Sicily, the Balkans, most of Italy, and some areas of North Africa. Turkish tribes began to migrate from central Asia to Anatolia in the 1000s. The Oguz Turks, who embraced the new religion of Islam, occupied a vast part of Anatolia during the 11th century. After their setback during the

Crusades, Turkish *gazis*, or Islamic warriors, fought against the Byzantine Empire and began to build the Ottoman dynasty. The Ottomans conquered the region and expanded their reign to the Christian Balkans. In 1453, the Ottomans conquered Constantinople, which was virtually the last stronghold under Byzantine rule. Constantinople was then rebuilt as the capital of the Ottoman Empire and the center of Sunni Islam.

The Ottoman Empire reached its peak of wealth and power under the rule of Suleiman the Magnificent in the 1500s. He controlled all or part of territory that included present-day Turkey, Iran, Iraq, Egypt, Israel, Syria, Kuwait, Jordan, Saudi Arabia, Albania, Algeria, Libya, Lebanon, Tunisia, Greece, Bulgaria, Sudan, Romania, Hungary, Yugoslavia, Czechoslovakia, Ethiopia, Somalia, Cyprus, and parts of the former Soviet Union. His vast empire reached into three continents and was noted for its system of justice and support of the arts, literature, architecture, and craftwork. The Europeans called him the Magnificent, but the Ottomans also referred to him as *Kanuni* or the Lawgiver. His legal influence by itself earned him an important place in Islamic history. A recent television series portrayed scenes of Suleiman lusting over his most coveted queen, Roxelana, and drinking goblets of wine. This TV series placed him in the center of a major row pitting secular Turks against Muslim conservatives. Even the actor who played Suleiman received death threats ("Controversial Turkish Television," 2011). For almost 6 centuries, the Turks lived in or near Europe and interacted with Europeans, assimilating parts of European culture. Sultan Suleiman's death in 1556 marked the end of a wonderfully creative era. The Ottoman Empire was the greatest military power in the world and successfully administered a multitude of ethnically and religiously diverse, settled and nomadic communities ranging from the Unitarian Hungarians to the Iraqi Turkmen (Mango, 2010). The empire began its decline with the loss of Hungary and the Crimea in the 1700s. In the next century, the Ottomans lost control of Egypt and most of the Balkans, and this was followed by the loss of Serbia, Romania, Cyprus, Algeria, and Tunisia.

In 1908 a coalition called the Young Turks attempted to restore power to the empire. However, instability in the region brought about drastic territorial changes and reduced the Ottoman holdings even further. The shrunken empire entered World War I on the side of the Central Powers in 1914. By the end of the war, the Arab provinces were lost, and a nationalist movement began. These events led to both the proclamation of a new nation and additional contributions to Turkish culture.

In 1923 the Treaty of Lausanne established the Republic of Turkey as we recognize it today. Mustafa Kemal Pasha, also known as Atatürk, renounced all prior conquests and introduced widespread, radical reforms to guide the country. *Atatürk* literally means "father of the Turks." His deliberate reforms transformed the diverse empire into a nation while shaping daily lifestyles for every Turkish citizen. Along with the internal modernization of the country, the republic turned toward Western principles and conventions. Turkey became a member of NATO in 1952 and has the second-largest standing force in NATO, after the United States, and the eighth-largest number of active troops in the world. It also became an associate member of the Common Market in 1963.

Turkish coffee was first introduced during the Ottoman Empire. In the 15th century, merchants from the Far East traveled along the Silk Road to trade their spices and other wares in European markets. To encourage trade and offer hospitality, hostels for travelers called caravansaries were built. As they passed through ancient Turkey, merchants bartered along the way and offered their products in exchange for hospitality. According to the strictest interpretation of the Koran, the sultans forbade the drinking of coffee because it is a drug. In spite of this restriction, drinking coffee became so popular that the palace rescinded the rule and allowed its consumption. Today, Turkish coffee is as popular as ever.

Islam and Secularity

One of Atatürk's most important reforms was the adoption of a constitution that encouraged secularism. Although an overwhelming number of Turkish citizens are Muslims (about 99%), other religions, such as Greek Orthodoxy and Judaism, are tolerated in Turkish society. During the rule of the Ottoman Empire, religion as well as culture was totally integrated with government, and Islamic world power was concentrated in Turkey. Atatürk and his followers felt strongly that adherence to the caliphate was an obstacle to the country's attempts to Westernize. Major changes resulting from secularism included a shift from Islamic to European legal codes, closing of religious schools and lodges, and recognition of the Western calendar rather than a religious one. Despite these sweeping changes, Islam still thrived, and in the 1950s religious education was reintroduced. Today the Turkish government oversees a system in which children are exposed to a measure of religion in schools and the clergy receive salaries from the government.

A Secular Nation

This distinction between Turkey and the other Islamic nations is noteworthy: Unlike most other Islamic countries, Turkey is a secular nation. Governments, schools, and businesses are operated independent of religious beliefs. Even traditional clothing, such as veils for women and the fez for men, were abandoned in the shift from Islam to secularity. Consequently, Islam does not affect daily Turkish life as much as it does in an Arab nation. Religious power over Turkish institutions is nonexistent, and this fact reflects a preference for association with other Western cultures.

However, as noted above, a growing political movement has evolved around the issue of making Turkey a theocracy comparable to some of the Arab nations. While Turkey has a Western-style system of government in which there are free elections, the military has often seen itself as preserving the constitution and has not been above overthrowing governments if it felt that the secular nature of the constitution was threatened. Since Prime Minister Recep Tayyip Erdogan and his political party, the Justice and Development Party or AKP (2002), came to power, the economy has prospered, numerous former and current military officers have been jailed for corruption, and the balance of power—formerly military first, then Islam, and then business—has shifted to give more power to the prime minister and business. In the summer of 2011, chiefs of staff in the military resigned en masse to protest the arrest of officers accused of trying to overthrow the government. For the first time, their successors were appointed by a civilian government. Tayyip Erdogan, who has led the country since 2003 and whose AKP won a decisive victory again in 2011, is considered to be the most successful politician of his generation. Ironically, in 1999, he was imprisoned for 10 months for reciting a century-old poem that the country's generals, responsible for enforcing Turkey's constitutionally mandated secularism, found offensive and capable of inciting religious hatred (Foroohar, 2011). One of the challenges facing the new government as this book goes to press will be the writing of a new constitution in the context of a representative government. This is seen as an opportunity for the prime minister to either move toward greater democratic freedoms as promised or consolidate his own power.

Although Islam does not influence state matters, its traditional practices, such as women wearing headscarves in public, have generated controversy. In 1999 Merve Kavakci, a Texas-educated politician in the Virtue Party, created an uproar by appearing in parliament in a headscarf. Almost immediately an appeal was filed with the Supreme Court to outlaw the Virtue Party for this and other assumed infractions. Furthermore, Mustafa Karaduman has become a successful businessman by establishing an Islamic-style clothing chain for women. One of his creations is the *nesrin*, an ankle-length skirt with a long jersey to which a hood is attached. Conservative Islamic women can easily take the hood off in places like parliament where it is banned (Zaman, 1999). The headscarf ban has become one of the most emotional issues in Turkey, signifying a power struggle between an increasingly wealthy middle class of observant Turks on the one hand and the secular elite of the judiciary and the military on the other (Tavernise, 2008). In 2010 the top military leaders boycotted a function where the wives of both the president and prime minister wore headscarves. In the cafes of Istanbul, people actively debate the pros and cons of allowing the veil, and some people see the issue as a clash between tradition and modernity and Islam and democracy.

The influence of Islam is also evident in the five times designated for prayer each day. Turkish Muslims do not necessarily converge on the mosque when the call to prayer is sounded, the way Catholics in such nations as Poland and Ireland flock to church for Sunday Mass at specified times. Islam is a religion in which individuals communicate directly with God without a need for intermediary spokespersons. Consequently those who pray at mosques do not need to coordinate their visits, although many arrange their visits to coincide with one or more of the five daily prayer periods. Afterward Turks may head to the coffeehouse for refreshments and socializing.

The Pillars of Islam

Five well-known pillars embody the essence of Islam. The first is acceptance of the creed, "There is no God but Allah and Muhammed is his prophet." The second pillar comes from the Koran, or Holy Book, and involves keeping life in its proper perspective. This can be done through praying five times a day to submit oneself to God's will. Third is the observance of the holiday of Ramadan by fasting during daylight hours for a month as determined by the lunar calendar, and fourth is giving *zakat* to support the needy equivalent to 2.5% of one's net worth. Fasting underscores humanity's dependence on God, teaches self-discipline, encourages compassion, and forces one to think. The final pillar is for those who are able to make the pilgrimage to Mecca at least once in a lifetime. It is understood that those who reach the holy city where God revealed himself have demonstrated their devotion.

In Turkish towns, the two most important places for social gathering, the mosque and the coffeehouse, are located in the town square. Throughout the world, inhabitants of small towns tend to be more conservative than city residents, and Turkey is no exception. As a result, the Turkish townspeople tend to follow their faith more strictly than their urban counterparts. Also, eastern and central Turkey is more religious than western Turkey, due in part to the diversity of the people living in the western region. Although there has been a resurgence of religious practices since the 1950s, Islamic fundamentalism remains a minor, if vocal, influence today. Nonetheless, even moderate Muslims have tried to revive some traditions that were eliminated with the arrival of a secular nation. The coffeehouse is often adjacent to the village mosque and may even provide a small operating fund or rent for the general upkeep of the mosque. In addition to rent, many coffeehouses occasionally collect donations from patrons to pay for the mosque's water and cleaning. As noted above, Muslims are called to prayer five times each day, although the frequency of prayer for contemporary Muslims is a function of both the level of piety and the availability of time. Thus a visit to the coffeehouse can also be considered a ritual ironically linked with the daily ritual of prayer. Furthermore, cleanliness is an important related Islamic value, and the owner of a coffeehouse typically squirts a bottle of water on the floor from time to time to keep the dust from rising. Some of the original popularity of coffeehouses was due to the Islamic prohibition of alcohol and the use of coffee as an acceptable substitute beverage.

Many other Turkish cultural values and beliefs, not associated with the coffeehouse, are derived from the Islamic faith. In particular, Muslims believe that the future will be better than the past. Village parents who struggle to support their children may rely on this optimism for decades. Also, the ideas that the soul lives forever and that people are responsible for their actions are important considerations for Muslims in accepting their lot in life.

Even today, 26% of employment is in the low-paying agricultural sector, even though it contributes only 9% of GNP. In contrast to their role in small towns, some of the beliefs and practices of the Islamic faith that are suitable for an agricultural people have become problematic in modern cities like Istanbul. For example, the Muslim Feast of Sacrifice—3 days of killing sheep, which are given in 3 equal portions to family members, friends, and charity—has horrified animal rights groups and created health issues in crowded cities. The Istanbul government has created several municipal sacrificial centers to decrease health problems and make the sacrifices as painless as possible.

The Ottoman Empire governed the people by Sharia, or Islamic law. Turks also adhered to moral and social rules, such as respect for their father, on a daily basis. In modern Turkey, however, unlike in purely theocratic Islamic nations, legal issues are not judged by one code alone. Likewise civil marriage ceremonies must be conducted whether or not there has been a religious wedding to obtain recognition under Turkish law. Civil code based on European models was introduced in 1926. Still, basic customs from the Ottoman days, just like the coffeehouse, have been carried over into modern Turkish society. Some Turks still refuse to accept interest accrued from savings accounts because such profits are prohibited in the Koran. Widely used Turkish phrases derived from Islam include *salaam* or *selam*, a friendly greeting that literally means "peace be upon you," and *mashallah*, which means "God protect you from harm." Both phrases are used in everyday language, in much the same way that U.S. Americans respond with "God bless you" when someone sneezes. Other examples include abstinence from or moderation in drinking alcohol, fulfilling oral promises, and using the catch-all expression "*Bismillahir-rahmanir-rahim.*" This translates to "In the name of God, the Merciful, the Compassionate," and is said when starting a task—be it a journey, a test, a wedding, or a meal.

Family Values

In Turkish tradition, the household extends beyond the nuclear family, and individuals are loyal to the entire family or kinship group. Women, especially, are expected to offer hospitality to all guests. If visitors knock on the door before or during mealtime, they are almost always invited to join the family in the dining room or at the kitchen table. As in mosques, Turkish guests offer to remove their shoes as a gesture of cleanliness on entering someone's home. Marriage decisions are influenced by families in rural areas, and in some instances dating is not permitted. Of course, these are merely generalizations about Turkish customs and do not apply to all Turkish citizens, particularly those living in large cities. Turkish compassion and hospitality come from the ethical aspects of the Islamic faith, as do racial equality and religious tolerance. Islam acknowledges the legitimacy of the other Semitic religions that preceded it but deems both Judaism and Christianity incomplete.

Part of the greatness of the Ottoman dynasty is attributable to Islam, which brought together different peoples and united them through spiritual means. When

Muslim warriors conquered an area, they did not kill the people, and they allowed residents to practice their religion, although as second-class citizens. Still, this was an advance over Christians in the Middle Ages, who frequently gave conquered people a choice of conversion to Christianity or death. Bernard Lewis (1995) points out that the Ottoman dynasty was much more socially advanced than Europe until the beginning of the 18th century, in large part because Europe practiced hereditary feudalism. While land was given for exceptional service in the Ottoman Empire, it provided only rent and space in which to live to the grantee; at his death, the land was not given to his heirs but returned to the empire.

The concept that every event in people's lives is predetermined has its roots in the religion of Islam. Like many other religions, Islam attributes circumstances beyond one's control to a supreme being. Muslims believe that people will act according to their own decisions under a given set of circumstances. For example, much of the younger population is migrating to cities to obtain jobs and better schooling. This trend does not reflect anyone's fate in particular, but people who decide to change their lifestyle by leaving the village subject themselves to Kismet, or chance. In other words, God meant for that person to move on and start a new way of life. If someone eventually relocates back to the village, that, too, is Kismet. This belief allows an individual's shortcomings to be more easily accepted.

God's Will

The Turkish orientation toward time goes hand in hand with the belief in destiny. It is easy to say that many Turks are not very time conscious, and one of the attractions of the coffeehouse is that customers can linger there if they so choose. Hosts and hostesses are concerned if their guests do not arrive promptly at the time given for an invitation to a social event, but they are very understanding. Delays at airports and train stations are not a cause for alarm. Polychronism best describes the Turkish ability to concentrate on different things simultaneously, whether at work, at home, or in the coffeehouse. Although schedules and appointments are important, especially in Western-oriented firms, people and relationships are also valued. To the polychronic Turks, time is intangible and supports the development and maintenance of long-term relationships. Elements of the past, present, and future tend to merge, and they permeate Turkish values and norms. However, large, multinational Turkish corporations place much more emphasis on being time-conscious, even if employees revert to polychromic behavior outside of work.

If Turks were asked to ponder the ideal position of their country in international dealings, they would probably refer to the halcyon days of the Ottoman Empire. In fact, some view Turkey's attempts in recent years to become a major regional player in the Middle East as a neo-Ottoman approach (Peet, 2010). Understanding the history of the country is crucial to understanding the Turkish mind-set, and a comparison of today and yesterday is vital. Conversely, Turks place much emphasis on what future generations will accomplish. This explains why parents want their children to get optimal educational opportunities, irrespective of cost and sacrifice. Kismet and time orientation are inextricably linked in Turkish culture.

Understanding the idea of destiny helps us to comprehend why time is relatively unimportant. In the United States, if a business project falls behind schedule, a firm risks embarrassment and scrutiny by consumers, investors, shareholders, and the government. In Turkey, the same type of delay is attributed to God's will and is more easily forgiven. Thus the phrase *Inshallah* ("if it is God's will") is heard quite often. A famous Turkish joke illustrates the degree of urgency in daily business:

> One day, a fellow named Nasreddin Hodja brought some material to a tailor and requested that he measure him and make a shirt from the material as soon as possible. The tailor measured him and said, "I am very busy but your shirt will be ready on Friday, *Inshallah.*" Nasreddin Hodja returned on Friday, but the tailor apologized that the shirt was not ready and said, "Come back Monday and, *Inshallah*, it will be ready." On Monday, Hodja went back to the tailor only to find out that the shirt was still not finished and was told, "Try again Thursday, *Inshallah*, and I promise it will be ready." This time Hodja wisely answered, "How long will it take if we leave *Inshallah* out of it?"

Recreation, Communication, and Community Integration

Coffeehouses became popular during the 16th century. The coffeehouse has always been a place to get information, especially when illiteracy rates were high. In those days, one person would read the newspaper to an eager audience. Throughout the reign of the Ottoman Empire, defense strategies were discussed and developed there. Until the middle of the 20th century, coffeehouses served as production and exhibition places for folk literature. Coffeehouses had battery-operated radios before they were introduced in homes, and the same was true when television arrived. Today patrons enjoy camaraderie when viewing a soccer match at the coffeehouse instead of watching it on television by themselves at home, and this pattern fits the group-oriented lifestyle of the Turks.

Turkish men go to the modern-day coffeehouse to become part of a group. They feel very comfortable when surrounded by friends and family and prefer the stability of belonging to an organization to individualism. And, as an old Turkish proverb states, 1 cup of coffee is worth 40 years of friendship. According to Bisbee (1951),

> The prime ingredients of the Turks' idea of fun and amusement seem to be relaxation, imagination, sociability and humor. Sitting is almost, if not quite, the most popular recreation of all. Turks sit at windows, in gardens, at coffeehouses . . . anywhere and everywhere they can see a pleasing view and relax in conversation. (p. 145)

In Turkey there is a relationship between collectivism and accomplishing the goals of the group. In small villages, the coffeehouse is often the setting in which important village decisions are made. Prior debate of the issue also takes place at the coffeehouse. A custom, *imece*, describes a Turkish social gathering at which everyone pitches in to help a neighbor undertake a large task, such as building a new home. In many instances of *imece*, the initial request for assistance and plans for the event are proposed at the coffeehouse. Turks prefer to approach problems in a logical but personalized manner, and they will discuss practical solutions at length in the coffeehouse. In small Turkish towns, the mayor can frequently be found at his second "unofficial" office, the coffeehouse. It is not uncommon to find community notices tacked onto a coffeehouse bulletin board. Typical examples are government announcements that crops will be sprayed with pesticides on a particular date or that a public hearing to discuss a new water project will be held. Messages are also left there for others who will eventually pass through; the coffeehouse is the information center in which most communication takes place, including political discussions and gossip. Being a "member" of the coffeehouse is considered important, regardless of the topic under discussion.

Women also have a need for affiliation; they get together at weekly coffees or teas at the homes of friends. The weekly coffee presents an opportunity to show some hospitality and become involved with others. Traditional Turkish hospitality extends to strangers as well, particularly in rural areas.

The group is highly valued, and individual identity is determined on the basis of group membership. Conformity to group norms and traditions is expected; trust and reliance within the group is important (Dindi, Gazur, Gazur, & Kirkkorpru-Dindi, 1989). In Geert Hofstede's (1991) 53-nation study of cultural values, it is not surprising that Turkey clusters with those nations emphasizing collectivism rather than individualism. In the more recent GLOBE study (House et al., 2004), which distinguishes between societal institutional collectivism and in-group collectivism, Turkey scores in the same band as the United States with respect to institutional collectivism but much higher, along with India, on in-group collectivism practices. These scores may very well reflect the unique position of Turkey as a geographic and cultural balancing act between the East and the West.

Collectivism at Work

Even at work, collectivistic values are expressed in unusual ways. At McDonald's the "employee of the month" is not selected for outstanding work. Rather, the selection is made on a rotational basis. Furthermore, because Turkey also clusters with high power-distance nations in Hofstede's (1991) 53-nation study (and this remains unchanged in the recent GLOBE study findings [House et al., 2004]), there is little, if any, two-way discussion with or participation by subordinates in many firms. However, Turkish managers link collectivism and power distance—and by extension a distinctive concept of employee participation—by telling employees that they are an essential part of the organization and that, as long as loyalty is shown, they will not be fired, even if performance is substandard.

As might be expected in a collectivistic culture, communication tends to be high context in nature. For example, if someone says, "It is very hot," people assume that the person wants a ride in their car. This indirect form of communication is common, even among very close family members.

Family gatherings are very important, as are deep friendships. Turks are nostalgic when it comes to family traditions and special occasions. Just as a man can stop by the coffeehouse whenever he wants, so too it is not considered impolite to drop in at a friend's home without an invitation. This is true regardless of economic, social, or educational status. Fostering good relationships requires time, and Turks feel that such time is always well spent.

Coffeehouses open early in the day, and for many Turks, they are the place to stop in before beginning the day's work. In the late afternoon, workers stop in prior to going home to their families. After dinner many men visit the coffeehouse to catch up on the latest news. In the summertime, customers sit outside on sidewalks or patios to escape the oppressive Turkish heat and catch an occasional cool breeze. In the winter, everyone gathers around the warmth of a stove or furnace in the coffeehouse. Just as the Italian piazza is the place to stroll to see others and be seen, the village coffeehouse provides a place for social gathering.

People Who Need People

In Turkish culture, involvement and interdependence are the ideal. Turks care about others, and they show their concern by stopping to help perfect strangers. People are important in Turkish culture, and most Turks will sympathize with those who are less fortunate. Above all, Turks pride themselves on hospitality and being helpful to strangers. The typical response to a traffic accident illustrates this aspect of Turkish culture. Within moments of the accident, everyone who witnessed the collision, along with those who did not, is on the scene. No one present would dream of minding his or her own business. Strangers then offer help, comments, and interpretations of the accident, and chaos results. If a vehicle breaks down at night, Turkish passers-by generally do not hesitate to stop and offer assistance to the driver. To ignore someone in distress would be considered indecent. By contrast, many U.S. Americans would not dare to stop for fear of threats to their personal safety.

However, these customs are decreasing in importance in urban areas, particularly Istanbul, which suffer from all of the problems associated with rapid migration from rural areas. As in other countries, residents of rural areas are drawn to the cities because of opportunities for work and diversity of experiences. Pockets of extreme poverty, many times in and around downtown areas, have arisen. Militant Islam, which was previously strongest in the rural areas, is on the increase in urban areas, at least in part because of such conditions.

Whether sharing small talk at the coffeehouse or offering hospitality in their homes, the Turkish people tend to be curious. Consequently, very little in people's lives is a real secret. Communication is the essence of Turkish existence. When one Turkish stranger meets another, one typically asks the other where he or she is from. Of even more interest is who the stranger's parents are and where they are from. The next few minutes are spent quizzing each other with questions like "Oh, my brother-in-law's uncle is from there. Do you know Ahmet?" or "Surely you must know Ali." "Turkish geography" is really a game played to discover to which clan the stranger belongs, as happens in other countries such as Israel, India, and Ireland.

A Male Domain

A Turkish coffeehouse is a place where men assemble throughout the day and throughout the year. Regardless of age, men gather at the coffeehouse to play back-gammon, share gossip, or just enjoy company. Young boys accompany their fathers and play alongside the tables until they are old enough to join discussions. Old men sit on wooden chairs and sip coffee while reminiscing, offering words of wisdom, and solving the world's problems.

A visit to the Turkish coffeehouse is a favorite pastime for male Turks of all ages. As in bygone eras, the village coffeehouse remains a center for all males, regardless of income, education, or social status. But this is less true in the larger cities, and the traditional coffeehouses are becoming associated with unemployed workers and those from the lower socioeconomic rungs of society. There is even sometimes a small stigma associated with frequenting such a coffeehouse, especially among adults who are assumed should be working full-time or going home to a family dinner.

A correlation can be drawn between the prominence of coffeehouses and cultural values in cities versus rural areas. In the larger cities of Istanbul, Ankara, and Izmir, life is hectic, and people have little time to sit and chat. However, Turkey is still an agrarian society in large measure; again, 26% of the workforce is in agriculture. People working outside industrialized areas are often limited by weather conditions and daylight. With extra time on his hands, a farmer may visit the coffeehouse, and it is a welcome diversion for a man out of work. Coffeehouses remain popular in rural areas where Turkish traditions and male roles are strong. The popularity of the city coffee-house, on the other hand, has declined as a new generation places less emphasis on traditional values and a greater emphasis on earning a living. Within the city, older citizens tend to be more devout and frequent the coffeehouse more than younger Turks, who often spend most of their leisure time on activities such as cinema, theater, and concerts as alternatives to the coffeehouse.

As cities become more cosmopolitan, coffeehouses in less populated locales are more likely to attract clientele than urban coffeehouses. The coffeehouse remains a cherished institution outside of the cities, where lower- and middle-class customers enjoy good coffee and good conversation, and city dwellers recognize its historical importance and speak of the coffeehouse fondly, even when they don't frequent one.

Male Dominance

There is no question that Turkey has a male-dominated culture, and the nature of such domination is ever present at the coffeehouse. According to the findings of the GLOBE study (House et al., 2004), Turkey had low scores on the dimension of gender egalitarianism practices, which indicates that the society generally believes that biological sex should determine the roles of members in homes, business organizations, and communities. While women are welcome, the coffeehouse has always been considered a male domain, especially in Anatolia where it may be rare to see a female customer. In major cities, on the other hand, anyone can go into coffeehouse and have a drink or two.

The Islamic origins of the population still influence the role of women. For example, most women pray at home rather than at the mosque. The killing of women and girls by relatives who believe that the females have brought shame to the family (honor killings) has plagued Turkey and other countries. In 2007, however, the Turkish government took unprecedented steps to campaign against this horrific practice by soliciting the help of imams, pop music stars, and soccer celebrities (Wilkinson, 2007c). In 2011, 13 European countries signed a Council of Europe convention in Istanbul on battling violence against women through providing hotlines, battered women shelters, and legal aid for abused women. Turkey reportedly spearheaded the effort. A moving 2010 German film, *Die Fremde* (roughly translates to "the Stranger" but titled as *When We Leave* for wider release), captures not only some of the issues relating to abuse of Turkish women but also the clash of immigrant cultures with the value systems of Western host countries (in this case Germany).

Even in Western-oriented Istanbul, which accounts for about 40% of Turkey's GNP, the separation of sexes is evident. During the day, there always seem to be eight men to every two women in public places, and at night, the number of women decreases significantly.

A long tradition of men as breadwinners, leaders of the family unit, and decision makers in local politics and matters of national concern exists in Turkey. As heads of the families, men in rural areas decide which crops will be planted and at which market crops will be sold. Village coffeehouses often become a market where brokers trade farm commodities. Within the clan structure, it is understood that sons will be in charge of the family and daughters will marry into their husband's family. As in other Western cultures, sons carry on their family name. Within the traditional family, a father's request is always obeyed, and Turkish fathers are especially protective of their daughters.

A Modest Environment

The simplicity of the coffeehouse itself is noteworthy. The furniture is basic, and the chairs are uncomfortable. A typical coffeehouse in a small village may consist of one small room, a kitchen, and several small wooden or aluminum tables and chairs. A smoky atmosphere from cigarettes or *nargile*, the traditional waterpipe, is unmistakable. Although each coffeehouse differs, the sounds are always familiar: Steady chatter, heated discussion, and hearty laughter can be heard above the clatter of cups and saucers, and Turkish music comes from a radio or TV. Likewise, the Turkish people are concerned more with substance than form. The true draw of the coffeehouse is the opportunity for release and self-indulgence. The release is only temporary, allowing escape from the stress or monotony of the moment, and the indulgence reflects the element of Turkish culture that says "experience life."

As noted earlier, Turkish life in the city is very different from that in the village. In the cities, neighborhood coffeehouses abound. However, the middle and upper classes in the cities tend to spend time at various elite establishments, such as bars or cafes, instead of being loyal to a particular coffeehouse. Apartment living is very popular in Turkish cities. Turks are less transient than U.S. Americans and tend to live in the same building for years, where they are surrounded by family and friends. Simply put, people are valued in Turkey. Respect for others is important; however, like other Mediterranean peoples, Turks have little fear of consequences for failing to respect laws. Along with liberal interpretations of traffic signals, patience is not a Turkish strong suit. A prime example is the early morning scene when workers try to catch a bus. It's "every man for himself" as people struggle on the downtown streets of Ankara to get on the crowded buses. In most other situations, however, Turks have considerable respect for the rights of others.

Coffeehouse Operations

The traditional coffeehouses are family-run establishments. Often the owner's son takes orders and delivers teas and coffees to the table. People should not expect to be served a meal there; however, patrons are more than welcome to bring in food. Many hungry patrons will first stop at a local carry-out for a freshly baked snack. *Simit*, a round flatbread topped with sesame seeds, is a familiar sight at coffeehouses. A coffeehouse owner does not mind food being brought into the coffeehouse because he knows that the more food eaten, the more drinks will be ordered. Unlike Turkish restaurants, coffeehouses invite customers to remain as long as they wish. Coffeehouses are also distinguished from cafes as places where table games like bridge and backgammon are played without the pursuit of any material gain. The coffeehouse is not a high-profit enterprise. By the same token, it is rare that a coffeehouse folds, because coffeehouses provide a valuable service to the community as a meeting place and information center.

Turkish coffee is always made in a special way. First the grains are ground into a fine powder, then water and sugar are blended with the powder, and finally the mixture is boiled over a flame. The three possible versions of Turkish coffee are *sade, orta,* and *sekerli,* which mean no sugar, some sugar, and more sugar, respectively. At the coffeehouse, the waiter will call out the orders to the kitchen so fresh pots can be made. When he returns, the waiter never seems to remember who ordered what. A running joke is that one day Atatürk, who is greatly respected by the Turks, went to a village coffeehouse with his entourage. The waiter took everyone's order and brought the coffees to the table. Atatürk was amazed that the waiter had gotten the order correct and told him so. When asked by Atatürk how he remembered, the waiter responded, "Yours is the only order that counts!"

Life Outside the Coffeehouse

Many activities occur outside of the coffeehouse, and we need to understand them as well and the manner in which they reflect cultural values. For example, observance of Islam in Turkey today has led to popular misconceptions about the role of women. Since the adoption of this religion more than 1,000 years ago, conservative ideas have evolved, including the seclusion and submission of women to men as a form of protection for them. At one time, women were expected to retreat to the harem out of deference to men. However, even in the harem, women had some degree of power in terms of training daughters and young sons in household management, arts and crafts, and religion. The harem was highly political; concubines were selected for sultans by their mothers, and royal marriages were arranged in the harem in those days. In 1925 the wearing of veils by Turkish women was officially discouraged. In the following year, Atatürk introduced civil marriage codes that abolished polygamy and established divorce and child custody rights for both men and women.

Women's Roles

As in earlier times, Turkish women have always been capable of subtly influencing their husbands' way of thinking. In Turkey women are brought up to show respect for their husbands, and they do not openly flaunt any power they may hold over their men. Turkish women rarely make firm denials of a husband's decision, yet they may quietly oppose decisions with which they are unhappy. In either case, the wife recognizes the needs of her husband's ego and is typically shrewd enough to offer small suggestions rather than demand compliance with her wishes. Many Turkish women possess an emotional inner strength and maturity that developed from the burdens of maintaining a stable family life under harsh economic conditions. This is particularly true for those who live in remote areas. In rural villages, women are responsible for meals, housework, and child care. Turkish kitchens are busy all day long as women prepare delicious meals of roasted lamb, rice pilaf, or other specialties. Throughout Turkey women take pride in a cooking style that intermingles Arabic, Greek, and European influences. An important development for women in the villages is that they have become responsible for working outside the home, too. External employment is often a necessity for women, who will work outside of their homes on local farms and in factories or will sell handmade items to support their families. Beautiful woven carpets, ceramic pottery, mosaics, and other items handcrafted by Turkish women are appreciated throughout the world. The women's determination in taking care of daily life affords them some measure of power over their husbands' behavior. Women who work in the fields cook, eat, clean, and even sing together.

Urban wives, who may be on a more equal educational footing with their husbands, may also affect men's behavior and take part in decisions as trivial as recommending what clothes a husband should wear or as monumental as deciding to risk a new business venture. Finally, career-oriented women reflect modern Turkish societal norms, which recognize joint decision making and cooperative patterns of husband-wife authority, along with traditional respect for the husband. It should be noted that families still supervise closely the activities of unmarried women, and strong attitudes prevail about the proper conduct for women.

Turkey was one of the first countries to give women the vote, more than 70 years ago, but most Turkish party leaders are men. In 2007 Turkish women launched a unique protest against their lack of representation in parliament that featured famous women pop stars and business leaders sporting fake mustaches in ad campaigns, sending the message that you had to be a man to be in parliament. Women represent about 14.1% of the parliament; this statistic is behind those of other Muslim countries such as Afghanistan (28%) and the United Arab Emirates (UAE) (23%). Women's associations in Turkey contend that there are two "faces" of women in their country: the democratic and Western-oriented women and the political party–driven women who are more conservative. According to the 2010 Global Gender Gap Index, Turkey ranks 126 among 134 countries. However, the 2011 election did see an increase in the number of women deputies in parliament, from 50 in the previous election to 78.

The Extended Family

Respect for parents is absolute. In turn, parents are expected to be concerned about their children's future. The extended Turkish family is proof of the respect afforded to elders. Grandparents, aunts, uncles, and cousins often live in the same dwellings or nearby as part of the core family unit. The notion of an assisted-living home for elders is nonexistent. Likewise, hired babysitters are unusual because family members care for children. Parents are willing to stretch the family budget to provide tutors or send children to better schools. Most parents feel obligated to give their children a moral education as well. Children are a continuation of a family's reputation, and famous children are an even greater source of pride for doting parents.

Boys and girls are brought up similarly with a few exceptions. Prior to reaching 7 years of age, boys are circumcised in a religious ceremony that symbolizes their ascent to manhood. Upon graduation from high school, men have a mandatory 18-month period of military service. Men who attend a university have the option of deferring their service until they reach 32 years of age. There is no compulsory service for women, although they are allowed to enlist for noncombatant positions if they desire. Traditionally, new brides became part of their husband's family only after they had produced an heir. Except in rare circumstances, this is no longer true. Today, Turkish daughters-in-law are immediately accepted into the family household. The family structure is important, and the divorce rate is relatively low. In Turkey, it is unusual for people to live on their own, unless they are students living in dormitories.

Education and Class

Another significant reform, the right to education for the masses, took place in 1924. Atatürk believed that education was an essential element of Westernization. Today education is seen as the legitimate discriminator for the social classes in Turkey. Elementary school is mandatory for all children. As in the United States, the school year begins in September and ends in June. In keeping with national policy, secularity is practiced. Although *laik*, or separation of church and state, is practiced, school vacations coincide with the Islamic holidays Ramadan and Kurban. In addition to monitoring regular schools, the Turkish Ministry of Education also controls religious schools to limit their influence. For those schools with limited resources, the school day is taught in half-day shifts. Wearing uniforms is required of young children. A dress code also requires neat grooming, including conservative haircuts for boys and hair ribbons for girls with long hair. Children learn respect for teachers at an early age. In the classroom, students normally stand whenever a teacher enters, and it is considered disrespectful to disagree with the teacher.

The curriculum includes mathematics, science, history, Turkish language, art, music, physical education, and morals. In larger towns and cities, tutors are often hired to complement formal school instruction. For those students who score well, the next year is spent at a private secondary school to learn a second language, most often English, French, or German. The language study is followed by 2 years of preparation for high school. Students attend high school for 3 years, and on graduation, those who wish to continue their studies at a university take a difficult entrance examination. Students who do not score as well on the initial placement exam attend a general secondary school, followed by entry into a vocational or technical school to learn a trade. Vocational students interested in entering a university are also invited to take the entrance exam.

The competition to attend universities is keen due to the limited number of universities in the country. Each year, about one fifth of the students who take the entrance exam are accepted. There is an obvious inequity in this system. Those who are privileged enough to have access to better quality academic resources have a better opportunity for admission to a university. Furthermore, within the universities, many disciplines have a limited number of student spaces available. Thus university students may aspire to a profession from which they are effectively barred, unless they are able to study for that profession abroad. While selection by an institution is competitive, interaction among students is cooperative. It is common practice for students to work together on homework. Students tend to take studying seriously and to appreciate their learning opportunities.

The Use of Humor

Humor is an important mechanism in Turkish culture and is a good way to make friends and maintain friendships, both in the coffeehouse and outside of it. Turkish humor is distinctive; Turks do not mind making fun of themselves. When things become too serious, a joke is welcomed to strike a balance and provide relief. The coffeehouse itself provides a similar relief from life's predicaments. Whether in political satire, television shows, or within the coffeehouse, humor is used frequently. For example, Turkish coffee is served in a small cup and has a thick, almost muddy, consistency; it is usually served with a glass of water. A popular joke involves differentiating between Turks and foreigners. The difference? Turks drink the water first to clean their palates; foreigners take the water after the coffee to wash it down.

Humor is taught early on, and folk heroes such as Nasreddin Hodja are loved by children and grown-ups alike. As a boy, the Hodja always had something clever and humorous to say in every situation. Hodja stories are well known and relate to everyday life in Turkey. A favorite story goes as follows:

> The Hodja was walking down the street when he noticed something glittering in the gutter. He ran over to pick it up and noticed it was a small metal mirror. He looked in it and said to himself, "No wonder they threw this thing away. I wouldn't keep something as ugly as this either!"

What makes the Hodja special is that he always expresses a note of encouragement and tries to live a happy life of honesty and simplicity. The subjects of his jokes run the gamut from religion to mothers-in-law to sultans and even to his own hearty appetite. Not only are his jokes retold at the coffeehouse, they often begin with "One day when the Hodja was at the coffeehouse . . . ." The proof of this character's popularity is that many people in Turkey like to claim that the Hodja was born in their village.

Humor is an effective communication technique and can even serve as a way to avoid confrontation and conflict. Turks are generally quite modest about their accomplishments. This makes sense because besides being impolite, boasting would tend to separate people from their groups. Instead, it is perfectly acceptable for good friends or family members to brag about others. Modesty complements the Turkish values of tactfulness and diplomacy. Turks prefer to avoid confrontation and to handle disputes indirectly whenever possible. Being direct is considered rude and insulting; directness goes against the respect Turks feel for other people (Dindi et al., 1989). Respect for authority is highly regarded and unconditional in many instances. In his 53-nation study, Hofstede (1991) showed that uncertainty avoidance epitomizes Turkish culture. However, this seems to have changed over the last several years because the GLOBE study (House et al., 2004) indicated a score of 3.63 for Turkey for society practices of uncertainty avoidance as compared to 4.15 for the United States and 5.37 for Switzerland, which had the highest score.

Looking Ahead

Turkey faces considerable challenges in the near future. The question of Kurdish independence still needs to be addressed for the estimated 12 million to 15 million Kurds who live in Turkey; the army waged a fierce war with them during the 1990s. In 2008, Turkish forces attacked the guerrillas of the Kurdistan Workers Party (PKK) by land and air over Iraqi sovereign territory and imprisoned at least 2,300 Kurdish activists since 2009. In general, however, the ruling AK party has had better relations in the last few years with the Kurds, both those within Turkey and the two Kurdish parties that jointly administer the autonomous region in northern Iraq that shares a border with Turkey.

Although the Turks would prefer further integration with Western Europe, Turkey has not yet been offered full membership in the European Union (EU), as "Turko-skepticism" continues over the AK party's more openly Islamist foreign policy ("Coming Apart?", 2006). Some Europeans are concerned that Turkey is shaping an independent foreign policy and becoming a major regional player. The government has tried to reintegrate the region by lifting visa requirements and promoting a Middle Eastern free-trade zone with the common free-trade area already agreed upon by Turkey, Syria, Jordan, and Lebanon (Shadid, 2011b). An independent foreign policy ("zero problems with the neighbors") gives Turkey more clout as a strategic player in the Middle East and the Muslim world, one that, many believe, the West would do well to cultivate and offer a seat at the table (Stephens, 2010).

Analyzing Turkey's future prospects, Peet observes in a special edition of the *Economist*, "The World in 2011," that while leaning toward the East, Turkey still needs to look West toward a liberal democratic Europe. Some vexing problems still need to be resolved. For example, disputes over Cyprus continue to strain Greek-Turkish relations, terrorism exists within Turkish borders, and Turkish minorities in the Balkan states are persecuted.

On the other hand, the future holds promise for Turkey. The end of the Cold War, growing support for full integration of Turkey into the EU throughout the world, and important Turkish energy resources provide hope for increased stability in the region.

Water projects on the Tigris and Euphrates Rivers will help provide better irrigation of Turkish farmland when completed. Trade with many of the EU countries and Russia now totals hundreds of billions of dollars each year. Trade between Turkey and Iraq amounted to US$6 billion in 2010, almost double that of 2008. In Iraq, Turkish companies are upgrading gas pipelines, refurbishing hotels, helping to build a 65,000-seat stadium and amusement parks, and have already built an international fairground in Basra, southern Iraq (Shadid, 2011a). Following the global economic crisis, which hit Turkey's trade with Europe (around half of Turkish trade), the "Anatolian Tigers" or small- and medium-sized entrepreneurs from Turkey's heartland have been looking at opportunities in Africa. According to Turkey's exporters association, Turkish exports to Africa have leaped from US$1.5 billion in 2001 to over US$10 billion in 2009 ("Ottoman Dreaming," 2010). The Turkish economy, which has merited inclusion in the G-20, has survived the global financial crisis well and is growing at a rate second only to China's (Mango, 2010). Together, these events demonstrate that Turkey possesses a good amount of strength and resilience and is poised to play a major role in the region. Although it may be a while before Turkey is accepted into the EU, EU membership may now be less attractive to the economically successful and proud Turks, with support falling in recent years to 38%, according to a poll conducted by the Italian foundation Compagnia di San Paolo and the German Marshall Fund of the United States in 2010. Surprisingly, support rebounded to 48% in 2011, but this figure is still much lower than the 73% in 2004 (Kalaycıoğlu, 2011).

This, then, is our portrait of Turkey, a traditional agrarian nation that is seeking to modernize rapidly. The coffeehouse reflects many of the important values and behaviors of the Turks, particularly the relationship between Islam and secularity, recreation, communication, community integration, male dominance, and the importance of substance over form within such a modest environment. Although Turkey is changing, its citizens still recognize the historical and cultural importance of the coffeehouse, even when they frequent it only periodically. Thus there will always be a place for the coffeehouse in Turkey, especially in the rural areas and small towns that still dominate life in this country.

CHAPTER 6

Dòn Gánh: The Two Sides of Vietnam

After the 1954 Geneva international conference, Vietnam was divided into two parts. On paper, North and South Vietnam were twin countries born at the same moment.

—Nguyen Cao Ky, former prime minister
of South Vietnam (1965–1967)

I n Ho Chi Minh City, an impeccably dressed businesswoman glides through the front doors of Louis Vuitton, ready to browse the store's new arrivals. On the edge of the city, women gossip as they sit by the side of a main road, displaying collections of brightly colored fruit and fresh baguettes for sale to the noisy stream of passing traffic. A land of serene beauty and bustling cities, Vietnam is a country of contradictions that continues to enchant visitors from around the globe. It is a nation in which modern design and ancient architecture, cutting-edge technology and traditional artisans coexist side by side. Vietnam exists in a delicate balance, symbolized by the vendors who traverse the streets of its cities and villages, all carrying their wares on a *đòn gánh* or a pole with a basket suspended at either end. As we will see, Vietnam seems to need to consider and manage adroitly the delicate balance between tensions or opposing dualities. These include North and South; individualism versus collectivism and harmony; change from the old to the new; life inside and outside the family; and inequality versus equality.

These carrying poles seem to be ubiquitous. They are of various lengths, and the size of the two baskets can be adjusted to the strength of the worker using it. Thus a carrying pole for a physically fit adult male will be different from that of a child. The pole is generally made of bamboo.

With 1,000 miles of coastline, Vietnam is about the size of California and home to 88.5 million, a population nearly one third that of the United States. GDP is US$90.6 billion, and GDP per head is US$1,050. About 90% of the country's population is ethnic Vietnamese, with about 2 million ethnic Chinese making up the largest minority. English is replacing French as the preferred second language. In 1954 the country was divided into two regions, north and south, linked by a long, narrow, mountainous area known as the center, or Hue region—the ancient capital of the Vietnamese kings. A country of great scenic beauty, Vietnam is geographically diverse. The 20% of the country that is level land is complemented by tropical lowlands, rugged hills, densely forested highlands, and the Red and Mekong River deltas. All contribute to Vietnam's rich agricultural tradition, and 52% of the population is involved in farming activities. However, agriculture provides only 22% of the GNP. Vietnam is bordered by China, Laos, and Cambodia in addition to the Gulf of Thailand, Gulf of Tonkin, and South China Sea.

Even a short-time visitor to this nation easily becomes entranced by its beauty. Halong Bay in the north, for instance, seems mystical; mountains are scattered throughout the bay, and some of these have fantastic caverns. Many Vietnamese consider it one of the Wonders of the Modern World. The hill tribes (the Hmong), living in the mountains of the far north, are a visual delight, especially on market day when they dress in their bright and colorful traditional manner. Hoi-An, Vietnam's chief port from the 16th to the 18th century and a UNESCO World Heritage Site, emerged unscathed by war. Its 844 buildings represent the traditional architecture favored by Chinese, Japanese, and Vietnamese traders of that era. These and many other delights await the curious traveller.

The Socialist Republic of Vietnam is a constitutional republic dominated by the Communist Party. As the governing body, the National Assembly elects both the country's president and prime minister; the president is the head of state, while the prime minister is the head of government. The majority of government positions are held by Communist Party members, who decide which candidates will run in elections and set the guidelines for all major governmental policy initiatives. Many consider the most powerful position in the country to be that of the Communist Party general secretary.

Buddhism is the main religion of Vietnam. Morrison and Conaway (2007) point out that the Communist government describes Buddhism as currently in decline, but it accepts the proposition that 70% of the Vietnamese are "strongly influenced" by Buddhist traditions. While 70% are nominally Buddhist, any Vietnamese, similar to their counterparts in some other Asian nations, tend to practice two or more religions, each for different occasions and purposes. Some still believe in traditional spirits of the mountains. In addition, about 10% are Catholic, a legacy of French colonialism and domination from the 17th century until 1954. Still, the major religious influence on Vietnam has been Buddhism and, to a lesser extent, Catholicism. At the same time, many customs that are distinctly Vietnamese manifest themselves at weddings and funerals and in ancestor worship. While these customs vary from region to region, a perceived core is regarded as uniquely Vietnamese. For example, a village funeral usually involves an ornamented carriage in which the deceased is placed and then is drawn by a few of the stronger villagers to the burial site.

The economy of Vietnam is a direct result of its recent history and political turmoil. Centuries of colonial domination and more recently the ravages of civil war have been exacerbated by the loss of Soviet financial support and the inflexible control of a centrally planned economy. While the modern economy strives for internationalization and decentralization, the government is still very involved in business with state-owned enterprises, which produce about 40% of GDP. The reform of the 1980s continues today as the government strives to modernize the economy and to produce a more competitive, export-driven industry. Vietnam joined the World Trade Organization (WTO) in January 2007 after a long negotiation process and in 2010 became a negotiating partner in the development of the Trans-Pacific Partnership trade agreement.

The economy faces challenges from high inflation (11.8% in 2010) and from falling foreign exchange reserves, an undercapitalized banking sector, and high borrowing costs. On the 2011 Index of Economic Freedom, Vietnam ranks 139th of 179 nations. As indicated previously, this scale integrates 10 measures, including fiscal soundness and openness to trade and investment, government size, business and labor regulation, property rights, corruption, monetary stability, and financial competition (T. Miller, 2011). The nation still needs to see significant improvement on the Index if the economy is to continue on a positive course.

History of Occupation

Vietnam has been under the control or influence of other sovereigns for much of its history, beginning with China, which ruled Vietnam for nearly 1,000 years from 111 BCE to 939 CE. Over this time China imparted knowledge, political institutions and systems, and the importance of education. Today, visitors to Hanoi can stroll through the grounds of the Temple of Literature, the site of Vietnam's first university, which was established in 1070 and opened officially in 1076. Originally, as in other Southeast Asian nations, Buddhist monks served as professors. As Chinese rulers integrated Vietnam politically and culturally into the Chinese Empire, they introduced Confucianism as the official ideology. Confucianism is frequently regarded as a religion but is more appropriately viewed as the Chinese code of conduct.

As a result of high migration during this period, many people in north Vietnam have Chinese ancestry. In particular, the Hmong people, a collective of Vietnam's largest ethnic minority who live in the mountainous area, are renowned for their striking traditional dress, with its intricate and brightly coloured embroidery. Patterns and jewellery subtly vary among subgroup members. As indicated above, tourists travel to the far north of the nation just to be there on market day. The language of Vietnam was influenced greatly by the Chinese, and until the 19th century, Chinese ideographic forms of characters were used as written Vietnamese (Ralston, Terpstra-Tong, Maignan, Napier, & Nguyen, 2006). Chinese art, architecture, and music all had their own effect on their Vietnamese equivalents.

The Chinese were responsible to a certain extent for the cultural values that have a foundation in ancient literature. Less than a century ago, mastery in literature, along with martial arts, gained one the highest status in society (Thang, Rowley, Quang, & Warner, 2007). The legacy of this system is the use of proverbs, sayings, and idioms in daily life that reflect the importance of education; for example, "If you want your children to be educated, you should love and respect their teacher" (Boston Public Schools, cited in Bempechat & Omori, 1990, p. 2). The Chinese were responsible to a certain extent for the cultural values present in ancient literature, including the key works of Confucius, Sun Tzu, and Lau Tzu (see Chapter 25).

The 17th century proved to be a period of French influence, which began when French Jesuit priests transcribed Vietnamese scripts into quốc ngũ, a Romanized language with a 27-letter alphabet. Quốc ngũ gained popularity in the 19th century and is the prevailing language in Vietnam today (Ralston et al., 2006). French colonization began in 1858, and by 1885 the French had effective control of the area. France gained control over northern Vietnam following its success over China in the Sino-French war (1884–1885). In October 1887, French Indochina was formed from Annam, Tonkin, Cochinchina (modern Vietnam), and the Kingdom of Cambodia; Laos was added later after the Franco-Siamese War. The French ruled as the colonial sovereign of Vietnam from 1862 to 1954. During this time, they changed the administrative, transportation, and school systems and contributed to growth in commerce and manufacturing. The French ruling class was largely Catholic and helped promulgate the French style of living. Colonialism did not improve the livelihood for the majority of the population; in the countryside, farmers struggled under the dual burden of heavy taxes and high rents. These farmers were, in effect, feudal serfs.

In 1940 during World War II, while France was defeated and partially occupied by Germany, Japan commenced border conflicts with the French colonial forces in Vietnam. After France fell to Germany, Japan sought a means of access through French Indochina to attack Nationalist Chinese forces near the border. With no support from the French authorities, Japan launched a ground attack. Two days later, Japanese aircraft bombed the port city of Haiphong, and the navy landed troops at the port. During 2 days of fighting, nearly 800 French troops were killed.

The Vietnamese Communists, led by Ho Chi Minh and Vo Nguyen Giap, commenced a resistance movement against the Japanese and French in late 1944 that was supported by the United States. General Giap, then a very young man, was trained by the U.S. Americans. He later became one of the most victorious generals in history, defeating the United States in the Vietnam War and defeating China, Japan, and Cambodia at different times. His victory over the French at the historic battle of Dien Bien Phu in 1954 is universally recognized as one of the 100 greatest battles in history.

The French Defeat and Division Into Two

As indicated above, the French suffered a historic defeat at the hands of the Viet Minh, also called the League of the Revolution and Independence of Vietnam, at the siege of Dien Bien Phu under the leadership of General Giap. At the time, the French were so confident of their military prowess that they set up their camp in a valley surrounded by large hills or mountains. The underresourced Vietnamese had only one strategic recourse: to take control of a mountain position with heavy firepower and shell the French constantly. At a horrific loss of Vietnamese life, the Vietnamese carried the individual pieces of a large gun up a mountain and were finally able to assemble it to begin the bombardment. Eventually the French were forced to surrender. This pattern of absorbing large losses because of Vietnamese patriotism in the face of overwhelming odds accounts for much of the military success under General Giap. The general also constantly reevaluated strategies that the Vietnamese had employed in past battles, regardless of whether they had resulted in victory or defeat.

We have already discussed some tourist highlights that reflect Vietnam's uniqueness. Among them, the miles of underground tunnels in which Vietcong lived while fighting the Americans in the Vietnam War stand out. One can now take a tour of these tunnels, many located around the former Saigon or Ho Chi Minh City, and Western visitors marvel at the ability of the Vietcong to live under such harsh conditions. It is not unusual for some Americans to begin the underground tour with the full expectation of finishing it, only to quit prematurely because of a sense of claustrophobia and physical discomfort.

Following the French military defeat, there was a peace conference in Geneva, Switzerland, in 1954. Laos, Cambodia, and Vietnam were granted independence, thereby ending France's domination in Indochina. At this time, Vietnam was divided in half. The south became the State of Vietnam led by Emperor Bảo Đại, while Ho Chi Minh led the Democratic Republic of Vietnam in the north. It was envisioned that the division at the 17th parallel, known as the Vietnamese Demilitarized Zone, would only be temporary.

However, Bảo Đại was ousted from the government of the South by Prime Minister Ngo Dinh Diem, who refused to hold the Geneva Accord–sanctioned elections. Friction grew between the North and South, and by 1958 the Vietcong (Communist-led guerrillas) had instigated clashes with the South Vietnamese government (Kahin & Lewis, 1967).

From 1945 to 1954, during the conflict between Vietnam and France, the South Vietnamese government received US$2.6 billion in financial support from the United States. By 1963 the United States had sent more than 16,300 advisors to South Vietnam, but despite this support, the Mekong Delta was lost to the Vietcong later that year. In 1965, U.S. involvement escalated, with President Johnson committing troops (536,000 in 1968) and commencing air strikes on North Vietnam.

In 1968, in what would later become known as the Tet Offensive, North Vietnam attacked South Vietnam during an official cease-fire for New Year celebrations (*Tet*). The massacres received widespread international media coverage and sparked demonstrations against intervention by non-Vietnamese in the war. It was considered a win by the North Vietnamese. President Nixon instigated "Vietnamization," a policy of American troop withdrawal from Vietnam to give the South greater responsibility for fighting the war. From 1968 to 1973, more diplomacy was attempted, and in January 1973, an agreement was achieved. The United States withdrew forces from Vietnam, and prisoners of war were exchanged. South Vietnam surrendered in April 1975.

In the Vietnam War, the first time the United States lost to a foreign adversary, it is estimated that between 2 to 3 million Vietnamese and 58,000 U.S. military died before the cessation of hostilities. It was the longest and most unpopular war in American history and left Vietnam in smouldering chaos with destroyed infrastructure, a decimated agricultural sector, a devastated population, and an unresolved civil conflict. To this day, the United States has been influenced by this defeat, and it casts a long shadow on the manner in which Americans talk about the formerly invincible fighting power of the American military and on the international policies their government pursues.

Millions of Vietnamese then fled their war-ravaged country. Work to address this humanitarian crisis was slow, with severe humanitarian and economic problems hampering efforts to rebuild the nation. At the end of the Vietnam War, the government commenced a large-scale campaign of collectivization of farms and industries. However, the policy was an economic failure and resulted in triple-digit inflation.

Supported by World Bank agrarian reforms of the 1980s, Vietnam's rural society made a fundamental shift from collective agriculture to family-owned land. From 1986, the *Doi Moi* policy of economic renovation put the nation on a path away from socialism toward a more capitalist model. The country's centrally planned economy was transformed into a state-managed market-oriented economy. Malarney (2002) argues that the goal of the socialist society involved strenuous efforts by the party and state to install a modern over a feudal outlook, a "scientific" over a "superstitious" mind-set. China had embarked on a similar model nearly 10 years earlier with comparable results (Thang et al., 2007). A survey by Ralston, Thang, and Napier (1999), in their study of nearly 800 Vietnamese managers, revealed a gradual merging of individualism and collectivism among Vietnamese managers. This change stimulated the national economy, and on January 11, 2007, Vietnam became the WTO's 150th member (World Trade Organization, 2011).

Throughout their intense efforts to create a new socialism, the Vietnamese state and the Communist Party constantly emphasized self-discipline, commitment, and concern for the nation over personal gain. Today many public education campaigns still take their cue from desirable moral characteristics identified by Ho Chi Minh: "frugalness, self-sacrifice, steadfastness, impartiality, disinterest in material perquisites, the rejection of arrogance and status-seeking, and the abilities to ask questions and recognize one's mistakes" (cited in Malarney, 2002, p. 54).

The Metaphor: The Dualities of *Dòn Gánh*

Vietnamese people say their country resembles two baskets of produce on either end of a carrying pole, a *đòn gánh*. We have already given a brief description of the metaphor. In this section, we will highlight the dualities that this metaphor encompasses.

Duality: North and South

In its simplest form, the *đòn gánh* highlights Vietnam's division into north and south. Although unified today, there are both subtle—and stark—contrasts between the two, including dialects spoken, climate (the south is significantly hotter on average), availability of food, and preparation of traditional foods. It's not unlike the differences we see when comparing cities on the east and west coasts of the United States. For example, visitors to the north will ask for *nem Sai Gon* when ordering spring rolls—a delicious bundle of shredded vegetables, seasoned, rolled in pastry, and deep fried— while waiters in the south will expect to hear *cha gio*, a crispy seafood or vegetable roll wrapped in lettuce and dipped in the sauce *nuoc cham* (Ray, Balasingamchow, & Stewart, 2009).

North Vietnamese culture has a distinctly French influence that extends from the cuisine and architecture to the language spoken. By contrast, the south has a more Western feel. Accents differ by region, and many consider the north to be more traditional and the south more dynamic. There are also more Catholics in the south, although only 10% of the population is Catholic, as indicated previously. Northern cuisine is known for its subtle flavors, central cuisine for its spiciness, and southern cuisine for its use of sugar and bean sprouts.

According to consumer research by The Nielsen Company (2009), Hanoians (those in the northern capital of Hanoi) are more collectivist and highly value the opinions of family and friends when making purchasing decisions, exhibit strong brand loyalty, and are keen to keep up with trends. By contrast, consumers in Ho Chi Minh City in the south tend to be more individualistic, are less likely to be influenced by others when making buying decisions, and show less brand loyalty or concern for keeping up appearances.

The Value of Harmony: Individual Versus Society

While representative of many things to Vietnamese people, the *đòn gánh* illustrates the importance and the ongoing struggle, particularly between north and south, to maintain harmony, as well as to balance personal needs against the demands of business and society. Given Vietnam's strong Confucian influence, it's unsurprising that citizens place a high value on etiquette to facilitate both personal and business inter-actions. As a result, it's critical that newcomers gain a swift insight into the nuances of polite society, particularly when attempting to negotiate an outcome in their own favor, whether it's understanding the correct place to sit during a business lunch or knowing how to accept business cards with both hands and a slight head bow.

The concept of "face," an individual's public image, is vitally important to the Vietnamese. In Western workplaces, it's not usual for managers to give direct, often frank, feedback to staff in an open forum. Within a Vietnamese context, managers must balance the need to give feedback against any potential loss of face, as extreme embarrassment can occur from public criticism or unfavorable remarks. Feedback is best dealt with in private and sometimes indirectly (E. D. Smith & Pham, 1996). "Loss of face is painful in any society, but unbearable in Vietnam. The Vietnamese have an expression: 'Better to die than lose face'" (Borton, 2004, p. 207). Similarly, Vietnamese people rarely go to court to resolve personal or business conflicts. Legal proceedings can affect brand and business image, two key elements for business success (Kohl, 2007).

The Confucian concepts of maintaining harmony and avoiding conflict and con-frontation can cause communication issues, and giving feedback is a balancing act. While negative feedback within a business or group setting may lead to loss of face, within the setting of close friends or family, giving feedback—no matter how frank—is a way of showing that you care about the other person. Vietnamese interpret the loss of face as having two sides, much like the *dòn gánh*. One side is keeping a distance from and respecting the independence of others, while the other is showing care and concern (Thang et al., 2007). A comment such as "It's a shame you're so fat" alerts a trusted family member or friend to potentially hurtful comments others could make, giving the loved ones the opportunity to take action and remedy the issue herself.

The Vietnamese concept of belonging originates in ancient Vietnamese culture and its Confucian overlay, but it has changed under years of socialism that closely links the importance of relationships within families, the village, an institution, and the nation (Borton & Ryder, 2000). When one travels to Vietnam, one is presented with two con-cepts that both are in harmony and conflict, the ideologies of Confucianism and com-munism. However, conflict seems more predominant in Vietnam than in China, given the large number of Buddhist temples in Vietnam despite the communism practiced by the government. Once again the duality is very evident, and a Vietnamese needs to manage it in the manner of balancing the *dòn gánh*.

Ho Chi Minh is seen in Vietnamese culture, particularly by the Communist Party, as an exemplar of political virtue. He is the ideal Vietnamese leader—a devoted revo-lutionary who lived a life of simplicity, avoided corruption, behaved in a fair and egalitarian manner, and put the nation and revolution above his own personal inter-ests. Party members and others often invoke the numerous moral adages coined by Ho during his life as a benchmark for social and political morality (Malarney, 2002). Ho put the revolution before his own relationships: "I am a professional revolutionary,

I am always on strict orders, my itinerary is always careful prescribed—and you cant devite [sic] from that route, can you?" (Green, 1996, "The Return of Ho Chi Minh").

In sum, a visitor is constantly aware of dual processes at play when visiting Vietnam, such as the traditional and modern economy, harmony and conflict, Confucianism and communism, and positive and negative feedback. These factors all work together and may eventually lead to the creation of a new Asian economic tiger.

Change: The Old and the New

Vietnamese are swift and flexible in adapting to change. They take a considered approach to fundamental change, and Western business associates need to be aware that Vietnamese people are "very Vietnamese, and very international" (General Vo Nguyen Giap, cited in Borton, 2004, p. 203). On the one hand, they are very adaptable, pragmatic, and receptive to change; on the other hand, many global businesses will not transfer their cultures and practices successfully to Vietnam due to many factors. Perhaps the most important factor is the match between the skills of the workforce and the products or services being produced. Vietnam is a developing nation and is at the low end of the technology scale. In the future, the Vietnamese are cognizant that they will have to be more flexible with incoming global business. They fully understand the dual reality of "cultural continuity and change" (Kohl, 2007, p. 2).

At the end of the Vietnam War, no one would have predicted that Vietnam, in the words of a former southern revolutionary, "has developed more in the last 10 years than in the previous thousand" (Borton, 2004, p. 203). Once again, duality between the forces of old and new comes into play. A recent visitor to Vietnam toured a village outside of Hanoi and met a former member of the Vietcong, the soldiers in the Vietnamese War involving the United States. This soldier had sustained serious injuries, and the visitor expected a negative answer when he asked whether the former soldier was happy with the eventual outcome of the war. Surprisingly, he indicated that he would have preferred for the Americans to have won, as they would have probably rebuilt Vietnam in a similar way that the United States helped rebuild Europe after World War II. The duality of patriotic pride at winning was balanced by a pragmatic assessment of what would have been better for Vietnam.

Change is a large and fast-moving part of contemporary society in Vietnam, and young Vietnamese live very different lives than those of their parents. Today 25.1% of the population is under 15 years of age. Given that tradition is so highly valued in Vietnam, we can expect change in cultural values will be gradual, but they will change more rapidly as individualism becomes more prominent and younger people assume positions of power.

Ecommerce presents a fascinating challenge for businesses entering Vietnam. Research conducted in Ho Chi Minh City highlights that businesses rarely rely on a shopping-cart model for online retailing. Websites generally direct consumers to bricks-and-mortar stores or stalls, which meet consumer preferences to inspect goods in person. If items are ordered online, clients generally pay on delivery so that they can immediately return unwanted items (interview with Rebecca Gardiner, June 28, 2011). Despite the fact that it's difficult to access Facebook within Vietnam without using a proxy server, many businesses rely on social media for an inexpensive online presence. URLs are discreetly displayed on brochures, business cards, and websites.

Commerce: The Supermarket Versus the Marketplace

As an agricultural tool, the *dòn gánh* exemplifies the importance of both the farming sector to the national economy and the cultural value of food within society. Despite the introduction of shopping centers and supermarkets to larger Vietnamese cities, vendors continue to use *dòn gánh* to transport goods to and from marketplaces and to make direct sales on the street. The traditional marketplace and modern global economy work in unison in Vietnam, and both have a voice.

Also, like many Asians in other nations, the Vietnamese are fond of all facets of doing business, whether it's negotiating in a market, managing an office, or navigating the global stock exchange. Vietnamese are great fans of bargaining, and they negotiate most prices from food to real estate. Expect Vietnamese to negotiate aggressively, but it is important to realize that high pressure and emotion have little place in business in Vietnam (Morrison & Conaway, 2007).

The *dòn gánh* also highlights the tension between subsistence farming and modern industry. Despite the industrialization of Doi Mo, agriculture remains the foundation of the Vietnamese economy. Vietnam is among a small handful of nations that do not import basic agricultural commodities, with local farming meeting domestic consumption needs.

Vietnamese membership in the WTO has brought its own *dòn gánh* to Vietnam. One basket contains limitless opportunities to pursue employment within the global economy, while the other holds enormous challenges for the national economy, especially the agricultural industry. While agriculture employs 52% of the workers, its contribution to GNP is only 22%. As Khoi (2008) points out, about 70% of the population lives in rural areas. This includes 13.2 million households, of which 11 million are directly involved in agricultural production. Over time this percentage is likely to shrink as the economy becomes more industrialized. Further, with two thirds of the population under 30 years of age, many young people choose to leave farming villages to pursue work in larger cities. This presents a problem for numerous rural families who rely on their children for labor and other family-related issues. There is a risk that traditional farming methods will be lost within a few generations.

Family: Inside and Outside the Family

In a collective community with tight social frameworks and self-functioning communities, the family is the nucleus of Vietnamese society, and individuals must balance their own needs against those of the family. Children feel a strong sense of duty to follow their parents' orders, which may include approval of a marriage partner. A Vietnamese proverb supports this way of behaving: "When entering a family, follow its practices." While the Western mind-set accepts a level of assimilation, it has difficulty embracing fully the collectiveness and totality of this obedience.

Vietnamese generally consider their own needs to be subordinate to those of their family and the broader community. Each person has his or her own place within the collective, which determines duties and responsibilities. As Borton and Ryder (2000) point out: "Relationships are not rigorously formalized as in some Asian cultures. In fact, some Vietnamese abandon right relationship in settings such as traffic and queues. Nevertheless, in the work setting, right relationship is omnipresent" (p. 21). Essentially, *right relationship* signifies that harmony is achieved and face is preserved by all. Further, like people in other Confucian cultures, the Vietnamese believe that respect for the elderly is an important virtue. Age carries experience and wisdom, and in the traditional extended family, the word of the father or grandfather is law.

By extension, managers in Vietnam often see their role as extending beyond normal Western employment practices, and they provide a great deal of social support. At times the manager becomes the uncle or auntie in employees' lives, helping out with investments, social life, and the selection of a spouse. In the state-owned sector, most managers tend to adopt a paternalistic approach toward their employees, exercising close supervision over subordinates. They often give a great deal of direction to ensure that the work is done well. In addition, managers often give priority to recruiting employees' sons, daughters, aunts, uncles, and parents to work in the company. This is seen as expanding the informal family to engender trust, harmony, balance, and happiness all around, with family members looked after both financially and emotionally (Quang & Vuong, 2002).

Vietnamese *Guanxi*

Vietnamese society is comprised of an interconnected network of personal relationships, all of which carry obligations on both sides. These mutual obligations are the underpinning of social order in Vietnam, so they are taken very seriously. Much as with the baskets of the *đòn gánh*, balance is required. The Vietnamese say, "If you want good-tasting food, then boil it well." The same can be said for doing business in Vietnam, where the nation's "slow-cook" business culture is in sharp contrast to the "time is money" approach of the American "fast-food" business culture (Kohl, 2007, p. 3). Outside of the family unit, business connections are among the most cherished relationships. Despite the fact that Vietnam is moving to a new economic model, knowing the right people is essential to getting things done, whether it is developing an existing business, launching a new business venture, or having a Vietnamese business partner.

Propriety and courtesy play a major role in personal and business relationships (E. D. Smith & Pham, 1996). When establishing a new venture, it may be some time before the business at hand is discussed. Instead, the early stages of networking focus on business partners getting to know each other's background, expertise, and character. Questions such as "How many people do you manage?" "How much is your operating budget?" and "How many managers work for you?" will establish your status in the eyes of the Vietnamese. A second phase of questions may focus on personal issues such as "Are you married?" "How many children do you have?" "What is your house like?" and, amusingly enough, "How much do you weigh?" as size can equate to wealth in some contexts. In a Western society, many may consider these questions to be inappropriate. However, in an Asian context, especially in Vietnam, these questions are asked in order to fully understand how you will work together and bring harmony and balance to business dealings. "By becoming acquainted and establishing a personal relationship with you, the Vietnamese are merely trying to understand you better" (E. D. Smith & Pham, "Personal Relationships").

Gift giving plays an essential role in developing relationships within Vietnamese business culture. Good business relationships are cultivated to strengthen interactions between businesses (Segon & Booth, 2010). When conducting business meetings in Vietnam, international business associates are expected to bring gifts for all official participants. Gifts should originate from the visitor's country of origin, not from Vietnam. A related important dimension of gift giving is the attention paid to seniority and status. A senior manager's gift should be of greater value that that of his or her subordinate, and gifts should range in quality according to status.

The *đòn gánh* is in evidence more than ever when one investigates the combination of the country's cultural specifics (local) and "best practices" (foreign). This combination, as Yeung and Tung (1996) suggest, should result in optimal benefits through capitalizing on multiplex *guanxi* and "developing fully polycontextuality among business partners and different cultures" (Thang et al., 2007, p. 125).

All cultures have different ways of establishing relationships, and what is evident in Vietnam is that at times, some relationships develop into widespread corruption as a result of nepotism, cronyism, and camaraderie in the absence of an effective legal system and social control norms (Thang et al., 2007). The "culture of envelopes," meaning money or bribes, has at times put a financial strain on the economic development of the new Vietnam. Whereas this was once the norm for doing business, as Vietnam enters the global economy more fully, this will be an issue that will need to be addressed on a case-by-case basis. Finally, the conflict between politics and family duty brings into perspective the issue of divergence of needs for Vietnamese. A local political official must toe the party line, but there is always pressure from family and the community to use his position for their advantage. This concept of nepotism, as discussed above, is to a certain extent culturally sanctioned.

Status: Equality/Inequality

Despite numerous changes, for all intents and purposes, Vietnam remains a hierarchical country. Under Confucian tradition, each person has a place and knows to whom to defer. As E. D. Smith and Pham (1996) point out,

Vietnamese society is outwardly egalitarian in accord with Marxist ideology, but continues to exhibit paternalistic, male-dominant attitudes in business and most official activities. So when Vietnamese women hold key positions, they are accorded the respect due that position, even if such is not the case in their personal lives. ("Gender Issues")

Women play an extraordinary role in business and head up ventures as diverse as market stalls, coffee shops, restaurants, tailor shops, employment agencies, and schools for English and even hold seats on the Vietnam stock exchange. Under communist ideals, women have equal rights under the law. However, despite female success in business, Vietnam is still a male-dominated country in both business and government (Morrison & Conaway, 2007). Vietnam ranks number 79 out of 135 countries on the World Economic Forum's Global Gender Gap Index for 2011 as compared to number 8 for the Philippines, which is the highest-ranking Asian country (Hausmann, Tyson, & Zahidi, 2011).

Food

The idiom "Have you eaten?" is a popular greeting in many Asian countries, including Vietnam, and is not unlike asking "What's up?" in the United States or "How's it going?" in Australia. Vietnamese food, with its unusual ingredients and styles of preparation, is distinct from both that of China and other Southeast Asian nations. It also defines the country and its people. Of particular note is the French influence on Vietnamese food, and French Vietnamese restaurants are popular in Vietnam and in the West. Ingredients are procured through daily trips to the marketplace, where visitors will see vendors selling raw ingredients and snack foods from their *đòn gánh*. The sharing of rice and several other dishes at a communal table is an important ritual for both family and business, and sharing food or drink with guests remains the primary means of building relationships. Serving tea from a small tea pot with small cups to guests is also an important ritual and has crossed into the business realm, although in more globalized Vietnam businesses, partners tend to go to restaurants rather than serve tea (Chambers, 1997). In Vietnam your host will take you to lunch or dinner. It is important to reciprocate by returning the courtesy and hosting a dinner at a well-known hotel restaurant.

According to De Mooij (2011), food has an important function in collectivist cultures, for "providing food and having food in the home for any guest who drops by is an important social value" (pp. 103–104). In Vietnam food is important for business interactions, and street food is an essential component of Vietnamese daily life. *Pho,* a noodle soup with a clear, meat-based broth, is considered by many to be a national dish. Other foods commonly consumed at these sites include other types of rice- or wheat-noodle soups, steamed glutinous rice, rice porridge, and sweet desserts.

In short, food is a large part of ritual celebrations in Vietnam, with vast feasts ushering in weddings and funerals. Alcohol is just as important as liberal amounts of food. Outside the main cities, this usually takes the form of locally produced rice wine, while metropolitan diners usually focus on beer or imported spirits. Banquets, large dinners, and family feasts are very important socially as they supply a context through which Vietnamese people are able to nurture social relationships. This is often accomplished by reciprocal banquets, family dinners, and feast invitations. Anniversaries of the deaths of family ancestors and the new Lunar Year or *Tet* are important occasions for families and communities to share food.

In conclusion, Vietnam's society is rapidly embracing the dynamics of a global economy while attempting to preserve its cultural heritage. The vendors weaving through the streets of this country's cities and villages are a constant reminder of a delicate balancing act. The tension between the past and future, the struggle to balance family life and the needs of business, and the competing needs of agriculture and high-technology business are issues faced by many countries around the globe. It's not surprising that this dynamic gem of a nation with a colorful and proud past is experiencing a period of rapid growth and attracting many of the world's leading brands. Still, we will continue to view Vietnam in terms of the basic metaphor of the *đòn gánh* or carrying pole with two baskets, each at one end, for many years to come.

CHAPTER 7

The Polish Village Church

Swept by converging streams of economic, political and social events, Poland has been affected by all. Yet she has remained stubbornly unique . . . she has absorbed much, resisted much, and remained very much herself. In many respects, Poland presents a remarkable example of continuity not often met within history.

—Sula Benet (1951, pp. 26–27)

Poland is still an overwhelmingly Roman Catholic nation, still conservative, and still religious, especially when compared with its European neighbors.

—Michael Slackman (2010b)

The first-time visitor to Warsaw, Poland, is frequently surprised by its modernity, as exemplified by the buildings in the central business district, many of which could easily be mistaken for buildings in U.S. cities. At the very modern Marriott hotel, businesspeople are constantly on their cell phones and BlackBerry devices or in intense discussions making deals. A few older buildings are left over from the communist era, but not many. Although Warsaw was largely destroyed in World War II, visitors would have a difficult time finding remnants of this destruction and the rest of Poland's past.

Yet Poland, with its population of nearly 39 million, is still a largely traditional society consisting mainly of small towns and villages. About 15% of the population is engaged directly in agriculture, although it contributes only 4.3% to gross national product. At least a third of the population resides in rural areas, and others live in towns close to the major cities of Warsaw, Poznan, and Gdansk. Moreover, many of the Poles in the large cities come from traditional rural areas and regularly visit them.

Currently this central European nation is making an exhilarating but disquieting and rapid transition from traditional to modern society.

In 2004 Poland became a member of the European Union (EU). Its economy has since grown significantly. Unlike the many other Eastern European nations, it weathered the Great Recession starting in 2008 successfully and investors worldwide are providing seed money for various large projects.

Given Poland's long and tortuous history, briefly described below, it is understandable that the Polish people are characterized by contradictions but are held together by a strong social system and a sense of shared adversity and experience. The Polish people are guarded in their manner of dealing with each other and outsiders and in their trust of institutions and people. Despite this guardedness, they possess a richness and depth of spirit that has helped them persevere through many shared adversities. Poland, since the collapse of communism in 1989, has been successfully struggling to find a place in the world as a free country and a self-determined people. The path Poland is now taking is very much influenced by the nation's peasant roots, a history of foreign power domination (including communism), and Catholicism. These three forces shape the image the Polish people have of themselves, their behavior, and their institutions.

The village church, found in virtually every Polish town, stands as a symbol of these three forces and presents a particularly appropriate metaphor for Polish culture. In each village, a church sits in a prominent location and serves as the focal point of town activity. The churches are the beneficiaries of much of the village money and attention. Some are as old as 500 years, and others were built since the collapse of communism. Church events are considered compulsory, and failure to attend is not viewed favorably. During holy periods, such as Christmas and Easter, residents attend the many church services held every day of the week. For services like the Easter Resurrection ceremony, held on the night before Easter, churches are packed, and people overflow into the street. As women, children, and the elderly find seats inside the church, men and older boys gather outside around the entrances to listen. Church personnel have adapted to these circumstances by sending a priest outside to administer communion at the appropriate time. Like the Malaysian *balik kampung* (Chapter 18), the village church is important as a focal point for Poles; pilgrimages back home for religious holidays are common. The church represents a safe haven from the forces of history that have shaped and at times attempted to destroy Poland.

However, while Poland is still an overwhelmingly Catholic country, there has been a marked decline in regular church attendance; only 41% attend Sunday mass regularly, especially since the death of the first Polish Pope in history in 2005, Pope John Paul II. During communist times, Russia did not allow the Polish church to involve itself in secular issues. In recent years, however, the church has supported conservative causes and political candidates, activity that has not endeared it to many of the more progressive elements in Poland. Some Poles have complained that the church recovered all of its property after the fall of communism, but ordinary citizens did not

(Slackman, 2010b). Still, the nation is overwhelmingly Catholic and conservative, and we can expect that the church's influence on moral matters, if not secular matters, will continue.

Historical Background

Whenever Poles want to explain some aspect of their work, they start by talking about Polish history. They are sensitive about Polish history and, as Edward Lucas (2006) notes, "prickly to a fault" about it, especially those who are older. History has played an important role in shaping the Polish way of thinking. The history of Poland is largely the history of peasants who were dominated by exterior groups (e.g., wealthy landowners, foreign powers, and communist leaders).

Premodern Times

From the medieval period (6th century) through the late 19th century, the people who farmed the land were predominantly serfs. Emancipation and refeudalization occurred several times during this period, which witnessed a continuing struggle between peasants, who sought rights and freedom, and landowners, who secured legislation to force the peasants to stay on their land so that they could exploit the peasants' labor for immense profit. The Polish bourgeoisie were perceived as a threat to these wealthy landowners. Landowners, therefore, encouraged Jews, Germans, and Armenians to immigrate to Poland and take technical jobs because these foreigners' economic prosperity did not pose a political threat.

As the bourgeoisie diminished in size, the population of Polish towns declined, and the power and tax base of the king fell. Landowners during this period became increasingly tied to specific German and Dutch bankers for capital. This left the landowners relatively powerful while they developed an increasing dependence on the core of the European economic system (northwestern European states). Some peasants during this period owned the land they worked, but they remained primarily subsistence farmers. To a great extent, the technology used in Polish agriculture remained primitive because of the ample supply of serf labor.

During the 16th century, Poland was large and powerful; the Polish state during the 16th through 18th centuries was run by a parliament that consisted of members of the Polish gentry, who selected the king. These wealthy landowners successfully maintained their independence and wealth through their employment of the *liberum* veto, a procedure giving any member of parliament the power to defeat any legislation with a single vote. Needless to say, few meaningful actions occurred. This procedure helped to maintain a balance in Polish politics and defined the strong individualistic values of the Polish gentry. It did, however, prevent Poland from amassing the strong collective behaviors required to fend off foreign invaders through political means.

This weakened state and dependence on foreign capital allowed Poland's relatively stronger neighbors—Russia, Prussia, and Austria—to partition Polish land beginning in 1772 and to assimilate it into their own borders. This partitioning of Poland ushered in an era of domination by these three great powers that lasted through the end of World War I. The result was the complete elimination of the Polish state. During this period Prussia, Russia, and Austria broke the power and wealth of the landowners. In addition, pressure throughout Eastern Europe forced the abolition of serfdom and redistributed land to foreign parties and to the peasants themselves.

Poland was formally reconstituted as a state in 1918. From then until 1939, Poland was a free country, and the distribution of land ownership to the peasants (land reform) was a primary political objective. A soaring population growth rate, coupled with a tradition of inheritance in which land was divided among all living children upon the father's death, led to the economic failure of land reform. The process resulted in lower production and lower profits from agriculture during the interwar period. Germany and Russia invaded Poland in 1939, marking another break in its independence as a nation.

The Communist Period

The aftermath of World War II brought a division of the spoils among the victors, namely the Western allies and Russia. Devastated by war, during which about 30% of its population died, Poland became a pawn in this process. Communism was adopted as the official state ideology in 1948, and despite its lack of general support among the Polish populace, Soviet government support for Communist Party leadership made significant resistance impossible. Economic rebuilding and a change in governmental priorities prompted postwar Polish leaders to divert resources from traditional sectors, such as agriculture, to industry (manufacturing, mining, service, and construction). Inadequate and unsupported reforms, however, produced a worsening economy and growing social discontent.

Collectivization of farming, a key tenet of communism, took place in Poland in the years 1949 to 1956. At its height, however, only 8.6% of total cultivated land was collectivized. A powerful peasant commitment to the land and often to a specific plot of land proved too strong for collectivization efforts.

For peasants, the farm was as much a social as an economic unit. Its output was produced for the satisfaction of family needs. Market pressures were counter to family consumption needs and demanded production increases, and they were often perceived as oppression forced upon them by Russian policies that the Polish government had to implement. Peasants often reacted to these pressures by refusing to increase production and producing only enough for family subsistence. Government agricultural policies had, ironically, succeeded in reinforcing the essential features of the peasantry. This fact gave the peasants power that could significantly disrupt the government systems, and they were seen as a threat.

As the state required more and more agricultural production, peasant farmers tended to resist through delaying tactics, highlighting their power over the government system. The government responded with greater pressure to collectivize, thus creating a vicious downward spiral of lower levels of production. In the 1950s, this process hit a crisis point when peasants lost their pride of ownership in their farms and became reluctant to improve or even to maintain them, resulting in low productivity and workforce apathy. Eventually the Polish government repealed its policy of collective farming.

Other policies were also met with strong resistance. The Poles' basic distrust of government systems produced an unwillingness to make sacrifices to turn the economy around. In addition, the socialist ideology on which the Polish social and political system was built altered the outlook of traditionally hardworking Poles, leading them to believe that it was the state's responsibility to provide for their households. When the state could not provide adequately for the Polish people, they became resentful. To compensate for the growing unrest, the government increased workers' wages fivefold between 1979 and 1986. The government was close to proclaiming state bankruptcy when it declared martial law in 1981 to quell growing unrest and calls for reforms by the Solidarity movement.

Solidarity and Independence

In 1989, spearheaded by the Solidarity movement and prompted by the weakening political and economic position of the Soviet Union, roundtable meetings in Warsaw resulted in the peaceful overthrow of the communist state in Poland and the beginning of significant economic, political, and social reforms that continue today.

It is against this backdrop that we explore Polish culture. The village church resides in the center of most Polish villages, exemplifying the central place that Catholicism plays in Polish life. In addition, the church's austere exterior and plush interior represent the contrasting nature of Polish identity, produced partially by the many years of foreign power domination and the partitioning of the Polish state. Finally, the village church endured and flourished during a period when religious worship was banned in Poland. Poles are very proud of this fact, and the village church stands as a symbol of the ability of the Polish people to survive during extreme adversity.

Central Place of the Catholic Church

The village church sits in the middle of the village, often in a place of particular prominence, such as the crest of a hill. This placement signifies the preeminence of the church in Polish life, both in the past and in the postcommunist period. As we have seen, the church has experienced a decrease in power and influence in secular matters. Still, it is difficult to overstate the importance of the Catholic Church in Polish culture. Hann (1985) goes as far as to say, "Polish has come to mean Catholic" (p. 10). Virtually every major holiday is religious in postcommunist Poland. Public processions of clergy and laypeople carrying religious banners and relics are the primary rituals in many of these celebrations. In these rituals, neighborhoods, youth, and Easter baskets are blessed. These occasions feature full Masses, sometimes lasting as long as 3 hours. In addition, Polish youth and adults celebrate "name days" rather than birthdays. These name days are set aside to celebrate the saints after whom many Poles are named.

The Catholic Church has played an important role for rural citizens in modern Poland. Parishioners continue to be a particular focus for the church. The first Polish Pope, John Paul, is currently in the process of being recognized as a saint, and the Polish people are proud that he is from their nation. During the period of peasant emancipation at the end of the 19th century, the church played an active role in acquiring freedom and land for the peasants, even though the Polish state was under foreign domination. This championing of the peasant cause positioned the church perfectly to play an active role in the creation of national sentiment, and it bound the Poles even more closely to the church. The result was that the parish became the focus for a collective Polish peasant identity.

The collectivizing influence of the Catholic Church is naturally accompanied by moral codes of conduct, including a belief in equality and fair division of resources and the church's sense of social justice. Also, the church has placed importance on collectivity over individuality and on suffering rather than short-term gratification of personal needs. Sacrifice is seen as the best means by which Catholics can find salvation. This belief has spread beyond religious life in Poland to permeate Polish views of national identity. It has given solace to a people who have suffered long periods of political and economic domination for centuries. Poles' search for explanations as to why they have had to suffer so terribly has generated a natural connection between them and the Catholic Church.

After World War II, Poland was unique among communist nations in that the Catholic Church and the symbols of Catholicism were not outwardly diminished by communist attempts to condemn and destroy them. In fact, commitment to Catholicism was probably strengthened by official condemnation, as were other aspects of Polish life. Polish peasants continued to abstain from meat on Fridays; to name their children after saints; and to marry, baptize, and administer communion in religious ceremonies. The Catholic Church also played an active role in the political life of peasants. It openly sanctioned much of the opposition to government policies in Poland. In addition, the church provided the structure to aggregate and articulate peasant interests, as a result of which devout Polish peasants were able to collectively oppose communism through their religious affiliation.

This peasant-church connection is further manifested in the almost spiritual link that the Polish people have with their land, as demonstrated by the All Saints Day commemoration celebrated every November 1. This commemoration is an amazing demonstration of respect for the dead that has turned into a cultural event. Its religious meaning serves to connect the Polish people both symbolically and literally to their roots and to the land. Many of the Poles who have moved to the cities within the last few generations travel back to their ancestral villages for this commemoration, and some of them visit the villages of both sides of the family. City dwellers with agrarian roots usually choose to be buried in the villages from which they came, further preserving the connection and the importance of family lineage and agrarian heritage. In addition, the family plots establish a permanent link of generation to generation in the village, a lineage that is literally "planted in the ground."

The Partitioning and Polish Identity

The exterior architecture of old and new churches alike is simple. New churches are large with brick or painted stucco exteriors. Old churches are rustic, made from meticulously matched split logs with steep, curved metal roofs. They are simply adorned with wood crosses and rosebud-shaped steeples. The inside of these old churches is like the inner light of the Polish people, filled with color, attention to detail, wealth of spirit, and surprise. But the church exterior hides the riches of golden altars, antique wooden carvings, and hand-painted walls. Still, the interiors of these village churches are not gaudy but simply elegant and rich with years of protecting the souls of the peasant people.

Like the contrast between the austere exterior and the rich interior of the village churches, the public and private lives of the Polish people are remarkably different and separate. This separation is in great part a result of the partitioning of the Polish state in 1772 by Russia, Prussia, and Austria and the resulting lack of Polish control over the Poles' own official business. Communism also contributed to this lack of control. It promised social peace and security in exchange for social control and private ownership of property. Poles desiring certainty and security after the perils of years of foreign invasions and rule, as well as the harsh consequences of World War II, entered into a social contract with the communist government. The Polish people, however, chose to focus on the welfare of close family and friends as opposed to a larger group, as the communist system required. The result of this social contract was an abdication of responsibility for much of the state of affairs that touched them directly. One example of this mentality is the upkeep of public property. In the socialist state, public property was theoretically the responsibility of everyone, but in practice, it was badly neglected. In this system, responsibility simply disappeared.

This does not mean that Poles do not care for their property. They do, in fact, take great pride in their possessions, even when they are simple. Most Polish homes and apartments have a room where visitors are welcomed and in which the residents display prized possessions, special glassware, and religious symbols in glass-enclosed display cases. But exterior spaces are not viewed with ownership or pride and thus do not elicit particular care.

Attention to Appearance

Poles value private ownership of property, and many village homes are "works in progress." Young men will begin building a home whenever money is available. Many Polish citizens working in other European nations send money home to support the construction of their homes, where they hope to live eventually. Houses are built in steps, and when one section is habitable, families move into this space. Other floors may remain as open shells until more money is available to complete them or the expanding family needs the space. Grandparents and even siblings are likely to work together on a house, sharing their money and efforts and eventually the finished home. Cohabitation by the extended family is common in Polish villages as well as in the cities. Despite the strong influence of the Catholic Church, Poles in cities such as Krakow and Warsaw tend to limit their families to one or two children, whereas village families are likely to have three or more offspring.

Poles are proud people who value appearances, particularly as they relate to their clothing. During the communist period, Poles did not have a good selection of apparel and had to settle for drab colors and poor styles. Today the individuality of Poles is reflected in their choice of apparel and the pride they take in wearing nice clothes. Young men and women in the cities wear designer fashions. Even when they may own only a few such outfits, they will wear them frequently and care for them meticulously. Older women can be seen on city streets in winter wearing a drab communist-era coat with a brightly colored (purple or pink) hat. Village women wear on their heads traditional scarves, which differ in design depending on the region of Poland. Such scarves are also frequently colorful.

Despite the attention they pay to their appearance, the face that Poles present in public is guarded and private, with smiles reserved for more informal and private moments between friends and family. People tend to mind their own business. In the cities, Poles are reluctant to get involved in the affairs of others. For example, if someone falls down in the street, Poles are unlikely to intervene unless it appears that a serious injury has occurred. Older women are the rare exception to this norm. Women who reach the status of grandmother are only too willing to render advice, particularly to younger women with children. Children are in the public domain, and Poles easily give advice on appropriate attire and discipline, as well as offers of candy or fruit. In addition, in the villages, involvement in the private matters of neighbors is quite common, though deeply resented by those who are the subject of the attention. Still, offers of assistance, when made without invasion of privacy, are welcomed and usually serve to generate a strong bond between the parties, which will be remembered and reciprocated.

Ironically, Poles identify strongly with Poland but feel that the Polish people tend to be lazy and quarrelsome (P. B. Smith & Bond, 1998). Poles' suspicions about their neighbors' intentions are based on a strong and pervasive distrust in Polish society, which is often connected with accusations of bribery or favoritism. Bribery is an ever-present phenomenon in Polish life. It is a source of jokes, folklore, and resentment, and it is often the explanation for the "way things are." Payments on the side are still necessary to receive adequate medical services and even entrance into universities. For example, to get into many universities in Poland, prospective students must pass a particular entrance exam. To pass these exams, they must obtain special tutoring from university professors because the contents of the exams are a closely guarded secret. Some Poles call the tutoring fees a bribe to the university professors, while others see them simply as payment for services.

However, bribery and related activities seem to be decreasing. In the 2011 ranking of 179 nations on the Index of Economic Freedom (T. Miller, 2011), Poland ranks 68th. This index includes the following measures: fiscal soundness and openness to trade and investment, government size, business and labor regulation, property rights, corruption, monetary stability, and financial competition.

Bribery Customs

Still, bribery permeates many aspects of Polish life, including the workplace. For example, Polish workers often use the expression "We came here on a rabbit," when bemoaning their particular lack of benefits or poor working conditions. This expression refers to refusal—or probably inability—to make some form of payment to their supervisor. Those who are favored and receive benefits or privileges are described as arriving "on a calf," the calf being the bribe to the new employer.

Bribery is just one manifestation of a system of privileges, power dispersal, and political access that is called *kumoterstwo* in the Polish language. *Kumoterstwo* is translated into English as "favoritism," but the Polish word tends to encompass a great deal more. Through a system of networks, the Poles rely heavily on social contacts for a number of official or unofficial services or products. Unlike U.S. networks, which often involve occupation or profession, these networks are based, first, on familial ties and, second, on economic or social standing. Such networks may be a necessary organizational tool for rural Poles, but they tend to generate resentment and suspicion among those who do not belong. Networks with power often require monetary payments for favors. Poles tend to view this system not as right or good but rather as a necessary fact of life. While the specifics are usually hidden under layers of denial, the general existence of this bribery-based system is fair game for discussion and ridicule. For example, in 2011 three employees of the Dutch company Philips International were formerly charged in Polish court for allegedly bribing Polish hospital managers to purchase Philips products. One of the accused employees is the former director of Philips Poland, and the prosecution indicated that the evidence suggested that this pattern of bribery had existed for years.

This form of social organization is a response to the difficulties associated with the communist state. At the end of World War II, Poles were subjected to a government that was ineffective and illegitimate in their eyes. Poles needed to find a way around the system. They relied on their traditional individualistic values and their dogged determination to guide their approach to dealing with their environment.

In brief, Poles live a dual life, public and private. Behaviors that are considered appropriate to "get things done" in the public sphere, such as bribery or deception, are not acceptable within the small private spheres of Polish life. Poles have learned to expect different rules for different situations and are able to compartmentalize their lives into these different spheres. The village church stands as a symbol of the divided lives that Poles live and the attempts to pull these two worlds together. Similarly the internal and external appearance of these churches also represents compartmentalization, a survival mechanism that has ensured the longevity of the Polish identity and the Polish spirit.

Survivors

The Catholic Church survived and even flourished during the communist period in Poland but not in other communist states. Like the Catholic Church, the Polish people have endured under great adversity. Today the changing economic and political context of democracy and a market system presents new challenges and opportunities for the Polish people. But this new world leaves Poles without a clear enemy and with a great deal of uncertainty.

Resistance to a common enemy is a key feature of Polish self-identity. During the long period of the partition of Poland, beginning in 1772, the governing powers (Russia, Prussia, and Austria) were viewed as enemies to be resisted. This resistance pulled Poles together for a common purpose and helped maintain their unique cultural heritage. During the post–World War II period, the enemy was communism and the Soviet influence over the political and economic system. Poles are proud of their history, which is marked by these dramatic periods of resistance to external enemies.

Most notably, Poles have resisted much larger and stronger armies with great valor. For example, Polish underground resistance during World War II was instrumental in providing the Allied forces with critical information, and the Poles were able to thwart many Nazi efforts through sabotage. Resistance to collective farming during the communist era is another key example. Finally, the efforts of the Solidarity Union and others were instrumental in hastening the collapse of communism. These collective efforts were encouraged by the Catholic Church, which supported resistance to communism and earlier had championed land reforms during the period of the partition of the Polish state. The Poles have always adapted and resisted, and it is precisely because of their ability to adapt well to their environment that their unique culture has survived.

Dark Humor

One way that Poles have adapted to adversity is through humor. Polish humor is dark humor that often pokes fun at the Polish condition. For example, Polish winters can be very harsh, with bleak gray skies and extremely cold temperatures. One joke goes:

> When the Germans were about to invade Poland during World War II, one Polish farmer was bemoaning to his friend the integration of Poland into the German state. The friend said to the farmer, "Well I don't think it is all that bad." The farmer looked at his friend in amazement. "How can you find good in this situation?" His friend replied, "Well, at least we won't have any more long Polish winters."

A second joke speaks to the lack of support Poles give to each other:

> Satan was showing a reporter around Hell. The reporter saw many deep pits with guards around the top of each. The reporter asked what they were. Satan said that there was a pit for each nationality of people. "Here are the Germans, over there are the Americans, and here are the Poles. . . ." The reporter noticed that the Polish pit did not have any guards around it. When he asked Satan why this was so, Satan replied, "Well, the guards are stationed at the mouth of each pit to keep people from crawling out. In the Polish pit, we don't have to worry about that, because whenever anyone tries to get out, a Pole from inside pulls him back in again."

These jokes are a common and a necessary form of social interaction in Poland, but it is not acceptable for foreigners to tell these same jokes. Rather, these jokes are reserved for Poles to turn the hardships of their lives into humor, which they can share.

As these examples imply, Polish people communicate in a high-context manner, especially when compared to U.S. Americans. A good example is the hugely successful commercial for Pollena 2000, a laundry detergent, made by the Polish company Pollena-Bydgoszcz (later acquired by Unilever). The commercial is based on *The Deluge,* a trilogy by the preeminent Polish writer Henryk Sienkiewicz that is still the most loved novel in Poland. The story takes place during the Swedish invasion of Poland in 1655, called the deluge. Two characters are twin brothers who were pretty good warriors, but only because of their physical strength and not because of their mental capabilities. Before getting involved in any fight, they would always ask their father, "*Ociec prac?*" meaning, "Father, should we fight?" The commercial takes advantage of the fact that *prac* also means to wash. So when the brothers ask their question in the commercial, the father answers, "Yes, but only with Pollena 2000!" In contrast, low-context German detergent commercials focus on the physical attributes of the product, which is typically discussed by two housewives who explicitly compare the quality of the wash; the majority of Polish TV viewers perceive these ads as dull and boring.

The collective efforts that so define the Polish people are usually followed by periods marked by extreme difficulties in managing and operating as a unified people.

Factions split off, and individual interests take precedence. Poles refocus quickly on the issues of their own families, leaving a disunity that often appears like anarchy. But it is also in these periods that the ingenuity of individual Poles is unleashed.

Market Opportunities

The opportunities of a market system have divided modern Poland along generational and geographical lines. Opportunities abound for young Poles, particularly in the cities. This generation had less exposure to communist ideology, and employers can more easily mold them. In fact, when Marriott was recruiting workers in Warsaw, one advertisement was tailored to this situation: "No experience wanted." Marriott did not want workers used to communism but, rather, young workers who would respond to the capitalistic incentives associated with high employee productivity.

In addition, younger Poles tend to be willing to take the risks associated with entrepreneurial activities. Compared to their older colleagues, they have traveled internationally much more and are much more comfortable using the English language, now generally recognized as the dominant language in international business. But change has been slow. For example, in 1989 Solidarity won the election after several years of political activity, and researchers established that Polish managers had made a slight but significant move from an autocratic to a participative leadership style from 1984 to 1989 (Jago, Mączyński, Reber, & Böhnisch, 1996). Nonetheless, Polish and Czech managers tend to be more autocratic than French, German, Swiss, and American managers (Jago et al., 1993). This latter study was conducted in the early 1990s and may reflect the Soviet influence on Polish and Czech managers, which over time has most probably decreased, especially in private companies that have adapted smoothly to capitalism.

Entrepreneurship is at the heart of the Polish spirit and has flourished since 1989. Poles can fix virtually anything by recycling parts from other items, often using their vast networks to procure or barter needed parts. Poles deal with their economic challenges by establishing small, sometimes one-man or one-woman, businesses to sell products of every kind. The roads into Poland from Germany have become makeshift markets, and Western Europeans travel along them to buy products of every kind from Polish entrepreneurs. Likewise, the grounds of the communist-era Palace of Culture and Science in the heart of the Polish capital, Warsaw, have become a flea market with rows and rows of concession stands. Many Poles now dream of being their own bosses, just as their forefathers dreamed of owning a farm. However, as noted previously, many Polish citizens have emigrated to other nations due to the lack of incentives and jobs.

The Church's New Role

The changing role of the church in Poland today is both positive and negative in the eyes of many Poles. Former Communist Party leaders, particularly in the Polish villages, now attend church regularly, thus uniting the village people under the church's steeple after many years of division. In fact, until recently former communists won federal elections, and many of them loudly proclaim their new adherence to the market economy. As Lucas (2006) notes, "Confusingly, the ex-communists are now the most ardent capitalists and the ex-dissidents often sound authoritarian" (p. 5).

But the church faces great difficulty in defining its new role in the lives of Poles. It has embarked on large-scale church development in Poland, and new churches are being built throughout the countryside. Many Poles resent this expansion of expensive churches when the needs of people are not being met as a result of changes in social services; for example, employment or welfare, health care, and education are no longer guaranteed.

While the church continues its role as a haven of resistance, it now serves as a moral barometer of the temptations of greed and selfishness that capitalism represents. This message has found some degree of acceptance, but many Poles, particularly the young, find that the opportunities that the market economy presents are alluring and key to their survival. Finally, many Poles feel the church has lost touch with the Polish people. For example, in 1995 Lech Walesa, the president and once-popular leader of the Solidarity Movement who was strongly supported by the Catholic Church, was defeated in his reelection bid by a former communist. His opponent's victory was accomplished with heavy support from Poles in the countryside, who voted against the church's wishes because they felt it just did not understand the issues they faced on a daily basis.

Yet the Polish people do not want to forget the past. In 1999 movies based on Polish history proved to be surprising box office successes, while American blockbusters faltered. Similarly, Poles love the opera *The Haunted Mansion,* by Stanislaw Moniuszko, not only because of the unique Polish *muzurhas* danced in it but also because of its explicitly favorable treatment of rural Polish life. This opera, written in the Polish language, was considered so subversive that it was banned during the Partition period. As might be expected, Frederick Chopin, the 18th-century romantic and nationalist Polish pianist and composer, is revered, and the home in which he lived until emigrating to France is an oft-visited museum.

To understand Poland in entirety, it is important to comprehend the transition to modern economic life as represented by Warsaw, its modern buildings, and its modern hotels such as the Marriott. Just as important, however, is to understand the traditional culture of Poland, which has withstood centuries of attack. There is no better way to understand this culture than to examine the traditional village church, using the features of the church's central place in the village to illuminate the partitioning of Poland and its influence on Polish identity (particularly in terms of public and non-public behavior) and the survivors' adaptations during periods of abrupt social change and transition.

CHAPTER 8

Kimchi and Korea

I think kimchi practically defines Korean-ness.

—Park Chae-lin, curator of
the Kimchi Museum (quoted in Demick, 2006)

As a child and young man in Seoul, Korea, I hated to eat kimchi and ran to McDonald's whenever possible. But then I studied for several years in the United States and sometimes had an uncontrollable urge to eat kimchi. Unfortunately the nearest restaurant serving kimchi was several hundred miles away, and many a weekend was spent traveling to and from it. I never realized the importance of kimchi and the feelings it engendered until I was deprived of it.

—Korean professor of economics
(personal communication, 2002)

Throughout its long history, Korea has suffered terribly at the hands of many nations—China, Japan, Russia, England, and France—whose armies invaded and ravaged it. After being occupied by British troops in 1860, the Koreans in vain tried to close off their borders to foreigners and, in the process, earned the epithet "the Hermit Kingdom." In 1910 Japan annexed Korea, which then suffered through 35 years of severe mistreatment until becoming independent in 1945. Although the Koreans were supposed to enjoy equal status with their Japanese counterparts, they were governed as a conquered people. For the first decade of Japanese rule, Koreans were not allowed to publish newspapers or to develop any type of political organization.

During the 1920s, Koreans were granted much greater latitude in voicing their opinions as a result of several large student demonstrations. The people gradually asserted themselves through various activities and organizations, including labor unions.

In 1937 the official Japanese policy of separate but equal treatment for Koreans came to an abrupt end, in large part because of the war between Japan and China from 1937 to 1945. Korea was mobilized for war, and hundreds of thousands of Korean men were conscripted to help the Japanese army, both in Korea and China. The Koreans were required to communicate in Japanese both publicly and in private homes, they had to worship at Shinto temples, and Korean children were encouraged to adopt Japanese names. All the Korean-language newspapers ceased production. In effect, Japan tried to assimilate Korea in every way imaginable with the intent of destroying Korean culture and identity.

Fortunately, Japanese rule of Korea came to end in 1945, and Koreans reasserted their culture with full force. Even so, their freedom would not be assured until 1957, as Chinese and U.S. troops occupied the country during the Korean War (1953–1957) between North and South Korea.

South Korea

This chapter concerns only South Korea, which became separate from North Korea because of the Korean War. At the time of separation, North Korea was the industrial powerhouse while South Korea was much more of an agricultural society. Today, however, years of communist rule have virtually destroyed the economic base of North Korea while South Korea has flourished. It is possible and even probable that reunification will occur eventually, given the very poor economic condition of North Korea.

South Korea today is a small country, about the size of Indiana, with a population of about 48 million. It is mountainous and possesses few natural resources. As in many developing nations, South Korea's cities have become very crowded. About 22% of the people live in Seoul and, if the suburbs are included, this figure rises to 35%. Economic growth since 1970 has been incredible, and South Korea is known as one of the five Tigers of Asia. While the 1997 Asian financial crisis created problems, especially in the financial sector, the economy recovered. However, the global economy began to deteriorate in 2008 during the global Great Recession, and Korea, along with many other nations, experienced major economic difficulties. It ranks 35th out of 189 nations on the Index of Economic Freedom, which suggests that it is a good nation in which to do business (T. Miller, 2011).

Fewer than 10% of the world's cultures can be considered overwhelmingly monocultural, with one dominant ethnic group, a common language, and a few very small minority groups. Korea is one such culture. Admittedly, this monoculturalism is under attack because of globalization, but Korea is still recognized as the most Confucian nation in the world.

Kimchi

Kimchi represents Korea in the same way that hamburger reflects the United States. Other than steamed rice, kimchi is the most popular food in Korea. Kimchi comes from a Chinese word translated as "immersing vegetables in a salt solution." There are literally hundreds of versions of kimchi.

Early forms of kimchi have been traced to the great wedding feasts held by King Shinmun, who ruled the country between 681 and 692 CE. Koreans probably created kimchi out of necessity. As mentioned above, Korea is a small country with few natural resources. The long winters made growing fresh vegetables very difficult. As a result, families would spend weeks in the fall harvesting their crops and pickling them in salt solutions (with other spices added for taste) to ensure they would ferment and be preserved for the winter, providing food for the family all year long. Kimchi includes ingredients such as Chinese cabbage, sea salt, sugar, crushed red chili, radish, chopped ginger, garlic, and green onions. Today Koreans buy ready-made kimchi in jars and cans. They still eat it with almost every meal, although fresh vegetables are now readily available at any time of the year.

A national museum in Seoul, the nation's capital, is dedicated only to kimchi. Given such facts, it is appropriate that kimchi should serve as our cultural metaphor for Korea.

The 60th Birthday

Korea is a classic authority-ranking culture, and this extends even to relationships in the family. However, because of its long periods of subjugation by other nations, Korea also emphasizes equality in many spheres of activity, including schools and work-places. For example, admission to private elementary schools is determined purely by lottery, which only one in eight children win. Such private schools offer a more diverse curriculum, including the study of English, than that provided by the elementary public schools. Many of the elementary public school children attend cram courses in English and other subjects after school to increase their future chances of success. Almost all the private school children enter the public system in Grade 7, but students must pass an examination to attend a high school where more classes are taught in English. These "foreign-language schools" send most of the students to South Korea's prestigious universities (Ramstad, 2007a).

A Korean's 60th birthday is important. Whereas in the United States, many people detest growing old and stop celebrating birthdays, Koreans tend to rejoice when reaching 60. Presumably all major life goals have been attained, and it is now time to relax and enjoy life to the fullest. The Chinese zodiac cycle is 60 years long, and Koreans believe that life runs in accordance with that cycle. Also, until recent generations, the estimated life span of those born in Korea was about 60 years. Thus the 60th birthday signifies that family and friends should gather to celebrate. Today the life expectancy of Korean men averages 74.5 years, and the ritualistic birthday party is frequently repeated on a man's 70th birthday and beyond.

Often the birthday party is held at the *k'unjip,* or "big house," the eldest son's household, where he lives with his wife, children, and parents. Through the eldest son, the family genealogy is traced from one generation to the next. He is responsible for caring for parents and conducting rituals in their honor, and his wife is expected to produce the male heir for the next generation.

Korea owes much of its values and culture to Confucianism, which was first introduced to Korea late in the Koryo dynasty, which ended in 1392. The succeeding Choson dynasty, which ruled until 1910, adopted Confucian philosophies as the state ideology. Confucianism is built on five relationships defining a hierarchical system in which there is a very high degree of power distance. These relationships are as follows:

1. Father and son: Governed by affection

2. Ruler and minister: Governed by righteousness

3. Husband and wife: Focused on attention to separate functions

4. Old and young: Organized on proper order

5. Friends: Faithfulness

These relationships are reflected in most activities in Korean society. It is significant that except for friends, the relationships are based on authority and subordination. Even the father-son relationship is governed primarily not by mutual affection but by the ability and willingness of the son to carry out his father's will. All of these relationships assume that the person in the superior position will act in a responsible manner, which will motivate the subordinate to react positively and in a similarly responsible manner. Confucius talks about the "ideal" man in this way, that is, striving to help others and the community but within a hierarchy. Thus Confucianism tends to create a particularistic culture in which people's behavior is motivated by their relationships with specific individuals. Koreans can be comfortable using different ethical values in different relationships, and they may be very uncomfortable with universalistic values such as those prevalent in the United States, where general rules of behavior apply to all, regardless of the situational relationships at hand.

The Family Model

Perhaps the key model or unit of analysis of Confucianism is the family and the mutual obligations that are central to it. In 2001, Lee Jong Dae, then chairman of the insolvent Daewoo Motor Company, was forced to lay off 7,000 employees. However, he took extraordinary measures to find employment for them, including holding a job fair, sending a personal letter to his counterparts at 26,000 companies begging them each to hire 1 of his fired employees, enlisting politicians to sell his cars, and abjectly bowing to a fired employee at the job fair and profusely apologizing for having to lay him off. Rarely, if ever, do U.S. American executives make such extraordinary efforts (see H. W. Choi, 2001).

If the son successfully carries out his obligations, which include hosting the 60th birthday party, he will be rewarded on his father's death, as he inherits the house as well as a greater portion of his parents' estate than his siblings. Naturally he becomes the family patriarch.

However, this emphasis on both functionality and male dominance creates some issues in the family, specifically an aloof relationship between the husband and wife and between the father and his children. There is a tendency for the father to be both aloof and critical of his children, and he frequently seems always to be expecting greater effort and results from them. For the wife, burdened with many familial obligations, the husband frequently does not provide adequate emotional support. There are now "daddy schools" that attempt to make husbands more responsive emotionally. Wives only attend the final session, during which each husband washes his wife's feet and massages them. Although most families are still male dominated and focused on functional relationships, the popularity of daddy schools has grown so much that it has been exported to the Korean population living in the United States. In total, about 200,000 husbands have attended in Korea and the United States, although about 10% quit before graduating (LaPorte, 2011).

The close relationship between the family and the nation is illustrated by pioneering government programs designed to attack the problems associated with a rapidly aging population. This demographic phenomenon is occurring in numerous developed nations, and few, if any, have attacked the problem as vigorously as Korea. Over 9% of Korea's population who are 65 or older are afflicted with dementia and related diseases, and the percentage is predicted to rise dramatically in future years. Korea has started a "war on dementia" by opening hundreds of neighborhood dementia diagnostic centers. Nursing homes have nearly tripled since 2008, and provision of day care and home care has increased fivefold since 2008 to include nearly 20,000 patients. The government is concerned that age-related diseases will undermine the respect traditionally accorded to age, and even children are actively involved in helping these patients (Belluck, 2010).

At dinnertime during the 60th birthday party, each of the five relationships is activated. The food is placed in the center of the table for all to share in a communal manner. Once members of the family are seated on floor cushions, the son's hardworking wife will fill the father's plate first, and kimchi will definitely be on it.

Confucian relationships demand that the father begin to eat first, followed by others in order of age. Ranking by age is critical and governs so much of Korean life that when Koreans meet a stranger, one of the first topics of conversation is each person's age so that each person can immediately assume the appropriate role in the relationship as the superior or the subservient. In comparison, asking a person's age in many Western cultures is considered intrusive.

With the exception of those who are friends, no one at this party (or anywhere in Korea) refers to others by name. Rather, titles are used to highlight hierarchical rankings. For example, the eldest son will be referred to alternatively as *son, big brother, husband, father, elder,* or *young one* throughout the day, depending on circumstances. The titles are so important that many at the party may not know the names of others. Supposedly some families separated during the Korean War could not reunite because brothers and sisters did not actually know each others' names, making a search impossible.

Strangers by Day, Lovers by Night

Many aphorisms mirror the Confucian perspective on male-female relationships, including the one in this heading, which is focused specifically on husbands and wives. Given the subordination of the wife, it is logical to expect that the wives and their daughters prepare the birthday feast and clean up. Men are expected to be good workers and represent the family in public. The women are to provide children (in particular, at least one male), care for the family, and be subservient in public.

First and foremost, the relationship between a husband and wife is functional. Romantic love is an afterthought that is nice but not critical, for the purpose of marriage is to carry on the family lineage by producing a male heir. Even today, although less often, marriages are often arranged, frequently by matchmakers. As might be expected, the husband and wife may know each other only slightly, if at all, at the time of marriage.

Because of the importance assigned to the functions of husband and wife, Korean families still want to approve or veto any potential union. Families tend to believe that successful unions are created when both husband and wife are of similar social and economic status. Also, ancestral heritage is usually critical when evaluating potential partners, for members of the same family clan, or *tongjok,* cannot marry. A *tongjok* includes families that share a surname and have a similar heritage dating back several generations.

Finding Partners

This emphasis on tradition causes many problems for younger people, as traditional Confucian practice is to separate males and females until marriage. In large cities such as Seoul, it is sometimes difficult to meet potential partners, and more affluent young people sometimes go to "booking clubs," spending hundreds of dollars in one night to engage in a stylized form of matchmaking. Men and women sit at separate tables, and when a man sees a woman he wants to meet, he asks a waiter to bring her to his table. Frequently she acts as if she is resisting but reluctantly accompanies the waiter to the man's table; the waiter may hold her arm firmly, thus signifying her resistance. In the event that she does not like the man when they meet, she can politely leave (see H. W. Choi, 2002).

A newly married woman leaves her parents' household permanently to join her husband's family, in which she ranks at the bottom, below all the other siblings. If she marries the eldest son, she will be required to care for both her husband and his parents. Her standing improves if she delivers a male heir.

In public, women traditionally have entered and exited elevators after men, helped men with their coats, and followed dutifully behind them as they walk down the street. Today such practices are decreasing. Further, as is represented by the yin and yang of the Korean flag, wives do possess power, especially at home.

As this discussion implies, women face difficulties in the workforce. The gap between median earnings of men and women is 40%, in comparison to a gap of 21% in the United States, even though nearly 90% of females attend college and 52% of females work. Apparently the lack of opportunity has motivated many women to seek opportunities outside of Korea. For example, of the 138 women golfers in the elite category of the Ladies Professional Golf Association (LPGA) in 2007, 34—almost a fourth—were Korean (Ramstad, 2007b).

Work Ethic

Korean men's status is a function of their occupation and the company employing them, and the strong Confucian work ethic requires that men work long hours. They are often absent from home as a result. At home the wife has more power than the husband: She manages the family finances, runs all the activities in the home, and takes care of the children. Some men become helpless at home. Hence, Korean widowers often remarry almost immediately after a wife dies, just to keep the household operating effectively.

Korea is noted for its strong work ethic, as we might expect in a Confucian culture. One international consultant was startled by the answer he received when he asked the top executives of a major Korean company what they believed to be their competitive advantage internationally: They enthusiastically cited the work ethic throughout the company. Koreans spend more hours on the job than their counterparts in any other comparably developed nation. Also, it is quite common for men at all levels of business to attend nightly functions with their coworkers and business counterparts. These functions often include not only dinner but late evenings of drinking and karaoke-style festivities.

There is a downside to this excessive emphasis on work, although it is largely responsible for Korea's remarkable transformation from a rural to an industrial nation since 1970. Today agriculture accounts for only 7% of employment, while industry accounts for 27% and services for 66%. However, the Southeast Asian Crisis of 1997 was accompanied by massive layoffs of workers, and many of them lost faith in the relationship between hard work and success/status. Similar issues surround the Great

Recession starting in 2008. The never-ending push for achievement is correlated with high levels of depression and the highest rate of suicide among developed nations who are part of the Organisation of Economic Co-operation and Development (OECD). A recent survey found young Koreans to be the unhappiest subset among nations in the OECD (McDonald, 2011). Subway stations in Seoul have barriers to prevent individuals from jumping on the tracks, and eight bridges have closed-circuit suicide-watch cameras. Mike Weisbart (2010), a U.S. American who is now a permanent resident in Korea, indicates that there is a reason why the words *ppalli-ppalli,* meaning fast, are among the first words that nearly all foreigners learn soon after arrival. One sociological explanation is that Korea has created a modern society in which many of its members live by traditional rules based on family status and shame (Rodriguez, 2007). When too much tension develops between these traditional values and life in the modern world, some Koreans may feel that they have let down their families and experience a feeling of shame, both of which are supposedly precursors to suicide.

Similarly, women work very hard to fulfill their many duties. Because their functions revolve around the home, Korean women tend to be evaluated on their ability to run a tight ship. The Korean home is almost unfailingly well maintained. Some Korean wives who have emigrated to Western nations do not like returning to Korea too often because of the onerous family responsibilities that are automatically thrust on them when they arrive.

Korean children also possess the strong Confucian work ethic. They help out at home and are expected to work hard at school. Korean children attend school 6 days a week, and even the younger students have 2 to 3 hours of homework a night. Like Japan, Korea has a literacy rate that is nearly 100%.

Kimchi's Public Role

The history of kimchi serves to highlight Korea's collectivist nature. As noted earlier, Korea has suffered many periods of foreign occupations, and during each, kimchi reflected the collectivist nature of Koreans, which was critical for survival. Families often had to hide food to protect it from foreign soldiers. Kimchi proved to be perfect for these resourceful people. Because it is a preserved food, Koreans could bury the kimchi underground to protect it from soldiers until the family was ready to eat it.

As in other Asian cultures, Koreans, when first introduced to one another, tend to ask "What company do you work for?" rather than inquiring about a person's title or occupation, which is of much more importance in the West. Also, people use their surnames first, followed by their individual names. Given such collectivism, it is easy to understand why Koreans have traditionally deemphasized individual stars in favor of team effort. However, an emphasis on individualism is emerging, as our discussion of Korean female golfers indicates. Hee Seop Choi (n.d.), first baseman for the Chicago Cubs, reflects this emphasis: "In spring training I'm in every newspaper [in Korea] every day. In the regular season, they watch it on TV. . . . My job is baseball. That's it. After that, I'll talk to my country. I'm happy to do that."

In Korea, what is good for the group is viewed as more important than what is good for the individual. This is a high-context society in which loyalty and the party line are valued more than the truth. Koreans are often uncomfortable with direct Western communication styles. Instead, from the highest levels of government to the house-hold level, people are expected to tell the "truth," which is not facts per se but rather thoughts and feelings conforming to traditional ideals and norms. The messages delivered, then, can be found not in what is said but in the implicit message underlying the spoken words.

Men and women are expected to control their thoughts and emotions and express only that which serves society best, as we might expect in a Confucian culture. For example, when asked to lie under oath to save a friend, more than 90% of people in Western cultures, such as the United States and Canada, but only 37% of the Koreans, would refuse (Trompenaars & Hampden-Turner, 1998).

The Irish of Asia

Koreans can be compared to the Irish because they tend to be more emotional than their Asian neighbors. Kim Sun Yang, a food scientist, addressed this issue of emotion-ality: "Koreans are very much like kimchi—hot tempered. . . . On the outside, both kimchi and Koreans might seem rude, but once you get to know them, they become long-lasting friends" (quoted in J. Solomon, 2001).

Korean kimchi tends to be more fiery than Japanese kimchi. Some estimates sug-gest that Japan produces 70% of the world's kimchi, which has motivated several Korean firms to develop and market creative brands of kimchi and sell them world-wide as the new salsa (J. Solomon, 2001). Any non-Korean company selling its kimchi in Korea leads to emotional reactions in defense of the native product. For example, a small Chinese-owned shop in Seoul began to sell kimchi at half of the cost of Korean brands, and farmers demanded that the government pass a law mandating high tar-iffs. The government was reluctant to do so, as it might cause a trade dispute with China (J. Solomon).

A good amount of this emotional expressiveness can be traced to Korean collectiv-ism and long periods of domination by foreign powers, during which Koreans spas-modically arose in fierce and open rebellion. But some of it is an outgrowth of Buddhism, which 25% of the population practices. The principle of the Middle Way that the Buddha advocated—keeping emotions under control, even to the extent of holding the body as quiet as possible under all conditions—is still dominant in South Korea. As discussed in Chapter 3 on the Japanese garden, such practices in combina-tion with traditional Confucian ideals tend to result in suppressed emotions that periodically flare up.

Given this perspective, it is easy to understand why Catholicism with its emphasis on rituals, collectivism, and shared emotional expressiveness has been much more successful in Korea than in other Asian nations. About 25% of the population, particularly those in the younger generation, practice it. Evangelical Protestantism is also popular, for similar reasons. Also, Christianity is viewed as less restrictive than Confucianism in terms of onerous family obligations, as exemplified by the activities at the 60th birthday party.

Harmony and "Face"

Collectivism and repressed emotional expressiveness are both related to *kibun,* the sense of well-being and harmony among people, which is central to the Korean way of life. The concept of *kibun* is closely related to "face." Taken literally, losing face means losing an eye, a nose, and ultimately the entire face and the person's life. Losing face is a very serious matter, and even minor criticisms in public are problematic. Unlike the Western concept of winning at all costs, face is a set of unspoken rules by means of which everyone's dignity and group harmony are preserved. Negotiations are frequently long and drawn out, simply to avoid losing face and to give face to others. Negotiations also involve a great deal of high-context behavior, including an abhorrence of saying no directly. Palliatives, such as "Perhaps we can consider this proposal at another time," or "That would be difficult," may really be the equivalent of no. Like the context-specific Chinese, the Koreans tend to study an actual situation at great length before agreeing to a course of action, and that study includes getting to know prospective business partners well before doing business with them. Unlike Westerners, who tend to start negotiating by taking a position and then modify it as they proceed, the high-context Koreans are frequently comfortable with an ambiguous position at the start that gradually coalesces into a position or conclusion near the end of the negotiations. U.S. managers listening to an audiotape of Chinese managers making a decision reacted incredulously because of this pattern of behavior, as did Chinese managers who listened to U.S. managers making decisions (Twitchin, 1991). Although no comparable analysis of Koreans and Westerners has taken place, we can reasonably expect similar findings, given the significant Chinese influence on Korea.

If Koreans like someone, they are prone to express this feeling more openly than their Asian neighbors. It is not unusual for a Korean businessman to take off his gold watch and give it to a Western visitor who has just said in passing that he likes the watch. Such actions are also rooted in Buddhism, which believes that the gift giver and not the recipient is the main beneficiary.

Just as kimchi reflects collectivism, it also mirrors the Korean trait of emotional expressiveness. Positive emotions tend to occur not only during the 60th birthday party but also at any meal where kimchi is served. But when the high-context nature of Korean communication is violated, especially when kimchi is on the table, the affront is serious and may well lead to an unpleasant and jarring emotional confrontation.

Business and Culture

Business in Korea is a direct reflection of the cultural values highlighted by kimchi. South Koreans have organized their business activities in a manner similar to that of the Japanese, who resurrected the outlawed *zaibatsu* after World War II and reconfigured them as the modern *keiretsu*. A *keiretsu* is a large consortium of companies, perhaps 300, that have overlapping boards of directors, one large bank, an import-export arm, and subcontractors. An example is Matsushita. In South Korea these groupings, which are heavily family based in terms of ownership, are called *chaebols*. An example is Samsung Corporation. Samsung's sales account for approximately 20% of Korea's gross national product, which is one measure of how important *chaebols* are. However, the operations of the *chaebols* are more reflective of Chinese culture than Japanese culture, because the Japanese stress employee participation to a greater extent. Like the Chinese, the Koreans tend to believe that power flows downward, and they act accordingly. This may be one reason why management and labor are more separate in Korea than in Japan (see Carroll & Gannon, 1997). Ownership in the *chaebols* is also less dispersed among non-family members than in the Japanese *keiretsu*. For example, Samsung is a family-owned company. Because of the Asian crisis of 1997, Korea has become a more open economy, but the *chaebols* are still important.

At work, Koreans have difficulty taking a risky position or making an individual decision. Nearly all action is taken by committees, which provide a buffer to prevent any one person from being responsible for decisions that later prove problematic. A few years ago, for example, Martin Gannon made a presentation at a conference in Korea, before which he described a few procedural activities, such as the placement of the podium, that would facilitate interaction. Although several people supposedly responsible for such activity indicated that everything would be done, in fact, nothing was. In various forms this aversion to taking individual action is repeated in many contexts.

In the public arena, Koreans provide others with very little personal space. While some of this behavior occurs because of crowded living conditions, it also is caused by adherence to cultural values. The respect for relationships and their governance of action applies only to known relationships. If a relationship has not been clearly defined, then Koreans act as if the relationship does not exist. When a relationship does not exist, Koreans will avoid action because they do not know the correct response. Instead, they will treat other people as if they do not exist, leading to no or limited personal space. For example, in such nations as Canada and the United States, lines are universally honored; in Korea, there is no respect for public lines. Instead, people push and jostle to get to the front of the line. In grocery stores, strangers bump into each other with their carts, and they don't even notice this slight inconvenience. By comparison, a fistfight might occur over a similar encounter in the United States.

In the GLOBE study of 62 national societies (House et al., 2004), Korea ranked last in terms of practicing gender egalitarianism and 49th in terms of valuing it, findings that reinforce our previous discussions. Similarly, Korea ranked 18th on the practice of assertiveness, as we might expect from the Irish of Asia, although 31st on valuing it. These findings suggest that Korea is experiencing a conflict between values and practices, most probably because of the rapid transformation of the economy. Still, the value of institutional collectivism remains strong: Korea ranked second on this dimension. Geert Hofstede's research (2001) generally confirms these results.

Boeing conducted a correlational study between Hofstede's scales and airline accident rates. Collectivistic nations experienced airline accidents at 2 times the rate of individualistic nations. When power distance and power were combined as one measure (low to high authority-ranking culture), the accident rate was 3 times as high for authority-ranking nations as for individualistic nations. Korea fits into this authority-ranking category. Malcolm Gladwell (2008) highlights the incidents of such accidents among Korean pilots in the following manner:

> To put that record in perspective, the "loss" rate for an airline like the American carrier United Airlines in the period 1988 to 1998 was .27 per million departures, which means that they lost a plane in an accident about once in every four million flights. The loss rate for Korean Air, in the same period, was 4.79 per million departures—more than *seventeen* times higher. (p. 180)

Based on such results, all of the major airlines introduced communication courses that would deemphasize power relations among members of an airline crew and emphasize that the crew was a team in which communication should be informal (for example, first names are used rather than titles and last names) and open. All crew members were to be treated as equals so that each team member's expertise would be given first priority rather than simply the power position he or she occupied. The pilot was ultimately responsible, but each team member was taught to communicate in such a way that the expertise of all was recognized. Such communication programs have been related to significantly decreased accident rates.

A Confucian Approach

In sum, kimchi's preservative nature and its historical role in safeguarding families in times of crisis and war make it an excellent proxy for the Confucian and collectivist nature of Korean society. Kimchi spotlights the Confucian ability to let time stand still, revere tradition, and create the hierarchical rules surrounding relationships. The use of kimchi to protect families reflects the importance of putting the good of the country and family ahead of the individual, protecting against risk, and understanding the value of the present moment.

However, this perspective on Korean culture may be too oversimplified. As globalization spreads, Koreans have tried mightily to preserve their heritage, but new international Korean superstars in sports, the increasing respect accorded women in the workplace, and the weakening of the financial system created by the *chaebols* in the face of the global economy and markets are slowly making Korea a new place.

Perhaps a supplementary cultural metaphor for Korea is the national flag, whose symbol is the *taeguh,* representing unity and harmony or what Korea essentially values. Still, the *taeguh* has two parts, the yin and the yang. In combination yin and yang connote harmony, but separately they represent opposites. Possibly the opposites better define modern Korea, because the contrasts and tensions in the culture have become more pronounced. These contrasts include the subordination of women in family relationships versus their hidden power in the household; the need for self-control balanced against the explosive volatility of individual emotions; and the hierarchy of power created by the Five Relationships vis-à-vis the collectivism that officially preaches at least a degree of equality among members of the group. Last, but perhaps the most potent contrast, is the pull of history and tradition and the push of globalization. Still, kimchi and its symbolic meanings capture a large part of Korean culture and behavior, and a visitor to this nation would be remiss to overlook its importance.

PART III

Scandinavian Egalitarian Cultures

I n egalitarian cultures, there is a high degree of individualism but a low degree of power distance (horizontal individualism). Status in this type of culture can be measured with interval statistical scaling; that is, a common unit of measurement allows one to say that individual B is 100% more important than individual A; that individual C is 100% more important than individual B; and therefore that individual C is twice as important as individual A on a particular dimension. But this type of culture does not recognize a true zero point such as zero money. Hence it is possible to compare individuals on one dimension at a time but not several dimensions, as there is no way to transform values to one common unit of measurement and arrive at a final score for each individual.

Still, there are various degrees of egalitarianism. Both the Hofstede (2001) study and the GLOBE study (House et al., 2004) have identified Scandinavian nations as a separate group of egalitarian national cultures that are reflective of the most extreme type of egalitarianism currently existing among nations. For example, in the United States and most other nations, a traffic citation for the same violation, such as paying $200 for being over the speed limit by 15 miles an hour, would uniformly apply to all. However, Scandinavian egalitarianism has been associated with the concept that those with more resources should pay more for the same violation than those with less resources. In some instances, the fine for driving 15 miles per hour faster than the speed limit has been more than $100,000. Why and how such concepts and practices have evolved in Scandinavia is the subject of this part of the book.

CHAPTER 9

The Swedish *Stuga*

But Sweden's strengths go deeper. Before the global economic crisis, academic studies had highlighted the superior performance of an economic model based on "consensus and long-run consistency," in the words of Karl Aiginger, director of the Austrian Institute of Economic Research in Vienna. The events of the past three years have only strengthened the case for a system in which politicians, businesses and trade unions agree on the best ways to support long-term economic growth—and then stick to them.

—Ralph Atkins (2010)

Few if any nations have manifested as firm a commitment to cultural values as Sweden. For 65 of the past 81 years, Sweden has been governed by the Social Democratic Party, which champions the values reflected in this quote. Since 2006 center-right parties have won national elections and have decreased some social welfare benefits, including very generous unemployment benefits that supposedly motivated some not to work. However, the Swedish model, which parallels the models followed in other Scandinavian nations such as Finland and Denmark, stresses generous welfare benefits, especially when compared to those of other developed nations such as the United States and Britain, and income equality. The International Monetary Fund (IMF) uses the Gini Index to measure income equality/inequality on a scale of zero to 1, with 1 representing extreme inequity. On this scale, it rates Sweden at .23, which puts it among the most equal nations; by contrast, the United States stands at .45 (Blow, 2011). Still, Sweden is a very good place to do business: It ranks 8th out of 179 nations on the Index of Economic Freedom (T. Miller, 2011) while the United States ranks 9th. In short, the government, regardless of which political party is in power, tries to balance the needs of a competitive economy with its commitment to the welfare of all citizens, a balance that has been the hallmark of the Swedish model.

Sometimes this commitment may seem excessive. Sweden has been generous in admitting foreigners suffering during wartime. Until 2008, Sweden admitted proportionately far more Iraqi refugees than any other nation. Immigration to Sweden has become more difficult since 2008 because of new regulations, motivated at least in part because of the burden it places on the social welfare system. Approximately 12% of Sweden's population is foreign born, with the Iraqis representing the largest group (Ward, 2010). Sweden ranks near the top among nations in terms of absorbing immigrants.

Admittedly there is much to admire in the Swedish model, and the *stuga* or summer/weekend home effectively symbolizes traditional Swedish values. While economic forces and globalization are causing a reevaluation of these traditional values, we can confidently predict that they will be maintained.

Sweden is one of the "three fingers of Scandinavia," located between Norway and Finland. In size, it is just larger than the state of California. Thousands of islands line the coast, and mountains form much of the northwest. Many rivers flow from the mountains through the forests and into the Baltic Sea. Sweden is dotted with lakes, and more than half of the country is forested. Although it rarely snows in the southern part of the country, the north has more than 100 snow days each year. The unique culture of the Swedes has resulted from the struggle to deal with and control harsh surroundings, and the outcome has been a stable society that is economically and socially the envy of many others.

The population of Sweden is 9 million. About 88% of the people are ethnic Swedes. In Sweden, about four out of every five couples are unwed. Under Swedish law, couples have the same rights to property and inheritance whether they are married or not. If Swedes marry, it is generally on the birth of a child. The divorce rate exceeds 50%. Sweden is a highly secular society. Although 95% of Swedes belong to the Evangelical Lutheran Church, most people rarely if ever attend church.

The standard of living is high in Sweden, as indicated above. Slums do not exist, and the crime rate is low. Free, compulsory education has raised the literacy rate to 99%. Sweden has a constitutional monarchy, and the head of government is the prime minister. Members of parliament are elected for 3-year terms.

An appropriate metaphor for Sweden is the *stuga* or summer/weekend home. Before showing how this metaphor accurately reflects modern Swedish society and its cultural mind-set, we need to provide some background about Sweden's history and form of government.

Early History

Sweden's recorded history begins about 500 CE, with a continuing series of minor wars and feuds. The Svea tribe, the largest at the time, gave its name to Sweden or *Sverige,* which means the Realm of the Sveas. About 1000 CE, the famous Vikings formed a tribe of superb seafarers known for their violence and success at ravaging Europe. But the Swedish Vikings soon turned their attention toward the east, setting up principalities in Russia and establishing trading relationships with the Byzantine Empire.

Domination of Sweden by German-speaking groups began in the Middle Ages. Missionaries from German-speaking regions, particularly those in the north, arrived in Sweden during the 9th century but were not successful in converting the Swedes to Christianity until the middle of the 11th century. German-speaking merchants conquered through commerce, as they were the main force in the Hanseatic League, which began in the 13th century. The League unified trade among several small regions and groups along the Baltic Sea, and it gained almost total control over Swedish trade and politics in the 13th century. Although no formal nation of Germany existed until 1871, German-speaking regions essentially ruled Sweden for the next few centuries using a modified form of European feudalism. Still, Swedish farmers held tightly to their ancient rights and privileges under Norse village ordinances and a tradition of Viking democracy, in which the chief was only the first among equals.

Sweden, Norway, and Denmark were united in 1397 as the Union of Kalmar, which was formed because their leaders felt that all of Scandinavia should be ruled by the same monarch, Queen Margareta of Denmark, to fight against German domination. The union was successful in defeating the Germans in battle and stripping some of their power, but German political and commercial influence continued for several centuries.

During the early 16th century, the Union of Kalmar was dissolved, and Sweden became an independent nation. About the same time, Sweden took the first steps toward parliamentary government. A national assembly (the *Riksdag*) was formed, consisting of four estates: nobles, clergy, burghers, and peasants. Gustav Vasa accepted the Swedish throne in 1523 and began the Vasa dynasty, which still rules the country. Gustav Vasa's achievements were remarkable and far-reaching. He supported the Swedish reformation to the Lutheran religion, succeeded in separating church and state for the first time, and strengthened the monarchy by making it hereditary. During the early years of the Vasa dynasty, Sweden became a major military power and sought to expand its trade and territory. The following years were filled with battles. Sweden became a formidable military power and conquered various parts of Europe.

Modern Evolution

The 18th century ushered in the Age of Enlightenment, a time of scientific discovery, growth of the arts, and freedom of thought and expression. In 1769 the Englishman Joseph Marshall, commenting on his travels through Sweden, reported that one could search "in vain for a painter, a poet, a statuary, or a musician" but admitted that "they were unrivalled" in the natural sciences (Jenkins, 1968, p. 63). Swedish leadership in the sciences extended beyond the Age of Enlightenment due to the Swedish talent for orderly classification and systematization. The world's first systematic registration of population statistics was begun in Sweden in 1749, and the census is still taken every year rather than every 10 years, as happens in the United States. In 1819 traveler J. T. James commented, "On the whole, with regard to science, there is no country in Europe which, in proportion to her numbers, has contributed so largely to its advancement as Sweden, and none where it is still so steadily and successfully pursued" (Jenkins, p. 78). Scientists today visit Sweden to gain access to her remarkable compilations of data.

The Age of Freedom followed in the 18th century, during which the *Riksdag* introduced a constitution limiting the power of the monarchy. This Age of Freedom witnessed the start of the transformation of Sweden from an agriculturally based nation to a trading nation. In 1809 the Treaty of Fredrikshamn was signed with Russia, resulting in the loss of Finland as part of Sweden. Norway separated into a sovereign state in 1905. In 1912 the three Scandinavian countries of Sweden, Norway, and Finland declared their agreement on a policy of neutrality, even during world wars.

Movement toward equality came fairly late in Sweden, but Swedes were much more progressive than their European or American counterparts after the movement began. In 1842 the *Riksdag* introduced compulsory education and elementary schools. Universal suffrage, including for women, was proclaimed in 1921. In 1971 the *Riksdag* became a single chamber, and in 1974 a new constitution gave the ruling monarch purely ceremonial functions.

Sweden's late Industrial Revolution in the early 1900s contributed to its swift rise from poverty to prosperity. The country had already established solid educational and transportation systems, which supported industrialization. Also, its valuable timber and iron, which were in great demand in Europe, provided money for expansion into new industries. Sweden had discovered early that a partnership of private and public interests was the best combination for both achieving economic success and benefiting as many people as possible. The evolution into a social democratic system had started.

Social Democracy

To understand modern Sweden, it is imperative to understand Swedish social democracy, which in Sweden is quite different from socialism or communism; it is a merging of the ideals of socialism and capitalism. This form of government is the hallmark of the Social Democratic Party. As indicated previously, all political parties accept many of the traditional ideas of social democracy within the framework of a more capitalistic and privatized economy.

More specifically, the government provides generous programs to make jobs available to all who wish to work, pensions for the elderly, sickness benefits for all workers, housing allowances, free education through college and university, almost-free medical care, and part-free dental care. Family benefits are abundant in Sweden. And, as the quote at the top of the chapter indicates, the government, industry, and trade unions work closely together on long-term plans to ensure economic prosperity. The government also provides child allowances for all children and gives advance payments for child support. Day care centers, called *dagis,* are offered by local authorities. All of these benefits are important in Sweden because about 90% of all Swedish women of working age are employed outside of the home.

Equal pay for equal work is another feature of egalitarianism in Sweden. Still, many occupations are clearly divided by gender. Swedish women face the same problems as those in the United States in trying to move up the corporate ladder. Sweden is also struggling with providing equality to immigrants. As indicated earlier, about 12% of residents are immigrants, many of whom came for political and humanitarian reasons, and they have difficulty achieving the standard of living that native Swedes enjoy. The government has made tremendous attempts to integrate immigrants and to offer equal opportunity, but there is a countermovement among some Swedes to restrict drastically the number of immigrants.

Furniss and Tilton (1977) stress six fundamental values of Swedish social democracy: equality, freedom, democracy, solidarity, security, and efficiency. This form of democracy in Sweden is often called the Swedish model and sometimes "humane capitalism"; it relies heavily on the close collaboration of business, government, and labor. Social democracy has created a society mostly free of the inequalities of capitalism and many of the inefficiencies of authoritarian central planning.

The Swedish word *lagom* is key to understanding the rationale behind social democracy. *Lagom* is untranslatable but essentially means both "middle-road" and "reasonable." The word (*lag* meaning group and *om* around) is said to derive from a circle of men sharing a single mug: it was essential that no one take more than his fair share in order to leave equal shares for all others. This word is representative of the foremost characteristic of Swedes: unemotional practicality. Swedes tend to believe that all problems can be solved rationally and satisfactorily through the proper application of reason. The Swedes have shown unusual thoroughness and ingenuity in translating their beliefs into social reality. The result of their efforts is a uniquely sensible way of life: a calm, well-ordered existence that is part welfare, part technological advancement, part economic innovation, and part common sense.

One advantage to this pursuit of *lagom* or rational thought and behavior is that arguments erupt less frequently than in most if not all other nations. When the rational Swedes begin the decision-making process, they have a strong tendency to find agreement. This allows the Swedes to reach a consensus quickly and act to solve the pending problem. In fact, Swedes are so zealous and efficient at attacking perceived problems in their society that they often will import not only ideas to solve problems but problems as well. Thus, John Kenneth Galbraith's (1958) *The Affluent Society* led the Swedish government to bigger and better spending programs to eliminate "public squalor," although it would be difficult to find anything in Sweden to fit Galbraith's image of American conditions.

Social democracy has been dubbed "the middle way" because it is a reasonable middle road between capitalism and socialism. Since social democracy is so consistent with the Swedish value of *lagom,* it has become much more than simply a model for economic planning. Social democracy is a functioning social system in Sweden as well as a political party. Therefore, even when the Social Democratic Party is not in power, Sweden is still a social democracy. As Kesselman et al. (1987) explain:

> Anyone who visits Sweden will quickly recognize that the influence of Social Democratic thinking extends beyond the 45 percent of the adult population who vote for the Social Democrats. To a remarkable extent, the Swedish Social Democrats have been able to define the problems on the political agenda and the terms in which these problems have been discussed by all major political parties. It is in this sense that social democracy might be described as the hegemonic force in postwar Swedish politics. (p. 529)

However, the downside of this model is that it is sometimes difficult to motivate employees, even to come to work. Labor costs, both direct and indirect, are high, and several large Swedish firms have moved some operations abroad to developing nations for this reason. Some firms have even moved their headquarters to another nation to avoid corporate taxes they regard as excessive. However, since 2006 the government has made it more desirable for employees to work than to be unemployed. Taxes, both corporate and personal, have also decreased but are still much higher than those found in the United States and many other developed nations.

The interesting paradox in Swedish social democracy is the seemingly contradictory goals of equality and efficiency. Modern Sweden, however, seems to have found a viable mean between equitable distribution of profits and economic performance, even given the problems described above. Milner (1989) believes that the "institutionalized social solidarity around them enables Swedes to feel secure and thus prepared to follow the market in the promising directions it opens up" (p. 17).

The ability to achieve both equality and efficiency may be a result of certain circumstances in Sweden conducive to a successful social democracy. Sweden's small size and relative cultural homogeneity allow for social and cultural consensus. International competitiveness is valued universally but is also seen as the means to secure the cultural value of equality.

The Swedish Summer Home

The dream of most Swedes is to spend the summer in the family *stuga,* the summer home. The typical summer home is a small wooden house, painted the traditional reddish-brown color that is a byproduct of copper mining. The doors and windows are trimmed in white, the facilities are modest, and the furniture is plain and simple.

Only the necessities are found in the summer home. Often, there is an outhouse, but otherwise there is no disturbance to the surrounding area.

More than 600,000 *stugas* are scattered everywhere in Sweden, around the lakes and in the countryside. No fences or "no trespassing" signs are to be found. Usually Swedes cannot see another house from their *stuga*, but sometimes clusters of homes make a small community. Most Swedes are only a generation or two away from the farm, so many can go back to the old family home. Some Swedes use the summer homes of friends or relatives, and others may have access to a *stuga* owned by their company.

The ideal vacation is spent at the *stuga* in June or July, communing with nature. Outdoor activities range from river rafting to walking or just sitting underneath a tree and reflecting on life. Swedes usually like to spend time alone or in small family groups at the *stuga*. The idea is quite different from the American "the more the merrier" vacation or the German vacation, during which activities take place on a regular and predictable basis so that no time is wasted. Swedes want to use this time to get away from it all, be alone with their thoughts, rejuvenate themselves, and refresh their ties to nature.

One Swedish graduate student in the United States began to wax enthusiastic about her upcoming vacation in Sweden to her American friends. She planned to spend an entire month by herself at her family's *stuga*, taking along only a few small necessities, a radio, a small rowboat, and numerous books she wanted to read. The Americans were incredulous, and one of them expressed the unspoken but unanimous group opinion: the month sounded more like a prison term than a vacation. While many Americans react this way, Swedes generally nod knowingly and approvingly when another Swede offers such an enthusiastic description of an upcoming vacation.

Sweden's best-known artist, Carl Larsson (1853–1919), focused primarily on the *stuga* and the informal country style it represents. His art reflects the admired lifestyle highlighted in Swedish magazines today and the simple lines of Swedish design that have made firms such as IKEA and Volvo world famous. IKEA, the Swedish multinational, seems to be a perfect reflection of such values, and its simple designs and furniture that can be assembled easily by a homeowner have proved to be popular in many nations.

As this discussion intimates, Swedish culture and values are mirrored in the metaphor of the Swedish summer home or *stuga*. The following characteristics of the *stuga* clearly reflect Swedish culture: love of untrammeled nature and tradition, individualism through self-development, and equality.

Love of Untrammeled Nature and Tradition

The national hymn in Sweden is *"Du gamla du fria,"* which concentrates not on glory, honor, or warfare but on a land of high mountains, silence, and joyfulness. Gustav

Sundberg, in his 1910 book on Swedish national culture, discussed this issue in the following manner:

> The most deeply ingrained trait in the Swedish temperament . . . is a strong love of nature. . . . This feeling is equally warm among both high and low—albeit not equally conscious—and this strong attachment to nature, which in some cases may produce wild unruly emotions, is on the other hand the most profound explanation of the indestructible power and health of the Swedish nation. (p. 104)

The Swedes' love and respect for nature is a strongly held value that has led to many laws that protect wildlife, parks, and waterways. The country has been termed a "green lung"—a place where you can breathe and enjoy the untouched countryside. Swedes were environmentalists long before it became fashionable, probably because of their intense love of nature and the desire to preserve the way it was when families lived on the farm. Sweden was the first nation to pass an environmental protection law, in 1909.

This preoccupation with nature stems in large measure from a centuries-long battle against the hostile elements in a vast, damp, cold, and sparsely settled land. It is not surprising that engineers are held in high esteem in Sweden, as their efforts are directed toward combating and controlling the forces of nature. Similarly the Nordic invention of orienteering is a result of this desire to combat the forces of nature. The orienteer is set down in a remote, unfamiliar location and challenged to find his or her way out with the help of only a map and a compass.

One of the least densely populated countries in Europe with only 20.2 people per square kilometer, Sweden has the space to provide ample outdoor activities of many kinds. Walking is a favorite pastime of the Swedes, and a long walk on the lakeshore or in one of the many national parks is a preferred way to commune with nature. Fishing and picking flowers, berries, or mushrooms are also on the back-to-nature agenda. It is regarded positively when employees return to Stockholm on Monday morning with the stain of berries on their hands.

For a true back-to-nature experience, Swedes like to go up north with a backpack and walk in the mountains for days. Some hikers follow well-established trails and stay overnight in cabins made available to all. Other hikers prefer to stay overnight in tents that they carry with them, and these hikers use only a map and compass to guide them. Another back-to-nature experience that Swedes love is rafting. The journey starts at one end of a lake where there are many logs from Sweden's huge timber industry. For a fee, participants make their own rafts from the logs and find their way downstream, where the logs are returned for use in the timber mills. The trip takes several days, and riders stop the raft at the side of the lake at night and make camp. This experience captures the essence of the idea of getting back to nature and living off the land.

Until relatively recently, Sweden was an agriculturally based society. About 90% of families lived on farms until the Industrial Revolution in the early 1900s brought workers to the cities. Sweden has changed quickly into an industrialized, city-based country, with only 2% of the population now employed in agriculture. Thus many Swedes remember life on the farm or have certainly heard stories about it. Ties to the farm are very strong and deeply personal. Although they enjoy everyday city life, most Swedes are still peasants at heart who could easily return to the ways of their ancestors, for the past is not too distant. Back-to-the-farm and back-to-nature romanticism constitutes a major part of Swedish culture. Swedes long for an escape to the country where they can remind themselves of a simpler time.

Furthermore, Swedes generally value tradition and still have a village culture. The Swedes deal with this paradox by spending the summer in the traditional village setting of the old family home. As Arne Ruth (1984) relates,

> The [Swedish] model presents the paradoxical spectacle of a nation possessing more of the outward trappings of modernity than any other society, yet at heart remaining the incarnation of Tönnies's mythical *Gemeinschaft.* With the cushions of tradition gone, the brutally modern forces of *Gesellschaft* throw the society's delicately balanced social structure out of gear. (p. 63)

Geert Hofstede's (2001) 53-nation study of cultures indicated that Sweden clusters with those countries emphasizing a small power distance between individuals and groups in society, a pattern that is typically found in a village setting. Swedes tend to be horizontal individualists who favor norms of equality over equity, in sharp contrast to the United States (see Törnblom, Jonsson, & Foa, 1985). Their individualism is manifested by their extreme self-reliance and avoidance of long-term relationships outside of the family. For example, Swedes tend to pay for a cigarette on the spot if they ask for one; living alone is common, even among the elderly; and Swedes who stay overnight at a friend's home bring their own sheets (see Daun, 1991). Thus, it is not surprising that commentators regularly report in their surveys that about 90% of Swedes like to live "as they please."

The Swedes have traditionally had the characteristics of practicality and rationality. When practicality conflicts with other values, practicality tends to win. This can be seen repeatedly in the setting of national policy. Staunchly neutral since its last war in 1814, Sweden can be said to avoid war largely because its citizens view it as impractical and, in the long run, not beneficial to any of the participants.

Individualism Through Self-Development

The summer home is a place to go for solitude and quiet individualism. Swedes escape into the nature surrounding the summer home to spend some time reflecting on life and getting in touch with their inner selves. In the untouched countryside, people can stroll for miles without coming across another human being. Great value is placed on this time for self-development. Managers complain about the unwillingness of workers to put in overtime so that they can pursue such activities. Currently most Swedes are entitled to 5 weeks of vacation a year, which they generally prefer to take in the summer. As noted above, absenteeism and excessive use of sick leave are problems for Swedish managers, although less so in recent years.

Swedes must work to afford to pay the high national sales tax, and a dual income is essential for a family to maintain the quality of life desired. Although Sweden is a "doing" culture and Swedes are achievement oriented, they tend to prefer jobs where they can develop as people, and they frequently look for jobs that are intrinsically interesting or that allow them to spend more time away from work. Decentralized decision making is valued and consistent with the ideals of equality and independence. Swedes are highly committed to quality of life and, thus, tend to value private time alone or with family as more valued or at least as valued as work.

Much of the emphasis on self-development is motivated by individualism. There is a common misperception that Sweden is a collectivist society because it is a welfare state. Swedes pay high taxes to fund a system where education, housing, health care, and many other programs are available to all. It is true that Swedes value equality, but they have come a long way from the farm. Modern Swedes tend to place individual interests before collective interests. Gustav Sundberg, a Swedish statistician, observed in 1912 that "we Swedes love and are interested in nature, not people" (Jenkins, 1968, p. 154).

In Hofstede's (2001) 53-nation study of cultural values, Sweden clusters with those nations emphasizing individualism, but it is obviously more collectivistic than the United States, which ranks first on this measure. Swedish individualism is different than American individualism, however, because Swedes desire individualism to facilitate personal development (horizontal individualism) whereas American individualism is more competitive in nature (vertical individualism).

The emphasis on community and family has eroded with the increased industrialization of Sweden. As a visiting American observed (Heclo & Madsen, 1987),

> Officially Swedish ideology is very good. Their attitude toward society as a whole and the world is generous. But the funny thing is that people don't care much about their neighbors. Swedes are so insular, self-contained. It's easy to be lonesome here. (p. 4)

This American experienced the typical treatment of visitors to Sweden: They are cordially and generously welcomed, but then the enthusiasm quickly ends. At heart Swedes are basically loners who are not accustomed to thinking in terms of other individuals. After the original courtesies are over, it is usually difficult to pursue the relationship on a deeper level.

Ironically the success of social welfare programs has fueled this move toward individualism. Many Swedes feel that paying high taxes absolves them of responsibility to other generations and to the needy. Likewise, teenagers in Sweden are encouraged to be independent, and they frequently travel outside of the country with friends. As a result, Swedish teenagers tend to be much more mature than the typical American teenager. A weaker bond between the generations has resulted. As Hans Zetterberg (1997) explains, "The milk of human kindness therefore flows less frequently from one human being to another; instead, it is dispensed in homogenized form through regulations and institutions" (p. 334).

An amazingly large number of organizations in Sweden exist to promote the interests of their members in a variety of areas. Close to 200,000 membership organizations create a dense social network of 2,000 associations per 100,000 people. An apparent contradiction exists between the Swede's preference for working toward a goal as a group and the individual isolation that is a national characteristic. The organizational system is accepted only because it is seen as the most practical and efficient way to get things done. Interactions among members are generally kept on a formal basis, thus preserving the individual's isolation.

Because the views of a single person are seldom voiced without first being digested by a group, many Swedish organizations tend to promote conformity. It has even been argued that the end result is a lack of individual initiative and creativity, although the success of the economic system and its businesses would suggest otherwise. Further, it is a difficult jump in logic to state that organizations cause the typically reserved affect of the average Swede. Rather, it is more likely that the organizations have allowed the natural temperament of the Swedes to be retained while satisfying the practical need for a public voice for their concerns.

Swedish individualism is further supported by an insistence on individual rights, which seems to extend even to trivial levels. When it rains, pedestrians who are splashed by a passing car have recourse in the rules. They take the license number, go to the police station, and file a complaint, indicating that their clothes were damaged. If the court finds that the driver did not take appropriate precautions, he or she is ordered to pay damages (in this case to have the clothes cleaned). Sweden also has a form of legal welfare that allows those who cannot afford court costs to pursue a civil case.

Given this emphasis on individualism and individual rights, it is little wonder that the Swedes invented the concept of the ombudsman, an official whose job is to process and negotiate issues on behalf of others. There are several types of ombudsmen. These include the equality ombudsman, who is largely responsible for promoting equality between men and women and for opposing discrimination against immigrants; the justice ombudsman, whose role is to ensure that citizens are treated fairly by governmental authorities; and the consumer ombudsman, who is responsible for ensuring that companies treat consumers fairly.

Equality

The summer home brings into focus most of the important values in Sweden, including equality. The ancient tradition of *Allemansratt,* or "everyman's right," permits anyone, within reason, to camp anywhere for a night or to walk, ski, or paddle a canoe anywhere. Fishing is generally free, but licenses, permits, or papers are frequently required. *Allemansratt* also allows Swedes to pass over any grounds, fields, or woods regardless of who owns them. Swedes are careful not to abuse this right and generally do not disturb the areas close to an individual *stuga.* They use common sense, but it is not illegal to pick berries, mushrooms, or flowers from any source. There are no laws of trespass; "keep out" or "private" signs do not exist. Equal access to the greatly loved nature in Sweden is representative of the value of equality in other aspects of Swedish life.

The egalitarian passion that has been almost as important as a moral force is termed *jamlikhet.* Success in the creation of an egalitarian society hinged on rapid economic growth and social democracy, and the national wealth resulting from the Industrial Revolution was distributed to all citizens through the guidance of social democratic policies. The goal was to organize society much as the Swedes would construct a machine. In pursuit of this goal, Swedes are constantly looking for new approaches or ideas that will make the societal machinery run better. For example, Sweden's distinctive and cutting-edge retirement systems automatically adjust monthly payments both upward and downward so that retirees do not become wealthier or poorer than working citizens.

An outstanding example of this egalitarian passion is the *dagsböter,* or "day fine," designed to equalize legal penalties in terms of income levels. A formula is used to calculate the fine based on income level, resulting in significant differences. For example, for the same infraction, low-income defendants may pay $1,650, whereas their high-income counterparts pay $12,150.

However, the Swedish machinery designed to achieve equality is quite complicated. Sweden could not be described as a simple and efficient machine. Rather, it is more like a Rube Goldberg invention: highly complicated and inefficient in the sense that many unnecessary steps and processes must be followed, but nevertheless the goals are eventually achieved.

The expression *krangel-Sverige* roughly means "red-tape Sweden," and it denotes a bewildering assortment of complications, regulations, procedures, and channels of authority. This does not imply that the system has broken down but merely that it is inconvenient for those who must deal with it. Swedes feel that the main function of the system is to operate; whether it gives pain, irritation, or pleasure to someone along the way is irrelevant to the main reason for its existence. Thus the Stockholm tramways regularly pass would-be passengers if the tramway is behind schedule because the function of a tramway is to meet the established timetable, and serving the public is only secondary. Similarly the medical care system is intended to deliver medical care. Because waiting in line does not seriously interfere with this goal, long waits to obtain medical care are viewed as not worthy of discussion.

In the past, the legendary Swedish *titelsjuka,* or title sickness, resulted in telephone listings that included Swedes' titles. Today, about 50% of the listings have titles following the names, but this is done for the practical reason of distinguishing people. The fact that the practice has declined is evidence of the desire for a society of strict equality. Comparable opinion polls indicate that only 2% of Swedes desire high social status compared to 7% of Americans and 25% of Germans (Triandis, 2002). Most Swedes now label themselves "middle class." The principle of universality means that all Swedes, regardless of social position, rely on the same network of services. Thus all have a stake in the quality and accessibility of services.

However, Swedes are demonstrating their individualism in distinctive ways. Surnames ending in *-son* (son of) are very common, with Johansson, Adernson, and Karlsson being most popular; of the 100 most common surnames, 42 end in *-son.* In recent years, younger Swedes have officially changed their surnames, demonstrating individualism (Tagliabue, 2011). On the other hand, egalitarianism is demonstrated in the game of golf. Sweden produces a disporportionate number of well-known golfers, in large part because golf courses at private clubs are much cheaper to play in Sweden than in the United States. The nation has 480 golf clubs, and no municipal clubs exist. Golf is not an elite and expensive sport in Sweden as it is in many nations, and more than 600,000 Swedes are registered golfers (Echikson, 2008).

On Hofstede's (2001) masculinity-femininity scale, Sweden is extremely feminine when compared to other nations in that 53-nation study, and this finding was confirmed by the GLOBE study (House et al., 2004). Femininity is defined as the extent to which the dominant values in society emphasize relationships among people, concern for others, and the overall quality of life. Such femininity and the emphasis on being a loner described above represent a paradox (both-and thinking rather than either-or thinking). This paradox is typical of value paradoxes that all cultures manifest (see de Mooij, 2011). Further, the characteristic of femininity is descriptive of the Swedes, but in some respects the society is changing. Relationships among people are becoming more distant, and concern for others is eroding due to increased individualism.

Such forces as globalization and immigration have resulted in a change in the ideological climate but not in the moral content of Swedish social policies; the issue is really the extent of the state's prerogatives versus individual and family rights. As early as 1984, Arne Ruth pointed out that the ideals and policies espoused by the Social Democrats needed to be updated and reinforced by new models:

A rationalistic futurism took the place of religion; social and technological change was felt to be not only unavoidable, but morally imperative. Antitraditionalism became, paradoxically, the dominant tradition. . . . Industrial organization and technological innovation are among the oldest and most formidable currents in Swedish culture. . . . There will need to be a new source for the cultural myths necessary to release once again the social energy that has for so long characterized the Swedish model. (p. 93)

Thus, the opposition to the Swedish model by the new breed of Swedes appears to be the result of the loss of a sense of community and heritage that occurred due to rapid industrialization. Sweden is now preoccupied with such domestic problems as high taxes to support the welfare system, alternative energy sources, a declining work ethic, the physical and social environment, globalization, and the purchase of Swedish firms by non-Swedish firms. Still, the unity of the Swedish mind-set is remarkable, as is the Swedes' devotion to untrammeled nature. We can expect that the Swedes will continue to emphasize the values and attitudes associated with their summer homes, particularly those of love of nature and tradition, individualism expressed through self-development, and equality.

CHAPTER 10

The Finnish Sauna

If sauna, tar, or alcohol doesn't help, you are sick to die.

—Finnish adage

Finns are reverential about the sauna. In the glow of the softly lit wood-lined space, they chat jovially or fall into a comfortable silence. The heat makes one welcome a dip in ice-cold water or a roll in the snow, as improbable as that sounds. Food and drink afterward never tasted so delicious. There is etiquette which has to do with practical and safety questions, but generous Finns will walk you through it. As is their method of rearing children, it's a window to the Finnish psyche.

—Anonymous Finn (quoted in Kaiser & Perkins, 2005)

F inland is located between Sweden and Russia on the Baltic Sea and has a population of 5.3 million. There are 15.7 people per square kilometer in comparison to 32.9 in the United States. The gross national product (GNP) per head is US$51,320, compared to a U.S. GNP of $46,350. On the Index of Economic Freedom, which combines 10 submeasures such as level of corruption and respect for property rights, Finland ranks 17 out of 179 nations, which means it is a very good place in which to do business (T. Miller, 2011). With 2 million saunas in Finland, the sauna density is clearly greater than that of any other country in the world. Most of the saunas are in the countryside, where 70% of the land surrounding the 60,000 lakes is forested. Finland also extends beyond mainland Finland into the Archipelago Sea with its 80,000 islands, which include the self-governing, Swedish-speaking Åland Islands province. Throughout Finland both Finnish and Swedish are official languages. However, most mainland Finnish-speaking Finns, who have taken obligatory Swedish courses in school, have only limited competence in that language.

The sauna began in the forests as a hole in the ground with hot stones and evolved into a small log cabin. The sauna metaphor is functionally and symbolically related to local and nature-focused values and customs. Over time Finns have moved from an agricultural environment next to the forests into urban environments. Urban living became significant only in the 1950s. As Finland has moved from an agrarian to an urban base, the countryside has remained not far away and more like a backyard down the road for many Finns. The recent administrative change from 415 municipalities to 336 municipalities has not affected the relative location of towns and cities: 67 urban, 74 semi-urban, and 274 rural. Helsinki is the largest city with a population of 591,112. Four other cities have a population close to 200,000 each, and 14 have more than 40,000 each. The Finnish government is currently integrating small towns into larger urban units to provide an economic base for improving social services.

The manifest or seemingly obvious functional roles of the sauna as a place of birth and physical cleaning during life and after death belongs to history, but the sauna's latent or hidden or symbolic roles have become an integrated part of most urban living units. Finns in urban places have easy access to saunas, which are frequently attached to homes or businesses. Small apartments are even integrating a modern "box" sauna into their limited living space. However, the dream and actuality of returning every summer to the sauna in a summer cottage have remained a key part of Finnish reality.

Saunas are located almost everywhere and play a role in the local social context, for example, as a family weekly ritual and as a gathering place for friends to discuss the local gossip and politics. The sauna is also used as a place both to relax and do business. As an illustration, Finnish businesspeople may well have a beer as they cool off after a sauna and then call clients to finalize business deals. Or they may discuss important business issues that they have had difficulty resolving during the regular workday. There are saunas in other nations such as Sweden and Ireland. However, the distinction between the manifest or apparent functional roles and the latent, hidden, or symbolic roles of saunas in Finland is distinctive, if not unique, and beyond comparison.

In this chapter, we employ the sauna as a cultural metaphor for Finnish values and practices. Using the sauna opens the door to an integrative discussion involving history, nature, the economy, social class structure, manager-subordinate relationships, communication norms, and so on. The three major themes associated with the sauna that we explore in this chapter are the transition from survival despite a harsh environment to political and economic success; apparent meanings and symbolic functions, that is, a secular "holy" place of equality; and communication and comfort with quietude.

As a Nordic and Scandinavian country, the Finnish welfare state overlaps with the Swedish metaphoric example focusing on the *stuga*. Finland has high taxes, universal health care, speeding fines related to income level, free education, and so on (see Chapter 9). Also, as equality-matching or egalitarian nations, Scandinavian nations have high scores in comparative rankings of nations on individualism and gender equality as well as low scores on power distance (see Hofstede, 2001; House et al., 2004). Hence this chapter focuses on those aspects of Finnish culture that differ from those of other Scandinavian cultures.

From Survival to Political and Economic Success

We begin with Finland's historical roots, which evolved into a Finnish Scandinavian society, and then turn to different aspects of Finnish culture where the sauna is often important. The roots of identity that are still active in the Finnish mind and culture are clearly the sauna, nature/forests, and survival, the last of which means that Finland has created political and economic competencies to achieve successful relations with both the neighboring countries that once ruled its territory and the globalizing world.

Whereas more than 90% of the world's nations are multiethnic, Finland is a relatively homogeneous country united by shared history, language, and religion. Finnish development has evolved via moving from "living at the mercy" of both nature and being politically dominated by other nations toward "living in harmony" with nature and a changing political reality.

This nation has experienced historical periods during which both a harsh natural environment and political domination by other countries, especially by Russia and Sweden, challenged it. It has turned these challenges into living in harmony with both nature and international political realities. Finland is a welfare society in which economic development has been a long-term process, bringing Finland to top international rankings as a very competitive, highly educated, and ethically outstanding society with a very low level of corruption. Its unique political history has evolved out of keeping the best from a centuries-long period of Swedish domination. For example, Finland maintained the Swedish legal system when it became part of the Russian Empire in 1809 as an autonomous region. It operated in a relatively independent fashion until it became a fully independent nation in 1917. During World War II, Finland defended itself against Soviet invaders, remained independent, and developed a postwar diplomatic rapprochement with its Soviet neighbor that allowed it to remain an integral part of Western capitalism and democracy.

History and Nature

To understand the roots of Finnish reality, it is important to begin with the relationship between "at the mercy of" and "in harmony with" nature. According to the mythic origins of the Finnish people, Väinämöinen, the poet eternal of the classic *Kalevala* songs, stood upon a barren island and asked Pellervoinen, the god of fields, to do the planting, sow the seeds, and sow them thickly in the treeless land (Friberg, 1988). The trees grew into forests. In the forest lived ancient Finnish tribes led by men and women alike. Historically the forest and nature have been the foundation of life for

Finns. Finns are well aware of the saying "At the mercy of nature." They clearly recognize both the inherent limits and opportunities of living in harmony with nature. Over time the traditional myths related to the forest have become less influential, but the dream of most Finns is to have time in nature and to sauna close to a lake at least every summer.

Out of the forest grew the sauna and a nation of sturdy farmers and crofters—landless farmers who were also "freemen"—in contrast to Russian serfs. They kept their noses to the grindstone, struggling against an arctic frontier and a difficult geopolitical-cultural frontier in which Russia was dominant. As children of the forest, Finns gradually carved out a zone of comfort by processing raw materials from the forest to sell on foreign markets—first tar and timber to European naval powers and later paper to European and American newspapers. Today Finland is a leader both in the paper and shipbuilding industries, and Finns build every fourth big cruise ship in the world.

Prior to the mid-1800s, the forest was easily interpreted as a primitive area with limited hope for economic development. However, technological innovations capable of turning natural resources such as wood into exportable products played a key role in Finnish economic evolution starting in the mid-1800s. These innovations also created a high demand for the resources that Finnish forests can produce, which has led to expanding Finnish paper-related production technology abroad. Being in harmony with nature—recognizing limits and opportunities—opened the door to long-term technical and economic development beyond reliance on nature-produced resources, even if organic agriculture is becoming more important in Finland.

If the forest represented the basis for and symbolism of innovation for a century and a half, the multinational, cutting-edge, high-technology Finnish firm Nokia created a symbolic message throughout Finland at the turn of the 21st century: Without innovation, there is no hope for economic success in a globalizing world for a small nation such as Finland. However, as noted below, Nokia has been experiencing some difficulty in recent years. Living in harmony with nature now requires benefiting from the development of both Finnish human resources and technology.

History and Foreign Control

Finland has a long history of both living at the mercy of foreign domination and developing competence to create a successful degree of diplomatic harmony with other nations. The Swedes came from the west in the 12th century and gradually turned Finnish tribes into a subordinated part of Sweden for 700 years. After the Napoleonic wars in the early 1800s, the European powers redrew the map of Europe and transferred Finland from Sweden to Russia. Unlike other parts of the Russian Empire, Finland benefited from an autonomous status as a grand duchy and retained the laws and Protestant religion from the Swedish era, which differed from Russian feudalism and Russian Orthodox Christianity.

During this period of autonomy in the Russian Empire, Finns developed their own culture and political institutions in the land where they had always lived. In essence, they created a Finnish—neither Swedish nor Russian—identity. The Finnish parliament gave every Finnish adult (male and female) the right to vote and, if elected, to be a member of Parliament during the period of "Russification"—Russian attempts to reduce Finland's autonomy at the turn of the 20th century. This movement toward egalitarian democracy, which occurred here before it appeared in any other country, supported Finnish determination to keep its autonomous rights to govern local issues. "Before this reform 70% of all adult people were outside suffrage," Professor Borg, formerly of Finland's Tampere University and a member of Parliament in the 1970s, told BBC News (Smith-Spark, 2006).

Movement toward egalitarian universal suffrage was a critical way to develop a sense of national unity to defend Finnish autonomous rights. Johan Sibelius, the most famous Finnish classical composer, reinforced Finnish identity by employing nature-focused motifs and patriotism to bring home these points. His symphonic poem, *Finlandia,* is the major symbol of Finnish determination to resist Russification.

Independence

Finland finally became an independent nation in 1917 after the collapse of the Russian Empire and the rise of the Soviet Union. The Finnish Parliament declared its independence on December 6, 1917, and the Soviet government recognized Finland's independence on December 18. However, Finland was politically unstable, and a civil war occurred between the "Reds" representing the ideology of communism and the "Whites" representing the ideology of conservatism in the first half of 1918. This civil war pitting Finns against Finns remains the most controversial and emotionally loaded event in the history of modern Finland.

After the civil war, the existence of a Soviet neighbor and possible revival of leftist extremism led to the distribution of part of privately owned land to landless rural inhabitants. At that time, the government believed that redistribution of farmland property was essential for preventing the growth of communism in Finland. One of the unique aspects of Finnish history is this partial land redistribution by conservatives, in marked contrast to outright land transfer and confiscation in communist countries to gain leftist support. Today many, if not all, economists believe that widespread ownership of property is a key determinant of successful economic development. Hernando de Soto (2000) titled his path-breaking exploration of owning property *The Mystery of Capital: Why Capitalism Triumphs in the West and Fails Everywhere Else.* Finland was decades ahead of many other nations because of land distribution to the landless.

After becoming independent in 1917, Finland slowly developed an economic infrastructure that made it possible to sell paper to the *New York Times,* which enabled Finland to be the only European country that paid its debts to the United States during the 1930s. The Finnish image of financial prudence was so powerful that one American newspaper published a picture of a man responding to a bill collector with the following question: "Who do you think I am, Finland?" (Berry, 1990, p. 53).

Just prior to World War II, Hitler "gave" the Soviet Union permission to "have" Finland. During the war, Finland claimed neutrality but was in fact allied with Germany and involved in the invasion of the Soviet Union. However, the Russian army defeated the Finnish army and confiscated some Finnish land, forcing 400,000 Finns or 11% of the population to move rather than be part of Russia. Still, Finland remained independent.

Against great odds Finland remained an independent country on the postwar Soviet border. It implemented a "harmony with political reality" strategy to move cautiously from "survival to success" (Jakobson, 1987, p. 7). The nation moved toward the West by emphasizing cautious "sauna diplomacy," sometimes even using the sauna as a place to find relaxation, goodwill, and some degree of equality between Soviet and Finnish diplomatic negotiators. For example, Kekkonen invited his Soviet counterpart to sauna where the two national leaders could free themselves, to some extent, from outside concerns. They discussed and sweated out problems in the sauna so that the Soviet Union and Finland would be in harmony, at least to some extent. The Soviet Union was eventually ready in 1973 to accept Finnish membership in the European Economic Community. This was the predecessor to the European Union (EU), which Finland joined in 1995.

During the Finnish presidency of the EU in 2006, the concept of sauna diplomacy was still active: The Finnish minister of foreign affairs was encouraged to invite the Greek and Turkish sides of the Cyprus issue to negotiate in a Finnish sauna.

The Strength of People

Throughout its history, Finland has been like a prickly juniper that bent when necessary but refused to break. Finland's strength has been in its people, particularly in their ability to accept limits when necessary and to maximize opportunity and cautiously move beyond those limits when possible. Shared survival against external political threats contributed to the creation of a social welfare society, successful economic development, a high degree of market competition, and a welfare state stressing social equality. In market-pricing cultures (for example, the United States and Great Britain), social welfare cohesion and competition are often believed to be a counterproductive combination. In contrast, an integration of social welfare cohesion and governmental policies stressing competitiveness has become the basis for Finnish success against external political challenges and international competition. Such success is distinctive in a nation with such a small population.

All of this historical development required *sisu*—a combination of guts, determination, and optimistic realism with moments of pessimism to survive against great odds. Morrison and Conaway (2006) indicate that this word is extremely difficult to translate but is sometimes translated as "never say die" (p. 162). *Sisu* has served Finland well with its traditional collective meaning, but the current meaning of the term has changed, referring more to individual will and determination as, for example, when a Finn wins an Olympic gold medal after falling down during the race. The current meaning of the term has also broadened to include brand names ranging from powerful trucks to one Finnish candy product labeled *sisu*.

Finland is one of the few euro countries with a government debt level under 50% of gross domestic product. Nevertheless, Finland is currently experiencing some economic and political challenges related to both the great global recession that began in 2008 and the EU's efforts to prevent the economic collapse of some euro members. In the 2011 elections, a populist party increased its representation from 2.5% to 19.5%, and its platform included a call for an anti-euro Finnish policy and less openness to immigrants. This party feels that the nation's money would be better spent on protecting Finnish social welfare. Nevertheless, the majority of the Finnish parliament is committed to the euro and willing to support other euro countries—but only if those countries accept stricter economic accountability and the private financial sectors carry a larger part of the burden. In addition to Finland, other EU countries such as France and Holland are also experiencing different levels of anti-EU and anti-immigration populist growth. In contrast to Finland, some EU nations such as Great Britain and Sweden have retained their own currencies, refused to support fully the euro-crisis countries, and are not under the pressure common to nations that use the euro as their currency. Finns justifiably believe that within the limits imposed by climatic, economic, and geopolitical realities, they have historically done it all on their own, and they have performed spectacularly.

Given the Finnish communication norm that modesty brings respect, Finns will rarely make this explicit when communicating with people from other cultures. Pride must remain active but under the surface. The Finnish saying "If you run away from a wolf, you will run into a bear" (Berry, 1994) resonates well with the deeply held Finnish value of finding ways to resolve seemingly impossible problems as soon as they appear and then to move forward. This fits in with Finland's new brand mission's focus on convincing Finns that they should become aware of and more actively communicate the strengths of Finland's culture to others, while remaining realistic about future challenges at home and abroad.

The Social Welfare State

An egalitarian sauna approach to diplomacy was integrated into the development of a social welfare state after World War II. Finland needed more children, healthy adults to work, attractive employment opportunities and wages to minimize the size of the small Communist Party in Finland, better education tied to future development, and a supportive governmental role in economic development. Today the differences between Finland and the other Scandinavian countries related to gender and social class equality are small. Still, there are other variations among equality-matching or egalitarian nations, including Canada and Germany (see Part IV). The GLOBE study (House et al., 2004) and the Hofstede study (2001) come to a similar conclusion about the uniqueness of the Scandinavian nations.

In 1871 writer and historian Zachris Topelius succinctly summarized the Finnish political objective, given its small size, harsh winters, and the desire to be independent of other nations: "To be neutral, to be self-sufficient, to have the freedom to look after one's own" (quoted in Mead, 1989, p. 15). Topelius's goals have been realized, as confirmed by international rankings of nations in terms of multiple indicators. Finland has consistently ranked at or near the top on each of them, for example, environmental sustainability; competitiveness; a low level of corruption; and the scores of 15-year-old students in mathematics, science, and reading.

The sauna, found around every corner, allows the Finns to relax briefly and build up energy among friends and fellow citizens before moving forward quickly once again to overcome almost overwhelming problems, which they have historically attacked with patience and vigor. As a result, the economy did not develop in terms of short-term responses to "quarter-to-quarter" stock market pressures. In the United States, small groups make decisions in a quick huddle and act on the basis of their best guess (see Chapter 16); in Finland the decision-making process is longer and more deliberative. Finland's president Tarja Halonen (2007) summarizes the Finnish innovative version of a "Nordic welfare society model": "In order to exploit the real benefits of research, we need to be patient and far-sighted and to invest in a sustained manner equally in education, science and technological development."

Sauna: A Secular "Holy" Place of Equality

Entering a sauna is often similar to entering a holy place full of the spirituality of nature. A Finnish proverb is that people should behave in the sauna as they do in church. The ideal associated with the sauna is a nonreligious cleansing of body and soul. Entering the sauna signifies leaving burdens and controversies behind, relaxing, and cleaning more than the surface of oneself. There is often a combination of privacy and togetherness that is taken for granted by Finns while being difficult for non-Finns to understand. For example, Finns often share comfort with quietude in the sauna, but at other times they also talk about private matters or humorously joke among themselves in a good-spirited fashion. In short, Finns are people comfortable with both quietness and with talking in different ways. Taking an argument into the sauna corresponds to taking one into a church service, which Finns regard negatively. However, discussing the matter as equals in a nonemotional manner, either after sauna or during it, is acceptable and frequently leads to successful resolutions. In some cultures, nudity is associated primarily with sex. In a Finnish sauna, by contrast, nudity has nothing to do with sex but with relaxation and the cleaning of the body inside and on the surface.

The word *sauna* is the only Finnish word that is used throughout the world. It moved into the German language after publication of a sauna advertisement: "If you want to experience heaven and hell simultaneously, go to a Finnish sauna" (Laaksonen, 1999, p. 279). For a moment, one can be at the mercy of too much water thrown on very hot stones but also feel in harmony with the relaxation that follows. During a summer tour of Finland, Robert G. Kaiser and Lucian Perkins of the *Washington Post* wrote about the sauna in an article titled "Finland Diary" and presented an unqualified positive viewpoint: "This, our first sauna experience, was everything promised: We finished feeling refreshed and invigorated. The wrinkles and bumps caused by days of hard travelling quickly disappeared from our bodies" (2005). A description of the sauna does not end, however, with reference to throwing water on hot rocks to send steam throughout the sauna. The sauna is associated not only with roots in history and a secular "holy" place of equality but also with the expression of values that exist throughout Finnish society.

Sauna Practice

Many families grow up in the sauna. A weekly ritual tends to reinforce togetherness. All members of the family are together until the children are teenagers. Sauna is more than just a time together; it is also a time during which everyone learns to enjoy respecting the quiet of others, even if some would prefer to talk, and to have something nice to eat and drink after the sauna. Whenever the children return home as adults, it is common that the sauna is ready for them, especially in rural areas where it is heated with wood rather than electricity.

Sauna is a weekly ritual for many and even a daily ritual for some Finns, and it is an essential ritual for Christmas and midsummer when the sun is visible between 20 and 24 hours each day. To have a midsummer celebration with family and close friends beside a lake in the forest without a sauna is incomprehensible. Even if most families live in urban areas with access to sauna, bringing sauna and nature together is the decided preference for summer vacations. Vacations outside of Finland occur usually in the dark autumn and winter.

All people are equal when they enter the sauna, and there are no visible symbols of social status. In business, there is a de-emphasis of social status, and everyone sits where they want to sit, whether a janitor or a CEO. Moments of egalitarian relaxation contribute to better superior-subordinate and human relationships. There is also an implicit link between the concept of equality in sauna and the responsibility to carry one's weight at work. As a consequence, there is an emphasis at work on the autonomy of subordinates. Once assigned a task, the subordinates become "self-bossed," possess individual responsibility to perform quality work, and contact the superior only when a problem arises. Such a participative managerial hierarchy with a "bottom-up" dimension facilitates autonomous development and allows Finns to create a vision for the future shared by all.

As suggested earlier, Finland shares its emphasis on equality with other Scandinavian nations. For example, fines for legal infractions are related to income levels, as the assumption is that those receiving high incomes must suffer as much as those receiving low incomes. In one situation, a Nokia executive was fined $71,400 for driving 18 miles over the speed limit. A low-income person might receive a fine only of $50 for the same infraction (Stecklow, 2001).

There are different interpretations of what it means to be Finnish. An American interpretation is aptly illustrated in the following incident. During a training session for three groups—Americans, Finns, and Swedes in a Finnish subsidiary in the United States—an American came to the consultant during the first coffee break and mentioned that there were problems with the Finns because they didn't talk much, if at all. This American didn't know what the Finns were thinking or hiding, if they ever thought independently, or whether they were interested during group discussions. In contrast, he said, the Swedes were easy to deal with because they talked, even if not as much as Americans. During the afternoon coffee break, the same American told the consultant that the Swedes were difficult because, after a decision had been made, they kept discussing whether it should be modified. In contrast, the American now felt that the Finns were easy to work with because they focused on the goal and, once a decision had been made, implemented it quickly.

The following day, the Americans politely raised a question about Finnish inability to make decisions, and the Finns politely responded that they felt the Americans also had a problem. The consultant then asked if there was perhaps a difference between "let's get the ball rolling" (which from a Finnish perspective might not be a good decision) and "let's plan carefully before the ball gets rolling" (which from an American perspective might prevent the ball from ever rolling). During the discussion, the American response was the following:

> For years we have been misunderstanding each other. Maybe long-term planning is what the Finns and Swedes have in common, but the Swedes just keep discussing after a decision has been made and the Finns seem to be silent during the planning process, yet there is no silence when they act on a decision. (Berry, 2009b, pp. 93–94)

This interpretation is consistent with the discussion in the next section of this chapter, "Communication: Comfort With Quietude," of the importance of Finnish active silence, which is often invisible to others. Active silence is when Finns are respecting and listening to others as they reflect while waiting their turn to talk. This active silence leads to creativity among the Finns. Even if talking is expected, Finns would say, it should be done at appropriate times, which Finnish culture often defines differently than other national cultures. For example, the Martti Ahtisaari–led Finnish team that participated in the United Nations discussion about ways to solve the Kosovo conflict was the last to talk, not only about their own ideas but also about those of others in the negotiation. Ahtisaari won the Nobel Peace award in 2008 for his activities in Africa, Asia, and Kosovo because of his approach, which directly reflects Finnish culture.

Gender Equality

Gender equality is rather high in Scandinavian nations, even if the ideal and reality don't always match. For instance, we encounter a paradox related to sauna and gender equality in business and political contexts: The sauna has traditionally symbolized equality, but typically the sexes do not sauna together.

However, women have significantly increased their leadership roles in business and politics and have assumed major leadership roles in the Finnish parliament. In 2007 Finland had a female president, and 42% of the parliament elected was female. Furthermore, the Finnish government has a tradition of gender balance for ministers, with more women than men in the period 2007–2011 and a female prime minister during part of that period. The 2011 government reversed the balance for ministers so that there is one more male than female.

Given the egalitarian emphasis in Finland, these results are not surprising. Even stories about ancient Finnish tribes living in the forest refer to leadership by men and women alike. As an autonomous part of the Russian empire, Finland was the second parliament in the world to give women the right to vote (New Zealand was first), and it was the first to give women both the right to vote and to stand for election. Sixty years after World War II, a postage stamp dedicated to the defense of Finland during that conflict focused on the active role of women supporting the Finnish soldiers. Hence the tradition among men of making important decisions without the active involvement of women during sauna negotiations has been reduced significantly.

Egalitarian Education

In contemporary Finnish society, the educational system is unique. It offers egalitarian educational opportunities regardless of the geographic location or the social background of the children. The Organization for Economic Cooperation and Development (OECD) conducts regular surveys as part of its Program for International Student Assessment (PISA). When the results from 2000 and 2003 are combined, Finland is at the top for learning skills among 15-year-olds for mathematics, science, and reading. In the 2006 PISA tests, Finnish students were at the top for science. In more recent years, Finnish students have consistently ranked at or near the top of students involved in such studies. All education in Finland is free up to the doctorate level, school teachers are highly educated, competition to be accepted into the university department of education is very strong, and salaries for teachers are determined at the national level with modifications according to the local costs of living.

This egalitarian focus in education is sometimes criticized for not challenging the most talented students enough. However, it provides a basis for advanced levels of education throughout society. In fact, educators from many nations travel to Finland to see firsthand "What Makes Finnish Kids So Smart" (Gamerman, 2008). According to Gamerman, Finnish teachers still favor traditional methods such as chalkboards rather than PowerPoint slides and other high-tech approaches, and the classes are somewhat chaotic and unstructured, but an intense focus on achieving high goals combined with strong teacher-student and student-student interactions within small classes are hallmarks of the system. For Finns, in contrast to Americans, "equality of opportunity" comes via "equality of condition" in education and health care.

Communication: Comfort With Quietude

Two Finnish academicians raised the intriguing question "Silence—myth or reality?" and responded: "The terminology [of English] may . . . be highly misleading depending on the type of culture that it is applied to" (Sajavaara & Lehtonon, 1997, p. 279). Finland is not a silent culture; it is a culture full of people "comfortable with quietude."

An American television program, CBS's long-running *60 Minutes*, produced a documentary on Finland called "Tango Finlandia." Words used by Finns to describe themselves in "Tango Finlandia" included *shy, silent, private,* and *brooding,* all of which can be very positive terms when translated back into Finnish. Thus it was startling for Finnish viewers to hear voiceover terms used by the American commentator that included *clinically shy, terminally melancholy, depressed, mourning, brooding,* and *isolated,* as well as the following judgment: "The national mission seemed to be not be noticed, grimly in touch with no one but themselves . . . a difficult time making even the most casual social contact" (Berry, Carbaugh, & Nurmikari-Berry, 2004, p. 267). This American commentary—a mirror rather than a window—epitomizes the incorrect ways many people from other cultures interpret Finnish comfort with quietness.

The Meaning of Active Silence

One of the challenges related to understanding other cultures and explaining one's own cultural ways to others is reliance on a shared international language, English, which carries multiple hidden cultural meanings for people from different cultures. As many Finns have emphasized in private conversations and writings on the subject, silence is not necessarily silence, even if the dictionary tells us so. There are various types of silences connoted by facial expressions, body motions, and even the length of each silence. Each type of silence expresses a particular positive, neutral, or negative meaning to those socialized in this fashion.

The English words *silent* and *shy,* which Finns often use to describe themselves to others, are often inaccurate when compared to what they actually mean in the Finnish language. This is especially the case when communicating Finnish comfort with quietude to people from cultures that are uncomfortable with silence. In many other cultures, these two words, *silent* and *shy,* can create negative images and suggest social disconnection. In Finland the words can carry negative meanings, but Finns interpret their active silence positively in terms of the following cultural meanings: communicating without words, listening, thinking, reflecting, pondering before acting or using words in important situations, and being in one's own thoughts and/or respecting the privacy of others even when surrounded by others. This positive Finnish interpretation of active silence, which is often difficult for outsiders to understand or even notice, corresponds to the combination of privacy and togetherness in sauna.

Movement back and forth between both comfort with quietness and comfort with talking is a natural Finnish way of being. There is no Finnish comfort with quietness if there isn't also comfort with talking when one has something relevant to say. What others might interpret as a "disconnected social void" can be full of Finnish respect for others, reflection, and a willingness to stand behind one's word. Sauna is a symbol of cleanliness that can be associated with the "cleanness" of society based on the subtle clarity of individual moral and physical responsibilities, for example, concepts of politeness and honesty.

In Finland, people make promises without using the word *promise.* They feel that the idea of pledging to do something is implied by the message itself. Similarly, Finns rarely use the word *please,* since courtesy is implicit. The meanings that are associated with the English words are considered to exist in the statements or requests themselves. As a result, Finns might be puzzled or suspicious when words such as *promise* or *please* are used. Conversely, native speakers of English might be confused or offended when English-speaking Finns fail to use such language.

Respect for privacy, communicating togetherness nonverbally, and being in harmony with a social or physical environment reflect deep Finnish comfort with quietness. For example, a U.S. American was driving a Finnish woman visitor through the Appalachian mountains to observe the beautiful fall leaves. She was silent and wrapped up in the enjoyment of the beautiful displays of leaves. Suddenly he stopped and demanded to know what was wrong. By contrast, a Finnish friend would have assumed that her quietness was a sign of deep feeling and reverence for nature. After listening to a recounting of this story, a Frenchman said that silence is like "the angle going away." It was not easy for him to understand that perhaps she was "with the angle" until asked "What is bothering you!" (Berry, Carbaugh, & Nurmikari-Berry, 2009, pp. 48–49).

The High-Tech Invasion

Finland became well-known as a high-tech nation in large part because of the great success of Nokia beginning in the early 1990s. The Nokia era of mobile phones added a new dimension to the Finnish communication style, even if the basics remain the same. Nokia's "connecting people" message can be interpreted by Finns in both positive and negative ways. One should not talk just to be talking, Finns believe, but a mobile phone call often means that the other person considers it important to talk. Therefore, they have a responsibility to make a full response. There is, however, a Finnish discomfort with the extent to which this modern connecting system invades the traditional desire to enjoy one's privacy. A common solution in many cases is to send a text message if appropriate and to talk when necessary. In this regard, people from other nations who keep their cell phones in their cars and strictly limit their use are probably comparable to their Finnish counterparts.

The sauna is still a place where one relaxes and enjoys harmony with nature. Still, as soon as people are out of the sauna, especially businesspeople, their mobile phones can be polluting the harmony of the relaxing postsauna environment and disconnecting the people who were together in the sauna. The phones allow businesspeople to go anywhere at any time but also reinforce the concept that the modern world is not the same as the natural world with which they are most comfortable. On the other hand, Finns who go abroad without access to mobile phone connections can feel very disconnected—not because they feel the need to call often but because of the unease that others can't contact them about something important.

Factors other than comfort with quietude influence communication, especially in business. Charismatic leadership, or expecting subordinates to follow leaders out of a blind faith in their exceptional power, can be counterproductive in Finland, even though it is highly valued in North America and Latin America. Finns value their unique "self-bossed" autonomy related to quality, honesty, equality, autonomy, independence, and responsibility. If leadership actively interferes with the expression of these values, Finns often feel that the possibilities for creativity are being denied.

Another factor influencing communication is that the Finnish norm is to allow other people to finish talking before saying something. Thus speakers do not overlap with one another, which demonstrates both a respect for others and a belief that quiet listening can often be a form of reflection. Hence silence, which is often understood in other cultures as agreement, is not necessarily the case in Finland. Finns might remain quiet if they disagree but don't have a good alternative to put on the table. From childhood, they are taught to never interrupt.

While the cell phone is pervasive in Finland, Nokia's fortunes have changed in recent years. At the height of its success, it actually contributed 4% to Finland's GNP. This contribution is now about 1.5%. The government is acutely aware of the importance of high-tech industries in a globalized world and is actively encouraging high-tech entrepreneurship in partnership with business firms and universities. At Aalto University, the nation's flagship campus, the Center for Entrepreneurship is sponsoring programs to help small high-tech start-ups. One such venture is Rovio Mobile, the maker of a hit cell phone game called Angry Birds, which has been downloaded 36 million times for US$1.00 per download (see ben-Aaron, 2010). In 2010 the government declared that Finnish citizens have a "legal right" to a broadband connection to communicate its commitment to equality and the Finnish future of high-tech.

Personal Style

Furthermore, Finns tend to stick to their plans, sometimes simply because of stubbornness but often because of the importance they attach to making a decision based on careful planning. To change a person's opinion in Finland, sharing quality information is more effective than using clever communication tactics.

Finns also prefer meetings based on premeeting preparation rather than brainstorming meetings. Those who talk the most are those who come well prepared. Similarly, listening to different ideas and opinions before speaking is esteemed. Everyone listens to a person who communicates meaningful information but is respectful of others' ideas.

Finnish values of quality can be seen in the sauna, especially when individuals are together but relaxing in their own ways, with the cleaning process going deep below the surface. This link between Finnish values and sauna can also be connected to the Finnish concepts of honesty and trust, which go beyond "don't lie/steal" to mean "stand behind one's words." For example, Finns tend to de-emphasize words such as *promise* or *please,* as discussed previously. The meanings are embedded in communication norms. Thus such words are often missing when Finns speak English. If a Finn has to say *please* or *I promise* in Finnish, everyone assumes that there are hidden problems of which they have not been apprised. Unfortunately, the Finnish reliance on a "grammar" of honesty and nonverbal politeness can easily hide, at least initially, such deep values as independence, responsibility, and politeness from outsiders.

Finnish comfort with quietude is one natural way to be in harmony with nature, one's self, and others. This comfort, which does not deny the importance of talking, frequently masks the complexity of active silence related to creativity and nonverbal communication expressive of both togetherness and respect for others. Initially a short-term visitor can easily be confused, especially when Finns fail to explain that their taken-for-granted active silence is full of respect for others. Similarly Finns might be initially confused when French people interrupt to show interest and Americans ask "How are you?" when walking past without expecting an answer. The more we realize how we (and others) talk about ourselves when talking about others, the more people "uncomfortable with silence" and people "comfortable with quietness" can begin to move beyond being at the "mercy of intercultural communication discomfort" toward "being in harmony with multiple ways of communicating" (Berry, 2009a, p. 78).

Most Liveable Nation

This, then, is Finland, a small nation with spectacular economic and political success that evolved out of a difficult natural and political environment. In 2007 Matthew Kahn, an environmental economist, ranked 141 nations in terms of a livability criterion, and Finland finished first followed by Iceland, Norway, Sweden, and Austria; the United States was 25th (Kahn & Lostys, 2007). Other studies have also rated Finland very highly in overall quality of life if not always first.

As this chapter has demonstrated, Finland is similar to other Scandinavian nations in terms of many values, but some of the differences are significant. They evolved out of the history and geographical position of the nation. In many countries, people refer to pessimism or optimism. The "Tango Finlandia" commentator from CBS's *60 Minutes* referred to "terminal melancholy" when describing Finns. As one Finnish student explained to exchange students,

> For us Finns *melancholy* means something like yearning, longing or even hope and desire. These are all positive words that live inside every Finn. Melancholy is a national characteristic rather than a symbol of depressed individuals. . . . There may be something like pessimistic streaks in Finnish culture, but the word *pessimism* is too strong. Finns are more like realists rather than optimistic or pessimistic people. We have our feet firmly on the ground, are hard working, and look forward to the future. But we realize that life is full of complexity. We must be prepared for difficult times even if we have hope in our hearts. (Berry et al., 2009, p. 42)

Finland's unique history helps to explain why Finns tend to emphasize realism, granted that there have been both very low and very high points over many centuries. And the sauna, which combines aspects of heaven and hell, is a realistic institution rooted in history and nature. It remains central to the Finnish way of life and offers examples of Finnish values related to communication norms, the quality of action, social equality and autonomy, and social and organizational responsibility.

CHAPTER 11

The Danish Christmas Luncheon

Christmas in Denmark goes on and on. The Danes really enjoy seeing their relatives.... Here in Denmark, there is no end to who you might meet for a Christmas lunch.... Everybody was dancing around the tree, holding hands and singing their lungs out. Even 80-year-old Granny was hopping about.

—Tom Gilbert, English researcher at
Copenhagen University (quoted in Henderson, 2010, p. 14)

D enmark, which has a population of 5.6 million, is an affluent and highly educated nation in which the gross domestic product (GDP) per person is $62,120, ranking it eighth among nations. It is a small country, about 10 times smaller than its neighbor Sweden, but with a long coastline of 4,545 miles. Since 1985 the population increase has been positive and fueled by immigration. According to the Danish government, relative to other European countries, Danish unemployment is low largely because of the increasing participation of women in the workforce. In recent years, knowledge-intensive industries have grown rapidly, and 86% of Danes have access to the Internet at home. It is an excellent country in which to do business: It ranks 8th among 189 nations in terms of the Index of Economic Freedom (T. Miller, 2011).

Denmark is situated in northern Europe, jutting out into the North Sea from Germany. Sweden and Norway are nearby. Denmark, Sweden, Norway, Finland, Iceland, and the Faeroe Islands in combination form Scandinavia. Although the Faeroe Islands and Greenland are part of the kingdom of Denmark, they are governed by home rule. The focus of this chapter is Denmark itself, which is composed of 406 islands. This peninsular country is linked by land to Germany and is flat, which has made the use of bicycles popular; former President Clinton was invited to tour by this means on one official visit.

The geographical location is accompanied by variable weather, which can be cold, gray, and rainy throughout the year. Probably because of its history, geography, and small population, this equality-matching and egalitarian nation has developed a unique culture.

Our cultural metaphor for Denmark is the Christmas luncheon or *Julefrokost*. Although numerous nations have Christmas-related festivities and parties, Denmark's luncheon has become a unique institution that provides insight into the Danish culture.

All or almost all businesses and organizations in Denmark host a Christmas luncheon, which typically occurs on one of three Fridays in December set aside officially for this purpose. Some businesses schedule the luncheon for other times, such as Saturday evening. Subways and railroads are open around the clock on these three Fridays to ensure that everyone gets home safely. The hosting organization generally provides the alcoholic and nonalcoholic beverages, while employees bring the food. The luncheon tends to begin about or after 1:00 PM; in many organizations, it starts in the early evening and extends late into the night, frequently ending at 2:00 or 3:00 AM. Traditional dishes include herring, rib roast, meatballs, rye bread, cheese, and rice pudding.

While the provision of public transit on these occasions suggests a nation that is conservative in terms of ensuring the safety of its citizens, the Danish Christmas party seems to differ little—at least superficially—from parties throughout the world at this time of the year. Denmark is a controlled culture in terms of emotional expressiveness and outlandish behavior when compared to many other cultures, although the Danes are more expressive than other Scandinavians, even to the extent of seeing themselves as the "Italians of Scandinavia." During the Christmas party, most inhibitions are overcome, and employees may even express inappropriate and possibly hostile feelings toward the organization, its management, and other employees. Overt sexual overtures and even extramarital affairs related to the party are not uncommon. These activities may not be forgotten, but they are condoned, although a major repercussion may well be widespread gossip.

A working wife attends her luncheon by herself while her husband babysits the children one weekend, and then they switch roles on another weekend. In recent years, spouses have tried to attend each other's luncheons, assuming they occur on different nights. In short, for one day a year, Danes are allowed to express thoughts and emotions that are seen as clearly inappropriate at all other times for all of the reasons provided in the rest of this chapter.

Interdependent Individualism

In some ways, Denmark faces many of the critical issues confronting all small nations. Queen Margrethe I of Denmark united Denmark, Norway, and Sweden in 1397. Norway belonged to Denmark until 1814, as did southernmost Sweden until 1658. Schleswig and Holstein in north Germany were also part of Denmark until 1864. Periodic wars led to a gradual diminution of both the military power and the size of Denmark.

During World War II, Germany invaded both Norway and Denmark. The German military demanded that all Jews in the nation wear armbands identifying them as Jewish. The Danish king, in a wonderful display of leadership, put on such an armband, and the citizens quickly followed his example. The Danes then attempted to secretly transport all Jews out of the country to the safety of neutral Sweden by a series of dangerous activities, saving about 95% of the 7,000 Jewish residents.

Denmark is clearly an individualistic nation, similar to its northern European counterparts, and is ranked 9th of 53 nations by Hofstede (2001) on this measure. However, its geography, small size, and historical experiences have helped to create a type of individualism that might best be characterized as interdependent. To some extent, this is borne out by the GLOBE study (House et al., 2004) in which researchers found that Denmark scored very low on in-group collectivism practices (indicating an individualistic orientation) and high on societal institutional collectivism practices (indicating a collectivistic orientation). Thus, we see some interesting differences on individualism at the individual and societal levels.

Denmark is a social democracy, like Sweden and other similarly inclined nations, and it provides all sorts of social services, facilitating a sense of equality among its citizens. Thus it is not surprising that Denmark is low on power distance and acceptance of risk; in the Hofstede (2001) study, it ranked 51 of the 53 nations on both counts, and the more recent GLOBE study (House et al., 2004) had an almost identical set of findings on the two dimensions. It is, however, a caring nation, as its social democracy suggests, and the Hofstede study ranked it third highest on femininity. The GLOBE study placed it fifth on gender egalitarianism, which is similar to Hofstede's masculinity-femininity dimension. Still, open and frank discussions and debates are encouraged, and many political parties represent various points of view, some of which lie outside of the social democratic framework. Such minority parties are generally weak.

Furthermore, as these extreme rankings suggest, it takes a delicate balance to ensure that individual expressiveness and group norms are both respected. Thus, even if Danes are wealthy, they play down this aspect of their lives, thus de-emphasizing the power distance between themselves and others even at the expense of individualistic expressiveness. For example, an affluent Dane might not have a large and ostentatious residence. Part of this self-effacement comes from the Lutheranism that pervades the culture, although few Danes attend church on a regular basis. The political system is rooted in social norms that are enforced by subtle peer pressure and the Lutheran heritage, which with its emphasis on community and distrust of ostentation reinforces modern social democratic policies (Kuttner, 2008).

The Danes are tolerant about everything except intolerance, which is one of the reasons that they were very surprised at the extreme negative reactions from around the Muslim world in 2005 to the decision of a newspaper, *Jyllands-Posten,* to publish cartoons depicting the prophet Muhammad. According to a study of 72 nations by scientists from Aarhus University in Denmark, the Danes are also among the least gelotophobic ("fear of being laughed at") nations in the world because of the high level of freedom of expression, which also explains why they found the negative reaction to the cartoons so puzzling.

Interdependent individualism as practiced by the Danes has been articulated by a few critical writers, including Nikolai Grundtvig (1783–1872), a Danish minister who studied in England. He observed that the educational community at England's Trinity College emphasized mutual respect, which was in marked contrast to the more authoritarian educational system then in place in Denmark. Fundamental to his way of thinking was that people must know themselves before they can know others, but this requires being able to say *we* and mean *I* at the same time. People must understand that they are unique and interesting without making the mistake of believing that they are the only individuals who are interesting.

However, other influential Danish writers have conceptualized interdependent individualism with a much more restrictive set of guidelines. Aksel Sandemose described the "law of Jante" in such a way in a well-known novel, *En flygtning krysser sitt spor.* Briefly, the protagonist commits a murder in his hometown, but readers learn that the conformist values in this hometown are essentially responsible for the murder, as these values destroyed the protagonist's ability to act against them. The law of Jante includes the following (Sandemose, cited in Gorman, 2011):

> Don't think you're anything special, Don't think you're as good as *we*, Don't think you're smarter than *we*, Don't convince yourself that you're better than *we*, Don't think you know more than *we*, Don't think you are more important than *we*, Don't think *you* are good at anything, Don't laugh at *us*, Don't think anyone cares about *you*, Don't think *you* can teach *us* anything. (p. 1)

The other side of this concept of *janteloven* is that companies may be open to innovative ideas from their customers; in business, this provides a fertile ground for citizen-driven product design. For example, the Danish company Lego is famous for tapping its customers to help develop its robotics kit (Fitzgerald, 2007).

Interdependent individualism is usually enacted in Denmark in a gentler manner than the Sandemose description suggests, but the essential point is that there is a tendency toward conformity, and the Christmas luncheon provides an escape valve that allows average citizens to express forbidden thoughts and emotions. For many Danes, and for many citizens of northern European nations, this valve is not sufficient to ward off the melancholia that may well be caused by the dreary weather, which lasts for long periods each year, and the social pressures on Danes, as suggested by the law of Jante.

Geographic Ambivalence

After the 1864 war in which it lost Schleswig and Holstein, Denmark was the second-smallest nation in the world. It could well have ended up as part of Germany after Germany became a nation in 1871, and Denmark certainly faced this threat again during World War II. It is well known as a small Scandinavian nation, but its culture can be considered a mixture of Scandinavian and German. Given all of the threats it faces, it is not surprising that Denmark joined NATO at the earliest opportunity, ahead of its Scandinavian neighbors; it also helped to found the United Nations after World War II. Its military is virtually nonexistent and is composed in large part of a medical corps set up to deal with national emergencies. Denmark is a member, but a relatively reluctant one, of the European Union (EU) and was known as the "footnote" member because of all of the items to which it would not give full approval, thus requiring footnotes noting Danish disapproval.

Commentators sometimes portray Denmark as the Italy of Scandinavia, suggesting that it has a much more relaxed approach to life than its neighbors. It is no accident that the famous Tivoli Gardens are located in Copenhagen and considered to be a symbol of Denmark. This 20-acre amusement park has more than 20 restaurants and regular musical shows. One American commented on the relaxed atmosphere when observing the Danes at an amusement park:

> There's a jovial warmth. Danes drinking their Tuborg or Carlsberg beer join for a song. Clothes and colors seem so varied and merry. Couples hold hands and eat their soft ice cream. Children run loose with pockets filled with candy. At those rare moments both the security and the spontaneity of life in Denmark cannot be exceeded. (Heinrich, 1990, p. 48)

In a study of international happiness involving 80,000 respondents, Denmark was the surprising first-place winner. According to Professor Kaare Christenson of the University of Southern Denmark, who was interviewed on the CBS newsmagazine *60 Minutes,* "What we basically figured out was that although the Danes were very happy with their life, when we looked at their expectations, they were pretty modest." Free health care and subsidized child and elder care may also play a role. According to Dr. Martin Seligman, the founder of the positive psychology movement, Denmark also ranked highest in Europe on a measure that went beyond happiness: the measure of flourishing. When people were asked not only about their moods but also about their relationships with others and the sense that they were accomplishing something, Denmark and Switzerland scored very high among 23 European countries (Tierney, 2011).

A generally relaxed atmosphere is counterbalanced by an emphasis on predictability, simplicity, and practicality. Danish lawns and flower gardens are carefully tended, and parks are clean. Danish-modern furniture is world famous for its simplicity and practicality. Similarly the educational system emphasizes science. Denmark's most famous scientist was Niels Bohr (1885–1962), a Nobel laureate in physics; only seven other nations equal or surpass Denmark in numbers of Nobel laureates in physiology or medicine.

One of the challenges that Denmark faces is an increasing shortage of labor. Young Danes are global citizens who take advantage of the great education in Denmark but then move to other EU countries, where taxes are much lower than the possible 63% upper limit in Denmark (Dougherty, 2007). This marginal tax rate results in income redistribution that makes Denmark almost the most equal society in the world but brings its own set of problems. Low-skilled immigrants consume a disproportionate share of public services. Although the Danes get a lot back for their taxes (unemployment benefits, pensions, health care), there is not much margin for complications, which may strain the budget in unexpected ways (Kuttner, 2008). The global recession has also begun to strain the welfare state, and in 2011, the government, struggling to keep its budget under control, reduced unemployment payments from 4 years to 2 years. In general, however, Danish history, its geographical location, and its small size all contribute significantly to a feeling of ambivalence, particularly geographically. Denmark is a small but prosperous and highly educated nation that actively seeks to be Scandinavian, European, and part of the world community.

Denmark wants to retain its unique culture but recognizes the need to be flexible and adaptable in a rapidly globalizing world. One example is the concept of "flexicurity" in the workplace, which essentially provides substantial unemployment and welfare benefits but imposes very few restrictions on hiring and firing by employers. The five key elements of the flexicurity model are full employment, strong unions recognized as social partners, fairly equal wages among different sectors, a comprehensive income floor, and a set of labor market programs supported by the government, which spends 4.5% of the GDP on customized retraining, transitional unemployment assistance, and wage subsidies (Kuttner, 2008). This is of course under strain following the global recession of 2008. Denmark's need for control and group effort is clear, as is the need for individual expressiveness, which should help it to adjust successfully. The Christmas luncheon is a critical vehicle for maintaining the balance between these competing demands.

Coziness

The Christmas luncheon emphasizes many cultural values that Danes stress, and perhaps the most important is making a social situation comfortable, cozy, and intimate (*hyggeligt*). This concept is closely related to the German concept of *Gemütlichkeit*, also translated into English in the same way. Coziness is a concrete demonstration of Denmark's geographic ambivalence, involving both Danish and Germanic features.

The luncheon is frequently elaborate, with everyone bringing dishes that are appealing and cooked at home, and the setting tends to include many lighted candles and sometimes a lighted fireplace. Everyone is encouraged to participate in the fun and enjoyment, not only for 1 or 2 hours, as is the custom in the United States, but for many hours. All willingly stay.

In Denmark most employees reside in the same city and work for the same organization all of their lives. This provides a sense of continuity and history that is lacking in many American organizations, and rituals and myths from the past are important. At the Christmas luncheon, it is not unusual for such organizational rituals and myths to appear, such as the company president leading a toast to good fortune in the coming year. Hilarious stories from the organization's past are often retold. All of these activities enhance the sense of coziness and commonality. This also reinforces Denmark's culture of workplace collaboration, which produces win-win outcomes for both corporations and their employees (Kuttner, 2008).

Throughout the year, and particularly during the Christmas season, Danes try to create a sense of coziness in their homes. Sometimes this sense of coziness is accompanied by an expression of patriotism befitting a small nation, for example, decorating the Christmas tree with the national flag. However, this is not done at the Christmas luncheon.

Originally the luncheon was a family affair held after Christmas. Sometimes an entire small village, of which there are many in Denmark, would hold a luncheon. Today, however, the Christmas luncheon has become the norm in business. Family-focused Christmas and after-Christmas luncheons at home, involving close friends and relatives, are similar to but different from the Christmas luncheon held at workplaces.

In summary, the features of the Christmas lunch highlight points of comparison and contrast with Denmark's Scandinavian neighbors (see Chapters 9 and 10). Its geography, small size, and history must be understood to fully comprehend the importance of the Christmas luncheon and of such key cultural values as interdependent individualism and coziness. While the luncheon has moved into the Christmas season and the workplace, it reflects values that are remarkably persistent and that are unlikely to change in a nation that is sensitive to its place in a globalized world economy.

PART IV

Other Egalitarian Cultures

In egalitarian cultures, countries tend to have a high tax rate that allows them to offer generous support for many social programs. There is a belief in such cultures that government is responsible for the welfare of all of its citizens and can solve many problems that business firms by themselves cannot. In Part III we described Scandinavian egalitarian cultures separately because of their unique features, such as the fact that legal financial penalties may be related to one's assets. In Part IV we describe other egalitarian cultures that have high tax rates supportive of many social programs: Germany, Ireland, Canada, and France.

CHAPTER 12

The German Symphony

The two sides are growing together, but it is not finished. It takes time. But today, there is one Germany, of course, one Germany. Not only geographically, it is one Germany by heart.

—Winfried Müller, eye doctor turned gallery owner in the former
East Germany, on referring to the two sides as East and
West Germany since their reunification in 1990 (Slackman, 2010a)

Germans, much like the Japanese and Chinese, represent a major challenge to American understanding, even though the largest group (about 30%) of Americans is of German descent. When Americans discuss Germans, they frequently describe them in terms of an excessive emphasis on rules and order. Sometimes, German emphasis on rules does stretch the bounds of credulity.

But rules in and of themselves provide only a very limited and stereotypical view of German culture. To gain substantial insight into the culture, it is important to understand the essentials of German history. Germany was not a nation until 1871, whereas many other European nations, such as Spain, England, Poland, Sweden, and France, had achieved this distinction several hundred years earlier. The Romans, whose empire was all-encompassing, feared and detested these "uncouth" peoples and left them alone after tribes led by Hermann the Cheruscan (known in English as Herman the Great) defeated them in 109 BCE. When other nations used the name *deutsch* or German, the connotation was pejorative (Schulze, 1998). Even the German mercenaries who fought in the American Revolution were objects of derision and considered ill-disciplined and lacking in courage. Finally, through the efforts of Frederick the Great and his father, a strong Prussia emerged between 1740 and 1780, and its military and governmental leadership led to the integration of many small kingdoms into the Germany of 1871. In fact, Germany operates as a federal confederation in which the 16 states are independent from one another on many issues, largely because of this historical background.

However, given its lack of an illustrious history, some Germans romanticized the 8th-century rule of Charlemagne, leader of the Holy Roman Empire, into what they called the First Reich. Such romanticism is found in most, if not all, nations as they seek to explain their past and its relationship to the present, but the grandiosity of the German perspective became distorted during Hitler's time. Although Charlemagne ruled almost all of Europe, his influence was brief, and his three sons began the division of Europe that led indirectly or directly to the creation of several European nations. Germany, being part of Western Europe but bordering Eastern Europe, became host to a large number of ethnic groups that settled within its boundaries.

The Second Reich began in 1871. This period was marked by militarism but also by rapid economic growth, an emphasis on education and culture, and the development of the first modern welfare system. Several German universities were recognized as among the best in the world; there was ample government support of the arts, including the symphony; and even Otto von Bismarck, the Iron Chancellor, demonstrated his generosity by championing the first modern social security system for retirees, ensuring that they would receive a government pension. However, Bismarck selected the age of 65 for pension eligibility because almost all citizens died before that age.

After World War I, the Versailles Peace Treaty of 1918 imposed extremely difficult conditions on Germany, resulting in great hardship and inflation in the 1920s. John Maynard Keynes, the great English economist, resigned from the Peace Commission because he foresaw the consequences of these conditions. A famous photograph in the 1920s highlighted the economic breakdown by showing a man using a wheelbarrow of money to purchase a loaf of bread. The depression of the 1930s only worsened the situation; numerous political parties vied for power, and street fighting involving these parties became common. Ironically Hitler, leader of the National Socialist Party, rose to power when Chancellor Hindenburg asked him to form a minority government, in large measure because most Germans at that time saw him as a source of stability and a counterforce to the street fighting and general uncertainty. This was the beginning of the presumptive 1,000-year Third Reich, whose atrocities and brief history have been abundantly documented elsewhere.

Postwar Evolution

Modern Germany began in 1945 when the Allies took control of Germany. The Anglo-American influence on Germany became evident in a flourishing democratic government, and a small number of parties began to vie with one another in open and free elections. This influence was also evident in the support of labor unions built in terms of Anglo-American collective bargaining. Finally, the Marshall Plan of

1947, which provided a financial base for effective business and commerce, secured the nation's future. For the first time in modern history, a defeated nation was not subjected to undue hardship but was offered the possibility of recovery. By the 1980s, Germany, although consistently portrayed as militaristic by the Western press, was in fact antimilitaristic. The standing joke in the 1980s in Germany was that the country had already won World War III: the economic war. There is a basis in fact for this assertion, as Germany far outstrips both the United States and Japan in terms of export sales per capita.

Today NATO, led by the United States, often criticizes Germany for its lack of interest in military preparedness and low level of involvement in NATO-led operations such as the strikes on Libya in 2011. The German government abstained from the initial UN vote authorizing the Libya campaign. Germany has an active military strength of 148,996 personnel and reserve of 355,000 and is Europe's largest economy. As such, it is expected to have a military presence in places like Afghanistan. However, as an outcome of its Nazi past, there is considerable opposition to wars (e.g., Iraq and Afghanistan) seen largely as U.S. problems; there is also a reluctance to send soldiers into battle (Whitlock, 2008).

Germany's system of social market economy (*Soziale Marktwirtschaft*), the main economic model used in Germany after World War II, with its extensive regulation of industry and commerce and high labor costs, has motivated some German firms to move their operations into other nations. In particular, small and medium-size firms (the *Mittelstand*) have been adversely affected, although such firms have been the backbone of German industry since World War II. In 2008 the *Wall Street Journal* argued that with the expected U.S. slowdown, Germany was the best hope for sustained growth in the euro-zone economies and that domestic demand from German consumers needed to increase to prop up the other ailing economies in the region (Emsden, 2008). A few years ago, the *Economist* wondered if Germany would go the way of Japan, and in late 2008, this economy slipped into recession along with the rest of the euro zone, thanks to an overreliance on exports and limited consumption at home. However, this very reliance on exports and rising domestic demand have been powering the largest economy in the 17-nation euro zone in the wake of the global financial crisis. Germany's GDP is US$3,649 billion, and it is the fourth-largest economy in the world after the United States, China, and Japan. It ranks number 23 out of 179 nations on the 2011 Index of Economic Freedom (T. Miller, 2011).

In Hofstede's (2001) study of 53 nations, the rankings of Germany were as follows, with 1 being the highest value: 43 on power distance, 15 on individualism, 9.5 on masculinity or aggressiveness and materialistic behavior, 29 on risk acceptance, and 11.5 (out of 35 nations studied) on long-term time orientation or the willingness to defer present gratification for future success. Similarly several surveys indicated that about 25% of Germans desire high social status, versus 2% of Swedes and 7% of Americans (Triandis, 2002). In the more recent GLOBE study (House et al., 2004), Germany scored in the middle on power distance, low on both in-group and institutional collectivism, in the middle on gender egalitarianism, low on risk acceptance, and high on future orientation. These findings are consistent with the cauldron of history out of which modern Germany emerged.

The Symphony Orchestra

As it was developing into a nation economically and politically, Germany was attentive to its culture and arts, particularly the symphony. The essence of Germany can be experienced through the sounds and sights of the symphony, which was created in the German territories in the 16th century. Its origins can be traced to the early Italian opera (Copland, 1939/1957). What originally started as chamber music or operatic accompaniment, with a few musicians and a relatively uncomplicated score, matured into full sections of woodwinds, brass, strings, and percussion with the occasional piano and a long list of creative sound effects. Certainly the most enduring achievements of composers from all areas have been accomplished in the symphony. Analogously, this endurance is reflected in the staying power of the German society and culture. German behavior as viewed through the symphony suggests that, although change may be slow, it will occur systematically and logically.

Haydn and Mozart developed many of the features of the symphony. Beethoven, however, single-handedly created a colossus that he alone seemed able to control (Copland, 1939/1957). The symphony lost all connection to its operatic origins. The form was expanded, the emotional scope was broadened, and the orchestra stamped and thundered in a completely new and unheard-of fashion. The composers following Beethoven added important innovations, including a cerebral emphasis and an atonal perspective. Today the symphony is as firmly established as ever, but this musical form was and will remain unfinished as innovations enrich it.

As for the musical instruments, single instruments had been played for centuries. However, prior to the 16th century, musicians had not mastered the art of playing together (Schwartz, 1938). Since that time nothing has matched the capacity of the symphony orchestra, which includes about 100 instruments and uses about four fifths of the range of human hearing (Schwartz). The symphony's power emanates through the sound of instruments originating from all over the world. Schwartz captures the historical significance of the symphony's musical instruments in the following summary:

Snake charmers from the Orient contributed the oboe. Ancient Greeks before Homer developed the primitive clarinet. Horns were probably first used in the religious ceremonies of the God-fearing Israelites. Conquering and militaristic

Rome brought trumpets to a high point of favor, while fifty generations later this same land took pride in its superb violins. At a late date, tubas sprang from Europe, and still later the saxophone and sarrusophone. Africa is famed for its drums and Greece for its pipes of Pan. (p. 5)

The music and performers are brought together by the conductor. A skilled baton unites the disparate personalities and talents of the musicians so that they perform as one, enacting the literal meaning of the phrase *in concert*. The various musical divisions of style and perspective, such as those between entire sections of strings and the brass and between the individual flutist and percussionist, are melded and molded by the conductor to produce a unified sound.

The orchestra, like society, is made up of individuals, each with his or her own likes and dislikes. However, for the greater good—the music—individual preference is subordinated to the demands of the conductor and the needs of the symphony. Not everyone can be a soloist, nor do all wish to be. In any event, solos are brief, and the orchestra as a whole soon picks up the music again. This disciplined or subordinated individualism—the voluntary submission of individuals to the whole, the guidance of the conductor, and the shared meaning of the music—enables the symphony orchestra to enthrall audiences.

Germans love symphonic music. Much as in the past, descendants of the aristocracy living in the old castles along the Rhine still arrange concerts of baroque and chamber orchestra music, played in secluded rooms illuminated only by intimate candlelight. These concerts transport listeners to an idealized Germany of old. Germans also frequent the symphony on a regular basis; the former West Germany, with its population of 66 million, boasts more than 80 symphony orchestras. Frequently visitors to small German towns and villages have the opportunity to attend symphonic concerts given by local musicians in churches, typically on Sunday afternoons and weekend nights and particularly during and around religious holidays such as Easter and Christmas.

This societal and cultural love of music has produced many of the world's great composers, including Haydn, Mozart, Schubert, Schumann, Bach, Händel, Strauss, and, of course, Beethoven and Brahms. It has also produced several world-class conductors, including Herbert von Karajan and Rudolf Kempe.

Many Germans play musical instruments as a hobby, and of those, many belong to informal musical groups that carry forward the tradition. From the horns of the Alps to big band to the operas of Wagner, music is an integral part of German life. German music is not only integral to the culture but it is taken seriously; it is not generally an outlet for emotion as it is in the United States and other societies. Music is foreground, not background. It is meant as a collective experience intended to enrich life. Even the audience at German symphonies reflects this seriousness, as its members normally dress more formally than is typical in the United States. Members of the audience listen intently to the music and are silent until a major movement of a symphony is completed, at which time they tend to respond enthusiastically but with decorum.

In this chapter we emphasize the following features of the symphony as being reflective of German culture and values: the diversity of musical instruments, the positional arrangements of musicians, the conductor or leader, precision and synchronicity, a unified sound, and the unfinished nature of the form.

Diversity of Musical Instruments

Prince Metternich, a 19th-century Austrian statesman, once remarked that the characteristic feature of the Germans was not unity but multiplicity (Cottrell, 1986). This observation still has considerable validity today. Germany is divided into an array of Germanic tribes and groups like the Celts, Romans, and Slavs. Historically and culturally, each of these ethnic groups evolved separately, and each continues to have its own characteristics. Since the 1950s the population of Germany has become more diverse. Millions of foreigners have migrated to Germany seeking employment, citizenship, or asylum.

One fact is fundamental to understanding this varied array of ethnicity: Throughout its long history, Germany rarely has been united (Solsten, 1996). Charlemagne's 9th-century Holy Roman Empire was more symbolic than real within a generation. Medieval Germany was marked by division. The Peace of Westphalia of 1648 at the conclusion of the Thirty Years' War left an exhausted Germany divided into hundreds of states. In fact, until the unification of West and East Germany on October 3, 1990, Germany had known only 74 years (from 1871 to 1945) as a united nation with one capital. As noted earlier, for most of the two millennia that central Europe has been inhabited by German-speaking peoples, the area called Germany was divided into hundreds of states. Like the musical instruments of the symphonic orchestra, the people of modern Germany can trace their ancestral lineage to a multitude of past and present countries and cultures.

The Force of Immigration

Historically immigration has been a primary force shaping demographic developments in Germany (McClave, 1996). After the first unification in 1871, a significant source of population growth was an influx of immigrants from Eastern Europe. Adding to an already ethnically diverse population, these immigrants came to Germany to work on farms and in mines and factories. This wave of immigrants was the first of several that would occur over succeeding decades.

Foreigners began arriving in West Germany in large numbers in the 1960s after the construction of the Berlin Wall. Since then, partly due to unification, the foreign population in Germany has increased substantially. Several million ethnic Germans from Eastern European countries, especially the former Soviet Union, began migrating to Germany with the end of the Cold War in Europe. As of 2010, Turks made up the largest group (more than 3.5 million) of registered foreigners living in Germany, followed by immigrants from European Union (EU) member states such as Italy, Greece, Portugal, and Spain. Because of the higher birth rate of foreigners, about 1 of every 10 births in Germany is to a foreigner. Likewise, Germany's law offers liberal asylum rights to those suffering political persecution.

Compared to the United States and its population, Germany is not a melting pot society, and Germans are not mobile. Many have stayed in the same geographic region and even the same house for generations. Germans are not accustomed to meeting and interacting with strangers at home, partly because most people live in apartments or small homes. As a result, they treat foreigners with a certain amount of wariness (Hall & Hall, 1990). Still, Germany's foreign residents remain vital to the economy, parts of which would shut down if they were to depart. Also, Germany has the ninth-lowest birth rate in the world, far below replacement (2.1) at 1.38 children per woman. This is problematic in a social democracy offering generous retirement benefits that are dependent on the taxes levied on current employees. According to the Federal Statistics Office, while 100 people of working age between 20 and 65 had to provide the pensions for 34 retired people in 2009, the same number will have to generate income for between 63 and 67 pensioners in 2060.

In October 2010, German chancellor Angela Merkel, speaking to the youth wing of her conservative Christian Democratic Union (CDU), suggested that multiculturalism had completely failed in Germany. She did clarify that she did not want Germany to be perceived as a country that did not welcome non-German speakers. The debate over immigration from Muslim countries was further fueled by an explosive 2010 bestseller, *Germany Does Away With Itself*, authored by Thilo Sarrazin, a prominent German banker and a former member of the Social Democratic Party (SDU). Sarrazin argued that Germany's Muslim population was responsible for some of the country's cultural and economic problems and would someday take over the state and society because of its higher birth rate. His arguments resonated with a large segment of the population. Nonetheless, Germany's demographic reality portends more rather than less immigration in the future.

Recently, Germany relaxed its citizenship laws. All children born in Germany automatically received citizenship at birth, provided that at least one parent was born in Germany or arrived before the age of 14 and has a residence permit.

Geographic Variation

Geographically Germany is also distinct. West Germany's absorption of East Germany enlarged its area by about 30%. The territory of the former East Germany accounts for almost one third of united Germany's territory. Now roughly the size of Montana, Germany is Europe's sixth-largest country, although the absorption of more rural former East Germany caused its population to be more sparsely distributed.

Germany has had difficulty integrating East and West Germany since they were reunited in 1990, as the costs were greatly underestimated. Until the global financial crisis of 2008, there was a persistently high level of unemployment, about 10% or more, particularly in the East. The unemployment rate has since decreased significantly to 6.9% in mid-2011.

Differing levels of economic success have led to tensions between the West and the East. Germany recently celebrated 20 years of reunification, and although the western states are wealthier and have about half the unemployment of the eastern states, most Germans agree that reunification was a good thing for their country. Incorporating more diversity into the new nation automatically created complexity, much as the addition of musical instruments does in the symphonic orchestra. However, although former East Germany was under a communist regime for about 40 years, values that were integral to German society such as orderliness, straightforwardness, loyalty, and integrity remained strong. This is one of the reasons that the GLOBE researchers (House et al., 2004) identified a Germanic cluster that included both former West and former East Germany, Austria, Switzerland, and the Netherlands (Gupta & Hanges, 2004).

Various parts of the nation are also quite diverse. Sunny and heavily Catholic Bavaria, for instance, seems to be worlds away from the colder and heavily Protestant north in both temperament and culture. Frankfurt, the financial capital of the nation, is more like an American city than a German city. There are several other large cities, each with its own character. However, this diversity is muted in many ways, including many citizens' preference to live in *Dörfer*, or small villages that surround the cities.

It is not to be denied that the large number of instruments in the orchestra creates complexity, in about the same way that the many forms of diversity (ethnic, geographic, religious) do in German society. Other features of the symphony address the need to control this complexity.

Positional Arrangements of the Musicians

When a symphonic orchestra is seated in front of the audience, the stage is crowded. To solve the problem of having large numbers of musicians on stage, and to make it easier for the musicians to play their instruments, the conductor arranges the seating into four separate sections: strings, woodwinds, brass, and percussion. This compartmentalized arrangement of seats helps to maximize the musical instrumentation and the quality of the sound, as does the seating of musicians within sections in terms of skill and responsibility (e.g., first violinist, second violinist, and so on).

Such crowdedness is mirrored in German society. Germany is about 66% of the size of France, the largest nation in Western Europe, and only 4% of the size of the United States. More important, it is a crowded nation relative to the United States: 230.5 residents per square kilometer versus only 32.9 for the United States. Viewed from the perspective of the symphony, it is easy to empathize with the compartmentalization of German society, represented by Germans' affection for privacy and respect for others. Apartment dwellers are wont to leave polite but anonymous notes asking their noisy neighbors to be quiet.

Just as the positional arrangement of the musicians in the orchestra separates them from one another, the home separates the individual from the outside world. Throughout the year—and most especially at Christmas—Germans greatly cherish the privacy and security of the home. In Christian Germany (about half of the Christian population is Catholic and half Protestant), Christmas remains a dutifully observed religious holiday, a time when *Gemütlichkeit* strongly prevails over the people. This word translates simply as "'comfort' or 'coziness,' but it has wider connotations—of the hearthside and deep content, of home cooking and family security" (Cottrell, 1986, p. 123).

Home as Haven

The home (*das Heim*) is at once a haven from the bustle and stress of the working world and a place where personal status may be more solid and unthreatened. It is a castle and a refuge from the outside world. Homes are protected from outsiders by a variety of barriers—fences, walls, hedges, solid doors, blinds, shutters, and screening—to prevent visual and auditory intrusion (Hall & Hall, 1990). Front yards, although beautifully maintained, are rarely used. Outside activities such as sitting in the sun or visiting with family are restricted to the back yard, away from the street and the eyes of others. The home is the most important possession to Germans, and life in the home with family is treasured.

Germans are extremely proud of their homes, and German homemakers spend a lot more time than their U.S. counterparts keeping everything spotlessly clean. Raj Pillai was informed by close German friends in Germany that they lived in mortal fear of neighbors dropping by, running their fingers over the tops of shelves, and inadvertently finding dust. In turn, Pillai's mother would make the servants clean and dust their home in India several times during the day when they had German visitors. In addition, it is remarkable to see some Germans, vacationing on the North Sea, shovel sand on three sides to a height of 4 feet to define the space on the beach that they will occupy for only a few hours.

Like the home, the door "stands as a protective barrier between the individual and the outside world" (Hall & Hall, 1990, p. 40). Germans tend to keep doors closed. Doors are often thick and solid, and their hardware heavy and tight fitting. The closed door preserves the integrity of the room, provides a boundary between people, and minimizes interruptions and accidental intrusions.

A related issue is the physical distance people keep between each other when talking to each other face-to-face. Germans keep more space between them than do individuals in nations such as France, Italy, and Thailand. This distancing may be a protective barrier and psychological symbol that operates in a manner similar to that of the home. In addition to maintaining physical distance, many Germans possess a distinctive sense of aural distance. German law actually prohibits loud noises in public places on certain days and times of the week. In one town, some residents filed suit against parents who allowed their children to play in the local playground during lunchtime and early evening. As noted above, Germany, particularly the western part, is a crowded country, and the emphasis on both physical and aural distances may reflect this fact.

Respecting Formalities

The compartmentalization in German society also is actualized in the German penchant for formality. Within the German home, family members abide by formal rules of behavior designed to give one another distance and privacy (Hall & Hall, 1990). These patterns of formality extend in adulthood to relations with friends and coworkers in the office. Germans tend to introduce themselves by their family name, as opposed to their first name. The use of formal and informal pronouns in the German language indicates the nature of this relationship. The familiar *du* (you) and first names are reserved for close friends and family. The difference between "close" friends and acquaintances is distinct. Those people at work or school whom Americans might label "friends" usually are referred to as "colleagues" by the more conservative Germans. This sharp distinction may be related to the socialization process throughout the German life course. Most Germans develop two or three close friends during their early years, relationships that often are maintained for life. It usually takes Germans a long time to categorize someone as a friend, but once this determination is made, they will treat this individual in a very special manner.

Although the following illustration is extreme, it helps to bring these concepts into perspective. An Irish professor and a German professor worked side by side for 3 years at an international agency in Brussels. Although they were of equivalent social status, their relationship was impersonal. In Germany the professor was formally addressed as "Herr Professor Doctor" followed by his last name, while in Ireland the Irish professor was called "Professor" or by his first name. Over beer one night the German professor indicated that he and the Irish professor could now be more informal and friendly with one another and that the Irish professor should feel comfortable addressing him as only "Doctor" in the future.

On a more serious note, under an obscure Nazi-era law, anybody who has not earned a PhD or medical degree in Germany is barred from using the title "Doctor." Seven U.S. citizens were recently subject to criminal probes for "title abuse" because it was *verboten* to go by "Dr.," although the legitimacy of the degree or the right to conduct research was not questioned. The correct form is to precede one's name with "Professor" and add the designation PhD after one's name, followed by the university affiliation (Whitlock & Smiley, 2008).

A similar emphasis on compartmentalization is found in the degree of politeness that Germans extend to acquaintances and strangers. Germans are careful not to touch accidentally or to encourage signs of intimacy (Hall & Hall, 1990). Gestures and smiling are restrained, and Germans do not generally smile at customers or coworkers. On the other hand, Germans do maintain eye contact in conversations to demonstrate they are paying attention. At times Germans may appear stiff, distant, and forbidding. However, this reserved nature should not mistakenly be interpreted as a lack of friendliness. They are usually gregarious after they get to know you.

Business Practices

These elements of compartmentalization, much like the positional arrangements of the orchestra, also extend to German business practices. Although Germans place a great deal of emphasis on promptness, delays in such areas as deliveries occur because of the compartmentalization of German life and business. Products may be delivered late without an apology. A salesperson may take an order and then leave on vacation without asking a coworker to follow up on the order (Hall & Hall, 1990). Likewise, problems in the shipping division of a German business may not be conveyed to the retailer and the customer.

Typical German business organizations tend to be more compartmentalized than American organizations, probably because of the high value attached to respecting status and power within the hierarchy. The owner of an insurance company constructed a building in Frankfurt in a form that is symbolic of this perspective. Each level of the building contains fewer people per square kilometer. The owner, surrounded by a few key staff people, occupies the top floor. The building itself looks like a line drawn at a 45° angle and is called "the ladder of success."

In recent years German business organizations have emphasized the use of cross-functional teams. Still, information flows less easily from one department to another in Germany than it does in the United States, as we might expect when privacy is so highly valued. As a result, quick decisions on business issues are difficult to reach. Inevitably, decisions often are made without the benefit of current information about fast-changing markets.

The importance of the German executive's office cannot be overemphasized. As in the United States and many other nations, the size of the office, the positioning of a personal secretary right outside of it, and related factors are key markers of status and hierarchy. But what is distinctive about the German office is that managers see it as inseparable from and as an extension of their personality (Hall & Hall, 1990). Hence the importance of closed doors, which visitors should generally avoid opening without permission. It is always a good idea to knock on a closed door and then wait to be admitted.

Furthermore, once inside the office, visitors should be careful not to violate the norms of physical space found in Germany by moving a chair too close to the manager's desk. Moving a chair closer and thus rearranging the office furniture is perceived as highly insulting. One German manager became incensed that visiting American salespersons would invariably move their chairs closer to his desk, presumably to establish a physical sense of intimacy in trying to finalize a sale. This executive took the extreme measure of bolting the visitor's chair to the floor, thus frustrating any movement that a visitor might attempt.

As both the Hofstede (2001) and GLOBE (House et al., 2004) studies confirmed, Germans tend to be risk-averse and are less comfortable with strange situations and newcomers than people of many other cultures. They also generally believe that it takes time and meticulous planning to do a job properly. Just as the symphonic orchestra must be rigorously rehearsed to achieve a unified sound, so too the German penchant for analyzing projects in depth means their levels of risk are accurately understood. This risk aversion may account for the extreme lengths to which German executives will go when analyzing business opportunities before committing to them.

As in many nations, generalizations about such issues as German formality and physical and aural distance need to be tempered by the fact that these characteristics are less notable among younger members of the culture. For example, German university students are quite informal in their interactions among themselves and with others, arrive late for class, and so on. However, once in a full-time position in business, these students tend to revert to the more formal styles of behavior that have been a hallmark of German culture.

Conductors and Leaders

Like the general direction provided by the symphonic conductor in the creation of the single, powerful sound of the orchestra, German leaders have provided direction and guidance to an often fragmented state. One study of 22 German orchestras showed that conductors who exhibited a transformational leadership style were more likely to have orchestras of high artistic quality and a collaborative climate among the musicians (Boerner & Freiherr von Streit, 2005). Historically, however, with the notable exception of Adolf Hitler, Germans have not reacted favorably to charismatic leaders who are intent on leading them to a new world order without any questioning of their authority (Hall & Hall, 1990). Rather, Germans have preferred visionary leaders who are mature and strong enough to delegate responsibility and decision making to competent subordinates throughout the hierarchy.

A notable exception was the charismatic, 39-year-old highly titled and wealthy German defense minister, Baron Karl-Theodor zu Guttenberg. In 2011 he was seen as a potential successor to Chancellor Merkel before he was forced to resign on charges that he had plagiarized his doctoral thesis in 2006. In a country where titles matter, he had to give up his PhD when the charges were shown to be true. The press had a field day describing him as "Baron Cut-and-Paste" and referring to "Guttenberg's printing press," but his popularity is still high. A yearning for charismatic figures was reflected in his enormous popularity, which was fueled by his aristocratic family background, polished manners, and impeccable wardrobe; his style overshadowed that of Chancellor Merkel (Habermas, 2010). Merkel, a pragmatic politician and a mother figure, is often described as the most powerful woman in the world but is seen as utterly lacking in charisma. She seems to fit the German preference for mature and strong leaders, especially in the wake of the global financial crisis and ongoing problems with several EU countries that are looking to Germany, as Europe's strongest economy, to assist them (e.g., Greece).

Frederick the Great, who ruled Prussia from 1740 until 1780 and was largely responsible for creating the basis of the German nation, epitomizes the classic German ruler. He survived the rigors of his Prussian military education to become a philosopher-king, famous for his taste in art, music, and literature. Frederick wrote poetry and scholarly essays, played the flute, composed concertos and sonatas, and maintained a regular correspondence with Voltaire. To this day, this ideal of leadership is emulated throughout German society. Corporate executives, for instance, tend to be more well-rounded than their American counterparts, and many of them are members of book clubs that make a serious study of science, literature, and philosophy; a large percentage of the CEOs of German industrial companies hold a doctorate.

Clearly, Frederick's visionary leadership resulted in reforms that transformed a previously fragmented state into a major European power. Similarly, corporate executives are expected to use this visionary but mature model of leadership as a model and provide the direction that organizational members desire. For example, German CEOs will generally tell foreign marketing executives to see their counterpart responsible for making decisions in this area. German managers expect a great deal of their subordinates and test them by pushing them to perform, but they do not hover (Hall & Hall, 1990). Adler (2007) describes Germany as a "well-oiled machine," with a small power distance and strong uncertainty avoidance. German businesses reduce uncertainty by clearly defining roles. In contrast to high–power distance cultures—where employees want their managers to act as decisive, directive experts—Germans expect their managers to delegate responsibility and decision making to competent subordinates throughout the hierarchy.

Pluses and Minuses

There are, of course, some drawbacks to this style of leadership. Martin Gannon attended several briefing sessions in Germany focusing on the Daimler-Chrysler merger. Some of the differences between the German and American companies, even after the merger in 1997, were noteworthy. Daimler had only four organizational levels, which is consistent with its emphasis on low power distance and delegation of responsibility, whereas Chrysler had nine. However, it was much more difficult for Daimler executives to take action, as their subordinates demanded the right to participate in the decision and, at times, to veto it. Also, the Daimler hierarchy was much more rigid, even to the point that middle managers would not dare to jump organizational levels lest they be viewed unfavorably. But the American middle managers had no difficulty offering suggestions and ideas to upper-level managers; even Robert Eaton, the Chrysler CEO who was largely responsible for the dramatic success of this company in the 1980s and 1990s, could be approached easily without fear of consequence. In the end, the merger failed, and Chrysler was acquired by a private equity firm. In 2009, the company required a major bailout by the U.S. and Canadian governments and Fiat of Italy, which now has a major stake in the automaker. Most analysts agree that the insurmountable cultural differences between Daimler Benz and Chrysler were partly responsible for the merger's failure, although the lack of synergies as well as competition from Asian automakers also played significant roles.

As indicated previously, the Allies strongly influenced Germany after World War II, and this influence can be seen in the area of leadership. Germany developed a unique democratic form of corporate governance termed *codetermination*. Unlike the single board of directors in American corporations, German firms with 2,000 employees or more by law must have two boards: a management board (*Vorstand*) and a supervisory board (*Aufsichtsrat*). The supervisory board must include some employees and labor union representatives. There is also a workers' council (*Betriebsrat*), which has the right to monitor and approve all corporate plans and actions. The *Vorstand* initiates an action, such as downsizing, but it must be approved by the *Aufsichtsrat* and *Betriebsrat* and finally by the national union. Needless to say, making decisions is slow and complicated, but once decisions are made, they are implemented quickly because of the consensus that has been achieved.

Currently there is a good amount of discussion about this system, and many believe that a single board of directors that can operate quickly is more appropriate in a fast-changing and globalized world. Similarly labor unions are losing members, and less than 25% of the workforce is now unionized. In 2006 the German software company SAP took steps to establish a workers' council with nonunion employees to protect its start-up culture, that of a global high-tech company that mainly employed college graduates.

Precision and Synchronicity

Perhaps the most critical features of the symphony are precision and synchronicity. Given the complexity of the music, the conductor stresses these two related characteristics. Everything must be done perfectly, and everyone must be willing to play their instruments within the boundaries of the musical score. Individual soloists are given ample opportunity to show their skills and abilities, but for the greater good of the orchestra, their solo time is short. Then they recede into the orchestra, once again merging their identities and personalities with other orchestra members. Unlike the opera, during which great singers clearly separate themselves from the chorus through memorable performances of arias, symphonic performers must willingly subordinate their individual selves to the greater good. Similarly, Germans tend to be individualistic, but their subordinated individualism is different from the competitive individualism found in the United States or the egalitarian individualism of Sweden.

Business Rules

There are countless examples of precision and synchronicity in German business. Most Germans are quite conscious of time and how to allocate it efficiently. To many Germans, there is no such thing as "free time." In a survey conducted by Martin Gannon, German respondents had difficulty with the category "I had free time on my hands," when asked to indicate why they were seeking a part-time position. Germans see a sharp distinction between work and leisure, but in both cases, they prefer that the time be used rationally and efficiently.

In both social and business life, tardiness is frowned on. Everyone is expected to arrive at least on time for a meeting and preferably 5 minutes early. Just as the soloist who comes in off cue may lose a position with the orchestra, the business-person who arrives late for a meeting may lose a client or miss important information. German meetings and negotiations are also long and tend to have well-marked stages. Unlike Americans, who like to get to the bottom line as soon as possible and follow the dictum, "Keep it simple, stupid," Germans love historical background and charts.

One American executive who was raised in Germany recalls a presentation he made to an American board of directors when he was unconsciously using the German perspective. He originally had planned to give a historical overview of a project for about 25 minutes, but he stopped short after 5 minutes when he noticed the vacant and bored looks on the faces of board members. Similarly a German executive who has lived in the United States for many years likes to point out how Americans and Germans would write a book about elephants, and we leave it to the reader to decide the national identity of the authors:

- *The Elephant: A Short Introduction in 24 Volumes*
- *The Elephant: How to Make It Bigger and Faster in 20 Minutes*

Precision and synchronicity also tend to influence communication. Germans communicate in a low-context manner; that is, they directly express their ideas both in written and oral form. Many American negotiators far prefer to deal with Germans than with members of high-context cultures, who indirectly and vaguely present their initial ideas. But Germans tend to use a deductive way of thinking that relies on past history and theory, in contrast to the Anglo-American inductive style that tends to use cases and examples to back up an argument. The basic German approach to problem solving is to deduct from a theory or small number of principles, whereas the American approach focuses on operationalizing a solution as soon as possible.

American businesspeople are frequently surprised when their initial ideas are met with a seemingly hostile response, but they are mistaken. In reality, Germans must be convinced that they are incorrect, and they are open to such an approach, but the solution must be backed up by logic, data, and consistency. Objective facts form the basis of evidence, and feelings are not usually accepted in business negotiations. Similarly Americans must be not only well prepared but also willing to discuss seemingly insignificant details. Precision and synchronicity must be honored, and one case study that is casually used to justify a course of action, or even a few case studies, are not ordinarily persuasive.

Similarly, words should mean exactly what they are intended to mean. An American might say, "I'll call you for lunch," without really intending to do so, but the German preference for precision and synchronicity requires that this statement be honored. Failing to do so will mark the American as insincere, careless in thought and habit, and culturally insensitive. An extreme example of miscommunication occurred in the Daimler plant in Alabama. German workers assigned to it showed up at their supervisor's home after the first day of work because they had interpreted the statement "Let's have dinner" in a very literal manner.

Perhaps the most extreme example of the German tendency to take words literally involves the late avant garde American music composer, John Cage, famous for such revolutionary productions as *4′ 33″* in which the performers sit silently on stage for 4 minutes and 33 seconds. A group of German musicians was pondering what Cage meant by "as slow as possible" (ASLSP) in his organ composition, *Organ 2/ASLSP,* which was originally written for the piano. They decided to repair a long-discarded church organ in Halberstadt and, starting in February 2003, began to introduce the notes very, very slowly; intermission is scheduled for 2319, and the entire performance is scheduled to last 639 years. The shortest notes last 6 or 7 months, while the longest last about 35 years (Wakin, 2006). The project is part serious endeavor, part intellectual exercise, and it is also a tourist draw in a town that is situated 2½ hours from Berlin.

Communication Styles

One distinctive feature of the German language is that the verb tends to be at the end of the sentence. Similarly the main point is often made at the end of a talk, meeting, or negotiations. Much like classical symphonies, meetings start slow, can last for hours, and ultimately build to a climax. At meetings and in negotiations, there is a slow but steady progress through easily recognizable stages during which timing; intonation; and control of voice, speech, and emotions are critical. Thus, in business as in music, sound, tone, modulation, and timing are key to a successful performance.

It is also helpful to demonstrate efficiency in communication, as this reflects precision in the manner in which the relationship will be established. For example, an American will tend to greet a German with "Hello, Thomas, how are you?" It is probably better to say: "Hello, Thomas, what can I do for you today?"

Finally, the emphasis on precision and synchronicity also applies to attire and dressing. Germans dress more conservatively than Americans, and it is helpful for Americans to look professional and act accordingly. Sitting at ease but upright, wearing clothes that are fashionable but do not take attention away from the matter at hand, and politely listening and contributing insight but without constantly interrupting the precision and synchronicity of the discussion—these techniques can enrich the communication process and relationship.

Education System

Germany's unity is also expressed through its educational system, which begins with the *Grundschule* or elementary school, where one teacher is sometimes assigned to the same group of children as they progress from Grades 1 through 4 or, in some states, Grades 1 through 6. Our discussion will assume Grades 1 through 4, although the total number of years of school is identical whether the *Grundschule* extends through Grade 4 or Grade 6.

After graduating from the *Grundschule*, students are assigned to one of three different types of school. In some German states, the teacher makes this assignment, while in other states, it is based on the results of a standardized examination. Given the importance of this assignment, it is quite common for German elementary students to have tutors as early as first grade to improve their chances of success. The assignment to a type of school largely determines each student's career; no other society separates its children at such an early age. It is possible, but somewhat difficult, to change from one type of school to another after the fourth grade.

The first type of school is the *Gymnasium*, or academic school, designed for those who want to pursue a university education. Students attend the *Gymnasium* from Grades 5 through 13, but they can leave after Grade 10 for a non-college-oriented career. If they pursue this option, their degree is equivalent to that of a

Realschule graduate as described below. Students in the gymnasium are required to pass a very difficult exam, the *Abitur*, before they can be considered for admission to the university, and admission is not automatic but depends on the number of available slots. Even those who pass the *Abitur* and are admitted are not granted admission to the entire university but only to one of its faculties. Thus, German university students have fewer opportunities than their American counterparts. Also, as the system is very much rigged in favor of class, it may be wasting a lot of the country's human capital. Today about 50% of German students attend *Gymnasium*, and most want to go on to university to study areas with an immediate career application such as information technology and business; however, universities offer few places in such programs.

After Grade 4, other students continue their education at the *Realschule* or "real-world" school through Grade 10. Some graduates then serve as apprentices for 2½ to 3 years while attending school 1 day a week. German industry subsidizes these apprenticeships and hires most of these students after they have completed them. Other *Realschule* students attend *Fachoberschule* (middle school) for 2 more years after the 10th grade and obtain a middle school degree; of this additional 2 years, 6 months are spent as apprentices. These students can attend traditional universities if they pass the *Abitur* or attend the *Fachhochschule* (specialized university) for at least 1 year. Normally, these graduates do not attend traditional universities but continue to pursue a university degree in these specialized universities, which emphasize four concentrations: technical, social sciences, science, and business.

After the *Grundschule*, some students attend the *Hauptschule*, and they can leave after Grade 9 without a degree. Most of them, however, leave with a degree and then serve as apprentices for 2½ to 3 years while attending school 1 day a week. These students also have the opportunity to attend the traditional universities or the specialized universities (*Berufsoberschule*) by going to school for 2 additional years and passing the *Abitur* examination. Many states may only have *Gymnasium* and one other form of school. There is also *Gesamtschule*, which combines all three school forms (*Gymnasium, Realschule*, and *Hauptschule*), but it is much rarer and often considered to be of lower quality than the traditional *Gymnasium*.

In recent years this system, while logically consistent and unified, has become strained. German parents want their children to graduate from the *Gymnasium*, much as American parents want their children to be in "gifted and talented" programs. Today more than 50% of students graduate from a *Gymnasium*, but many of them cannot achieve the career success historically associated with such graduation because of their overwhelming numbers vis-à-vis available opportunities. Also, far too many graduates from traditional universities specialize in professions such as law and medicine, and the universities are overcrowded.

Clearly, this educational system reflects the German penchant for order and unity. The sequence of schools mandates particular steps for students to attain the necessary education for whatever they prefer to do occupationally in support of the German effort. In a sense, Germans subordinate some individuality to this system so that all of society may benefit. Like musicians in the orchestra, Germans do their individual parts within the order imposed by this educational system to make the national effort successful.

At present there is a great debate over the relative merits of the German educational system when compared to the American approach. In 2001 Germany experienced what has come to be known as the "PISA shock." PISA refers to the Program for International Student Assessment, a survey done by the Organisation for Economic Co-operation and Development; it compares educational achievement in different countries. Germany scored 21st in reading and 20th in math and science among the 31 countries assessed (Siegele, 2006). This was largely attributed to the performance of its "migration-background" students. In 2009 the scores improved to some extent, but Germany was still outstripped by several Asian countries and other European countries. The U.S. score exceeded that of Germany in reading but was far behind in math and science. Reforms are underway, and it is believed that in the long run, Germany may have to do away with its three-tier system because of demographic changes and increased demands from German business. In contrast, the American system seems much more responsive to changing needs, and it is much easier to change career directions in the United States than in Germany. The CDU proposes a merger of the two lower-level schools into a new school model, called the *Oberschule*, or "upper school," which has already been implemented in some federal states. However, there is opposition from other quarters. With regard to university education, university tuition fees have been abolished in several German states, especially those led by left-leaning governments.

A Pattern of Order

The subjugation of the individual for the good of the whole also was evident in policies to procure German military personnel. Even in light of geopolitical changes in post–Cold War Europe, Germany maintained a military force structure based on a policy of conscripted service. It came to an end on July 1, 2011, to make way for a smaller and more professional army. Although conscription had long been rejected by a majority of the younger generation, the *Bundeswehr* (Army) was accepted by the majority of Germans as an instrument for defense and maintaining peace (Fleckenstein, 2000). The ability of German youths until recently to engage in a form of national service for the public good is analogous to the subjugation of the separate instruments to the unified sound created by the symphonic orchestra.

Germans also manifest their unity in their love for flowers and gardens. The window sills of most German houses are lined with flowers. German gardens often contain a variety of vegetables and fruit trees, which are placed in a systematic way. Germany as a whole is dotted with thousands of small villages and sprawling urban centers, separated by fields or grasslands plowed and maintained, likewise, in a systematic and orderly manner (Cottrell, 1986). The same can be said of the vineyards that dominate much of the land in southern Germany. This ordered beauty is appreciated throughout Germany.

Furthermore, the extremely efficient rail and road networks tend to emphasize this sense of unity. There is a clear parallel between the efficiency and unity of these networks and the predictability, regularity, and unified sound of the symphony. Chronometer-like timing, precision, and conformity underlie both music and transportation activities. On seeing these German transport systems—more than 4,500 miles of *Autobahn* (high-speed highways) and *Deutsche Bahn* or nationalized railroad with its luxurious Trans-European expresses and fast, reliable intercity services—it is difficult to believe that, for centuries, German transportation systems lagged far behind those of other West European countries (Cottrell, 1986). In addition, foreign travelers to Germany will find that trains rarely leave their originating station late or fail to arrive at their destination on time.

Festivals and Celebrations

Just as the symphonic orchestra unites individual musicians, the tradition of folk festivals unites the German population. Literally thousands of festivals take place in Germany each year. They range from village feast days to "elaborate civic displays of organized chaos" (Cottrell, 1986, p. 118). Typically these festivals include beer, abundant food, brass bands, dancing, and colorful parades. Although it may seem at first that carefree festivals run counter to the dour German stereotype, such communal activities actually are among the most popular and oldest of traditions, and they reinforce the feelings of group solidarity.

Most German festivals have a religious origin. *Karneval* is a Catholic celebration, a period of frivolity and deliberate self-indulgence before the period of Lenten fasting, which is predominantly celebrated in the Rhine area. In the 15th century, when ascetics criticized Germany's wild and unrestrained pre-Lenten celebrations, a churchman reasoned in defense that "a wine barrel that is not tapped will surely burst" (Cottrell, 1986, p. 118). To this day his comment remains as good an explanation as any of the extraordinary way millions of Germans can, once a year, suddenly cast aside inhibitions and everyday formalities and throw themselves wholeheartedly into the madcap fun of *Karneval* (also called *Fasching* and other regional names).

Nothing else in Germany compares with the sheer overindulgence of *Oktoberfest*, traditionally celebrated in Bavaria. This festival and many wine festivals celebrate the earth's yield of crops. Throughout the wine-growing districts, there are concerts, fireworks displays, dances, and nonstop pouring of wine. Germans fondly continue old traditions that give autumn a truly magical air, and thus they are reminded of their unity as a people. Today, *Oktoberfest* celebrations are almost as ubiquitous as Saint Patrick's Day festivities in the United States, and they bring together U.S. Americans of German origin and their non-German counterparts in festivities that all enjoy.

Similarly, sporting events are festive and bring Germans together regularly. In contrast to sports in the United States, sports in Germany are not sponsored or organized by the schools. Instead, youngsters join sports clubs to engage in athletic competition. According to the German government, one person in three is a member of a sports club in this sports-loving nation. Soccer and tennis attract millions of participants and spectators. The World Cup tournaments revive nationalistic sentiments and both the waving and the "waiving" of the flag. Some taboos regarding exhibitions of national pride have started changing, although some leftist groups make it their business to "capture" flags. In 2010 one proud Lebanese immigrant, Ibrahim Bassel, unfurled a giant 60-by-15-foot German flag over his storefront and kept replacing it after it was repeatedly torn down (Angelos, 2010). The German Football Association is the biggest individual sports association in the world with 6.7 million members in 26,000 clubs. Germany also has lovely hiking trails all over the country. One of the more enjoyable activities in Germany is to hike up to a mountaintop restaurant. Even traditional U.S. sports, such as football and basketball, are beginning to attract more participants, and ice hockey is rapidly gaining in popularity.

Two common elements run through all of these activities. First, they are enjoyed at all levels of society; second, they tend to be organized into, or at least enjoyed, in groups. These aspects of sport may provide relief from workplace stress while providing Germans with the sense of group identity that they enjoy. Unlike their U.S. counterparts, most German workers have ample leisure time to enjoy these many activities, as the average number of hours devoted to work is much lower in Germany and holidays are much longer and more frequent.

The Unfinished Symphony

Many of the great German composers, such as Beethoven and Brahms, bequeathed to posterity unfinished symphonies, and scholars love to debate what the composers intended and how they planned to realize their intentions. Similarly Germany is a work in progress.

Because of the unification of East and West in 1990, one of the chief aims of the constitution, national self-determination for all Germans, has been achieved. However, Germans of the now-enlarged Federal Republic feel as if they inherited a huge estate that is proving to be more of a liability than an asset, at least in the short run. Unification may be described as a marriage of two partners from totally different backgrounds that started with a short honeymoon followed by a period of recriminations (Kettenacker, 1997). West Germans are said to expect gratitude; East Germans, an attitude of charity and caring. Both, however, are unreasonable propositions.

In recent years, the east has been very gradually catching up to the west, and Germans have embarked on a search for a "new" national identity that will shelter them from their worries and anxieties and overcome their loss of direction. Two decades after reunification, many in the eastern states feel as if they're immigrants in their own country and that their values are delegitimized. The young were able to build new lives and the elderly received pensions, but the in-betweeners who grew up in a communist state were expected to succeed in a new system for which they were ill-prepared (Slackman, 2010a). Furthermore, Germany continues to struggle with the ideas of integration, multiculturalism, and the role of *Leitkultur* or guiding national culture (Slackman). Germans are also increasingly disenchanted with the idea of being the bankers of last resort to troubled EU countries. Although it is in Germany's national interest to have a strong EU, it is a hard sell to the German people, who feel that the countries that need to be bailed out have been careless with their economies.

Soul-searching, always a favorite German pastime, can no doubt be recognized as more justified than ever. Germany's comparatively short history as a nation-state since 1871 is the master key to understanding its political culture, from which a new identity must be distilled (Kettenacker, 1997). Clearly World War II and its aftermath changed Germans in very material ways. Almost all of these changes have been positive, including German leadership in the EU, economic prosperity, and successful implementation of new organizational approaches in government and business. But like many European nations that are now part of the EU, Germany has dual allegiance to both the nation and the EU. At least some surveys have suggested that proportionately fewer Germans identify primarily with the EU than do citizens of other nations. Polls in 2011 showed that a majority of Germans had little faith in the EU and the euro (see, e.g., "Some Friday Afternoon Polls"). There is nothing wrong about such feelings, provided that Germany continues to maintain its expected leadership role in both the EU and NATO. Otherwise, the peace and prosperity of the world could be jeopardized.

Looking through the lens of the characteristics of the symphony, we can speculate on the nature of German culture and changes it will experience over the next several years. While the population will continue to diversify, other factors will also be critical. There are clear generational clashes in Germany, as in many European nations with an aging population. Currently, the proportion of Germans over 60 years old is 26%, but this proportion will probably rise to about 34% by 2040. After Japan (44.7 years), Germany has the highest population median age at 44.3 years. About 18% of Germany's immigrants are over 55. In an interesting twist on this problem, Germany is struggling to provide for immigrant Turkish pensioners who unexpectedly decided to stay on in the country instead of returning to their homeland (Kresge, 2008).

Germany has weathered the global financial crisis better than most Western countries. It has a strong manufacturing sector and export-led growth, and its unemployment levels are below that of the United States. It wields enormous financial clout in the EU. It is the undisputed global leader in solar energy, and German infrastructure is among the best in the world. According to a McKinsey *Germany 2020* report, Germany will continue to be one of the biggest beneficiaries of the growth of Brazil, Russia, India, and China, together known as the BRIC economies, with the biggest drivers of economic strength being the manufacturing and processing industry sectors (McKinsey & Company, 2008).

It seems safe to predict that Germany will continue to emphasize the characteristics of the symphony, such as positional arrangements, compartmentalization, subordinated individualism, precision and synchronicity, and unity or a unified sound. Although parts of Germany are changing while other parts sustain traditions, we can expect that there will always be a symphony. Surely, the country that gave the world Beethoven's "Ode to Joy" will transcend its current challenges.

CHAPTER 13

Irish Conversations

We Irish have had a long, unyielding love affair with language.

—Edna O'Brien (quoted in Arana, 2002)

Ireland, or the Republic of Ireland, only became a freestanding nation in 1922 after a revolution that began in 1916. Britain, which governed Ireland for hundreds of years, finally yielded and accepted the independence of the Irish nation. Northern Ireland chose to remain as one of the four separate nations in Great Britain. For many years there was tension and even guerrilla-type military actions involving Ireland and Northern Ireland. Ireland is primarily a Roman Catholic nation, while Northern Ireland is primarily Protestant, and some of the tensions were related to religious preferences. However, economics also played a decisive role, as Northern Ireland was wealthier than Ireland until recently and received more favorable treatment from Great Britain than did Ireland. Dublin, Ireland's capital, is only 90 miles from Belfast, Northern Ireland's capital.

Right after the revolution's success, conservative forces in Ireland, led by its long-serving political leader Eamon De Valera, essentially "wrapped Irish patriotism together with Catholicism, agrarian traditions and the Gaelic language, and they won the day" (Shorto, 2011, p. 45). The relationship between the Catholic Church and Ireland was highlighted in the first words of the country's constitution: "In the Name of the Most Holy Trinity." De Valera and the archbishop of Dublin, John Charles McQuaid, co-authored the initial draft of the constitution.

The conservatives viewed modern life suspiciously, established a generous social welfare system that placed a heavy tax burden on those working, and did not encourage entrepreneurship or innovation or even industrialization. For decades Ireland remained an agrarian nation, although the situation today is quite different. Dublin, for example, provides approximately 40% of Ireland's gross national product (GNP), and about a third of the total population lives there. Crime, drug use, and other urban ailments are now prevalent in Dublin and other cities. As a result of the emphasis on maintaining an agrarian nation, Ireland did not advance economically as quickly as many other European nations until it became part of the European Economic Community in 1973, the predecessor of the European Union (EU). Ireland's economy grew very rapidly when the EU was founded in 1993. In the EU, wealthier nations subsidize the economic development of poorer nations, and Ireland was one of the first members to benefit from this policy.

For much of its history, both from 1922 to 1995 and prior to 1922, many more people left Ireland than came permanently to Ireland, primarily because of a lack of jobs. From 1995 until 2009, this pattern was significantly reversed, and Ireland became known as a "Celtic Tiger" because of the rapid growth of its economy. Unfortunately, the global economic recession starting in 2008 had a very negative impact on Ireland due to the risks its banks had taken in making loans to home buyers and businesses. Almost everyone, including bank executives, later regretted the banks' actions in fomenting an economic bubble.

The European Central Bank and the International Monetary Fund insisted the Irish government accept very stringent conditions to obtain a loan from them to mitigate the crisis. One clear indicator of the severity of their approach is that in 2011, the unemployment rate in Ireland was well over 10%, and some projections forecast a rise to 25%. Another is the significant increase in taxes that citizens must pay to service the public debt. The Economic and Social Research Institute, a Dublin think tank, estimated that 100,000 people would emigrate from April 2010 to April 2012, more than 2% of the population of 4.4 million, to obtain work and escape the draconian situation (Chazan & Thomson, 2011).

As indicated above, the three pillars of Irish culture are rural heritage, its language, and the Catholic Church. Even as late as the 1960s, most of the Irish lived on farms or in small communities, and Dublin was a very provincial city in comparison to other European capitals. In 1950 the gross domestic product (GDP) per capita was only $2,500; today it is $60,460. This rapid and successful transformation occurred for several reasons, including Ireland's movement away from a high-tax, socialist economy beginning in 1990; its willingness to attract large multinational corporations through tax breaks and the lowering of tariffs; and its entry into the EU (Peet, 2004). But this transformation is now threatened by the global financial crisis and what Ireland must do to manage it internally. Still, the 2011 Index of Economic Freedom ranks Ireland 7th of 179 nations, which means that it is a good nation in which to do business (T. Miller, 2011).

Although about 40% of the population attends Sunday Mass regularly and almost 90% claim they are Catholic, the Catholic Church no longer has the power and prestige that it flaunted and exercised for generations. There has been a marked decrease in the number of individuals studying to be priests and nuns. Some causes that are cited for this situation include increased secularism and prosperity and, particularly, the exposure of priestly abuse of children (Daniszewski, 2005a; Shorto, 2011). Still, the close linkage between the state and the Catholic Church is such that the Catholic Church still manages and staffs the elementary schools, even though the state subsidizes them. It is also reflected both in Ireland and other nations, including the United States, when people refer to themselves as "Irish Catholics" just as frequently as they use the term "Irish" (Shorto).

Only one of the three pillars of Ireland, the Irish language, Gaelic or *Gaeilge*, is increasing in importance, this after nearly going extinct. The Irish refer to this language as *Irish* to distinguish it from the Scottish form of Celtic or Gaelic. In the *Gaeltacht* or Gaelic-speaking area of Ireland, which includes 60,000 people, all English versions of geographic names and place names were replaced by Gaelic versions in 2005, and the English language no longer has official standing on signposts, legal documents, or government maps. All students in Ireland must study the Gaelic language for 13 years and receive more than 1,500 hours of instruction in total. There are 1.5 million who say that they speak Gaelic, and 337,000 use it daily. About 5% of all Irish children attend schools where only the Gaelic language is used. A Gaelic-language TV station has 100,000 viewers daily, and people listen to pop music on a 24-hour Gaelic-language radio station. Even some graduate university programs, including at least one master's of business administration program, are taught only in Gaelic. Unlike most other European nations, Ireland has two official languages, English and Gaelic. Thus, the hope of sustaining Irish culture may be vested in its language (Daniszewski, 2005b), particularly as the other two pillars decrease in importance.

It is a truism that the use of language is essential for the development of culture and that most if not all cultural groups take great pride in their native languages. Thus, it is not surprising that voice is one of the four essential elements of the metaphor for Italy: the opera (see Chapter 21: The Italian Opera). In the case of Ireland, brutal English rule over several centuries essentially made the Irish an aural people, whose love of language and conversation was essential for the preservation of their heritage. More specifically, the intersection between the original Irish language, Gaelic, and English has made the Irish famous for their eloquence, scintillating conversations, and unparalleled success in fields where the use of the English language is critical, such as writing, law, politics, and teaching.

An outstanding example is Garret FitzGerald, the former president of Ireland who made the first overtures to Great Britain and Northern Ireland in the 1980s that resulted in a marked decrease in animosity between Ireland and Northern Ireland. He was a journalist for several international newspapers, a professor of economics, a philosopher, and an eloquent speaker. At his death, the *Economist* stated the following:

> If you had the good fortune to sit next to Garret FitzGerald at dinner—wrapped round by his natural warmth and curiosity, as well as numbed by the sheer volume of Dublin-tinctured words that tumbled out of him—you might learn many dozens of mind-bogglingly arcane facts. ("Garret Fitzgerald," 2011, p. 91)

He could surprise people by his adroit turn of phrase, for example, "That is all right in practice, but will it work in theory?"

Early History

The Celts or Gaels conquered Ireland and its native inhabitants, the Firbolg, several centuries before Christ. They split Ireland into various kingdoms, whose petty kings usually ruled over a local group of clans. During this period, a belief in magical powers was a central element of the culture, and even today many of the landmarks and traditions in Ireland can be traced back to this time of belief in magical creatures.

Ireland escaped the rule of the Roman Empire due to its distance from Rome. Saint Patrick, who had previously been captured and enslaved, returned to Ireland in 432 CE and had great success in Christianizing it. When the Roman Empire fell in 756 CE, Europe plunged into its Dark Ages, but Ireland's Golden Age of learning and scholarship began and lasted until the 11th century. As Thomas Cahill (1995) showed in his best-selling history, the Irish essentially saved European civilization through an emphasis on scholarship and its preservation. In 795 CE, the Vikings from northern Scandinavia started to invade Ireland, founded settlements along the coasts, and established Dublin as their capital. Eventually, the Irish united under the high king, Brian Boru, and defeated the Vikings at Clondarf in 1014 CE. The Vikings were allowed to remain in their seaport towns, intermarried with the Irish, and in time were absorbed by Irish culture.

Starting about 1160 CE, the English, sometimes at the invitation of petty kings, became increasingly involved in Ireland's affairs. However, the English who settled in Ireland were quickly absorbed by the culture through joint business ventures, intermarriage, and a perception that England was too distant from Ireland to be controllable. In 1366 the English passed the infamous statutes of Kilkenny as a defensive reaction against this absorption, and they outlawed intermarriage and concubinage between the English and Irish and the use of Gaelic by both the English and "the Irish living among the English" (Beckett, 1986). The English were even forbidden to use Irish names and dress, and laws were passed excluding the Irish from positions of authority. These statutes tended to be disregarded in Ireland when first passed, but many came to be strictly enforced in later centuries.

In 1534 Henry VIII began to exert strong English control over Ireland. His successors initiated a plantation policy, seizing Irish lands and encouraging Protestants to settle in the country in an attempt to make the nation Protestant. There were several Irish revolts, but they were beaten down. The 10-year revolt starting in 1641 was particularly important, as 600,000 people died during it, and eventually Puritan leader Oliver Cromwell put it down mercilessly and brutally. Cromwell kept a diary describing the joy that he experienced at inflicting so much pain on the Irish for the greater glory of God. Some Irish still hate Cromwell today. Ironically, today the English and Irish are working together amiably in the EU.

English Oppression

The Irish eventually sided with James II, a Roman Catholic who became King of England but was forced from the throne in 1685, at least in part because he had abolished many anti-Catholic laws. Although he tried to regain his throne, he and his Irish supporters were defeated in the Battle of the Boyne in 1690. For the next two centuries, conditions among Irish Catholics, which had been deplorable, got worse. The English seized additional land, and by 1704 the Irish held only about one seventh of the land in Ireland. A series of penal laws were passed so that Catholics could not purchase, inherit, or even rent land; they were also excluded from the Irish Parliament and the army, and they were restricted in their right to practice Catholicism. Also, Catholics were barred not only from the one university, Trinity, but even from most of the schools in which English was the language of instruction.

To counteract the assault on their culture, the Irish employed illegal schoolmasters who taught in Gaelic in "hedge schools" or schools hidden from sight behind hedges; sometimes classes convened in the homes of the students. Because schoolmasters did not have access to many school materials or even classrooms, almost all of this education was oral in nature, involving memorization, oral presentations, and debates.

Between 1782 and 1798, the all-Protestant Irish Parliament ruled the country. It restored to Catholics their right to hold land and lifted restrictions on the practice of Catholicism. However, the Irish still did not have political rights, and most continued to live in wretched conditions. Moreover, the Irish Parliament was dissolved in 1801, and when Ireland attained independence in 1922, the nation was ruled from Parliament in London, which included a small number of Irish members of parliament (MPs). In 1828, largely through the efforts of one Irish MP, Daniel O'Connell (the Great Liberator), Catholic emancipation occurred, and the penal laws governing the Irish were relaxed.

There were periodic rebellions—in 1798, 1803, 1848, and 1865. Although unsuccessful, they helped to lay the foundations for final independence in 1922, largely sparked by the Rebellion of 1916. Although all of these rebellions were unsuccessful, they reflect the Celtic trait of accepting nobility in death for a righteous but doomed cause.

In 1831 the English established a national school system in Ireland in which only the English language could be used. Irish children had to wear a wooden baton around their necks. If they were heard talking in Gaelic, the teacher would make a mark on the baton, and their parents usually beat them at home because the parents' opportunities to work and thus survive were completely in the hands of the English. Many of the Irish began to discard Gaelic, at least in public. Patrick Pearse, an Irish patriot who was later executed because of his leadership of the 1916 uprising, characterized the educational system as a "murder machine" designed to stamp out Irish language and culture. Furthermore, Britain had set up a mercantilistic system that made the Irish dependent on one crop, potatoes. When that crop failed, the Great Potato Famine of

1845–1849 occurred. The English refused to provide any significant assistance to the Irish because of their belief in a free market economy and thus allowed about 1 million people out of a population of 9 million to starve to death.

This event has often been compared to the Holocaust during World War II. Even before the famine, conditions among the Irish had become so deplorable that satirist Jonathan Swift argued eerily in "A Modest Proposal" that Irish babies should be killed and eaten. Some of his modest proposals, such as using the skin of the babies to make gloves and boots, resemble what actually happened in the Holocaust.

Ireland as we know it today began to emerge in 1916, when a small group of Irish patriots commandeered the General Post Office Building in Dublin on Easter Sunday. The English executed the 15 leaders of the rebellion, and this sparked a war against the English that led to the modern division of Ireland into two parts, the Protestant north with a minority Catholic population and the Catholic south. The focus of this chapter is the Catholic south, which occupies five sixths of the land.

Identifying Links

It is said that everybody knows everybody else's business in a country village. Ireland and its culture still reflect this village-like perspective and mentality. Whenever the Irish meet, one of the first things they do is to determine one another's place of origin. The conversation usually helps to identify common relatives and friends. Given the wide circle of friends and acquaintances that the Irish tend to make, it is usually not difficult to find a link.

Ireland's size is little more than one hundredth of that of the continental United States. It lies to the west of Great Britain and is economically tied to that country. Ireland has four major cities: Dublin, Cork, Limerick, and Galway. In the early 1970s, more than 60% of the workforce was employed in agriculture, but today only 6% are found in that line of work; 26% of the workforce is in industry and 68% in services. Ireland is a high-tech leader in the EU and its workforce is young, although it is beginning to become more mature due to prosperity and the resultant higher life expectancies. More than 20% of the people are under 15.

The importance of conversation to the Irish makes it a fitting metaphor for the nation. However, to understand the metaphor fully, we need to explore the intersection of Gaelic and English. Then we can focus on an essential Irish conversation, praying to God and the saints. The free-flowing nature of Irish conversation is another of its essential characteristics, as are the places where conversations are held.

Intersection of Gaelic and English

The Irish tend to enjoy simple pleasures, but the complexity of their thought patterns and culture can be baffling to outsiders. They generally have an intense love of conversation and storytelling, and they have often been accused of talking just to hear the sound of their own voices. The Irish use the English language in ways that are not found in any other culture. They don't just give a verbal answer; rather, they construct a vivid mental picture that is pleasing to the mind as well as the ear. When the transition from Gaelic to English occurred, the Irish created vivid images in Gaelic, a language whose meaning is often ambiguous, and expressed them in English, a direct language whose meaning is generally clear even to those who learn it as a second language. The vivid imagery of many Irish writers originated in the imaginative storytelling that was historically a critical part of social conversation.

Gaelic was, to the Irish, a graphic, living language that was appropriate for expressing the wildest of ideas in a distinctive and pleasing manner. Frank McCourt's (1996) popular *Angela's Ashes*, with his description of growing up in extreme poverty during the Depression in Limerick, is a perfect example of this use of language. Almost everyone who has read this book comes away feeling as if they are actually with McCourt as he goes through his dire experiences.

As indicated previously, Ireland remained relatively bucolic until the 1980s. Eamon De Valera and his conservative followers were advocates of rural life, and they vehemently resisted efforts to industrialize and modernize Ireland. Given this situation, it is easy to see how the talent for conversation as an art form was maintained, as there was not much else to do for recreation. And, while Irish cuisine has improved markedly in recent years, conversation among many of the Irish is at least as important as, if not more important than, the food being served. Visitors sometimes notice that the Irish seem to forget about their food until it is almost cold.

If, however, an Irish person admonishes a compatriot for eating too much or too quickly, the witty reply is frequently to the effect that one never knows when the next famine will occur. Such "slagging matches"—in which a comment is made at the expense of another person, then a witty retort is made, followed by a series of such interactions—are much loved by the Irish. Moreover, this emphasis on the primacy of conversation is in contrast to practices found in some other cultures, such as the Italian and French, where both the food and conversation are prized.

Important Writers

If the size of the population is taken into account, it seems that, since 1870 or so, Ireland has produced many more prominent essayists, novelists, and poets than any other country. This prominence reflects the intersection of the Gaelic and English languages and the aural bias of the Irish. They have also produced great musicians, who combine music and words in a unique way. Conversely, the Irish have not produced a major visual artist equal to those of other European countries, and their achievements in science are modest.

Countless examples could be used to illustrate this intersection, but the opening words of James Joyce's (1914–1915/1964) *Portrait of the Artist as a Young Man*, in which he first introduced the technique of stream of consciousness, aptly serve the purpose:

> Once upon a time and a very good time it was there was a moocow coming down along the road and this moocow that was coming down along the road met a nicens little boy named baby tuckoo. . . .
>
> His father told him that story; his father looked at him through a glass; he had a hairy face.
>
> He was baby tuckoo. The moocow came down the road where Betty Byrne lived: she sold lemon platt.
>
> > *O, the wild rose blossoms*
> >
> > *On the little green place.*
>
> He sang that song. That was his song.
>
> > *O, the green wothe botheth.* (p. 1)

Several points about this brief but pertinent passage deserve mention. It expresses a rural bias, befitting Ireland, and it reflects the vivid Gaelic language in which Joyce was proficient. Also, it immediately captures the imagination but leaves readers wondering what is going to happen: They must read further if they want to capture the meaning, and it seems that the meaning will become clear only in the most circuitous way. Furthermore, although the essence of the passage is mundane, it is expressed in a captivating manner. Readers are pleasantly surprised by the passage and eagerly await additional pleasant surprises. In many ways this passage is an ideal example of the manner in which Gaelic and English intersect. Although some of the modern Irish and the Irish who have immigrated to other nations such as the United States and Australia may not be aware of these historical antecedents, their patterns of speech and thought tend to reflect this intersection.

Perhaps the most imaginatively wild of the modern Irish writers who incorporate the intersection of the Gaelic and English languages is Brian Nolan, who wrote under the names Myles na gCopaleen and Flann O'Brien. Nolan wrote some of his novels and stories in Gaelic and others in English. Even the titles of his books are indicative of this imaginative focus, for example, *The Poor Mouth: A Bad Story About the Hard Life* (O'Brien, 1940/1974). "Putting on the poor mouth" means making a pretense of being poor or in bad circumstances to gain advantage from creditors or prospective creditors, and the book is a satire on the rural life found in western Ireland. Nolan's masterpiece, *At Swim-Two-Birds* (O'Brien, 1939/1961), sets the scene for a confrontation between Mad Sweeny and Jem Casey in the following way:

Synopsis, being a summary of what has gone before, FOR THE BENEFIT OF NEW READERS: Dermit Trellis, an eccentric author, conceives the project of writing a salutary book on the consequences which follow wrong-doing and creates for the purpose

The Pooka Fergus MacPhellimey, a species of human Irish devil endowed with magical power. He then creates

John Furriskey, a depraved character, whose task is to attack women and behave at all times in an indecent manner. By magic he is instructed by Trellis to go one night to Donnybrook where he will by arrangement meet and betray. . . . (p. 1)

The remaining characters are sequentially introduced in the same imaginative way.

Memorable Sounds

In the area of music, the Chieftains, who have been performing together for more than 40 years, represent the distinctive approach of the Irish to music. Their songs, played on traditional instruments, are interspersed with classic Irish dances and long dialogues that sometimes involve the audience. Similarly Thomas Moore, who lived in the 19th century, is sometimes cited as the composer who captured the essence of the intersection of the Gaelic and English languages in such poetic songs as "Believe Me If All Those Endearing Young Charms," which he wrote as lyrics to accompany a traditional Irish folk tune for a woman whose face was badly scarred in a fire:

Believe me, if all those endearing young charms,

Which I gaze on so fondly to-day,

Were to fade by to-morrow, and fleet in my arms,

Like a fairy-gifts fading away,

Thou wouldst still be ador'd, as this moment thou art,

Let thy loveliness fade as it will,

And upon the dear ruin each wish of my heart,

Would entwine itself verdantly still. (Moore, 1808/1841, p. 259)

A reminder that the Irish are different from the English and Americans is their brogue. When the conversion from speaking Gaelic to speaking English was occurring, this brogue was an embarrassment for many Irish. The English looked down upon these "inferior" people who were unable to speak "proper" English (Waters, 1984). Today the brogue is prized by the Irish and appreciated throughout the world, but it is clearly in decline as the Irish move away from their rural heritage.

Given that Ireland is a nation in which unhurried conversation is prized, it is logical that there is a balance between the orientations of "being" and "doing." Although the

Irish have enthusiastically accepted change in recent years, they still express astonishment at the "doing" entrepreneurial activities of their 44 million Irish American counterparts, who have made Saint Patrick's Day, a holy day in Ireland, into a fun-loving time for partying that embraces all people (Milbank, 1993). The Irish generally take life much more slowly than Americans, who tend to watch the clock constantly and rush from one activity to another. No matter how rushed the Irish may be, they normally have time to stop and talk.

However, urban living has significantly influenced this placid pattern of behavior. In 1969 Martin Gannon visited a slow-moving but entrancing Dublin in which people would walk you to the building when you asked for directions. During a recent visit to a now crowded and busy Dublin, he experienced difficulty obtaining similar information from pedestrians, some of whom clearly signaled their unwillingness to talk through lack of eye contact and hurried steps.

The Irish also tend to place more importance on strong friendships and extended family ties than Americans do. When they first arrived in the United States, many early Irish immigrants settled near other friends or relatives who had preceded them to the United States and developed a reputation for being clannish. But slowly the Irish love of conversation and curiosity about all things led to their interaction with others and their Americanization.

Prayer as Conversation

Prayer or a conversation with God is one of the most important parts of an Irish life. As noted above, more than 90% of the population is Roman Catholic, and regular attendance at Sunday Mass is about 40%, which is one of the highest figures for regular weekly attendance among nations. Many Catholic households contain crucifixes and religious pictures, which serve as outward reminders of people's religious beliefs and duties.

Furthermore, prayer is accompanied by acts of good works that stem directly from the strong ethical and moral system of the Irish. They are recognized as having made the highest per capita donation to relief efforts in countries such as Ethiopia, and they are quick to donate their time, energy, and even lives to help those living in execrable conditions. The extent of the crisis in Somalia in the early 1990s, for instance, was first reported to the United Nations by Mary Robinson, then president of Ireland, and an Irish nurse was killed after arriving in Somalia to help out.

The Irish state relies on the works of the Catholic Church to support most of its social service programs. For example, most of the hospitals are run by the Catholic Church rather than by the state. These hospitals are partially funded with state money and are staffed with nuns, when possible. The state has very little control over how the money is spent, especially because it lacks the buildings and the power to replace the church-run system that was in place when the state was formed.

Religious Influence

As indicated previously, the national school (state) system is also under the control of the various religious orders in Ireland. It is the primary source of education for primary school children. The state funds the system, but the schools are run by local boards, which are almost always controlled by the clergy. There is a separate national school for each major religion. Local Catholic national schools are managed by local parish priests, while Protestant vicars have their own separate schools. Many of the instructors in these schools are nuns or brothers who work for little pay; thus, costs are much lower than in a state-operated school. In exchange for lower costs, the Irish state has relinquished control. The schools are really the church's last line of defense because it has the ability to instill Catholic morality and beliefs in almost every young Irish child in the country.

Many Irish begin and end their day with prayer. This is their opportunity to tell God their troubles and their joys. One of the more common prayers is that Ireland may one day be reunited. This act of talking to God helps to form a personal relationship between the Irish and their God. It is difficult to ignore the dictates of God because He is such a personal and integral part of the daily Irish life. God is also present in daily life in the living personification of the numerous priests and religious brothers and sisters found in Ireland.

Entering the religious life is seen as a special calling for the Irish. In the past, when families were very large, it was common for every family to give at least one son or daughter to the religious life. An Irish mother's greatest joy was to know that her son or daughter was in God's service, and this was prized more highly than a bevy of grandchildren. Vocations to religious life have decreased in recent years, and many churches rely on priests from such nations as Mexico and Nigeria.

In the Republic of Ireland, unlike Northern Ireland, there are few problems between Catholics and members of other religious groups. In fact, Catholics enjoy having the Protestants in their communities and treat them with great respect. In one rural area where the Protestant congregation had dwindled, the Catholic parish helped the Protestants with fundraising to make repairs to their church. This act of charity illustrates the great capacity for giving that the Irish possess. Historically many of the Irish were not greatly attached to material possessions and were quite willing to share what they had with the world, although materialism has increased significantly in recent years.

A Free-Flowing Conversation: Irish Hospitality

Conversations with the Irish are known to take many strange turns, and participants may find themselves discussing a subject and not knowing how it arose. Also, not only what is said but also the manner in which it is expressed is important. The Irish tend to be monochronic, completing one activity before going on to another one, yet they cannot resist divergences and tangents in their conversations or their lives. They often feel that they are inspired by an idea that must be shared with the rest of the world, regardless of what the other person may be saying. The Irish tend to respect this pattern of behavior and are quite willing to change the subject, which can account for the breadth of their conversations as well as for their length.

Like their conversations, the Irish tend to be curious about all things foreign or unfamiliar, and they are quick to extend a hand in greeting and to start a conversation, usually a long one. It is not unusual for the Irish to begin a conversation with a perfect stranger, but for most of the Irish there are no strangers—only people with whom they haven't had the pleasure of conversing. The Irish do not usually hug in public, but this in no way reduces the warmth of their greeting. They often view Americans as too demonstrative and are uncomfortable with public displays of affection. They tend to be a hospitable, trusting, and friendly people. Nothing illustrates this outlook more than their national greeting, *Céad mile fáilte* or "One hundred thousand welcomes," which is usually accompanied by a handshake.

In addition, the Irish are famous for their hospitality toward friends as well as strangers. As Delaney (1974) points out, "In the olden days, anyone who had partaken of food in an Irishman's home was considered to be secure against harm or hurt from any member of the family, and no one was ever turned away" (p. 103). This spirit of hospitality still exists in Ireland. In the country the Irish tend to keep their doors unlocked and open. People who pass by or ask for directions may be invited inside to have something to eat or drink. It is not unusual for the Irish to meet someone in the afternoon and invite that person to their home for supper that evening, and this happens in the cities as well as the country. Meals are accompanied by great conversation by both young and old.

Many of the Irish don't believe in secrets, and even if they did, it would be hard to imagine them being able to keep one. They seem quite willing to tell the world their business and expect their visitors to do the same. However, the Irish feel that Americans are much too willing to divulge sensitive information. As the Irish saying goes, "You can get a lift with an American, and by the time you separate, you know much more about the person than you care to know."

However, the Irish are often unwilling to carry on superficial conversations. They enjoy a conversation that deals with something of substance and are well-known for breaking the often-quoted American social rule that one should not discuss politics or religion in public. The Irish enjoy nothing more than to discuss these subjects, hoping to spark a deep philosophical conversation.

Places of Conversations: Irish Friends and Families

There is no place where the Irish would find it difficult to carry on a conversation. They are generally quite willing to talk about any subject at any time, but several places have a special meaning for the Irish. Conversation in the home is important for an Irish family. Conversation is also one of the major social activities of an Irish public house or pub.

Family Dinners

The typical Irish family tends to be closely knit, and its members describe their activities to one another in great detail. Mealtime in the Irish household should not be missed by a family member, for the conversation if not the food. Supper is the time of day when family members gather to update one another on their daily activities. The parents usually ask the children about their day in school and share the events of their own day. One of the most famous Irish American families, the Kennedys, stayed true to this tradition in their new homeland. Dinner table conversations at Joe and Rose Kennedy's table became dinner seminars on politics and policies, and the children were quizzed on what they had learned that day. This practice has continued through generations of Kennedys.

The Irish have always held education and learning in high regard. Teachers are treated with great respect, and their relatively high salaries reflect their worth to the community. Ireland has a literacy rate of 99% due to compulsory national education.

A frequent topic of conversation at family dinners is news of extended family, friends, or neighbors. The Irish have an intense interest in the activities of their extended family and friends, but this interest isn't purely for the sake of gossip. They generally are quick to congratulate on good news and even quicker to rally around in times of trouble or need. When someone is sick, it is not unusual for all the friends and family of the person to spend almost all of their time at the hospital. Friends help the family with necessary tasks, and they entertain one another with stories and remembrances. Many of the Irish have a difficult time understanding the American tendency for the nuclear family to handle emergencies and other problems by itself.

Weddings and Wakes

This practice also holds true whenever there is a death in the community. Everyone gathers to hold an Irish wake, which combines the viewing of the body with a party that may last for 2 or 3 days. There is plenty of food, drinking, laughing, conversation, music, games, and storytelling. Presumably the practice of a wake originated because people had difficulty traveling in Ireland due to poor roads and nonmechanized means of transportation, and the wake afforded an opportunity not only to pay respect to the deceased but also to renew old friendships and reminisce. Although the problems of travel have been solved, the Irish continue this ancient way of saying good-bye to the deceased and uplifting the spirits of those he or she has left.

An event that is as important as the wake is a wedding, a time of celebration for the entire family and neighborhood. Customarily a big church wedding is followed by a sit-down dinner and an evening of dancing and merriment. Registry office weddings are very rare in Ireland, as might be expected in this conservative and Catholic-dominated nation.

Irish parents tend to be strict with their children. They set down definite rules that must be followed. Irish children are given much less freedom than American children, and they usually spend all day with their parents on Sunday and may accompany them to a dance or to the pub in the evening. Parents are usually well acquainted with the families of their children's friends and believe in group activities. The tight-knit social community in which the Irish live makes it difficult for children to do anything without their parents' knowledge. There is always a third cousin or kindly neighbor who is willing to keep tabs on children and report their behavior to the parents, some of whom have even managed to stretch their watchful eyes across the Atlantic to keep tabs on children living in the United States. This close control can sometimes be difficult for young people, but it creates a strong support network that is useful in times of trouble.

Pub Life

A frequent gathering place for men, women, and children is the local pub, given that the drinking age is not enforced throughout most of Ireland. Most pubs have two sections: the plain, working-man's part and the decorated part, where the cost of a pint of beer is slightly higher. In the not-too-distant past, it was seen as unbecoming for a woman to enter a pub; there are still some pubs in which women are comfortable only in the decorated part, and women typically order half-pints of beer while the men order pints.

Pubs tend to be informal, often without servers and with plenty of bar and table space. Young and old mingle in the pub, conversing with one another and trading opinions. The Irish are raised with a great respect for their elders and are comfortable carrying on a conversation with a person of any age or background. They tend to be a democratic people by nature. Although they may not agree with a person's opinion, they will usually respect him or her for having formed one.

Irish pubs are probably the sites of the liveliest conversations held in Ireland. Ironically, the number of pubs per capita has declined dramatically in recent years, in large part because of the movement against excessive alcoholic consumption; new, strict laws; and the powerful association of pub owners, who lobby against new licenses. The Irish tend to be a sociable people who generally don't believe in drinking alone. This pattern of behavior has often resulted in their reputation for being alcoholics. In fact, the Irish consume less alcohol per capita than the average for the EU, but there are at least two distinct groups: those who do not imbibe at all and those who do so, sometimes to excess.

Admittedly many Irish drink more than they should, but the problem often appears worse than it is because almost all of their drinking takes place in public.

Furthermore, coworkers and their superiors frequently socialize in pubs, and they tend to evaluate one another not only in terms of on-the-job performance but also in terms of their ability to converse skillfully in such a setting. The favorite drink of the Irish is a strong black beer, Guinness. It is far more popular than the well-known Irish whiskey.

Even more important than a good drink in a pub is good conversation. The Irish are famous for their storytelling, and it is not unusual to find an entire pub silent while one man holds sway. It is also not unusual for someone to recite a Shakespearean play in its entirety from memory or to quote at length from the writings of such Irish writers as James Joyce and Sean O'Casey. In Ireland and in other nations to which the Irish have emigrated, there is a tradition of reading all of James Joyce's famous and path-breaking book *Ulysses* on Saint Patrick's Day in pubs.

Many a heated argument can erupt in a pub. The Irish seem to have a natural love of confrontation in all things, and the conversation doesn't even have to be about something that affects their lives. They are fond of exchanging opinions on many abstract issues and world events. During these sessions at the pub, the Irish sharpen their conversational skills. While these conversations can become heated, however, they rarely become violent.

Irish friends, neighbors, and families visit one another on a regular basis. As indicated above, rarely if ever is one turned away from the door. Family and friends know that they are welcome and that they will be given something to eat and drink. It is not unusual for visitors to arrive late in the evening and stay until almost morning. Such visits are usually not made for any special purpose other than conversation, which is a mainstay of the Irish life no matter the setting.

Ending a Conversation

A conversation with an Irish person can be such a long and exciting adventure that a person thinks it will never end. It will be hard to bring the conversation to a close because the Irish always seem to have the last word. Ireland is a country that welcomes its visitors and makes them feel so comfortable and accepted that it is hard to break free and return home after an afternoon or evening of conversation.

Geert Hofstede's (2001) research profiling the value orientation of 53 nations confirms many of our observations. Ireland is a masculine-oriented society in which sex roles are clearly differentiated; it ranks 7th of the 53 nations on this dimension. However, the more recent GLOBE study (House et al., 2004) contains a more nuanced profile. Ireland ranks 3rd of 62 national societies on a comparable value measure, gender egalitarianism, with lower rankings indicating greater male domination. Thus, Irish values stress that males should be dominant, as only 2 other of the 62 societies, England and Sweden, are higher. But in the *practice* of gender egalitarianism, Ireland ranks only 39th, with lower scores indicating greater male domination, suggesting that changes to gender roles, such as wives working full-time, are leading to a discrepancy between attitudes and actual behaviors. Further, Ireland is not an acquisition-oriented society, as Hofstede's classification might suggest, but a society in which there is a balance between "being" and "doing."

Also, Hofstede's (2001) study of cultural values indicates that Ireland clusters with those countries emphasizing individualism, ranking 12th of 53 nations, as we might expect of a people who are willing and eager to explore and talk about serious and conflict-laden topics. Individualism is expressed through conversation on issues that affect society; it is also expressed through writing, art, and music. Music is itself a means of conversation, and Ireland reportedly has one of the highest numbers of musicians per capita of all countries. Still, the Irish tend to be collectivistic in their emphasis on the family and religion and their acceptance of a generous welfare system and strong labor unions.

In short, the Irish tend to be an optimistic people who are ready to accept the challenges that life presents, although there is a melancholic strain in many of the Irish that is frequently attributed to the long years of English rule and the rainy weather. The Irish usually confront things head-on and are ready to take on the world if necessary. They can be creative in their solutions but also stubborn when asked to compromise, and they tend to be truly happy in the middle of a heated but stimulating conversation. Given their history and predilections, it is not surprising that people of Irish descent prefer personal situations and professional fields of work where their aurally focused approach to reality can be given free rein, even after they have spent several generations living in countries such as the United States and Australia.

CHAPTER 14

The Canadian Backpack and Flag

Many a Canadian nationalist harbours the bizarre fear that should we ever reject royalty, we would instantly mutate into Americans, as though the Canadian sense of self is so frail and delicate a bud that the only thing stopping it from being swallowed whole by the U.S. is an English lady in a funny hat.

—Will S. Ferguson, Canadian writer and novelist (2007, p. 198)

Whenever I come to Canada I think the world should be simple. People are nice. They're decent. There's lots of space. Angry identities assumed in tougher climes morph into gentle ones beneath the wide Canadian sky.

—Roger Cohen (2011)

Canada is the world's second-largest nation in size, the first being the new Russian Republic. Its population is about 33.2 million; about 90% live within 125 miles of Canada's border with the United States. Canada is a nation of open spaces. Canada has a GDP per person of US$45,070, which is nearly the same as the U.S. GDP per head of $46,350. Canada also ranks 6th of 179 nations on the 2011 Index of Economic Freedom, which means it is a very good place to do business in terms of such measures as corruption and governmental red tape (T. Miller, 2011). The climate in most Canadian cities is comparable to neighboring regions of the United States, but the empty spaces of northern Canada are very cold. Throughout the nation winters are cold and summers brief.

An apt metaphor for Canada is the Canadian maple leaf flag, which countless Canadians unobtrusively sew onto their modest backpacks and suitcases. Amid the bewildering variety of suitcases at the baggage claim of any major international airport, one occasionally sees a Canadian backpack, sturdy but a bit frayed around the edges. Its most notable feature is a sewn-on patch displaying the Canadian maple leaf flag; such a bag symbolically and emphatically proclaims: "I am definitely not a U.S. American." This is a typically indirect way of Canadian communication, especially when contrasted to that of U.S. Americans, and only rarely will one encounter a straightforward statement of hostility like the one found in the opening quote.

But this backpack also conjures up other messages. The bag's modesty reflects the Canadian bias for egalitarianism, and its flag suggests a personality that is indirect and suggestive in communication. The backpack also suggests that Canadians are willing to accept others as equals, even if different. In all likelihood the average Canadian probably owns more copies of the national flag than the average citizen of any other nation. A 2007 poll by Ipsos Reid for The Dominion Institute conducted before Canada Day showed that most Canadians feel attached to the maple leaf (87%), the beaver (74%), hockey (73%), and the "mountie" (72%) as unifying Canadian symbols. The percentages were smaller for the French province of Quebec, where only 66% indicated that they felt attached to the maple leaf. Canadians older than 55 were also more likely to display the flag than those aged 18 through 34. The largest such poll was conducted in 2008 for the Department of Citizenship and Immigration and The Dominion Institute by the Ipsos Reid Institute, and the top contenders were the maple leaf, hockey, the flag itself, and the beaver in that order. The youngest bracket of 18 to 34 felt more attached to iconic places like the CN Tower and Toronto, whereas Canadians 55 and older felt more attached to historical events.

The Canadian flag appears on lapel pins, cereal boxes, bumper stickers, bathing suits, and, of course, army surplus backpacks. This may seem curious to those who know Canadians to be polite and somewhat reserved in nature, but a need to sew their flag onto their backpacks and elsewhere is an undeniable feature of Canadian culture. In short, the bag and its flag combine to form an apt metaphor for our Canadian neighbors.

In this chapter we will examine three aspects of this metaphor: egalitarianism and outlook, the Canadian mosaic, and clear separation from their U.S. neighbors. Before doing so, however, we briefly trace some historical facts without which Canada is difficult to understand.

Historical Background

The history of Canada cannot be separated from the history of other nations, particularly Britain and France. The British formed one of the first chartered trading companies in the world, the Hudson Bay Company, in 1670 as a way to organize and profit from trade as well as to promote exploration and settlement of Canada and other lands. French and English colonists fought numerous battles over the territory that is now Canada until France officially ceded its claims in the 1763 Treaty of Paris. During the American Revolution, thousands of British loyalists fled to Canada, drawing the colony closer to the British crown.

In 1867 the Dominion of Canada was established as a self-governing member of the British Commonwealth. Until 1965 the official Canadian flag was the British Union Jack, at which time the maple leaf flag replaced it. The modern nation of Canada was forged by the experiences of World Wars I and II; more than 60,000 Canadian soldiers were killed in World War II out of a population of 8 million.

Because of World War II, Canada and the United States began to cooperate closely. Their soldiers fought side by side for 3½ years, and afterward these two nations were among the small number that had not been completely shattered by the war. Most important, Canada and the United States worked together to rebuild Europe and supported one another through trade. Canada and the United States share the world's largest undefended border and do more business together than any other two nations. The United States accounts for about 77.7% of Canada's exports and 52.4% of the country's imports.

Egalitarianism and Outlook

The Canadian soldier's backpack was part of his standard gear in warfare, able to hold the bare essentials for life under extreme conditions: blanket, tent, rain gear, cup, cooking pot, can opener, rifle-cleaning kit, and little more. The modern version includes much of the same equipment. Although today more than 80% of Canadians are city dwellers, easy access to splendid scenery and challenging trails has made hiking, trekking, and canoeing national pastimes. Many Canadians, especially among the older generations, have worked in the interior as loggers, road builders, miners, and related occupations in Canada's resource-based economy. Even today, younger city-dwelling Canadians spend a summer or two planting trees in the nation's parks or working at some other job in the wilderness that requires life to be lived out of a backpack.

Such experiences have contributed to a sense of egalitarianism and a conservative outlook, both for Anglo and non-Anglo Canadians. Similarly, other than the presence of the prominently displayed maple leaf flag, the most striking feature of the Canadian backpack is its lack of striking features. Discerning U.S. backpackers might go to REI or a similar store to choose from a number of models featuring the latest lightweight waterproof fabrics, snazzy color schemes, and a hefty price tag. Most Canadian backpackers will simply go to the closet and pull out the trusty and well-used model. They silently rejoice in its utility and the fact that they do not have to spend a large sum of money like their U.S. counterparts, which appeals to their generally frugal nature.

Canadian backpackers will, of course, make a purchase if necessary, but then they will select the plainest possible color. Canadians avoid flashy displays of status or wealth, instinctively forgoing material possessions that would seem like an attempt to be better than others.

The conservative English Canadians also avoid open expressions of emotions and feelings, but the French Canadians may be less reserved, gesture more expansively, and stand closer during a conversation. Although they are extremely polite and friendly, Canadians tend to be more like the English in their preference for internalizing problems and concerns as opposed to the U.S. tendency to "let it all hang out." It is no accident that the national animal of Canada is the beaver, given the nation's vast natural resources. Beavers survive primarily by working together in colonies and building impregnable lodges. The colonies, or lodges, consist of one or more family groups, and beavers in one colony generally have little contact with those in another colony except when danger approaches. Then the beavers loudly warn neighboring colonies and try to escape through one of the two tunnels they have constructed.

Canadians tend to be more diplomatic than U.S. Americans, often preferring to accept situations that are not to their liking rather than to call attention to them with complaints and demands for better treatment. Canadians who are served the wrong dish at a restaurant might go ahead and eat it, whereas U.S. Americans would demand the correct dish. Similarly, a Canadian book was published some years ago with the modest title *Your Guide to Coping With Back Pain* (Fine, 1985). The publisher decided that the book would never sell in the United States using this title, so there the title was changed to *Conquering Back Pain* (Fine, 1987).

Canadians emphasize good manners and conflict avoidance but not at the expense of truth. This approach may not be fully desirable in a business meeting where open expression of needs and concerns is vital to the identification and resolution of problems. Similarly Canadians may find it difficult to initiate an unpleasant conversation with their superiors or business partners. Although polite and indirect, Canadians are more direct in communication than their Asian and Latin American counterparts, with their discourse lacking the complexity of meanings that are characteristic of these cultures. Thus Canadian communication patterns overlap with and are similar to but different from those of the more direct U.S. Americans.

Another manifestation of the Canadian sense of egalitarianism and fairness is the country's support for universal health care and the social safety net. Compared with the United States, services are much more evenly distributed in Canada, which is more in line with the social democracies of Western Europe. Michael Moore, in his celebrated documentary *Sicko* (Moore & O'Hara, 2007), focused on these differences, suggesting that life expectancy was higher in Canada, Britain, and France than in the United States because of their respective health care systems.

Moore did not point out, however, that a Supreme Court Justice in Canada had opined in 2005 that many Canadians suffer from chronic pain while they wait for treatment and some die before they receive it. Wealthy Canadians often travel to the United States to obtain high-quality health care. In 2010, Newfoundland premier Danny Williams, an independently wealthy former lawyer and businessperson, travelled to the United States for heart surgery, provoking both anger and sympathy from his constituents. The other downside is that Canada's total tax burden is much higher than that in the United States, and this progressive tax system encourages highly paid individuals to cut back on their workloads or to move out of the country. Still, most Canadians accept this tradeoff, which reflects their egalitarianism and conservative outlook. To ensure that people receive adequate health care, they prefer using modest backpacks to spending money on flashy items.

The Canadian Mosaic

Canadians are taught from an early age that no person is inherently any better than any other, and this sense of equality pervades much of the Canadian perspective on social status and Canada's place in the world. Canadians have a strong appreciation of foreign cultures and have actively encouraged immigration from around the world for the past several decades. In fact, Canada is often dubbed "a global village in one country." Although Canada has much open space to fill, immigration also stems from the Canadian people's sense of equality and fair play. Canadians are sensitive to the suffering that occurs in overcrowded, poverty-stricken lands. Canada receives most of its legal immigrants from three main sources: people with skills who immigrate for economic reasons, people with relatives already in Canada, and refugees from around the world that Canada has traditionally accepted due to a fairly liberal policy on political asylum. These immigrants help make up the famed Canadian mosaic.

The diversity of cultural backgrounds in Canada is breathtaking. Its immigrants come from more than 200 countries and territories of birth. At least 16% of the Vancouver area's 1.8 million people are Chinese, and airport signs and oral instructions are in both Chinese and English; approximately another 14% of Vancouver residents come from other parts of Asia. Similarly more than 10% of Toronto's population is either Chinese or Filipino. Canada has large numbers of immigrants from China, India, Southeast Asia, Eastern Europe, the Caribbean, and other places. Toronto and Vancouver have two of the biggest Chinatowns in North America. Immigration represents about 60% of the population growth in Toronto and Vancouver, and this trend is expected to continue. Canadian businesses are focused on reaching these ethnic markets, especially the Chinese and South Asian markets. It is estimated by Statistics Canada (2008, Figures 28 & 40) that by 2017, roughly 1 in 5 Canadians will be a member of a visible minority; in Toronto and Vancouver, this figure rises to about 1 out of every 2. Thus it is not surprising that Toronto has not only a very large Chinatown but also large neighborhoods that are overwhelmingly Greek, Indian, Italian, Portuguese, Caribbean, and Ukrainian.

In some ways Canada is changing the new arrivals, but they are also changing Canada. The distinctive Canadian personality lives on through the values passed down through schools, businesses, and other institutions, which help to shape the newcomers into Canadian citizens. However, Canada emphasizes the creation of a mosaic of cultures rather than the U.S. melting pot (Andrews, 1999). This approach is officially recognized in the Canadian Multiculturalism Act of 1988, and Canada is proud of the fact that it became the first country in the world to adopt an official Multiculturalism Policy in 1971.

Some Anglo Canadians resent the large influx of immigrants, but their polite and friendly nature for the most part allows them to neutralize this feeling, although an economic downturn could bring negative feelings to the surface. In 2011 Statistics Canada reported that hate crimes had increased in 2009 in both Toronto and Vancouver and most other parts of Canada. Just over half of the hate crimes were motivated by race and ethnicity, followed by religion and sexual orientation. According to Rob Gordon, director of Simon Fraser University's School of Criminology, "in 2008, there was a global economic crisis which, I think, had a major impact on many centres in Canada" (M. Robinson, 2011). A troubling statistic, according to the report, was that the majority of crimes were committed by the 12–17 age group.

In general, however, the Canadian economy has advanced significantly because of its large number of immigrants, and immigration has made Canada one of the richest countries in the world. Other nations, such as Japan and Italy, are suffering economically because of declines in their populations and an increase in the average age, but Canada readily accepts people who can contribute as workers, skilled professionals, managers, and consumers. Multiculturalism in Canada is a doctrine and part of the national Charter of Rights and Freedoms, which is very different from the situation in Britain or France or the Netherlands. Of course, integration is a much greater challenge for "visible" minorities, and according to government statistics, "satisfaction with life" decreases from first to second generation for these minorities.

Canadians as Non-U.S. Americans

Although Canadians and U.S. Americans cooperate significantly with one another in many areas, Canadians dislike being mistaken for their neighbors to the south. Many of them are not happy that U.S. fast-food chains, books, and films are much more popular than their Canadian counterparts, and the Canadian government periodically considers legislation that would restrict the sale of U.S. books, magazines, music, and films. In fact, Canadian TV and radio stations are required by law to carry a specified amount of "Canadian-only" material, which is defined as being at least partly written, produced, presented, or otherwise contributed to by people from Canada. The government subsidizes significantly the activities of Canadian artists and companies, but the

North American Free Trade Agreement (NAFTA) and the World Trade Organization preclude exclusion of non-Canadian goods and services.

A 28-year-old Canadian actor became a cultural hero in the late 1990s when he spontaneously spoke the following words, subsequently made into a Molson Beer ad, at a coffeehouse open-mike night:

> I am Canadian. I'm not a lumberjack or a fur trader. I don't live in an igloo, eat blubber, or own a dogsled. I don't know Jimmy, Suzie, or Sally from Canada, although I'm certain they're really really nice. I have a prime minister, not a president. I speak English and French, not American. And I pronounce it "about," not "a-boot." I can proudly sew my country's flag on my backpack. I believe in peacekeeping, not policing; diversity, not assimilation. And that the beaver is a truly proud and noble animal. A tuque is a hat, a chesterfield is a couch. And it's pronounced zed. Not zee. Zed. Canada is the second-largest land mass, the first nation of hockey and the best part of North America. My name is Joe, and I am Canadian. (Molson Canadian Beer, 2000)

Throughout the nation Canadians lined up to shout the rant or their version of it into microphones set up on the ice between periods during hockey games. The Joe Canada discussion was a daily feature in the nation's editorial pages, and most Canadians agreed that a little national pride was a good thing. Ironically, however, Joe's day of fame was deflated when he moved to Los Angeles to seek work as an actor due to poor job prospects in Canada. Some critics felt that Joe should have carved out a separate Canadian identity instead of focusing on the "not American" aspects. However, the ad spawned many parodies and imitations in Canada and around the world. In 2007 the Muslim American Society created a video entitled "I am a Muslim," which took many lines from the Molson beer ad and applied it to Muslim stereotypes.

Similarly a popular Canadian TV weekly show, *This Hour Has 22 Minutes,* satirized U.S. ignorance by interviewing unsuspecting U.S. Americans with such questions as the following:

> Do you think Canada should join North America? It's a big story up north. Care to comment?

> Should Canada outlaw the slaughter of polar bears in Toronto?

However, the creator of this show and its interviewer, Rick Mercer, commented tellingly on the show's appeal:

> Canadians spend a huge portion of their social life trying to define what it means to be Canadian. Americans never spend any time trying to define what it means to be American. Canadians have an identity crisis. We look like Americans. We sound like Americans. We know everything about Americans. They know nothing about us. . . . We find that funny. (Brown, 2001)

There could be several explanations for this non-U.S. American (but not anti-U.S.) bias. Canada was formed principally by those loyalists who left the United States during the American Revolutionary War. The more activist U.S. outlook contrasted sharply, and still contrasts sharply, with the more conservative Canadian outlook. Whereas the U.S. constitution protects life, liberty, and property, Canada's constitution emphasizes "peace, order, and good government." U.S. comedians frequently use Canada as the butt of their jokes, as in Robin Williams's famous rendering of the song "Blame Canada" from the movie *South Park: Bigger, Longer & Uncut* (Parker & Stone, 1999) or the comment widely attributed to Comedy Central's Jon Stewart: "I've been to Canada, and I've always gotten the impression that I could take the country over in about two days."

Also, it is difficult to be the much smaller and less prosperous neighbor of the United States. U.S. teams have won the Stanley Cup, hockey's highest honor, consistently since 1993. Given that hockey is Canada's national sport, this is particularly difficult for Canadians to accept. In 2011 Vancouver Canuck fans rioted and took to the streets with torches following their team's loss to the Boston Bruins in the final game of the Stanley Cup. However, most of the players on the U.S. teams are Canadians, which assuages the damage. Unfortunately, the greatest hockey player of all time, Wayne Gretzky, was traded to the Los Angeles Kings in 1988 because the Edmonton Oilers could no longer afford his salary; many Canadians considered the trade a national calamity. The 2010 Vancouver Winter Olympics hockey showdown between Canada and the United States in the gold medal round ended in a thrilling golden goal in overtime by Canada's Sidney Crosby. This gave the host nation, which also won the most gold medals at the Games, a grand victory in the sport so intertwined with the nation's identity. Whatever the explanation or explanations, Canadians are definitely not U.S. Americans. This may well be the essence of Canadian culture, defining itself in terms of what it is not.

However, the similarities between Canadians and U.S. Americans are much greater than the supposed differences. Both cultures tend to be individualistic, and both prefer a direct, low-context form of communication in which accomplishing goals is more important than process or getting to know one another before doing business. The manners of English-speaking Canadians are very similar to those of English-speaking U.S. Americans, but French Canadians may exhibit less reserve, and wealthy Hong Kong Chinese with Canadian citizenship have their own business etiquette reflecting their identity.

Some Canadian firms have a well-deserved reputation for being aggressive and successful in international business. In recent years, in the context of the volatility in the world's oil prices as a result of growing demand and instability in some key oil-producing countries, Canada's vast reserves of oil sands in the province of Alberta hold considerable potential for North America. The oil sands contain reserves (approximately 170 billion barrels) that are second only to Saudi Arabia's reserves and are likely to contribute to the energy needs of Canada, the United States, and other markets for many decades to come. Contrary to popular perception, Canada is the number one supplier of oil to the United States.

Following the global financial crisis, Canada emerged with deficit and debt ratios which were far lower than those of the other G8 countries and a relatively stable banking environment. Some argued that the reason the Canadian banking system did not require a bailout lay in Canadian bankers' tendency to be "boring but in a good way" and Canada's penchant for being conservative in all things. Writing in the *Financial Times*, noted financial journalist Chrystia Freeland (2010) suggests, however, that the real reason lies in Canada's highly restrictive mortgage market. All mortgages with less than 20% down payment are insured, and variable-rate or interest-only mortgages are almost unheard of, as is negative return on equity.

Free trade between the United States and Canada has benefited both, particularly Canada, in terms of balance of net exports. A large number of Canadians have become successful in the United States because of unlimited opportunities for success in a country with a population that is almost 10 times that of Canada. These include but are not limited to William Shatner, Donald Sutherland, Celine Dion, Martin Short, Justin Bieber, and Ryan Reynolds.

Still, Canadians revel in pointing out the differences, even to the extent of sewing the maple leaf flag in the middle of their backpacks. Presumably, Canadians see themselves as the middle point of a distribution in which the brash U.S. Americans are on one end and the withdrawn English on the other, although the reality is much more complex.

And the complex reality of Canada is epitomized in the difficult relations between the Canadian English and Canadian French. Most of the generalizations in this chapter apply particularly to the English, but there are two French-speaking provinces, Quebec and New Brunswick. The locus of the hostility is Quebec, which historically has been much poorer than the English-speaking provinces. In 1995 Quebec held a provincial referendum about separation from Canada, and the final vote against was extremely close: 50.5% to 49.5%. Victory would have cast doubt on the concept of the nation of Canada, and only through a heroic flag-waving effort were the Québécois convinced to stay. Subsequent opinion polls indicated a fall in support for independence, and the Parti Quebecois (PQ), which was pro-independence, suffered defeat in the 2003 provincial election. As this book goes to press, polls show that about 40% support independence and the PQ is expected to win the next election, which could raise the possibility of another referendum. In general, French Canadians claim to feel more Canadian when they travel outside their country than within the country itself.

Ironically, 1995 was the year of a well-financed campaign celebrating the 30th anniversary of the Canadian maple leaf flag. The issue of separation is still lurking in the background, but the continuing influx to Quebec of people from non-French cultures and an improved economy have blunted or at least postponed the threat of separation. Furthermore, in 2006 Parliament agreed that the Québécois should be considered a "nation" within Canada in a gesture that was largely symbolic.

Anglo Canadians have been economically dominant since their arrival in Canada, and the new mosaic (including the French component) will probably enlarge the economic pie and prosperity but increase cultural diversity. As this happens, new and perhaps conflicting cultural symbols will emerge, such as the Chinese family altar (see Chapter 26). However, according to a Dominion Institute poll conducted in 2007, 7 out of 10 Canadians believe that their common history, heroes, and national symbols are responsible for their success as a nation. A recent nationwide survey conducted by the Montréal-based Association for Canadian studies showed that "learning about Canadian history" scored number one among the ways that Canadians felt that they could develop attachments to their country. Interestingly, in what was dubbed as the "Celine Dion phenomenon" by Association for Canadian Studies executive director Jack Jedwab, most Canadians felt that watching Canadian stars succeed internationally had a powerful influence in maintaining citizens' pride and possibly unity (Boswell, 2011). Therefore, at least for the foreseeable future, we believe, the maple leaf flag sewed on the modest backpack will serve as an effective cultural metaphor for this vast land and complicated culture, which appear to have a very bright future.

CHAPTER 15

French Wine

Wine making is really quite a simple business. Only the first 200 years are difficult.

—Baroness Philippine de Rothschild
(quoted in Rachman, 1999, p. 91)

Behind the bustling terrace cafés and bright municipal blooms of springtime, France is not a happy place. Tense, fearful and beset by self-doubt, the French seem in a state of defiant hostility: toward their president, political parties, Islam, immigrants, the euro, globalisation, business bosses and more.

—"Reforming Gloomy France," 2011, p. 27

To describe French culture, it is useful and perhaps essential to consider French wine, the best of which is considered preeminent throughout the world. French viticulture has produced many of the leading wine practices for centuries and has created many of the most well-known grape varieties, including cabernet sauvignon, chardonnay, pinot noir, syrah, and sauvignon blanc. Wine has played a vital role in determining the economy, traditions, and attitudes in France. It has shaped the country's disposition, weaving a common thread through all the varying walks of French life. Just as there are more than 5,000 varieties of French wine, so too the French have a variety of idiosyncrasies and personalities, many of which are puzzling to outsiders. Beneath these differences, however, is a culture that unifies the people and their institutions. Accordingly, wine appears to be an appropriate metaphor for describing and analyzing the French culture.

However, as noted in the second opening quotation, France today is feeling gloomy. Some of the reasons apply to other nations as well, such as the United States and many other European nations. For example, there is a fear that rampant and unregulated globalization will destroy jobs; a fear that the euro, the common currency of the European Union (EU), will be destroyed; and a backlash against immigrants. Still, France is in 2011 gloomier than most other nations. In a multination survey, less than 20% of the French replied "better" to the following question: Do you think that 2011 will be better or worse than 2010? By contrast, the comparable figures are as follows: Nigeria, 80%; China, about 62%; Sweden, about 46%; and the United States, about 41%. Of the 12 nations surveyed, France ranked lowest in terms of a positive response ("Reforming Gloomy France," 2011).

Still, the first opening quote suggests that France, like wine, is a complex culture that seems simple to understand but in reality is not. It has taken centuries for the French to develop a nation that is the model for numerous nations because of its emphasis on the concepts of life and liberty. The United States is the only nation in the world that has added the pursuit of happiness to its constitution.

In many ways the French wine industry represents the classic tradeoff between globalization and cultural identity. France has been the leader in wine production among nations for centuries and is still regarded as the producer of the best wines at the top end of the market. But government regulation of French wine making has done serious harm in the form of fragmentation of the industry into many small growers who cannot take advantage of economies of scale found in other wine-growing nations, a confusingly large number of wine categories, and poor and inadequately funded marketing campaigns. The Bordeaux region of France by itself has 20,000 different producers, yet Gallo, based in California and the world's largest wine company, spends more than twice as much on advertising as all the Bordeaux wine companies together. The wine industry has also grown in many other nations, such as Australia and Chile, over the past few decades. Still, the preeminence of French wine, particularly of the finest vintages, is universally acknowledged. Furthermore, French companies have established joint ventures in such nations as China and India that now produce superior wine at a reasonable price, and it is a mark of distinction to carry the French name on the wine bottle.

To focus this discussion of French culture within the metaphor of French wine, five principal elements of wine will serve as a guide: pureness, classification, composition, suitability, and maturation.

Pureness

To more fully appreciate the metaphor, we must first understand what wine is, what its origins are, and how it is made. A wine's characteristics are the summation of its past development within a given environment. Viniculture is the precise and patient process that further shapes the grape's transformation into wine. Fine wine is considered to be the distillation of 2,000 years of civilization. It is understandably viewed as an object of great pride; a survivor of nature's caprices and uncertainties; a product of patience and modesty; and, most important, a symbol of friendship, hospitality, and *joie de vivre*.

Vital to the quality of the wine are the soil, climate, vine type, and the viniculturist who tends the wine-making process. The complex interplay of these factors determines whether pride or disappointment reigns once the wine flows from its bottled womb. Soil and climate nourish growth in mysterious ways that defy chemical analysis. Contrary to what might be expected, the vine thrives in the type of soil in which little else will grow. Climate and vine type must complement each other so as to produce healthy grapes, and the viniculturist must make sure that the timing of harvest and maturation is meticulous and accurate. Vines are interbred, making it difficult to classify the wine produced because the offspring may resemble their parents or display entirely new characteristics. The wines recognized as the world's greatest—those that cost more than $100 a bottle—come from grapes grown in only a few select vineyards in France.

The art and science of viniculture also influence the wine's personality. Experience, diligent patience, and effort are required to propagate the wine through its various stages of cultivation. The *vendange*, or harvest period, brings a sense of urgency. A delay of even 12 hours between harvest and preparation for fermenting can spoil both taste and aroma. After transfer from vats to bottles, the wine continues its aging process. Age, then, influences personality development, with great wines requiring more than 50 years to mature to perfection.

A Perfect Land

The French, much like U.S. Americans, have a romantic view of their country as being special and unique. Like a flawless bottle of vintage wine, France displays perfection in the land and its people. The French have mentally massaged the image of their borders into a hexagon, perfectly situated midway between the equator and the North Pole, balanced in soil and climate. Symmetry, balance, and harmony—it all coalesced into one great land because the French supposedly willed it. This perception of symmetry and unity in the physical dimensions of this geographically diverse land is more wishful thinking than reality.

The north and the south disagree as to the origin of the French people. In different parts of the country people have different identities: The northeast identifies with the German and Swiss, the northwest with the English, the southwest with the Catalans and Basques, and the southeast with the Italians. Perhaps, then, the quest for unity has deep and stubborn roots in a past in which the French have been an aggregate of individuals struggling to forge themselves into a single entity.

One source of tension is that Muslims now number about 5 million in France out of a total population of 61.9 million. This is the largest Muslim community in Europe. Poverty and joblessness are much greater in Muslim communities and other immigrant communities, such as the Roma, than in non-Muslim communities. The tension results largely from the colonial legacy of France, particularly its acceptance of Algerians as French citizens after the Algerian War during the 1950s and the acceptance of members of other former French colonies. In French cities with large Muslim populations, it is now common to see Muslim women wearing the burka, which is a combination of a veil covering the face (the niqab), a headscarf, and loose-fitting robes covering the remainder of the body. In 2010 France outlawed the wearing of the niqab or face veil from public places in accordance with the principle of strict separation of religious and public arenas. France had previously banned the wearing of headscarves, yarmulkes, and other visible religious symbols from the public schools.

Nevertheless, some of the tension is clearly productive. One example is the Muslim desire to eat halal hamburgers, that is, hamburgers made in accordance with Muslim law. There is no difference between the taste of halal and non-halal hamburgers. However, a French competitor of McDonald's, Quick, which had only one third of McDonald's market share, decided to introduce halal hamburgers. Sales boomed. Similarly, films stressing either an Algerian viewpoint or French viewpoint about the Algerian War have helped each side to consider their joint issues from the other's perspective. In addition, the fact that French voters elected Nicholas Sarkozy, the child of a Hungarian father and mother with Greek Jewish roots, as president suggests a degree of open-mindedness that is greater than that in many other nations.

Historically, the French tend to give the impression that France is the center of the universe around which the rest of the world rotates. (Many other nations have expressed a similar belief in their superiority. China, for example, was called the Middle Kingdom, and for many centuries the Chinese drew maps of the world with China as its center.) One can quickly learn to resent the French belief in their cultural superiority along with their lack of immediate friendliness. But they readily defend their position in part by noting that international business and diplomacy were conducted in the French language until World War I and that French art, literature, and thought remain pervasive in education and society.

The extent to which the French defend this supposed superiority is extraordinary. A commission must decide which foreign words can be a part of the official language; the proceedings of conferences are required to be published in French, even when English would suffice; and the seventh summit devoted to the French language was held in 1997 in Vietnam, which France formerly ruled but in which only about 1% of the population speaks French. In the 11th summit, held in Bucharest, Hungary, in 2005, former prime minister Jacques Chirac warned of a unilingual world in which the dominance of English would limit cultural creativity and variety.

Historical Roots

The earliest traceable ancestry of the French people begins with the Celts, a Germanic people who later became known as the Gauls. They planted an extensive empire, which was subdued by the invading Romans under Caesar in 52 BCE. For the next 500 years, the Gauls were repeatedly subjected to invasions by other Germanic tribes and, last, by the Franks, who emigrated westward across the Rhine. Out of the Middle Ages and its feudal system emerged the Renaissance (rebirth), a time of increasing wealth and power for France but also of continuing turmoil.

A golden age burst forth in the person of Louis XIV, the Sun King, who proclaimed, "*L'état, c'est moi*," or "I am the state." He orchestrated his rule from the extraordinarily lavish Palais de Versailles, and during his reign, France expanded and built an impressive navy. Its language was spoken and its culture was emulated all over Europe.

But the Sun King allowed a widening gap to develop between the wealthy and the poor, and in an increasingly financially stressed economy, that gap exploded in the French Revolution of 1789. The quest for *liberté, égalité, fraternité* first resulted in the brief rule of Napoleon III. He fostered a more organized France by enforcing the Code Napoleon, which gathered, revised, and codified a vast, disorderly accumulation of laws, both old and new. Unfortunately the oppressive restrictions that Napoleon III placed on laborers, peasants, and women are still felt today.

In the 20th century, France was heavily affected by World Wars I and II. Although a victor in World War I, France lost nearly 2 million men. World War II still lives in the memories of many French people as a time of hopelessness and disgrace under German occupation.

Troubled Years

The history of French wine has also endured notable difficulties. From 1865 to 1895, a disease called *Phylloxera vastatrix* destroyed virtually every vineyard in France (Vedel, 1986). This was a tragedy of major proportions that adversely affected thousands of wine growers. But, even in such dire circumstances, the French did not lose their resolve. After toiling for months, they discovered by trial and error that a viable solution was to graft French vine strains onto American stocks that were resistant to the disease. Forced into a corner, the French came together to save the industry. In subsequent years the vineyards regained their health, and the wine industry flourished once again.

Even from this brief overview, it is apparent that the lives of the French people have been planted, uprooted, and replanted throughout history. The conquering Romans left the French with a sense of pageantry and grandeur as well as an affinity for control and bureaucratic organization. The Romans introduced the concepts of centralization and a complex bureaucracy, which have taken root in French hearts and minds. France's present concept of grandeur was first thrust on the French people in the time of Louis XIV. From this epic era emerged the idea that the French were guardians of cherished universal values and that their country was a beacon to the world. The French saw themselves as favored, as possessors of ideas and values coveted and treasured by the rest of mankind. As the French poet Charles Péguy is said to have written, "How maddening, says God, it will be when there are no longer any Frenchmen."

It is true that the purest, finest wines must be grown in special soil. In this sense the French consider France to be a pure and proud country. Accordingly, those not born and raised in France need to guard against forming quick and negative first impressions without understanding past trials and tribulations as they relate to the formation of the French culture.

Classification

As noted earlier, France produces 5,000 varieties of wine precisely classified so that impostors cannot pass for superior wines. This insistence about nomenclature bestows on wine a pedigree that is displayed on each label. Through fermentation and the aging process in the bottle, wine develops its final personality, blend, and balance.

Although wine is classified in excruciating detail, those who are not connoisseurs might dare to divide it into four major classes: the *Appellation d'Origine Contrôlée* wines, which are the best and most famous; respectable regional varieties, known as *Vins Délimités de Qualité Supérieur*, which are quite good for everyday use; the *Vins de Pays*, which are younger, fresher wines suitable for immediate consumption; and the *Vins de Table*, which lack taste and pedigree.

Similarly French society is clearly stratified and divided into four principal and generally nonoverlapping classes: the *haute bourgeoisie*, which includes the few remaining aristocrats along with top business and government professionals; the *petite bourgeoisie*, owners of small companies or top managers; *classes moyennes*, or the middle classes—teachers, shopkeepers, and artisans; and *classes populaires*, or workers.

People may know their place in society, but that does not imply that they feel inferior to others. The French are comfortable accepting and living within the confines of this classification system rather than resisting it. Workers in the *classe populaire* are just as accepted for their contribution to society as officials in the haute bourgeois class. This norm extends to French attitudes toward outsiders. Visitors to France sometimes have difficulty relating to the French, who can be just as ethnocentric as anyone else, for the French tend to behave independently of others who mistakenly expect tacit cooperation from them in an undertaking. The reason for this outlook is quite simple. In the French mind, France and a person's own particular social class tend to come first. The French interpret the phrase *tout le monde* (literally, all the world) to mean all who are French or, even more specifically, all who are in their particular social class. Outsiders are countenanced but not openly welcomed.

Creating Order

Rules, regulations, and procedures give certainty, definition, and order to French life along with guaranteeing the preservation of a particular quality of lifestyle. Still, *savoir-vivre* facilitates life, meaning there is a certain way to do something no matter what the situation is or how trivial it may appear. The rules provide an avenue for security where a threat is presupposed and certainty where fears and doubts exist. Consequently nothing is left to chance. Even as Napoleon codified civil law, Antonin Carême (1833) codified gastronomy in his five-volume *L'Art de la Cuisine Français au Dix-Neuvième Siècle*. Nothing has been omitted or forgotten; even slavery was codified, and it resulted in more humane treatment of slaves in France and its colonies than in England or Spain and their colonies.

On the other hand, *savoir-vivre* can lead to preoccupation with form over substance, transforming every aspect of life into a ceremony. Preoccupation with form is evident in the French sense of style and fashion and their flair for elegance. Some first-class French hotels have decrepit furniture, yet the rooms have such charm that all is forgiven and overlooked. Image, and the stress on the sensual, is more important than the facts in business advertisements as well. French advertisements tend to be attention getting. They concentrate on creating a mood or a response instead of informing (Hall & Hall, 1990). French advertising campaigns must first produce pieces of art before trying to be effective. This is why many of the French believe that U.S. advertisements are not very good—the messages are too straightforward for French tastes. At least to many French commentators, American ads, when compared to French ads, are boring and predictable (Haley, 1996). Similarly it is no accident that the French subway system has reproductions of classic paintings on display at major stations.

That the French love classifying things is apparent not only with regard to wine but also with regard to the classification of people by title and in their fastidiousness with regard to and insistence on politeness and attention to social forms. Like labels pasted on wine bottles, labels that are applied to people stick. There is little room in French society for impostors and little fluidity in crossing class barriers. The French pay attention to status and titles and expect others to do likewise. Correct form must be followed. For example, when introductions are required, the person who makes an introduction must be of the same status as the person being introduced. In a business meeting, it is essential that the person with the highest rank occupy the middle seat. The importance paid to social standing is so great that even salary takes second place. Likewise, when honor is an issue, keeping one's word has more value than profit (Hall & Hall, 1990). Given this situation, it is little wonder that many people who seek social mobility have migrated to countries such as Canada and the United States in recent years.

On the 2011 Innovation Index, France ranked 18th among nations in the world while the United States ranked 1st. While there is a movement to reform the education system so that children from poorer families are given the same opportunities as those from affluent families, the top half of French students match the standards in writing, mathematics, and science of the very best performers in the 20 most developed nations of the Organisation of Economic Co-operation and Development (OECD; "*Bac* to School," 2007). However, on the 2011 Index of Economic Freedom, France ranks only 69th of 179 nations (T. Miller, 2011), which suggests that France is a moderately difficult nation in which to do business.

Cartesian Legacy

Like the viniculturist, the French generally have a need to control and refine life and to order the universe. A significant portion of this desire can be attributed to the thinking of Descartes, whose desire to make humanity the master of nature led him to ponder a rational meaning of the universe. Because he elected to discover this meaning without leaving his study, due to his belief that "I think, therefore I am," his findings were not always accurate. But that did not matter to him as long as he was convincing. He has been described as the "intellectual father of the French preoccupation with form" (de Gramont, 1969, p. 318). One example of Cartesian thought would be a general who devises a perfect battle plan with incomplete knowledge of the enemy's strength and capacity and suffers defeat—but with style and elegance.

The legacy of the Cartesian method can also be witnessed in life's most commonplace occurrences. Preoccupation with shaping, organizing, and magically transforming raw material into a work of art is evident in food shop windows, where displays of colorful and elaborately prepared casseroles and desserts could vie with paintings in the Louvre as master-crafted creations. In sum, Descartes, who is frequently described as the founder of modern philosophy, left nothing unexplained, and neither do the French today.

French businesspeople are no less concerned with form. Presentations are given from the heart, and the French display eloquence much more than U.S. Americans do. Their obsession with form shows in their belief that how one speaks makes as much an impression as what one says. The French love to discuss abstract and complex ideas spontaneously, in detail, and at length so that agendas, efficient use of time, and conclusions appear to have less importance.

In addition, French business tends to be highly centralized because of the enduring influence of the Romans. The person atop the hierarchy is most important and wields power in many, if not most, decisions. Thus the French tend to bypass the many intervening layers of bureaucracy and appeal directly to the pinnacle of power. The French manager with authority demonstrates it physically; the manager's desk is placed in the center of the office. Those with the least influence are relegated to the far corners of the room. It is little wonder that change in French organizations tends to come from the top downward, not from the bottom upward (Crozier, 1964). Behavior in France today mirrors Crozier's findings, at least anecdotally.

Managerial Style

Such a centralized social structure lends itself to the acceptance of autocratic behavior. Managers, therefore, display almost total control over their subordinates. In fact, French managers are often accused of not delegating authority, instead sharing vital information only within their own elitist network. As a result, lower-level managers can have great difficulty moving up the corporate ladder.

This tight inner circle of upper management can be likened to the tight inner circle of the highest-quality wines that win awards year after year. Only those wines from the best regions with the best color, brilliance, and taste can gain the status of *Appellation d'Origine Contrôlée*—the highest distinction available. In the same way, gaining a top management position frequently requires education at the finest of schools and upbringing in the most affluent regions.

This high level of centralization can be regarded in a positive light, as it serves to maintain unity. The French remain a diverse people who tend to be proud of and loyal to their respective regions of origin. Throughout history the French have strived for unity, but they tend to detest uniformity, for they are a people who generally love to differ. For example, when the United States went to war in Iraq, several European nations were lukewarm in support of this action. Among these nations France was most prominent, even to the point that some Americans organized a boycott of French wine that led to a significant decrease in sales. The answer to this dilemma of integrating diversity of opinion and unity of action may be in the modern autocracy of centralization. People who exist in a hierarchy of niches can find their own niche, security, and sense of belonging among members of the same social class.

Understanding France's hierarchical business structure can be instructive to American business managers. Just as the best bottle of wine is saved for presentation only to the most distinguished guests, so too should the most polished proposals be saved for presentation to a top manager in a French corporation. Efforts to persuade lower- and middle-level managers may prove frustrating, as few final decisions can be made without approval from the top.

In addition, one should be aware of how the French handle meeting unknown colleagues at a typical business lunch. Uncertainty brings unease and implies a lack of control, for it entails a threat that must be thwarted. The lunch, then, gives the French time and opportunity to reflect, study, and learn who outsiders are and how they can be expected to behave in various situations. Pleasure and business are intertwined, for there is no better way in the French person's mind to open up communication and understanding than with a leisurely repast of food and wine (Hall & Hall, 1990).

Interestingly, however, the average amount of time devoted to lunch during the busy day has decreased from 90 to 40 minutes, suggesting that the globalization of business has influenced even the diehard French. Similarly, the number of French brasserie cafes has decreased from more than 200,000 in 1960, when the population was 46 million, to about 50,000 today, when the population is 69.1 million. Even the average number of gallons of wine consumed per French person per year has declined. In France it is now common to drink wine only on special occasions, when dining out, or on the weekends but not at every lunch and dinner.

Classifying Behavior

Perhaps the best attempt to categorize and classify different types of French behavior was completed by the anthropologist Edward T. Hall (1966). According to Hall, France is at the middle of his context dimension, with Japan and the Arab countries representing high-context behavior while Germany and the United States represent low-context behavior. The French are high context in the sense that they frequently do not need explicit and/or written communication to understand one another. However, they tend to emphasize low-context behavior in the form of excessive bureaucratic rules and regulations. Everything is spelled out explicitly in written form and is typically repeated orally so that the message is clear. This seemingly contradictory behavior reflects the Roman emphasis on centralization and bureaucracy and, at the same time, the innate desire of many French people to know one another deeply before transacting business.

Hall's framework may help to explain why the French tend to evoke strong emotional reactions in many short-term and long-term visitors to their country. Frequently visitors complain about the rudeness that greets them in France, a complaint not unlike those voiced by some visitors to the United States. This rudeness or directness in speech among the French seems to represent both low-context and emotional behavior, which is interpreted, correctly or incorrectly, as rudeness. Conversely, other visitors paint an opposite picture of the French, describing them as concerned about their feelings and welfare and as going to extreme lengths to demonstrate hospitality and friendship. This may represent more high-context and emotional behavior.

In both instances it is best to reserve judgment, as initial external manifestations of behavior can be misleading. For example, the French tend to smile at someone only after they know a person for some time, a cultural practice that is centuries old. This can be a major problem in any situation but particularly in a service-related industry. Today it is common to teach "surly" waiters and clerks in France to smile and speak in a friendly tone, even to new customers (Swardson, 1996).

Composition

Many experts on wine emphasize that it is extraordinarily intricate and complex and even inconstant in quality from one year to the next, as it involves many factors and ingredients such as climate, harvesting at just the right time to capture the ideal smell and taste, competitive pricing, and marketing. And so it can be said of the French. Who they are has been determined by their ancestry, the region of the country where they were raised, and the social and educational systems that have influenced them. Their society is changing, and so are they. Perhaps their adaptability is an outgrowth of their complexity. The French tend to do many things at once, and they do everything with alacrity—especially in an urban setting such as Paris, where the pace is rapid. In this sense the French are polychronic. This pace encourages quick decision making and contributes to impetuousness. For example, in a highly centralized structure, many businesspeople try to skirt cumbersome intervening layers of hierarchy to accomplish their objectives, even when doing so poses some risk to their own careers.

To the consternation of U.S. Americans trying to do business in France, the French tend to tolerate disruptions for the sake of human interactions because, to them, it is all part of an interrelated process. This makes planning difficult, even for the French. After all, given life's uncertainties, one never knows what obstacles may prevent promises from being kept.

Still, Edward T. Hall (Hall & Hall, 1990) points out that the French tend to be monochronic—doing one activity at a time—once they have defined a goal they wish to attain. This simultaneous emphasis on polychronism and monochronism is, once again, a reflection of the fact that France is at the midpoint of the high-context/low-context continuum. Given this intermediate position, it is easy to understand why foreigners have difficulty comprehending French behavior.

Work and Play

The French work hard and prefer to be their own bosses, although few have this opportunity, given their country's relatively rigid social structure and governmental regulations. At the very least, most French people would like to be recognized as leaders, even if what they lead is the smallest unit in the organization.

By law the French must devote 5 weeks, including all of August, to vacation. About 40% of them spend this time in vacation spots such as the Côte d'Azur. Holidays, like food and wine, are taken seriously, and the French tend to prepare carefully and meticulously for them.

Weekends tend to be devoted to family matters. Of the 85% who ascribe to Catholicism, fewer than 15% attend Mass, usually on Saturday evenings or Sunday mornings. Saturday afternoons are often reserved for shopping. In regard to religion, some argue there is an antichurch sentiment; others disagree, asserting instead that the French have no particular persuasion on religious matters and that they are more irreligious than antireligious. This is probably the true state of affairs, given the justified pride that the French manifest toward their magnificent cathedrals such as Chartres, which are found throughout the country.

Geert Hofstede's (2001) analysis of 53 nations in terms of cultural dimensions tends to confirm this profile of the French and the apparent contradictions that emerge when the metaphor of wine is employed. Not surprisingly, the French tend to accept a high degree of power distance among individuals and groups in society and to dislike uncertainty, preferring to be in familiar situations and to work with long-term colleagues. But the French also tend to be individualistic and even iconoclastic, and they cluster with other nations who value a high degree of individualism.

Still, Hofstede (2001) shows that France is a feminine society in which aggressiveness, assertiveness, and the desire for material possessions are of much less importance than the quality and pace of life. The French have deep-seated needs for security and getting along with insiders, colleagues, and family members. In short, the French accept centralization and bureaucracy but only insofar as these forms of organization allow them to be individualistic and buffer them from life's uncertainty so that a high quality of life can be maintained. The GLOBE study (House et al., 2004) is in remarkable agreement with the Hofstede study in terms of these findings.

Conversational Style

An integral part of maintaining a high quality of life in France is conversation. Like French business, however, conversation is not without classifications, rules, and hierarchical structure. By way of contrast, this is quite different from the free-flowing Irish conversational style. Just as the process of making wine is complex, intricate, and meaningful, so too is the art of French conversation. The French seem to feel an innate restlessness, wanting to explore every conceivable issue or topic through lengthy and lively conversation. Whether the topic is politics, weather, history, or the latest film, contrasts and controversy challenge the French intellect and raise their spirits.

Many consider the French to be argumentative—no one more so than the French themselves. They can be quick to criticize, but this is often only to stimulate discussion. Few French people are satisfied by mere superficial discourse. If a conversation is worth beginning, like the production of a tasty Burgundy, it is worth cultivating into a meaningful discussion.

For example, late one evening in the small town of Dijon, a U.S. American caught a cab to save himself a 25-minute walk. No sooner had he sat down than the cab driver quickly blurted out, "*Ah, vous êtes Américain?!*" Not expecting such quick questioning, the American cautiously replied, "*Oui, je suis Américain . . . pourquoi?*" The cab driver responded excitedly that he had never been to the United States and wanted to learn more about it. Conversation continued briskly and was quite philosophical at times. The cab driver was mostly interested in comparing the respective styles and mannerisms of the U.S. Americans and the French. Meanwhile, time—and the money meter—was ticking away. The passenger knew pretty well the different ways to get home, and the cab driver's route was not one of them. Finally, after 30 minutes or so, the cab arrived at its destination. The U.S. American was a bit angry that the ride had taken so long and was worried that he didn't have enough money. Just as he reached for his wallet, the driver said abruptly, "*S'arrête! Je ne veux pas d'argent. Merci pour la conversation,*" and, after a pause, "*Bonne nuit.*" What did this mean? "Stop! I don't want any money. Thank you for the conversation. Good night." Other Americans have had similar experiences.

The finest wines result from following carefully a detailed, meticulous set of rules (H. Johnson, 1985). If one of these rules is forgotten or ignored, the quality of the wine will be greatly diminished. The same is true of speaking and conversation in France. Even small mispronunciations have the unnerving effect of fingernails scraping on a blackboard. Conversation is a highly developed art and follows very specific rules.

Not surprisingly, the French language is governed by a seemingly endless (and annoying, in many eyes) set of rules. For example, all French nouns are either masculine or feminine, and articles and adjectives must agree. Verbs have so many different endings and participles that they are almost impossible for many nonnative speakers to keep track of. Proper sentence structure often places the verb at the end of the sentence, as opposed to its beginning or middle, a practice that is sometimes difficult for English speakers to grasp.

There are two very different forms of addressing a person in French. The second-person singular, *tu/toi*, is reserved for only the closest of friends and family members of the same age or younger. *Vous*, which is the second-person plural as well as singular, is used on a more formal level. Care needs to be taken in using *tu* and *vous*, as the wrong usage can spoil a conversation or jeopardize a relationship at an early stage. Until you know a person well, the *vous* form should be used. As you become better acquainted, an occasional usage of *tu* is not considered offensive. But only much later, when friendships have thoroughly developed, should you use the *tu/toi* form regularly—but not with elders or superiors. Among the younger generation a more informal conversational style is rapidly replacing these formal rules, although even young people revert to the more formalized style once they join the full-time workforce.

Relationships

An implicit conversational rule is that to smile at someone you don't know and say hello is frequently considered provocative, not friendly. On the other hand, to pass a friend on the street or bump into family acquaintances without offering conversation would be considered rude (S. A. Taylor, 1990). These differing interaction styles for different levels of friends in France are not so common in the United States, where a friendly hello and small talk are the norm.

Like a glass of vintage Bordeaux, the family tends to be important to the French because it is a source of acceptance, nourishing them in the midst of life's vicissitudes. The French often look to their families for emotional and economic support. Similarly, as when the horrible disease struck the wine industry in the late 1800s, wine growers look to each other in times of trouble. Likewise, ordinary French people vigorously supported the resistance of wine growers who eventually forced the large American firm, Robert Mondavi, to sell the land on which it planned to harvest wine grapes in southern France in 2001. Relationships among family members are close. Family bonds are strengthened by eating weekend meals and taking extended holidays together. These are times for catching up on family matters, planning, and simply enjoying each other's company.

Paradoxically, although French people can be very romantic about love, the concept of marriage and children tends to be approached in a businesslike, practical manner. Children are considered the parents' obligation, and children's behaviors directly reflect proper (or improper) upbringing. French parents are not as concerned about playing with children as they are about civilizing them (R. Carroll, 1987). Parental guidance continues through adolescence and often through university. In fact, it is not uncommon for parents to help their children out considerably with housing or other expenses, even after marriage. It sometimes seems that the French support their children financially until they are stepping on their beards.

The French are very private with regard to their homes, so an invitation to dinner implies a high level of intimacy. The home is mostly reserved for family or very close friends. Restaurants are used for acquaintances and first-time get-togethers. One should never ask to visit a French home if not invited, and if you want to stop by for some reason, telephone first.

Women's Role

Furthermore, similar to a fine vintage selection patiently awaiting its proper time for opening and enjoying, the women's movement in France has been in no great rush to achieve full equality, even though many women are now prominent in business, politics, and the professions. French women see themselves, and are regarded as, the equals of men—equal but different. Presented with opportunities to play the same roles as men, women have shied away from doing so. Accordingly, many milestones in women's rights came about much later in France than in other countries. Only in 1980 did the Académie Française admit its first woman member. Until 1964 a wife still had to obtain her husband's permission to open a bank account, run a shop, or get a passport, and only in 1975 and 1979 did further laws remove inequalities in matters of divorce, property, and the right to employment. The negative U.S. American reaction to then-president Bill Clinton's relationship with Monica Lewinsky was puzzling to the French, and one prominent French politician formed a group to support Clinton. The French countenance the fact that many politicians, such as former president François Mitterand, have a second, unofficial family. Thus, given the Frenchwoman's tendency to prefer femininity over feminism, it is not surprising that the growth of the women's liberation movement has been relatively slow in France. This movement will most likely be just as successful in France as in America, but like the best wines of France, its growth will be patient and organized.

Suitability

The most meaningful occasions in the French person's life often center on food and drink. Certain wines "marry" certain foods; furthermore, the type of wine served dictates the shape of the glass. The wine must be drunk properly with one's hand on the stem so as not to warm the liquid. A fine wine must be gently swirled, checked with a discerning eye for clarity, sniffed to detect bouquet, and tasted critically before it can be served to guests. Meals can last for hours, consisting of several courses served in proper sequence and with appropriate wines to match each course.

This challenging and often controversial business of pairing wine with the proper food requires much mating and matching, contrasting and complementing (H. Johnson, 1985). In the same way, the French people constantly struggle to find a political system that is the best match for the nation. During the Third Republic alone, from 1872 until 1940, France had 102 governments, while the United States had only 14 over the same period. In the 12 years of the Fourth Republic, from 1946 until 1958, there were 22 governments.

People and Politics

On three separate occasions since 1981, France was governed by what the French term "cohabitation": a president, responsible primarily for defense and foreign policy, from one political party and a prime minister from another party. In all three instances, the two were directly at odds with each other on many issues, particularly over nationalizing private industry versus privatizing a number of state-run organizations.

Part of the reason for such political instability is that the president, with the consent of the prime minister, has the power to dissolve the national assembly at any time except during a crisis. This would be the equivalent of a U.S. president telling the 535 members of the Senate and House of Representatives that their jobs have been terminated. Dissolution of the assembly can also operate another way: That is, the president or prime minister can resign voluntarily, causing a new round of national assembly elections to take place. Such upheaval and constant change make matching the government (wine) with the people (food) extremely difficult.

Internationally, France has been careful to guard its individual sovereignty. For example, in 1966 President Charles de Gaulle informed the North Atlantic Treaty Organization (NATO) that France was going to withdraw its land and air forces from NATO to maintain sovereignty over its own territory. In 1982, when U.S. president Ronald Reagan was planning an air strike on Libya, French President Mitterrand refused to allow U.S. aircraft to fly over French air space. Similarly France was vigorously opposed to the Iraqi war that the United States led in 2003, ostensibly because it viewed the action as unauthorized by the United Nations. As indicated previously, this created anti-French feelings in the United States and anti-American feelings in France, even to the extent that some U.S. restaurants renamed french fries. However, Nicholas Sarkozy, who was elected prime minister in 2007, has taken several steps to smooth over the relations between the two nations. For example, France strongly supported the United States in its quest to replace Muammar Gaddafi, ruler of Libya, in the spring of 2011.

Paradoxically, the French welcome governmental instability. They tend to be proud of their wide range of active political parties—six in all. Abundant political choice is consistent with the concept of French devotion to individual freedom. Furthermore, the political process is helped along by a free press and a love of political discussion. It is little wonder that France averages about 10,000 public protests of all types a year (Fleming & Lavin, 1997).

The related issues of immigration and racism have been in the political spotlight. Although the percentage of immigrants in France has remained relatively constant at about 7% during the past 25 years, immigrants are disproportionately economically deprived and unemployed. There is also tension between Catholics, who make up the majority of the population, and Muslims and Jews, some of whom do not want to assimilate into French culture. In 2002 Jean-Marie Le Pen, an avowedly racist politician heading the National Front political party, actually won the first round of the presidential election, although he ultimately failed in his quest. Pen's daughter,

Marine, has succeeded her father as the head of this revitalized political party and may win the first round of the forthcoming presidential election handily.

The French seem determined to maintain their governmental system despite the frequent controversies it engenders. Many observers point out that no matter where you set foot on French soil, you will find yourself engaged in political discussions. Thus, although the wine and food of French politics don't always suit each other, their very unsuitability stimulates conflict and a spirited involvement of the citizens in the political arena.

The Maturation Process

Viniculturists strive for disciplined growth, tirelessly pruning and training the vines to conform to their will (R. Carroll, 1987). This disciplined growth is also reflected in the French educational system, which is strictly controlled by the state. Children begin their education at the age of 6, with many enrolling in preschool by age 2. Unlike other countries such as Japan, where promotion from one grade to another is generally automatic, French students do not advance until they attain certain skills. The result is that children of widely varying ages are in the same class. French education is known to be rigorous, with 30 days of the school year tagged for examinations. But unlike the *vendange* or harvest and its intense preoccupation with accomplishing its mission in 12 hours, young students must focus their developing minds on 35 intense hours of instruction each week. Mercifully, the French have a short school year.

For children who continue in the school system, educational growth is controlled so as to be directed toward a certain diploma. The teachers who tend their crops of young students decide their academic paths—and ultimately their careers. There is a tendency to stress mathematics because proficiency in that area is seen as a key to success and guarantees treatment as a member of the elite. Today the most able children are being trained as scientists, technologists, and businesspeople to operate in an international culture. Some critics feel that this preoccupation with mathematics reaches into inappropriate realms of study such as music classes, which also require mathematics proficiency. As indicated above, the best French students compare favorably to their counterparts in other OECD nations in terms of mathematics, language, and the sciences. This bodes well for France's continued high ranking on the Innovation Index.

Destiny Determined

The destiny of less able or privileged children is to glean careers from the leftovers. Parents of these children lack the education and influence to mold a bright future for their offspring. In a real sense, social status more than anything else determines children's educational opportunities or fate. The elite, who understand the importance of education, begin to prepare their children early in life to attend the *grandes écoles* (elite universities similar to American Ivy League universities) and *universités* or *facultés* (specialty colleges and universities, e.g., in journalism), and this practice tends to reinforce existing sharp social class differences.

Educational choices are limited in other ways. It is difficult for those who do not belong to the upper social groups to have any freedom of choice in their vocations. Rather, the system early on categorizes them and shapes and defines their destinies. One young Frenchman, son of a successful flower shop owner who had built his business selling flowers on the street, did not want to carry on the family business. Because of the intense competition in his country, he was convinced that he had no chance of going to the *lycées* (elite secondary schools) or *universités*, *grandes écoles*, and *facultés*, which most privileged students attend. As a result, he pursued educational opportunities in the United States, which were better than his choices in France. Immigrants to France, such as those from Algeria, have frequently reached the same conclusion, namely that their educational and career opportunities are very constrained. Many live in the poorer districts, and some of these immigrants have been involved in violent riots in recent years to protest the system.

This elite approach to education has been widely criticized, as it tends to lead to a narrow perspective on problems, both in business and government. For example, the 5,000 graduates of the elite École Nationale d'Administration (ENA) tend to dominate government bureaucracies and then, later in life, frequently become chief executives in the firms they once regulated.

Acquaintances and Friends

The French tend to take many things seriously, even life's joys. Among the French, one of life's greatest pleasures is friends; therefore, friendship is taken seriously, as might be expected of a society emphasizing high-context behavior. Friendship must be carefully cultivated and tended over the years. The growth of friendship is a slow and deliberate thing. The French are critical of the quick and seemingly casual manner in which U.S. Americans make and discard friendships. Such behavior is uncouth—not unlike chugging a glass of wine when a sip is appropriate. A friendship, then, is not to be taken lightly, but like a carefully selected wine, it is to be savored and enjoyed to the fullest. A good wine and a good friend—they are the joie de vivre.

A helpful guide to building meaningful friendships in France is to recognize the parallels of this process to cultivating wine: Don't rush the process but instead allow quality to improve over time. That is, approach the relationship in a high-context manner. For Americans venturing into France for the first time, it is important to acknowledge that the American conversational style is quite different from the French conversational style. Whereas Americans tend to have many small conversations with a number of people, the French prefer fewer conversations on much deeper levels.

For example, a U.S. businessperson had been in France just over 3 weeks, working on a 1-year project, when he came into contact with a French colleague critical to the success of the project. The two naturally had to spend a great deal of time together. The U.S. American appreciated this opportunity to brush up on his French-speaking skills, as his colleague was a traditional French person who supposedly did not speak English. The U.S. American did his best to communicate effectively but often felt frustrated that he couldn't express himself clearly and feared that he might convey the wrong message unintentionally. Then suddenly, after 4 or 5 weeks of such effort, the two were preparing for a business meeting when the Frenchman said, "You can speak in English if you would feel more comfortable." The U.S. American was astonished. The Frenchman then explained that the French are cautious in dealing with foreign business colleagues and are careful not to overexpose themselves before a more serious, respectful relationship is established. In recent years many politicians and businesspeople have become comfortable speaking English to their monolingual American colleagues.

Health and Fitness

Another area where maturation, as well as adaptation, appears in France is in the country's gradual response to the health and fitness craze sweeping from the United States into European countries. Traditionally the French have shown a disdain for such trends, choosing continued adherence to national pastimes such as fine wine and cuisine. But times are changing. Nowadays, joggers are everywhere: in the Parc de la Tête in Lyon, on the coastal roads of Brittany, and at the foot of the Eiffel Tower. Smoking, traditionally popular in France, has become decidedly unchic, and tobacco consumption has dropped sharply. The government has taken advantage of this social change by passing a law that makes smoking more difficult in public places.

By most accounts the health craze began about 1990. There are Gymnase Clubs in many cities, all filled with people eager to trim down or get into and stay in shape. As if this were not enough, today's French are actually concerned about what they eat. They are subscribing to nutritionist services in record numbers, and the book *Eat Yourself Slim* (*Je mange, donc je maigris!*; Montignac, 1987) was a best seller for more than a year. Recently a French doctor created the Dukan diet, which has become popular not only in France but in other European nations and the United States. Thus, it is not surprising that overall wine consumption has declined. Ironically, while the French have increased in body weight in recent years, comparatively speaking weight gain is a minor issue when France is compared to other developed nations. For example, in 2007 a best seller in France and around the world was *French Women Don't Get Fat* (Guiliano, 2005).

The Changing Portrait

As our discussion implies, the French have a predilection to think in terms of greatness. This is understandable, given the glories of their past in such areas as music, art, philosophy, and innovation. Greatness also applies to the reputation the French have developed and maintained in the wine industry. French wines are the best, a fact that the whole world acknowledges, and for the French, that acknowledgment tends to extend to their other accomplishments and to themselves as well. The assumption of greatness tends to be instilled in the French from birth, even in the most rustic villager.

Undoubtedly the French imagine greatness to be part of their future. In an era of technological upheavals, they are excelling in high-tech areas. De Gaulle exhorted his compatriots to shape their own destinies independently of the United States, to find their own place in the sun, and to become a nuclear power in their own right. This they have done with lightning speed, making rapid advances in numerous areas of importance. They enjoy an impressive network of highways, and more than 75% of the nation's energy is provided by nuclear power.

Economic Constraints

Sometimes, however, the French penchant for going it alone hurts the economy. For example, the French developed Minitel, which just a few years ago was the world's largest database, connecting every conceivable service in Paris and some other cities, as well, by computer. However, the French were slow to use the World Wide Web as an alternative. Today use of the Web is widely accepted and employed.

With the building of the Concorde, the French married high-tech grace and excellence; the supersonic jet was, indeed, a work of art on wings. Ironically the Concorde was a joint project with the British, but people commonly attribute the accomplishment to France, not Great Britain. Could it be because prestige and grandeur seem typically French? However, due to poor market demand, the Concorde was decommissioned in 2003.

The famous Train à Grande Vitesse (TGV) is the bullet-shaped orange train that streaks past vineyards and villages at more than 170 miles per hour. Riding the TGV at night with blackened windows is to experience complete absence of motion. To incorporate both transport and motionlessness in this train is typical of French creativity: mastering nature, striving for perfection, and blending unlikely and diverse elements.

In spite of its various wrinkles, the societal system in France functions well, giving its citizens a safety net that cuddles them like a blanket at birth and softens the unpleasant jolts life can bring in old age. It provides 98% of its citizens with a level of medical care and benefits unknown to U.S. Americans and citizens of many other nations. Income is guaranteed to those over 65 even if they have never worked, and the wealthy collect, too, for it is their right under the law.

The French would revolt if this system was taken from them, but it is costly. While benefits are being cautiously pared to reduce a large federal deficit—for example, the retirement age of government employees was recently changed from 60 to 62—pension benefits are almost equal to an average wage. Moreover, mothers and babies alike get free care with the goals of boosting the sagging birth rate and elevating standards of living.

An Evolving Culture

Even as wine has a maturation or aging process that alters its personality, so do the French. Also, just as the flavor of wine changes with different blends of ingredients, France's cultural composition is evolving. The French have experienced many changes in their history, and more will follow. France is one of the few European countries that actually encourage assimilation by granting citizenship to all who are born on its soil. Recently, many have emigrated from France's former colonies. Well over 100,000 political refugees have been allowed into the country. There is resentment, prejudice, and discrimination against these newcomers, as noted previously. Still, France is one of the few nations that has welcomed so many outsiders and refugees.

However, while the face of France is slowly changing in numerous and complex ways, short-term and long-term visitors to this country will most likely continue to have strong emotional reactions to the French. The French most likely will continue to invest a great amount of time nurturing relationships, being wary of outsiders, being sensitive to social class differences, accommodating themselves to the centralized bureaucracy, and being individualistic and iconoclastic. While such activities may appear on the surface to be contradictory, they reflect an approach to life that welcomes, and even thrives on, many different and contrasting ideals. The secret of being able to accommodate such difference is moderation, and wine offers good training in the exercise of moderation. Healthy in itself, it must be taken with restraint, as in excess it can cause serious problems.

In more than 2,000 years of wine cultivation, French wine makers have accumulated a wealth of experience from which they have learned successful techniques and procedures. Throughout the history of viniculture and cultural development in France, the quest for quality has mobilized the collective energy of the French people. While nature ensures that each vintage is different, the human element at each step along the way determines the ultimate outcome. The best wines are objects of great pride and, at the same time, offer lessons in patience and modesty. In this respect the French obsession with rules, procedures, classifications, and form help to develop a product—and a culture—that is world renowned. Thus, whatever paths the people of France choose to follow, the metaphor of composing a fine wine will continue to give insights into their fundamental motivations and system of values.

PART V

Market-Pricing Cultures

Market-pricing cultures assume that it is possible to compare individuals using a ratio scale; that is, there is a common unit of measurement and a true zero point. In this way, it is possible to compare individuals on several dimensions simultaneously and even to transform all of the scale values into one final score for each individual. The true zero point is zero money; everything is judged and evaluated in terms of this point.

A stark reminder of this cultural orientation occurred in the opening days of the 2003 invasion of Iraq. For a day or two the Allied Coalition (the United States, Britain, and Australia) suffered few if any casualties, the strategy was dubbed "Shock and Awe," and the bombing of Iraq was intense. On CNN and other television stations, war coverage was immediately followed by an optimistic report about the U.S. and world stock markets, which rose significantly on the assumption that the war was going to be short. By the third day, however, Allied casualties and Iraqi resistance began to become significant, and war coverage was immediately followed by a pessimistic report on the stock markets, which had lost significant value as investors began to sense that the war would be longer than anticipated. The war finally ended in 2012. Regardless of one's stance on the war and the suitability of following news on the fighting immediately with news of the stock market, it is clear that market-pricing mechanisms were accorded great prominence.

CHAPTER 16

American Football

Indeed, the growing complexity of business makes many corporate managers shy away from baseball as a metaphor. Baseball, more than most other major sports, is structured in ways that promote the emergence of improbable heroes. . . . Many business leaders see their game as more like football, with its image of interdependent players with multiple skills cooperating to move the ball down a long field 10 yards at a time.

—Jonathan Kaufman (1999)

The game of football, though, simply explodes. From the moment the ball is passed backward through the legs of the center to the quarterback, 22 players are in constant motion trying to execute complex instructions, each intimately involved in the way the play will be resolved. No writing can really capture such intricacy; it must be seen.

—"American Football" (2006, p. 95)

The game of life.

—Headline of *Los Angeles Times* article (Goldstein, 2004)

When you don't understand the rules, it just looks like big men running around wrestling.

—Alan Paul (2007)

Baseball is where we were. Football is what we have become.

—Mary McGrory, journalist, quoted in *The Billion
Dollar Game* (Allen St. John, 2009, epigraph)

Business writers and pundits seem to be of the unanimous opinion that football (U.S. version; soccer is called *football* in most of the world) is the appropriate cultural metaphor for understanding U.S. Americans and U.S. business behavior. Geoffrey Colvin (2002), a *Fortune* columnist, analyzed the large number of U.S. corporate scandals since 2000 by comparing the complex rules of football to the complex accounting rules and laws that U.S. executives and citizens would like to evade. By comparison, devotees of European soccer watch a simpler game with only half of the number of rules, most of which are stated as principles that the referees use to make calls in a manner similar to the more general accounting principles governing European business. Appropriately, Colvin titled his article "Sick of Scandal? Blame Football!" In 2003 Colvin followed up with an article titled "For Touchdown, See Rule 3, Sec. 38," in which he reiterated his beliefs:

> We Americans like the idea of a national pastime, so let's hold a retirement party for baseball as it relinquishes the title.... We all know America's real pastime is NFL football.... The reason is that NFL football is the most legalistic, rules-obsessed, argumentative, dispute-filled sport on the planet, and that means we Americans simply cannot get enough of it. (p. 34)

The intent of this chapter is to demonstrate that, if you don't understand U.S. football, you will have difficulty understanding U.S. culture and the manner in which business is practiced by U.S. Americans. Social critic Camille Paglia (1997) presents a similar argument, encouraging women to study football rather than attend feminist meetings. Shiflett (2000) echoes these sentiments by suggesting that presidential candidates should simply insist that football viewing be made mandatory for U.S. youth, as it "embodies and promotes the very values many parents seek for their offspring."

Apparently both U.S. males and females are in agreement that football is the most popular sport in the United States: At least 68% of the nation's sports fans, and 57% of female sports fans, love football (Conty, 1999). As the *Economist* ("In a League," 2006) states: "It remains the most popular of the four big American sports on almost every measure, from opinion polls to television ratings" (p. 63). Super Bowl Sunday has replaced Christmas as the national holiday on which families and friends gather together for parties to watch the winners in the two football conferences, the National

Football Conference and the American Football Conference, play a single game for championship of the National Football League (NFL). Allen St. John (2009) highlighted the importance of Super Bowl Sunday in the title of his popular book: *The Billion Dollar Game: Behind the Scenes of the Greatest Day in American Sport—Super Bowl Sunday.* Similarly the trial of O. J. Simpson on charges that he murdered his wife and her friend was billed as the "trial of the century" in large part because it involved a football idol.

However, not everyone is enamored. Columnist George Will (2006) declared that football manages to combine two of the worst aspects of national life: violence and committee meetings. Journalist Alistair Cooke described it as a cross between medieval warfare and chess ("Punctured Football," 1993).

This chapter describes U.S. football in terms of the following topics: the tailgate party; pregame and halftime entertainment; strategy and war; selection, the training camp, and complex plays/the playbook; individual specialized achievement within the group; aggression, high risks, and unpredictable outcomes; huddling; and the church of football and celebrating perfection.

The Tailgate Party

A professional U.S. football game typically starts with a tailgate party, a uniquely U.S. phenomenon. Some fans drive hundreds of miles to attend the game, and everyone arrives at the parking lot fully prepared for an outdoor party. They quickly unpack their barbecue grills, food, beer, and soda. Friends may cluster together, but they are sure to share their food and thoughts about the home team and its opponent with other fans in the vicinity. After the party, almost everyone is ready to attend the game. But not everyone. Many times in freezing weather, some fans stay in the parking lot in heated vans to watch the game on TV, presumably because they can see the game better, although they could have watched the game on TV at home.

High school football in some states such as Texas is, as the saying goes, the game of life. People in small towns and cities talk constantly and sometimes obsessively about each game for days and weeks before it occurs. In 2005 one father in Canton, Texas, severely wounded the school's football coach, Gary Joe Kinne, ostensibly because the coach had cut his son from the team. Several years ago, one Texas mother planned the assassination of her daughter's chief rival for a coveted spot on the cheerleading team. Such incidents, however, are rare, and most citizens look forward to cheering their sons onward and participating in the tailgate party, for which they prepare elaborately.

At the college level, the tailgate party takes on additional social functions. For instance, at a University of Michigan tailgate party, fans who have never attended the university but identify closely with it wear blue to reinforce the team's motto, "Go Blue." Entire families, from grandparents to 5-year-olds, will arrive at the tailgate party with everyone dressed completely in blue, and some vans are covered in blue as well. Frequently a part of the parking lot is set aside for special alumni groups, such as the class of 1980, and not only are friendships renewed but financial contributions to the university are encouraged.

After the game, all fans hurry to get out of the parking lot as quickly as possible. They drive safely but are not above cutting off another driver they met for the first time and with whom they had been friendly during the tailgate party. All conviviality is forgotten, especially if the team has lost. Fans return to the normal fast pace of U.S. American life in which getting ahead, even at the expense of cutting off another driver, is a strong cultural value.

Pregame and Halftime Entertainment

Before the game and during halftime, there is entertainment on the field. Let's look in on one particular case. There must be at least 300 performers on the field before the game, each with a flag and a lavish smile, all synchronized down to the slightest move. The sun is glittering on the dancers' shiny outfits, and the wind makes the flags dance to the beat of the drums and the sounds of the horns. The sky is clear except for a Goodyear blimp circling high above the outdoor stadium where the New England Patriots, one of the most successful teams in professional football history, play their home games. Although it is freezing and snow begins to fall, the fans are so responsive that they react spontaneously to anything and everything that occurs. They cheer the cheerleaders! They cheer the announcer! They cheer other fans! They even cheer the beer vendor! These fans are seriously committed to having a good time this Sunday afternoon.

The crowd seems to be homogeneous; fans are wearing the same colors, supporting the same team, and hoping for the same outcome. Yet every fan has added a personal touch to this weekly extravaganza. One man has painted his face with the team's colors. A younger guy in front of him has a huge banner with a witty message that indicates his frustration with the coach. Everybody is eating, yet no one is particularly engaged in this feast. They are just continuously munching and crunching while focused on doing something else.

The cheerleaders gather on one side of the field and intensify their dance routines. The music is suddenly blasted, shaking one's body. A bomb, yes a bomb, explodes on the field, igniting a thunderous roar from the crowd. Smoke fills the air, and the middle part of the field becomes virtually concealed. As the smoke clears, a car seems to appear on a podium right on the 50-yard line. Yes, it is a car. Now that the view is unclouded, one can see a Honda standing gallantly on a wide podium surrounded by dancers and models. The Honda jingle is played on the stadium's loudspeakers, the crowd is singing along, and then the announcer proudly proclaims Honda is one of the major sponsors of this week's game. Just as the announcer ordains, the reliable Honda Civic is driven away, followed by the dancers who are still frolicking and prancing in a marketing celebration.

Then the mood becomes serious. The military color guard marches with the U.S. flag to the center of the field and plays the national anthem while one of its members sings the words, accompanied by the voices of many fans, all of whom stand respectfully. During periods of war, this period of silent awe takes on renewed energy. If this mood is violated, fans are not happy. For example, at the various Super Bowls, popular singers have been selected to give their renditions of the national anthem, and periodically these singers are roundly and publicly criticized for disrespecting the anthem and what it is supposed to convey—namely awe, respect, and honor.

At halftime, the Patriots' marching band comes onto the field to perform a spirited and complex series of moves and themed musical numbers under the leadership of the band's director. Accompanying the band are others, including a person carrying the team's flag, cheerleaders, and twirlers. When the second half starts, the home crowd is again ready to cheer on its beloved team.

The halftime entertainment, which is similar to the short breaks found at work— the coffee break, the celebration and presentation of awards for outstanding and/or long employee service, and so on—is over. It is now time to become serious once again and return to the action on the field.

Strategy and War

After the sponsor is announced (and never before), the stage is set for the actual game of football. A sport that captures many of the central values of American society, football has steadily become an integral component of the community. Football in the United States is not only a sport but also an assortment of common beliefs and ideals; indeed, football is a set of collective rituals and values shared by one dynamic society. The speed, the constant movement, the high degree of specialization, the consistent aggressiveness, and the intense competition in football, particularly professional football, all typify American culture.

Strategy is fundamental in football, war, and American business. Zbigniew Brzezinski (2000), a native of Poland who became a U.S. citizen and eventually former President Carter's national security advisor, was initially puzzled by football until he was able to define the roles of the various actors in terms of war and strategy. First, there are the owners of the teams, who host special guests in elaborate skyboxes during the game. They can be nasty dictators, aloof monarchs, and variations thereof. Next are the coaches or commanders in chief, who are the CEOs or generals responsible for the team's strategy and oversight of all activities. The head coach is assisted by 9 or 10 assistant coaches, each of whom specializes in a particular area, such as defense and passing. Other coaches sit high in the stadium to provide detached and immediate observations and information to the head coach through their electronic headsets. The head coach calls most if not all of the plays that the quarterback and the offensive team execute. Then there are the quarterbacks, who are the field commanders making last-minute tactical decisions. Finally, the home front or spectators play a key role in cheering on and energizing the home team while demoralizing the enemy.

Football is more like chess than the Chinese game known as Go (see Gannon, 2008, chap. 6). As in chess, the objective is to wear down and destroy the enemy or opposing team totally. Just as the game of chess ends with the loser's pieces removed totally from the board, so too in football the winner is exalted while the loser is quickly forgotten. In Go, the objective is to conquer as much space on the board as possible while rendering the opponent powerless. However, saving face or the dignity of the loser is also important, as the winner may someday need his or her help, and it is considered best not to create an eternal enemy who may arise from the ashes to oppose you. For this reason the powerless opponent still has pieces on some of the board. In contrast, saving the dignity of the loser is of minor concern in football.

In business, it frequently takes several years for a firm to create a new business model against which other firms have difficulty competing. Examples include the cost advantage of 3% to 5% provided by Wal-Mart's efficient supply chain or General Electric's movement starting in the 1970s from commodity/low-profit products to high-margin differentiated products. Similarly football has had several such business models, including the no-huddle offense pioneered by the Buffalo Bills and the one-back offense (freeing up the other back to become a receiver) pioneered by the Washington Redskins.

Bill Walsh, head coach of the San Francisco 49ers for 10 years, created one of the most successful strategies by having the quarterback use many short passes, which had a higher probability of being caught and a lower probability of being intercepted. He and other coaches also realized that they needed to protect their quarterbacks more strongly, as their injury rate was alarming and finding talented recruits for this position is difficult. Soon the left tackle protecting the quarterback's blind side rose in stature and compensation, and in some instances his salary is higher than that of the quarterback, usually the highest-paid player (see M. Lewis, 2006). This approach is consistent with the U.S. emphasis on linking pay directly to performance.

Selection, the Training Camp, and the Playbook

It is often said that selecting the right people for the job and training them about company expectations is the best guarantee of a firm's success. Companies devote enormous resources to selection and training. For example, U.S. companies spend more on training and education than do all of the U.S. business schools combined. This emphasis on selection and training is mirrored in the practices of professional football teams. Their coaching scouts tour the entire country and the world evaluating college and semiprofessional football players and even high school players. The NFL administers a draft in which each team in turn, starting with the one with the poorest record in the previous year, selects players. The team's coaching staff has thoroughly evaluated all of the players in the draft in terms of the team's needs and strategies and selects draftees accordingly.

Once selected, players arrive at each team's summer camp to learn the numerous complex plays in the playbook. There are three specialized teams, each with 11 players: the offense; the defense; and the special teams, some of whose members are extremely specialized. For instance, one player may only kick field goals. The field is 100 yards long, and after the opening kickoff, the offense is given 4 plays in which to win a first down by advancing 10 yards, gaining it the right to another 4 plays. Each field goal is worth 3 points and is not attempted unless the offense faces a fourth down and a low probability of scoring a touchdown, which is worth 6 points; a successful kick after a touchdown is worth 1 point, although a run or a pass into the end zone is worth 2 points.

Every player is a specialist and responsible for specific actions during a particular play. These plays are complex and sometimes number 200 or more. Each coach has a playbook describing each play in detail, and during summer camp, players are expected to learn these plays thoroughly. At times some players have complained that the plays are so complex and numerous that they are confusing and hard to remember. Still, for the team to be successful, each player must know not only the intricate rules governing the game but also the the particular team's complex plays.

Individual Specialized Achievement Within the Team Structure

Some researchers, such as Hofstede (2001), have ranked the United States ahead of all other nations in terms of individualism, that is, identifying one's needs and interests and making decisions accordingly. The opposite end of this same scale is collectivism, that is, identifying primarily with the group and its needs. Such a perception is only partially accurate. Americans are also group oriented, and being part of a group or network and identifying with it is essential for success in almost all areas of life. Within the group structure, however, specialization is exalted, and everyone is expected to add value to the final product or service.

Similarly, it is no accident that the undergraduate business and master's of business administration degrees originated in the United States. American business schools moved away from the prevailing non-business-oriented model, which emphasized areas such as liberal arts and religion, in the early 1900s to specialize in the functional areas of business such as finance, accounting, and marketing.

Emphasis on belonging to a group does not mean that everyone receives the same rewards and compensation. Depending on special qualifications, some players, such as the quarterback and the left tackle protecting him, are rewarded much more handsomely than others. Similarly, rewards in U.S. business are much more unequal than in all or most other nations, with some CEOs making 500 to 600 times more than the average salary in the firm. This trend has accelerated since 1960, when the comparable ratio was about 30 to 1. Americans believe in equality of opportunity but not equality of outcomes. In comparable surveys involving five nations (the United States, Germany, France, Britain, and Italy), U.S. respondents were far less likely to agree that it is more important for government to guarantee that no one is in need and far more likely to indicate that government's role is to provide freedom to pursue goals (Parker, 2003). Life, liberty, and the pursuit of happiness is the ideal. If the company or team is successful, everyone benefits financially, but just as in football, all players benefit but to unequal degrees.

However, a recent survey of college-educated workers in the top quarter of wage earners in their respective nations indicates a more nuanced approach, at least in this subgroup. When the researchers asked respondents in 22 nations to indicate whether they agreed with Milton Friedman's famous statement that "the social responsibility of business is to increase profits," the United States ranked only 9th ("Milton Friedman Goes on Tour," 2011, p. 63). The respondents expressing the most agreement were from Saudi Arabia (84%), followed by those from Japan, India, South Korea, Sweden, Indonesia, and Mexico. Only 56% of U.S. Americans and 43% of respondents from Great Britain agreed, even though these are typically classified as market-pricing cultures.

There has always been a belief in the Horatio Alger myth in the United States; that is, one can lift oneself out of poverty through individual efforts and become a CEO or U.S. president. Football strengthens this belief, as many of the stars are assumed to have unbelievably superior skills and abilities that lead to success. Ironically, a special report in the *Economist* ("Ever Higher Society," 2004) reviews the mounting evidence that since 1970, it is more difficult to move from a lower social class to a higher class in the United States than in Europe. In 2008 the Organisation of Economic Co-operation and Development (OECD) issued a study of economic inequality in 20 developed nations that confirms the United States now leads all of these nations in the level of inequality among its citizens.

Football is a team sport, yet the individual is glorified and celebrated. The extent of individualism in football seems to be unsurpassed by that in any other team sport. All the major trophies in football are named after individuals who have contributed to the sport. There are the Heisman trophy, the Vince Lombardi Super Bowl trophy, and many other awards that extol the individual. As indicated previously, every player has a particular role to play. The play's success depends on how well all the players perform, yet there is frequently one player who exerts extra and unusual effort. This distinguished player is seen as making the play happen and receives most of the accolades for doing so. However, he typically does not receive all of the accolades, as clearly team coordination and effort are also required for success. Thus other players and sometimes the entire team are lavishly praised. There is, in effect, individualism within the team structure.

The New England Patriots exhibit the fusion of individuals within a team structure more than other teams. Its members have refused to be photographed individually but will pose for team photos. Similarly, Tony Nicely is the CEO of the highly successful

GEICO Insurance Company, part of Berkshire-Hathaway, and he has acted in a similar manner. The esteem in which Nicely is held is captured by the legendary Warren Buffett, the founder of Berkshire-Hathaway, who publicly commented that Nicely is a shareholder's dream ("Potential Heirs," 2011).

Extreme Specialization

Professional football teams are actually multimillion-dollar corporations subdivided into departments and divisions, each with a large, highly specialized staff. Each member of this football "organization" has one very specialized task. Each squad has its own coach or coaches, and there are also medics, trainers, psychiatrists, statisticians, technicians, outfit designers, marketing consultants, and social workers, all with specific duties and assignments. There is even a person assigned to carry the coach's headphone wire throughout the game so that he will not trip on it! Professional football epitomizes specialization for many Americans. The plays in football are complex and precisely executed athletic routines; the players' movements and maneuvers are designed to achieve a high level of physical perfection; and the NFL, in general, embodies all that is impeccable and optimum in the American mind: profits, fame, and glory.

Even the equipment is highly specialized; no other sport in the world provides such specialized equipment. Similarly, it seems as if every American carries around a gadget of some sort to do some kind of task. Look at the football player! He wears a helmet, shoulder pads, neck pads, shin guards, ankle pads, and thigh guards to protect himself; he wraps antistatic nonadhesive tape around his wrists and fingers for support; and he wears state of the art astro-rubber shoes for artificial turf or evenly spiked fiber-saturated shoes for grass fields. Then each type of player has his own distinctive equipment: The receivers wear grip-aligned synthetic gloves to catch the football; the linebackers wear tinted-glass face masks (shatterproof, of course) to protect their eyes from the glare; and the cornerbacks wear ultra-light reinforced plastic back pads to maximize their speed. Even the coaches have their own specialized gadgets: They use sensitive cellular devices to communicate with the statistician and the assistant coaches watching the game from seats high in the stadium.

The "families" within a single football team are the different groups of players forming a "squad," each of which is one family that includes a group of players with similar attitudes and traits. Each player relates primarily to his squad. As indicated previously, there are three squads on every football team, each with its own distinguishable characteristics and values. The defensive squad is usually the most aggressive and violent; the offensive squad includes the higher-profile, higher-paid players; and the special teams squad is characterized by big plays and high intensity. It is amazing how players try to fit into their particular squads' cultures, even to the extent of using nicknames such as "the Hogs" to describe a squad.

Even though football's rules and regulations are constantly changing from one season to the next, the basic values and ideals of the sport have changed very slowly over the years. In U.S. society, innovation and modification are encouraged and sought, but usually not when it comes to values and ideals. U.S. values, like those of football, have developed rather slowly, and few radical shifts in ideals have taken place over the past two centuries. Coaches such as the late Bill Walsh who develop innovative strategies are esteemed, as are entrepreneurs and CEOs such as Microsoft founder Bill Gates and investor Warren Buffett. Equality of opportunity, independence, initiative, and self-reliance are some of the values that have endured as basic American ideals throughout history. All reflect a high degree of specialized individualism that expresses itself within the structure of a team.

Competition as a Goal

As this discussion implies, competition seems to be more than a means to an end in the United States; it has apparently become a major goal in and of itself. Just as over half the rules and regulations in professional football deal with protecting and enhancing competition in the league, so too American antitrust laws and regulations were essentially created to safeguard competition and equality of opportunity for individuals and groups. U.S. ideals and values trace their origin to successive waves of European immigrants. These diverse immigrants often came into heated conflict with each other. Although hostility could be intense when immigrants first arrived, feelings of animosity were not usually expressed through violence because the immigrants were tired of wars and bloodshed. Rather, these feelings manifested themselves in competition, specialization, and division of labor.

Each geographical area in the United States specialized in a particular category of production: the Northeast in manufacturing, the Midwest in agriculture, and the West in raising cattle. Even within parts of the country that specialized in agriculture, there was further specialization. The more fertile regions of the United States (for example, Idaho) specialized in raising different crops than those grown in the less fertile (but more populated) South. The distinct, highly specialized immigrant communities were still competing with each other economically, but their use of the law of comparative advantage propelled them to focus their efforts on one particular domain of production in which they excelled.

Thus communities were involved in a new kind of war, one that once and for all was designed to settle the scores between Protestants and Catholics, Poles and Jews, English and Irish, and Germans and Danes. Competition prevailed, and the battles of the Middle Ages were refought in the United States but with new weapons and for new spoils. Each community frequently believed that it carried the burden of proving its own superiority through bigger dams, larger statues, more crops, and greater wealth. The legacy of competition continues to flourish in U.S. society today, but with more restraint.

European immigrants, although distinct and dissimilar, shared a deep suspicion of authority. They assumed that authority impedes competition and foils specialization, both for individuals and groups. Their main reason for fleeing Europe in the first place was corrupt and oppressive authority and/or government. Systems of checks and balances were developed in the United States primarily to protect the people from rulers who might control the economy, dictate religion, or dominate political power.

Similarly, the NFL uses a system of checks and balances during a game. There are two sets of referees, one on the field equipped with whistles and flags and the other in the review booth equipped with a videocassette recorder and a color TV. If one team does not like a call that a referee on the field makes, it can appeal to the review judges, who watch the play on video and make a final judgment.

Technology and Tools

Technological development is a catalyst to competitive specialization. Technology is a key ingredient in the efficient competitive specialization required by an intensely capitalist society such as the United States. Similarly technological development plays a key role in the NFL. The weight machines that professional football players use, the cameras and satellites that follow them, and the specialized equipment that they wear are integral to their athletic performance and reflect the U.S. fascination with tools and machines.

The reason behind this fascination with tools is simple: America has historically been short on labor and long on raw materials. To use the abundance of raw materials available, U.S. Americans had to substitute machinery and equipment for unskilled labor. The success of highly mechanized industry in the late 1800s influenced U.S. Americans to continue to develop technology. To U.S. Americans, technology was empirically proven to stimulate growth and success, and their dependence on machines grew stronger as the number of U.S. patented inventions increased. A recent manifestation of this focus is the continuing success of Silicon Valley and the emergence of high-technology industries.

U.S. Americans are typically not influenced greatly by extended kinship or family groups; the nuclear family is the locus of activity and identification. In many ways U.S. families are like the three squads in football mentioned earlier. A football player relates primarily to his squad and only secondarily to the team. Similarly U.S. Americans relate to society through nuclear families and not kinship groups. As a general rule, U.S. children are taught to relate primarily to their nuclear family at a young age; they learn through the example of their parents that the nuclear family is the integral part of their lives. U.S. Americans normally encourage independence, self-reliance, and initiative in their children. Children are raised to believe that a rich, healthy, happy, and fulfilling life can be attained by almost anybody as long as they are willing to follow certain steps and procedures. The U.S. egalitarian spirit is nourished in children's spirits and accentuated in their minds by parents eager to help their children be successful. As a result, when children have matured to the adult stage, they tend to believe that success (wealth, health, and happiness) is an individual's responsibility and duty. U.S. society frequently views people who are poor, unhealthy, or unhappy as having failed to avail themselves of the opportunities offered.

As indicated earlier, U.S. Americans believe in equality, but only equality of opportunity; personal successes and failures are attributed directly to the individual (see Stewart & Bennett, 1991). Many if not most U.S. Americans tend to see poverty and misery as largely self-induced. When citizens lose their jobs, the United States provides far less unemployment coverage than do many other developed nations. *Business Week* ("Jobless Pay," 2010) reported that the United States compares very poorly with the following nations in terms of replacing previous compensation with combined unemployment pay and state benefits during the first year of unemployment: Norway, 72%; Spain, 69%; France, 67%; Canada, 52%; Turkey, 46%; Japan, 45%; South Korea, 31%; the United Kingdom, 28%; and the United States, 28%. Stewart and Bennett (1991) point out that making the individual responsible for all actions, some of which are beyond his or her control, makes life difficult for the average U.S. American, who must be constantly vigilant to maintain self-sufficiency.

U.S. Americans are not honored for past achievements but for what they are currently accomplishing; in this sense their personalities tend to be constantly in a state of flux and evolution. Even during a closely contested football game, the TV sports commentators tend to begin to praise the first team that gets a big lead, only to reverse themselves immediately when the second team catches up and surpasses the first team. It is as if the commentators are trying to predict the final score of the game and align themselves with the winner by praising the winning team unconditionally and ignoring or, worse yet, heaping mounds of criticism on the losing team.

Openness to Change

One of the major results of this orientation toward achievement is that U.S. managers are generally very open to change and are constantly introducing new programs with which they can identify and for which they can claim much of the credit; it is not sufficient for them only to build on the programs of their predecessors (Kanter, 1979). They tend to jettison programs just as quickly, however, and the United States is famous for both the fads that it introduces and the short-term orientation of its managers.

In short, competitive specialization, both for each individual and the groups in which he or she participates, appears to be the most evident feature of the United States. Generally speaking, the notion of "specializing to compete" is the principal ideological ideal that U.S. Americans endorse, practice, safeguard, and promote worldwide. Competitive specialization is the tool with which U.S. Americans tend to tackle life's main challenges. This tool is often serviced and maintained with high levels of emotional intensity and aggressiveness. From this perspective it is not surprising that most U.S. Americans, when asked what they do, immediately describe their occupation or profession, unlike the Japanese, who tend to respond with the name of the company in which they work (see Chapter 3).

Aggression, High Risks, and Unpredictable Outcomes

The similarities between real life in the United States and a professional football game are astounding, especially in terms of the warlike atmosphere that pervades this sport. Football closely parallels the extroverted and sometimes even belligerent U.S. society. According to the Myers-Briggs Type Indicator, which is the most widely used personality scale in the United States, 75% of American males and females are extroverted and aggressive in personal relations (Keirsey, 1998). While such extroversion is in large measure a positive feature of U.S. life (Barnlund, 1989), the United States is a leading country in terms of indicators that profile the negative aspects of extroversion and aggressiveness. For example, 308.8 million U.S. citizens own an estimated 240 million guns. As the noted political scientist James Q. Wilson (2007) points out, this fact in and of itself does not confirm violent aggression. However, he also points out that the non–gun homicide rate is 3 times higher in the United States than in England. Relatedly, the United States leads the world in terms of the number of prisoners as a proportion of the population at 1 per 100. As the *Economist* notes ("Too Many Laws," 2010), no other developed nation is nearly as punitive as the United States: Britain's rate of incarceration is only one fifth of America's, Germany's is one ninth, and Japan's is one twelfth. If those on parole or probation are included, then in the United States 1 adult in 31 is under "correctional" supervision.

U.S. Americans recognize instinctively the link between life in America and what happens on the football field. Violence and aggression are part of football's appeal to U.S. society, and they both correspond to real life. Aggression, which is often interpreted as energy and intense motivation, is encouraged in the United States. Analogously, aggression is celebrated in football. The teams compete with one another, players on the same team compete for starting positions, and even the fans compete for better tickets.

In the early part of the 20th century, there was a movement to outlaw football as a college sport because of large numbers of permanent injuries and deaths. Future U.S. president Woodrow Wilson, then president of Princeton University, led a group that changed the rules to make the game safer, thus saving college football from extinction. Similarly, while some U.S. states have moved to outlaw popular mixed martial arts contests, which are fought brutally in a cage with few rules, defenders of these regulated struggles point out that 63 deaths have occurred in football between 1993 and 2006 and only 2 deaths have resulted from mixed martial arts; furthermore, these deaths took place in unregulated contests in Korea and Russia (Schrotenboer, 2006).

Recently there has been increased concern about the long-term impact of playing football on the players' health. Under special scrutiny is brain damage. Steps are being formulated to mitigate this serious health problem, but the fact remains that football is a dangerous sport. Loss of bone cartilage, crippling arthritis, and other permanent injuries are also common.

Survival of the Fittest

This type of individual competition and aggressiveness seems to be particularly suited to the United States. Richard Hofstadter (1955) graphically describes why social Darwinism or the survival of the fittest individual was a social philosophy that appealed to U.S. Americans at the turn of the 20th century:

> With its rapid expansion, its exploitative methods, its desperate competition, and its peremptory rejection of failure, post-bellum America was like a vast human caricature of the Darwinian struggle for existence and survival of the fittest. Successful business entrepreneurs apparently accepted almost by instinct the Darwinian terminology which seemed to portray the conditions of their existence. (p. 44)

Given its violence and aggression, one might question why football has such pervasive popularity in the United States. It has, however, compensating characteristics, including its expression of deeply held U.S. values. Also, the complexity of football intimately involves football aficionados in every play, and they easily see analogs in their daily and business lives. Fans and experts compare statistics on each player and team along numerous dimensions, and they have developed a highly specialized vocabulary for doing so. A week before a major game, sports radio programs featuring call-ins from fans with decided opinions and vast knowledge are popular, and follow-up programs after the game use the same format. Having the knowledge to participate in these conversations creates a sense of in-group solidarity, and the clueless spectator is ignored.

Just as important is the highly unpredictable nature of the game. One team may be in total control of the game in the first half, only to wither and die through attrition or succumb to revitalized offensive and defensive/aggressive play of the opponent in the second half. Football is one of the most unpredictable sports games in the world. For example, a 2-minute warning is sounded before the end of the game, when play is paused briefly. When play resumes, it is not unusual for a seemingly defeated and discouraged team to score two touchdowns, creating a tie and taking the game into overtime or even winning outright. Similarly, one team may be losing 35–0 at halftime only to come back and win. In the 2008 Super Bowl, the Patriots were seeking a historic finish to an undefeated season of 19–0, but they lost in the final minute of the game to the underdog New York Giants, who used a modified no-huddle offense to save time (see "Huddling" below).

Expect the Unexpected

Furthermore, although each player is expected to perform a particular action in each play, the unexpected happens so frequently that the individual player must be creative. The best players can implement an inventive tactic on the fly that, despite its riskiness, may be successful and bring the crowd to its feet. For instance, a play designed for a run may be altered to include a pass when the designated runner is surrounded by the defensive team. All of the players, both on offense and defense, must then adapt to the new situation.

There are, as we have seen throughout this chapter, many reasons to study football and to watch it. Among these reasons, complexity, risk taking, and unpredictability rank high.

Huddling

Another characteristic that differentiates football from any other sport in the world is the huddle, in which the offensive team comes together as a group before each play to hear what play they will execute. There is no other sport in the world where one sees the huddle before every play. In the huddle are different players from diverse backgrounds and with various levels of education. All have agreed that the only way to accomplish a certain task is to put differences aside and cooperate objectively to achieve a certain goal. After the game, every player returns to his own world, living his own life in his own way. That is the essence of the melting pot, a diversified group of people who forget their differences temporarily to achieve a common goal. As early as 1832 Alexis de Tocqueville drew attention to this facet of the U.S. perspective (as quoted in L. C. Miller & Hustedde, 1987):

> These Americans are the most peculiar people in the world. You'll not believe it when I tell you how they behave. In a local community in their country a citizen may conceive of some need which is not being met. What does he do? He goes across the street and discusses it with his neighbor. Then what happens? A committee comes into existence and then the committee begins functioning on behalf of that need. And you won't believe this but it is true. All of this is done without reference to any bureaucrat. All of this is done by the private citizens on their own initiative. (p. 91)

Can a football team afford the luxury of eliminating the huddle? In most cases, no. However, the 1991 Super Bowl, one of the best Super Bowls to date, featured the Buffalo Bills, who did not huddle after each play, and the New York Giants, who did. It was a very close game that was decided only in the final minutes. The no-huddle Bills were able to use this approach only because of the expertise of their outstanding quarterback, Jim Kelly. Once again, an individual was able to shine within the group context. Still, the final result was that the huddling Giants won. The final verdict is not in, as other NFL teams have since employed the no-huddle offense successfully, but only sparingly thus far. Similarly, most if not all groups and organizations in the United States employ a version of huddling to handle their problems and achieve their objectives. Wal-Mart, for instance, pioneered the daily 10-minute early-morning meeting at which all stand so as to get down to business quickly, shorten the meeting time, and then go out and execute the plan. This company also pioneered Saturday morning motivational breakfast meetings at which awards are given to individual employees and managers and everyone shouts company cheers such as "In Sam we trust," in honor of Wal-Mart's late founder, Sam Walton. This is similar to what happens when a football team wins its league championship or, better yet, the Super Bowl, and the winning team is traditionally honored by a parade in its hometown.

Business Groups

The U.S. concept of huddling to coordinate activities is quite different from the Japanese sense of community within the organization. The Japanese normally socialize with coworkers after work, and if a major problem occurs, they will sometimes go off-site for an evening of drinking, dinner, informal camaraderie, and finally the discussion of the problem at hand and how to address it. Periodically they will repeat such sessions until the problem is solved. Other nationalities, such as the Chinese and the Koreans, also have similar practices involving frequent group activities after working hours. U.S. Americans, on the other hand, tend to huddle together in a business meeting specifically to address and solve the problem at hand, after which they scatter to complete their other work-oriented activities. If additional meetings are necessary, they are normally conducted in the same fashion.

As Daniel Boorstin (1965) has so persuasively shown, the lone cowboy or lone frontiersman is a poor metaphor for the United States. Rather, as adventuresome U.S. Americans moved westward to pursue a better life, they came together frequently to form temporary associations or teams to solve specific problems. However, given the rapid mobility of U.S. society—a characteristic still dominant today—relationships among members of these groups tended to be cooperative but only superficially friendly; there was no time to develop deep friendships. The United States is the classic "doing" society whose members are primarily interested in building and accomplishing goals. The focus in the United States is on accomplishing present goals to ensure a safe future; little attention is given to past activities and history. Europeans and Asians frequently complain that it is very difficult to establish deep, personal relationships with U.S. Americans. As a general rule, U.S. Americans commit themselves intensely to a group effort but only for a specified and frequently short period of time. Unlike many Europeans, who live, work, and die within 30 miles of their birthplaces, U.S. Americans frequently huddle in temporary groups as they change jobs, careers, geographical areas, and even spouses throughout their lives.

In football the huddle divides the game into smaller sets of tasks that, when accomplished, successfully lead to the fulfillment of victory. A team is divided into independent jobs, which are realigned during short periods of position reassessment and fueled by continuous tactical evaluation. The huddle phenomenon in U.S. culture—meeting together to subdivide a large task into smaller related jobs that are accomplished one at a time—is illustrated in the way that U.S. Americans tackle problems. Any intricate situation is broken down into smaller issues, which are then addressed one at a time. U.S. Americans tend to believe that any problem can be solved, as long as the solution process has a specific number of steps to follow and questions to answer. Likewise in football, no matter how complicated a situation may be, teams are convinced that they can overcome it through a standardized planning process.

Manufacturing System

The U.S. American system of manufacturing (ASM), a system that developed as a result of Frederick Taylor's time-and-motion studies at the end of the 19th century, is the huddle of American economic history. It reflects how the U.S. mind is tuned. Just as the huddle in football facilitates a standardized planning process for a specific situation, the ASM facilitates a standardized manufacturing process for different products.

The ASM emphasizes simplicity of design, standardization of parts, and large-scale output. U.S. Americans introduced the concept and use of mass production as a direct consequence of their intense use of machinery. Whereas it took a group of German workers 1 week to masterfully produce 10 high-quality shotguns in the 1800s, the same number of U.S. workers, with the help of standardized parts and ready-to-assemble components, produced in 1 day many more shotguns at less cost. U.S. products throughout history have generally been known not for their elegance but for their utility, practicality, and cheapness. The U.S. culture is one that respects machines and considers them critical to civilization. In fact, one of the major U.S. contributions to the development of society has been its emphasis on ingenious tools and technology, including the personal computer, the telephone, the photocopy machine, and the iPad.

U.S. society directly relates standardization to the ranking of individuals. Many decisions depend on ranking via a standardized process (often based on statistical analysis) in the United States. Usually there is no time to judge people subjectively. Stewart and Bennett (1991) point out that many "being" or high-context societies rank or rate employee performance in an absolute sense so as to save face; for example, Jones is a superior or good performer. However, U.S. Americans in their "doing" mode typically compare individuals to one another when evaluating performance. Standards are relative and not absolute, and an employee may well be replaced when someone else ranks higher.

General Electric, for example, pioneered the use of such a forced rating system, and other large U.S. American corporations have imitated it: 20% receive above-average rewards, 70% average rewards, and 10% few if any rewards, with some of the bottom group being advised to leave if earlier warnings did not lead to positive changes in performance. General Electric is also the only multinational firm in the world that has a public tournament for the position of CEO, which must be vacated at age 65. Four or five long-time GE executives are selected and announced 2 years before the current

CEO's departure, and their performance is closely scrutinized. Once the new CEO is announced, the other candidates typically depart. This Darwinian system, however, has encouraged other large firms to hire the rejected CEOs because GE thought so highly of them that they were asked to participate in the tournament.

Academic Competitiveness

Even in an academic setting, students in the United States are often evaluated and compared relative to each other. Students' grades are plotted as a curve of relative performance (usually a bell curve). This curve determines the students' final reported grades.

As might be expected, U.S. Americans normally want to know what the bottom line is so that they can objectively make a decision. This perspective is particularly disconcerting in U.S. schools and colleges, where many students want to know only what will be on the final examinations. The egalitarian character of the United States, together with the fast pace of life, necessitates one form of standardized ranking or another when assessing a certain situation. Such rankings are accepted by individuals, who still huddle and work together within the group structure.

Although many U.S. Americans consider mathematics boring and tedious, all forms of standardized rankings involve figures and numbers. When ranking quarterbacks, for instance, the NFL standardizes the ranking process by defining different numerical categories that cover all aspects of the position. Each quarterback has certain numbers and figures, ranging from "percentage of pass completions" to "interceptions over touchdowns" to "number of yards passed per game." The quarterback's livelihood depends on those numbers. To negotiate a raise, a quarterback has to improve his numbers, and when a quarterback is benched, it is often due to unsatisfactory numbers. Similarly, at least 13 million Americans belong to virtual football leagues in which participants select players from different professional teams; at the end of the season, the participant whose virtual team has amassed the most points, defined by each virtual league differently, wins the jackpot. Such leagues even have a draft at the beginning of the season.

Numbers have an immense impact on the decision-making process in American society, whether it is a financial market analysis, a college recruitment program, or a political decision. U.S. politicians are very sensitive to polls (which are nothing but bottom-line numbers), even to the extent that there is always a statistician on any major political staff. Similarly, a dependence on aptitude tests is crucial in the U.S. education system. Academic institutions normally require that students take one kind of standardized test or another. Although the admission decision is based on a larger number of criteria, the aptitude test score is extremely influential. Just as a college football player's "numbers" are the arguments on which he is judged for professional recruitment, so too the student's aptitude test scores frequently are the decisive factors for college acceptance or rejection and for the quality of the colleges to which he or she is admitted.

Saving Time

This whole notion of standardized ranking evolves from the U.S. perception of time. Time is not thought of as a continuous and abundant commodity. There is frequently no time for conducting numerous specialized or personalized tests when judging recruits. There is only one standard test, to be taken once every so often, because naturally time is limited. Analogously, the sport of football is based on the notion that time is limited, and teams are continuously trying to beat the clock, particularly near the end of the game after the 2-minute warning has been given.

There is almost always a time limit in the United States, and the huddle phenomenon in football reflects this time shortage. There is a specific time limit for the huddle before each play. Football players often rush into or out of the huddle in an attempt to conserve time. Similarly, U.S. Americans constantly have a stressful feeling that time is running out and therefore they must talk quickly, walk quickly, eat quickly, and even "rest" quickly.

A concrete manifestation of this emphasis on a time limit is provided by speed dating, which originated in the United States. Young and not-so-young unmarried adults do not have time for traditional dating, so they attend sessions at which each of them talks consecutively with 30 to 40 members of the opposite sex, each for 3 minutes. An official sounds a bell after 3 minutes to signal that it is time to talk to another person. At the end of the evening, each person is free to accept or reject an offer for a longer meeting. Given that McDonald's established the first nationally successful fast-food chain, the *Economist* fittingly titled an article on this phenomenon "McDating" (2002). The popularity of speed dating in the United States is so high that the practice has spread to many other nations.

When talking, U.S. Americans have mastered the art of developing acronyms for time-consuming words such as *economics* (*econ* for short). The concept of extended formal names—for example, Herr Professor Doktor—is not only anathema to egalitarian U.S. Americans but also runs against the grain of their time-saving efforts. Any combination of words that forms a name or a title of some sort is promptly diminished to fewer letters so as to save time when saying them. The National Football Conference and the American Football Conference are never referred to as such, but rather they are efficiently called the NFC and the AFC. The Grand Old Party is the GOP, *madam* is *ma'am*, President Kennedy is JFK, the federal bank is the Fed, *amplifier* becomes *amp*, and best of all, *howdy* is the time-conscious way to say "How do you do?"

Due to the prevailing notion that time is scarce, when improvident news events occur, especially scandals such as the O. J. Simpson trial or former President's Clinton sexual mischief, they are vigorously discussed and energetically debated in U.S. society—but not for long. U.S. Americans do not have much time to dedicate to one news event. As Hall and Hall (1990) have shown, U.S. Americans are monochronic, doing one activity at a time rather than several activities. After intensely analyzing one major event for a short period, U.S. Americans become distracted and begin to focus on a new event. In recent years, however, because of the pervasive influence of computers and related activities such as the use of social media, U.S. Americans seem to have become more polychronic in terms of multitasking, as have the citizens in many nations.

Time is also limited in the United States because there are so many things to do in a lifetime. Society develops technologically at horrendous speed, and it is difficult to keep up. One has to be continuously on the move. This is the United States; there is little time for contemplating or meditating. Ideally one succeeds at an early age, and success in the United States is often impersonal and lonely. And the trend has accelerated: In 1985 U.S. Americans shocked pollsters when they indicated that they each had on average only three personal friends; in 2006 the number of friends had decreased to two (McPherson, Smith-Lovin, & Brashears, 2006). Similarly, de Mooij (2011) points out that Japanese advertisements tend to employ single-person ads presumably because there is a desire for individualism, while in the United States the opposite situation prevails; that is, groups at a party or a bar are emphasized in the idealized world presented in ads because of too much individualism and loneliness in real life.

Football provides that sense of belonging and the brotherhood/sisterhood atmosphere that success lacks, and the huddle is the ideal time-efficient approach for handling problems either in football or at work. The popular belief that the top is often lonely, however, does not inhibit most U.S. Americans from pursuing higher levels of achievement because life, they believe, is a test of self-reliance and independence.

The Church of Football and Celebrating Perfection

Robert Lipsyte, a well-known journalist, titled his 2007 article "The Church of Football." This arresting title captures the esteem and awe in which most U.S. Americans hold both religion and football. U.S. Americans attend church regularly when compared to many citizens of European nations. However, a Pew Foundation study indicates that, in recent years, 44% of adults have abandoned ties to specific religions or switched religious affiliations. The Pew Foundation study profiled the major U.S. religious affiliations as follows: Evangelical Protestant, 26.3%; Catholic, 23.9%; mainline Protestant, 18.1%; historically black Protestants, 6.9%, and other/unaffiliated, 24.8% (Kang, 2008).

The legendary Vince Lombardi, who took over as coach of the Green Bay Packers after the team had posted a 1–12 win-loss record in 1960, is an example of a leader who linked hard work, religious beliefs, and success closely. When he met the team for the first time, he thanked the Packers for allowing him to be their coach. Then he followed up by saying, "Gentlemen, we are going to relentlessly chase perfection, knowing full well we will not catch it, because nothing is perfect. But we are going to relentlessly chase it, because in the process we will catch excellence" (quoted in Schaap, 2008, p. 8). The adage "Winning isn't everything; it's the only thing" is also attributed to Lombardi. This relentless focus on perfection and winning led the team to capture five NFL championships from 1961 through 1967 and the first two Super Bowls in 1967 and 1968. Today Lombardi is revered by long-time football fans and coaches of all stripes.

Similarly the new immigrants had a utopian vision for the United States. The ideals that the nation symbolized were and still are considered sacred and perfect. Unlike in other major societies, U.S. values are based on written materials that are believed to be inviolate and perfect, namely the Constitution and the Declaration of Independence. U.S. history is an ongoing battle to preserve the perfect values and utopian ideals incarnated in these documents.

With that in mind, one can understand why the portrait of the United States in the minds of the immigrants was actually a utopian image. Charles Sanford (1961) encapsulates the essence of this image:

> The Edenic image, as I have defined it, is neither a static agrarian image of culti-vated nature nor an opposing image of the wilderness, but an imaginative com-plex which, while including both images, places them in a dynamic relationship with other values. Like true myth or story, it functions on many levels simultane-ously, dramatizing a people's collective experience within a framework of polar opposites. The Edenic myth, it seems to me, has been the most powerful and comprehensive organizing force in American culture. (p. vi)

For centuries the United States was "utopianized" by people fleeing persecution, subjection, tyranny, and oppression. America the concept was actually an attempt to create utopia. America the value encompassed all that is perfect: strength, wealth, phi-lanthropy, family, children, and glory. This is utopia. Analogously football personifies that unblemished portrait. Professional football is a symbol of the U.S. utopia realized.

Founding Documents

It is very important to note that the Declaration of Independence and the Constitution, the basic written sources of U.S. values, were created by individual human beings, not gods, prophets, sacred apostles, or holy emperors. From this fact one can understand why the United States ceremonially glorifies the individual. The common belief in the United States is that individuals are capable of doing anything they want to accom-plish. Individual achievements, whether earning a degree or scoring the highest number of field goals for one game, are considered precious and are entitled to com-memoration in one type of ceremony or another. Ceremonial celebrations of more significant accomplishments, such as winning a major party's presidential nomina-tion or the Super Bowl, become automatically a reflection of the U.S. pursuit of perfec-tion and utopia.

When retired NFL players are selected to the Football Hall of Fame, the most prestigious honor in professional football, the induction ceremonies celebrate both the individuals selected and the country that bestowed such perfection. The high sense of nationalism felt around professional football is ceremonially reflected before the start of each game, as we have seen. The national anthem is played and sometimes sung by a celebrity, and the fans proudly sing along; the flag procession precedes every football game, and representatives from the Army, Navy, and the Air Force carry American flags and assemble on the field. Apparently there is nothing worth celebrating more or nothing more perfect than the United States. In the United States, sporting events in general and professional football games in particular are in essence ceremonies that celebrate how perfect teams can be, how spectacular the nation is, and how well the system works.

It is little wonder that the Super Bowl, watched by about 100 million U.S. Americans and by millions of other fans throughout the world, has become the major family holiday in the United States. At the first Super Bowl in 1967, there were vacant seats. Because of such factors as adroit marketing and promotion of this event, it is now very difficult, if not impossible, for average people to purchase a ticket, even if they can afford it. The shortest TV advertisements cost more than $1 million per showing during the Super Bowl, and the halftime show is spectacular. In the city where the contest is held, parties begin a week before the game, and invitations to them are scarce. In fact, there are so many glitterati, public relations specialists, and businesspeople who attend the parties but skip the game itself that the *Wall Street Journal* recently headlined its article on the event "What Game?" (Karp, 2008). In essence, the Super Bowl epitomizes the relationship between basic cultural values and material success.

Russell H. Conwell—the first president of Temple University, a Methodist minister and famous orator—provided an apt expression of this relationship between religion and material success in his "Acres of Diamonds" sermon, which he delivered more than 10,000 times throughout the United States in the late 19th century:

> I say you ought to be rich; you have no right to be poor. . . . I must say that you ought to spend some time getting rich. You and I know that there are some things more valuable than money; of course, we do. Ah, yes. . . . Well does the man know who has suffered that there are some things sweeter and holier and more sacred than gold. Nevertheless, the man of common sense also knows that there is not any one of those things that is not greatly enhanced by the use of money. Money is power; money has powers; and for a man to say, "I do not want money," is to say, "I do not wish to do any good to my fellowmen." It is absurd thus to talk. It is absurd to disconnect them. This is a wonderfully great life, and you ought to spend your time getting money, because of the power there is in money.
>
> Greatness consists not in holding some office; greatness really consists in doing some great deed with little means, in the accomplishment of vast purposes from the private ranks of life; this is true greatness. (quoted in Burr, 1917, pp. 414–415)

Even today, leaders of mega-churches in the United States, such as Joel Osteen, link religion and worldly success by explicitly stating that God wants each of us to succeed in a material way.

The celebration of nationalism is evident not only in football but in most areas of socializing in the United States. On television, which U.S. Americans watch while socializing, many commercials are tied directly to nationalism, and innumerable marketable products or services are related to patriotism. In general, U.S. Americans perceive their nation to be young, successful, and prestigious. By associating products with the United States, marketers aim to relate the youthfulness, beauty, and sex appeal of the United States to their own products. For example, here are the words of a Miller beer commercial:

> *Miller's made the American way,*
>
> *born and brewed in the U.S.A.,*
>
> *just as proud as the people . . .*
>
> *who are drinking it today,*
>
> *Miller's made the American way.*

The jingle is accompanied by pictures of smiling U.S. American faces and happy U.S. American children, all of whom are joined in a dramatic celebration of the perfect beer brewed by the perfect country. In the background and throughout the commercial, the U.S. flag is flying gracefully, symbolizing flawlessness. There is basically nothing stated about this beer other than that it is pure American. Well, that's enough for many U.S. consumers. The utopian U.S. character is partial to success, popularity, and prestige.

Nationalist Beliefs

Sometimes nationalism generates ethnocentric behavior in the United States. In football, for instance, the Super Bowl is referred to as the "world championship" in spite of the fact that only U.S. teams compete in it. To many U.S. Americans, the United States is the world or at least the best part of it. The globe revolves around the United States, and the poorer members of the international community are protected by U.S. financial and military force, as confirmed by the ongoing military operations in Afghanistan.

However, such confidence has been questioned in both the United States and elsewhere in recent years. As globalization has proceeded, other nations such as Brazil, China, and India are rising in influence. Even the U.S. preeminence in technology is in question, as about 50% of the patents filed in the United States come from foreign-owned firms and foreign-born inventors.

Still, the economic success and military might of the United States often induce egotistical reactions to international events among its citizens. These narcissistic feelings are frequently evoked by the media's persistent portrayal of and fascination with the world's disasters and mishaps. To the U.S. media, "no news is good news," and therefore the outside world is often reported as volatile, violent, and miserable. The positive features of foreign countries are rarely highlighted. Because average U.S. Americans are continuously bombarded with news of famines, wars, violence, and political turmoil from the outside world, they are frequently not aware of the pleasant and fascinating features of other nations. This ethnocentrism is so extreme that many U.S. Americans believe that their country is the safest and most prosperous country in the world, even when the facts do not support such a conclusion.

Religious Affiliation

As indicated previously, religion is held in high regard in the United States, and the U.S. utopia is not complete without the practice of religion. More than half the U.S. population attends church regularly. Only a few other nations, such as Ireland and Poland, surpass the United States on this measure. More than 400,000 churches in the United States appeal to all types of religious beliefs. Although the country is primarily Christian, there are numerous other denominations. Also, billions of dollars are spent on church-related activities. For example, it is often said with some justification that the Vatican would be in grave financial difficulties if U.S. Catholics decreased significantly their level of financial support.

In many ways, the church of football incorporates the values of all of U.S. churches, even when conflicting dogmas and creeds impede the possibility of mergers. During games and in interviews, coaches and players invoke God and religion as the source of their success. Coaches have followed the late Vince Lombardi's lead by espousing a football gospel of hard work, team integration and effort, religious inspiration, perfection, and worldly success. However, if a coach or player violates the ideals, members of the football church renounce him, as in the cases of fabled NFL player O. J. Simpson, currently in prison for multiple felonies, and legendary coach Joe Paterno, who was fired from Penn State after one of his assistant coaches was arrested on charges of abusing children.

Just as team managers try to relate to and identify with society through religious ceremonies, so too U.S. Americans participate in religious activities to belong to a social group. For the early immigrants who left their families and possessions, religion reestablished their social life in the United States. To these new immigrants, moving to a different society entailed a weakening ethnic identification and rootlessness. Religion thus became a means of identification and belonging for U.S. Americans, and churches and religious organizations frequently formed political pressure groups to achieve goals that helped their members and were compatible with their beliefs.

By way of summarizing this discussion of U.S. culture, it is possible to relate the football metaphor to Hofstede's (2001) five dimensions of culture described in the first part of this book. As indicated previously, of the 53 countries in Hofstede's original study, the United States ranked 1st on the importance that its respondents attached to the belief in individualism. As we have seen in this chapter, however, this individualism is aggressive individualism enacted within the rules and structure of the team or group. The United States also clustered with those countries that accepted and even relished a high degree of risk in everyday life and that manifested a high degree of masculinity or an aggressive and materialistic orientation to life. Also, U.S. Americans demonstrated a preference for informality, low power distance between individuals and groups, and weak hierarchical authority. In light of our discussion in this chapter, these findings are not surprising.

Many throughout the world still view the United States as far better than the countries in which they live, despite the global financial crisis of 2008 that threw the American economy into recession and put many Americans on the unemployment rolls. The United States still attracts large numbers of immigrants, many of them illegal, who are willing to put up with the hardships of life in the United States because of the opportunities that are available to those who work hard and strive for success. When they arrive, they tend to experience a distinctive form of culture shock resulting from the interplay among the factors described in this chapter. Much of this culture shock is encapsulated in common U.S. sayings and aphorisms, and we end by highlighting some of them:

- Life is just a bowl of cherries.
- Let's get together and work on this problem.
- It's not violent. It's energetic, dude!
- It's lonely at the top.
- Get out of my face!
- Gotta run man—maybe we'll talk later.
- America . . . Love it or leave it!
- Where there's a will, there's a way.
- One step at a time.
- It's never too late.
- You're from Nigeria? Is that a city in Germany?
- Hi! How are you? (As he or she walks by not really wanting or expecting an answer)

CHAPTER 17

The Traditional British House

An Englishman's home is his castle.

—old English proverb

We shape our buildings, and afterwards our buildings shape us.

—Winston Churchill, October 28, 1944 (in Keyes, 2006, p. 19)

I n the early 1990s, an MBA class on cross-cultural management and behavior had an extended discussion about a possible cultural metaphor for Britain. Try as they might, two students—one U.S. American who had lived in Britain for 10 years and one Brit married to a U.S. American—had been unable to identify one possible metaphor, even after a semester's work on the topic. Finally, the U.S. American started to compare her experiences in the United States and Britain. She likened U.S. Americans to independent atoms that periodically come together to accomplish a specific goal and the British to individuals connected through some sort of "invisible glue." According to the U.S. American, the British appear to understand the manner in which their destinies are inextricably linked; they have little, if any, need to be explicit about their basic values and why they behave as they do. The British student immediately saw how this invisible glue was closely associated with the traditional British house, and serious work on this cultural metaphor then began.

Britain's long and illustrious history lends credence to this cultural metaphor, and the heroic manner in which the British people rallied in World War II, when the nation was bombed and heavily damaged, reinforces it. Britain is the only major industrial nation that does not have a permanent written constitution; it does not even have an official flag. Supposedly everyone knows what to do, and they do it. But there have been some critical changes. Britain, once the most centralized of European nations, is going through a devolution of power, as evidenced by the fact that Scotland has a parliament and Wales has an assembly, both created in 1999. In May 2011, the Scottish National Party became the first single political party to gain the majority of the seats in the Scottish Parliament, and it intends to hold a referendum seeking independence for Scotland within the next few years. Also, membership in the House of Lords is no longer a matter of heredity.

David Cannadine (1999) depicts three models of Britain, the first of which supports the invisible glue concept: It is a nation whose people are linked closely by shared values and expectations. However, the second model focuses on a nation divided along three class lines: the upper class, the perpetually striving middle class, and the lower class. Cannadine's third model is the bleakest: Britain is really two nations, one very privileged and one socially disadvantaged. In this chapter, we explore the relevance of these models to modern Britain.

The Traditional House

First we need some understanding of a traditional British house, which is built to stand the test of time. It reflects the local materials, which tend to be stone, brick, flint, or combinations. Houses hundreds of years old and a few buildings thousands of years old are still standing and functioning in their original capacity. A few properties proudly display signs indicating that they were mentioned in the Domesday book, the great land survey commissioned by William the Conqueror in 1085 after he invaded Britain in 1066.

Much of the essence of Britain and her people can be sensed from the fortitude and durable style of their buildings. The design of a British house is traditional and blends with the others around it; the foundations are firm and strong; the floor plans are often similar to one another. Like the British people, the traditional house holds few surprises. A British person could find his or her way around a three-bedroom "semi" (semidetached house or duplex) anywhere in the country. They are often based on the same tried and tested design. The British way of life is reflected in their traditional houses. They change very slowly except for some gradual chipping away or eventual weathering over the years. There is usually one "right" way to do things, and most if not all citizens know what it is—no one has to be told.

Putting up a modern California-style wood house with an open and unusual floor plan surely does not meet this need. Perhaps due to the legendary British weather, a timber-frame house of any sort would tend not to meet with approval and could make financing and insurance difficult to get. In fact, even when the population was sparse and forests abounded, houses were made of stone, not wood. A house, like a way of life, should have strong foundations, be familiar and unchanging, and be built in tried and tested ways, the British believe.

Close Connections

Former prime minister Margaret Thatcher was fond of referring to U.S. Americans as her first cousins, and U.S. Americans reacted positively to this and similar statements. In fact, this strong sense of identification is justified, as surveys focusing on many countries show that the British and U.S. Americans tend to cluster together in terms of basic values and attitudes. As Winston Churchill once shared with a group of Harvard University students, the great Otto von Bismarck, who brought several countries together in a united Germany, is said to have observed toward the close of his life that the most potent factor in human society at the end of the 19th century was the fact that the British and U.S. peoples spoke the same language.

These shared values show up in behaviors. For example, U.S. American law, government, and social mores are rooted in their British antecedents. Britain and the United States have been staunch allies for more than 100 years, the "special relationship" cemented during World War II through the extraordinary collaboration between Prime Minister Winston Churchill and President Franklin D. Roosevelt. However, there are significant cultural differences that surprise and confuse U.S. Americans when they consider their "cousins," the British.

It will be helpful to examine the British culture in terms of the metaphor of the British house. We will examine the "laying of the foundation of the house" evident in British history, as well as the political and economic climate of today. Next, we will look at the "building of the brick house," which naturally includes the various elements of growing up British. Last, we will describe "living in the traditional brick house," including some cultural patterns found in business and social situations.

History, Politics, Economics: Laying the Foundations

First, let us identify Britain geographically. A number of terms are used when discussing this area, such as the British Isles, Great Britain, Britain, and the United Kingdom. We will be discussing Britain, which is synonymous with Great Britain, consisting of England, Scotland, and Wales. These make up the larger of the two islands that lie off the northwestern coast of Europe. The smaller island is made up of the Irish Republic (a separate country) and Northern Ireland, which is a part of Britain. Britain reluctantly increased its control over Northern Ireland in the early 1970s, imposing direct rule in 1972 because violence between various Protestant and Roman Catholic elements had been increasing for more than 30 years. Recently some of the animosity has declined, and Northern Ireland now has a government in which Catholics and Protestants share power. Although the term *United Kingdom* includes Northern Ireland (since 1922), Great Britain does not.

Britain's early history is one of a succession of invasions and immigrations from tribes such as the Celts, Romans, Angles, Saxons, and Jutes, many of whom were warriors, barbarians, and pirates. The date when Britain was first inhabited is unknown, but parts of a woman's skull found at Swanscombe in Kent were dated at about 300,000 years ago.

The Years of Empire

Britain's history from the middle 1500s to the 1950s is a story of empire building and domination that many nations have tried to emulate without success. For many years the territory ruled was so vast that "the sun never set on the British empire." According to historian Niall Ferguson (2002), the British empire, begun as a counterbalancing force to other European empires such as Spain, was a great modernizing force in history that led to the spread of liberal capitalism and parliamentary democracy around the world.

The British have left their mark on many of the foreign lands over which their flag has flown in a variety of ways. One of the most obvious is the fact that the accepted international business language or *lingua franca* across the world today is English. More than 350 million people speak it as their first language, and another 450 million claim it as a second language. Also, even when English is not spoken as either a first or second language, global business is so reliant on it that inventive, basic ways of communicating in one's native language and to a minimal degree in English have been created (e.g., Chinglish and Spanglish). Many former British colonies set up their parliamentary and legal systems to emulate the British system, including freedom of the press, and still look to the British for advice and consent in their own affairs. In fact, the Magna Carta, which was signed in 1215 in Runnymede, England (considered the birthplace of modern democracy), has influenced one of the most important documents in world history, the U.S. Constitution.

The rate of immigration to the home country of Britain from former colonies and Commonwealth countries continues to rise, and experts predict that Britain's population will increase to more than 70 million in the next 20 to 25 years. Many of these immigrants have settled permanently in Britain, and more than one quarter of the population of central London is of African, Asian, or Caribbean origin. Britain has lagged behind the United States in passing equal opportunity laws and opening up job opportunities for ethnic minorities. However, many Brits do not mind living close to others of different social classes and different ethnicities and frequently marry across class and ethnicity, a result supportive of the invisible-glue perspective: Council houses (low-cost housing) are often found in affluent parts of town.

Most 19th-century Britons were better educated and much richer than most other Europeans. Across Europe, people set out to dress like the British, talk like them, and imitate their manners. Even the fashion of wearing black, which survives in our contemporary evening wear, came from British style in the 1830s. "It's their confidence," Aldous Huxley (1951) said of them in *Antic Hay*, "their ease, it's the way they take their place in the world for granted, it's their prestige, which the other people would like to deny but can't" (p. 38) that made them admired models. The adoption of British ways was so universal that it was unquestioned. People automatically chose the best, and the best was considered British (Barzini, 1983).

For hundreds of years, there was a tacit admission of British supremacy in almost every regard. Furthermore, there was universal admiration and envy of their wealth, power, sagacity, and brutal ruthlessness when necessary. There was a certainty that Britain knew best; that its overwhelming power and wealth would take care of most of the world's military, political, and economic problems; that private problems could be controlled by the British moral code and rules of good manners; that Britain could prolong the status quo indefinitely; and that there was nothing to worry about (Barzini, 1983). This is the heritage of the British people—the foundation on which the rest of the traditional house is built.

As noted in Chapter 1, culture can vary along several dimensions, including time or whether a society is past, present, or future oriented. It is easy to see why the British would emphasize the past far more than U.S. Americans (Trompenaars & Hampden-Turner, 1998). The traditional pageantry and ceremony of Britain's political structure is built right into the walls and shell of the house—without it, the house would certainly not stand as tall and proud.

Government and Politics

Britain's government, considered one of the world's most efficient, is based on Acts of Parliament. There is a written constitution (although it is sometimes said that Britain has an unwritten or uncodified constitution), which is quite different from the permanent U.S. Constitution in that it consists of the Acts of Parliament, court judgments, and European treaties existing at any one time. Within Parliament, the House of Lords basically acts as a review body and can delay but not veto acts passed by the House of Commons. Thus real power rests with the House of Commons. Precedent or common law is used only when there is no legislation concerning a major issue or no clear legislative intent. Common law, however, is widely used. It is frequently assumed by the British that everyone "knows" the rules, so most citizens receive positively the application of common law. Contrary to the fundamental U.S. American assumption that supreme authority must never be vested in a single institution, the British Parliament exercises supreme power over both the figurehead monarchy and the courts. Like a load-bearing wall, it accepts full responsibility for governing in Britain. More recently, treaties with the European Union (EU) make EU law, in some cases, superior to British law. Britain does not use the euro as its currency, which helped the nation economically during the global recession starting in 2008.

In a different way, the monarchy is a vital part of the political scenario; panoply and pageantry distinguish every ceremonial phase of royal processions. This enduring display of pomp simultaneously manifests the people's unity and strengthens it. The official opening of Parliament involves a ceremony over which the queen presides, and each week she meets with the prime minister to discuss current national issues. The past, present, and future are united in the crown and the monarch. The monarchy is one of the things that makes Britain unique, and even many of its former colonies welcome the royal family with open arms and respect. Without the presence of the royal family, some of the mortar that holds the traditional British house together might surely decay. In 2012 the Queen will have been on the throne for 60 years. In 2011 she became the second-longest reigning British monarch after Queen Victoria, who reigned for 63 years.

Periodically the monarchy is criticized, particularly in terms of being a feudal institution not appropriate in modern times, but the public strongly supports it. For example, 1 million or more citizens turned out to watch the wedding of Prince William and Kate Middleton in April 2011, and about 26 million watched on television. The BBC website crashed and ran more slowly than usual because of the numbers of people who tried to access it on the royal wedding day. The wedding generated almost as much interest "across the pond" in America, and an almost equal number of Americans watched the event on televisions; some even held royal wedding watchers' tea parties.

There are two main political parties in Britain: Labour and Conservative (Tory). A third party, the Liberals (started in 1859) now known as the Liberal Democrats (or Lib Dems), works toward social justice and has recently espoused the idea of making Britain carbon neutral by 2050. Britain has a representative form of government. In a national election, people vote for their constituency member of Parliament (MP), and that person represents them. It is quite possible and has happened that the majority of votes go to a party that has a minority of seats in the House so that it does not win the election, because winning is determined by the number of party-affiliated MPs elected. Elections can be called by the government at any time within 5 years of the last election. This policy gives the party in power a political edge because it can, within limits, arrange that an election take place when public support for the government is greatest. To offset this, a vote of "no confidence" in the prime minister and his or her party can force a reelection at any time. The historic May 2010 general election produced a hung parliament (in which no party commanded a majority in the House of Commons), and a power-sharing deal was reached between the Tories led by David Cameron and the Lib Dems led by Nick Clegg, who serve as prime minister and deputy prime minister, respectively.

Voting is often along party lines; thus personalities often play a less important than in U.S. politics. Voting is also often allied to social class, so it is fairly common for citizens to vote the way their parents did and the way their neighbors do. In addition, political parties are generally farther apart ideologically than U.S. American parties, and changes in government can result in noticeable changes in policy. For example, the election of a Conservative government led by Thatcher resulted in the privatization of nationalized industries, the reduction of income taxes, and the rewriting of trade union legislation. Prime Minister Tony Blair's government, however, after the

Labour Party had lost four general elections between 1979 and 1997, adopted a "third way" and billed itself as New Labour, adopting some free-market and Thatcherite policies. The ruling coalition led by Prime Minister Cameron and Deputy Prime Minister Clegg set out to remake Britain in the wake of the global financial crisis. Their main goals are to eliminate structural fiscal deficit by 2015 and devolve the power of the state over public services ("The Uncivil Partnership," 2011).

In addition to elected officials, there exists a whole matrix of official and social relations within which power is exercised called "the establishment." This elite web includes such diverse interests as Oxford and Cambridge Universities (Oxbridge), the British Broadcasting Corporation (BBC), and wealthy, high-society individuals known as the "great and the good." It is a difficult network to break apart because of the different forms it may take under different circumstances. Some say that this network has lost some of its clout, whereas others feel that it just keeps changing shape. U.S. Americans may be familiar with the portrayal of the British civil service as consisting of long-suffering officials fighting against the whims of ministers in changing governments, portrayed so effectively in the BBC series *Yes Minister*.

Economic Divisions

There is some support for the belief that social structure at the top levels of society has changed. The *Economist* has compared the educational backgrounds of those who held the top 100 jobs in Britain in 3 years: 1972, 1992, and 2002. In 1972 and 1992, the percentages who had attended the elite public schools (67% and 66%) and either Oxford or Cambridge (52% and 54%) were very close, but in 2002 the corresponding figures were 46% and 35% (see "The Ascent of British Man," 2002; "How Britain's Elite," 2002). A YouGov poll conducted for the *Economist* in 2006 revealed that the key identifying markers of class were occupation, address, accent, and income in that order. Only 28% of those surveyed expected to end up in a different class than the one into which they were born ("But Did They Buy," 2006). In a comprehensive study of class in Britain conducted in December 2010, the research company BritainThinks investigated the social attitudes of the middle and working classes. The study showed that only 24% (compared to 67% in the late 1980s) identified themselves with the working class and people who are struggling financially consider themselves to be below the working class. Members of the working class are more likely to feel isolated and marginalized, whereas members of the middle class are more likely to feel as if they are a part of the larger community (Rentoul, 2011).

Economically, Britain can be divided into two parts. Those who live in the south (within a few hours' drive of London) consider it to be superior in sophistication, wealth, and social status (much to the chagrin of the others). This perception is somewhat accurate due to the predominance of service, high-tech, and other growth industries in the south. The north of Britain is associated with heavy industry, engineering, mining, and unemployment, although a lot has changed with revitalization of cities such as Manchester and Liverpool, the latter of which was anointed European City of Culture 2008. Parts of the north still experience high unemployment, where traditional industries such as steel, coal mining, and textiles have contracted. The differences between north and south were celebrated in the acclaimed social novel *North and South* by Elizabeth Gaskell (1855/1995), which was adapted for television in 1975 and 2004.

Long after their empire dissolved, the British were still considered the moral leaders of Europe. After World War II, they felt they had earned the right to be the third superpower in the world since the country had paid so dearly in terms of human life and physical destruction of property and the British had shown tremendous courage. However, in 1955 they stood aloof from or outright objected to attempts to unify Europe. While British opposition has softened in recent years, Britain still resists the idea of a unified Europe. Britain is a member of the EU, but it has not accepted the use of the euro, the common currency.

The British could have collaborated with other European nations on many occasions to formulate a unified Europe in their own interest, but many British leaders found it unthinkable to risk losing the country's full identity. Britain has tended to be a jealous guardian of its freedom, proud of its solitude. The British prefer to be victims of their own mistakes rather than to trust the judgment of other people (Barzini, 1983). In fact, the UK Independence Party (UKIP), the fourth-largest party in the UK, is dedicated to withdrawing Britain from the European Union because it believes that participating is bad for Britain's economy and prosperity. It would prefer to replace Britain's participation in the EU with trade agreements and treaties of corporation (UKIP, 2010). In the wake of the debt crisis necessitating the bailout of Greece, Prime Minister Cameron vowed that UK taxpayers would not be asked to bear the burden of the bailout because, "thank god," Britain had stayed out of the euro.

We have taken a look at the British character as exemplified in the traditional, rigid, but long-lasting houses and suggested that a strong sense of history is the foundation on which society rests today. Shared traditions and beliefs, like mortar, bind people in a national identity. National fervor now often runs along Scottish, Welsh, and Irish lines. The English tend to be more reserved in their expression of nationality, as brazen exhibitions of patriotism often evoke unpleasant reactions from the others. The Welsh dragon and the Saint Andrews cross of Scotland, on the other hand, fly with pride. Now we will look at the social mechanisms—socialization processes and the educational system— that sustain these feelings.

Growing Up British: Building the House

Due to the prestigious foundations of British history, foreigners still expect the British to show something of their ancient firmness, resourcefulness, diplomacy, leadership, and certainly good graces. How do the British continue to instill some of these admired virtues into their society? How do they put the bricks together atop the foundation to raise their children British?

It has been said that all Britons have a few ideas firmly embedded in their heads that exactly and universally give them the answers about how to be perfectly British. This has allowed them, throughout history, to know exactly what their compatriots would expect them to do and how to go about doing it. For the most part there is only one right way to do just about anything—from greeting guests to waging war.

Children Behave

Above all else, most British families bring up their children to behave. Inquiries about children will often be about whether they are well behaved rather than whether they are happy. It is assumed that they need to be controlled and not spoiled. A great importance is placed on learning proper manners. George Mikes, the Hungarian-born British humorist, is supposed to have observed, "On the Continent people have good food; in England people have good table manners."

The British are taught at an early age to control spontaneity, and because children can be embarrassingly spontaneous, the emphasis is on keeping them quiet so they don't bother adults. For example, it is rare to see children in a restaurant in the evenings. Children who do not know their place are thought to be not well brought up. Behavior equated with showing off or boasting meets with disapproval. After all, children are meant to be seen and not heard. This emphasis on manners and the importance of being aware of one's responsibilities increases with age.

A result of this restraint is the well-known British reserve in adults. In fact, following a survey in 2006, the British Heart Foundation suggested that the famous British reserve motivated 42% of the people polled to adopt a "wait and see" attitude before calling for help with chest pains. This resulted in a massive billboard campaign showing a man with a belt tightening around his chest and the caption, "A chest pain is your body saying call 999" ("British Stiff-Upper Lip," 2006). Britons have many things in common, and a respect and strong desire for privacy are primary among them. This sentiment is so strong that the British often appear to others as distant and aloof, as though they are building walls between themselves and others to create their own space within the brick house.

This need for privacy is a defining factor and one of the dimensions along which cultures differ. The expression "We like to keep ourselves to ourselves" is particularly British (Glyn, 1970, p. 176). Glyn notes that even in the case of child care, babysitters need to be hired because relatives will generally not help or interfere, although rising costs and modern life have a way of changing social mores. He also observes that even on trains, the British will frequently not sit near someone when a more secluded seat is available. In a crowded fast-food restaurant, if people are forced to share a table, they will often act as though the other party is not present. Striking up a conversation with a seatmate would generally be considered an invasion of personal space, although this restraint is more characteristic of people living in the south of the country.

There are practical reasons for the British insistence on private, personal space. Britain is a crowded country, and space must be used efficiently. The average population density in Britain is about 251.5 people per square kilometer, which is considerably higher than that of most of its Western counterparts (e.g., the United States has 32.9 people/square kilometer; France has 113.8 people per square kilometer).

Unlike other Europeans, the British prefer houses and are not great flat (apartment) dwellers, but their houses are small by U.S. standards and closer together than in the United States. Just as there are partitions of rooms within the house, the British also grow hedges around their gardens to separate their space from neighbors and to keep out the eyes of passersby. The British tend to keep work and leisure completely separate, much as the living areas and bedrooms of the traditional two-story house are separated by downstairs and upstairs.

A good neighbor is one who is friendly at a distance and who does not intrude. Because physical distance is often not possible, the only available protection of personal space is psychological distance. One should always phone ahead before visiting a British home—dropping in unannounced would generally be unwelcome. Also, frequent social telephone calls tend to be regarded as an intrusion.

Emotional outbursts (except at times of genuine crisis) are seen as "soppy" or as evidence of an unstable personality. From childhood onward the British are admonished to keep a "stiff upper lip," referring to pursing the lips to prevent an outburst. Even good friends may never be as intimate as in many other cultures. However, this may apply differently to the different classes, with genteel restraint being seen as definitely more upper-class than lower-class British. John Cleese (of Monty Python fame) made this point entertainingly in the film *A Fish Called Wanda* (Shamberg & Crichton, 1988) when he said to his U.S. girlfriend, played by Jamie Lee Curtis:

> Wanda, you make me feel so free. Do you have any idea what it's like being English? Being so stifled by this dread of doing the wrong thing, of saying to someone, "Are you married?" and hearing "My wife left me this morning . . . ," or saying, "Do you have children?" and being told they all burned to death on Wednesday.

The British must endure a lot of weight from their lofty heritage. Although the foundation is strong and deep, the walls and especially the exterior of the British house and personality must seem to be effortlessly indestructible and imperturbable.

Privacy and Pubs

Inside the house, private space is also cherished. The British do not generally like open-plan living areas. Instead, rooms are separated and divided by walls and doors that close. Although houses are relatively small, family members are thus ensured private space. Still, Edward T. Hall (1966) points out that the smallness of the houses effectively precludes children from having their own rooms, as is the norm in the United States. He argues that as adults, the British do not have as great a need for separate offices as do members of some other cultures. Even members of Parliament do not always have their own offices.

All of this talk of privacy and reserve should not be taken to mean that British people are unfriendly. They are by and large friendly people and make the most gracious hosts. If you ask people for help, even on the street, most will give it cheerfully. U.S. Americans, on the other hand, are often seen by the British as coming on too strong and too gushy, as being insincere, and as getting too personal too soon. Although the British enjoy the privacy of their own small homes, they also enjoy the camaraderie of the local pub. Nearly every large and small town throughout Britain has at least one pub, many of them hundreds of years old. This is where many British do most of their socializing with coworkers and friends. It is a favorite pastime to share a few beers after work, with subordinates and bosses mingling, although wine is slowly but surely replacing beer with the advent of the gastropubs. In fact, pubs can almost be thought of as a substitute for the living room in a traditional house because Britons tend not to entertain in their own homes as frequently as U.S. Americans.

Pubs generally serve various kinds of beer—ale, stout, lager (having replaced ale as the best-selling British beer), or bitter—by the pint or half pint. Beers are served at room temperature and never cold, which would disguise the flavor. Most other drinks are served without ice and, if you ask for ice, you will be given a cube or two. Social changes and tough times have taken their toll on pubs. According to the British Beer and Pub Association (BBPA), there are around 52,500 pubs today compared to 58,600 pubs in 2005. Alcohol consumption has fallen by 13% since 2004 as a result of tax increases and public health messages. Some pubs are trying to adapt by opening around 7:00 AM instead of the usual 11:00 AM to serve coffee and breakfast to young families, pensioners, and office workers ("Two Pints of Lager," 2010).

Orderliness, patience, and unexcitability are hallmarks of British behavior, although in recent years these traditional characteristics are being strongly challenged by hordes of beer-guzzling football (soccer) fans who regularly invade other countries with fervent displays of nationalism. Unique to the British is the idea that many a problem can be solved over a good cup of tea; the English love their tea. The British prefer to see each task through until completion, regardless of the priority one might assign to it. For example, if you approach a hotel desk where a clerk is alone attending to some paperwork, he or she will finish the current task unhurriedly before attending to you. There is nothing between the ordinary and a true state of emergency for most British.

Class Structure

There is a wide range of living standards in Britain, from some of the worst slums in Europe to grand estates. Roles and statuses are generally well defined. Still pervading this stratified society are distinctions among the working class, the middle class, and the elite upper class. In numerous surveys over time, the British themselves reinforce these divisions by assigning themselves more than 90% of the time to one of these classes without prompting. As the recent study referred to earlier showed, in the wake of the global financial crisis and recession in Britain, people who are struggling to make ends meet are increasingly assigning themselves to the "poor" class. By contrast, most U.S. Americans, including many who would be considered working class in Britain, describe themselves as middle class.

One is born into a class in Britain, and it is difficult to move from one class to another. Once again, tradition rules, whether it be in one's house plan or social class. Family background, especially one's accent and use of language, tends to determine the type of education one receives and hence one's career. In the past, it was not unusual to see job advertisements that explicitly required a public school (the equivalent of U.S. private schools) education. Indeed, the playing fields of Eton contributed to most of the officer corps of the British Army in World War I. As noted above, social mobility is decreasing for the population overall, even if the social structure of the top 100 positions in Britain has changed in recent years. When Prince William got engaged to Kate Middleton, the fact that she was a "commoner" brought Britain's class distinctions to the fore, with one newspaper commenting on her progress from the "pit to the palace" in reference to her coal-mining ancestors and another speculating about her fitness to be queen someday. Some observers saw this as evidence that despite the rise of commoners such as Richard Branson and J. K. Rowling to great wealth, Britain is still very much a society where status is measured by birthright and breeding (Faiola, 2010).

Although real disposable income overall has increased in recent years, so too has income inequality. This same pattern holds for other nations, especially those involved significantly in the global marketplace. In 1979 the top 20% of British households had 43% of all earned income, whereas the poorest 20% had only 2.4%. In 1996 the corresponding percentages of earned income had increased to 50% and 2.6%, respectively. In 2006/2007, according to the National Statistics Office, the original income of the top fifth of households was 15 times greater than that of the bottom fifth before taxes (£72,900 per household compared with £4,900) and 4 times greater after accounting for taxes and benefits (£52,400 and £14,400, respectively). Such facts reinforce Cannadine's (1999) third model, in which Britain is divided into two nations: the haves and the have-nots. Even Cannadine's second model, focusing on a three-class nation, seems to have a good amount of support. If anything, the distance between the top 20% and everyone else seems to have increased. However, a recent study by John Hills of the London School of Economics found that the widest gaps among social groups (e.g., various ethnic minorities, men and women) have diminished over time ("Reversing Inequality," 2010).

The British are experts at classifying each other's social status by noting tiny details of speech, manners, and dress. George Bernard Shaw wrote in the preface to

Pygmalion (1912/1916) that "it is impossible for an Englishman to open his mouth without making some other Englishman hate or despise him." *My Fair Lady*, an adaptation of *Pygmalion* that is one of the most popular musical comedies ever, humorously but accurately emphasizes the importance of language and accents. The British can still identify regional accents and therefore where the speaker is from and his or her class. The discrimination that this once produced may be fading, however, because regional accents can now be heard in professions and walks of life that were once reserved for the upper class only. For instance, while there was a time when only "proper" upper-class English would be heard on the airwaves, particularly on the BBC, regional accents are becoming more acceptable and are heard in all areas of broadcast. This may be indicative of a broadening and deepening of the middle class in society, raising the level of some of the working class.

Language Speaks

Even so, the use of the language (and other behavior) can be telling of class. Alan Ross published a popular version of his 1954 article "Linguistic Class-Indicators in Present-Day English" under the title "U and Non-U," referring to upper-class and non-upper-class language (1956; see also Ross, 1969). Many of the distinctions have faded with time, but some are as true today as ever. For example, "I worked very hard" is U, and "I worked ever so hard" is non-U. "Half past ten" is U, and "half ten" is non-U. In terms of style, rugs or a plain carpet are U, and wall-to-wall patterned carpet is non-U; putting milk into tea cups first is non-U, but offering it after the tea has been poured is U. Another non-U expression that tends to puzzle foreigners is "He wasn't half angry," which means he was extremely angry, or "He isn't half handsome," which means he was exceedingly handsome (Braganti & Devine, 1992). Even the use of terms for meals of the day may differ depending on one's social class; non-Us sometimes employ the terms *dinner* to indicate lunch and *tea* to indicate dinner.

T. R. Reid (2000) points out that U.S. Americans possess a distinctive advantage: The British cannot classify them by their speech, which tends to cut across class distinctions. As he states, "In Britain, the way you talk speaks volumes about you—your economic status, your school, your ancestry, your career prospects." An interesting recent development has been a negative reaction to the proper English that has so distinctively separated the social classes. It is estimated that there has been a decline from 5% to 3% of speakers who use the clipped manner of speaking that is frequently associated with Oxford and Cambridge Universities. However, there is a significant increase in the demand for "better" speech that masks or softens regional speech patterns, particularly in business settings and presentations (see "Accents: We Want to Talk Proper," 2002).

Of course, the British seem to believe that U.S. Americans do not speak English at all and find their language a sloppy adaptation of it. According to Professor David Crystal (2011), one of the world's foremost experts in English, the future will usher in a situation where people will have to learn two varieties of the language, one spoken in their home country (e.g., India and China) and another that is a standard international version of English. Apart from using different grammar and pronunciation, the British and U.S. Americans can confuse each other with their use of different words. For example, in Britain, you'll hear *flat* rather than *apartment*, *chemist* rather than *drug store*, *lift* rather than *elevator*, *solicitor* rather than *attorney*, *ring up* rather than *call* (which means to visit in person in Britain) or *phone*, and *boot* rather than *trunk* of a car. One colleague was driving with his American father through rural England when they saw a sign advertising a "boot sale," whereupon his father immediately concluded that it was a sale for cheap shoes. Our colleague informed his dad that the English organize boot sales to sell old stuff from their car boots (or trunks), similar to yard/garage sales in the United States!

Some segments of the population have developed entirely different speech patterns that may not be easily understood by other British (or other English speakers). The best known is the working-class Cockney population, officially those born within hearing distance of the Bow Bells that ring from the Church St. Mary le Bow in the east end of London. These people have developed "rhyming slang," some of which has passed into general usage. If a man talks about the "trouble and strife," he is referring to his wife. To say "I didn't say a dicky bird" means "I didn't say a word." Understanding Cockney rhyming slang is yet more difficult when the conversion is one step further removed. For example, "loaf of bread" stands for head, but the whole phrase is not used, just "loaf." So if someone tells you to use your loaf, you are being told to think clearly or to use your head. Another popular expression is "Blimey!" which translated means "God, blind me if I tell a lie," and is used throughout Britain as a common exclamation.

Educational Policy

British educational policy has changed considerably over the past 25 years, but the old system and its influence are still evident. Tenure has been abolished at the universities, which are ranked on a series of criteria used for determining future funding. As noted above, the number of university graduates has increased, but it is still extremely difficult to get into the top-rated universities, and many graduates are dissatisfied with their jobs. In December 2010, students rioted in London after Parliament passed a bill tripling university tuition to US$15,000 per year, a bargain compared to US$50,000 per year at some private American universities. Some 50 demonstrators broke away from the previously peaceful demonstrations in central London and attacked the car carrying Prince Charles and his wife, the Duchess of Cornwall, as they looked on in horror at this uncharacteristic British behavior. Tuition was free until 1996 and has been steadily rising since then, but the 200% increase to take effect in 2012 left many students feeling betrayed and shut out from a university education and better job opportunities (Jones, 2010).

Today many children attend U.S.-style "comprehensive" high schools or secondary schools for children of all abilities. But the nature of the secondary schools is still very important. Whereas U.S. Americans tend to identify a person's social standing at least in part by the prestige of the college attended and rarely think about the secondary school, the British give approximately equal weight to the college and secondary school. Public secondary schools (which in the United States are called private schools) existed and still exist for children of affluent parents or those able to win scholarships. These were often founded by trade organizations, for example, the Merchant Taylors' boys school in London and the school for both girls and boys founded by The Worshipful Company of Haberdashers. Others, including Harrow and Eton, provide more than their share of entrants to the prestigious Oxford and Cambridge Universities. There is an ongoing clamor for the provision of more seats in these universities for state school graduates. Recent data show that in 2009–10, Oxford and Cambridge, with 54.3% and 59.3%, respectively, had relatively low participation from state school students among universities. According to the Sutton Trust Charity, five schools send more pupils to "Oxbridge" than 2,000 others combined, with private schools winning out over state schools when students have similar results (Berg, 2011). The reputation of the school attended accompanies one through later life, and the more prestigious it is, the more doors it opens. These more prestigious schools often have ties or scarves with certain colors or patterns associated with them. Wearing them is considered an earned honor, and it would be a major faux pas to wear a tie or scarf to which one is not entitled. The popular series of Harry Potter books by J. K. Rowling and subsequent movies show off the vaunted British school system in a positive light.

Just as the mortar holds the solid British house together, so the socialization processes, class distinctions, and educational system described above represent the floor plan of the traditional British house. It is within this framework that the British people live, work, and play. But once any house has been built, people live in it in their own way. We will now look at some dimensions of British everyday life, such as work habits, etiquette, humor, social customs, and leisure activities.

Being British: Living in the House

Most travelers expect to find the British stuffy and starched. Indeed, that is one side of the coin: the gentleman wearing pinstripes and a bowler hat, carrying a furled umbrella, greeting another with "I say, old chap," and the like and the oh-so-proper lady shopping at Harrods and having afternoon tea with dainty little cups and rich pastries. Flip the coin, however, and you will find goths, punks, emos (short for "emotional") who fit their respective categories based on music, clothing, and lifestyle preferences, as well as other less noticeable eccentricities. Indeed the modern young generation has certainly become more adventurous in its sartorial tastes.

Furthermore, you may offend the Scottish (or Scots) or the Welsh if you do not respect their differences, even though Britain encompasses England, Scotland, and Wales. Many variances, such as food preferences and specialties, appear superficial, but others are more substantial. For instance, Scotland has its own legal and educational system, which is patterned after the German system (see Chapter 12); Wales finds its identity in its own language, and official documents and websites are bilingual.

Although there has long been a strong connection between church and state, outside Northern Ireland religion plays little part in the everyday lives of the British. King Henry VIII declared himself the equivalent of the pope when he created the Church of England, but about 38% of the British population claim to have no religion. The rest of the Christian population, if pressed, would probably say that they are "C of E" (Church of England, or Anglican). Roman Catholicism is set to become the dominant religion of the country for the first time since the Reformation thanks largely to immigration (Gledhill, 2007). Among ethnic minorities, Islam is poised to take over as the most practiced religion, with about 3% of the population identifying themselves as Muslim. Despite this wide spectrum, the British are considered a relatively homogeneous group of people. We will focus here on the similarities among them, not their differences. For instance, they all share the same constantly wet weather, which often serves as a convenient conversation starter. The benefit of all the rain is that it produces some of the lushest, greenest land in the world. Perhaps to enjoy this aspect of life, the Scots invented the game of golf in the 14th century and still have some of the most desirable courses in the world. At one point, the Scottish king outlawed golf because the citizens were devoting too much time to it and not enough time to archery and preparation for battle.

Maybe this constantly wet weather is what the British mean by "making the best of a bad lot." If things go wrong (or the weather happens to be lousy), the right thing to do is to make the best of it. Doing so will be admired. The British tend to think highly of anyone who suffers setbacks and perseveres; whether success comes is less important.

"It is not whether you win or lose that is important, but how you play the game." The British really mean this and will even applaud the opponent for making a good play in a cricket match. In fact a lot of conversational phrases have been spawned from the game of cricket. For example, in Britain "It's just not cricket" is used to indicate that something has been handled unfairly. Draws (ties) are quite acceptable in British cricket matches. In the United States, on the other hand, the rules are often such that tiebreaking is essential. Also, the heart of the British tends to go out to the underdog, the player who is in a lost and hopeless position such as that of the man playing for a draw in cricket, who must stay at his post until the close of play.

Sports and Leisure

Again, however, these generalizations must be tempered. In recent years the British have not won many international events; it is more than 70 years since an Englishman,

Fred Perry, won the men's singles at Wimbledon. And the loutish behavior of some English soccer fans caused the *Economist* to identify them as "England's Shame" (1998); the phenomenon has also been labeled "the English Disease" in recent years. According to Professor Eric Dunning, an expert on football hooliganism, the behavior is a relic of empire and an example of aggressive nationalistic posturing. Still, most of the British follow the pattern set by their ancestors when it comes to fair play.

Whereas cricket tends to be a middle- and upper-class sport, popular in public schools, soccer (it is called football in Britain) is a working-class sport. And, just as elite public schools, clubs, and universities have their own scarves or ties associated with them, which are earned and worn with pride, so too scarves are available in soccer team colors. These scarves may not be earned, but they can be seen trailing from car windows on Saturdays as enthusiastic fans travel to watch "away" matches.

Regarding sports as a leisure activity, the British tend to be keener spectators than active participants. They invented many of the sports the world plays today: football (soccer), golf, tennis, badminton, and rugby. Indeed, the all-American sport of baseball is based on the old British city game of "rounders." The British tend to be loyal fans and as sports mad as U.S. Americans. They talk about it, read about it, gamble on it, and turn out in the worst weather to watch their local teams.

Those who have the financial resources spend much of their leisure time "in the country." It is considered the utmost luxury to have a house in the country, and most Britons yearn for this. In the smallest towns and villages throughout Britain, houses may still be addressed by their names instead of street numbers. These names are usually descriptive and may include the name of the original owner. Examples might be Hawthorne's End, Cadbury's Cottage, or Dunroamin (where the well-traveled person has finally settled). This is a quaint carryover from the days when people referred to all addresses this way and streets were unpaved and unnamed.

An important leisure priority for the British is a respect for nature. The British generally like to walk, sometimes around the block but in a garden or country setting is better. Another way of getting close to nature is to create your own garden. However modest the patch of ground in front or in back of the brick house, there is another traditional element: the English garden. It is not called a *yard*, which signifies a dusty concrete patch like a school yard, but a *garden*, which implies flowers and grass. The British are renowned for beautiful gardens, which may be elaborate or small but usually consist of a patch of lawn surrounded symmetrically by colorful flowers and shrubs. Of course, these gardens do not suffer from lack of rain and tend to be wonderfully lush.

Celebration and Ceremony

Ceremonies and holidays offer an interesting example of how the past-oriented British hold on to age-old attitudes and traditions. A large proportion of Britain's oldest surviving customs come from towns and cities, and these customs are bound with a long and complex history (Kightly, 1986). Local celebrations are widespread; there are more than 7,000 fairs annually, and many a village has a yearly festival celebrating the day of the patron saint to whom its parish church is dedicated. Founder's days are common as well, with institutions such as schools, hospitals, and alms houses honoring their benefactors annually. Such celebrations reinforce the same conservative traditions that the British house embodies.

One favorite tradition is Guy Fawkes Day, which is celebrated each November 5 and is dedicated to the memory of a traitor who tried to blow up the houses of Parliament. Bonfires are set, a straw doll to symbolize Guy Fawkes is set atop, and spectators cheer as it burns to ashes. At a Guy Fawkes bonfire, people chant the rather morbid poem: "Penny for the Guy, poke him in the eye, stick him in the fireplace, and watch him die."

British humor seems to run the spectrum of possibilities. Despite their well-recognized reserve, the British have a basic aversion to seriousness and prefer to lighten most events with humor. On the one hand, there is the dry, satirical humor that one would associate with Noel Coward. At the other end of the spectrum, the British love the broadest slapstick, replete with rude jokes and outrageous behavior, such as in *The Benny Hill Show* and *Monty Python*. Even in dignified settings such as Parliament, high-spirited bantering finds its way into many otherwise dull negotiations. In one celebrated instance, an MP had to apologize to the Parliament after its members voted that he must retract the statement "Half the members of Parliament are asses." He apologized by saying that "half the members of Parliament are not asses," and then sat down. This skillful display of biting humor disarmed his adversaries.

Perhaps this love of humor comes directly from their culture, where a direct display of feelings is suppressed. Humor distracts from embarrassing or tense situations that might otherwise be difficult for the British to handle. Just as the windows in a traditional home bring in light and fresh air, humor changes the atmosphere and relieves tensions.

One of the more popular British sitcoms both in Britain and in the United States, where it is carried on public television, is *Keeping Up Appearances*. This sitcom focuses on only one topic, with variants thereof: social class differences. Some commentators, both British and U.S. American, have heaped unqualified praise on this show, and the reader is encouraged to see it not only for its great humor but also its incisive depiction of social class differences. The British pride themselves on their dry wit, and it must have come as a surprise to them that they ranked seventh in a 2011 worldwide poll to rank the world's funniest people conducted by Badoo.com, which is based in England. The Americans came in first, and the Germans came in last (Casciato, 2011).

Fashionably Late

In social and business situations alike, one should be right on time or up to several minutes late, but never early. The British institutionalized the idea of being "fashionably late," usually interpreted as being 10 to 20 minutes late. If the British arrive early for an appointment, they will often wait in their cars or outside until the agreed-upon time. However, with the advent of mobile phones (and the ability to make apologetic calls or send a text message), almost two thirds of Britons admit to being regularly late for appointments. According to David Holmes, a social psychologist at Manchester Metropolitan University, the modern generation considers lateness to be more of a norm than a social breach to be avoided (Rose, 2006).

The old notion of the British being unable to relate to you unless you have been properly introduced by a third party is out-of-date. Increasing informality in this area is becoming more common, but the British reserve may still shine through, giving the impression of coolness or indifference. Nevertheless, first names are used almost immediately in business and social situations among people of the same level. People of a much lower status in business or socially will usually address their superiors by an appropriate title and surname. In some cases, men may be heard calling each other by their last names only, but this is simply a carryover from public school days and need not be imitated.

The expression "How do you do?" is a common greeting in Britain. It is not an inquiry but evokes the same response, "How do you do?" and nothing more. Also, the British think using the expression "Have a nice day" on leaving someone is strange and see it as a form of command—although with the invasion of many American fast-food chains, the phrase is being heard more often. The British tend to be more circumspect in their conversation than others. They avoid being direct for fear of offending someone. In fact, they often phrase definite statements as questions. For instance, they may say, "It gets dark in the evening, doesn't it?" No one is expected to answer the question. These examples confirm the off-quoted adage that the British and the U.S. American share a culture but are separated by language.

Politeness and modesty are the hallmarks of the British in social conversation. Do not be surprised if, after you pontificate at length about the history of Poland to a new acquaintance, you find out much later that he or she is an expert scholar in this area. It would be impolite and immodest for the acquaintance to point that out to you at the time. Most likely you will have to learn these facts from another mutual acquaintance.

In all forms of communication, whether oral or written, subtlety, imprecision, and vagueness are typical. Exact facts and figures are avoided. Anyone can find obvious examples of this in the local newspapers, where trends are expressed in "more" or "less" but not in terms of how *much* more or less. U.S. Americans, conversely, prefer precise figures and rankings (see Chapter 16).

Work Habits

The British view of work tends to be pragmatic but less so than the U.S. view. Britons prefer "muddling through," which usually results in finding the most expedient rather than the most innovative solutions. The French, who prefer to emphasize pure theory, sometimes have difficulty understanding the perspective of their more empirically inclined British counterparts. Similarly the Germans, who prefer a deductive form of thinking, contrast sharply with the inductive British.

Paradoxically, the average Briton will obey any rules that are spelled out or stated in exacting detail. Their strong sense of order and tradition dictates that they do what is right, and written instructions and legal signs indicate what is right. Unlike in many other countries, where rules and laws may or may not be obeyed depending on the circumstances, it is a common sight in Britain to see lines of people and cars waiting patiently in a way that would make members of other more hurried and anxious cultures cringe. It is understandable, then, that the British would shy away from having too many rules and written laws because they would tend to obey them strictly.

Most Britons prefer to work for other people rather than for themselves. Only about 10% are self-employed. Overall, in the business environment there is more formality between different levels in the hierarchy, which is more rigid than in America, and formality in dealings between employee and superior is greater. Adler (2007) gives an example of a U.S. executive who went to London to manage the company's English office. This executive noted with annoyance that visitors had to go through several people—the receptionist, the secretary, and the office manager—before seeing him. The English explained that this was usual procedure and without it the executive's status would be compromised.

Similarly, Laurent in a classic study (1983) analyzed diversity in concepts of management among executives in 12 Western countries. Twice as many British as U.S. managers felt that hierarchical structures exist so that everyone knows who has authority over whom, and twice as many British thought that there was an authority crisis. The British were also more in favor of well-defined job descriptions, roles, and functions. This is consistent with living in the traditional British house, with its floor plan divided into many small rooms, each with a designated purpose.

Trade union membership has declined in recent years, but about 26% of the British workforce is unionized. The relationship between unions and management tends to be adversarial, but in recent years the unions have deemphasized the use of the strike weapon.

The most important abilities of managers are seen as conducting meetings efficiently and having good relations with subordinates. It is a convention that instructions should be disguised as polite requests. Combined with British reserve, this makes for a distant relationship in which both sides are constantly on their guard. Fairness is the most important arbiter of management style.

Meetings, in general, are a significant part of the workday in Britain. Business decisions are typically made jointly and usually discussed, ratified, or implemented at a meeting. These meetings are generally informal, beginning and ending with social conversation, and individuals are expected to make a contribution, even if it is only in the form of questions. Ideas and opinions are normally encouraged, but their value to the group depends heavily on the status or seniority of the person stating them.

Egalitarian and Individualist

Hofstede's (2001) study points out that the British accept only small power distances between individuals and believe that all people should have equal rights. The GLOBE study (House et al., 2004) confirmed that England had undergone a significant cultural change since the 1970s, moving from a traditionalist society to one that is being challenged by a liberal culture in which individuals are expected to succeed on the basis of merit. The GLOBE researchers suggest that business leaders of the future will not succeed by using an authoritarian approach but by understanding how to provide energy, vision, and inspiration.

Although the British are seen as more individualistic than collectivist in Hofstede's study, individualism in the British sense tends to find its expression in eccentricity and nonconformism rather than initiative and competition. Also, the British are often uncomfortable and unwilling to take a stand unless they know that the group consensus will support them. Efforts to avoid disharmony among group members will smooth over all but the most fundamental disagreement. For this reason, even as consumers, the British will frequently accept indifferent treatment from businesses with little complaint. Such acceptance may reflect social class differences. If a customer does complain, the response will quite likely be a patient explanation of why the customer is wrong and how the business's actions are justified.

The British also normally prefer to work within the security of a group with which they can identify. They feel motivated when they see the work as useful to themselves and see others striving to achieve the same goal. The basis of social control in Britain, as in most Western nations, is persuasion by appeal to the individual's sense of guilt at transgressing social norms and laws. Indeed, this works particularly well in Britain because of the strong sense of tradition—a belief in the right way to do things and "not letting the side down."

Most British identify hard work, education, ambition, ability, and knowing the right people as the means to get ahead. However, these factors often must be accompanied by regularly moving from one company to another to achieve success. This is due to the fact that in many organizations, one must still wait for a higher up to be promoted, move on, or pass away to make space for an employee promotion.

Women make up nearly 50% of the workforce in Britain, which is much higher than in other European countries, even though Britain provides low maternity benefits and little child care support. Economic necessity has driven women into the workforce. Because they are paid less than men and many are willing to work part-time, companies are happy to have them. Do not expect to find a significant number of them in the higher levels of management or in technical careers. For instance, only about 20% of the information technology workforce is female. Women still feel that the glass ceiling is alive and well and that men are much more favored for promotion in today's Britain. However, one of Britain's strongest leaders in modern history, Prime Minister Thatcher, was known throughout the world as the "Iron Lady." Women who find themselves in positions of authority can and do demand respect. In fact, far more women than men in Britain are training to become doctors, and women are found to be better at generating financial returns ("The Importance of Sex," 2006). Recent information released by the Office of National Statistics, however, indicates that women are losing full-time jobs much faster than men as companies downsize during the Great Recession that started in 2008. The situation is exacerbated by the elimination of thousands of state jobs, held largely by women.

The Royals

Speaking of respect, no one draws more than the queen. There is a magical and mystical quality about the royal family, and especially the queen. As might be expected in a tradition-bound society, the most glamorous and somber events involve royal processions. The queen's coronation was complete with decorative pomp and pageantry, a ritualistic anointment with oil, and crowning.

More recently, however, the scandal pages and gossip newspapers have been filled with the less noble actions of various members of the royal family. This is nothing new: Throughout the history of the royals (or any family so unrelentingly examined), there have been some demonstrations of less than perfect behavior. However, in a democratic society, it is also no surprise to find a constant questioning of the necessity and future of the monarchy: Should the throne continue to exist? Should the royals pay taxes? And so on. In answer to these charges, one must remember that in the queen are embedded notions of history, tradition, civility, and national pride, and one third of the British population still dream of meeting her (Michon, 1992). However, the royal family did begin paying yearly taxes in 1992, which implies a narrowing of the gap between the royal family and the ordinary citizen.

The British people hold the royal family and the tradition of the monarchy very dear in their hearts and minds, and the queen and her nobility are constant reminders of the brilliant past of the British empire, the worldwide respect and awe afforded her and the nation throughout the world, and the hope and dignity of the future. The untimely death of Princess Diana in 1997 reinforced the popularity of the monarchy. It also caused many British to display their emotions much more than they normally do, and commentators are still trying to discover why the British were willing to let down their "stiff upper lip." By and large, this emotional display was probably more the exception than the rule. The excitement that was recently generated by the wedding of Prince Charles and the late Princess Diana's son, Prince William, to Kate Middleton and the enthusiastic reception the young couple received on their overseas visits is perhaps an indication that the monarchy is being rejuvenated. The British put on a grand ceremony like no other country on Earth. The world continues to be fascinated with all things British and young British royalty as it is rebranded for the 21st century.

In conclusion, our discussion of the British suggests that they tend to be steadfast and traditional in orientation, and the traditional British house is an apt metaphor for understanding the country and its people. A report, specifically commissioned by Prime Minister Gordon Brown in 2008 to assess the strategic challenges facing Britain in coming years, concludes that the country is uniquely positioned to succeed if it harnesses the skills and talents of its people and provides them with opportunities throughout life to face the challenges of globalization. It remains to be seen to what extent Britain's success will be determined by the aftermath of the global financial crisis; the draconian spending cuts proposed by the government; and, in particular, debt crises in various European countries, which pose a threat to the stability of the EU and other economies. However, change in Britain does not come rapidly, and it will probably not do violence to the traditional, favored ways of the past. The British people cohere strongly to a set of cultural values that are uniquely theirs, that have served them well in the past, and that—with modification—should help them adapt successfully to a rapidly changing world.

PART VI

Cleft National Cultures

A cleft nation is one in which the major ethnic groups are so clearly separate from one another in terms of values that it is difficult to form a national culture. These groups tend to be insulated from one another, particularly if they do not share the same or similar religions and value systems. In some cases, one may have difficulty identifying a cultural metaphor expressive of the major values of all of the ethnic groups living in such a nation. However, it was possible to identify cultural metaphors for all of the nations treated in this part of the book.

We have categorized Italy as a cleft national culture not because of ethnic groupings but, rather, because the north and south are radically different from one another in terms of value orientations such as collectivism and individualism. It is generally felt that the greatest novel about Italy, The Leopard (di Lampedusa, 1958/2007), reflects the sharp differences between the north and south. While this is a simplistic interpretation, there is truth in this characterization, even among those who feel that Sicily is in the boot of Italy and only partially representative of the south. As we will see, it is less difficult to classify the other nations as cleft cultures.

CHAPTER 18

The Malaysian
Balik Kampung

*We solve problems through unity and friendship. Malaysia is one nation
with one people. Our strength lies in our unity and is drawn from our determination to involve Malaysians from all religious and ethnic backgrounds
in the progress and prosperity of our nation.*

—Former prime minister Abdullah Badawi (March 2, 2008)

A few years ago in a faculty seminar at the Universiti Kebangsaan in Malaysia,
Martin Gannon was explaining the concept of the cultural metaphor, that is,
an activity, phenomenon, or institution with which all or most individuals
of a cultural group closely identify and that reflects underlying values. However, in the
case of a nation or national culture, these individuals would be its citizens. As
explained in Chapter 1, ideally the activity, phenomenon, or institution should be
unique or distinctive, and preferably it should be difficult for outsiders to understand
how it expresses underlying values. Some faculty members immediately observed
what many foreign visitors to Malaysia also experience, namely that the three major
cultural groups—the native Malays (about 65% of about 28 million people), Indians
(7%), and Chinese (26%)—seem to be so different from one another that it is nearly
impossible to identify such a national cultural metaphor.

Indeed, Samuel Huntington (1996) has argued that a national culture such as that
in Malaysia is cleft: Its various ethnic groups are so separate that it is difficult to unite
them into a common culture. Gannon pointed out that if a nation's citizens cannot
identify one cultural metaphor about which there is general agreement, the possibility
that the nation will survive in its current form is highly uncertain. From this perspective,

former prime minister Mohammed Mathadir's emphasis on Asian values, although sometimes anti-Western in tone, expresses a search for cultural metaphors.

After a spirited discussion, Rozhan Othman, a professor of management and marketing at Universiti Putra Malaysia, suggested that the *balik kampung*, the periodic return to the village, would probably be a representative cultural metaphor. As he explained, the patterns of behavior associated with it tend to be defined and predictable across all three cultural groups. For instance, when the nation was waging war against internal communists a few decades ago, police would wait outside a village and allow a prominent communist to have the festival dinner during *balik kampung*, after which they immediately arrested him.

Malaysia gained independence from the British in 1957. It has evolved from a rubber and tin economy to one of the world's emerging industrialized nations in a little more than 50 years. It is similar to many developing nations undergoing rapid industrialization, particularly those in Southeast Asia where ethnic groups are so sharply delineated. Almost half of the nation's population lives in urban areas, but many of these city residents are newly or recently arrived. Hence their attachment to traditional and rural values is understandable. In fact, the capital city of Kuala Lumpur with its world-famous and iconic Petronas Twin Towers has been described as a city whose sections loosely represent groups from specific rural areas and even villages.

In 1995, to ease pressures in the overcrowded capital city, the government decided to build Putrajaya (named after the country's first prime minister, Tunku Abdul Rahman Putra) as a garden city of the future about 25 kilometers (15 miles) from Kuala Lumpur. The city, which plays the role of the federal government administrative center, is part of the Multimedia Super Corridor project of the Malaysian government and is designed to be environmentally friendly and to showcase modern and Islamic architecture. Across the lake from Putrajaya is Cyberjaya ("Cyber Success"), which aspires to be Malaysia's Silicon Valley and is home to 500 information technology companies and two universities. Today, Malaysia is one of the world's most advanced Muslim nations and ranks 53 out of 179 countries on the 2011 Index of Economic Freedom (T. Miller, 2011).

Malaysia's history greatly influenced the occupational structure and separation of its various ethnic groups. The British, as part of their divide-and-rule policy, brought in Chinese to work as laborers in the tin mines, and these workers were not allowed to acquire land. The most promising alternative was to engage in trade, and today the Malaysian Chinese are one community of the expatriate Chinese who reside in many nations. Most of the Chinese are both Confucian and Buddhist. In contrast, Indians were recruited to work either as laborers on the rubber plantations or as laborers and clerks in the railway service. Indians working on the plantation live in villages in estate housing apart from the Malays; those in the railway service tend to live in towns. Hinduism is their main religion. The Malays as a general rule live in villages and work either as rice farmers or as fishermen. Almost all of them are Muslims.

Thus these three ethnic groups were separated not only by their languages, religion, and traditions but also by their occupations and geographical concentrations. These separations were magnified by the British practice of opening up English schools mainly in the towns; rural schools, which tended to be Malay and Indian, used the native languages, Malay and Tamil. Before 1957 only those who had acquired an English education had the opportunity to advance to tertiary education. This requirement restricted the possibility of achieving social mobility through education for Malays and Indians.

As might be expected, these sharp divisions facilitated the race riots of 1969 against the Chinese, who over time had become wealthier than the Malays and Indians. In response, the government devised a system of equal opportunity called *bumiputras* or "sons of the soil" to help the Malays; the Indians were not included, however. This policy seems to be working for the Malays, at least partially, although cronyism is a major problem in the awarding of government contracts. Companies seeking a listing on the local stock exchange are required to have a *bumiputra* shareholding of at least 30%. The policy has also given rise to so-called Ali Baba arrangements in which a Malay serves as a front to obtain the license and a Chinese businessperson runs the enterprise.

In 2010, Prime Minister Najib Razak initiated reforms waiving this requirement in 27 service and financial subsectors in order to attract foreign investment. In what has come to be called "Najibnomics," the prime minister, who took over in 2009, has been trying to enact economic reforms so that Malaysia can continue as a global economy and to keep voters happy. In the process, he may end up alienating both foreign investors and his political base. Malays are not pleased with his attempts to reform the *bumiputra* policies of the past.

In 2011 the World Bank reported that the policies pursued by the government have been a critical factor in the brain drain of non-*bumiputras,* who make up a majority of the Malaysian diaspora (Sani, 2011). This finding was based on interviews conducted in conjunction with Harvard's Kennedy School of Government. The largely Chinese interviewees identified lack of opportunity and noninclusive policies as the reasons they left Malaysia for Singapore and other countries. Many Indians—who on average have higher incomes than the Malays—have experienced great difficulty; the rubber plantations no longer provide employment for most of them, and they have been forced to live in shantytowns near major cities where they can obtain work. They also resent the "creeping Islamization" in the country as evidenced by the demolition of "unauthorized" Hindu temples built during the colonial era and the strict guidelines about the building of non-Muslim places of worship. In recent years, the country has witnessed a series of interfaith disputes following decades of harmonious ties among Malaysia's ethnic groups. In 2009 scores of Muslims marched with a severed cow's head (cows are sacred to Hindus) to protest the government's plans to build a Hindu temple in a largely Muslim neighborhood. The site was later moved, and 12 Muslims were fined as punishment for organizing the protests. In 2010, following a court verdict that the word *Allah* could be used by Christians in Malay language publications, firebomb attacks broke out in non-Muslim areas.

Political parties tend to be based on the three ethnic identifications, and the prevailing attitude seems to be "let sleeping dogs lie" because the economy by and large has been prosperous over the past 35 years. There are, however, some worrying signs. For example, many Chinese withdraw into ethnic enclaves and send their children to Chinese schools, thus depriving them of interactions with children from Indian and Malay cultures. They are also a large part of the brain drain referred to earlier. About 90% of Chinese children attend Mandarin-language state-financed schools, and 70% of young Indians are taught in Tamil. Malaysians, therefore, become used to segregation from an early age. In fact, 50 years after independence, it is sometimes lamented that the different races eat, learn, work, and socialize separately, giving the lie to the idea of one united Malaysia.

Three characteristics of the *balik kampung* are highlighted in this chapter, namely returning to nearby roots, authority ranking, and reinforcing basic values and behaviors. We treat each of them in turn. As we will see, the *balik kampung* is a cultural metaphor that encourages the integration of these three major as well as minor ethnic groups.

Returning to Nearby Roots

Immigration has many effects, among them physically separating individuals from their root culture by thousands of miles. This can be a heart-wrenching situation, as the plaintive songs of immigrants to the United States and other nations during the 19th century attest. For almost all such immigrants there was no hope of ever returning to the root culture, so they were forced to adopt new values and behaviors to meet the demands of their new situation. In contrast, Malaysia represents a nation undergoing rapid industrialization but one in which the immigrants to the cities are from nearby rural areas, a pattern found in many developing nations. Thus describing a cultural metaphor for Malaysia should prove helpful for other such nations as they modernize.

Returning periodically and regularly to their rural roots nearby is our first characteristic of *balik kampung,* for ironically the diversity of Malaysia's ethnic groups provides a metaphor apt enough to describe the Malaysian culture. In many societies, differences in religion and tradition are sources of divisiveness. But in Malaysia religious and traditional celebrations provide rituals common across all ethnic groups. During such festivals, *balik kampung* is very prominent, although it obviously occurs at other times as well. During these celebrations, major cities, which are normally teeming with people, are transformed into veritable ghost towns.

For example, from 1996 through 1998 the major Muslim festival Hari Raya ("the day of celebration") and the Chinese New Year fell on consecutive days, and cities were deserted in favor of the villages for several days. During the Hindu Deepavali festival or Festival of Lights, a similar pattern emerges. *Balik kampung* is more than just traveling away from the hectic city to enjoy a few days in a serene village. It represents a critical integrating element of the Malaysian value system, that is, the attachment that Malaysians have to their origins and families. The rituals performed during religious festivals help to shed light on the importance of *balik kampung* and the values associated with it. A significant feature of *balik kampung* is that it provides an occasion for the entire extended family to get together, and family members typically gather under one roof for the celebration. In most Malaysian families, this means three generations: grandparents, parents, and children. For some families the living room is transformed into a huge bedroom. Currently, the police are partnering with some neighborhoods so that Malaysians can "*balik kampung*" during their specific holiday without worrying about their vacant homes, as neighbors and the police participate in joint patrols to keep their homes safe. This practice has recently been tried out very successfully in the Selangor state in Malaysia.

Religious rites play a critical role in the celebrations of the three ethnic groups. The festivals provide a time for reflection, atonement for past sins, and personal reformation. Among the Malays, the Hari Raya represents a victory over self and temptations after fasting during the whole month of Ramadan. As Muslims, the Malays pay the *zakat*, a form of alms, to purify their wealth and property; they also seek forgiveness from each other on this day. Among the Indians, the Deepavali Festival or the Festival of Lights commemorates the victory of Lord Rama, who was reunited with his wife Sita following a 14-year exile and after having killed the demon king Ravana. This is the most popular interpretation and is recounted in the epic poem *Ramayana*. Another interpretation for the celebration is the success of Lord Krishna, one of the three main Indian gods, in killing the demon Narakasura. The common theme is the triumph of good over evil. Indians begin this festive day by taking a bath in oil to symbolically wash away their sins.

A ritual common to all three ethnic groups during these festivals is the audience with the elders. Among the Malays, the children take turns kneeling before the parents to pay their respects and seek forgiveness. The Chinese take turns bowing before the parents and wishing them a happy New Year. In some traditional Chinese families, each child presents the parents with a small cup of tea and wishes them good health. Among the Indians, the children kneel before their parents and seek their blessing. In all three traditions, the eldest child begins the ritual, and the other children then join in. Age is important in determining status and position in the family.

In all three traditions, children are given gifts of money. The Malays and Indians have adopted the Chinese practice of putting the money in small paper envelopes called *ang pow*. Gifts are also exchanged among relatives, neighbors, and friends. Among the Malays and Indians, the gifts are usually in the form of food and special delicacies made by the family during the festival. Among the Chinese, a favorite gift is mandarin oranges. Deceased parents and grandparents are also explicitly remembered. Many Malays will stop to clean their parents' or grandparents' graves and offer prayers after going to the mosque. Among the Chinese and Indians, family members pray for the departed ones at the family altar in the home.

After performing the prayers, having breakfast together, and greeting the elderly, the three ethnic groups begin visiting others in quite a similar manner. On the first day of the celebration, they mainly visit their relatives and neighbors. Only then do they visit friends, and the Malays generally do not do such visiting until the second day.

A common practice across all ethnic groups is having an open house during the festivals at which all Malaysians are welcome. Anyone can come for a visit without making a prior appointment and be assured that he or she will be welcomed. In many instances, the festival dinner becomes a multiethnic celebration involving friends, colleagues, and business acquaintances from all three ethnic groups. The Hari Raya celebration lasts 1 month, the Chinese New Year 15 days, and the Deepavali 1 week. Although some Malaysians have adopted the practice of having visitors on specific days during these periods, visitors are welcomed at any time. Even the king, prime minister, and ministers have open houses on specific days.

Although we have been emphasizing the festivals, many Malaysians do *balik kampung* monthly and even weekly because it is relatively easy to return to their nearby roots. Parents use these periods to remind their children of their humble origins and teach them the courtesies of traditional Malaysian culture.

Authority Ranking

Using Alan Fiske's (1991a) typology, we can describe the three ethnic groups as cultures emphasizing authority ranking; Triandis and Gelfand (1998) employ the term *vertical collectivism* in a similar fashion. According to Fiske, members of authority-ranking cultures are able to rank individuals in terms of power and prestige, but there is no common unit of measurement; that is, the data points are ordinal rather than interval. For example, 2 is greater than 1 and 3 is greater than 2, but 3 is not 2 times greater than 1. This tends to give rise to powerful leaders whose orders are accepted without question, as the power of leaders becomes exaggerated in the minds of followers, who have difficulty calculating the exact amount of power that a leader possesses. However, such leaders are required to take care of group members in return for such unquestioned loyalty. Behaviorally, authority-ranking cultures manifest themselves in elaborate bowing in which the lower-ranked person bows more deeply than does the superior. However, in recent years the handshake, which signifies equality, has replaced or supplemented the traditional bow. This is true of most Asian cultures. There is a much stronger psychological relationship found in authority-ranking organizations than in Western organizations, where only rational-legal authority bonds individuals to one another (Weber, 1947).

Thus Malaysians are very conscious of and sensitive to status in an organization's hierarchy. This is consistent with both Hofstede's (1980a, 1991) finding that Malaysia is a high–power distance nation and the more recent GLOBE study (House et al., 2004) where Malaysia scores relatively high on power distance. In business dealings, it is customary to send someone of equal rank to deal with the counterpart from another organization. Failure to do so will normally be interpreted as not showing proper respect to authority and tend to vitiate future business dealings.

Similarly the importance of age as an authority-ranking device is reflected in the honorary title *Dato,* which accompanies an award bestowed by the king; it literally means grandfather. In Malaysia this indicates that the person is wise and honorable, even if the person is relatively young or middle-aged, and Malaysians are expected to call this individual by the honorary title. It is difficult to imagine a middle-aged Western person who would be comfortable with such a title.

Also, other phrases tend to emphasize the importance of age. Among the Malays, elders are considered as *lebih awal makan garam,* which translates as "having tasted salt earlier." The Chinese say *wo' che' yen tuo' kuo ni che' fan,* which translates as "I have eaten more salt than you have eaten rice." Furthermore, it is expected that the younger members of a family will not start eating until the elders have begun. There are even rules for order of movement when walking, although these are not as strictly enforced today. In all three communities, politeness also requires that a person should never sit with feet pointed directly toward someone, especially someone older.

Even within the extended family, all three ethnic groups employ specific titles for family members according to ranking and position. These titles are much more complicated than those used in Western nations. For instance, the Malays refer to their uncles and aunts not by name but by rank: The eldest uncle would be termed *Pak Long,* the second uncle *Pak Ngah,* and so on. These and similar terms tend to reinforce the concept of authority ranking and high power distance. Addressing Malaysians properly while doing business is a complex matter for Westerners who are unfamiliar with the naming practices in Malaysia's various ethnic groups. Most businesspeople should be addressed by their proper title and name, and it is better to err on the side of formality and follow the lead of your Malaysian host.

Reinforcing Common Values

As countless immigrants have discovered, it is difficult to maintain the values of your root culture when thousands of miles separate you from home. To hold onto these values, it is important to reinforce them, at least on a periodic basis. As our discussion has already indicated, such reinforcement is possible with the *balik kampung,* particularly in the area of authority-ranking symbols. However, the *balik kampung* goes far beyond authority ranking, as it is a dynamic forum in which common values and behaviors are reinforced. Some of these are family-focused collectivism, maintaining harmony and preserving face, reaffirming religious traditions, and adjusting to other cultural groups.

Family-Focused Collectivism

The individual's relationship with the family is considered critical in all three groups, and this translates into a close relationship between the family and community. Among the Malays, living harmoniously and cooperating with other families in the village are important, for in the recent past the only way that families could work the rice fields was by pooling their labor and resources. Such working together is known as *gotong royong* among the Malays, and it is also practiced during weddings and funerals. Neighbors will work together to prepare the food and setting for the wedding celebration. Likewise during funerals, neighbors will help one another prepare the grave and make arrangements. This is one reason why there are so few professional funeral services in Malaysia.

Being part of immigrant communities, Chinese and Indian families tend to emphasize the importance of their relationships with the clan and trade association. In the recent past, it was only through such self-help organizations that these two groups were able to pool their capital to help each other start their businesses. Thus events such as weddings and funerals tend to reinforce basic values common across all three groups and constitute a major reason for periodically completing a *balik kampung*.

The importance attached to collectivistic values is particularly highlighted by the *pok chow* system found among Chinese laborers. *Pok chow* literally means gang contracting, and it represents a group of workers who get together by mutual consent. A *pok chow* group is essentially a work group whose members decide on their own rules, division of work, the remuneration given to each worker, and even the election of the leader (Hamzah-Sendut, Madsen, & Thong, 1989). In recent years, Western firms have employed a similar system, self-managed work teams, which collectivistic systems have emphasized for centuries, and it is little wonder that both Hofstede's (1980a, 1991) study of 53 nations and the GLOBE study (House et al., 2004) of 62 cultures indicate that Malaysia is highly collectivistic.

Most Chinese and Indians in Malaysia are third- or fourth-generation Malaysians and cannot be described as classic first-generation immigrants. Likewise, many Malays today live in urban areas and no longer rely on agricultural activities. Still, studies indicate that a great emphasis on collectivism remains in all three groups (Md. Zabid, Anantharaman, & Raveendran, 1997). Thus it is not surprising that Malaysians tend to prefer a participative approach to decision making, both at work and outside of it. In negotiations compromise and collaboration are preferred to confrontation and the winner-take-all approach that seems to be common in the United States. This emphasis on moderation is called *chung* among the Chinese (Wang, 1962), and it reflects the Koranic concept of *ummatan wasata* among the Malays. As indicated previously, authority ranking reinforces collectivism, and all of the age-related rituals during *balik kampung* tend to keep it alive.

One of the most interesting results of collectivism is that Malaysians have a tendency to hold an entire group, and sometimes a nation, responsible for the misconduct of a person or a few people from that nation. As such, criticism by the media or nongovernmental groups from a foreign country about human rights or environmental issues is attributed to the country as a whole. Westerners tend to find such behavior as bordering on paranoia. To Malaysians, the experience of being exploited and humiliated during colonial rule has made them wary of losing face due to criticisms meted out by foreigners.

Harmony and Face

While *balik kampung* reinforces family-focused collectivism, it also serves as a means for maintaining harmony and preserving face. In a highly collectivistic culture, great importance is attached to maintaining harmony and building relationships; self-centered individualism, which would detract from these activities, is normally viewed in a negative manner. One of the important ingredients in building harmony is to avoid doing anything that can disgrace and humiliate others.

Preserving respect and dignity is fundamental to understanding Malaysians. Among the Malays, this is termed *maruah,* while the Chinese refer to it as "face" and the Indians use the closely related term *thanmanam.* Face is the unwritten set of rules that everyone is expected to follow to preserve individual dignity and group harmony. Whereas the West and East both seek to protect and preserve face for all, people from Asian nations such as Malaysia also attempt to *give* face so that everyone is a winner, at least to some degree. One never knows when additional interactions with others will be necessary, which is another reason for giving face.

To maintain harmony and preserve face, Malaysians have developed elaborate courtesies and rituals. The *balik kampung* provides an important venue within a social context in which to preserve face. If a personal offense or slight has occurred, an individual can attempt to correct it during, before, and after *balik kampung,* as happens during family meetings involving younger adults and their elders. At the very least, the individual can offer prayers and alms as a way of alleviating a sense of shame. While Malays seek forgiveness from one another, they are not expected to mention, and usually avoid mentioning, any specific mistake or error. In this fashion harmony is maintained while debate over specific issues is avoided. Members of collectivistic cultures tend to respond more to a sense of shame at having hurt others than to a sense of guilt, which seems to be more important in Western nations.

Malaysians are sensitive about maintaining face and will try to avoid disgracing others, particularly in public. In extreme situations, some Indians consider suicide preferable to accepting a loss of face, which motivates others to protect them from experiencing it. Similarly it is common for a Chinese businessman to withdraw from negotiations if he feels that the outcome will make him lose face. Westerners need to be aware that sometimes they may receive a quick yes during negotiations while their Malaysian counterparts are actually finding an appropriate way to deliver a polite and final no at the end of negotiations without engendering a loss of face for anyone.

Malaysians frequently defer to the more senior or elderly member of the organization, who will generally be the first to speak at a meeting. As suggested above, however, the most senior person is expected to be responsible and should respect his juniors. At least partially for this reason, heated debates tend to be uncommon, and it is expected that the most senior member will consult with subordinates, although he may withhold critical information if he feels doing so is in the best interests of the group. If you are a member of a delegation, it is important to line up in order of importance so that the most important or senior person is introduced first.

All three ethnic groups emphasize the need to be polite even while disagreeing. An abrasive and confrontational style is problematic. Speaking with a raised voice, shouting, and swearing are inexcusable, as the person subjected to this kind of behavior will suffer a loss of face and the instigator will experience a loss of respect that is difficult if not impossible to recover. Speaking in calm, gentle tones is highly valued, and it is never appropriate to point at anyone with a forefinger or to pound a fist into the palm of a hand to make a point.

Thus Malaysians engage in a great deal of high-context communication, and this includes avoiding the word *no* when disagreeing with another person (Hall & Hall, 1990). Westerners commonly believe this is dishonest and annoying, but Malaysians are simply trying to avoid damage to a relationship. As stated earlier, a deeply ingrained culture of politeness demands that a Malaysian not disagree openly; therefore, the word *no* is rarely heard. Differences tend to be stated in a tactful and polite manner. Heated debate tends to be uncommon. Often, a polite but insincere yes is simply a way to avoid giving offense and preserve face. Likewise Malaysians sometimes use subtle and indirect words to convey their meaning, for example, using proverbs and idiomatic expressions. It is little wonder that Westerners frequently employ third parties to clarify communication during negotiations. No is often conveyed through these third parties.

Malaysians also use third parties, but they do so when they expect that the outcome of a particular negotiation will be potentially embarrassing. Among the more traditional Malays, it is common for arranged marriages to occur, and the man's parents will send the third party to the woman's parents to inquire about her availability. If for some reason the woman does not want to consider the man as a potential groom, both families have avoided an embarrassing situation. Only after the woman's parents have responded positively will the parents from both sides meet so that his parents can propose that a wedding take place.

An anecdote may help to highlight the elaborate and complex ways in which Malaysians communicate. A hostess was entertaining her guest at a dinner at home. The guest was hungry and was hoping to have another helping. However, she noticed that there was no more food at the table. Rather than asking for another helping directly, she complimented the hostess on the beauty of the plate that had been used to serve food. The hostess noticed that the plate was empty but did not want to say that there was no more food. Rather, she showed the pot used to cook the food to the guest. She then explained to the guest that she had cooked the food in the equally beautiful pot, thus showing the guest that the pot was empty. This enabled the guest to understand that the food was finished without the hostess being forced to say so. Of course, this anecdote is exaggerated, but it does indicate the lengths to which Malaysians will go to maintain harmony and preserve face.

Similar communication patterns can be found in many situations. For example, during *balik kampung* both the visitor and host know that serving food is part of the festival. Yet the visitor will always make it a point to tell the host not to trouble himself or herself with preparing something. Likewise the host will always apologize for not making adequate food preparations, even though the meal is elaborate and sumptuous. Malaysians also engage in the practice of using rhetorical greetings similar to the British "How do you do?" Malaysians will ask, "Have you eaten?" or "Have you taken food?" even if they don't expect to offer food, and the polite response is "Yes," whether or not you are hungry. Similarly, you are not expected to reveal the details of your itinerary when asked, "Where are you going?" A simple "Nowhere important" will suffice.

Religious Values

We have already suggested that the *balik kampung* is particularly important during religious festivals. Malays will offer special prayers on the morning of the Hari Raya, as will the Chinese on the eve of the Chinese New Year and the Indians on the morning of Deepavali. All generations of a family will participate in these religious rites.

As Muslims, Malays pray five times each day, and this practice is continued during *balik kampung*. Malays engage in prayer services when someone moves into a new house or when a firm occupies a new building. Likewise, a Malay organization usually celebrates its success by having its employees offer a thanksgiving prayer to Allah. Many Chinese shops and offices have an altar for the owners to offer prayers, and, as indicated in Chapter 26, Chinese homes frequently have family altars. At some work sites, some Chinese workers will build their own altar.

Among the Indians, the same attachment to religion is evident. In some factories, a Hindu altar featuring several prominent Indian gods is erected so that Indian workers can pray at work. The Indians are similar to the Chinese in that they tend to offer prayers in the morning and evening, and they are similar to the Muslim Malays in that Friday is a special prayer day. Many Indians either fast or observe a vegetarian diet on Fridays, even during *balik kampung*.

One interesting new phenomenon in this progressive Muslim nation is the unprecedented popularity of a reality TV show called *Imam Muda* or "Young Imam." It is an *American Idol*–style serious search for the country's most eligible young religious leader. Ten young men in sharp black suits are judged on a variety of tasks such as the reciting of Koranic verses, washing of corpses, counseling young couples, and slaughtering sheep according to Muslim practices. At the end of each round, one person is sent home. The last one standing wins a scholarship to the al-Madinah University in Saudi Arabia, a job leading prayers at a Kuala Lumpur mosque, and an expense-paid trip to Mecca to perform the Hajj pilgrimage (Hookway, 2010). It is so popular that the second season in 2011 was opened to competitors from other Muslim countries in the region. Islam is the most widely practiced religion in Southeast Asia with more than 240 million followers.

We have already described gift-giving practices during the festivals. Westerners are frequently surprised by the degree of gift giving that occurs in Asia, and many Western businesspeople have belatedly requested that their home offices airmail a large number of gifts that they can give to their counterparts at various ceremonies and dinners. All three ethnic groups engage in a great deal of gift giving, as it is viewed as an ideal way to maintain harmony and save and give face. As described earlier, gift giving is a common practice among Malaysians during *balik kampung*, at least partially for these two major reasons.

There is, however, an element of reciprocity in this relationship. The person given the gift cannot refuse it, as this would involve a loss of face. At the same time, he or she is now obligated to the person giving the gift. Among the Malays this is called *hutang budi*, which roughly translates into a debt of deed. The person receiving the present need not reciprocate immediately but is expected to remember the *hutang budi* when the giver asks for assistance at a later date.

This custom of reciprocating is important in building long-term relationships. Non-Malaysians may find this practice exploitative, especially when practiced by some Malaysian businesspeople seeking favors. However, refusing a gift is ill-advised. Rather, the recipient should reciprocate immediately by giving a gift of similar value, which signifies that *hutang budi* has been paid.

Of course, religious sensitivity and custom should be observed when giving gifts. Malays do not appreciate alcoholic beverages as gifts or food containing pork. Meat should come from animals slaughtered in accordance with Islamic rites. Similarly the Chinese give gifts in even numbers, for example, a pair of pens rather than a single pen. However, the Indians prefer their gifts in odd numbers. Among the gifts that should not be given to the Chinese is a clock, which is considered a bad omen, as the Cantonese word for *clock* also means "to go to a funeral" (Craig, 1979, p. 37). There are other "dos and taboos" that can be easily learned by consulting books specializing in this area (see, for example, Morrison & Conaway, 2006).

Coming Together

Thus far we have emphasized practices and behaviors that reinforce common values and behaviors across the three groups but that occur only within each group. But *balik kampung* also exemplifies a certain paradox about the Malaysian culture, for through it each of the three groups reinforces not only its identity but also the larger identity of being Malaysian. Malaysians of all groups and religions will join their fellow Malaysians to celebrate the respective festivals. There is evidence that certain customs formerly practiced by one ethnic group during the festivals have been adopted by the others. In a similar fashion, a Malaysian may comfortably switch languages in one sentence. For example, the first two words may be Tamil, the next three English, the next three Malay, and the last one Chinese.

In employment, more organizations that formerly hired from only one ethnic group have expanded to include two or three of the groups. This is partly because of the governmental *bumiputra* policies but partly because a nation undergoing rapid industrialization needs to employ its citizens as productively as possible. As suggested above, Prime Minister Najib Razak wanted to put Malaysia on the path to becoming a high-income nation by 2020. To this end, he enacted reforms, identified US$444 billion of private sector–led projects to champion, and promised to change the *bumiputra* policy. The cost of the *bumiputra* policy is becoming too high because of the backlash and brain drain among the other ethnic minorities and lack of sufficient innovation, research and development, and entrepreneurship. The government is trying to reverse this brain drain by turning Johor on the southernmost tip of peninsular Malaysia into an Asian hub for Western education. Famous English colleges (e.g., Marlborough College) are building replicas of themselves in this part of Asia. In return for putting up a lot of the money to finance these educational institutions, the Malaysian government wants universities to teach subjects such as engineering because they will be most useful to Malaysia. However, in order to attract foreign students, the government has had to waive restrictive regulations that govern the country's own universities, and this does not sit well with local students ("A Reverse Brain Drain," 2011). The Malaysian people also want reforms in the election system. The Coalition for Clean and Fair Elections, also known as *Bersih* ("clean" in Malay) is comprised of 62 nongovernmental organizations and has been actively agitating for a major overhaul of the process.

Despite these deep rumblings, the general approach taken by Malaysia to nation building also reflects an emphasis on the mutual adjustments of the three ethnic cultures so that harmony is preserved. Before his retirement in 2003, long-serving Prime Minister Mahatir Mohamad (or Dr. M as he is popularly known) declared that Malaysia should attempt to forge a united "Malaysian nation" by 2020. To this end, the government initiated a new national service program to bring thousands of young Malays, Chinese, and Indians together to do community service, intermingle, and discuss the future of their country.

Another example of mutual adjustment is that while the Malay language has been adopted as the national language, Tamil and English are still widely used. Mandarin and Tamil vernacular schools continue to operate, and many are funded by the government. The state-owned TV station has regular news broadcasts in Malay,

Mandarin, Tamil, and English. Although Islam is the state religion, freedom to practice other religions is guaranteed by the constitution. Anyone traveling through Malaysia will come across mosques, temples, and churches throughout the nation. Unlike some nations in which only the festivals of the majority are public holidays, the following are classified as public holidays: the Muslim Hari Raya celebrations, Chinese New Year, Buddhist Wesak, Hindu Deepavali, and Christmas.

This, then, is Malaysia, whose underlying values are expressed in the *balik kampung* of the three major ethnic groups. In many ways Malaysia and, to a lesser extent, other Southeast Asian nations such as Thailand and Singapore represent ideal laboratories for demonstrating that ethnic groups seemingly radically different from each other can be forged into a common identity over time. The *balik kampung* with its emphasis on returning to nearby roots, authority ranking, and reinforcing common values is critical in this endeavor. Thus far the *balik kampung* has helped to integrate rather than separate the three groups and aided Malaysia in its pursuit of what Berry (1990) has identified as ideal: allowing individuals to maintain their own cultural identities while simultaneously adopting new values supportive of the cultural identity of a larger group, such as a nation. The ideal of a united Malaysian nation is still a work in progress, but values and practices are in place to address the grievances of minorities and propel this multiethnic democracy toward that goal.

CHAPTER 19

The Nigerian Marketplace

A stroll through the alleyways of any West African market makes clear that most goods bought and sold by the "mama benzes" and "marché mamas" aren't exactly part of the technologized global marketplace. Rather, they're the products of West African, and particularly Nigerian, industry.

—Amy Chua (2003, p. 108)

Nigeria is a dream worth striving for because we are unique among Africans. All we need to do is revamp the system by which we elect our leaders, devolve power from an overweening central government to local authorities, diversify our sources of revenue, make corruption and election rigging crimes punished by death for now (desperate times call for desperate measures). This way we'll be on our way to becoming an economic powerhouse of global dimensions. That's the Nigeria I live for. Otherwise, I'll be living in France by now. One thing I fear the most is that my children will grow up in the Nigeria of today.

—Austin Inyang, Lagos, Nigeria, weighing in on a BBC News
website dedicated to discussing what it means to be
Nigerian 50 years after independence

Nigeria represents both the hope and the despair of Africa, a continent ruled by European colonial powers for much of the 19th and 20th centuries. Nigeria itself was ruled by Britain until 1960 and has been an independent nation for 52 years. Although the country is rich in natural resources, its ruling classes have squandered them irresponsibly. Nigeria is Africa's leading oil producer with revenues of $59 billion in 2010. Oil has been both a blessing and a curse. Corruption is widespread; Transparency International, in its annual survey of corruption among nations, consistently ranks Nigeria as among the most corrupt nations. Most government revenue comes from oil, making the economy particularly vulnerable to fluctuations in demand for oil. However, the *Economist* ("The World in Figures," 2010) forecasts a growth rate of 5.8%–7.0% based on the performance of the oil sector and strong performance by non-oil industries. Nigeria ranks 111th out of the 179 nations on the 2011 Index of Economic Freedom, as compared to other African nations such as Mauritius (12th) and Botswana (40th; T. Miller, 2011).

Nigeria's 151.5 million people constitute a little more than half of the population of West Africa and make Nigeria Africa's most populous country. Gross domestic product (GDP) per person is about US$1,370 per year, which is just about 24.1% of South Africa's GDP per head of US$5,680. Nigeria is among the lowest in national rankings on the World Bank's Human Development Index with a ranking of 51.1 in 2010. Of the Nigerian population, 70 percent live on less than US$2 per day, while members of Parliament are paid huge salaries. Furthermore, Nigeria's tropical weather subjects its citizens to a higher incidence of disease than residents of the more temperate parts of Africa. Along with many of its African neighbors, including South Africa, Nigeria has a low life expectancy of about 48 years as compared to 75+ years in the world's developed countries.

For almost all of its postcolonial history, the nation was ruled by the military. When he became president in 1998, General Abdulsalam Abubakar forthrightly described the nation's plight in the following way: "Currently, we are the world's 13th poorest nation. Given our resource endowments, this sorry state is a serious indictment" ("First Things First," 1998). In 2000 he handed over power to a democratically elected president, Olusegun Obasanjo. Ironically, it was Obasanjo who, as military ruler in 1979, had supported the first democratically elected government in Nigeria's history. Unfortunately that government was short-lived, and military rule returned after 1983. The April 2007 election of Umaru Yar'Adua had many logistical problems but marked the first time that political power was transferred from one civilian government to another and bodes well for postindependence Nigeria's future. Mr. Yar'Adua died in 2010, and his vice president, Goodluck Jonathan, took over as acting president in 2010; Goodluck was then elected in April 2011 in an election that won general approval from international observers.

As a modern political entity, Nigeria came into existence in 1914 when the British, under the leadership of Frederick Lugard, amalgamated three of their West African colonial territories: the Colony of Lagos, the Southern Nigeria Protectorate, and the Northern Nigeria Protectorate. Each of the three territories, in turn, had been constructed by the British out of a diverse collection of indigenous kingdoms, city-states, and loosely organized ethnic groups through treaties or outright conquest. Thus Nigeria as a geopolitical entity was, in effect, a creation of British imperialism. Nigeria remained a colony of Britain until it gained independence in 1960. Sir Ahmadu Bello, the premier of the Northern Region at independence and a "founding father," called the amalgamation "the Mistake of 1914," and some Nigerians to this day blame their problems on this "mistake." Others acknowledge, however, that the British were only part of the problem. As the great Yoruba leader, Obafemi Awolowo, who worked closely with the British, put it, the population was not ready for independence, lacking a "sense of civic responsibility" (quoted in Cunliffe-Jones, cited in Kaplan, 2010).

Archaeological evidence attests to millennia of continuous habitation of parts of what is now Nigeria. One of the earliest identifiable cultures is that of the Nok people, who inhabited the northeastern part of the country between 500 BCE and 200 CE. The Nok were skilled artisans and ironworkers whose abstractly stylized terra-cotta sculptures are admired for their artistic expression and high technical standards (Burns, 1963). High-quality bronze art at Ife and Benin City in the southwestern parts of the country also predated the arrival of Europeans in the region. Over the centuries, successive waves of migration along trade routes into Nigeria from the north and northeastern part of the African continent swelled the population, which eventually became organized along tribal lines into kingdoms, emirates, city-states, and loosely organized ethnic groups. This was the setting the early European adventurers, notably Portuguese navigators, found when they first made contact with the people of the coastal regions in the 14th century.

The marketplace is an appropriate metaphor for understanding the culture of the people of modern Nigeria. In this context, the marketplace refers to the physical areas of a city, town, or rural village where indigenous commercial activities are concentrated. According to a report in the *Economist*, the Onitsha market in southern Nigeria looks as busy each and every day as any main street in a rich country during the Christmas shopping season. The shops are stacked high with goods, the streets are jammed with customers, and many call this the world's biggest market ("Africa Rising," 2011). Around 3 million people visit daily to buy commodities like rice, high-end goods like computers, and everything in between. The marketplace metaphor has a special significance because the bulk of the history of the region up to modern times can be summed up in one word: *trade*. Many of the ancestors of modern Nigerians first migrated to the region along trade routes; the slave trade was primarily responsible for the arrival of Europeans in large numbers; and after the abolition of the slave trade by the British in 1808, the need to enforce abolition and to replace the trade with legitimate commerce was a primary motivation for the British to maintain a presence.

For centuries before the arrival of the Europeans, the marketplace was the community center for a town and the surrounding settlements. It was the center of commerce, the local town hall, and the main social center all rolled into one. This characterization is still true in the rural areas where about two thirds of the Nigerian population still lives. Market networks link many towns and villages. The networks consist of major markets held on specific days and attract traders for miles around. In the past, such networks were the conduits through which new commodities, outside influences, and immigrants reached local communities.

The characteristics of the Nigerian marketplace that stand out include its diversity, its dynamism, and the balance between tradition and change. Each of these strongly reflects modern Nigerian society.

Diversity

The typical Nigerian marketplace, especially in the bigger towns, is a sprawling, usually bustling place where virtually every commodity is available. As a general rule, the market is divided into rows of covered stalls, with a narrow aisle separating each row. Each row of stalls is assigned to a specific commodity, ranging from perishable foods to household electrical appliances. Sellers of similar commodities often unite to form market associations to look after common interests. The marketplace is where the vast majority of people shop for their daily needs. This is the case even in the urban centers where there are modern department stores. The roadside stalls, called *Buka,* also represent an opportunity for a good meal; the best local cuisine is to be found here. Commodities in plentiful supply include fresh meat and fish, vegetables, household goods, electrical appliances, jewelry, building materials, clothing, and traditional medicinal herbs. Nearly everything is available either wholesale or retail. In addition to commodities, the marketplace offers services, which include privately operated taxi and bus services to any part of town, heavy hauling, appliance repair, custom tailoring, and secretarial services.

The major marketplaces are usually centrally located, with a network of roads linking most parts of the town to the market. Intercity transportation hubs are usually located in close proximity to the main markets. The wide range of goods and services available and the size, relative importance, and modern nature of each market compared to others in the area are aspects of diversity that evoke the diversity of Nigeria as a whole.

The diversity of the Nigerian culture is one of its hallmarks. In a country about the size of Texas and New Mexico combined, there are about 300 ethnic and subethnic groups, with as many distinct languages and dialects. Often a dialect is clearly understandable only to the inhabitants of a town and its immediate environs. Just as the marketplace is clearly divided into sections by commodity and into subgroups by market associations, so too is Nigerian society clearly delineated by ethnic and language differences. But just as the separate commodity sections form an integral whole to serve a common clientele, so too does Nigerian society try to forge a national identity out of the widely diverse ethnic groups artificially joined into a nation by the British.

The heterogeneity of Nigerian society is physical, social, religious, and linguistic. Each ethnic group is concentrated in clearly defined geographical areas that its people have occupied for centuries. The same is true of the subethnic groups. Two large rivers, the Niger (from which the name of the country was derived) and the Benue, form a Y that divides the country into three parts. Each of the three parts is dominated by one of the three main ethnic groups: the Yoruba, the Hausa-Fulani, and the Ibo (or Igbo). The Yoruba are the only major ethnic group with a traditional aristocracy, and these elites are the most influential. Although the power and influence of the aristocratic class has diminished over the years, they are still a major social force in Yoruba society. Yoruba-speaking ethnic groups also dwell beyond the Nigerian border in the Benin Republic.

The Ibos are located primarily east of the Niger. Although they are more densely concentrated in their primary geographical area, they are more fragmented politically than the Yoruba or the Hausa-Fulani. The Ibos are notable for their business acumen and strong work ethic. They also have a long tradition of democracy and express strong antimonarchy sentiment with the common name Ezebuilo, which roughly translates as "A king is an enemy" (Achebe, 2011).

The Hausa-Fulani occupy most of the area to the north of the Niger and the Benue, an area more than twice as large as the two southern regions combined.

In most cases, differences in physical features among ethnic groups are not significant enough to reliably distinguish a member of one group from another. In the past, permanent facial markings were used to distinguish members of ethnic groups. Their primary purpose was to identify friend or foe in battle rather than to serve as bodily decoration. The practice of facial markings has been largely abandoned in modern times. Today names and attire are more reliable indicators of ethnic membership than physical attributes.

The Social Structure

With so many different ethnic groups and languages, it would seem that defining the contours and structures of this highly heterogeneous society is impractical. Admittedly it is difficult, but it is not impossible. There are several reasons for this. First, despite the great number of ethnic groups, four of them—Yoruba (21%), Hausa and Fulani (29%), and Ibo (18%)—comprise nearly 70% of the Nigerian population. As the Hausa and the Fulani have intermixed over the centuries, they are now commonly regarded as a homogenous group.

Second, the correspondence between language and ethnic group varies. Several groups may speak essentially the same language and have similar cultural characteristics but prefer to identify themselves as separate entities due to differences that span centuries. For instance, the Yoruba have at least 20 subethnic groups, each of which vigorously protects its separate identity.

However, modernization and the federal government's adoption of policies that promote a sense of national identity have gradually resulted in the emergence of some common national characteristics. Examples of such government intervention include the establishment of English as the official language of government and commerce throughout the country, the practice of posting some federal employees to states other than their own, and the requirement that all graduates of postsecondary institutions complete 1 year of national service. The influence of the mass media, especially television, has also helped to break down cultural barriers among ethnic groups.

Nigeria has a long way to go in terms of interethnic harmony, however. Interethnic mistrust is deep and is a primary reason for the repeated failure to establish a viable Western-style democracy since independence, giving the military an excuse to establish authoritarian regimes for long periods of time. Although most Nigerians are patriotic and genuinely want their country to work, deep-rooted ethnic allegiance often takes precedence over national allegiance. As a typical example, the Egba are among the 20-odd subethnic groups of the Yoruba, but when the chips are down, an Egba considers himself an Egba first, a Yoruba second, and a Nigerian last. In the distant past, members of subethnic groups fought bitter fratricidal wars among themselves. Territorial expansionism, control of trade routes, and the desire to cash in on the lucrative slave trade were among the reasons for conflict. Writing in *My Nigeria*, Peter Cunliffe- Jones, grandson of Nigeria's last colonial governor, Hugo Marshall, suggests that his grandfather made a terrible mistake by not forcing the Yoruba and Hausa leaders (representing the major southern and northern tribal groups) to adopt a truly national constitution. Instead, they were allowed to adopt a federal structure that created regional power centers (cited in Kaplan, 2010).

International Comparisons

Geert Hofstede (2001), in his landmark analysis of the cultural differences across 53 countries, did not include a single black African nation. This was not because the multinational corporation in which the analysis was completed (IBM) had no subsidiary in any of them, for there was one in Nigeria during the period of the study. But IBM, along with several other multinational corporations, later chose to leave the country rather than comply with a new federal decree requiring 40% Nigerian equity in certain classes of foreign business investments. This policy illustrates an important aspect of the Nigerian psyche: a strong sense of national honor and self-worth. While Nigerians in general admire and actively attempt to emulate Western economic and social development, they are quick to take offense at real or perceived condescension on the part of Western expatriates.

The recent GLOBE study (House et al., 2004) included Nigeria and found it to be high on power distance, high on both institutional and in-group collectivism, medium on gender egalitarianism (classified in the same band as China, Germany, and the United States), and relatively high on uncertainty avoidance or risk aversion. Traditionally, a large power distance exists between social classes and between superiors and subordinates in most Nigerian ethnic groups except the Ibos. If the four major ethnic groups are ranked in order of power distance, the Hausa-Fulani would most probably score the highest, followed closely by the Yoruba, and trailed by the Ibos. The Hausa-Fulani are overwhelmingly Sunni Muslims who have adopted much of the Islamic world's rigid social order and way of life. The Yorubas' high power distance is tempered considerably by opportunity for upward mobility based on individual achievement. The Ibo were noted as an egalitarian society for centuries and have largely remained so.

Collectivism and high uncertainty avoidance are more evenly applicable to the bulk of Nigerian society regardless of tribal affiliation. Virtually all the disparate ethnic groups believe in the extended family system. Hometown associations are formed with the express purpose of improving the infrastructure and facilities in the community. For example, during the early years of national development, it was not unusual for a community to sponsor the overseas studies of promising local students in the hope that they would return to serve the community. Nigerians also score relatively high on uncertainty avoidance or risk aversion, preferring to deal with people and situations with which they are familiar.

However, some research suggests that the business-oriented Ibos are more individualistic than the other major ethnic groups. That is, they explain their success or failure in terms of their own abilities, whereas other Nigerian ethnic groups emphasize luck or the situation (see Smith & Bond, 1998). Given this research, we would expect that the Ibos would have a longer-term time orientation and would be more willing to sacrifice short-term enjoyment to attain long-term goals. The GLOBE study (House et al., 2004) classifies Nigeria as scoring relatively high on a future orientation toward societal practices. The authors were surprised to find that many developed countries scored lower on future orientation than developing countries. They argue that emerging and lower-income nations may "see a stronger need for taking a long-term perspective and sacrificing for the future because they must cope with scarce and limited resources" (Ashkanasy, Gupta, Mayfield, & Trevor-Roberts, 2004, p. 305).

In general, Nigerian society is heavily patriarchal, and both its dominant religions proclaim the superiority of males to females. Because of the taboos associated with open discussion of sexuality among women and girls, many women suffer silently from sexually transmitted diseases. According to data from the Nigerian government, Nigeria accounts for 10% of the global HIV/AIDS burden. There are thousands of HIV orphans, and life expectancy for both men and women has declined over the last decade.

However, there are some notable differences among the three major ethnic groups. The Hausa-Fulani, true to their Muslim religion, tend to consider women as subordinate to men in virtually every respect. This is not the case among the Ibos and the Yoruba, where women have traditionally faced relatively little opposition to their entrepreneurial spirit.

Social Dynamism

Nigerians have often been characterized as resourceful, pragmatic, entrepreneurial, and energetic (Aronson, 1978). In this context, social dynamism refers to the energy, vigor, and adaptability of Nigerian society. These qualities are readily observable at the Nigerian marketplace, which bustles with activity, especially on Saturdays when most families do the weekly grocery shopping. Traders hawk their wares in cadences particular to their commodity. The bargaining is energetic, with the burden being on the customer to negotiate a fair price. While many items have fixed prices, most do not, so the smart shopper must come to the market fully armed with knowledge of the latest fair prices. The shopper must also be savvy about the various shady characters who are attracted to the marketplace. The typical seller, in turn, has perfected the art of keeping a poker face in order to extract as much profit from the sale as possible without antagonizing the customer.

Many shoppers have favorite stalls that they repeatedly patronize. Such repeat buyers are often taken care of quickly, with the minimum of negotiating necessary to arrive at a mutually acceptable price. In recent years, sellers seem to have concluded that the time and effort spent on haggling are not worth the extra profit and have started to place a fixed price on as many items as possible. Prices are usually set by market or trade associations, and changes are frequently communicated by word of mouth several times a day.

Doing things quietly is not the Nigerian way, whether it is an argument, a political discussion, a celebration, or a sad occasion. Just as the market bustles with a cacophony of sights and sounds, so too do Nigerians complete most activities with gusto. The dynamism of Nigerian society is reflected in the business and political landscape, the attitude toward education, the manner in which the people celebrate holidays and family events, and their favorite leisure pursuits.

At independence, Nigeria's economy was engaged almost exclusively in the production of food for home consumption and commodities (e.g., cocoa, groundnut, and palm oil) for export. The vast deposits of oil and natural gas had not yet been discovered. Since then, successive governments, including the military regimes, have made the development of the industrial sector of the economy a priority.

Oil-Based Economy

Just as the local marketplace bustles from dawn to dusk with activity, so too Nigeria's more formal economic scene bustles with complicated deals and contracts. Nigeria has considerable crude oil and natural gas resources and has been a member of Organization of Petroleum Exporting Countries (OPEC) since the 1960s. This natural wealth has provided the resources to modernize the economy, especially during the boom years of the 1970s, when vast amounts of new crude oil deposits were being discovered in the coastal areas at the same time that prices of crude oil were steadily rising in the world market. At this time, the federal government took steps to ensure greater Nigerian participation in such key economic activities as banking, insurance, manufacturing, and oil production, which were then dominated by foreign companies or their local subsidiaries. According to some accounts, although the performance of the non-oil sector is growing, the country is still largely dependent on oil and gas earnings, and the origin of the non-oil growth is difficult to identify. As long as oil prices continue to rise, it will be difficult to estimate the long-run sustainability of Nigeria's upswing.

Unfortunately, only a small fraction (less than 10%) of the population controls much of this wealth. Many analysts see a direct link between crude oil and corruption and strongly argue for the creation of a system that will prevent politicians from having access to petrodollars. It is estimated that about US$400 billion has been siphoned from Nigeria's treasury since independence, making it very hard for the country to succeed despite its advantages (Achebe, 2011). The wide gap between the rich and the poor is a major concern for Nigeria's economic planners. For many years the federal government dominated and closely controlled the economy, but in recent years it has recognized the detrimental effects of meddling too much and has moved toward the establishment of a freer market.

The Nigerian political arena is not for amateurs or the faint-hearted, just as the marketplace is not for those who are not versed in the fine art of haggling. Politics in Nigeria is a rough-and-tumble game, and only the fittest survive. Politicians, including ex-presidents, are sometimes put in jail on questionable charges.

However, unlike the situation in many African countries, Nigerian political leaders are less inclined to impose a single-party state. The electorate is too sophisticated for that. Modern Nigeria is a federation of 36 states and a new federal capital, Abuja, which is located near the geographical center of the country. The states are further divided into 774 local government areas. The political framework is similar, by design, to the federal system of the United States, but the institutions and requirements reflect the needs and experience of the country. The federal government consists of an executive branch, a legislative branch, and a judicial branch. Each of the 36 states is similarly organized.

Officially Nigeria is a Western-style democracy, but the threat of authoritarian rule is never far away, and there have been several military coups. Nigerians are accustomed to waking up to a brand-new government that has taken shape overnight. They have learned not to let political instability interfere too much with their daily lives and business activities. One of the challenges for President Goodluck Jonathan will be to bring greater stability to the turbulent Niger Delta region, where kidnappings of foreign oil workers, gang warfare, and militant activity are quite common. This is despite the fact that billions of dollars of oil money have been funneled to this region under a federal formula that favors the oil-producing area. In fact, a ghostly high-rise hotel, a luxury shopping-center-in-waiting, a mostly empty large hospital, and incomplete housing projects dot the landscape, and out of US$30 billion in supplemental oil revenue funding, almost US$22 billion remains unaccounted for (Nossiter, 2011). Elsewhere, schools crumble and people live in squalor. This then is the paradox of Nigeria today.

Education System

Many of the traders and craftspeople in the marketplace are graduates of apprenticeships. In the same manner, Nigerian society believes that a sound educational system will provide the energy that will propel the country into the industrialized age. Parents who have the means hire private tutors, send their children to prestigious schools that may be far away from home, and give up their own comforts so that their children can do better than they have. Like the political system, the education system is patterned after that of the United States. One reason is that many of the policy makers in government were educated in the United States. However, Nigeria's federal government performs abysmally in the area of education.

Education is free and compulsory up to the sixth grade, but most students choose to go further, if they have the means. English is the official language of instruction. It is introduced at the primary school level and used exclusively at the secondary and postsecondary levels. The government, recognizing the value of a high level of literacy to rapid development, has tried to take advantage of oil wealth to implement a free education policy at all levels. It has not been able to achieve this objective partially due to the sheer size and cost of the educational system, which is government controlled at all levels. Admission to postsecondary institutions is limited and extremely competitive. Although these institutions continue to expand, they are currently not capable of admitting all the students who qualify for admission.

Furthermore, Nigerians are not shy about making a public scene when the need arises, just as the haggling in the marketplace is sometimes done with rancor whenever either party steps over the line of decorum. Arguments are typically carried on in a loud and animated manner, but they rarely lead to physical combat. Bystanders eagerly offer their own loud opinions about the ongoing dispute. The urban centers, especially in the south, are overcrowded, and there is a constant influx of students and job seekers from rural areas. Competition is intense for nearly everything. Jobs, housing, transportation, and other daily necessities of life are in scarce supply in the cities, even though cities receive a disproportionate share of federal development budgets.

So believing that it is a jungle out there, the smart urbanite steps out each morning prepared to survive another hectic day. Western expatriates usually, but not always, are untouched by all this hustle and bustle of daily life because they tend to live in the quieter, wealthier neighborhoods built in colonial times when the government and larger foreign companies built residential reservations for their expatriate staff.

Leisure Activities

Not everyone goes to the market to shop. Some go to take in the scene, browse, or meet friends. Nigerians take their leisure seriously and try to find the time to indulge in their favorite leisure activities. They are keenly interested in sports, and their preferred sporting activities reflect their dynamism. Wrestling was a popular sport in many parts of the country before the arrival of the Europeans. It is still popular, as is boxing. But neither comes close to the interest in soccer, as both a participatory and spectator sport.

Checkers is popular among the lower working class, and the game is typically accompanied by friendly banter and bets (nonmonetary). A favorite way to relax is to be in the company of friends who can trade war stories about the vagaries of daily life, pass on the latest social gossip, and solve the country's problems. Nigerians in general do not seek isolation and solitude; in fact they avoid them as much as possible.

Holidays and ceremonies are an important aspect of Nigerian culture. Both the Christian and Islamic holidays are nationally observed, as are local community festivals, some of which have been celebrated for centuries. Some local festivals were of a pagan nature but are now largely stripped of religious significance. Common ceremonies include weddings, the naming of a new child, and funerals. Such ceremonies often are lavish affairs, depending on the wealth of the celebrants. Ostentatious display of wealth is the norm, and the rich often welcome the opportunity to make a brash, bold, in-your-face statement to the world that they are rich and not ashamed to show it. Everyone knows what the status symbols are: the big wedding or funeral, the chauffeured car, the expensively tailored suits, and the big houses complete with servants quarters. There was even a time, during the oil-boom years, when owning your own jet was on the list.

Holidays provide a respite from what many in the populace regard as the rat race of daily life. Even the marketplaces are silent and empty on the major holidays. The favorite way to spend a holiday is to hold a feast or to attend one. Either way, holidays provide an opportunity to congregate and socialize with good friends.

Only a small percentage of the population, mainly the wealthy elite, enjoy recreation and leisure in the Western sense. They may play tennis or golf or go for a swim. At exclusive country clubs, admission is usually based on wealth, connections, and social status. The vast majority of the population does not have the means or the time to indulge in Western-style leisure, and the average Nigerian does not go on a road trip just to see the country or go for a hike in the woods just to commune with nature. In the cities Nigerians tend to frequent the ample nightclubs, movie houses, restaurants, and private clubs.

One form of recreation that is changing Africa is Nigeria's film industry, otherwise known as Nollywood. According to a report in the *Economist,* Nollywood, which is second only to its Indian counterpart Bollywood, produces about 50 full-length features per week. The influence of Nigerian films is so pervasive in Africa that Ivorian rebels are reported to have stopped fighting when a shipment of DVDs arrived from Lagos. Zambian mothers observed that their kids talk with accents learned from Nigerian television, and the president of Sierra Leone drew crowds at campaign rallies after inviting a Nigerian screen goddess to join him. However, this has generated a backlash not only from cultural critics who worry about the "Nigerianization" of Africa but also from other African governments, which have instituted protectionist measures in the form of high fees required of visiting actors, producers, and directors. Film plays an important role in fostering understanding across the different cultures on the continent and is replacing music and dance as the dominant medium. Overall, the success of Nollywood has spurred competition from other African countries and is perceived as the voice of Africa, an antidote to Western media portrayals of the continent ("Lights, Camera, Africa," 2010).

Balancing Tradition and Change

Modern Nigerian society is markedly different from the cultures that existed before outside influences began to take hold in the early 19th century. Nowhere is this more noticeable than in the way the center of political and economic power has shifted from local traditional rulers and their councils of senior chiefs to the educated elite, business magnates, politicians, and the military. No country wants to be an island, isolated from all outside influences. If outside influences threaten to engulf aspects of the society that are cherished by its members, however, then it is necessary to take actions to preserve them. This is true for modern Nigeria, which seeks to modernize without sacrificing cherished traditional values.

Among the facets of daily life that rulers in precolonial times tightly controlled were the local marketplaces, especially the most important ones. Among the Yoruba, for instance, the largest and most influential markets were situated in front of, or in close proximity to, the king's official residence, and they were called *oja oba* (the king's market). In some areas, the official title of the local head chief was *loja* (owner of the market). Virtually all markets are now administered by local government councils, which are popularly elected bodies. Although control of the markets has shifted from traditional rulers to the people, these rulers are still regarded in many places as the titular heads of the markets, especially in rural areas. Changes in market administration are indicative of the broader changes that have occurred in Nigerian society as a result of modernization.

Other notable aspects of culture and tradition that have changed considerably over the years include religious preferences, the traditional family compound, dating behavior, language, sports, and leisure pursuits. However, the changes are not universal. As a general rule, the rate of change in the urban centers has far outpaced that in the rural areas.

Power and Influence

In precolonial days, power was heavily concentrated in the hands of local kings and their chiefs. Palace intrigues and territorial expansionism through intertribal warfare were common. Again, an exception to this situation was the Ibos, whose egalitarian social structure did not allow for the concentration of power in any one individual or small group of rulers.

Although their power and influence have been largely curtailed by the establishment of more democratic political systems, traditional rulers still play an important role in their communities. They are regarded as the custodians of their people's legacy and identity, and they are usually at the forefront of the fight to defend traditional values against Western influence. In addition, some senior local traditional rulers, especially in the north, have learned to exert influence behind the scenes. Moreover, northern Muslim traditional rulers also tend to be their community's religious leaders.

Thus some senior traditional rulers have become even more powerful than if they still had direct political power. But they are no longer referred to in English as *king*. The most common English term used is *traditional ruler*.

When a traditional ruler dies, the eligible candidates campaign vigorously to win ascendancy to the throne, for there is almost never an automatic line of succession. Candidates are drawn from traditional ruling families, and only the adult male members are eligible. In some areas the chieftaincy is rotated, by tradition, from one ruling family to another.

Traditional rulers are selected by a council whose members are invariably called kingmakers, consisting of the senior chiefs in the community. The selection process varies from community to community. It is worth noting that while the selection process has largely remained unchanged, the criteria for selection have changed markedly over the years. Today candidates with adequate formal education who have distinguished themselves in a professional field are favored.

Church and Family

Major changes have occurred in the area of religion. The first religious incursions came from the north, when the Fulani under Usman Dan Fodio overran the Hausa and other northern states in the 18th century. The conquerors forcibly established Islam in the city-states that dotted the region. Usman Dan Fodio would have carried out his vow to expand his jihad (holy war) all the way to the sea if the British, who were then establishing a presence in the south, had not put a stop to his ambition (Burns, 1963). The early European explorers and traders entering the country from the south were quickly followed by Christian missionaries. Today only a small percentage of Nigerians still adhere exclusively to indigenous animist religions. About 50.4% classify themselves as Muslim, 48.2% as Christian, and 1.4% as other.

Many did not find the spirituality they needed in what they considered the sterile form of worship of the European Christian sects. Some were also turned off by the perceived condescension of the Christian missionaries. Indigenous Christian sects founded and led by Nigerians soon began to proliferate, especially in the Yoruba-dominated western region. Notable sects include the Cherubim and Seraphim sect, the Apostolic Church, and the African Church. What these indigenous sects have in common is a form of worship that is reflective of Nigerian society: less formality in worship, singing and dancing to lively indigenous Christian music, spontaneous audience participation during worship services, and a deep personal relationship with God. Today some of these sects are increasing their memberships at a rapid rate.

While the general population has welcomed many of the inevitable changes that have accompanied modernization, it has perceived others as socially regressive. An example is the way the traditional family compound has changed. In the past, as the male children in a family became adults, they were given plots of land adjacent to the family home on which to build their own houses in preparation for starting their own families; female members of the family were expected to get married and become members of their husbands' families. Today young adults are more likely to move to the cities, first to further their education, then to work or engage in business. In the cities, the relative scarcity of land and the high cost of building construction make family compounds impractical. The result has been a decline in allegiance to the larger kinship group. Urban centers continue to grow in size and population while rural areas stagnate or shrink.

Weddings are usually major events, with members of the extended family on both sides in attendance. Alternatives for weddings include holding them in the local magistrate court, a church, or mosque or having a traditional wedding in which the bride and groom wear Nigerian dress and Nigerian music plays in the background. Many couples choose a combination of the traditional wedding with one of the other alternatives. Most brides take their husband's surname immediately after marriage. Divorce was at one time rare but is becoming common due, in part, to the pressures of modern life and the decline of the family compound.

Language Evolution

Like the family structure, linguistic patterns have changed considerably. Because of waves of migration of young people from rural areas to urban centers, many of the 300-odd ethnic languages are now spoken by as few as 10,000 people. The three main languages—Hausa, Yoruba, and Ibo—are spoken by more than 65% of the population. It is telling that after 52 years of nationhood, very few Nigerians are interested in learning to speak another ethnic group's language.

Also, urban versions of the major languages have developed. For instance, *Lagosian* is the term given to the style of Yoruba spoken in Lagos, the former capital, which is in Yorubaland. Lagosian is a stylized version of spoken Yoruba, peppered with English words and considered by young Yorubans to be the most sophisticated version of the language. Yorubans also have a tendency to add an *o* at the end of words to add emphasis. When this is extended to English, words such as *sorry-o* are shouted to someone who suffers a misfortune (Harris, 2008). The Yoruba language is distinctive in that it is tonal, similar to Chinese. It is the only tonal language in Africa and has three tones.

Another urban language is pidgin English, which is spoken chiefly by the lower working class. It cuts across ethnic lines, providing a means of communication among the disparate ethnic groups that live and work side by side in the large urban centers. However, the Nigerians' English (a quaint combination of Victorian-era vocabulary and grammatical and syntax structures of indigenous languages) has given rise to some concern that they will not be understood in a globalized world. Eateries are *chop houses,* street children are *urchins,* a dead or jailed robber is often said to have met his Waterloo, and the infamous Nigerian email scams are committed by the "Yahoo-yahoo boys" (Harris, 2008).

Just as some markets have remained in the same location for centuries, selling many of the same traditional foodstuffs throughout that time, so too have some beliefs, practices, and social norms endured the onslaught of centuries of outside influence. Aspects of Nigerian culture that have survived colonialism and modern influences largely intact include seniority and authority relationships, social roles and status, a rigid class structure (where it existed), orientation to time, view of work, early socialization, the extended family system, and traditional festivals.

Seniority Rules

A strict system of seniority governs normal interpersonal relations. Children, for instance, are expected not to look their parents or elders directly in the eye while being scolded. This expected deference applies to any interaction in which one party is significantly senior to the other. The prerogative to use first names is granted only to close friends and superiors. It is considered an insult for a younger sibling to address an older sibling casually by the first name unless they are very close in age. An age difference of just 1 year is enough for an older individual to expect to be addressed respectfully.

A common way to address a superior respectfully is to precede the first name with a respectful salutation. Among the Yoruba, one way to do this is to precede the first name of the older sibling with *buroda* (derived from *brother*) or *anti* (derived from *auntie*). Both terms have English origins, and it is not clear how the Yoruba began to use them as a means of conveying deference. Parents are invariably addressed using the local equivalents of the Western *Dad* or *Mom*.

This seemingly stratified ordering by age group and seniority reflects the high power distance discussed previously. The larger the age difference or seniority, the greater the amount of deference expected. Methods of greeting seniors, parents, and other adults vary among ethnic groups, but they generally involve some bowing of the head, if the greeter is male, or bending of the knees, if the greeter is female.

In return for deference, the seniors are expected to guide, lead by example, and generally be supportive of their subordinates. Although the major criterion for determining seniority in social situations is age, there are instances where the senior in a situation is the younger person. In the workplace, for instance, a supervisor may be senior to much older workers from whom he or she may expect the deference accorded to seniors.

In business situations and among the educated, Western greeting behavior is more prevalent than traditional greeting behavior, but traditional greetings are still expected where the age or seniority gap is significant. This requirement does not extend to subordinate expatriates, who are routinely excused from traditional greeting requirements in favor of Western ones. Superior expatriates are not accorded traditional greetings either, not because they are not considered worthy but perhaps because they do not expect such traditions to be observed.

Work Attitudes

The Nigerian's attitude toward work is a study in contrasts and points to a deep-seated social problem that retards economic progress. On the one hand, entrepreneurs work prodigious hours to build and maintain their businesses. On the other hand, the average wage earner wants to put in as little effort as possible. Because the first group often must hire the second, conflict results. The attitude of workers is not a manifestation of an inherent laziness; it seems to be a manifestation of a lack of faith in the system. Many workers simply do not believe that advancement on the job is based on performance. They have been conditioned to believe that favoritism, nepotism, and other unfair methods are the usual means of advancement. This attitude is further reinforced by the fact that seniority (length of service) rather than performance is a common criterion for advancement, especially in the civil service. The effect of this attitude on national productivity is not difficult to fathom.

The same deep distrust of the establishment is the reason why Nigerians of all stripes dislike paying taxes. Wage earners cannot avoid having their taxes withheld, but entrepreneurs can and do work around the tax system without feeling the least bit guilty. The widespread incidence of official corruption and mismanagement is often cited as justification for cheating the government out of taxes. Quite a few entrepreneurs convince themselves that they can use the money for the public good better than government bureaucrats.

Women's Role

The role of women has not changed significantly over the years. They continue to bear the brunt of child care and household responsibilities, in addition to holding down jobs or running their own businesses. The typical Nigerian husband considers it beneath his dignity to perform household chores. There is often a clear delineation between the kinds of tasks, commercial activities, and jobs that men and women do. This distinction is very much in evidence in the Nigerian marketplace, where women far outnumber men both as traders and customers. The casual observer might infer from this that the marketplace is a female domain, but this perception is inaccurate. Although women have always outnumbered men in the marketplace, the men have wielded the real power behind the scenes. It was noted above that the marketplace was administered formerly by the local head chief and more recently by elected local government councils. Both the head chieftaincy and the councils are male-dominated institutions. The true picture is that while women dominate at the retail level, men dominate at the production, wholesale, and administrative levels of the market structure. In addition, some commercial activities are perceived to be either male oriented or female oriented. Sometimes there appears to be no logical reason for the distinction other than the mere fact that the activity has been a male or female preserve for as long as anyone can remember. For instance, butchers are almost exclusively male while fishmongers are almost exclusively female. Female-oriented activities are purposely avoided by men, and male-oriented activities are often closed to women, either overtly or covertly.

Women have been active in local and national politics for years, dating from the early colonial period, when market women rioted to protest the imposition of taxes on women. Politics in Nigeria is still largely male dominated, but women are making steady progress. The one area where women have distinguished themselves is in commerce. This is also just about the only area where society has given them wide latitude. The homes, streets, and markets of Nigeria are alive with women trading, and many women have built large-scale trading enterprises with little outside aid. An example is Monica Adeola and her Gorgeous Look embroidery shop in Lagos, which caters to diverse customers—the stay-at-home moms and the young professionals and laborers who are part of the growing middle class in Africa (Connors, 2011). However, Nigeria ranks 118th out of 134 countries on the World Economic Forum's 2010 Global Gender Gap Index, which measures the disparity between men and women in areas such as economic participation, educational attainment, and political participation. In comparison, South Africa ranks 12th and Iceland ranks 1st.

Overt or covert discrimination against women persists, however, because the typical Nigerian man, in the final analysis, was not raised to regard women as equals. Polygamy is legal, but it is neither encouraged by authorities nor tolerated by women. It is no longer fashionable among the educated class and has been steadily declining in recent years, except in the Muslim north.

Extended Families

The decline of the family compound has not resulted in a parallel decline in the extended family system, which is a cherished aspect of African societies. Both near and distant relatives are embraced as full members of the family. The extended family is the African parallel of Western social welfare systems. Members of extended families take care of one another, find jobs for young members, band together to help members in times of sorrow or hardship, intervene to solve marital problems, and celebrate one another's successes. When a member gets married or otherwise has a reason to celebrate, there is no need to send out formal invitations to extended family members because everyone knows they are invited and expected to attend.

In addition, Nigerians have always tended to be conscious of status differences. In the Nigerian marketplace, some retailers achieve prominence and become unofficial deans of the market or leaders of the market associations. Social status is important to Nigerians, but status consciousness is not the same as supporting a rigid social stratification system. In the past, the highest status was accorded to the king, followed by his chiefs. Other people of status might include war heroes, successful traders, or great farmers. Today, as in the past, Nigerians, especially men, aspire to be recognized by their community as people of "timber and caliber," which is a popular term connoting high status and integrity. Status can be earned through education, success in business, philanthropy, exemplary character, leadership qualities, or any combination of these. However, wealth by itself does not automatically confer status. The community may shun a wealthy man of dubious character and negligible philanthropy.

In modern Nigeria, one of the most sought-after status symbols is a chieftaincy title, which is considered to be higher in status than an earned doctoral degree. When an individual with an earned doctorate becomes the chief of his hometown, he may use the title *Chief,* followed by the title *Dr.* in brackets (as in Chief [Dr.] XYZ). A chieftaincy is highly valued because it is an affirmation by the community that the conferee is a community leader.

Although chieftaincies are of various ranks and importance, all conferees are eligible to use the title *chief.* There are separate title lines for men and women, for women also can be chiefs. Traditional rulers see two clear advantages in the modern chieftaincy system. It encourages successful citizens to be philanthropic because that is an important criterion for becoming a chief. Furthermore, it promotes the preservation of traditional culture and values, since it co-opts the conferee into the traditional structures of the community.

Ironically, the increasing popularity of chieftaincy titles has threatened the integrity of the institution. Many successful Nigerians feel incomplete without being recognized by their hometown with a chieftaincy. As a result, rumors of payoffs, favoritism, and award of chieftaincies to ineligible individuals sometimes surface.

The desire for status carries over into the workplace. Prestigious job titles and impressive offices are prized. People are often defined by what they do for a living and how high they have risen in their profession. However, most people work simply as a means of earning a livelihood; the concept of work for its own sake is not widely valued. And, as suggested previously, evidence of large power distance is prevalent throughout the workplace. Subordinates are expected to show deference, but it is not uncommon for superiors to have strong informal relationships with some immediate subordinates. The size of the power distance is roughly proportional to the vertical distance between the two parties on the organizational chart.

Perspectives on Time

Another area that highlights the balance between change and stability is that of time. There is a common misconception among Westerners that Nigerians, like many Africans, do not pay much attention to the clock. Nigerians are quite capable of going by the clock, and they are pragmatic enough to recognize when they should do so. In senior-subordinate relationships, subordinates are expected to be prompt, and they usually show up at the appointed time. Workers, despite their attitude toward work, usually report to work on time. Schoolchildren are routinely punished for arriving late to school. Nearly everyone who can afford a watch has one. Still, when possible, Nigerians are much more relaxed about time schedules than U.S. Americans.

However, certain economic and social conditions have contributed to a relaxed approach to time. In rural areas, there is usually no need to watch the clock because the pace of life is slow. In the cities, severe traffic congestion and an unreliable public transportation system make it difficult to foresee how long a trip across town will take. Although city dwellers readily start off early to arrive at their jobs or schools on time, they do not feel pressed to do the same for casual social engagements. Everyone understands the difficulties of being on time, so they are not offended when appointments are missed. Just as the trader at the market patiently waits for the next customer when business is slow, so too does the Nigerian host wait patiently for guests to arrive. Thus Western hosts should not be surprised if their Nigerian guests show up hours after the appointed time without apologizing profusely for the delay. However, when the issue is business, Nigerians will try their best to be prompt and apologize for being late.

There is a significant contrast in culture and values between the younger, college-educated generation and older generations, which as a rule are less educated. The older generations are more conservative in their views and are alarmed that traditional values are rapidly eroding among the younger generations. The elders fully support economic and social progress, but not at the expense of cherished traditional values.

Religious Conflict

In trying to strike a balance between tradition and change, perhaps the greatest difference is between the Muslim north and the largely Christian south. Most of the values, culture, and traditional institutions in the Muslim north have survived intact; it is ultraconservative compared to the Christian south. The typical northern Muslim, regardless of age group, is not impressed by Western manners, culture, and values. Muslims are more likely to identify with the culture and values of the Islamic world. Thus a Muslim community leader in the north is more likely to address a community meeting in either Hausa or Arabic than in English, even if both he and his audience speak English fluently. In fact, one of the threats to stability is the emergence of an Islamist group called *Boko Haram* (meaning "Western education is sinful") after sectarian violence in 2009. The group would like to see a wider application of Sharia law ("Northern Nigeria," 2011).

Some observers characterize the southern educated elite as trying to be more Western than Westerners. There is an element of truth in this observation. It is not unusual, for instance, for English to be the first language of the child of an educated southern elite rather than the parents' ethnic language. There is a stark contrast between the mainly Muslim north and the Christian and animist south: literacy rates are two thirds lower in the north than in Lagos in the south, income per head is 50% lower in the north, and fewer than 5% of the women are able to read and write in some northern states ("Northern Nigeria," 2011).

One of the greatest issues facing Nigeria is conflict between Muslims and Christians, particularly over the imposition of Sharia or strict Islamic law in the

Muslim communities; Christians are supposedly not subject to it. Penalties can be devastating, for example, having a hand removed for stealing $30. Only a few nations such as Saudi Arabia and the Sudan follow Sharia. In the year 2000, Sharia was introduced, and more than 2,000 people died in fighting between Christians and Muslims in the northern state of Kaduna; about half of this northern state is Christian, unlike most of the Muslim north. In 2002 another 220 people died in fighting between Christians and Muslims over the issue of having the Miss World Pageant in Nigeria during Ramadan. Such occurrences, while not the rule, are not rare.

The imposition of Islamic law in several states has deepened religious divisions and caused interfaith violence to erupt and separatist aspirations to take root. It has also caused thousands of Christians to flee. The announcement of the April 2011 election results was followed by violence in the northern stronghold of Mr. Jonathan's main opponent, General Muhammadu Buhari. The election results revealed a religious geographical divide with Jonathan doing very well in the predominantly Christian south and his opponent sweeping the predominantly Muslim northern states.

Throughout this chapter, we have attempted to offer an accurate portrayal of the people and culture of Nigeria. Like a snapshot, it does not include all the detailed nuances of this highly diverse society. Still, the image of the marketplace is critical for understanding traditional and modern Nigeria. It is an appropriate metaphor for many African nations that face the gigantic task of integrating diverse ethnic groups as they seek to modernize without losing the cherished aspects of their traditional cultures.

Most of the world and especially U.S. Americans know of Nigeria because of the email and other Internet-based scams that aim to part "gullible Americans" from their money. However, there is much more to Nigeria than this. The African continent as a whole has around 300 million people who earn incomes in excess of their basic needs, up more than 60% from a decade ago, according to the African Development Bank. Estimates suggest that Nigeria's informal economy is at least as big as the country's formal economy, which is about US$200 billion (Connors, 2011). Jeffrey Sachs, director of the Earth Institute at Columbia University, visited Nigeria during the week of President Goodluck Jonathan's inauguration. He suggests that there are five reasons for optimism: political reforms since 1998, democratic elections, the global wind in Nigeria's sails through trade links with Asia, development of best practices and advanced technologies, and Nigeria's commitment to tackling extreme poverty and disease (Sachs, 2011). He is very optimistic about the country, which he believes is on the verge of an economic takeoff. In a June 2011 report, two Morgan Stanley economists even made the bold prediction that Nigeria's economy had the potential to overtake South Africa's by 2025 and become the largest on the African continent (Mazen, 2011). With this in mind, we hope that this chapter provides a more complete picture of the fascinating subcultures that make up this populous and oil-rich African country.

CHAPTER 20

The Israeli Kibbutzim and Moshavim

The feuding over these stark hills, ridges, and valleys south and east of Bethlehem, a 27-square-mile region that includes the Nassar farm, is emblematic of the decades-old Israeli-Palestinian conflict—a struggle rooted in land.

—Richard Boudreaux (2007)

Israel goes out of its way to display its ugliest side to the world by tearing down Palestinian homes or allowing rapacious settlers to steal Palestinian land. Yet there's also another Israel as well, one that I greatly admire. This is the democracy that tolerates a far greater range of opinions than America. It is a citadel of civil society.

—Nicholas D. Kristof (2010)

As the opening quote by Nicholas D. Kristof suggests, Israel is a land full of stark contradictions. It is, in one sense, a classic cleft culture in which various ethnic and religious groups experience great difficulty living comfortably with one another (Huntington, 1996). Although most citizens are Jewish, the nation seems to be composed of tribes with radically different viewpoints and lifestyles, and 10 or more political parties vie with one another at any given time. Psychologically, it is more difficult to live in Israel than in many nations that have resolved or at least minimized their ethnic and/or ideological/religious differences, and various estimates indicate that 1 million Israelis out of a total population of 7 million and possibly many more have either emigrated permanently or live outside of the country on a semipermanent basis. However, many of these exiles will not openly admit that they are very reluctant to return to Israel permanently. Israelis would tend to view such an admission as traitorous or worse.

A perfect example of this psychological conflict and identity crisis is the comedy routine of a well-known Israeli trio, HaGashash HaChiver. An Israeli couple goes on a tour of the United States and stops to visit a relative's friends who had moved to the United States several years earlier. When the visitors ask their hosts when they plan to return to Israel, the host says: "You have caught us literally sitting on our suitcases, all packed and ready to go; we are just waiting until our son finishes college, and then we will hurry back to our beloved Israel." When the visitors inquire about the son's age, they are astonished to learn that he is "already 3 years old."

Before discussing the cultural metaphor of Israel, the kibbutz (kibbutzim in the plural) and its close cousin, the moshav (moshavim in the plural), we will provide some historical material that will shed some light on this small and complex nation. Although Israel was founded in 1948, its short history is as complicated as or more complicated than that of many older nations. Given its contradictions, it is difficult to identify a cultural metaphor that is expressive of the nation's basic values and, as suggested above, its conflicts. We have chosen the kibbutz because it is so intertwined with the nation's history and values, but some of these values have changed and are changing, at least in major segments of the population.

Zionism, Types of Judaism, and the Palestinians

Israel's place in history is directly related to its geography. This small country lies on the eastern coast of the Mediterranean. It is only 260 miles from north to south and averages 60 miles from east to west, sharing borders with the Arab nations of Lebanon, Syria, Jordan, and Egypt. The country's landscape is marked by abrupt changes from mountains to plains and from fertile green areas to harsh deserts. The diversity of the scenery is immense—there are more than 15 distinct geographical regions. Israel's population is 7 million, and 20% of its citizens are Palestinians.

The history of Israel has been characterized by a unique geopolitical position and frequent oppression. At various times it has been ruled by Christians and Muslims. In their early history, the Israelites, in contrast to the tribes surrounding them who believed in polytheism, worshipped only one God. For this belief they suffered persecution and enslavement, thus creating the condition for their flight from Egypt under Moses's leadership. Christianity and Islam trace their origins to Judaism and this belief in only one God; Muslims hold that Mohammed ascended to heaven from Jerusalem, while Christians maintain the same belief about Jesus, thus making the city sacred for all three religions and a source of conflict among them, particularly between Islam and Judaism. What sets Judaism apart from other major religions is its search for meaning in all aspects of life (H. Smith, 1991).

The opening of the Suez Canal in 1869 significantly increased the geopolitical and economic importance of the Middle East, and Jewish immigration began to grow significantly. Most of the newcomers came not for religious reasons but because of Zionism, a unique modern national and ideological movement.

Zionism, born in the last half of the 19th century, was the movement for the redemption of the Jewish people in the land of Israel. It derives its name from the word *Zion,* the traditional name for Jerusalem and the land of Israel. The movement gained strength because of the continued oppression and persecution of Jews in Eastern Europe and increasing disillusionment with their formal emancipation in Western Europe, which had neither put an end to discrimination nor led to the integration of Jews into the wider society. The Zionist movement aimed at attaining an internationally recognized, legally secured home for the Jewish people in their historic homeland.

Inspired by Zionist ideology, increasing numbers of Jews immigrated to Palestine at the end of the 19th century. These early pioneers drained swamps, reclaimed waste-lands, founded agricultural settlements, and revived the Hebrew language for every-day use. It was at this stage that the kibbutzim became intertwined with the history of Israel, as they were founded by the Zionists seeking to create a new society for the Jewish people.

The first kibbutz was founded in 1909, and there are now approximately 270 of them. Although many kibbutzim are still engaged in farming, others are involved in industrial activities. They are highly enterprising. For example, many have branched out into environmental businesses that have become highly successful (Wainer, 2010). They currently include about 110,000 individuals, down from a peak of 125,000 in 1990. However, the influence of the kibbutzim and their demo-cratic and egalitarian character on Israeli society is vastly disproportionate to their modest numbers.

The basic principles of kibbutz life are community ownership of all property, abso-lute equality of members, democratic decision making, the value of work as an end as well as a means, communal responsibility for child care, and primacy of the group over individuals. However, there are many pressures on the kibbutzim, and the moshav allows for private ownership of some property and for more individual freedom; the moshavim now account for more than 30% of all kibbutzim. Because of economic hard times, approximately 75% of the kibbutzim charge for meals, about 82% require pay-ment for electricity, more than 25% have introduced salaries based on sliding scales, and more than 30% charge for health care (Leggett, 2005). In this chapter, we will describe the kibbutzim and include some final remarks about the moshavim.

Previously, members of the kibbutz received no pay for their work. The commu-nity provided all their essential needs: food, shelter, clothing, medical care, and education. Children are raised with their peers, meals are usually eaten in the kibbutz dining hall, and members convene once a week to discuss and vote on issues. Jobs rotate among members. All positions of authority—such as those of the chief execu-tive of the kibbutz, plant managers, and supervisors—change every 2 or 3 years. Power is not permitted to accumulate in the hands of individuals. The kibbutzim range in size from 100 to 2,000 members and are small enough that the individual's role in the community is visible and tangible.

Because of the kibbutz's relative success as a social, innovative, political, and economic enterprise, it has attracted worldwide attention. Also, the kibbutz is a vehicle for obtaining insight into the Israeli character and the mythology from which the Israelis draw their self-identity. The perception of the kibbutz as an ideal existence stems from the initial goal of the founders: that the kibbutzim would be the core of society, rather than only an alternative.

A New Country

To understand the kibbutz fully, we need some historical background. After the Ottoman Turks were defeated in World War I, Britain took control of Palestine. Until World War II, consecutive waves of immigrants arrived, and an infrastructure of towns and villages, industry, culture, and health, educational, and social systems was developed. The kibbutzim were close to their Palestinian or Arab neighbors and had fairly good relations with them at the time. Meanwhile, immediately before and during World War II, Jews in Europe suffered immensely in the Holocaust; an estimated 6 million perished. Renewed calls for an independent state were raised.

In 1947 the United Nations General Assembly adopted a resolution calling for the partition of the land into two states, one Jewish and one Arab; 54.5% of the land was allocated to Israel and 45.5% to the Palestinians. On May 14, 1948, the state of Israel was declared. On the very next day a combined Arab force committed to the destruction of the new state attacked. Although Israel was badly outnumbered and suffered the loss of 1% of its entire population, it won 6 months later. About 700,000 Palestinians became refugees, most of them fleeing to UN camps in neighboring Arab nations, camps that still exist. These refugees became a pawn of the neighboring Arab nations and Israel in the political and military conflicts since 1948. Poverty is widespread and deep among all Palestinians.

In 1948 and immediately thereafter, the new state of Israel faced the daunting task of turning Zionist ideological dreams into reality. Immigrant absorption was an immediate priority. In its first 3 years, Israel welcomed 678,000 immigrants, many from the Arab countries, and in the process doubled its population. The nation's economic growth over the next decade was truly remarkable, especially in light of the fact that Israel has few natural resources and does not even have water in some major areas of the country. With the development of sophisticated farming and irrigation techniques, orchards and groves bloomed in even the most arid regions of the country. Tens and hundreds of new towns and agricultural settlements came to life, modern industrial plants were built, roads throughout the country were paved, and a modern army was equipped virtually from scratch.

This success could not have occurred without outside help, which has continued to this day. By 1991 Israel had become the single largest recipient of charity, grants, and assistance per capita in the world, the bulk of it from the United States. The U.S. government allocates more of its foreign aid to Israel than to any other nation; Egypt receives the second-highest amount.

Continuous War

In 1956 and 1967, Egypt moved aggressively against Israel, but in both wars Israel emerged as the victor. The 1967 war, also known as the Six-Day War, resulted in a devastating defeat for Egypt, Syria, and Jordan, as Israel gained possession of the Sinai Peninsula, Gaza Strip, the Golan Heights, the West Bank of the Jordan, and East Jerusalem. For the first time in 2,000 years, Jerusalem was again under Jewish sovereignty. However, the country relaxed its military posture, and the Egyptians and Syrians attacked again in 1973, this time on Yom Kippur, the holiest day on the Jewish calendar. Israel was caught by surprise, and although it won the war, losses were significant. In recent years there have been *intifadas* or uprisings by the Palestinians accompanied by guerrilla warfare and suicide bombings within Israel. Extremists in the Palestinian Territory and in the neighboring Arab nations vow to destroy Israel, which makes negotiations between political leaders from Israel and the Palestinian Territory extremely difficult.

Today Israelis are in the awkward position of living in a cramped geographical area within which the Palestinians also live, but separately. In the early 1980s, Israel withdrew from the Sinai and in 2006 from Gaza. It is doubtful that Israel will ever give up the strategically important Golan Heights, as it provides one third of Israel's water and is a buffer against invasion. Still, as Tolan (2006) points out, the Palestinians have fared even worse in terms of space, and some Israeli proposals would provide less than 20% of the original Palestinian objective of the whole of Palestine. There are, as indicated previously, Palestinians who are Israeli citizens (approximately 75% of Israelis are Jewish, 21% Arab or Palestinian, and 4% other minorities), and they fare better than the others. Still, there is discrimination against the Palestinian citizens, whose homes in the West Bank and East Jerusalem are sometimes confiscated and bulldozed by the Israelis to make way for Jewish settlers. The Palestinian Israelis have recourse to legal remedies, but their suits often fail. Also, the Israelis have built a wall separating Israel from the Palestinian Territory, thus creating an aura of overt hostility and perpetual warfare. For example, when there is high tension between Israel and the ruling Palestinian Authority, Israel will shut off its borders and not allow Palestinians to cross them, even to go to their jobs in Israel.

Further, Amnesty International has frequently cited Israel for violating the basic rights of the Palestinians. In the 1980s and early 1990s, there was great hope for and movement toward a genuine Palestinian state by both the Palestinians and Israelis, and it looked like the Oslo Peace Accord of 1994 would be the basis of a solution to this long-festering problem. However, this hope was dashed when an ultra-Orthodox student in 1995 shot and killed Yitzhak Rabin, the prime minister who led this effort. An increased level of deadly conflict between the Israelis and Palestinians followed, with the Palestinians suffering much more than the Israelis. As this book goes to press, there is a good chance that the UN will support the Palestinian Territory's petition for statehood.

Within Israel, many Palestinian or Arab Israeli citizens report feeling uncomfortable and threatened, and they have suffered unprovoked attacks. Even Israelis are divided on the issue of the poor treatment accorded non-Israeli Palestinians, and many Israelis also champion the movement for Palestinian self-rule and peace. An unlikely source of support for better treatment of the Palestinians has emerged with the creation of Rabbis for Human Rights, which has helped them recover some land through lawsuits in Israeli courts, despite fierce opposition from other groups in Israel. In fact, one of the great tragedies is that businesspeople on both sides of the conflict have actively attempted to create a Mideast economic community in which trade and commerce would flourish, but so far to little avail.

Religious Conflict

To complicate matters even further, Israeli citizens manifest a great variety of religious beliefs or lack thereof, which is one of the key reasons why there are so many political parties in the nation. The population of the Israeli Jews (excluding the 21% who are Israeli Palestinians and the 4% belonging to other minorities) is sharply divided along religious lines: 9% are ultra-Orthodox, 11% religious, 13% religious-traditional (that is, they are religious Jews who regularly attend synagogue but do not adhere strictly to all of the dictates and laws followed by the first two groups), 25% nonreligious-traditional (that is, they attend Jewish services episodically but are nonreligious, even to the point of being agnostic), and 42% secular.

Thus many Israelis are secular and even agnostic or atheistic in their beliefs and do not participate actively in Judaism or attend synagogue. At the other extreme are the ultra-Orthodox Jews who demand rigid adherence to all aspects of Judaism, including strict dietary laws and the cessation of all business activities during the Sabbath. They are also called the *haradim*, or those in awe of God. There have been instances in which such Jews have demanded that females sit in the back of public buses, separately from males. These Jews believe that religious laws and regulations should be given precedence over the secular legal system, at least in some instances. They refuse to serve in the military until the age of 24 and receive subsidies from the government to preserve Judaism. Other Israeli groups vary between these two extremes in terms of their adherence to tradition and change.

Jews in Israel are not differentiated by synagogue affiliations as much as by the manner in which they relate to the land and state of Israel (Friedman, 1989/1995). There are no Reform Jewish synagogues in Israel as there are in the United States and elsewhere. Members of such synagogues follow Judaic practice but in a much looser form than that found in Conservative Jewish counterparts. There is a much greater acceptance of outsiders and other points of view in the Reform Jewish synagogues. Although many Jews marry non-Jews—the percentage of intermarriage in the United States exceeds 50%—members of Reform synagogues tend to do so more than other Jews.

One of the issues surrounding Orthodox Jews is that the government supports their intense focus on religious study and observance. When the state of Israel came into existence in 1948, there was a shortage of rabbis and others who knew intimately Jewish history and its practices. Today, however, many of these adult males who are perpetual students receive government subsidies to study Judaism, and many of them live below the poverty level. Over 60% of ultra-Orthodox Israelis do not work compared to 15% in the general population, and when the prominent Rabbi Chaim Amselem suggested that they were a drain on the economy, his comments caused a major uproar (Kershner, 2010). The same situation exists among ultra-Orthodox women when compared to the female labor force (21% versus 50%). Also, the ultra-Orthodox have larger families, thus perpetuating poverty across generations. The Taub Center for Social Policy Studies released a report that shows, if current trends continue, 78% of primary school children in Israel will be either ultra-Orthodox or Arab Israelis by 2040 (Kershner). Unfortunately the Arab Israelis also have high levels of poverty and unemployment. Israel's labor force participation rate is only 55%, one of the lowest in the world. Given that about 30% of Israel's population is either Arab Israeli or ultra-Orthodox, the situation seems untenable.

Fortunately, other parts of the Israeli economy are doing very well. Once population is taken into account, Israel leads all other nations in the number of start-ups and the size of its venture capital industry. However, high-tech industries account for 40% of Israel's exports but only 10% of its employment (see "Beyond the Start-Up Nation," 2010, p. 60).

In this chapter the focus is on the Israelis, although clearly their troubled relationship with the Palestinians at least needs to be spotlighted.

To return to our cultural metaphor, debates about the viability of the kibbutz in a globalized economy reflect the intense debates among the various tribes of modern Israel, as we will see. Probably no other institution is as uniquely Israeli as the kibbutz, the collective farm that played a critical role in the Jewish settlement of Palestine and later in establishing and developing the Jewish state. As Lawrence Meyer (1982) describes it, "The Kibbutz is the ultimate symbol of pioneering Labor Zionism, the institutional embodiment of the dream of returning to the land, working it, receiving sustenance from it, and reviving an ancient culture in the process" (p. 327). As indicated above, the kibbutzim are making significant advances in green industries and have inspired the transfer of knowledge to create entirely new industries, such as the insight that then-nonexistent heart stents could be based on the drib-irrigation systems that kibbutzim members used to create conservational water systems in farming.

With this understanding of both Israel's and the kibbutz's origins in mind, it is possible to see how the kibbutz reflects many of the essential features of Israeli society and the Israeli character. First, the explicit social and ideological values to which the kibbutzim adhere are also manifested in Israeli society, although to a lesser degree. Also, the small size of both Israel and the kibbutz is related to specific behavioral outcomes, and the traumas that the Israelis have experienced have led to the evolution of a distinctive worldview and personality profile both in the kibbutzim and Israeli society. It is these points of comparison between the kibbutz and Israeli society that we will highlight.

Explicit Values

Most if not all societies possess explicit values that their members share, at least to some degree. In Israel these values are explicit in the kibbutz and, correspondingly, in Israeli society. They include democracy, egalitarianism, socialism, a group-oriented mixture of socialism and individualism, and a deep connection to the land.

One of the main features of the kibbutz is its practice of direct and total democracy. Almost all decisions and rules are voted on by all kibbutz members, and no major decision can be made by only one or a few individuals. Analogously, democracy is a deep-rooted Jewish value. Having to confront many perilous situations as a group rather than as atomistic individuals, the Jews developed a self-deprecating sense of humor that deflated pretentiousness and heightened a feeling of social democracy, out of which evolved political democracy. The concepts of social and political democracy were brought to Israel by immigrants from Western countries, but mainly by the East European immigrants who founded most of the kibbutzim before the establishment of the State of Israel in 1948. The successful preservation of political democracy occurred in part because of the disproportionate influence of kibbutz members in Israeli politics.

Formally, Israel is a parliamentary democracy consisting of three branches. The executive branch (the government) is subject to the confidence of the legislative branch (the Knesset, Israel's parliament), and the judiciary branch, whose absolute independence is guaranteed by law. The 120-member Knesset is elected every 4 years. The entire country is a single electoral constituency, and Knesset members are assigned in proportion to each party's percentage of the total national vote. In this way even very small parties that succeed in gaining only 1% of the votes are represented. This system of voting was a result of a preference for a government that would reflect not only one party but the consensus of at least half a dozen. Hence the system lends greater leverage to small and even miniscule factions and interest groups, and a good amount of bargaining occurs among the parties, some of it quite dishonorable. In 2011, for example, there were 66 out of 120 members in the ruling but minority coalition (consisting of six parties) in the Knesset plus noncoalition members from seven additional parties. In terms of membership, the smallest party had three members, and three other parties had four members. (See "Can the Doves Take Off Again?" 2011.) By contrast, the United States and only three other nations employ a "first past the post" system in which the party winning over 50% of the vote wields the most power. Debates in the Knesset are sometimes vitriolic.

Bargained deals often result in undemocratic concessions to religious splinter groups, which hold the balance of power between the main political blocs. Such concessions have led to strict Sabbath laws and laws such as those prohibiting the raising and selling of pork, civil marriage, and divorce. Many of these laws are unacceptable to a large portion of the Israelis, especially to those who are secular and cleave to Judaism's culture but do not regularly participate in religious activities or attend the synagogue. Still, on the 2011 Index of Economic Freedom, Israel ranks 43rd of 179 nations, which suggests that corruption and excessive bureaucracy are relatively low.

Although Israel is not a theocratic state, there is a significant overlap between the government and Judaism. As indicated previously, rabbinical law prevails in such matters as marriage, divorce, and the Sabbath, and sometimes there are conflicts between state laws and religious laws. For example, the Old Testament dictates that every 7 years, farmers should let their fields lie fallow. Modern Israeli farmers meet this requirement by technically selling their property to a non-Jew through the auspices of the local chief rabbi, who holds the check for 1 year and then destroys it. This formal practice has met the letter but not the spirit of the Old Testament since the founding of the state of Israel. However, one of Israel's two chief rabbis, Yona Metzger, changed this system by allowing local rabbis to decide whether the food raised in the 7th year was kosher; a determination that it was not would severely hurt the farmer. This issue became so important that the Supreme Court ruled that, if a local rabbi decided that the food was not kosher, an additional, more flexible rabbi would be appointed (Khalil, 2007). In 2010 dozens of well-known rabbis signed a religious ruling against the rental or sale of property to non-Jews. Although there was a backlash against this proposal, the fact that so many prominent rabbis signed this religious ruling brings into focus the constant tension between the secular government and Judaism.

The Army's Role

A prominent example of how important democracy is to Israel is the status of the army within the society. Although necessity has turned the army into an essential part of Israeli life, Israel is far from being a military society. Israelis spend a large portion of their adult lives in the army, both during their compulsory 3 years of service and then during at least 30 days a year as reserve soldiers, but they remain very much civilians. The Israeli army is highly professional, with a basic discipline similar to that of many other armies, but it is always the first preference to train the soldier by example, not by order and punishment. Amos Elon (1971), an Israeli author, points out:

> The army is not an aristocratic institution, as it continues to be in some democratic countries. There is no deliberate attempt to break the will of recruits. It is a citizen army, and the gap between officers and men is minimal. There are few privileges of rank. The Israeli military code bluntly states that officers have no privileges whatsoever, only duties. Officers are usually addressed by their first names. There are no fancy uniforms. . . . Military titles are used in writing, but rarely in verbal address. The use of such titles in civilian life after retirement is frowned upon. . . . Job turnover among officers is unusually rapid and the army is almost never a lifelong occupation. Most officers are weeded out soon after they reach forty. This practice has helped to prevent the establishment of a military class. (p. 252)

Hence, the Israeli army exists out of necessity, not out of choice. It combines the needs that evolve out of Israel's memories of its tragic past of persecution, the constant state of war or fear of it, and its small size with the wish to maintain a democratic society that will not be controlled by any elite. Thus far, Israel has been successful in maintaining that combination.

The kibbutz is close to the ideal of an egalitarian society. The equality of all people within the small, enclosed society of the kibbutz is one of its most fundamental principles, and the periodic rotation of critical and powerful roles is one effective way of preserving egalitarianism.

Likewise, the egalitarian principle is basic to Israeli society. In Hofstede's (2001) study of cultural values across 53 nations, Israel had the second-lowest score on the dimension of power distance or the belief that inequality among members of a society should be emphasized. The more recent GLOBE study (House et al., 2004) indicates that only 5 of 61 societies promote the *practice* of lower power distance more than Israel. Still, this study also indicates that Israel scored near the middle of these 61 societies in terms of *valuing* lower power distance, a finding that accords with the objective data indicating growing inequality. In fact, Israel has become one of the most unequal societies in the world. About 25% of Israelis live below the poverty line—including one third of all Israeli children. Among people 65 and older, Israel has the highest rate of poverty in the Western world. One major reason for this state of affairs is the acceptance of all Jews who wish to immigrate to Israel, many of whom come from poor and impoverished nations.

The Role of Power

Twenty centuries of oppression have made Jews skeptical of the indiscriminate use of power. Many Israelis find the mere striving for power to be objectionable. This has caused a basic disrespect for authority, which is a main characteristic of Israeli society. The anarchist strain found in Israel also has its origins in the Marxist and socialist ideas that the first pioneers espoused, for some envisioned an entire society based on a network of collective agricultural and industrial associations involving a minimum degree of coercion and a high degree of voluntary, reciprocal agreement. Although this vision did not materialize, belief in egalitarianism continues to this day. Voluntarism, rather than formal authority, is highly regarded throughout Israeli society, and especially so in kibbutzim and cooperative movements. Members spend a relatively large amount of time on voluntary activities, such as serving on different committees and working extra hours. A high percentage of kibbutzniks serve in the elite units in the army and as officers; it is almost a social norm to volunteer for these assignments.

Some Israelis are worried that the simultaneous growth of prosperity and inequality will lead to greater individualism and a weakening of the collective spirit (Waldman, 2007). Some kibbutzim members are selling some of their property; their small homes are now dwarfed by the mega-mansions that wealthy Israelis have built alongside. While the number of applicants from the kibbutzim for combat units has actually increased, the six wealthiest cities vary in the enlistment of 18-year-olds in active combat units from 37% to 60%; historically the kibbutzim have registered far higher rates of recruitment.

Furthermore, the ideological basis of the kibbutz is socialism, whose basic tenet is that the major means of production and distribution are managed and controlled by the community as a whole, and this is actively practiced in the kibbutz. Members live according to a system whereby each person works as he or she can and receives what he or she needs. Almost all needs are met by the kibbutz, including food, shelter, clothing, medical care, child care, and education. As noted previously, the cash-strapped kibbutzim are now charging their members for some of these services.

A similar type of socialism exists in Israeli society at large. The concept of national responsibility for basic health, housing, and social welfare is a given. Even the influx of hundreds of thousands of Ethiopian and Soviet Jews has not led to a fundamental renewed questioning of priorities, although the costs are enormous. Education is free, and health insurance is set at a price all people can afford.

Group Versus Individual

Another key value in the kibbutz and Israeli society is the primacy of the group over the individual. From the outset of the Zionist movement until the proclamation of the state, the theme was consistent: The purpose of the Zionist movement was the redemption of the Jewish people. The movement, and later the state, focused on the group rather than the individual. Moreover, the early pioneers arriving in Palestine firmly believed in this socialistic approach, and they quickly realized the value of group cooperation as they attempted to make the land habitable.

Many of these pioneers were not accustomed to manual labor, were weakened by malaria and other diseases, and suffered from the hostility of some Arabs. To overcome such obstacles, making the group more important than the individual was not only desirable but absolutely necessary. This experience had the same effect on the Israeli society as a whole, although to a lesser extent.

Currently the demands made on the individual in Israel are great because of the continuing tenuous security that the nation faces, which implies that survival rests on the cohesiveness of the group. Therefore, each Israeli must sacrifice some individuality to meet these demands. Mandatory military service is required of both sexes, taxes are among the highest in the world, and Israelis can take only a small sum of money out of the country to invest elsewhere. The ultimate betrayal in the eyes of Israelis is to leave the country permanently. A similar attitude toward people who left the kibbutz to live elsewhere formerly existed. People who grew up in the kibbutz and decided to pursue a different way of life found they were rejected by the group, although this rejection was not always conscious (Bettelheim, 1969). This reaction is much less intense than it used to be, partly because a relatively large number of young people choose to leave—between a third and a half of each age group, and sometimes even more.

The relative unimportance of the individual is most apparent in encounters with the bureaucracy, which is a hassle in most nations. However, the Israeli system presents itself to Israeli citizens not as a guardian and servant but as a warder. The stories about the indifference and callousness of the Israeli bureaucracy are legion. Almost every contact with a government or public agency involves standing in line for a long time, and having to wait in several queues to arrange one matter is quite common. The combination of constant demands on the individual and an unpleasant bureaucracy leads to a resistance to authority that manifests itself in a disregard for whatever seems unessential to the general safety or survival. For example, cheating on taxes is a common practice.

Admittedly individualism has increased significantly in recent years. Only 2% of the workforce is now in agriculture, and most Israelis live in and around cities. In Israel 20% of the workforce are university graduates, second only to the United States. It leads all nations in terms of the percent of engineers in the workforce. Erez (1986) dramatized this movement toward individualism in a well-controlled study in which she manipulated leadership style across three Israeli organizational cultures. In the kibbutzim, collectivism was the highest, and participative management was most effective in this setting. In the public sector, however, delegative management was most effective. But in the private sector, which was the most individualistic, directive leadership was most effective. Today Israel's economy is increasingly integrated with the activities of other nations, and its private sector is growing rapidly. Given this situation, we can expect to see individualism increase and conflict between variously individualistic and collectivistic groups to rise.

Other Values

It can be seen, then, that while the instinct for self-preservation has given rise to social discipline, there is still a widespread, almost compulsive resentment of any regimentation. The result is a peculiarly Israeli mixture of self-reliant individualism and a socialistic readiness to cooperate. This interplay between individualism and collectivism is also portrayed in Hofstede's (1991) study of 53 nations, where Israelis scored near the middle on the individualism-collectivism dimension. In the more recent GLOBE study (House et al., 2004), however, Israel ranked only 49th of 61 societies in valuing institutional collectivism, thus suggesting that Israel has moved toward more individualism since the Hofstede survey, completed 1968–1973.

A deep connection to the land is another value held both by the kibbutz and the Israeli society, even though agriculture represents only 3% of gross national product. This connection stems partly from the knowledge that land is necessary for survival and protection and is partly the consequence of a rebellion against generations of Jews who had no real connection to any land. Israeli land was poor in many ways, but the vigor of Israelis' agricultural efforts has been overwhelming. The people of the kibbutzim have shown their love and connection to the land through working it and making it fertile and blooming. In Israel at large this connection has been shown through the attempts to settle as much of the land as possible, even in the most remote areas.

Size and Behavioral Outcomes

The kibbutz and Israel are small, both geographically and in population. As indicated previously, Israel's population is 7 million, 20% of whom are Palestinians, and the distances between cities are very short. Driving from the Mediterranean to the border with Jordan takes 1½ hours. Both Haifa and Jerusalem are an hour's ride from Tel Aviv. More than 80% of the population is concentrated in this small triangle. Much of the country is uninhabited desert, and it is consequently even smaller than it appears on most maps, where it is about the size of New Jersey.

As a result, both in the kibbutz and Israel, specific behavioral outcomes occur that are not common in larger organizations and societies. Relations of all kinds are much more intimate than in larger entities. In the kibbutz, children spend almost all of their time with the same group of peers throughout childhood. Because there are typically only a few hundred people in the kibbutz, adult members interact with the same people almost every day. Similarly in the larger Israeli society, people tend to maintain a relatively steady and intimate group of friends, but with a relatively large number of acquaintances and contacts on the periphery.

Families also are close-knit. Small geographical distances lead to easy access and relatively frequent visits and gatherings. This sense of closeness also manifests itself in the responsibility many parents feel toward their adult children. If parents can afford it, buying an apartment for sons or daughters when they get married is a common practice, and financial help frequently continues even after that stage. Moreover, children tend to expect this help because of the high cost of living.

Given the country's small size, maintaining anonymity and privacy requires hard work. It is extremely difficult for individuals to achieve anonymity, and intimate details about someone's past and present are common knowledge, even in the larger urban centers. There are 337 people per square kilometer in Israel, whereas the comparative figure in the United States is 32.9. This intimacy establishes a strong sense of community.

Furthermore, this physical and emotional closeness leads to a heightened intensity of experience. Tragedy rarely remains isolated within the narrow confines of the family but spreads to wider social circles. In the kibbutz, with its communal dining room and similar collective arrangements for hundreds of members, this is obvious. But it is often true also in the towns, where news travels fast and immediately affects even apparent strangers. Each death in war electrifies the country as though it were the first, drawing strangers closer to one another. At such moments, the sense of cohesion is so strong it makes the country seem more like a large village than a state.

Finally, the mass media powerfully dramatize this state of affairs, and Israelis are obsessive consumers of radio, TV, and Internet news. It seems that no people in the entire world tunes in to the news as often, as regularly, and with such fervor.

Traumas, Worldview, and Personality

The Jews have experienced proportionately more traumas than most if not all major cultural groups. Two modern traumas that have had an enormous influence on the Israeli worldview and personality, both in the kibbutz and outside of it, are the Holocaust and the continuing struggle with their Arab neighbors. More than 6 million Jews, or about one third of all Jews then living, perished in the Holocaust during World War II, and the memory of this event remains vivid in Israel. Furthermore, the Holocaust had an enormous impact on the process of creating the state of Israel. As Elon (1971) points out, it

> caused the destruction of that very same Eastern European world against which the early pioneers had staged their original rebellion, but to which, nevertheless, Israel became both an outpost and heir. Because of the Holocaust there is a latent hysteria in Israeli life that accounts ... for the prevailing sense of loneliness, a main characteristic of the Israeli personality. (p. 199)

This sense of loneliness helps to explain the obsessive suspicions, especially of outsiders, in both the kibbutz and in the society at large and the urge for self-reliance at all cost in a world that never again can be viewed as safe and secure. Clearly the Holocaust left a permanent scar

> on the national psychology, the tenor and content of public life, the conduct of foreign affairs, on politics, education, literature and the arts. . . . The notoriously lively bustle . . . and seemingly endless vivacity of Israeli life merely serve as compensatory devices for a morbid melancholy and a vast, permeating sadness. . . . It crops up unexpectedly in conversation; it is noticeable in the press, in literature, in the private rituals of people. (Elon, 1971, p. 199)

It is little wonder that the term "gripe parties" is employed to describe many social gatherings.

There are countless public and private monuments to the Holocaust. Israelis do not let themselves forget. One day a year is devoted to mourning for the victims. The public commemoration serves a need to reassert the group and demonstrate its continuing vitality. However, as older generations die, they are replaced by others who often do not use the Holocaust to justify questionable actions, particularly the harsh treatment of Palestinians. And younger Israelis are focused not so much on remembering the Holocaust as on making Israel into a modern nation that is comfortable with different nationalities and perspectives.

Most Israelis believe wholeheartedly that the Holocaust was possible simply because the Jews had no country of their own and consequently lacked a means of resistance. To them, it is proof that the earlier Zionist theme of a need for a land was absolutely correct. The Holocaust also explains in part why Israelis are willing to endure most hardships imposed by their government with hardly any protest.

Arab hostility has helped to sharpen the outlines of the picture of utter loneliness drawn by the Holocaust. Since independence in 1948, Israelis have lived in a state of geographic and political isolation unusual in the modern world. Most countries today share common markets or at least open borders, a common language, or the same religion, but Israel does not. Also, it does not have military, political, or economic allies in the region. This claustrophobic isolation has given rise to a pessimism that is a main feature of the Israeli personality. It is a root cause of Israeli stubbornness and largely explains why earnest reprimands from other nations have little effect.

The kibbutz, although in a completely different way and for different reasons, is also isolated in many ways from the Israeli society as a whole, choosing to keep to itself. Although egalitarian in their own society, kibbutzniks tend to view themselves as elite, and this view about the kibbutz is also held by some Israelis. Their social systems, such as education, are almost completely separate. They also are not much influenced by criticism that comes from the outside, feeling that others who have not shared their experiences cannot judge them.

Because memories of the Holocaust are so alive, Arab threats of annihilation achieve just the opposite of their original intention. Such threats have kept Israelis wary and ready for combat long after the initial period of pioneering enthusiasm waned, and they have increased Israeli resolve, inventiveness, cohesion, vigor, and a nervous but fertile anxiety. Being under threat has also helped foster the sense of shared social purpose. Cohesion and unity are also strong in the kibbutz, although like other Israelis, the members of the kibbutz are the harshest critics of their own community.

Ironically, Zionism in its early period was predicated on faith in peaceful change, which is one of the major reasons why the members of the kibbutzim had good relations with their Arab neighbors. The discovery that this was nearly impossible to achieve has profoundly affected the Israeli worldview. Redemption has become intertwined with violence on a continual basis, and the resulting dissonance is now a part of this worldview, creating an outlook that is a combination of the hopeful and the tragic.

A Fatalistic Approach

The never-ending state of war has brought about an awareness of *Ein Brera*—there is no choice. This viewpoint reflects a fatalistic attitude. Zionists, the former rebels against their fate, have come to accept continual warfare. This fortress mentality was certainly not part of the original Zionist dream. Again, however, some younger Israelis are questioning the need for such constant vigilance. Young people accept their military responsibility, however, with an unreflecting, elemental urge to preserve the Zionistic vision of their elders.

However, as might be expected in such a small land whose citizens are constantly living under a state of siege, claustrophobia has emerged as a major problem. This claustrophobia, combined with a sense of adventurism, drives many Israelis, including kibbutz members, to trips outside of Israel, ranging from the conventional 2-week tours in Europe to exotic trips that may last for months and years. Kibbutzim members, given the small size of the relatively confined society in which they exist, can experience this sense of claustrophobia even more intensely than other members of Israeli society. Many young people go off to explore the life outside the kibbutz, working and living for 1 or 2 years in the city. The sense of claustrophobia is in part the reason why some choose not to return to the kibbutz, as it is the reason why some Israelis choose not to live in Israel.

There are, naturally, factors besides trauma that help to form the Israeli worldview, two of the most important being immigration and religion. Israel is rife with contradictions, such as pessimism and optimism, fatalism and determination, and so forth. One of the most salient of Israel's contradictions is the composition of its population. Many of its citizens are native born, but the rest are immigrants from across the world: Europe, Asia, Africa, North America, South America, and Australia. Even many of the native-born Israelis are only one or two generations removed from their immigrant past. Most immigrant societies face problems resulting from serving as a melting pot for widely divergent backgrounds, but in Israel there is a noticeable distinction between the Ashkenazim Jews and the Sephardim Jews. The Ashkenazim are those Jews from Eastern and Western Europe, America, and Australia. Their religious practices follow the Germanic or Central European rites of Judaism. The Sephardim Jews represent those following the Spanish rites of Judaism. The early Zionists and the founders of the state were almost all Ashkenazim.

The Sephardic Jews, now approximately half the population, include those who emigrated from Islamic countries in the Middle East and North Africa and who came to Israel after it was established as a state. It also includes Jews from such nations as Portugal and Spain. The Sephardic Jews had to enter a modern Western society when many of them had significantly lower literacy rates and education, were short on professional skills, and had very little money. The largely Ashkenazi establishment, unlike the newer immigrants, was socialist and secular, and it tried to transform the mostly traditional Sephardim to be more like themselves. Although a large number of the Sephardim prospered in their new country, many did not. By the 1960s it became clear that a "second Israel" had emerged, and there is a real gap between the two groups. This has resulted in a campaign aimed at improving the conditions of and opportunities for the Sephardic Jews.

In a definite manner, the kibbutzim represent part of this status problem. Almost all their people are of European descent, and in many ways they represent an Ashkenazi elite, which unofficially was reluctant to have the newer immigrants join its ranks. However, this is slowly changing, and today the kibbutzim are much more accepting of these immigrants and their offspring.

Religion and State

The other major issue affecting the Israeli worldview is religion. As discussed previously, serious conflict exists between religious and secular Israelis, and this explosive issue has not been resolved but merely shelved temporarily. In fact, it has been impossible even to reach an agreement in Israel over the most basic question: Who is a Jew?

Given such strong opinions and points of view, it is not surprising that these groups clash fiercely over the relationship of religion to the state. While the secular Jews want the state to be completely separate from religion, the religious Jews want them to be intertwined. Another clash is over allowing young men from the ultra-Orthodox, non-Zionist group to avoid service in the army, especially in the combat units, which the Zionist Jews bitterly criticized. Most of the kibbutzim are decidedly secular, and their founders actively rebelled against everything represented by the Judaism in their native Eastern Europe. In this sense the worldview of the kibbutzim is similar to that held by secular Jews, who constitute the largest group in the population.

Thus far, we have emphasized the internal character or personality of the Israelis, but this should be related to their overt behavior as well. The common perception is that Israelis are impolite, arrogant, and brash. A classic example of this behavior is the high-risk, macho manner in which Israelis drive. They do not keep much distance between cars because of a fear that someone will cut ahead of them. Drivers honk at each other if the car in front of them does not move within a nanosecond of the traffic light turning green. Furthermore, this arrogant behavior is exhibited in the way people cut corners in their business and personal dealings and in the impolite manner in which customers are frequently treated. This roughness of Israeli culture reflects the way Israeli society works, and it is not deliberately directed at the outside but is rather a spillover from anxiety and internal frictions. Many U.S. American Jews visiting Israel experience great difficulty relating to the Israelis because of this brusqueness.

Tom Friedman, in his vivid portrait of the Mideast (1989/1995), interviewed a prominent Israeli historian, Yaacov Shavit, who neatly summed up what living in Israil entailed:

> "I must tell you," he confided, "I just came back from two years in Germany. It was paradise. It was Germany, but it was paradise. No news. No one waiting for the Messiah. It was so relaxing. Here, you live in a very dynamic state. You are always involved in everything. Always listening to the news. You can't escape the utopian aspirations of the left or the messianic expectations of the right. You can never relax. People are always arguing about your identity. People are always asking you to decide. Are you a Jew? Well, what kind of Jew? Are you a Zionist? Well, what kind of Zionist? You turn on the television and people are arguing about the borders, about the boundaries between religion and state—nothing is ever settled here. You just can't relax." (p. 289)

Friedman relates that Noga, Shavit's 17-year-old daughter who was preparing the lunch, broke in at this point and said: "Dad, that is the fun of the place." As Friedman states, it looked like Shavit would prefer a little less fun. Friedman argues that the most amazing aspect of the world's only Jewish state is the fact that it was built and managed to stay together given such wide ideological and religious chasms.

In part, this behavior stems from the constant feeling of insecurity, the simultaneous need to suppress it, and the need and desire to go on about daily life and behave normally. Such contradictory needs fuel repressed tension, which builds up over time, between the desire to admit fears and worries and the belief that it is not appropriate, helpful, or "masculine" to do so. To put such tension in perspective, Friedman (1989/1995) relates a joke about two Jews, one of whom asks: "Are you an optimist or a pessimist?" The second replies: "I am an optimist, of course. I am certain that today will be better than tomorrow" (p. 273).

Personal Style

Also, this behavior is partly a result of a Mediterranean influence—Italians behave in a similar manner. Israelis are quick to react, to scold, and to act impolitely but also quick to calm down. Still, this is only surface behavior. This harshness on the outside combined with a soft inside is the reason why the image of native-born Israelis is portrayed by the *sabra*—a cactus plant with thorns on the outside but a delicate inner part. Correspondingly there is relatively little violence in terms of rape, murder, or extortion, and the streets are safe at night.

Israelis are generally very direct people. As Joyce Starr (1991) describes it,

> They are eager to get down to business, to get right to the heart of things. The little extra graces that give the Middle East its charm and style are seen by Israelis as useless decorations, impediments that only waste time. Everything is up front, without pretense, and matters are stripped down to bare essentials. Israelis almost never phrase things with "I think" or "It seems to me," the classical American way of avoiding hurting the other. They will simply attack with "you are wrong." (p. 45)

In studies of the prisoners' dilemma, an exercise in cooperation, Israeli men are more uncooperative at the early stages of negotiation than most men from other nationalities. *Dugry,* an Arabic term now part of Israeli slang, reflects a similar orientation among Israelis, as it means "Don't take offense, as I am going to speak frankly and be critical, so get ready, but realize it is not personal." There are actually management programs that train Israelis to be polite to U.S. executives, who are not very tolerant of blunt criticism.

In addition, informality is the norm in Israel. People introduce themselves to strangers using first names. This behavior is repeated almost everywhere: First names are used between employees and employers, schoolchildren and their teachers, and soldiers and their commanders. As noted previously, Israelis seek to deemphasize status and power distance between individuals, and they have little patience for formality or protocol, for complicated rituals or procedures. Israeli men rarely wear a suit and a tie. This informality is associated with a display of openness and frankness that encourages people to speak their mind and offer their opinion freely to another without feeling that they are being presumptuous for doing so. It is also associated with the way people socialize with each other—it is common to simply drop by a friend's house without calling in advance. When someone says "Why don't you drop by?" they actually mean it.

Both the directness and the informality are essential ingredients of the kibbutz way of life. Because status differences are greatly if not totally deemphasized, and all matters are subject to debate and participative decision making, the weekly meetings create a platform where opinions are usually expressed freely, including opinions about the members themselves. Informal social relationships are easy to maintain because the physical size of the kibbutz is so small. Informal clothing can actually be a source of pride.

Finally, Israel is a classic "doing" society in which people act proactively to control situations and overcome problems. Although U.S. Americans like to think of themselves in a similar fashion, the Israelis far outshine them: They have an uncanny ability to improvise, and they are at their best when doing so. Israelis pride themselves on their ability to fashion solutions to both mundane and desperate problems as they occur. In part, this ability comes from their historical experience when Jews didn't have rights and the only way to survive was to look around for a shortcut.

More recent experience, that of overcoming many difficult and complex problems in a very short time as Israel became a state, has strengthened this ability. Jeanne Brett (2001), in a study of negotiation among international MBA students at Northwestern University, showed that Israelis (pragmatic individualists) are more effective than Germans (cooperative pragmatists) or the Japanese (indirect strategists) in terms of achieving favorable outcomes for themselves. However, she also points out that even though they are hard, individualistically oriented bargainers, Israelis paradoxically achieve success in large part because they are more responsive to the needs of their negotiating adversaries, thus leaving both parties more satisfied with the outcomes than occurs with German and Japanese negotiators. Given such insights, Martin Gannon asked an Israeli hotel to refund payment on his credit card for 5 of 6 nights— he didn't dare to ask for a total refund—even though he had booked through a website because of its lower prices and knew that he had agreed to pay for all nights if he cancelled. He told the hotel manager that his 2011 spring trip to Israel, Jordan, and Egypt had been cancelled due to the Egyptian uprising and he had planned to stay at the hotel prior to the tour. The hotel manager concurred and charged him only for 1 night.

Within the kibbutz, the ability to improvise was developed to its highest form. Many of the kibbutzim possessed only scant resources, so their members learned to use all of them in inventive ways. Without such improvisations they might well have failed. Part of the fame that modern Israeli agriculture has acquired worldwide for its inventiveness can be traced to the experiences the kibbutzim had to face.

Together with being an action-oriented society, Israel is also an intellectual society. A high percentage of people have university degrees, and the number of books bought per capita is one of the highest in the world. This trend also exists in the kibbutz, and one way kibbutzim try to maintain a high cultural level is through special cultural events, either produced internally or brought from the outside.

A Changing Culture

As organizations change, so too does the culture in which they exist. The most popular model for looking at organizational change and growth is biological or evolutionary; that is, organizations go through distinct stages. Edgar Schein (2010) has described a three-stage model. First is birth and early growth, during which the main ideas and sources of inspiration come from the founders and their beliefs. These ideas serve as the "glue" holding the organization together. During the second stage, organizational midlife, members feel less commitment to the organization and key goals and values, which results in a crisis of identity. If an organization is to achieve the third stage, organizational maturity, and become even stronger, it needs to redefine its goals and values to meet the expectations of a changing world. In effect, the kibbutz is experiencing an organizational midlife crisis; correspondingly, so too is Israel.

In particular, most Israelis are not willing to work the long hours that kibbutzim require, although they frequently feel that their children should spend at least 3 months working on a kibbutz to reconnect with the country's past. The moshavim have become a popular alternative because they are characterized by a lower degree of ideological fervor, the ownership of private property, and some rights for individuals, even to the extent of benevolently accepting the fact that some members want to leave permanently.

Fortunately, the ideological rigidity of the founders of both Israel and the kibbutz has eased considerably, and the new generation is responding to a changing world. In the kibbutz, the rigid rules for living with the bare essentials have changed dramatically. Life has become more prosperous, and members now have all or most of the modern appliances in their own rooms, are able to take more vacations abroad, and so on. These changes parallel those in the larger Israeli society, which has become more materialistic.

Another dramatic shift in the kibbutzim is industrialization. Israeli agriculture has reached its upper limit, mainly because of the lack of water. By 1980 Israel was using all its replenishable water supply (Meyer, 1982). Today, many of the kibbutzim have at least one factory, employing on average 50% of the members. Some kibbutzim are engaged in tourism and such service-oriented activities as managing hotels and weddings. As indicated previously, Israel's high-tech and venture capital industry is ranked number one in the world, adjusted for population. This transition from agriculture occurred because of a belief that the future lies in industry and elsewhere. Still, it has been accompanied by problems. Economic decisions in the kibbutz have become more complex, and it is harder for all members to participate in all decisions because of a lack of knowledge necessary to understand the issues. And, as noted above, many kibbutzim have suffered economically in recent years.

There is also a definite shift in the kibbutzim, and particularly the moshavim, from an emphasis on group effort and collective well-being to one combining such group effort with recognition of individual needs, privacy, and family. Many kibbutz members, and correspondingly many Israelis, demand more freedom for self-expression and individual preferences. One result in the kibbutz has been the decline in the practice of collective child rearing, which was once synonymous with kibbutz life and an essential expression of the ideology. Another manifestation of this trend is the larger flexibility kibbutzim show toward people who want to be able to pursue careers they freely choose.

Although the kibbutzim are still well represented in the Israeli parliament or Knesset, their influence has declined in recent years. The Labor Party, championed by the kibbutzim, was replaced by the more conservative Likud Party as the leading political party in 1977. In fact, in 2011 there were only 8 Labor Party representatives in the 120-member Knesset. This ascension of the Likud Party was not only a signal event but a symbolic one, as it stood for the movement away from some traditional values of the kibbutz, particularly the emphasis on creating people who want to adhere to group norms rather than to lead. Today the leadership of the kibbutzim mainly sets an example and is not involved in politics.

The kibbutzim have been an absolutely essential part of Israel's struggle to survive, and their values have been a bellwether for the country. If the kibbutzim and Israeli society are to achieve and maintain the third stage of maturity, it would probably be wise to rekindle the spiritual and moral heritage of the kibbutzim throughout Israel in some form, for their basic values were and most probably are indispensable for continued growth and success. Israel, now a global leader in some areas such as technology and higher education, is seeking to balance individual desires and national imperatives, and using the kibbutz and moshav as a starting point for discussion may be wise.

CHAPTER 21

The Italian Opera

The only form of theatrical music that is at all controversial ... is the operatic form.

—Aaron Copland (1939/1957, p. 133)

In March, Italian senator Paolo Amato joined placard-waving citizens furious over the removal of an iconic painting from Florence's famed Uffizi Gallery. While protesting the loan of Leonardo da Vinci's "Annunciation" to an exhibition in Japan, the senator took an unusual step: He wrapped himself in chains, looped them around a post outside the museum entrance and snapped the padlock shut. The stunt was the dramatic, even operatic conclusion to a noisy conflict raging for weeks.

—Christopher Knight (2007)

MILAN—La Scala opened this week with a new and in many respects outstanding production of Wagner's 'Walküre.' No matter how much opera has declined as a popular pastime in this country, the start of the season remains the grandest event on the Italian cultural calendar, attracting glitterati and heads of state. ...

It's more than a social event. It a political and symbolic one too, and in the end countless Italians care, or profess to, about the quality of the music. The performance is big news. There's no equivalent elsewhere in Europe, or in America.

—Michael Kimmelman (2010)

taly celebrated its 150th year as a modern nation on March 15, 2011. Among developed European nations, only Germany is younger. However, unlike other newly founded nations, Italy is exceptional in the ambivalence that many Italians feel about the nation. Its regions are clearly different from one another, and citizens tend to identify with their regions first and nation second ("Happy-ish Birthday," 2011).

Still, Italy for centuries has had a well-deserved reputation for excelling in the areas of painting, music, and living life fully with a general sense of style and vivacity. Other nations excel at waging war and creating economic prosperity for most of their citizens. However, Italy is a laggard economically, particularly in comparison to such members of the European Union (EU) as Germany, France, and the Scandinavian nations. Some causes include high taxes to support social programs such as early retirement from government work, a low rate of labor force participation, low productivity, the continuing influence of criminal groups such as the Mafia, widespread corruption, tax evasion, a huge public debt, and inefficient government. Just in the area of tax evasion, one reliable estimate indicates that unpaid taxes are equal to 27% of Italy's gross domestic product (Kahn & Di Leo, 2007). On the 2011 Index of Economic Freedom, Italy ranks only 87th of 179 nations (T. Miller, 2011).

To make matters worse, much of the prosperity in Italy since World War II has occurred because of dramatic success that small, entrepreneurial firms in the north have experienced. Because of competition from China and other nations and the increasing power of large multinational corporations, such small Italian firms have faced serious problems in recent years. There are only about 47 large firms in Italy, with its population of 58.9 million, while Britain with a similar population (61.0 million) has approximately 129 (Peet, 2005).

Italy is about the size of Florida but is less fertile and less endowed with natural resources. The country is divided into two main regions. Continental Italy consists of the Alps and the northern Italian plain, while Mediterranean Italy encompasses the Italian peninsula and the islands. The Apennine Mountains run directly down the peninsula's center, and its northern range almost completely cuts off the north from the south. This geographical division has led to extreme regionalism, and many Italians view Italy as two separate nations: the wealthier, industrial north with a population of 40 million, and the poorer, more agrarian south with a population half that size.

North and South

Political scientist Robert Putnam (1993) has empirically and convincingly demonstrated that the civic traditions of the north and south of Italy originated from different sources and that these traditions have persisted for centuries. In the 11th century, King Frederico established an autocratic form of government in the south that was both politically and economically successful, but over time his successors corrupted it. The Mafia arose as the middleman between the kings and the people and tended to reinforce corruption. In the north, by contrast, a centuries-long legacy of civic involvement through both guilds, which stressed education and apprenticeship programs, and democratic elections has held corruption in check. Today the north of Italy continues to be successful, even though it is under duress because of globalization. However, the south languishes in poverty, even though millions of dollars have been devoted to eradicating it. There is even a group, the Northern League based near Milan, that periodically seeks to divide Italy into two separate nations. However, this movement is more quixotic than real, as the economically prosperous north depends heavily on emigration from the south for its workforce. Moreover, the north and south are closely linked to one another culturally, as noted below, even though there are regional differences.

Although Italian culture is justifiably renowned, it is in danger of extinction, as are the cultures of some other developed nations. Italy's fertility rate (1.4) is far below the replacement level and is one of the lowest in the world. Italy has the third-oldest population among nations in terms of median age (43.3 years), following Japan and Germany. Still, the population is large, and these trends may reverse. Also, many people want to immigrate to Italy, and in fact countless illegal aliens cross its borders daily. Thus, while Italy will probably change, its cultural base should be relatively secure, at least for the foreseeable future.

Italy has been historically victimized by natural disasters: volcanoes, floods, famines, and earthquakes. It is a geologically young country, most of which cannot be categorized as terra firma, and so many mudslides have resulted in loss of property and life, both in the past and in recent years, that the Italians nickname the nation "landslide country" ("Hand of God," 1998). As a result, Italy exudes an aura of precariousness (Haycraft, 1985/1987). Italians tend to accept insecurity as a fact of life. This acceptance may help to explain why they seem to be able to enjoy life more for the moment and are willing to accept events as they happen. Italians tend to feel that if something is going to happen, it will, and not much can be done about it.

Italy's history is filled with many culturally rich and influential periods, including the Roman Empire and the Renaissance. As noted previously, the country emerged as a nation-state in 1861, much later than many other European nations such as France and England, as a result of national unification known as the *risorgimento* or revival. Before unification, Italians never quite identified with the many foreign cultures that conquered and ruled them. This is a possible explanation for Italians' historic contempt for the law and paying taxes. And even though Italians have been strongly influenced by foreign rule, they have managed to create a culture that is distinctly their own.

The Opera Metaphor

To understand Italy, it is helpful to look at the opera, the art form that Italians invented and raised to its highest level of achievement. It is the only art form for theatrical theater in which almost all of the words are sung rather than spoken. Musical forms that have evolved from the opera include the English operettas of Gilbert and Sullivan and such U.S. musicals as *South Pacific* and *Oklahoma.* However, these derivative forms have proportionately many more spoken rather than sung words in comparison to opera.

The opera represents most, if not all, of the major characteristics of Italian culture. It is a metaphor for Italy itself, as it encompasses music, dramatic action, public spectacle and pageantry, and a sense of fate. It may be tragic or comic, intensely personal or flamboyantly public, with the soloists and chorus expressing themselves through language, gesture, and music and always through skilled acting. A larger-than-life aura surrounds operas, and the audience is vitally engaged in the opera itself, showing great emotion and love toward a singer whose talents are able to express the feelings that Italians tend to share. Operas and operatic songs reflect the essence of Italian culture, and Italians embrace them with an emotional attachment that less dramatic peoples might find difficult to understand. Opera has decreased in popularity among the public, in large part because of the high costs of production and the resulting high ticket prices. Still, nothing can match opera as an apt expression of Italian values. Therefore we chose the opera as our metaphor to understand Italian culture.

Using this metaphor, we focus on five distinctive characteristics of the opera and demonstrate how they illustrate Italian life. These characteristics include the overture; the spectacle and pageantry itself and the manner in which opera-like activities are performed in the daily life of Italians; the use and importance of voice to express words in a musical fashion; externalization, which refers specifically to the belief that emotions and thoughts are so powerful that an individual cannot keep them inside and must express them to others; and the importance of both the chorus and the soloists, which reflects the unity of Italian culture (chorus) but also regional variations (soloists), particularly between the north and the south.

The Overture

The overture was such an influential innovation that it inspired the development of the German symphony. Essentially the orchestra sets the mood for the opera during the overture and gives the audience an idea of what to expect. Typically the overture is about 5 minutes long, and it frequently includes passages that are emotionally somber, cheerful, reflective, and so forth. At various points the overture is quick, moderate, or slow in tempo, and it employs different instruments to convey the sense of what will happen in the various acts—usually three—into which the opera is divided.

Italian culture emphasizes overtures. It stands somewhere in the middle of the continuum between U.S. low-context culture and Asian high-context culture. U.S. Americans tend to ignore the overture and get down to business quickly. Many Asians, on the other hand, devote a significant amount of time to getting to know their negotiating counterparts before doing business with them. Italians take a mid-way position on the issue of personal trust and knowledge, but they do tend to convey their feelings and thoughts at least partially at the beginning of the relationship. The other party has some understanding of what will unfold, but it is only a preview that is imperfect, as the unexpected frequently occurs.

There are regional differences in the manner in which the overture is performed in daily life. In Milan, which has been influenced by its proximity to Switzerland and Germany, there is a tendency to shorten the overture. Still, it occurs, even in the small-est cafe that has only a few tables and a modest menu featuring sandwiches. The sandwiches are presented in a colorful and appetizing manner, and *paninis*—invented in Italy—are frequently featured, as are various forms of coffee and espresso. There may be just a few moments of conversation with the owner, but they are pleasant, like the display of food. Department stores feature the same pattern of behavior, and customers tend to interact with the salesperson much more in Italy than in the United States.

In the south, the overture can be much more involved. When looking for a pair of shoes, for example, the buyer frequently visits a shop and indicates to the owner that a mutual friend suggested he or she make a purchase there. This information leads to a pleasant conversation and perhaps the offer of a cup of espresso. Frequently no purchase is made, or expected, on the first visit. When the buyer visits a second time, the same pleasantries occur, and he or she may or may not make a purchase. However, both parties expect that a purchase will occur if the buyer visits the shop for a third time. At this time the real negotiations or opera begin. Both parties—and the audience—have a good idea about the outcome, but expressions of emotion, various uses of argument and persuasion, and different tones of voice facilitate the final outcome or sale. This strengthens the general sense of living life fully and with vivacity. Still, the unexpected can and does occur, as fate is a critical element in the mix.

Pageantry and Spectacle

By and large, Italy is a land of spectacle and pageantry. Italians tend to be more ani-mated and expressive than most if not all other nationalities. Many Asians, for example, attempt to minimize emotions and gestures when communicating with oth-ers. Italians, particularly those in the south, enjoy communicating in an expressive manner. The level of noise in Italy tends to be high in public places, and people tend to congregate rather than to be isolated from one another. Also, some bystanders do not mind becoming part of the action. For example, a driver stopped by a police officer for excessive speed may be debating the issue while a crowd vocally supportive of the driver's plea for mercy offers comments. In one situation, a bus driver argued with a mother that her son, who at 6 feet tall was obviously not a child, should pay the adult's rather than the child's fare, but he also had to argue with the many other passengers who vehemently came to her defense.

Once the overture is done and the curtain goes up, the audience is greeted by a set so visually stunning that it elicits applause. This is the beginning of the pageantry and spectacle. These play such an important role in Italian life that people and things frequently tend to be judged first and foremost on appearance. Barzini (1964), in his classic portrait of the Italians, points out that the surface of Italian life, playful yet bleak and tragic at times, is similar to what has occurred in Italian history and has many of the characteristics of a show. It is, first of all, unusually moving, entertaining, and unreservedly picturesque. Second, all of its effects are skillfully contrived and graduated to convey a certain message to, and arouse particular emotions in, the bystanders. Italians are frequently great dramatic actors, as we might expect of the creators of the opera. Recent portraits of Italy in best-selling books, such as *Under the Tuscan Sun* by Frances Mayes (1996), reaffirm Barzini's descriptions, suggesting that cultural change in Italy is occurring slowly in many areas.

The first purpose of the show is to make life acceptable and pleasant. This attitude can largely be explained by the circumstances of history, both natural and man-made, where four active volcanoes, floods, earthquakes, and continuous invasions by outsiders have created a sense of insecurity. Italians tend to make life's dull and insignificant moments exciting and significant by decorating and ritualizing them. Ugly things must be hidden, unpleasant and tragic facts are swept under the carpet whenever possible, and ordinary transactions are all embellished to make them more stimulating. This practice of embellishing everyday events was developed by a realistic group of people who tend to react cautiously because they believe that catastrophes cannot be averted but only mitigated. Italians prefer to glide elegantly over the surface of life and leave the depths unplumbed (Barzini, 1964).

The devices of spectacle do not exist simply because of the desire to deceive and bedazzle observers. Often, to put on a show becomes the only way to revolt against destiny and to face life's injustices with one of the few weapons available to a brave people, their imagination. To be powerful and rich, of course, is more desirable than to be weak and poor. However, it is frequently difficult for the Italians, both as a nation and individually, to have either power or wealth.

The Importance of *Garbo*

This eternal search for surface pleasures and distractions is accompanied by *garbo*. Although this term cannot be translated exactly, it is the finesse that Italians use to deal with situations delicately and without offense. *Garbo* turns Italian life into a work of art. Italians tend to have a public orientation, are willing to share a lot, and are used to being on stage at all times.

As this description suggests, many Italians wish to portray a certain image to those around them. This is termed *la bella figura,* which Brint (1989) has defined as the projection of a confident, capable face. Wilkinson (2007a) expands on this definition by pointing out that *la bella figura* represents the Italian obsession that allows substance to be ignored in favor of style; it is the art of public performance.

The importance attached to impressions is shown in the basic document of the Italian republic, the constitution. In the U.S. Declaration of Independence, the first of the self-evident truths is that all men are created equal. In the Italian constitution, the first basic principle is that "all citizens are invested with equal social dignity" (Levine, 1963). Similarly many Italians would rather sit inside their home than go outside and make a bad impression. Wilkinson (2007a) describes the extreme pursuit of *la bella figura* in Italy among those who are wealthy but not sufficiently wealthy to pay for what, from their perspective, is expected. There is even a social club that allows them to rent a prestigious car for an afternoon or to obtain an impressive but temporary collection of paintings on their walls for a party. While such ostentatious displays are common in other nations, Italy seems to outshine many if not all of them in this regard.

A large number of Italians pursue *la bella figura* through material possessions. Giving a good impression, not only by one's demeanor but with material wealth, is important. Various explanations have been offered for this tendency, including years of domination by foreign nations, overcrowding in various areas, and natural disasters. Whatever the explanation or explanations, it seems that the creation of a show through an eternal search for pleasures and distractions is an attempt to deal with the difficult realities of everyday life.

A reliance on spectacle and *garbo*, or turning life into a work of art, helps people solve most of their problems. Spectacle and *garbo* govern public and private life and shape policy and political designs. They constitute one of the reasons why Italians have excelled in activities in which appearance is predominant. During medieval times, Italian armor was the most beautiful in Europe: It was highly decorated, elegantly shaped, and well designed. However, it was too light and thin to be used in combat. In war the Italians preferred German armor, which was ugly but more practical. Similarly, on the occasion of Hitler's visit in 1938, Rome was made to appear more modern, wealthy, and powerful with the addition of whole cardboard buildings, built like film sets.

Italians tend to believe that "anybody can make an omelet with eggs" but that "only a genius can make one without" (Barzini, 1964, p. 91). For example, warfare during the Renaissance, as it was practiced outside of Italy, consisted of the earnest and bloody clash of vast armies. The army that killed more enemies carried the day. But in Italy, warfare was an elegant and practically bloodless pantomime. Highly paid leaders of small companies of armed men staged the outward appearance of armed conflict, decorating the field of battle with beautiful props: flags, colored tents, horses, and plumes. The action was accompanied by suitable martial music, rolls of drums, heartening songs, and blood-chilling cries. The armies convincingly maneuvered their few men back and forth, pursued each other across vast provinces, and conquered each other's fortresses. However, victory was decided by secret negotiations and bribes. It was, after all, a civilized and entertaining way of waging war. Although this approach often left matters as undecided as warfare practiced elsewhere, it cost much less in money, human lives, and suffering.

Church Ritual

The operatic pageantry of Italian life also occurs in the rituals of the Catholic Church, which still exercises considerable political and cultural power ("By Hook or by Crook," 2007). Italians prize these rituals for their pageantry, spectacle, and value in fostering family celebrations more than for their religious significance. Many Italians view the church, much like the opera, as a source of drama and ritual but not authority. Although they do not attend church regularly, the church still exerts a strong cultural and social influence on their behavior, and almost all Italians identify themselves as Catholics.

Furthermore, the spectacle of Italian life is apparent in the area of communications. Italians tend to be skilled conversationalists. Onlookers can frequently follow a conversation from a distance because of the gestures and facial expressions that are employed to convey different emotions. Similarly one can understand many of the actions that take place in an opera without fully understanding the words the actors are singing.

Although Italians tend to be emotional and dramatic, decisions are influenced rarely by sentiments, tastes, hazards, or hopes but usually by a careful evaluation of the relative strength of the contending parties. This is one of the reasons why, when negotiating even the smallest deal, Italians prefer to look each other in the face. They read the opponent's expression to gauge his or her position and can thus decide when it's safe to increase demands, when to stand pat, and when to retreat.

Transparent deceptions are employed to give each person the feeling that he or she is a unique specimen of humanity, worthy of special consideration. In Italy, few confess to being "an average man." Instead they persuade themselves that they are "one of the gods' favoured sons" (Barzini, 1964, p. 79).

The operatic Italians must always project a capable face to the world. Therefore, they prefer to engage only in work that will create the image of confidence and intelligence. In Italy, middle-class people tend to work once they have a profession and not while still in high school or university. In fact, many lower-level jobs such as waiting on tables are full-time and not readily available to students, a practice that is also common in other European nations. In the universities, students specialize immediately in their first year and do not dabble, as is the custom in the United States. However, there is no set term for most university careers—for example, 4 years devoted to undergraduate work and 3 years to law school—so many Italians spend more time in school than do their U.S. counterparts.

Business Negotiations

Pageantry and spectacle also apply to business presentations and negotiations. When presenting ideas during negotiations, managers are expected to ensure that the aesthetics of the presentation are clear and exact; they should demonstrate a mastery of detail and language and be well organized. Polish and elegance count for a great deal. However, although pageantry is important in business presentations and negotiations, Italians also tend to expect good-faith bargaining.

Most, if not all, Italians feel that it is infinitely better to be rich than to seem rich. But if a man or a nation does not have the natural resources necessary to conquer and amass wealth, what is he to do? The art of appearing rich has been cultivated in Italy as nowhere else. Little provincial towns boast princely palaces, castles, and stately opera houses. Residents of some small coastal villages have completed elaborate paintings on the rocks that can be seen from the sea to give the illusion of wealth and prosperity. In spite of economic difficulties, many Italians wear good clothes, drive late-model cars, and dine at expensive restaurants. However, some of these people may have few material possessions. Decoration and embellishment transform the realities of economic insecurity, uncertainty, and a scantily endowed land into a spectacle of illusion.

The pageantry of Italian life is highlighted by its lack of a rigid social hierarchy. There is no permanent and rigid class structure in Italy. Rather, there are conditions on which a person is judged. These include occupation and the amount of authority a person has in that role, education, ancestry, and, in most instances, wealth. However, the major focus is on social behavior. The Italians term this focus *civilta* or the extent to which someone is acculturated to the norms of the area or region (Keefe, 1977). These norms include styles of dress, manners, and participation in the local community.

Position in the social hierarchy can be clearly judged by the amount of respect members of the community show to a person and his or her family. However, respect is also associated with age and family position. Younger people will almost always show deference to older people, just as children show respect for parents.

Class consciousness and the social hierarchy will inevitably change as a result of industrialization, massive migration to urban areas, low birth rates, an aging population, and the Americanization of Italian youth. However, certain titles still command much respect. These include doctor, lawyer, and professor. Many people feel honored to speak to or have affiliations with someone holding such a title and will refer to him or her in a respectful, subordinate manner.

One final example of pageantry is appropriate, especially because it shows how some other cultures are similar to that of Italy (see Chapter 23: The Mexican Fiesta). Once a year in every village and city there is a celebration in honor of its patron saint (*santo patrono*) in which a parade is featured. The statue of the saint is placed in the lead position in the parade, followed by the clergy, members of the upper classes, and then all other citizens. A celebration follows in the piazza or town center. This traditional festival and parade strengthen the village's feeling of solidarity and permit people to escape from their regular routine in a dramatic, spectacular, and fun-filled manner.

The reliance on spectacle must be clearly grasped if one wants to understand the Italians. Spectacle helps people solve most of their problems and governs public and private life. It is one of the reasons why Italians have always excelled in activities in which impressions are important: architecture, decoration, landscape gardening, opera, fashions, and the cinema.

Voice

Italians tend to believe that their language, a derivative of the Tuscan language, is the most beautiful in the world. Much of the beauty of the Italian language derives from the fact that it has a higher proportion of vowels to consonants than all or most languages, which gives it something of a musical effect. Italians put great emotion into their language, speaking with passion, rhythm, and changing tonality. It is the quality of the way people speak that is of utmost importance, and this bias is replicated in the opera in strikingly different voice registers, such as the soprano and the bass. And, like the opera, the sound and cadence of the communication play a role at least equal to the content of what is said in getting the message across. Italians are often much more interested in engaging and entertaining their listeners than in conveying their thoughts accurately.

Given the importance of the Italian language, it is interesting to note that 44% of the population spoke regional dialects alongside the Italian language as late as 2000. However, as television's influence increased, the Italian language has become the norm, although many still speak regional dialects ("Happy-ish Birthday," 2011).

Perhaps the most difficult operatic singing is associated with bel canto, or beautiful singing, introduced by the romantic Italian composer Vincenzo Bellini. This form of music requires extraordinary exertion and ability on the part of the singers, especially when they are singing together to express their thoughts and emotions. Bel canto is so difficult a form of opera that only a limited number of singers can perform it effectively, and only Italian composers have been successful in writing music in this style.

Italians tend to talk louder than many other nationalities, but more so in the south than in the north. At meetings or informal gatherings, individuals often talk simultaneously and begin to raise their voices without realizing that they are doing so. Stories are told with passion, anger, and joy. The air in Italy is filled with so many voices that one must frequently talk in a loud voice to be understood, thereby increasing the total uproar.

Speech and Gesture

Oral communication in Italy is something of a show itself. Speaking is punctuated by elaborate gestures, befitting the Italian operatic tradition. Whatever the section of the country, Italians talk with their hands. Quick, agile, expressive movements of the hands, arms, and shoulders contribute emphasis and sincerity to the spoken words and facial expressions. For instance, a man thinking about buying fish in a market empties his imaginary waist pocket when he is told the price and walks away without a word (Willey, 1984).

However, the gestures are not, as many believe, unrealistically exaggerated. In fact, the gestures are so realistic that they may be unapparent. The acting of the opera singers, directly derived from the Italian's natural mimicry, contributes to the erroneous impression of excessive exaggeration. In reality, Italian gestures are based on natural and instinctive movements and can therefore be understood by the inexperienced at first sight. Many of these gestures have been traced back to classical antiquity (de Jorio, 2000).

In addition to gestures, Italians sometimes employ flattery and polite lies to make life decorous and agreeable. The purpose is to reduce the turbulence of day-to-day living and to make life more acceptable. Flattery somehow makes the wariest of men feel bigger and more confident, similar to the larger-than-life opera singer. This perspective accounts for the fact that Italians sometimes make promises they know they cannot fulfill. Small lies can be justified to give pleasure, provoke emotion, or prove a point. This applies not only to the businessman who swears with soulful eyes that he will deliver his product on a certain day (and does so a month later) but also to officers of government cabinet rank. Ministers will promise an appointment, will confirm it and reconfirm it, but on the appointed day will find an excuse for evading the appointment. Casualness toward promises is part of accepted Italian behavior.

Contentious Spirits

Contentiousness is generally not far below the surface of the Italian personality. This argumentativeness surprises many because it is discordant with the usual Italian demeanor. Yet the accusatory words shouted by offended drivers, the sidewalk conversations that often sound like arguments, and the tedious monologues by Italians reciting some imagined wrong they've suffered testify to the argumentative side of Italians. For most Italians controversy is a hobby or a sport, something in which they take immense pleasure (Levine, 1963).

Italians are frequently portrayed as joyful people with an operatic song on their lips. This is not completely accurate. They can also be rather somber, just as many of their operas end in death and tragedy. This dark side is emphasized through humor, which tends to be more insulting than witty. Humor generally implies the ability to detach oneself from the object of wit. However, the Italians tend to be passionate people who easily identify with what they are talking about.

Italians make up for this type of humor by analyzing everything around them through conversation. Talking is a great pastime for most Italians, who frequently meet in cafes to discuss the latest news. Privacy is frequently lacking in any Italian community, even though Italians say they mind their own business. Unlike the reserved English person, an Italian is apt to tell an acquaintance of a half-hour's standing all about his or her financial status, family health problems, and details of current emotional attachments. The Italian love of conversation as a pastime usually limits the chances of something secret staying so for very long, and it is this love of conversation (and voice) that is intimately related to externalization, the fourth characteristic of the opera.

Externalization

Externalization refers specifically to the fact that feelings and emotions are so overwhelming that people must express them to others. It also refers to the assumption that the event is more important than the actions of one individual, which is consistent with the Italian reaction to catastrophes and uncertainty described previously. That is, the drama is of more significance to the viewers or community than to the individuals involved because of its symbolism and generality. This pattern of behavior is the opposite of the Anglo-Saxon mode, which emphasizes that people should control emotions and not express them or, as the British say, keep a stiff upper lip (see Chapter 17). At Italian funerals, for instance, there is no shame in showing emotions, and both women and men cry openly and profusely to express what they feel. Although infrequent, it is not unusual in Italian villages in the South for someone to express grief at a funeral by throwing themselves on top of the coffin. Similarly a major victory such as a World Cup Championship is accompanied by a tremendous amount of noise, large gatherings in piazzas, and communal festivities at which everyone talks excitedly and simultaneously. Although there will be some drinking, the Italians do not tend to celebrate victory in this way as much as do the English and U.S. Americans.

Given their emphasis on externalization, it is generally not wise to ask Italians: How do you feel? Unlike Anglo-Saxons, who will usually give a cursory reply, the Italians may well describe in minute detail all of their aches and pains, what the doctors have prescribed for them, and even the most intimate details of any operations they have experienced.

Because of the importance of drama in everyday life, Italians place the piazza at the center of every town and village. It is the stage on which people gather to share conversation and relate experiences. The actions that take place in the piazza are minor dramas of Italian life. Most people do not schedule meetings with others, but everyone knows that gatherings will occur at regular times at the piazza, usually around noon and at 5:00 or 6:00 PM after work, and it is thus easy to see old friends and acquaintances and make new ones. This pattern of strolling (*fare la passeggiate*) is in sharp contrast to the German *spatziergang,* which occurs primarily on Sunday afternoons. Even in Italian cities where there is no central piazza, it is well-known that certain avenues serve as substitutes, and village-like behavior is replicated along them. On these avenues are many outdoor cafes at which people meet and greet one another, and sometimes there are even small, open-air areas with benches that are miniature replicas of the village piazza. As might be expected, Italy has far more bars and restaurants per capita than comparable European nations. An Italian doctoral dissertation has wedded the importance of externalization with changing cultural circumstances by suggesting that the large piazza is more descriptive of southern Italy whereas bars (and the adjoining small parks) are more descriptive of northern Italy (Venezia, 1997).

The View From the Piazza

Italians tend to be great spectators of life. The show at the piazza can be so engrossing that many people spend most of their lives just looking at it. Cafe tables are often strategically placed in such a way that nothing of importance will escape the leisurely drinker of espresso. Remarkably, an old woman once died at her window, and 3 days passed before any of her neighbors thought that something might be wrong with the immobile figure.

Foreigners are frequently impressed by the fact that many Italians seem to be doing their jobs with whole-hearted dedication and enthusiasm. This does not mean that Italians do everything with efficiency, speed, and thoroughness. Rather, they frequently complete their jobs with visible pleasure, as if work were not humankind's punishment. However, when the visitors look closely at the actions of Italians, they realize that many Italians have a theatrical quality that enhances but slightly distorts their actions.

In the opera, the best example of externalization is the crowd scene. There are so many crowd scenes in Italian opera that some writers have identified them as one of its essential characteristics. Members of the crowd are the chorus relative to the lead singers, and dynamic interplay takes place between the lead singers and the chorus. This interplay is analogous to the behavioral dynamics in a small village in which there is a problem and everyone comments on it in the piazza.

Most Italians have little, if any, private life. Everything of importance occurs in public or is at least discussed in public. There is no word for privacy in the Italian language, and information is widely shared. There are some regional differences, as northern Italians tend to be more reserved than southern Italians. However, once a person is perceived to be a member of the community, it is assumed that he or she will externalize, at least to some degree, when in public.

Business confidentiality can be a problem in Italy. Everyone discusses secret business negotiations with friends and family as well as the press. Therefore leaks are common for most large business deals. The media in Italy are volatile and speculation prone due to people's interest in their neighbors' activities. Hence ordinary business dramas become a theater with a large audience of spectators. Furthermore, to uncover corruption and tax evasion, the government has dramatically increased the use of wiretapping of phone conversations in recent years, which makes keeping secrets even more difficult. The Italian think tank Eurispes estimates that the government spent nearly US$1.6 billion on nearly 200,000 phone call intercepts between 2000 and 2005 (Wilkinson, 2005).

La Bella Figura

We have already indicated that dressing is important to Italians, as it represents pageantry and spectacle in the form of *la bella figura*. Dressing is also an aspect of externalization, as it is an outward expression of the emotions that Italians want to convey. Italians dress differently in public than at home at least in part for this reason. In the business environment, clothing is well tailored and sophisticated. Through their clothing Italians externalize the feeling of confidence.

Many aspects of daily life yield opportunities for drama. A well-known example of externalization is Italian driving behavior. In the larger cities such as Rome and Naples, drivers blow their horns impatiently, swear at one another, gesture colorfully, and drive in a dramatic and seemingly reckless manner. To Italians, such behavior is normal because it allows them to communicate with others even when behind the wheel. Even when two drivers get out of their cars to confront one another, they rarely come to blows, although their gestures, body movements, shouts, and the torrent of words would lead the onlooker to believe that blood will be spilled. The drama of the occasion is what gives Italians emotional satisfaction.

Even politics takes on a dramatic and entertaining edge, especially during elections. Television coverage of such events is said to have somewhat of a carnival atmosphere (Brint, 1989). Such an atmosphere reflects the Italian penchant for pageantry, voice, and externalization. Even though the Italian political system is changing radically, as discussed below, we can expect that such drama will continue to be part of the political process. Silvio Berlusconi, the three-term (former) prime minister, clearly exemplified this emphasis on drama. A prosperous businessperson before becoming prime minister, he was sued countless times and even attempted to have the constitution changed so that the prime minister could never be charged criminally. Berlusconi was criticized for inappropriate sexual behavior many times, and before his resignation in 2011, prosecutors submitted evidence to Parliament documenting orgiastic parties at Mr. Berlusconi's residence purportedly involving underage females ("A Party Animal," 2011).

Feelings and emotions are expressed through both direct communication and subtleties in Italian culture. The Italian history of natural disasters and foreign invasions has created a fear of the unpredictable. This fear can be detected behind the Italians' peculiar passion for geometric patterns and symmetry that can be easily destroyed (Barzini, 1964).

Weddings are considered the highlights of life and constitute an excellent example of externalized behavior. In fact, the wedding scene is quite common in Italian opera.

Italians often save for a lifetime to marry their daughters off in an appropriate manner. Guest lists frequently include the entire village. The wedding ritual is often something of a mini opera, beginning with the bridal party traveling in open automobiles to the church, with relatives and friends following. The success of the wedding ritual is judged by the number of cars, the size of the crowd, and the feast served. Parents are content to spend years of savings and even get into debt to correctly carry out their social obligations. This society may, in the eyes of outsiders, be living at a subsistence level, but it carries on ancient traditions with real satisfaction (Willey, 1984). Throughout the wedding ritual, the emotions of sadness and joy are expressed by all. It is not uncommon for both the bride and her father to be crying while walking down the church aisle.

Family Ties

The family and the extended kinship group are the basic building blocks for externalization. Familial relationships tend to be close and emotional, and the behaviors found in the piazza are replicated within the family. The family is generally seen as one's greatest resource and protection against all troubles. For example, children are critically important, and normally everything is done for them, even to the extent of satisfying their smallest wishes. Parents often go without comforts to pamper their children and to see that they go to school and reach a higher rung on the social ladder. This attitude can be directly linked to the constant influx of foreigners who compete with the Italians for jobs, to rapidly changing governments, and to the overwhelming natural disasters that have characterized Italian history. Of course, externalization plays a part in this support as well, as the family views its children as public expressions of its values and lifestyles.

The Italians themselves see the irony and humor in having family relationships that seem excessive. A few years ago a best-selling book, *Mammoni* or "Mamma's Boys," was widely discussed in Italy, and there was even a segment about it on the U.S. television news show *60 Minutes*. It is estimated that 40% of Italians between the ages of 30 and 34 still live at home, and of these males far outnumber females at a ratio of 2 to 1 (Peet, 2005). Some unmarried male Italians in this age group also live independently but come home for dinner every night. One mother ironed her son's clothes, including underwear, and shipped them to him weekly by bus. One town was thinking about introducing a tax on unmarried males over the age of 25.

But it is not only male children who are doted upon. Italian mothers will prepare a weekly meal for their children who live as far as 500 miles away. These meals are transported to these adult children, some in their 40s and 50s, on a bus hired only for this purpose. As one of the mothers said, "The umbilical cord was never cut." This practice now involves thousands of meals each week (Meichtry, 2011).

Furthermore, family connections are often extremely important for handling problems and getting ahead. Outside the family, official and legal authority is frequently considered hostile until proven otherwise. Closeness within the family is transferred to outside relationships and brings a personal edge to most social interactions. This helps to explain why Italians are so demonstrative and why men feel almost no hesitation to show affection to one another.

In the Italian business environment, family contacts tend to be necessary to run a successful company. An example of the importance of contacts is the general lack of hiring policies. Hiring is usually accomplished through personal connections and recommendations. Many corporations select people not on the basis of their skills but on the basis of their relationship with employers and their families. Smith and Bond (1998) have reviewed national preferences for various selection techniques, and Italian business is distinctive in that the interview by itself is the preferred alternative, even though this method when used by itself has been shown to be the least effective of all techniques.

The family remains the center and stronghold of Italian life, despite modern trends; the role of each member is understood and performed as elaborately as any Italian opera. Although men are the official leaders of the families while women are subordinate to them, the reality of family life is much more complex. The main character in the family, who might be compared to the lead tenor, is the father. He is in charge of the family's general affairs. But while he holds center stage, his wife is an equally important figure, like the lead soprano. Although the Italian father is the head of the family, the mother is its heart. While yielding authority to the father, she traditionally assumes control of the emotional realm of the family. The mother usually manages the family in a subtle, almost imperceptible way; she soothes the father's feelings while avoiding open conflicts. However, the woman of the house frequently has the last unspoken word. The factors that determine the strength of the family are placed in the hands of women. Wives engineer appropriate and convenient marriages, keep track of distant relations, and see to it that everybody does the suitable thing, not for individual happiness but for the family as a whole. The fact that women form the predominant character of Italian life can be seen through many small signs. For example, popular songs frequently highlight the role of mothers, and in some years more new songs are devoted to mothers than to romance.

Gender Issues

However, Italy tends to be a man's world. When a child is born, the proud parents tie a blue ribbon to the door for a son, but only sometimes do not-quite-so-proud parents of a girl put out a pink ribbon. The principle of male superiority is less strictly enforced in the north than in the south, as in Sicily, for example, where in some villages unmarried women are supposed to sit indoors during the day when unchaperoned.

Divorce and abortion have been legalized in Italy. Legal abortion symbolizes the loosening of state control over individual morals and the breaking of the hold of the Catholic Church over the family. In 1974 civil divorce became legal, but it seems to be more a symbol of social independence than anything else. Not many marriages have actually ended in divorce. For example, there are only 0.8 divorces per 1,000, one of the lowest rates among nations.

Many Italians view divorce as unacceptable because it chips away at the foundation of the family and entire clans. Others argue that it has not increased in popularity due to the fact that, without husbands, most women would be in dire financial straits. This argument is losing merit as industrialization ushers women into the workforce and gives them financial independence. Divorce, however, is still viewed seriously. If a man leaves his wife, sometimes the ex-wife will move in with the husband's family while he is ostracized, especially in the south.

The family frequently commands everybody's first loyalty. Italians raise their children to be mutually supportive and to contribute to the family. Separation from the family is generally not desired, expected, or easily accepted. Things that create conflict in Italian families may be sources of celebration in other cultures. Some normally joyful events that may cause operatic sadness are a job promotion that necessitates moving away from the family into another Italian region, acceptance into a prestigious university in a foreign land, and marriage. While these experiences may be sources of personal growth for the individual, they are likely to be experienced negatively if they weaken the collective sense of family. Many Italians view education and vocational training as secondary to the security, affection, and the sense of relatedness the family has to offer. Personal identity tends to be derived significantly from affiliation with the family, as well as from one's occupation or personal success. Family connections are extremely important for handling problems and getting ahead. Italians, not wanting to work for outsiders, often start family businesses. The business naturally adds to the solidarity of the family.

As noted previously, the north of Italy has been successful economically, and much of this success is due to the existence of small firms specializing in particular products. Moreover, these firms both compete and cooperate with one another. If one firm cannot honor an order, a neighboring firm will help it produce the product so that the commitment can be kept. At the same time, firms will cut prices to move ahead of neighboring competitors. These types of close business relationships echo family and village patterns, which are also expressed in the opera.

Personal Style

Sex for Italians, especially men, is seen as the essential life force (Newman, 1987). While honor is a quality all strive to achieve, virility and potency are still the basis on which many men are judged. This is confirmed by the fact that an adulterous wife is considered to be a direct reflection on her husband's lack of manliness. For many Italians, the ideal man is not necessarily intelligent or well off but rather of good character and physically and sexually strong.

Most Italians do not put much faith in what others say. Everyone is considered to be an outsider except members of the family. It is not surprising that Italians, living as they have always done with the insecurity and dangers of an unpredictable society, are among those who find their main refuge among their blood relatives. This overall suspicious attitude may be partially due to a quality on which Italians place high value, namely cleverness. Because of constant change and struggle, those who can survive through enterprise, cunning, imagination, and intelligence are held in high esteem by others. In other words, many Italians admire those who can create the most imaginative show. Minor deceptions, cleverly and subtly executed, are acceptable even if not necessary. Because everyone is trying to outsmart everyone else, the population as a whole is placed on the defensive. Visitors to Italy often comment on this feature of Italian life. For example, it is common practice to shortchange customers, sometimes significantly. If, however, the customer questions the transaction, the correct amount and profuse apologies will be offered immediately and without question.

While the family is the group that above all else influences the individual, another important group, the political party, can be the difference between employment and unemployment. Italians move from group to group, feeling little remorse when doing so because they tend to be skeptical of all groups besides the family. Members of groups often create powerful coalitions that are used to gain power and influence. These subcultures, groups, and parties allow for intergroup bargaining that creates coordination and cooperation among all involved.

Sometimes these powerful coalitions lead to widespread corruption. The worst example of corruption in Italy's history was exposed beginning in 1992 when a company in Milan refused to give a kickback, a regular business practice that is estimated to add 15% to 20% to the final price of goods. However, in this instance, public officials vigorously pursued various leads involving large numbers of prominent people. More than 1,200 businesspeople were indicted, and many served prison time, as did several Mafia members and two former prime ministers; some committed suicide in prison. While these and related activities seemed to weaken the Mafia, even more virulent and violent criminal organizations became prominent in the south: the Camorra and the 'Ndranghera. There has been a backlash against the reform movement, even to the extent of limiting the use in Italian courts of evidence gathered abroad and decriminalizing convictions for false bookkeeping.

Italians of many persuasions would like to see the emergence of a genuine two-party system, which is normally associated with much less corruption. Still, the sense of family and coalition behavior is so strong in Italy that we can expect many of the behaviors described in this chapter to persist. For example, we can expect that many job referrals and recommendations will still be based at least in part on family connections, much more so than in the United States.

Problematic Attitudes

Externalization also influences the management style of Italians. There is little delegation of authority or effective communication between the different levels of management in most Italian firms. Employees have little say about decisions concerning the company or about their own work. In fact, superiors are likely to cut off emotionally the ideas and suggestions of subordinates.

One final example of externalization is somewhat disturbing, as Italy is experiencing difficulty integrating the large number of legal and illegal immigrants flooding into the country, particularly those from the African nations of Morocco, Nigeria, Senegal, and Tunisia. The poorest Italians are most affected in that they feel that these immigrants are taking jobs away from them. Atrocities have included the burning of immigrants and the hanging of a 16-year-old immigrant. Many Italians are upset by this trend and, in true Italian fashion, have externalized it dramatically in newspapers, on television, and in the traditional piazza. Although such outbreaks of violence occur in many societies, Italians are confronting the problem in an open manner involving everyone in the society, and solutions are gradually being implemented.

Externalization is directly related to the mixing and balancing of diverse elements in both the opera and Italian society. Because the entire community or audience is involved in the unfolding of the drama, several elements involve numerous individuals. It is not an accident that the Italians have not specialized in one-person stage shows or dramas. Thus Italy, while primarily stressing individualism, is oriented toward specific aspects of group behavior or collectivism. Although individuals might not give the country as a whole much consideration, they place great importance on local and regional affiliation. This is directly related to the next characteristic of the opera, the influence of soloists and the chorus.

Chorus and Soloists

When Italians created the opera about 1560, there were no soloists. The first great Italian composer, Claudio Monteverdi, basically used different parts of the chorus to express ideas and emotions. However, singers vied with one another for the spotlight, and gradually soloists became prominent. Today it is difficult to conceive of an opera without great solo performances, which may help to explain why Monteverdi's operas are so seldom performed. This tension and balance between the chorus and soloists epitomize the struggles between regions, as each region retains certain easily perceptible characteristics, even if there is a major overriding division between the wealthier north and the poorer south. Most Italians define themselves by the town where they were born. These regional differences are similar to the chorus and soloists in operas. Soloists represent regional differences in the culture, whereas the chorus is the embodiment of the overall Italian culture. The Italian word that expresses the idea of belonging first to a town, then to a region, and third to a nation is *campanilismo*, derived from *campanile*, which means "bell tower." It refers to the fact that people do not want to travel so far as to be out of sight of the piazza church steeple.

Because of industrialization, northern Italians have had the benefit of a thriving economy and relative prosperity. In contrast, southern Italians, who have relied on farming for their livelihood, have tended to be poorer and less educated. The people from these two regions are similar in that they love life and enjoy creating the illusion of a show. However, they differ in that southerners tend to cling to past ways of living whereas many northerners look toward the future.

To most northerners, wealth is the way to ensure the defense and prosperity of the family and close friends over the long term. Northerners are perpetually trying to acquire wealth in its various forms. They want a job, a good job, and then a better job. They also want the scientific and technical knowledge that will ensure better paid employment and advancement. Many southerners, on the other hand, want above all to be obeyed, admired, respected, and envied. They want wealth, too, but frequently as an instrument to influence people. Southerners are preoccupied with commanding the respect of the audience throughout the many operas of life. Many southerners, be they wealthy or poor, want the gratitude of powerful friends and relatives, the fear of their enemies, and the respect of everybody. Southerners seek wealth as a means of commanding obedience and respect from others (Barzini, 1964).

A Culture of Death

In the south the culture centers around death. The Italians worry that the operatic drama of life will fall apart when a family member dies. The experience of dying and the fear of not being able to react properly to such an event has motivated southerners to create a complex strategy to enable them to face and conquer death (Willey, 1984). The strategy encompasses hundreds of beliefs, customs, and rituals. The purpose of these rituals is to reestablish contact between the living and the dead because, according to southern beliefs, the family includes both the living and the dead. Each family member has reciprocal rights and duties. The dead have to protect the living, and the living have to keep alive the memory of the dead, and people tend to attach great value to these obligations. Thus, in the early 1980s, a parish priest in one Calabrian village thought he would discourage long local funeral processions by levying a special fee per kilometer on the family of the deceased. His bishop promptly transferred him to another part of Italy (Willey).

This distinction between north and south is easily found in Italian operas, which tend to depict the characteristics of one region or the other. For example, *Cavalleria Rusticana* by Pietro Mascagni represents a classic southern opera with its emphasis on humble folk, suspicion, and revenge. In contrast, Giuseppe Verdi's *Tosca* emphasizes the north, as it takes place in elegant urban settings in which important personages display more subtle and complex feelings, although no less passionate (and perhaps even more so) than those found among the southerners.

Education has been a major mechanism for bringing about the modernization of Italy and minimizing regional differences. By diffusing the national culture through the teaching of one Italian language and by raising literacy levels, Italians have stressed cultural unity and deemphasized regionalism to a greater degree than in the past.

Different Ways of Doing Business

Although many of the differences between "the two Italys" have been defused and minimized through time, business dealings differ between the two regions. Working with people from northern Italy, a low-context subculture that emphasizes written rules and agreements, is much like dealing with U.S. Americans or Germans. To negotiate effectively with northern Italians essentially means communicating with them in a straightforward, sophisticated manner. Social talk should be kept to a minimum as the parties get down to business. When negotiating with people from southern Italy, a high-context subculture in which oral communication and subtle nuances are stressed, visitors must spend time establishing rapport with their counterparts. Long-term relationships are important to southern Italians, and trust must be built up before business dealings become truly effective.

In spite of these subtle differences, most Italians use a collaborative style of negotiating in that they will continue a dialogue until everyone's needs are met. Part of this style is due to the emotional nature of many Italians. Communication involves much more than words. The emotional nature of Italians enables them to see past the words spoken to the emotions felt. This insight helps them empathize and understand the needs of those with whom they negotiate. Such aggressive yet emotional Italians want to please everyone, including themselves. Therefore, a collaborative style of negotiating is common throughout Italy.

Similar to the operatic importance of both the chorus and soloists, regional differences combined with the overall Italian culture helped Italy gain economic strength during the 1970s and 1980s. This strength resided in the proliferation of small-scale commercial and industrial enterprises, usually family run, as noted previously. People whose families used to be southern farmers brought their deep-rooted traditions to the north and entered the commercial marketplace. The tradition of keeping ownership within the family, combined with the skills of managing a diverse product mix and willingness to work long hours, enabled the new entrepreneurs to compete effectively with their European neighbors. However, as noted earlier, such small firms now face increasing competition from China and elsewhere and do not enjoy the scale of operations of large multinational corporations, which are becoming more and more common throughout the world.

As indicated previously, Italy is facing major economic problems. Some governments in villages and even large towns do not have the money to manage critical services. For example, in 2007 Naples experienced a garbage strike during which accumulating piles of garbage created a major health crisis. To maintain a leading role in the EU, Italy must change this situation. Since the Great Recession starting in 2008, short sellers in stock markets have targeted Italy, Spain, Greece, and Portugal as particularly vulnerable. It is even possible that habitual government overspending in these nations may undermine the euro as a common currency. Whatever the eventual outcome, we can expect the Italians to address these problems in their distinctive, if not unique, operatic manner.

Chorus and Culture

The characteristics of the chorus and soloists can also be applied to other aspects of Italian culture. Italians tend to be individualistic, yet they place importance on the group. As we have seen, the family is the primary group that influences individuals. Whenever important decisions are made, the individual usually consults with family members to get their opinion and evaluation of the situation. Although the family's opinion is important, however, the individual makes the final evaluation. This is similar to the relationship between the chorus and soloists in the opera. The chorus frequently gives the soloists facts and opinions about the drama unfolding on stage, yet the soloists are the ones who dramatically decide how to handle the peril or situation, even when their decisions lead to disaster and tragedy.

The influence of the group is also felt in the business environment. In business meetings, people will externalize their feelings and opinions about a subject. They will listen to everyone's ideas and freely give their own opinions. Business meetings tend to be productive in Italy due to the openness displayed by everyone. However, like the chorus and soloist, the decisions coming out of a meeting are frequently made by one or two dominant or domineering people. In spite of the influence of the group, Italians tend to be aggressive and materialistic individualists due to their bias toward spectacle and externalization.

In the opera there is inherent inequity in the amount of fame given to each of the soloists. The same is true in the Italian economy. Today poverty still exists in some areas, particularly in the south. While Italian industry has been successful since the end of World War II, success is not shared equally by everyone. Because northern companies believe northern and southern work ethics differ, they are reluctant to locate branches in the south. The large migration of workers from the south to the north has left behind people who are not willing to give up customs and traditions that have been followed since early European civilization. Still, although the Italian culture consists of many regional subcultures, the modernization of Italy has begun to unify them. Italian culture is steadily changing to one where the melodies of the regional soloists blend into a harmonic chorus.

In this chapter, we have not explicitly treated the Italian orientation toward time, space, and the other culture-general concepts (see Chapter 1). As the discussion of the piazza suggests, Italians tend to be more polychronic than monochronic, performing many activities simultaneously. In Geert Hofstede's (1991) study of the cultural values of 53 countries, Italy clusters with those countries emphasizing a large power distance between groups in society; that is, Italians tend to accept the fact that some groups are and perhaps should be more powerful than others, and they act accordingly. The GLOBE study (House et al., 2004) confirms this feature of Italian life as evidenced in daily practices. Italians also try to avoid risk and uncertainty in everyday life, preferring friends over strangers and familiar over new or strange situations, as their behavior in the piazza and externalization would confirm. Although the family and kinship are important, Italy tends to cluster with those countries that are more accepting of individualism and aggressive, materialistic behavior, which reflect their externalized bias.

This, then, is Italy. It is still a grand and larger-than-life society whose citizens love pageantry and spectacle, emphasize a range of voices in everyday life, externalize emotions and feelings, and feel a commitment to the town and region of the country in which they were born. Italians have had a difficult history. Institutions have changed, rulers have come and gone, and people have to survive—and do, thanks to their personal, unofficial relationships. In Italy life is the theater, each act carefully played out for everyone to witness. From this perspective, the opera is not only helpful but possibly essential for understanding Italian behavior and culture.

CHAPTER 22

Belgian Lace

"I decided to put Belgium on eBay; 63 bidders, and we ended up at €10 million. But it was very symbolic, and it was like nothing happened after 100 days and all of a sudden, there was a man who sold his country on eBay. And wow, I was just famous for five minutes, I think it was called."

—Belgian journalist Gerrit Six speaking with National Public
Radio host Scott Simon (2011) about his frustration
with political deadlock in Belgium

Belgium is a small country slightly larger than the state of Maryland, with just over 10.5 million people. The distance between its farthest points is 175 miles. Given its size and population, the casual observer should be careful not to underestimate its importance to and interrelatedness with Europe and the world. The bitter tensions between the two major ethnic groups, the Wallonians (French speaking) and Flemings (Dutch speaking), are considerable, and the manner in which they address and resolve them may reflect in many ways approaches to the ethnic and national cultural tensions across the European Union (EU). In June 2010, the country held general elections, which resulted in a stalemate with the Flemish national party emerging triumphant in Flanders and the socialists winning in Wallonia. In February 2011, after the country overtook Iraq's record of 249 days without a government, people tried to hold on to their sense of humor by staging special events to honor the milestone. Some students in Leuven feasted on free frites and downed Belgian beer, and 249 individuals planned to strip naked in Ghent (Castle, 2011). As this book goes to press, a new Belgian government has been sworn in on December 6, 2011, after a record 541-day impasse. Prime Minister Elio Di Rupo, a French-speaking Socialist, will be leading a coalition of Socialists, Christian Democrats, and Liberals.

To understand Belgium and even some of the tensions within the EU, it is helpful to describe this nation in terms of the metaphor of lace. Just as the gifted lace maker takes fine threads from many spindles and weaves them into a fabric with a beautiful but strong pattern, so too history, geographic position, and religion have woven the Belgian culture into a diverse and complicated design, similar to that of all of Europe.

Before doing so, however, let us explore Belgium's turbulent and fascinating history. For hundreds of years, the people of Belgium, both the Flemish (of Dutch ancestry) in the north and the Wallonians (of French ancestry) in the south, were ruled by a number of other nations. Over the last 500 years Austria, Spain, France, and the Netherlands ruled, at one time or another, the area that is now Belgium. Although indigenous nationalistic movements sought to create the nation of Belgium from time to time, it was finally established in 1830 thanks to the machinations of Lord Palmerston, arguably the most influential foreign affairs minister that Britain has ever produced. He wanted to create a buffer zone between the Germans and the French in the event of war between these two nations and in the process to provide England with some breathing space before she was forced to enter any conflict. Lord Palmerston's instincts were unerringly correct, as Belgium was the site of some of the bloodiest battles in both World War I and II, and without this buffer zone it is conceivable and even probable that Germany would have overwhelmed both the French and the English (Tuchman, 1962).

The Flemish and Wallonian cultures, existing side by side, have given birth to a sense of Belgian pride. At multinational or world-class competitions, a Belgian is a Belgian and the entire country unites to watch the performance, regardless of which side of the language border the participant or team originated (Schrank, 2008).

Wallonian Versus Flemish

Still, it cannot be denied that conflicts and tensions exist between the Wallonians and the Flemish. Unlike many other cultural groups living in one nation or area who escalate these differences into bloody confrontations and war—for example, the fighting between the Catholics and Protestants in Northern Ireland or that among the Croatians, Bosnians, and Serbians in the former Yugoslavia—the Wallonians and the Flemish have patiently addressed their differences in a systematic way since 1968. Today Belgium is a federation of states in which the central government has relinquished almost all of its power except in such areas as finance, defense, and international relations. There are, in fact, a bewildering number of parliaments: One is for the nation in its entirety; one for Brussels (an international city in the middle of Flemish-speaking Flanders, in which 80% of the residents nevertheless speak French); one for Wallonia; one for Flanders; one for the tiny German-speaking community; and even one for French speakers regardless of location. The impasse following the June 2010 elections reflects an inability to find common ground between Flanders, the wealthier Dutch-speaking region in the north that wants more autonomy, and Wallonia, the poorer French-speaking region in the south. The stalemate has negative financial implications for the country, as it has been warned by rating agencies such as Standard & Poor's that its credit rating is in jeopardy.

Admittedly, attempts to resolve the ongoing ethnic and regional tensions have led to some bewildering outcomes. In Brussels, the capital, some streets receive only Flemish-language cable TV, while adjoining streets receive only French. Belgium's embassies abroad have three separate commercial attachés. Although these means of governing amid ethnic tension may seem contrived and unduly complicated, they are far preferable to the alternative of war and destruction. Protests are relatively civil and even tinged with some humor and self-mockery, as the protests against the government stalemate indicate. One Belgian, as reported above, posted the country for sale on eBay—but the listing was pulled after attracting a bid of US$13 million. Flemish protesters slashed signs with names in both Dutch and French and paraded coffins symbolizing Belgium's demise.

Still, there is a serious movement among some prominent Wallonians to argue for national disintegration so that the Flemish region can unite with the Netherlands and possibly parts of France and Germany ("Could Flanders," 1997). This has caused concern in other European nations where there are also secessionist movements (e.g., Spain). Whatever the eventual outcome, Belgium serves as a useful model that other nations—and even groupings of nations such as the EU—with diverse cultural groups can study and at least partially follow to avoid such alternatives, and this model closely resembles our metaphor of Belgian lace.

History of Lace

Lace first appeared in the late 15th century in Flanders and Italy. It was originally used as a modest ornament for undergarments. By 1600, lace had become a fabric of utmost luxury and a key article of trade and commerce. Nobility from all over Europe began to enhance their clothing with lappets and cuffs of lace. Dresses were soon adorned with lace overlays and shawls. Beyond clothing, lace began to drape tables, windows, and bed linens. Lace was a sign of social status and wealth. As a lace-making center, Flanders established itself as a prominent industrial region within Europe.

Bobbin lace, first introduced in Flanders, requires the weaver to manage hundreds of bobbins in creating a single piece of lace. Systematically and rhythmically, the threads from the 10 to 20 sets of bobbins are braided around brass pins skillfully affixed to a cardboard pattern to form a geometric or pictorial design. The design incorporates a delicate balance of lace and space that is best exhibited when the lace is placed on a dark background fabric such as deep-colored velvet or satin. During the Renaissance, lace making emerged as both an industry and an art form, as the following passage confirms:

> Form became more important than color; instead of intricate effects of limitless expansion, designers stressed clarity, symmetry, and stability. In the decorative arts, the new spirit was most noticeably expressed in sharp distinctions between pattern, background, and frame. No minor art form embodied Renaissance ideals more fully than lace. (Benton, 1970, Vol. 13, p. 85)

Traditionally, the best lace makers were cloistered nuns. Emperor Charles V (1500–1558) decreed that lace making should be a compulsory skill for girls in convents throughout Flanders. To create a square foot of lace with an intricate design may require hundreds or even thousands of hours. Legend has it that some nuns would spend their entire lives producing lace for the pope's robes. Although lace is no longer a predominant industry in Belgium, and machine-produced lace is the norm, the Belgians still take great pride in this traditional art form; most homes have at least one piece of handwoven lace on a table or displayed in a frame.

Many Belgians can hold up a piece of lace and tell if it was handwoven or machine made, the approximate retail value of the piece, and the region of the country where the piece was produced. The texture and pattern of the lace have regional characteristics. For instance, in Brugge and Turnhout the texture is delicate and the patterns are ornate, whereas in St. Hubert the thread is coarse and the design simpler. Hence lace from Brugge might typically be used as a table runner between meals, and lace from Saint-Hubert might adorn the edge of the tablecloth used during a meal.

We selected Belgium's famous lace as a metaphor for this country because it encapsulates the beauty of this land of contrasts where different cultures coexist in relative harmony, where individualism is compatible with the control of very strong family values, and where cooperation and harmony win out over competition and the people are quietly proud of their traditions and heritage.

A Land of Contrasts

The beauty of lace can be fully appreciated only when contrasted with woven cloth and dark background. Just as lace interweaves contrasting elements of a complex design into a single structure, so too many contrasting elements are interwoven in Belgium, a small country that recognizes three languages and includes two major cultures, three official regions, three flags, two major economic centers with separate industries, and three distinct geographic landscapes. The starkest contrasts for Belgium are linguistic and political. In addition, other areas of contrast include the following:

- The struggle between individualism and the need to belong to a group, conform to societal rules, and have strong family ties
- The dichotomy between working and social welfare
- The differences between urban and rural areas
- The desire for art and beauty but also a penchant for practicality

Just as a lace maker integrates contrasting designs in a masterpiece, the Belgian government attempts to integrate separate cultures into a unified republic, despite each of the three major regions having its own parliament.

A Land of Three Languages

The Belgian government recognizes three languages through regulations regarding the conduct of education and commerce within the areas populated primarily by native speakers. In Flanders, the northern portion of the country bordering the Netherlands, business and education are primarily conducted in Dutch, the native language of the Flemish people, who comprise about 58% of the Belgian population. In Wallonia, the southern portion of the country bordering France, business and education are primarily conducted in French, the native language of the Wallonian people, who constitute about 31% of the Belgian population. In Limburg, a very small area bordering Germany with about 1% of the population, German is the native language. To be impartial and economically viable, merchants, educators, government officials, and others in the capital city of Brussels conduct business in Dutch, French, or English, depending on the mutual preference of the participants.

Brussels is at the crossroads of Europe, and many multinational firms have established European offices there in recent years because of the unification of the European Community in 1992. At any given time, about 5% of the population of Belgium is foreigners. The complex federated governing structure of the nation can cause confusion, especially for the newly arrived foreigner. The city of Brussels, one of the two capitals of the European Parliament, is technically not equivalent to the Brussels region, although geographically they are the same. It is understandable why some visitors call Brussels the capital of confusion (Waxman, 1993).

In Belgian schools, children are first required to study the native language of the region in which they live for at least 8 years. They are also required to study a second language, which could be Dutch, French, English, or German, for at least 4 years. It is not uncommon to meet a Belgian, usually a Fleming, who is proficient in each of the four languages as well as others. However, Belgians are proud of their native languages and cultures. If two headstrong Belgians, a Fleming and a Wallonian, have to communicate, they will usually defer to English because the Wallonian will probably not be able to or want to speak Dutch and the Fleming will not condescend to speak French to a Wallonian if it can be avoided.

In everyday life, the impact of these linguistic differences varies significantly. Those who reside deep within Flanders or Wallonia may not be affected by them at all. By contrast, Belgians living closer to the language border or in Brussels must deal with language differences daily. For instance, new regulations in some municipalities near NATO headquarters require that public land can be sold only to Dutch speakers or those who show a willingness to speak the language. One man reported that police failed to respond to his French-language request to investigate a disturbance. Belgians tend to appreciate the use of their languages and will generally warm up to outsiders more quickly if an attempt is made to learn at least one of them. Although many Belgians deal with language differences every day, it is in poor taste for a foreigner to point out the differences or to wonder aloud why the differences cannot be resolved through diplomacy.

The oldest Catholic university in the world, the University of Leuven, located 20 miles east of Brussels in Flanders, illustrates the consequences of the language conflict. For hundreds of years, the university served both Flemish and Wallonian students and scholars, using French as the official language on campus. After World War II, linguistic tensions began to mount, causing sporadic scuffles in cafes around the university. Over more than 20 years, the hostility evolved to the point that the university was divided into two campuses: one in Leuven (Flanders) and one in Wallonia. This separation divided not only students and faculty but also resources such as the library collection. Books were literally divided by title, with those in the first half of the alphabet staying in Leuven and those in the second half going to the new campus. Conducting research now necessitates visiting two campuses, but this cumbersome and inefficient solution is preferable to engaging in linguistic conflict.

Region Versus Nation

As an extension of the dual languages and cultures of the Flemish and Wallonians, the country has three prominent flags: the tricolor of black, yellow, and red, representing the Belgian country; the Flemish lion; and the Wallonian rooster. Most Belgians identify more emotionally with the flag of their respective cultures than with the tricolor flag of the nation. The Flemish lion is the symbol of the Flemish resistance to French domination over hundreds of years.

While regional and ethnic identification is clearly important, Belgians do identify themselves as Belgian when outside the nation and come together on critical social issues. For example, 300,000 Belgians—as a proportion of the total population, the equivalent of 7.7 million U.S. Americans—rallied against the seemingly careless and perhaps corrupt manner in which the judiciary handled a chilling case involving a pedophile ring that had killed four young girls. This small country produced two top-10 tennis players in Justin Henin and Kim Clijsters, who came from different regions of the country but generated great national pride and enthusiasm when they played on the international stage.

Belgium is a constitutional monarchy divided into three republics: Flanders, Wallonia, and Brussels. Each republic has its own representatives in the central government or national parliament and its own divisions of the national political parties, which are also divided into subparties by language. Each subparty operates autonomously yet generally follows the same political agenda as the parent party.

The two largest political parties are the Christian People's Party, whose members are primarily Flemish and Catholic, and the Socialist Party, whose members are less strict Catholics and non-Catholics and more likely to be Wallonian. These two parties are also responsible for publishing most of the major newspapers in Belgium (five of seven) and supervising social facilities for youth, sports confederations, care of the aged, hospitals, savings banks, and unions. Much of the workforce is unionized. Successful administration of the trade unions and other social programs depends heavily on social stability. Due to the extensive influence of these two political parties in the life of the average Belgian, other political parties have not gained a significant foothold. Most voting districts are split along French- and Dutch-speaking lines. The Francophone Socialist (PS) and Flemish Nationalist (N-VA) parties won the largest proportion of seats during parliamentary elections in June 2010. The N-VA became the country's largest party, winning 27 seats compared to 4 in 2007, indicating growing support for regional autonomy in Flanders.

However, a right-wing, anti-immigration, secessionist political party, the Vlaams Blok, created in 1978, started gaining popularity in the 1990s. On November 14, 2004, the party changed its name to Vlaams Belang (Flemish Interest). Vlaams Belang, which won 13% of the Flemish vote in the elections of 2010, pursues independence for the Dutch-speaking part of Belgium. In several European nations (e.g., France and Spain), similar political parties have been campaigning against the free entry of immigrants into their nations.

Individual Versus Group

Belgians tend to be very individualistic. Hofstede's (1991) cross-cultural study ranked Belgians 8th out of 53 nations on this dimension. It is considered a major accomplishment for young adults to become established in their own houses, apart from the family. Hard work is also valued, as it is seen as providing an incentive for individuals to get away from the home. Still, even when the young leave the immediate family, they do not venture far geographically, usually living within 30 miles of their parents' home. This practice creates strong family/community ties.

Belgian individualism is also displayed in a preference for owning one's own home. Despite the great expense, about 65% of Belgians own the place where they live, residences that range from condominiums to suburban-country homes. A person's home is his castle, and Belgians tend to take great pride in the cleanliness of their homes. Early in the morning, it is common to see people sweeping their porches and walkways. While a U.S. American might use a garden hose to wash down a sidewalk, a Belgian would typically use a bucket and a scrub brush. This preference may be traceable to the historical shortage and high cost of fresh water. Belgians also tend to take short baths; use soapy water to wash the dishes and then wipe the soap off with a towel, rather than rinsing them with water; and drink soda water, juice, beer, or wine rather than tap water or anything made with tap water.

Just as each region of Belgium has a distinctive style and texture to its lace, so too are condominiums and row houses often organized and decorated distinctively, reflecting the tastes of their owners. Unlike England's traditional houses (see Chapter 17), the interior layout of a Belgian row house cannot be assumed from its exterior appearance. In Flanders it is common for extended families to construct the exterior brick walls of a new or remodeled home.

While Belgians tend to be individualistic, their family orientation is strong. The family plays a central role in daily life. Family activities and meals are highly cherished. Most Belgian children go home after a long day at school, do their homework, eat dinner, help with chores, and spend time with their families. Family time often includes reading or watching television. Programs are broadcast in French, Dutch, German, and English, usually with subtitles in a second language. Because the state owns the Belgian television stations, there are few commercials.

Family Life

On the weekends many Belgian children participate in scouting programs. Sunday lunch is usually the biggest meal of the week. The meal will normally take place at the same relative's house every Sunday, and family from the immediate area will all attend. If a husband and wife live close to both in-laws, they will frequently rotate Sundays between the two families.

Mothers often work. Out of a total workforce of over 4.4 million, more than 1.9 million are women; however, women typically are found in traditionally female occupations such as nursing and secretarial jobs. Few have completed a university education or occupy top management positions. Day care is heavily subsidized by the state.

Families often spend weekends and vacations together, traveling to the Belgian coast for short stays and to Spain or the Riviera for longer stays. In the warm months, camping in the Ardennes (mountains in southeast Belgium) is a frequent pastime.

When a couple marries, the woman takes the name of the man and connects it with her maiden name, so that if she is a Smith and marries a Jones, her married name becomes Mrs. Jones-Smith. Especially in Wallonia, it is not uncommon for a couple to live together until the woman becomes pregnant with their first child, at which time the couple will revert to Catholic tradition and get married in church. Due to Catholic influence, divorce is rare and only recognized after years of separation. However, the economy, more than the Catholic Church, has influenced the size of families. The socially correct family size is two children, and a family has received a perfect gift from God if the two children are a boy and a girl.

In the family it is typical for the father and the eldest son to be the ultimate decision makers. Mothers usually administer discipline and rule household matters. Since about 1970, much has been done to emancipate women through legislation. Although legal equality has been mostly achieved, however, it will take time to eradicate the convictions and prejudices that have been nurtured for so many years. Moreover, the gender-based segregation of half of the country's elementary classes (primarily in parochial schools) reinforces the traditional view of women's role (Verleyen, 1987), although this is changing.

Aside from family, over their lifetimes Belgians will have only a few truly close friendships. Unlike the United States, where people tend to be quick to establish friendships, the Belgians generally require a great deal of time before relationships mature. Most people with whom Belgians interact regularly will remain simply acquaintances, even after many years (see also Chapter 12: The German Symphony).

Consensus and Compromise

Belgians normally hold their right to privacy and their own opinions sacred. As lace makers have a range of motions with which they pull thread from their bobbins and weave it around the brass pins, so too the Belgians seem to have similar ranges in their varied activities. Still, rarely does a Belgian stray far from the group by taking an extreme position. Belgium is generally a country of consensus, compromise, and cooperation. However, eccentric artists are revered as the embodiment of the eternal voice of protest, as long as they are not hostile or confrontational. For the individual, however, exclusion from the group can entail loneliness, pain, and, more often than not, material poverty (Verleyen, 1987).

Overarching the individualism of each Belgian is a set of common political rules that have governed public policy and conduct for decades. This set includes the following:

- The monarchy and Brussels are untouchable; in other words, all else could change, but there should still be a monarchy and Brussels should still be the capital.
- European unification and the EU are to be advocated without any reservation. As noted above, however, the political party Vlaams Belang advocates the breakup of the EU.
- The authority of NATO and Belgium's ally, the United States, may be the subject of frequent criticism, but they also enjoy the privilege of inviolability.
- Prosperity is to be shared and not to be used as a justification for confrontation or class struggle.
- Labor strikes should not be allowed to jeopardize the existing economic order.
- Privacy and personal liberty are not to be impeded in any serious way (Verleyen, 1987).

The varied types of occupations and pastimes enjoyed by the Belgian population present yet another area of contrast. Belgium has a long tradition of agricultural activity. The central area around Brussels has rich soil and flat terrain conducive to farming, yet only 2% of the workforce is agricultural and only 1% of the gross national product comes from farming. The population is increasingly concentrated in urban areas and engaged in industrial and service activities. Nonetheless, Belgians vigorously defend and subsidize their traditional agricultural base. Although Belgium has the 17th-highest population density among nations at 344 per square kilometer, urban planning has helped to ensure that most urban areas are pleasant.

Industry and Business

In the past few years, a great debate has raged over national subsidies to the mining and steel industries located particularly in the Wallonian region. Many believe there is no prospect of these industries ever regaining their former status or profitability and assert that governmental support should be rechanneled toward expanding industries that can compete in the EU and worldwide.

Belgians must attend school from age 6 to 18. Programs are rigorous, and most children have at least 2 hours of homework every night after 8 hours of school. To pass from one level of education to the next, each student must take an exam. The results of the exams determine what schools the student may attend and what vocation the student may undertake. As in Germany, students begin studying for a vocation in their early teens. When they leave secondary school, most begin internships in their chosen vocations or go straight to college. Belgians are highly educated and skilled craftspeople.

The contrasting fortunes of the north and south of Belgium have undergone a dramatic change over the last century. In 1830 French was the official language of the Belgian kingdom. The nobility spoke French; government proceedings and church services were conducted in French; and the wealthiest citizens, Wallonians, spoke French. Therefore French came to be perceived as the cultured language. Conversely, the Flemish were perceived as the uncultured and poorer members of Belgian society. Some Flemish families remain embittered over stories that their ancestors, foot soldiers in World War I, died simply because they could not understand the commands of their French-speaking superiors. As fortunes shifted from the coal and steel industries in Wallonia to the shipping and international trade industries of Flanders, the Flemish found themselves in a position to demand recognition of their language and cultural heritage.

Over the last decade Flanders has continued to prosper, while most of Wallonia has been devastated by high unemployment and by depression. "Today old factories dominate the gray landscape" where once "a kind of provincial snobbery was polished to a fine sheen" (Sciolino, 2007). In Wallonia unemployment is of a structural nature, whereas in Flanders unemployment is more cyclical. This and other differences between the two regions threaten to tear the delicate lace that constitutes Belgium into different sections.

Immigration Issues

In general Belgians are hard-working people, just like lace makers who may work nearly 1,000 hours on an intricate piece of lace that measures only 1 square foot, investing not only time but pride in the quality of their work. Today, most Belgians are moving heavily into service and diplomatic industries, leveraging their native skills to meet global economic demand. Because of the great pride that they take in their work and craftsmanship, regardless of how depressing the prospect of long-term unemployment might be, many Belgians would prefer to draw unemployment than do work below their level of training or skill. Therefore immigrants from third-world countries are viewed as necessary to correct a temporary labor imbalance.

Typically immigrants are brought in from North Africa and Turkey to work in the mines and do other menial jobs that Belgians reject. These immigrants are given access to many government social programs, such as medicine and welfare, but they are ineligible to vote and are rarely allowed to become citizens. Although Belgians tend not to warmly welcome third-world foreigners, antiracism legislation makes discriminatory public expressions against immigrants punishable by law. Furthermore, although the Belgians feel that third-world immigrants are only needed temporarily, long-range forecasts show that the Belgian population is shrinking because of low birth rates and emigration while the immigrant population is increasing. As mentioned earlier, social tradition has led most Belgian families to have two or fewer children despite the fact that the Catholic-influenced legal system prohibits abortion and most forms of birth control.

Urban Versus Rural

Another sharp contrast is between urban and rural settings. The Belgian countryside is green and lush due to abundant rainfall and high humidity throughout the year. As one drives through Belgium, one sees long stretches of rolling green hills dotted by little white farmhouses. Older farmhouses have the barn on the first floor and the family lives upstairs, and the farmer plowing a field with his large workhorse is a frequent sight. At times like these, it is hard to imagine that Belgium ever entered the 20th century, let alone the 21st.

The cities typically look like medieval fortresses, many with a wall surrounding them, interrupting the gentle slope from urban to suburban to rural. There are no U.S.-style suburbs in Belgium. An aerial view at night would show roughly circular areas of dense lights surrounded by thin networks of lights along major highways and a few spots of light in rural areas. This view might resemble the contrasting lace made around Brussels, in which densely woven patches are delicately connected by threads to other densely woven patches.

Inside the cities, one finds further contrasts between modern industrial facilities and the grandeur of older architecture. In Brussels, the Atomium, a large structure built during a recent world's fair, resembles a giant silver atom. Its elevators take visitors up for a view around the city. The NATO buildings, among others, are modern and efficient. By contrast, the Brussels town square, the Grand Place, is surrounded by cobblestone streets and buildings with ornately carved facades, and it draws the visitor back to the city's origins in the 16th century.

In recent times, more than two dozen groups have formed to reenact life in the Middle Ages. This movement is so strong that "juvenile delinquents in Flanders have been allowed to atone for their misdeeds by making the Chaucerian pilgrimage to Santiago de Compostela, in northern Spain, 1,250 miles, on foot, carrying backpacks and accompanied by a guard" (Bilefsky, 2007a). According to Herman Konings, a Belgian behavioral psychologist who studies national trends, the medieval craze can be attributed to a strong desire to return to a more glorious past. The country, divided between Dutch-speaking Flanders in the north and French-speaking Wallonia in the south, is experiencing anxiety about its identity. This anxiety will probably increase in the future (Bilefsky).

Beauty Versus Practicality

A final area of contrast in Belgian culture is that between a love for art and beauty and a sense of practicality. Obviously most lace is beautiful and artistic, but it is also designed to adorn clothing and linens rather than be simply admired. The artistic history of the country is evidenced by the prominence of museums, theaters, and artistic venues. In Belgium there seems to be a museum for everything. The largest is the open-air museum at Bokrijk. Rural buildings from various centuries have been excavated from all over and painstakingly rebuilt here. Many retirees dress up in authentic costumes of the times and display the tools and crafts of the era from which the buildings come.

The Rijksmuseum in Antwerp has one of the finest collections of Flemish art in the world. Flemish art was the world standard from the 16th through the early 18th centuries. Exemplified by Brueghel, the van Eycks, and Rubens, Flemish art used the vivid colors and figures of the Italian Renaissance but rendered the human figure less elongated, plumper, and more realistic. Typical signs that a painting comes from the Flemish era are rosy red cheeks and the presence of lace on the clothing in portraits or on the table in a still life.

Inside many of the oldest churches in Belgium, one can find wonderful works of art, most with no apparent security systems attached. For example, it is not uncommon to locate a work by Rubens, van Eyck, or van Dyck hanging in an obscure village church where the doors are never locked. Some of these churches appear old and worn on the outside, but inside they have beautifully carved vestries and pedestals for the priests to stand on. Hung on the inside walls of many churches are works of art representing the 12 stations of the cross. Most of the churches were constructed so that the lighting is primarily natural and from candles. The art here was created to inspire the worshipper rather than simply to be admired, so the idea that someone might steal these works from the churches is absurd to the average Belgian. The oldest churches are all Catholic, each having a statue of the Virgin Mary with blazing little white candles all around her. When Belgians, even nonpracticing Catholics, are troubled by work or family matters, they often light candles for Mary.

The school system strongly supports the study of art history. Schoolchildren flood museums throughout the school year for lectures and sightseeing. Early lessons stress the importance of Belgian artists, nearly to the exclusion of others. This emphasis on art is initiated at a young age and is carried forward throughout most Belgians' lives. The people of Belgium do seem to have painting "in their blood" and seem to like hearing themselves described as a nation of painters. Belgium is proud of its artistic past and for good reason.

Another example of Belgian practicality is the site where the Battle of the Bulge was waged in World War II. This battle was a major victory for the Allied forces and has been a major tourist attraction for many years. The site is marked by a large circular monument with pillars listing the names of the dead in that battle, resembling a modern Stonehenge. The monument is surrounded by rolling hills, which during tourist season are meticulously covered with rows of white crosses to mark the resting places of the dead. After tourist season (September–April), the crosses are removed and cows are pastured on the hills.

Control

Lace production requires strict and complex controls to avoid flaws. In addition, there must be balance between the spindles and the thread and between the patterns in the cloth. This emphasis on controls and balance is similarly found in the Belgian preference for controlling behavior, interacting with friends and colleagues in familiar situations and surroundings, and leading a balanced life. In Hofstede's (2001) cross-cultural study of 53 nations, Belgium ranked 6th in terms of avoiding uncertainty. Belgians tend to exhibit this high degree of control and uncertainty avoidance in several areas, including lifestyle, transportation, social conventions, rules and procedures, and stress management. Belgians tend to be suspicious of anyone who would change his or her adopted schedule or routine. Most Belgians have a deep-rooted attachment to what is called a "3-by-8" schedule: 8 hours for work, 8 hours for play, and 8 hours for sleep. Modern management proposals to change the organization of work so as to increase industrial output are frequently opposed. Many who own small businesses work longer hours, but they also tend to live over their shops so they are never far from home and family. Most shops and businesses are closed on Sunday, although since the Catholic Church changed its policy to allow parishioners to attend High Mass on Saturday evening, more Belgian businesses have Sunday hours. Still, Belgium ranks 32nd out of 179 nations on the Index of Economic Freedom (T. Miller, 2011) and has a relatively high gross domestic product per person of US$47,090.

Transportation

To avoid uncertainty, political and linguistic borders are well-defined and mapped. Savvy travelers can usually determine which region they are in by the first reference on the city and street signs. However, this can all be very confusing to the visitor, as a sign may list two or more names for the same place, for example, Antwerpen (Dutch), Anvers (French), and Antwerp (English). In the city, most maps and signs will say Antwerpen. However, if the map consulted came from Wallonia or France, the city would be marked Anvers.

Belgium has several large ports, including Antwerp, the second-largest port in Europe. To accommodate the huge amount of trade from its port cities, Belgium has designed the largest transportation system in the world for a country its size. Like the threads in a piece of lace, the highways, railways, and canals in this system connect every city and village in the country, allowing goods to flow efficiently all over Belgium and into the rest of Europe.

Major roads are constructed in a hub-and-spoke fashion, with roads encircling larger cities (the hubs) and other roads extending toward other major cities (the spokes). Many road signs in various languages accommodate industry and travelers. As one drives along the spokes from one city to another, the name of the road will change halfway between the cities. For example, should one take the Mechelen road from Brussels to get to Mechelen, halfway there the name of the road will change to the Brussels road, indicating that the traveler is now closer to Mechelen than Brussels. Changing road signs can severely complicate the trip of inexperienced travelers, especially when languages change as well. However, this practice is orderly to the Belgian mind, just as the pattern and texture of a piece of lace is set by its origin.

As one drives over the cobblestone roads of the inner city and occasional dirt roads in the country, there are no stop signs. It is assumed at every intersection that the driver to the right has the right of way, no matter what the circumstances. Therefore, technically at every intersection drivers need look only to the right before proceeding, and Belgians will sometimes grow quite impatient with travelers who stop to look in all directions before proceeding.

One of the most interesting jobs keeping some Belgians away from the unemployment office is that of road worker. Many city streets are paved with cobblestones. Road crews can be seen working on a small area at the side of the road, digging up the cobblestones, placing them in a pile, cleaning them carefully, and then relaying them. However, the stones are not simply replaced in a haphazard fashion. Rather, they are laid in an orderly pattern similar to the manner in which lace is arranged, often with some artistic, geometric design. Hence this job, although seemingly menial, appeals to the Belgian sense of industry, beauty, and practicality.

Social Rules

In social settings, Belgians are generally formal in their interactions with others and employ a number of explicit rules. For instance, when greeting others, the surname is the proper way to address all but close friends. The casual manner in which first names are used in many countries would probably offend most Belgians. This formality is common in business and social settings, even with neighbors and acquaintances.

Formal titles are used in many business and social settings in lieu of the full name; for example, *Monsieur* or *Mijneer* for a man, *Madame* or *Mevrow* for a married woman, and *Mademoiselle* or *Jevrow* for a single woman. It is important not to use *Monsieur* or *Madame* with a Flemish speaker; instead, Mr., Ms., Miss, or Mrs. is the preferred form. Titles are also used in many subordinate-superior relationships, such as student to professor or employee to boss. Both the French and Dutch languages incorporate formal and informal manners in which a person can be addressed. Informal address is used when addressing a child, but adults generally need to know one another well before communicating in this way. Among younger people and in business with English-speaking partners, however, much less formality prevails, and using first names is common practice.

Greetings are also an extremely important part of the social ritual. Handshakes are the norm unless the two parties are good friends. A person will typically shake hands with everyone when meeting and again before leaving the gathering. Belgians will often lament if they do not have a chance to shake hands before parting. In addition, women greeting either men or women in an informal manner will generally kiss three times on alternating cheeks.

Belgians are conscious of social rituals such as gift giving. Gifts are given at any type of social visit, and not to present a gift is seen as rude. However, gifts are normally not a part of business relationships. A typical gift when one is invited to dinner is flowers (except chrysanthemums, which signify death), a small box of chocolates, or an unusual fruit such as a pineapple. If the visit extends to a number of days, it is common practice to offer a gift for each day spent. Acknowledgments and thanks are made in writing for any gift received, even birthday and holiday cards. In Belgium, new year's cards are sent in lieu of Christmas cards.

Almost all social gatherings are somewhat formal. When alcoholic beverages are served, it is customary to wait until everyone is served and then, with some ceremony, to raise one's glass to each person in turn, catching his or her eyes and wishing him or her *gezondhiet, santé,* or the like. Likewise, it is customary to wait for everyone at the table to be served before eating. Just before taking the first bite of food, everyone says *smaaklijk* or *bon appétit* or, in other words, wishes everyone else a tasty meal. Written invitations are frequently sent to dinner guests, even to close friends, and a formal four-course meal is normally prepared. Afternoon tea can also be a formal event.

People, including close friends and family, seldom drop by another's house without first telephoning. Neighbors also observe this protocol, maintaining a high level of formality when interacting. All this formality, however, does not keep Belgians from visiting each other. They normally love to socialize; they just like to plan ahead when someone is coming. Their plans often include going to the bakery on the corner to get a special dessert to serve with tea, which may be traditional tea or herbal tea.

When one enters a Belgian home, one generally finds an unheated entryway with stone or linoleum flooring where coats are hung and wet shoes are kept. By contrast, the living area of the house is generally warm and cozy. Thoughts of putting on a cold coat and wet shoes may explain why guests stay so long on winter nights.

Belgians tend to require certainty and privacy in social settings as well as in everyday life. In Belgium almost every door has a lock. In a home or a business, this means that even cabinets and closets can be locked. In business settings, it is appropriate to keep office doors closed and to knock on a door and wait for an answer. A homeowner may need 50 keys to guarantee privacy and security. In the older buildings of some universities, there is a light above the professor's closed office door. When a student wants to see the professor, he or she must ring a bell, in response to which the professor activates the light's color to indicate whether the student should come in (green), wait a few minutes (yellow), or go away (red). While this may seem extreme, it appeals to the Belgian sense of practicality, and the same system is used in some other northern European nations to some extent. Further, there is a comparable but not widespread practice in U.S. business offices where those working in a cubicle will place a red, orange, or green ball on top of the cubicle to alert potential visitors: red (not available), orange (available but busy right now), and green (available).

Public Gatherings

Certainty is also highly desirable in social agreements. For Belgians, their word is their bond, and promises must be kept. However, beneath all the formal rituals and procedures, the Belgian people tend to be friendly, laid-back, and good-natured. To see this side of their personality, one can go to a local pub and observe the closeness of the relationships and abundant consumption of beer. Beer is not only a cherished drink but a source of pride for Belgians. Most Belgian cities have at least one brewery, and the smell of the hops hangs in the damp winter air. Belgians will make beer out of most any grain and wine out of most any fruit.

Another place where Belgians are sure to congregate is at the local *frituur* or french-fry maker's shop. In most neighborhoods it is a place to escape from the cold weather and to learn all the latest gossip. Belgian french fries, *frits* (pronounced "freets"), are thickly sliced and fried once at low heat long enough to soften them. Then they are allowed to cool completely before being fried again in very hot lard. The result is a crispy outside with a soft inside, much like the bread in the bakeries. Frits are served in a paper cone with a choice of 20 or more toppings, including stew meat (usually horse meat with a beer gravy), curry sauce, and "sauce American," which is ketchup. They are as popular in Belgium as hamburgers are in America.

Before lace makers arrange the spindles and thread to begin weaving a piece of lace, they design the pattern on cardboard and carefully punch brass pins in the cardboard pattern to guide the thread during weaving. Similarly, one manifestation of high uncertainty avoidance is that Belgians have regulations and customs that act as brass pins to guide behavior in most situations. They tend to dislike the government and police officers, but they love order and so tolerate the intrusion. Dealing with government offices is tedious. There are specific papers and experts for everything. First one must figure out what paper to fill out for the needed service, and then the trick is to figure out what building and what window has the expert who can process the paperwork.

Citizens of the EU are not required to carry visas, but most Belgians carry personal cards or business cards with their family name, home address, and telephone number, which they can exchange or leave with a note on the back if they miss meeting someone. It is also obligatory for every Belgian citizen over the age of 12 to carry an eID or electronic identification card. In 2009 a "KidsID" was introduced for children under 12 on a strictly voluntary basis to enable them to enter "youths-only" chat sites and keep predators at bay.

Living With Stress

Hofstede (2001) demonstrated a strong correlation between high uncertainty avoidance and high anxiety and stress. This characteristic is manifested in Belgians in several ways. One is that they are a "doing" society; people are busy all day long, typically rising early. Many Belgian sayings refer to the judicious use of time; examples include "Time is money," "Make hay while the sun shines," and "Time heals all, so get back to business" (Verleyen, 1987, p. 55). Belgians try to prepare for everything so that nothing can go wrong. Much of this feeling may be attributed to their geographical location and historical lack of control over invading armies. The North Sea on the west is Belgium's only natural boundary. Therefore any emperor conquering the continent generally started in Belgium (the Low Countries) and moved on from there, as did Bismarck in the 19th and Hitler in the 20th century.

The religious orientation of the Belgians also contributes to their need to be constantly busy. Catholic doctrine places high importance on good works and personal industry in this life to ensure a comfortable station in the next. About 75% of Belgians are Catholic. Historically, Belgium produced more nuns and priests per capita than any other nation in the world. Although religious intensity has declined since World War II and most Belgians do not attend church regularly, a majority are still educated in Catholic schools.

Because Catholicism is the official religion of Belgium, the state heavily subsidizes Catholic parishes, priests, and schools. The constitution guarantees freedom of religion, and most major religions can be found somewhere in Brussels. But for most Belgians, religions other than Catholic are for foreigners. In September 2010, the Catholic church in Belgium was rocked by an official inquiry's finding that widespread sexual abuse of children by priests had taken place over several decades. The 200-page report contained details of abuse and torment by members of the clergy that went back to the 1950s. Church attendance, which was already below 10%, is likely to decline even further in the face of these revelations.

One result of the great effort that Belgians make to follow tradition and avoid uncertainty is minor mental breakdowns. It's not uncommon to call on them for an appointment and be put off because today they are having a *zenuw inspanning,* a Dutch phrase translated as a nervous strain. Typically this means they overslept, overexerted themselves, or generally aren't prepared to face the world for a while. When they feel a breakdown coming on, Belgians will call a doctor who will routinely prescribe tranquilizers and bed rest. In Belgium medicine is socialized and easily obtainable, although quality is often questionable. The health care infrastructure is immense, given the size of the population. Home visits by doctors and nurses are common, and paramedic support is widespread.

Cooperation and Harmony

While weaving a strand of lace, the lace maker must always focus on the symmetry of the design. A careful balance is maintained to ensure that neither the lace nor the linen overpowers the other. The overall effect should be one of harmony, with no stray ends or spaces to mar the unity of the structure. Each movement of the lace maker may be quick and concise but is always within a small range of motion. There are no extreme movements.

Furthermore, lace itself is a subtle and unobtrusive material. Traditional lace, being all white or ivory, is used to neutralize the bold colors of background material, to soften the hardness of wooden tables, or to balance an object visually. The carefully balanced nature of lace with its neutralizing and nonextreme tone is reflected in the Belgian approach to the world, especially in continuity, statesmanship, and modesty.

Belgians exert a great deal of energy maintaining continuity, the status quo, balance, and a set standard of living for all. They normally work to ensure that their internal cultural and linguistic differences do not disrupt daily life, squelching conflicts by remaining neutral or by reaching mutual consensus among the involved parties. Throughout its existence, Belgium has had linguistic tensions of varying intensity. Yet these tensions have never escalated to violence or bloodshed. When necessary, concessions were made and tempers were defused so that tensions would be carefully balanced. In lace making, this means the threads are held tightly to reduce both the slack and the potential for gaps or holes that might weaken the durability and quality of the cloth.

The Middle Road

Although Belgians can do little to control the weather in their country, the moderate climate seems to reflect their approach to life: Take the middle road between extremes. Due to the Gulf Stream off the coast, the climate is mild, ranging from about 35°F in the winter to about 75°F in the summer. The weather is frequently cloudy and/or rainy, with little snow and few fully sunny days. However, a winter day with clouds is preferable to a cloudless day because the clouds tend to insulate the land.

The middle road between extremes is also where Belgian managers can usually be found. Subordinates will refer to managers using formal titles and last names; however, managers will seldom stand out because of appearance, conspicuous consumption, or attitudes that might separate management from line workers, as frequently happens in the United States. Again, to Belgians wealth is to be shared rather than flaunted.

Furthermore, the Belgian balancing and peace-making approach to life is repli-cated in a competitive (or not-so-competitive) nature. Belgians tend to be cooperative more than competitive. Their social and economic structure is designed to actually lessen the competitive drive. For instance, the socialized system of government ben-efits provides full health care and monetary subsistence for all citizens. Furthermore, there is no time limit on eligibility for unemployment, as long as the person appears at the appointed time each week at the unemployment (labor bureau) office and regu-larly applies for openings in her or his stated occupation. The appointed time changes each week to prevent working around the appointment. There are, however, propor-tional benefits with an upper limit.

Recently there has been discussion of limiting the unemployment allowance to 5 years, but as long as the government can afford it, Belgians will probably not limit this subsidy. Most citizens feel that a certain standard of living is a social right, regard-less of a person's ability to find a job for which he or she is suited. Needless to say, the unemployment subsidy, social security/health care system, and other socialized ser-vices in Belgium are largely responsible for one of the highest tax rates in Western Europe. Although Belgian workers tend to be highly skilled and hard working, thus creating a situation in which there is high productivity per worker, the tax rates are so high that the cost of labor almost offsets productivity.

Another factor of Belgian society that induces a less competitive nature is that the salary earned in many jobs does not vary to reflect effort and performance. For instance, a professor who instructs classes, devotes an inordinate amount of time to research, and publishes regularly will not be paid any more than a professor who maintains a much more relaxed lifestyle. Other than a sense of personal achievement, which is not necessarily highly valued, there is little reward for working harder than the average professor or coworker. There is a greater emphasis on cooperating with colleagues than on climbing over one another to get to the top.

Born Negotiators

Furthermore, Belgians share a great tradition of statesmanship and the ability to negotiate on behalf of others. Peter Paul Rubens, the Flemish painter, was a legendary statesman whose greatest efforts were in fostering international cooperation. He was hired by royalty and wealthy merchants to paint portraits of others. While he had the subject seated for long periods of time, he was paid to put forth the philosophy or argument of his benefactor. For example, he was sent by Philip IV, king of Spain, to paint Charles I, king of England, all the while negotiating a trade agreement between the two nations. This is one reason why Rubens painted about 1,600 royal portraits.

Modern Belgians have carried forward this tradition. The cooperative nature of the Belgians is again apparent in their approach to the European Community and the world. Belgium's linguistic and cultural diversity made it an ideal model for the "EU 92" negotiations. Due in part to this unique status, Brussels was selected as one of the two capitals of the EU. In 1967, for many of the same reasons, NATO moved its headquarters from Paris to Brussels. Belgians are also joiners, and there is an association for every need. Due to Belgium's cultural traditions and unqualified acceptance of these international organizations, its balanced nature, and its central location, Brussels has become one of the most important international areas in the world.

In addition, international corporations seeking to expand into European markets have flooded over the Belgian borders over the past 30 years. About 40% of Belgian industries are foreign owned. In an interesting twist, the maker of the "king of beers" in America, Anheuser Busch (Budweiser and Bud Light), agreed in 2008 to a US$52 billion takeover by the Belgian brewer InBev SA (Stella Artois, Beck's and Bass) in a merger that has created the world's largest brewery. The Belgian government offers international groups major tax incentives to bring central offices or high-tech activities into the country. Despite generous wages, high manufacturing costs, and exorbitant personal tax rates, companies have sought out manufacturing facilities in Belgium to take advantage of the transportation infrastructure and friendly economic climate. Thus, another element that the Belgians seemingly balance effortlessly is the internationalization of their small country while maintaining their own identity.

A Proud People

Finally, although the Belgians have many reasons to be proud and boastful, people outside the country are rarely aware of Belgian accomplishments. For instance, many readers may not have been aware of the importance of Belgium to lace and vice versa before reading this chapter. Also, it is not generally known that Belgians produce some of the best beer and chocolates in the world. Belgium ranks consistently among the top 20 nations of the world with regard to per capita gross domestic product. Despite Belgian prominence in international circles, many people are still unfamiliar with the country. Most people struggle to name prominent Belgians after fictional detective Hercule Poirot and beloved comic strip hero Tintin, who is enjoying great success in the 2011 Steven Spielberg film *The Adventures of Tintin*. The reason underlying this lack of international recognition seems primarily to be the Belgian approach to life. Belgians are not generally boastful, tending not to expound on their capabilities and accomplishments. Indeed, they act much like a small piece of lace on the collar of a garment; they bring out the best qualities of those with whom they work without being flashy or calling attention to themselves. Some view this approach as an inferiority complex of sorts, but this idea is contradicted by the definite pride that Belgians feel toward different characteristics of their country. Belgians do not feel they are less important or worthy of praise, as an inferiority complex would suggest. In fact, the case is quite the opposite: Belgians tend to believe that the country can and will be an integral player in the EU and the world. The typical Belgian emphasizes the role Belgium plays as coordinator and peacemaker among international markets, sometimes sacrificing publicity and recognition in favor of achieving concord amid tension.

In short, Belgium is as complex as its renowned lace, and its citizens have learned to meet the challenges posed by the interactions that must occur among its cultural and linguistic groups. Citizens have a tradition of self-mockery and irony, which has helped them deal with challenging situations such as the recent extended lack of a federal government. While this country has been internationally recognized as an independent state for fewer than 200 years, its past has been rich. Its future is delicate, intricate, and complicated, just like the lace for which the nation is well known. Belgium adds character and richness to the EU, just as a small piece of lace adds beauty and depth to a well-crafted garment. While there are tensions between the Wallonians and Flemish, we expect that Belgium will remain a country united not only by its lace but also by its long-standing rational manner of approaching ethnic diversity.

PART VII

Torn National Cultures

Some nations have experienced major assaults on the core values of their cultures. That is, they have been torn from the cultural roots that had nourished them for decades if not centuries. We provide two outstanding examples of such nations in this part of the book, Mexico and Russia. As indicated throughout the book, each nation can fit into more than one category or part of the book, and this is true of Russia and Mexico. But if readers desire to plumb the depths of what a torn culture really means, they can benefit from the analysis of these two nations.

CHAPTER 23

The Mexican Fiesta

The solitary Mexican loves fiestas and public gatherings. Any occasion for getting together will serve, any pretext to stop the flow of time and commemorate men and events with festivals and ceremonies. We are a ritual people, and this characteristic enriches both our understanding and our sensibilities, which are equally soft and alert. The art of the fiesta has been debased almost everywhere else, but not in Mexico. There are a few places in the world where it is possible to take part in a spectacle like our great religious fiestas with their violent primary colors, their bizarre costumes and dances, their fireworks and ceremonies, and their inexhaustible welter of surprises: the fruit, candy, toys, and other objects sold on these days in the plazas and open-air markets.

—Octavio Paz (1961, p. 47)

Mexico celebrated the 200th anniversary of the beginning of its struggle from Spanish domination in 2010, but the mood was far from festive (Thomson, 2010a). Its government has been openly fighting the powerful drug cartels since 2006, and over 30,000 citizens have been killed in this violence. Although the Institutional Revolutionary Party (PRI) lost in the 2000 national election and was turned out by the voters after 71 years of continuous rule, subsequent governments have not performed well. To compound matters, the global economic recession has been particularly difficult for Mexicans. It is little wonder that most Mexicans greeted the delay of two celebratory projects (an independence park and a monument) to mark the anniversary with a stoic shrug.

Mexico represents a classic torn culture, that is, one torn from its roots by invaders and disasters such as widespread famine (Huntington, 1996). In Mexico's case, this process has occurred several times, most recently beginning about 1990 as this nation's leaders began to make it a major player in the global economy. There are three distinctive cultures in Mexico: the Indian culture, the Spanish culture, and the *mestizo* culture of mixed Indian and Spanish ancestry. About 60% of the population of 107.8 million is *mestizo* and 30% pure Indian (Amerindian) or predominantly Indian. The Indians are descendants of the Mayan and Aztec empires. Finally, about 9% are of Spanish ancestry. As might be expected, there is implicit but imperfect ordering of these three groups in terms of status: Spanish, *mestizo,* and Indian.

Sometimes this ordering leads to conflicts. For example, some business firms have fallen on hard times because Spanish and *mestizo* owners and managers have found it difficult to work together, and Indians have experienced many forms of discrimination. In more recent years, there have been attempts to alleviate the plight of impoverished Indian groups.

Still, the threefold distinction is a critical part of Mexican culture and is celebrated at the well-known Plaza of Three Cultures in Mexico City where Hernando Cortés, the conqueror of the Indians, built a Spanish church in 1521. The church was built on and around the site of an ancient pyramid structure constructed by the Indians. A marker at the church succinctly describes the three-partition culture: "On August 13, 1521, heroically defended by Cuanhtemoc, Tlateloko fell into the hands of Hernando Cortés. It was neither a triumph nor a defeat; it was the painful birth of the *mestizo* nation that is Mexico today."

When talking about Mexico, it is important to distinguish between the northern states bordering the United States and the nine states of the south and southeast, which account for nearly a quarter of the population. These nine states tend to be more rural and poorer than the rest of the country. Over time, however, all of Mexico has advanced in terms of many measures. For example, since 1960 the number of years that the average Mexican child spends in school has increased from 2.6 to nearly 8 (M. Reid, 2006).

Mexico, like its fiestas, is a complex blend of reality, tradition, art, and people. The fertility rate per woman is 2.2, which indicates that the population will remain relatively stable for the foreseeable future. Mexico City, the capital, has a population of 19.5 million and is the fifth-largest city in the world. Most Mexicans identify with their Indian or Spanish heritage. Spanish is the official language of Mexico, although many in large urban areas understand English. As many as 100 Indian languages are still spoken in parts of Mexico. Mexico is about three times the size of Texas or one fifth the size of the United States.

Mexico is several thousand years old and still influenced significantly by its past. For example, plans to build a subway line under the capital's main plaza were cancelled when it was discovered that construction would destroy hidden remains of the Aztec empire. The past is celebrated in numerous statues, in streets named after past—including pre-Hispanic—heroes and historic dates, and in the calendar. For example, the entire month of September is devoted to ceremonies commemorating

Mexico's independence from Spain. However, as noted, the 200th anniversary of independence from Spain was muted because of preoccupation with current problems. This devotion to the past is also revealed in the fact that the Mexican government spends more of its budget on anthropological research than does any other country.

Even the official past remains of current interest. Interviews and newspaper columns highlight news a half century old. Symbols are sometimes taken from prehistoric times. A 1978 monument to police officers and firefighters who died in the line of duty was a statue of Coatlicue, goddess of the earth and fertility, with a fallen Aztec warrior at her feet. Important figures of Mexican history have been divided into good and evil and personify concepts such as heroism, nationalism, and revolutionary ideals or cowardice, treason, greed, and repression.

Thus, the past is important for understanding Mexican thought and action. As such, a brief review of Mexican history is essential to a comprehensive understanding of the Mexicans and their culture.

Historical Background

When Cortés arrived in 1519, Mexico was populated by hundreds of indigenous tribes, including the Aztecs, the Incas, and the Mayas. It took only 2 years for Cortés to conquer the indigenous people in the name of Spain. Although most of the indigenous people were wiped out by the conquest and European diseases, those remaining were instructed by the Spanish in the Catholic faith during the colonial era. The silver mines and the people of Mexico were exploited and the riches sent back to Spain.

After victory over Spain in the War of Independence (1810–1820), Mexico began a period of independence and turmoil that lasted another 100 years. By 1853 half of Mexico's territory had been acquired by the United States, mostly in the Mexican war. This period featured unstable leadership and exploitation of the poor peons by the elite landholders, who made the peons virtual slaves on the hacienda farms. One leader during this time was Benito Juárez, notable in part because he was pure Zapotec Indian.

When the Mexican revolution ended in 1920 after 10 years of intense fighting between various factions representing the large landholders and the poor, presidential elections began. The government attempted to break up the Catholic Church, which was a large conservative landholder, and a constitution was drawn up separating church and state. The church was not allowed to hold land, and priests could not vote, although religion remained inseparably woven throughout the lives of most Mexicans. Land holdings of the church and large landholders were taken away and given to the peasants and indigenous people under land reform measures.

Catholicism in recent years has decreased in popularity, with nearly 100% of the population identifying as Catholic in 1960 and about 85% doing so today. Protestantism, particularly of the evangelical variety, has correspondingly risen from nearly zero to 6%. Some reasons for its appeal to the poor include its firm stance against alcohol and its more open and less hierarchical approach. Anti-Catholic films highlighting the faults of the clergy have become popular. *El crimen del Padre Amaro* has become one of the most popular films in Mexican history; it relates the true tale of a 19th-century priest who violated his vows of celibacy and paid for an abortion that resulted in the death of a poor young woman.

In spite of the beneficial outcomes of the Mexican revolution ending in 1920, many problems remain today, including poverty, unemployment, a high birth rate, an inadequate educational system, inefficient industry and agriculture, a high foreign debt, and a variable economy lacking financing capabilities. In some ways the economic situation has improved markedly over the last 90 years, in large part because of the discovery of oil. Also, the North American Free Trade Agreement (NAFTA) increased trade between Mexico and the United States, which buys 80.1% of Mexico's exports. NAFTA, established in 1994, is controversial, as it has benefited larger Mexican firms much more than the smaller firms. Still, given all of its problems, Mexico received a relatively high rating among nations on the 2011 Index of Economic Freedom: 48 out of 179 (T. Miller, 2011).

One political party, the Partido Revolucionario Institucional (PRI), dominated politics for 72 years. In 1988 a near-loss by the PRI marked a turning point in Mexican politics, and viable opposition parties became a reality, culminating in the PRI's defeat in the national elections in 2000. The PRI had experienced several scandals, and it no longer has unquestioned authority to operate as it wishes. Its leaders had attempted to maintain an aura of gravitas and imperial mystery, but now they must compete against one another and members of opposition parties in U.S.-style elections.

Although this chapter generalizes about the culture of Mexico, in reality the culture is not uniform. There are five more or less distinct regions (Kras, 1989). The northern border region has been influenced by its proximity to the United States and the presence of many foreign-owned businesses under the *maquiladora* program, in which foreign businesses ship parts into Mexico, use Mexican labor to assemble the products, and ship the products back out of Mexico free of tariffs. People in the north tend to be more aggressive and independent than other Mexicans.

The central region is characterized by more traditional, conservative, autocratic, family-owned businesses. In the southeast region, people are more relaxed. There are more plantations and less industry. Business is paternalistic and autocratic. A large indigenous population lives in this region.

The capital, Mexico City, comprises the fourth region, and it boasts about 40% of Mexico's gross national product. Gross domestic product per head is US$10,230, less than 25% of that of either the United States or Canada. Although it is overcrowded, it is very much a modern, cosmopolitan city.

The fifth region consists of the areas along the Gulf of Mexico, which are rich in oil.

The mixture of the indigenous population and the Spanish population is nearly complete, resulting in what Mexicans call *mestizos*. Despite the tragedy inflicted by the conquistadors, the Catholic faith helped the indigenous population assimilate into the

Spanish culture. Traditional indigenous religions have blended with Catholicism, resulting in a uniquely Mexican culture that is reflected in the people's religious beliefs and practices. The mixing of these two cultures (Indian and Spanish) can also be seen in distinctive architecture, the language, and many other aspects of people's lives.

For example, during the fiesta of the Day of the Dead, people flock to the graveyards to put flowers and food on the tombs of their relatives. These symbolic gestures combine the Catholic concept and the ancient Indian concept of the afterlife. One day each year, people dress up like peasants and take their children to the cathedral to be blessed. In front of the church are booths where children get their pictures taken. In the backdrop of these booths and in the children's costumes are visible signs of the indigenous backgrounds of Mexicans.

The Mexican Fiesta

Although there is much more to life in Mexico than the fiesta, many aspects of the fiesta can be related to Mexico to more fully understand its culture. According to the Mexican Department of Tourism, the number of official fiestas varies yearly between 500 and 600. Fiestas are held for a variety of reasons, including celebrating historical events such as Mexican Independence Day; reinforcing the traditions of individual towns, cities, and states; honoring Catholic saints and practices; paying homage to special foods and crops found in a particular region; and recognizing birthdays, baptisms, weddings, and graduations. As such, the fiesta is an appropriate metaphor through which to view Mexico.

One broad-based and partially inaccurate stereotype is represented by the popular tourist ads having the tagline "Come to the land of the fiesta." Such ads feature seductive girls dressed in sequins and ribbons dancing with beautiful boys to romantic guitar music. This fiesta represents that of the movies, tourists, and perhaps a big town project. The real Mexican fiesta is the country fiesta—the more remote and difficult it is to get to the fiesta, the more attractive the celebration.

The pure pleasures of the simple life can be experienced at a fiesta: indigenous, native dances in beautiful costumes and people dancing happily about. The fiesta gives Mexicans the opportunity to enliven and enhance their existence: They can see people from their neighboring towns, sell a few ornaments, party, and enjoy the camaraderie of friends and family members. Even the most modest fiesta produces a particular mood, full of humor and energy. The fiestas are a blend of beautiful costumes, language, bustling activity, and aimless walking around.

In the tropical coastal towns, rural fiestas are especially festive. Although fiestas have humor, they are not good-humored or consciously funny. If they are dramatic, it is unplanned. The participants may not understand fully the ceremonies and rituals, even when they have been involved with the fiesta for years. A fiesta cannot be likened to a big block party. It is irrational, mysterious, and moving.

Generally, the state of Oaxaca in the south has wonderful fiestas with beautiful regional costumes, flower arrangements, and tall *castillos* (towers) of native fireworks.

The people of Oaxaca are predominantly Indians who share grace, calm, and worldliness. They are quite interested in new people and new ways. The state of Chiapas, the scene of revolutionary activities in recent years, has pagan ceremonies that may be alluring and frightening to outsiders. Other regions only eat, sing, dance, and drink, leaving religious meanings behind. This is especially true of the tropics, which are devoted to the present. Given the diversity of fiestas, each of them must be experienced, not simply observed.

However, in more recent years at least some fiesta traditions have faded. Even the Fiesta of the Dead on November 1 is changing. This fiesta highlights death as transformation rather than as the end of life. In this way it stresses the importance of family history. But the U.S. celebration of Halloween is being grafted onto the Day of the Dead, and in the process many traditions have been discarded ("Mexico, Haunted," 1999).

Four important aspects of Mexican culture are revealed in the fiesta. First, the primary focus of the Mexicans is on people, and the fiesta offers them a chance to be with and enjoy the company of family, friends, and community. Second, religion is a pervasive influence in the Mexican's life, and the abundant religious fiestas are a chance for Mexicans to communicate with God. Third, experiencing the present is important to Mexicans, and the fiesta is an opportunity to do this. Last, within the social order Mexicans find freedom, and within the social order of the fiestas Mexicans exhibit this freedom.

Primary Focus on People

People are of paramount importance in Mexican culture. A fiesta is a time to enjoy the company of family and friends. It also forms a bond among all Mexicans, uniting them into a common people. Mexico is collectivist, and within a tight social framework members of the in-group, particularly those in positions of authority, are expected to look after everyone else in exchange for loyalty. Gabrielidis and his research team (Gabrielidis, Stephan, Ybarra, Dos Santos-Pearson, & Villareal, 1997) found that the collectivistic Mexicans display concern for others and use accommodation and collaboration more than the individualistic U.S. Americans do. As a whole, Mexico is an authority-ranking or vertical collectivistic but paternalistic culture in which a good amount of social distance exists between superiors and subordinates. Paternalism is manifested in various ways, such as the *aguinaldo* or Christmas bonus, which can be as much as 3 months of the recipient's salary. But in some areas, such as those bordering the United States, individualism is becoming stronger.

The basic building block of society is the immediate family. In more rural areas, several generations live together in the same house. Children are encouraged to stay dependent on the family and not leave home. The family spends most of its nonworking hours together, and the children go everywhere with the parents. Babysitters are rarely if ever used, except by the minority of the population that is rich enough to afford servants. The family is an informal welfare system in Mexico. If a cousin cannot afford to feed the children, the rest of the family will provide the groceries. Mexican families tend to regard homelessness among relatives very negatively and will do as much as possible to give family members a roof to sleep under.

The fiesta is a chance to enjoy the company of the family. Some fiestas even extend the family. Godparents (*madrina* or *padrino*) are selected for baptisms and other important festive ceremonies in a child's life. To be chosen as a godparent is an honor and responsibility. A child can have different godparents for each ceremony, with new ones added to existing ones rather than replacing them. Because these godparents will be present for every important occasion in the child's life, this practice actually extends the family to include the godparents and their families. *Compradazco* connotes coparenthood shared by the parents and the godparents. A Mexican friend likened *compradazco* to a network of invisible lines linking many houses or families into one big family.

Friends are also important in Mexico. Once a person becomes a friend, he or she becomes one of the trusted members of the in-group. Friends almost become a part of the family, as in the case of *compradazco*. Friends of friends also become part of this network. Friends are often called by familial titles such as *brother*, *sister*, and *cousin*.

Relationships Rule

Mexicans are ruled much more by relationships than by abstract concepts. Mexicans will interrupt whatever they are doing at the sight of a friend or a relative. Diminutive endings such as *-ito* or *-ita,* which mean small, are often tacked onto the ends of names or words to suggest affection, for example, *Silvita* instead of *Silvia.* These endings are also used to minimize problems and save face.

Mexicans tend to hire relatives and friends over strangers, no matter what the qualifications or achievements of each, although this is less true in the more modern businesses. In Hofstede's (2001) study of 53 nations, Mexicans were found to have a high need for uncertainty avoidance, indicating that they feel threatened by uncertain situations and strangers and try to avoid them. Therefore, knowing someone before hiring or doing business with him or her is important. The old adage "It's not what you know, but whom you know" is taken literally. If business must be done with strangers, much time is spent getting to know them before any deals are made. Mexicans are not loyal to an organization, but they are committed to the people in the organization.

Considering the central role the family plays in Mexican life, foreign executives must take the concerns of the employee's family seriously. For example, they might show interest and concern when an employee is absent due to illness in the family. Understanding family ties is an excellent way for foreign managers to comprehend subordinates' behavior and to develop good relations with them.

Mexicans tend to view success in terms not of achievement but of affiliation. It is important to be someone who is important to other people. Achievement is, however, more important in larger, more modern companies. The uniqueness of each person as an individual is highly valued, even though these individuals are an integral part of a collectivist culture. Mexicans refer to *alma* (the soul) or *espiritu* (the spirit) to describe this inner individual.

It is important to protect this soul or dignity or honor. Managers should rarely, if ever, criticize subordinates in front of their friends or family. Praise is important to Mexicans. Mexicans tend to be consensus seekers and will lie to avoid hurt feelings and confrontation. Avoiding the placement of blame on anyone is important. In Spanish, people do not break things; instead things just break—*se lo rompió*. Lies and truth are not absolute. Mexicans will frequently say what you want to hear to avoid confrontation and the loss of someone's dignity, even if what is said is not the complete truth. When asked directions, Mexicans will sometimes give a false answer rather than say they do not know. When they beg one's pardon, they say, "Pretend it never happened, *señor*."

Michael Agar, a cross-cultural anthropologist who was asked to facilitate relations between U.S. Americans and Mexicans involved in a joint venture, recalls vividly how the Mexicans perceived the U.S. Americans. After working with U.S. businesspeople all day, the Mexican executives went out for a drink, and one of them said *el capo* as he waved an imaginary torero's cape before the bull or, metaphorically, the U.S. Americans, and the other Mexicans laughed uproariously. The Mexicans perceived themselves to be too polite and sophisticated to tell the U.S. Americans to their face that their behavior was boorish. However, this politeness was a major reason that the joint venture eventually failed, for the U.S. Americans became exasperated when the Mexicans indicated that meeting a deadline was "no problem," only to fail to do so repeatedly. The U.S. Americans bluntly told the Mexicans that they had lied, and the Mexicans were insulted. Given the communication and negotiation styles of U.S. Americans and Mexicans, such outcomes are frequent.

Mexicans tend to view humans as a mixture of good and evil. Possibly because of this perspective and the gray area between truth and lies, one can encounter occasional obstacles where someone may need to be rewarded to gain cooperation. Analogously, in the fiesta one often dons a costume and a mask. The mask allows an escape from reality without the loss of dignity. Octavio Paz (1961) even argues that the Mexican is "a person who shuts himself away to protect himself; his face is a mask and so is his smile" (p. 29). From Paz's perspective, Mexicans tend to mask painful realities, hiding more than they reveal.

Communication Style

Nonverbal communication is important in most, if not all, cultures. In Mexico, gestures, facial expressions, glances, posture, and clothing all reveal important facets of the culture. Greetings and salutations take a long time and are often full of handshakes, hugs, kisses, and pats on the back. There is more physical contact between members of the same sex in Mexico than is common in the United States. Men greet each other with an *abrazo* (embrace), whereas women may kiss on the cheek. Overall, Mexicans employ more physical closeness and smaller interpersonal distances than their counterparts in the United States.

Thus U.S. Americans may withdraw from Mexicans during interactions, communicating emotional or social distance. Mexicans may seem overbearing to U.S. Americans. Body language is also different between the two cultures. Mexicans tend to use more of the trunk of the body while North Americans use the head and neck. Mexicans use their hands extensively to illustrate and emphasize what they are saying.

Neat clothing and appearance are also important because they show respect. In Mexico, clothing and jewelry are representative of the country's great ethnic diversity. The type of attire indicates a person's region or ethnic background. In hats alone, the diversity is wonderful. Upper-class Mexicans distinguish their status by wearing fine clothes, expensive jewelry, and fancy hairstyles. The concern with being respectable or *decente* is revealed in clothing.

Conversation is an art in Mexico, and the manner in which things are said is as important as what is said. The speaker beats around the bush in a dramatic and flowery style and often repeats things. Allusions and double meanings are a delight to Mexicans. Cultures differ in the importance they place on words to convey information (Hall & Hall, 1990). U.S. Americans and Northern Europeans place great emphasis on words. In Mexico, context is more important, and Mexicans may view a statement as honest in one situation but rude in another. Knowing who says something and how it is said are vital to understanding what is meant.

Meetings often become social events in which participants simply enjoy each other's company. There is a lot of emotion and passion in any conversation. When a Mexican man courts a woman, for instance, he typically expresses flowery praise of her beauty. Similarly in the fiesta, extreme joy and sorrow are exhibited.

The language often says more than it means. For example, "*Mi casa es su casa*" literally means "My house is your house," but in reality it means "You are welcome in my house." When Mexicans are pleased to meet you, they say they are *encantado*; that is, they are enchanted to meet you.

Education and Training

By and large, schools have emphasized theoretical concepts and social competence. Intellectual pursuits such as philosophy, science, and the arts are important, whereas practical applications have been less so. This practice often leads to problems in business when subordinates are charged with implementing a plan but have insufficient skills to do so. Thus international managers must realize the importance of training their subordinates, especially given their tendency to be agreeable and not to question authority.

In recent years there has been an increase in the importance of practical training. For example, Monterey Tech (ITESM) produces a large number of first-rate business and engineering students, and some of its programs, such as the MBA program, are ranked among the best in the world. This university also provides a year of remedial work for undergraduates who fail to measure up to its tough entrance standards but are admitted on a probationary basis.

The Emphasis on Religion

The significance and number of religious fiestas demonstrate the importance of religion to life in Mexico. The religious fiesta gives participants an opportunity to communicate with God. In addition, some fiestas that are nonreligious in purpose have religious features.

An important fiesta is Carnival, which is celebrated before Lent. Another celebration, the feast day of Our Lady of Guadalupe, is one of the more important religious holidays: The country celebrates the anniversary of the day when the Virgin Mary is said to have appeared on the hill of Tepeyac (now part of Mexico City). On the 9 nights before Christmas, Mexicans act out Mary and Joseph's search for lodging in Bethlehem. Every night after these ceremonies or *posadas,* the children play the *piñata* game. Holy Week, the week before Easter, is celebrated with fiestas. In addition, each city or village has an annual fiesta for its patron saint. During the religious fiestas, Mexicans pray and light candles in the churches.

In addition, family fiestas celebrate the traditional rites of passage, including baptism, first communion, and marriage. The whole family, including the godparents and their families, is present for these fiestas, which frequently begin with a church service during which Holy Communion takes place.

Even some fiestas that are not religious in purpose have aspects of religion. A fiesta for 15-year-old girls, *quinceañera,* is similar to the sweet-16 party or coming-out party in the United States. It is social in origin but includes a service in the church with communion, a multicourse meal, and dancing, preferably to a large band's music. This is one of the most important fiestas in a girl's life, and the girls attending wear expensive, elaborate dresses while the boys accompanying them are in suits and ties. Families devote a good amount of money to this fiesta, and those lacking sufficient resources will take extraordinary measures to ensure that their daughters experience the delight of *quinceañera.* For example, a single mother with four children whose income was derived solely from cleaning homes in the United States sewed the dresses and suits that the major teenage principals in the festival wore at the church service, hired a band of local Mexican musicians, prepared most of the food, and managed the entire festival in honor of her daughter. This *quinceañera* started at 10:00 AM and did not end until 3:00 AM the next day.

What God Wills

Mexicans tend to believe that life is beyond their control. What God wills, happens. The common expression "*si Dios nos presta el tiempo*" means "if God lends us the time." The expression *ni modo* means "no way" or "tough luck." Many Mexicans generally consider nature to be dominant over people. When problems are encountered, Mexicans will tend to modify themselves rather than try to modify the environment. For this reason, class lines are not easily broken, and problems are often minimized. Similarly the mask in the fiesta is a means of modifying the self to deal with reality. But the mask also embellishes reality and adds a creative dimension to life that is missing at a typical U.S. American cocktail party and even during official holidays such as U.S. Independence Day.

Because many Mexicans tend to believe life is beyond their control, they tend to share a fatalistic attitude. They also exhibit a fascination and even an obsession with death. The newspapers are full of gory, morbid stories. This obsession is reflected in fiestas. The Day of the Dead, also called All Souls Day, is celebrated with a fiesta to honor and remember the dead. People bring food and flowers to the tombs of deceased relatives. Some people even set a place at the table for the dead. Candy skulls with a person's name on them are purchased and eaten or given as gifts. To Mexicans this cheerful celebration is for both the living and the dead. Of course, other seemingly distant cultures have similar traditions (see Chapter 26 about the Chinese family altar).

Mexicans tend to believe that death is only part of a larger picture. This belief may stem both from indigenous religions and Catholicism. In the circular Aztec calendar stone, the center contains the sun god with two snakes. Supposedly human sacrifices were made on this stone to pay back the gods so that the continuous regeneration of life could continue. Christianity also views death as a transition between two lives. Although some have argued that to the modern Mexican, death is no longer a transition, Mexicans still tend to view death as an integral and inseparable part of life. This belief in communion with the dead is an outgrowth of a belief that the past is not dead. Similarly fiestas are a time of death and rebirth for Mexicans in that the fiesta revitalizes and strengthens them. Thus fiestas are a source of continual energy and renewal for the Mexican people.

The bullfight, which is clearly a ritual emphasizing bravery in the face of death rather than just a sport, is often a part of fiestas (see Chapter 30: The Spanish Bullfight). The death dance of the bullfight is an expression of the Mexican preoccupation with death. Also, bullfighting is an exhibition of *machismo,* in that the *torero* must show that he is not afraid of death. At some fiestas, there are other opportunities to show courage in the face of death, as when men hold onto the end of long poles and rotate like a Ferris wheel either vertically or horizontally around a tall center pole.

Effects of *Machismo*

Machismo is an important concept in Mexico. Manliness and virility are greatly admired, and perhaps even more admired is authority. Although there are now genuine competing political parties, strongmen such as trade union bosses are still the most powerful personages in the majority of Mexican towns (Sullivan, 2002). It is important for men to exhibit masculinity and stoicism at all times and to show that they are not afraid of death. Male children are more exalted than their female counterparts. Boys are expected to act like little men and are told to look after the family when the father is away. One day each year families take their children to the cathedral to be blessed. When they have their pictures taken outside the cathedral, they draw mustaches on the boys to make them look like men.

A Mexican male's insecurity is manifested by his fear of betrayal by women. One generic anthropological explanation suggests that because Mexican mixed bloodedness began with the mating of Spanish men and Indian women, male-female relationships were based on the concepts of betrayal by women and conquest by men. The macho man must protect himself against betrayal, just as the conqueror could not fully trust the conquered.

The male worship of the female ideal is illustrated frequently by adoration of the Virgin and adulation of one's own mother. The wife, however, is sometimes viewed as a sexual object. A husband who is faithful and affectionate shows vulnerability and weakness. Having mistresses lets the man conquer before he is betrayed. Wives, resentful of their husbands who have mistresses, are sometimes too attentive to their sons. Sons, in turn, view their mothers through the lens of the feminine ideal yet tend to adopt their fathers' ways once married.

Women, like men, spend most of their time with members of their own sex. At social gatherings, they stay close to their husbands or mingle with other women. Rarely do they spend significant time with other men. A female seeking a career runs into obstacles. The traditional role of mother and homemaker makes choosing to pursue a career a difficult matter. Women remain central to the family, reliable in a society where illegitimate children, broken homes, and absentee fathers are common.

While they seek security, Mexicans can be introspective. Fiestas provide an emotional outlet from their solitude and self-restraint. They provide a release that is not found elsewhere.

Experiencing the Present

Although most Mexicans are very much influenced by the past, they live for the present. The fiesta allows them to stop and enjoy the moment. It is an escape from work and poverty. The fiesta is a release of the soul.

The Mexican concept of time is relaxed, and there is always plenty of it. In such polychronic time, more than one thing goes on at once (Hall & Hall, 1990). Mexicans call this *la hora Mexicana* (Mexican time). Interruptions and tardiness are common, and deadlines are flexible. Absence after a long weekend is institutionalized in *San Lunes* or Saint Monday, and this is accepted as an explanation for absence. Many projects are never seen to completion. People are expected to be late to social occasions, and hosts actually plan on this eventuality. Arriving on time is considered rude. Many Mexicans are dismayed over North American invitations that state in advance what time a party will be over.

Even though Mexican bus or taxi drivers may have paying passengers, they will sometimes stop to give a friend a ride to an unscheduled destination. This view of time is also exhibited in communication, which is often spontaneous and simultaneous, and ideas flow from many directions. What some term the *mañana syndrome* stems not from Mexican laziness or inefficiency but rather from a different philosophy of time. Disasters are considered unavoidable, *ni modo*.

However, sometimes other factors, such as the importance of authority, override the cultural expression of time. One U.S. trainer on his first trip to Mexico experienced this phenomenon. He was ready to start his class, but not one of the 50 managerial trainees was in the room. Wanting to be polite, he waited 30 minutes before starting, at which time about half of the class was present. When he complained to his Mexican superior about the lax approach of the trainees, the Mexican startled him by saying, "It is your fault." The explanation was that the trainer should start class on time, even if no one was in the room, and everyone would be there forthwith because he was the figure of authority. He did so in the second class, and within 10 minutes all the trainees were in their seats. In all subsequent classes, the trainees were in their seats when class began.

There is more pressure to be on time and to produce in larger, more modern companies. Strict adherence to time schedules is important for modern companies, but U.S. executives must be patient with the Mexican attitude toward time. They must plan for time slippage and the unanticipated.

Finding Happiness

Mexico is a country of extremes, both in terms of geography and rigidity of the social class structure, which often makes a Mexican's life hard. However, Mexicans frequently know how to find happiness in even a difficult life. They have developed the ability to find a silver lining in any cloud. The fiesta is a time for Mexicans to find joy, and the mask worn at the fiesta allows them to do this.

Mexicans have a plethora of expressions for their displeasure with work. They say *"El trabajo embrutece,"* or "Work brutalizes," and *"La ociosidad es la madre de una vida padre,"* or "Idleness is the mother of the good life." Even the word for business, *negocio,* connotes the negative of leisure; that is, work is completed only for the purpose of obtaining leisure (Fisher, 1988). Although many Mexicans work hard, they value leisure time spent with their family and friends more highly than work. Again, they tend to be more motivated by affiliation than by achievement, and their emphasis is on being rather than doing. Work is done only because it has to be done, a concept in stark contrast to the Protestant work ethic, which holds that work is good in and of itself. Mexicans need a balance between work and leisure, which requires them to leave some jobs until "*mañana.*" For this reason, some foreigners stereotype Mexico as the land of *mañana.*

One reason for the deemphasis on work is that success in life is frequently based not on achievement but on personal relations. Career advancement often occurs because of personal contacts rather than achievements. Hard work does not necessarily lead to success or prosperity, and many Mexicans work hard all their lives only to live in dire poverty. There is no strict dichotomy between work and leisure. Mexicans like to have friends and relatives working with them to make work more fun, a phenomenon that Thais would describe as *sanuk* at work (Chapter 2). Many businesses are run by the family, and they hire other family members and friends before they hire strangers.

Mexicans tend to deemphasize the future, and little long-term planning occurs except in the larger and more competitive firms. Each day is taken as it comes. This is due in part to the unstable economy. Follow-through on projects is often difficult to obtain. Concepts such as quality control are uncommon in all but the largest, most modern companies.

Freedom Within the Social Order

Mexican society is hierarchical (vertical collectivism), and everyone has a role within the society. Mexico has a high score on Hofstede's (2001) power-distance dimension, meaning that the society accepts without question an unequal distribution of wealth and authority; the GLOBE study (House et al., 2004) confirms this finding. Thus the distinction between the two forms of the word *you* in Spanish is noteworthy. *Tu* is informal and used between friends, and *usted* is formal and used to show respect to superiors or elders. This distinction is, however, not unique to Mexico; many other nations employ it.

In the smaller villages, people fill specialized roles within the community. This hierarchy can be clearly observed in the patriarchal family structure in Mexico. The father is the authority figure, and traditionally the mother's role is to love her children and husband and to lead a life of self-sacrifice for them. Children are taught to obey their father and mother. Just as the parents take care of the children, so do the more affluent members of a family take care of the poorer members. When a family holds a fiesta, the wealthier members are expected to pay for a large part of it. It is common for Mexicans working in the United States to send money home to help pay for a younger sibling's schooling, a sister's coming-out party, and many other things. Such aid is in the billions of dollars and rivals government aid in terms of its magnitude. Similarly it is expected that Mexicans in the United States will send money to less affluent relatives to help pay for the family fiestas. Because of the current poor job market in the United States, many workers have returned to Mexico, thus decreasing the amount of remittances sent from family members in the United States to Mexico.

At work, there is a rigid hierarchy where the subordinates traditionally do not question the boss. A problem typical of authoritarian administrations is that Mexican subordinates tend to withhold negative information, even if it is important, and convey only good news. Everyone knows his or her role and conforms to it. Similarly the government is bureaucratic, the Roman Catholic Church is hierarchical, and schools are traditionally structured in an authoritarian manner so that questioning is not encouraged. This stratification began before the coming of the Spaniards. Today, absolute authority within the hierarchy is beginning to break down, especially in the cities, as larger businesses move toward more participative management styles.

Traditional Versus Modern

As this discussion implies, conflicts sometimes arise between traditional values and modern life. In one family, the older brother had started a promising business and hired the next oldest brother to be his chief salesperson, and the latter complained to the father that his older brother was not paying him the promised salary but a much lower one. When the father asked the older brother about the matter, he was incensed and indicated that he would indeed pay his brother all that he owed him—to the detriment of investment in the growing business—but that he would immediately fire him, regardless of the impact on the family. When the father communicated this information to the younger brother, he withdrew his request for the promised salary until the business became more stable.

Status is important to the Mexicans. Impressive academic degrees or titles command respect. Title usage reinforces the sense of hierarchy within Mexican society. At low levels of the bureaucracy, the use of *licienciado* for a university graduate is common. It requires wearing a suit and tie and implies influence. The head of an office is not *licienciado* So-and-So but *el licienciado,* as if he were the only one. *Maestro* is often used for plumbers, painters, and carpenters and for senior officials teaching at the university.

Members of the elite were formerly drawn from purer Spanish backgrounds and were proud of their light skin and Spanish heritage. Although there are now elite from the indigenous and *mestizo* populations, there is still a preference for lighter skin and eyes. For the most part, being Indian is defined culturally rather than racially in Mexico. A person is considered Indian only if he or she speaks the language and practices the culture of the Indian. In the revolution of 1910, the indigenous heritage of Mexico was glorified and even celebrated in an attempt to erase the stigma applied to Indians.

Structure and security form a curious amalgam with freedom in Mexico. Everyone knows his or her role and will usually not violate it or challenge another's role; people are careful not to trammel one another's dignity. Yet there is not as much pressure for conformity as there is in less hierarchical societies. Mexicans have the freedom to do what they want as long as they do not affront others or go beyond their role in society.

Jobs offer security to Mexicans, and they consequently enjoy freedom at work. As previously mentioned, Mexicans feel free to be absent from work on Monday, with the only excuse necessary being that it is "Saint Monday." Children feel secure and warm in the family structure, yet because they are so loved, they have more freedom to do what they want to do.

Mexicans as individuals may feel freer from guilt and obligation than U.S. Americans. It is not the individual that is guilty; the group shares the blame. The obligation is not the individual's but the group's. Also, the Catholic religion allows Mexicans to become free from sin by asking God's forgiveness in confession. Again, friends and family usually take care of those in their group who are in need.

Chaos in Structure

During a visit to a large cathedral in Mexico City, this freedom and even chaos within the structure and order could be clearly seen. Although the Roman Catholic Church is hierarchical and structured, what went on inside this cathedral was not. People came in to pray independently and left at their leisure without reference to leadership from the priest. This was true in the main chapel as well as the many side chapels. A woman knelt beside a priest at the front of the church, apparently having her confession heard completely independently of everything else happening in the cathedral. The chairs, seemingly well used, were in disarray instead of in neat rows. Within the church's hierarchy there is security and freedom.

The fiesta is a chance to observe this freedom, and in some ways fiestas are a celebration of chaos. Sometimes participants will become inebriated and exhibit rowdiness and related behaviors. Roles, hierarchies, norms, and laws vanish; for example, the poor dress up like richer members of society. Everyone dresses up in gaudy costumes and becomes someone they are not. During the fiesta, it is almost as if people are free to choose which mask they wear. Although they indulge in freedom and chaos during the fiesta, however, they by and large operate within accepted norms of behavior.

Mexicans easily identify with the song of longing written by Jorge Negrete, a Mexican who became homesick in Cuba and penned the following well-known words:

Mexico beautiful and beloved,

If I die far from you,

Tell me I am sleeping,

And bring me back here.

Mexicans have changed over the years and will continue to do so. Mexico currently faces many challenges, particularly chaos related to the drug wars and economic problems associated with the global slowdown since 2008. In the cities and larger corporations, Western concepts such as achievement and rigid schedules are becoming more common. Larger corporations are less autocratic and paternalistic than smaller businesses. This may be due in part to the fact that many of the larger corporations are owned by foreigners. Although these changes are visible, they represent only a small part of the culture of Mexico. For the most part, Mexico is composed of smaller, more traditional businesses, with a much more traditional culture. Throughout the years the fiesta has been, and will remain, an integral part of the Mexican culture. And the fiesta will endure as a metaphor describing the importance Mexicans place on people, religion, experiencing the present, and the freedom that exists within a hierarchical social order.

CHAPTER 24

The Russian Ballet

Russia is an exceptional place. In the 20th century, over a single lifetime—70 years—it saw three civilizations. Each of the first two was rejected by its successor, forcing people to renounce their convictions. You can imagine the chaos of ideas and beliefs in their hearts.

—Edvard Radzinsky (2006)

Ballet is a dance executed by the human soul.

—widely attributed to Alexander Pushkin

Russia represents a classic case of a torn nation (Huntington, 1996), as it has been severed from its social, economic, and cultural roots not just once but four times in its tumultuous and long history, and three of these pivotal periods have occurred within the past 70 years. The first period began in the 12th century when the Tartars or Mongols from central Asia invaded and brutally subjugated the country for 400 years. In the early 18th century, Peter the Great initiated the second period when he began to westernize Russia while deemphasizing Asian influences. He defeated his chief enemy, the Swedes; created the Russian navy to facilitate trade in the landlocked nation; and constructed Saint Petersburg (later Leningrad) out of swampland to connect Russia by land with the West. However, prominent Russians emphasize the exceptionalism created by their Slavic heritage and ethnicity, and they portray Russia as neither Asian nor European ("Russian Exceptionalism," 1996).

In the third period, starting in 1917, the Russian Revolution wrenched the nation from rule by the czars to communism, and the results were disastrous socially, economically, and culturally. Millions of people were imprisoned and died; Russia lost more soldiers and civilians in World War II than all other nations combined (an estimated 50 million of the 100 million); the economy became extremely weak after World War II as the Russian government poured most of its resources into military and atomic weapons; priceless Christian Orthodox churches were destroyed; and religious worship was banned. Ironically the Western press after World War II tended to portray Russia as having a vibrant economy, but part of this image was based on the "Iron Curtain" that stood between the West and Russia, which made good information difficult to obtain.

Thus, just a few years prior to the formal dissolution of the Soviet Union in 1992, the West was ignorant of many of the realities of Russian life. During these years former president Mikhail Gorbachev led a movement toward Western capitalism, and two new words entered the English language: *glasnost* (openness) and *perestroika* (restructuring).

A tumultuous fourth period in the nation's history, starting in 1992, was initially marked by optimism and hope. Elections involving candidates with widely different philosophies and agendas became possible, and a free press encouraged debate. Economic reforms were supposedly based on Western capitalism. However, they failed miserably. For example, to make Russians into capitalists, the government gave Russian citizens small shares of stock in formerly nationalized companies, which had been privatized as part of the largest privatization effort ever undertaken. At least 6,000 large and mid-size firms were involved in this experiment; by comparison only about 8,000 firms worldwide were privatized in the 1980s. However, most of these firms failed to meet the exacting competitive standards of early-stage capitalism, at least partially because of the antiquated technology used in many industries, and most of the shares became worthless. Simultaneously, a small group of businesspeople gained control, frequently in a questionable manner, over the most profitable parts of Russian industry, and they purchased the stock certificates of profitable companies for a pittance from ordinary citizens who were unaware of their value. Corruption and crime became rampant. Some U.S. businesspeople seeking to do business in Russia in the early 1990s were shocked at the open manner in which bribes were sought.

In 2000 Vladimir Putin became president. Largely because of Russia's oil and gas preserves, the economy began to improve. However, the government has been taking away many of the rights, such as genuine political elections and a free press, that the creation of the new Russia in 1992 encouraged. In 1988 under former president Gorbachev, about 5% of the national political leadership was *siloviki* (literally, those who work for or used to work for the "ministries of force" or *silovye ministerstva*) or those with career military and security backgrounds such as in the former KGB (the Russian spy agency). Today, they hold political power in Russia and work for 22 agencies, the best known of which is the Federalnaya Sluzhba Bezopasnosti (FSB), a successor to the KGB. No matter their institutional affiliation, all *siloviki* have a special type of training that sets them apart from civilians. This training provides them the skills, motivation, and mental attitude to use force against other people (Illarionov, 2009).

According to a new book, *The New Nobility* by Andrei Soldatov and Irina Borogan, the FSB has become a sprawling intelligence-gathering empire, both within and beyond Russia's borders, and it employs at least 200,000 personnel (Lucas, 2010). Although Putin relinquished the presidency in 2008, he was elected to the newly created and supposedly largely ceremonial post of prime minister, and he is widely believed to be directing Russian government and his handpicked successor, President Dmitry Medvedev. As was widely expected, Putin has announced plans to run for the presidency again in 2012.

There is also concern that the Russian economy will experience an economic bubble if oil and gas prices fall significantly, as Russia is the world's largest energy exporter. Russia does not have any leading multinational firms that can compete globally, and its smaller businesses tend to be inefficient. Furthermore, there is a general consensus that the Russian state is performing very poorly in many areas such as public safety, health, corruption, and the security of property rights when compared to other nations (McFaul & Stoner-Weiss, 2008). Russia's economy is growing at a much slower pace than its fellow BRIC countries (Brazil, India, and China). In 2010 it experienced the worst drought in at least half a century. On the 2011 Index of Economic Freedom, Russia ranks shockingly low at 143 out of 179 nations, below the other three BRIC countries and just above Ethiopia (T. Miller, 2011). Life expectancy, at 61.9 years for males, is the lowest among all developed nations.

After the fact, it is easy to see how mistakes occurred when Russia as a torn nation gyrated quickly from one civilization to another, especially since 1917. This chapter focuses on the culture of Russia, acknowledging that culture is influenced by, and influences, social infrastructure and economic practices.

We focus on Russia, with its population of 141.8 million and a land mass that is almost double that of the United States. A Commonwealth of Independent States consisting of 12 states was established to reformulate the Soviet Union without the economic or political costs of union, but it has virtually disintegrated, even though politicians are seeking to revive it. Russia's population is about equal to that of the other states in the Commonwealth combined, the largest of which is Ukraine with a population of 45.9 million. Moscow is located in the western region of the nation, and Saint Petersburg is situated to the northeast of Moscow.

An Apt Metaphor

Russian ballet provides an apt metaphor for Russia for several reasons. Russia has excelled at producing ballet of the highest and arguably unsurpassed quality. While Russians did not create ballet, they enriched this art form immeasurably. It seems appropriate that a torn nation should be represented by a cultural metaphor that did not originate there. Furthermore, since 1992 and until recently, Russian ballet experienced political intrigue, lack of funding, and some low levels of performance, thus mirroring the nation's troubles. At the current time, however, there are attempts to reinvigorate Russian ballet, the major ballet companies are now performing frequently outside of Russia, and the famous Bolshoi Theatre has undergone a major renovation.

To better understand Russian culture, we will take a look at three important characteristics: echelons, theatrics and realism, and the Russian soul. These elements also apply to our metaphor and help to distinguish this art form from its counterparts in other lands. Seeming larger than life, Russian ballet represents the complexities of Russian culture—the grand expression of aristocracy and the gentle beauty of a countryside.

Russian ballet means many things to many people. Some consider it the type of instruction given at the famous Bolshoi and Kirov academies; others identify Russian ballet with specific eras and performances. Those who witnessed the sumptuous performances of Diaghilev's *Ballet Russe* in the early 20th century surely identified his productions as "the Russian ballet." And audiences familiar with specific works such as *Swan Lake* and *Sleeping Beauty* proclaim these magnificent dance programs as Russian ballet. Essentially, all of these definitions are correct. As we will soon learn, the words *Russian ballet* evoke feelings of tremendous joy in anyone who is familiar with the finesse and style of the assured dancers associated with any part of this art form.

A brief background on the evolution of ballet in Russia gives us insight as to why the ballet remains so important to Russians today and explains why Russian ballet enjoys its excellent reputation throughout the world. Ballet in its modern form originated from court dancing in Italy during the Renaissance period. Although many U.S. Americans today think of ballet as a feminine occupation, in the 17th century, male dancers dominated spectacles for an audience of Italian nobility. Ballet emerged in the next century as a pantomime dance to the fascination of wealthier Europeans. In France, royalty participated in this form of entertainment by assuming starring roles. As ballet gained popularity throughout Europe, performances became theatrical and were enjoyed by the public at opera houses.

Like Louis XIV, who established an academy in France to improve the art, Peter the Great during the 17th century encouraged the development of social dance in an attempt to increase Russian awareness of the outside world. His determination to transform Russia into a powerful empire was achieved through modernization using Western Europe as a model. Russians have always had a great love of dancing, and when ballet was introduced in Russia in the 17th century, they responded enthusiastically. The monarchy placed emphasis on the arts by paying dancers salaries, who became known as "artists of his Imperial Majesty."

During Peter the Great's reign, one of the most significant changes in Russian ballet was the elimination of cumbersome robes to permit dancers freer movement. In 1736 the city of Saint Petersburg, the capital of Russia at that time, became the home of the Imperial Russian Ballet. Two years later, Empress Anna, who was also fond of ballet, sponsored the first school at her Winter Palace with the goal of developing professional Russian dancers.

A Flourishing Art

With the assistance of French and Italian choreographers, ballet flourished in the 18th century in Saint Petersburg, Moscow, and Warsaw. Perhaps the most influential of those who staged ballet compositions was French-born Marius Petipa, who in the late 1800s created such masterpieces as *Swan Lake, Sleeping Beauty,* and *The Nutcracker.* Among the legacies of the Russian ballet is its tradition of brilliant composers, such as Tchaikovsky, who collaborated with Petipa to create the music of those well-known ballets, and Prokofiev, who wrote the stirring music that accompanies the ballet of *Romeo and Juliet.*

Although ballet lost much of its vitality in Western Europe during the 19th century, Russia preserved the tradition and elegance of the art form. In 1909 Sergei Diaghilev revived the splendor of classical ballet with his *Ballet Russe,* or "Russian ballet" for Parisian audiences. His company was hailed as the "most exciting artistic force in Europe for the next twenty years" (Clarke & Crisp, 1976, p. 27). Sadly Diaghilev's extraordinary *Ballet Russe* did not survive his death in 1929, due to lack of either a school to develop new talent or a permanent theater to call home.

After the revolution in 1917, the "artists of His Imperial Majesty" in the former Saint Petersburg adapted to the socialist way of life, as did the rest of Russian citizens. Russian dancers became state employees of state-owned companies. The world-renowned Mariinsky Theater in Saint Petersburg became the famous Kirov Theater in Leningrad (the former Saint Petersburg), named in 1934 for the Bolshevik revolutionary Sergey Kirov after he was assassinated. Inside Russia, this company is now known as the Mariinsky Ballet Company; however, foreign audiences are still familiar with the Soviet-era name, Kirov. Likewise, the Petrovsky Theater, home of the Imperial Ballet in Moscow, was renamed Bolshoi, signifying that which is big or grand and capturing the dramatic and grand style of the Bolshoi performers, which is different from the refined and controlled style of the Kirov dancers. Thus, the Bolshoi and Kirov represent two distinctive styles.

In fact, ballet became more popular than ever as the government discovered that ballet could express the problems and ideals of a socialist state. Soviet promotion of socialist realism emphasized all types of artistic creativity, and citizens were encouraged to attend cultural events. To match the public fervor for ballet, an infrastructure was developed for its expansion. A. Y. Vaganova, a legendary ballerina from the old Imperial Ballet, was called on to create a training program for dancers, and it eventually produced the finest dancers in the world. She was responsible for much of the physical richness of Russian ballet, and her method of teaching is still widely used throughout Russia. Other maestros such as George Balanchine and Mikhail Fokine inspired eager students, including the magnificent Anna Pavlova, Vaslav Nijinsky, and Galina Ulanova. More than 40 new ballet companies were formed, and theaters were built throughout the Soviet Union. Gifted female pupils hoping to become prima ballerinas were provided with free academic and artistic support. Soviet teachers also searched for boys with strength, agility, and stamina who wished to pursue careers as members of a ballet troupe. Even today, a retired Russian male dancer usually retains his special status as *premier danseur.*

In spite of recent difficulties, Russian ballet serves as the standard for the rest of the world. This measurement is based on its fine traditions of classical ballet and intense national commitment to preserving and improving the art form.

Echelons of the Ballet

Clear echelons of status and privilege exist within the ballet company. At the very top is the prima ballerina, the prominent star of the troupe. Years of schooling and practice alone do not set one dancer apart from other dancers. The principal dancer must possess a natural gift of virtuosity and inner beauty. As is true in other nations around the globe, Russian citizens revere such accomplished individuals as national heroes. Although she is the most famous personality within her industry, the ballerina does not necessarily receive the largest salary. However, her status as number one dancer allows the ballerina much greater privilege than almost any payment could. Similarly the producer, choreographer, and conductor are held in high esteem.

The next level within the ballet company consists of the director, set designer, and costume designer, revered not only for the titles they hold but also for their personal reputations. Then there are those who report to the director—specifically the production, stage, company, and wardrobe managers; musical arranger/director; set design assistant; makeup director; light designer; and dance captains. Many of these individuals possess the ambition and potential to become experts or even members of the elite. Furthermore, there is the corps de ballet or the members of the ballet company who perform dances. They constitute by far the largest of the groups. Finally, supporting musicians and various technicians, who specialize in everything from lighting to makeup, are at the bottom of the hierarchy. They sustain the other classes or groups both within and outside of our metaphor.

During the Soviet era, the government provided ample financial support for ballet, and the echelons received rewards commensurate with the rank ordering described above. Privileges were selectively awarded and were given primarily to members of the Communist Party, about 20% of the total population. Many prominent members of ballet companies received ample rewards because of their association with ballet and, by extension, the Communist Party. Hence being a member of the ballet was associated with privileges that were denied to most citizens. While the echelons still exist in the ballet, the rewards are fewer, given the inability of the government to fund the arts at previous levels. However, some new funding has been found from worldwide tours that have made Russian ballet much more accessible to non-Russians. Members of the Bolshoi have even performed in Las Vegas.

As the discussion of the four periods or eras of this torn nation implies, Russia historically has been an autocratic nation in which the few at the top ruled with an iron hand, and echelons of power and prestige were created in accordance with this perspective. For example, even though Russia under communism proclaimed the doctrine "From each according to his ability, to each according to his needs," those who were members of the Communist Party received preferential treatment. Currently there is some concern that Russia could revert to its former ways, especially if most citizens begin to feel that the costs of capitalism outweigh the benefits. In contrast, the basic meaning of the echelons in Russian ballet is that outstanding, honest, and open performance is rewarded. It is easy to see when a dancer performs at a superior level, and the common citizen proudly identifies with such performance and culture. But the popularity that Prime Minister Putin enjoys, even though many of the rights of Russian citizens have been taken away in recent years, suggests that having a military and security background leads to favorable treatment. The somewhat passive acceptance of state control is changing as Russians have been shocked in recent years by the bold assassinations of journalists opposed to the regime. In fact, Russia is considered to be one of the most dangerous places in the world for journalists. It also appears to be a dangerous place for dissidents, as evidenced by the lengthy prison sentence (since 2003) for the country's most famous dissident, Mikhail Khodorkovsky, once Russia's richest man, on reportedly bogus tax and embezzlement charges. The parliamentary elections in December 2011 brought thousands of young people into the streets because they believed that the elections were rigged. These were among the biggest protests in recent years, and it appears that many Russians are becoming frustrated with endemic corruption and authoritarianism.

In business, senior Russian executives still have a tough time speaking freely about issues, as American consultants have discovered. Professor I. K. Adizes, speaking in 2010 at the 10th anniversary of the establishment of executive development programs at the Academy of National Economy of the Russian Federation in Moscow, observed that Russian companies are very centralized and that some Russian executives still favor the "imperial culture" characterized by surrender to authority. Interestingly, D. J. McCarthy, Puffer, and Darda (2010) investigated entrepreneurial leadership styles based on interviews with 130 Russian entrepreneurs over a 5-year period, as reported in the *Harvard Business Review*. The results showed that a large majority of these entrepreneurs had adopted an open leadership style similar to that of U.S. entrepreneurs. Their research supports a convergence theory of entrepreneurial leadership style across cultures. In some sectors, it appears that the idea of echelons is giving way to shared leadership and teamwork.

Russians tend to possess a strong sense of dignity and composure. Even though the lower classes may never experience the thrill of seeing a performance, Russians share a great pride in the reputation of their form of ballet as both enchanting magic and a symbol of magnificence. The very Westernness of ballet reflects Russian dignity and superiority, regardless of one's personal class status. Historically the most prestigious of dance companies was the Bolshoi Ballet, which is based in the Bolshoi Theater in Moscow and tours throughout the world. The newly refurbished and renovated Bolshoi Theater with its iconic neoclassical facade was reopened to much fanfare in

October 2011. Bolshoi management is trying to keep its traditional audience with a focus on classic ballet, while at the same time introducing some innovations such as inviting foreign choreographers to work with its dancers. The Bolshoi has even hired an American as a lead dancer, causing some controversy in the Russian ballet community. The Moscow Academic Choreographic Institute, better known as the Bolshoi School, is formally affiliated with the ballet company and is located adjacent to the theater. Less famous but sharing an equally superb tradition of dancers, teachers, and choreographers is the Mariinsky (Kirov) Ballet Company, which in recent years has outshone the Bolshoi. This company and its school descend directly from Empress Anna's Imperial School and ballet company and still make their home in the same building in Saint Petersburg today.

Drama and Realism

Audiences throughout the world recognize Russian ballet as the most spectacular form of dance. No other art form requires such a combination of elegance and simplicity. Russian ballet is distinct from ballet of other national origins due to its singular innovations, which were developed from classical ballet foundations. While ballet stagnated for many years in the West, Russia along with the rest of the Soviet Union cultivated its theatrical resources to develop unimpeachable superiority over all other national ballets. Only the pageantry of the Italian opera rivals the brilliance of the Russian ballet, and only the Spanish bullfight compares with its drama. The pursuit of perfection in Russian ballet has been an inspiration to thousands of audiences and become a permanent part of Russian culture and pride.

Audiences feel the vitality of the corps de ballet during the most dramatic moments of the performance. Throughout the ballet, dancers seek audience approval by delivering increasingly lofty performances. Sometimes the audience will respond to a dance so positively that a dancer will step out of character and take a bow, something that rarely happens in the West. In the final scene, the dancers pour their last remaining energy into the dance to make an unforgettably grand impression on each and every spectator. Each member of the company strives to be remembered in the minds of the audience as a glorious image of movement. In response, the audience expresses approval in the form of applause, flowers, and ovations. The dancers offer their performances, again and again, in return for audience gratification.

Like the dancer who makes a personal attempt to appeal to people in the audience, the ordinary Russian citizen tries to make an impression on those who are in a position to help. The most efficient way to accomplish anything is through personal favors. Rather than jeopardizing careers by assuming risk or showing initiative, some Russians will avoid taking responsibility or other action that may be construed as controversial, especially when jobs are scarce. Similarly the interchange between the dancer and the audience is symbolic of the basic exchange between total strangers in mundane matters. Whether the dancer gives pleasure to those who watch and is rewarded with faithful appreciation from the audience or two citizens or firms barter with one another, each participant offers the other one something that the other desires.

Just as some Mexicans use the fiesta to escape a mundane existence, so too do Russians place great value on the theatrical component of the performing arts. Films, plays, and the ballet offer opportunities for diversion. The ultimate cultural fantasy involves a melodramatic storyline surrounded with extravagant scenery and fancy costumes. The greater the pull on the heartstrings, the more Russians tend to love the performance; this sentimentality is a rare self-indulgence in this culture. Like the ballet company, which relies on theatrics to please the audience, the Russian shopper uses drama to persuade the clerk to decrease the price of an item. An indisputable part of Russian culture is the custom of bargaining and negotiating to beat the system. Similarly at an early age, students learn to supply the "right" answer in the classroom. Sharing of answers is tolerated, and children become adept at skirting authority with minimal confrontation.

As might be expected in an autocratic and authority-ranking culture, favoritism and corruption have been and continue to be used extensively to get around the system. Transparency International ranks Russia number 154 out of 178 countries on the Global Corruption Perceptions Index for 2010. Disobeying laws, even to gain mere trifles, is a part of Russian culture. It is little wonder that firms must have their own private police forces. Friends and connections are important, and many Russians have developed complex networks of relationships that allow them to survive in an unpredictable world. A great deal of effort is required to create and maintain these relationships in the hopes that benefits will result. Russians are continual gift givers, hoping to influence future generosity on the part of others. Such behavior is not likely to change, even with the qualified acceptance of competitive markets in which there is a level playing field.

Russians initially tend to take extreme views and offer few concessions when negotiating. If a foreign opponent makes a concession, it is perceived as a weakness. Unlike U.S. negotiators, Russians have little authority to make on-the-spot decisions and prefer not to make decisions spontaneously. Chess is a national pastime, and much of the relative strength of the many regional and world champions from Russia comes from their ability to think ahead. Players rely on strategic planning, whether offensive or defensive, to consider potential repercussions, similar to what Russians do when negotiating.

The Vodka Pastime

Furthermore, many consider drinking vodka a national pastime. Drunkenness is accepted as a socially approved method of entertainment and escape that is helpful in coping with years of suffering and hardship. Russians respect the need to drink thoughtfully or sorrowfully. At the same time, they join together in triumphant discovery—singing, laughing, and forgetting time. Especially in rural areas, drinking is a part of any type of festivity. Despite severe shortages, Russians manage to make a memorable feast out of nothing. Kitchen tables are the most likely setting for sharing conversation and vodka with friends. Throughout this culture a tenderness, even an affection, is shown by sober people to those who have overindulged. Everyone seems to understand the Russian need to consume vodka, although alcoholism is a widespread problem that has been linked to many social ills, including the premature deaths of Russian males. In the last decade, the consumption of vodka declined by a third and was replaced by a 40% rise in consumption of beer. However, in 2011 the parliament passed a law classifying beer as an alcoholic drink in order to battle a 24-hour drinking culture in Moscow and other major Russian cities. New rules prohibit the sale of all forms of alcohol on all forms of transport and at airports and railway stations. They also ban advertising on television, radio, and billboards.

Patience Yields Rewards

Russians are patient in working out compromises. Whereas time is a precious resource for American negotiators, deadlines often go ignored in Russian negotiations. Budgets and production schedules have traditionally been difficult to meet, and the prevailing attitude has been "Why bother?" Within the bureaucracy, it is apparent that citizens are used to tolerating long delays and complacency.

Compromise is not always necessary for achieving goals; compassionate appeals may be equally effective. Yale Richmond (2003) describes the time that he arrived at his hotel in Moscow hungry, after a long plane flight, only to learn from the woman in charge of guest services that the currency exchange office was closed for the day. He was traveling alone, did not have any rubles, and therefore would be unable to pay for dinner. When asked, she had no suggestions to offer. Instead of retreating, Richmond chatted with this complete stranger about his trip, the weather, his family, and her children, and eventually he returned to the subject of his hunger. This time she reached into her own purse and lent him some rubles until the next day. Although he did not expect to bargain with the woman, he approached her as another human being, and she responded with kindness. This is a common experience in Russia.

Realistic Depictions

Haskell (1963, 1968) makes several points about the role of realism in Russian ballet. First, Russian choreography tends to emphasize realistic interpretations through the expressions of characters, as noted in the part of Albrecht in *Giselle*. Whether Nureyev or Vikulov played the role, it was played with such vivacity that the transition from self-centeredness to remorsefulness over his lover's suffering was evident to the viewer. Also, spectacle is subordinated to the human values in the story. In Russian versions of *Sleeping Beauty*, the scene in which Princess Aurora falls into her slumber is choreographed with more than 100 dancers on stage. However, even in the midst of a host of dancers, the audience can sense a real interaction among the principal dancers. Another Russian contribution to the world of ballet is a reliance on experts for accurate set and costume design. Leon Bakst, famous for creating lavish sets and costumes, was the first to tie his depictions to historical information relative to the era in which a ballet took place. Thus Russian costumes have always been able to boast a thread of truth, and sets on the Russian stage have likewise lent credibility to the ambience of the ballet.

It is well known that idealism is important to most Russians. During communist rule, atheism was the official policy on religious affiliation, as party ideology was supposed to replace spiritual doctrine. Official pressures made it risky for most of society to participate openly in religion, but an underground system of belief survived. Since the adoption of a 1990 law allowing religious freedom, many Russians have renewed their interest in the traditional values of the Orthodox Church. In 1991, for the first time in more than 70 years, the Orthodox Christmas Day (which does not coincide with December 25) was proclaimed a national holiday in Russia.

Realism also plays a role in everyday life in Russia, as people attempt to survive daily obstacles. Connections, or personal contacts, are easily the most valued perquisite for the privileged. Knowing someone who is able to influence an outcome is the way to get things done, and this is an accepted way of life in Russia. For example, pulling strings is an effective way to arrange the swap of apartments between strangers and acquaintances.

Connections can also be serious business, as in the case of a doctor willing to recommend a surgeon to a patient who wishes to circumvent the bureaucratic health system. (It is generally acknowledged that the public health system totally collapsed in the early 2000s. Only recently has the government focused its attention on this area, with some good results.) The ultimate accomplishment of parents is to secure better educational opportunities for their children; special arrangements for admission to a particular school can be made outside of that school's formal admission system. Regardless of the type of favor asked, it is understood that a return favor may be redeemed at a later date.

Another dramatic tool borrowed from a ballet performance is the use of *vranya,* or bluffing, and it is consistent with Russian historical norms. *Vranya* is best characterized by the statement "You know I'm lying, and I know that you know and you know that I know, but I go ahead with a straight face and you nod seriously." It is publicly distasteful for most Russians to admit that anything has gone wrong. Social ills have been repressed in an attempt to maintain the image of Russian superiority.

Personal Qualities

From a foreign perspective, Russians have been characterized as serious and unexpressive, betraying no emotion in public. They hold a reputation for hardiness and stoicism. Often this external toughness comes across as coarse indifference or pushy discourtesy to the visitor. In the brusque surliness of service people and glum faces of crowds full of impassive stares, foreigners find the gruff, cold impersonality they expect. But this exterior is *maskirovannoye,* a false front. The stereotypical demeanor is part of the drama of Russian culture. Underneath the mask is a raw humanness that could not be more real.

Ballet is much more than a dance on stage; it is a marvel of choreography, music, costumes, and lighting that create a distinct mood for each audience. Choreographers express ideas through every dancer's movements, whether they are presenting a precise theme or leaving an audience free to use its imagination. Composers write scores to accompany the beautiful technique of ballet, and orchestral conductors lead musicians to perform scores at the proper tempo, rhythm, and volume for dancers. Wardrobe designers and lighting experts use specialized knowledge of their crafts for ballet productions, and visual artists also contribute to the mood by designing sets to provide the proper backdrop for each dance. Finally, trained, athletic dancers combine flexibility, strength, and balance to perform a series of dances that often tell a story for spectators of all ages.

A final consideration of this characteristic of Russian culture is the seeming contradiction of drama and realism. On the surface, these principles appear to be opposites. Herein lies one of the major dichotomies within the culture. Theatrics project a contrived atmosphere, while realism is the rejection of visionary ideals. One of the more puzzling aspects of Russian culture is the illusion of disparity. Russians are categorized as both lazy and hardworking; they want to have money, yet they despise it. Russians seemingly want to get money rather than earn it. A well-known Russian fairy tale tells of Emelya, the youngest brother in a family and a fool who was famous for being idle and lying on top of a large stove. He did not have to go anywhere because his stove could carry him and his wishes were fulfilled by magic. He even ended up marrying the tsar's daughter. Today, a restaurant chain in Saint Petersburg is named after this character.

Russians are depicted as being uninterested in building relationships (Adler, 2007) and at the same time as "warm and helpful" after new relationships are formed (Richmond, 2003, p. 3). This is because they tend to deem people either friends or strangers and treat them accordingly. A common saying in Russia is "100 friends are better than 100 rubles."

Denied religious freedom for more than 70 years, Russians still possess faith and hope. Russians tend to be both dreamy and pragmatic; they place great value on the work of writers, artists, and dancers. This nation's contribution to world literature and the performing arts is priceless. Like members of other cultures, Russians are faced with choices about priorities.

Russians' roles in their public and private relationships also seem to conflict. In their public roles, Russians are characterized as careful, cagey, and passive; in their private lives, they are depicted as honest and direct. Foreigners describe Russians as suffering, unruly, and stoic; they are also known as cheerful, generous, obedient, and hospitable. With friends, unlike in public, Russians feel free to pour out woes to one another and are not burdened by the need to disguise the realities of disappointment or pain. Like people of other nationalities, they can be publicly pompous and privately unpretentious, either caring or unkind. Perhaps the great novelist Fyodor Dostoyevsky described it best as "half saint and half savage."

The Russian Soul

From the 12th century until the time of Peter the Great, and then from 1917 to 1992 during the Communist era, Russians were isolated from the rest of the world. Two events, the Tartar (Mongol) invasion and the Ottoman conquest of Constantinople (modern Istanbul), abruptly halted commercial, religious, and cultural exchanges with other nations and limited Russia's development for centuries. Russia had relatively little need for trade because it was self-sufficient in agriculture; most of its interaction with other nations related to land disputes. From the Russian perspective, territorial expansion resulted from victories over foreign invaders. At one time or another, Teutonic knights, Lithuanians, Poles, Swedes, French, Germans, and Asian groups invaded Russia, which has no natural border defenses. On all sides, fear of invasion by neighboring adversaries led to a Russian preoccupation with state security. A tradition of citizens, both peasants and nobles, serving the state evolved from fear of the hostile powers that surrounded Russia. In subsequent centuries, Russian rulers purposely limited foreign influence on the empire, and as a result, people met later attempts to introduce new methods and technologies with skepticism. Putin, for example, although he and former President George W. Bush were friendly on a personal level, reacted very negatively to Bush's plan to station nuclear weapons in Poland, which borders Russia. Russia's 2008 military incursion into Georgia, which is seeking to join NATO, seemed to be partially based on the fact that Georgia had been a part of the Soviet Union. In general, Putin has used Russians' strong belief in words and symbols to promote a Stalinist vision of Russia as an isolated fortress surrounded by enemies ("The Long Life," 2011).

Today Russian distrust persists, as indicated by their feelings about Western influence. Also, Russia is concerned about the rising importance of China, with which it shares borders. As we might expect, Russians want to be independent of foreign influence, and this is refracted in the concept of the Russian soul, which basically reflects the desire for distance so that the culture can be preserved, as it has been for so long. The idea that distance is essential for survival is a characteristic of Russians, even today. As a people, Russians are considered self-reliant, strong willed, and possessed of inner resources.

Although it may seem that so many years of tsarist regimes and the iron fist of communism would have stifled the outward expression of such inner qualities, in fact individual perseverance and creativity have thrived in spite of absolute rule.

Undoubtedly many Russians have been entrepreneurial since 1992, but the inadequacy of infrastructure, such as effective laws and banks, and the increased intrusion of the Russian government into the private sector have stymied their efforts. One in six Russian businesspeople has been prosecuted for an alleged economic crime over the last 10 years, and with acquittals close to zero, the many defendants are at the mercy of corrupt members of the justice system and must serve time in prison ("The Long Life," 2011).

Each member of a Russian ballet troupe must endure laborious training on a daily basis and possess unfailing discipline to perfect the art. Classes, rehearsals, and performances compose an exhausting routine for Russian dancers; this cycle requires a dancer's complete attention on the world of dancing with little time for much else. This distance or separation from everyday life allows dancers to put all of their energy into the dance. Orthopedic surgeons, masseurs, and medication have become part of the reality of contemporary ballet; physical demands often require dancing through aches and pains. Relying on Russian self-determination, each dancer is able to achieve total concentration, fueled by the passionate intensity of the Russian soul. The result is unmatched excellence in both technique and artistry.

The Russian soul is a mixture of intense feeling; it is emotion, sentiment, and sensitivity combined. It is triumph over seemingly insurmountable troubles or sadness arising from the discovery of stark truth. Over the years much has been written about the magical and mystical nature of the Russian soul. What is known as something mysterious seems to boil down to this: At the very core of individual Russian expression is the enigmatic principle, or soul, that places absolute value on decency, respect, honesty, and moral goodness. Part inherited and part learned, the stony resolve of the Russian people is unlike any other, and it can be interchanged with human compassion in the blink of an eye. Creative, electrifying, and daring, the Russian soul is the source of inspiration within the dancer.

There seems to be a strong relationship between the severe Russian winter and the Russian soul. To keep warm, the entire family would sleep together on top of the *pech* (Russian fireplace and stove), and to survive under such harsh conditions, it was necessary for everyone to work closely together. A strong in-group orientation developed in which people expressed emotions openly and automatically helped others; it was a classic generic culture of community sharing in which collectivism was high and power distance low. For example, the U.S. coffee break is designed to "help people get through a day" or "wake up," but the Russian tea break is really about continually reconnecting emotionally with others (Ries, 1994).

A Contact Culture

Probably because of the harsh winters, which were instrumental in facilitating the defeat of both Napoleon and Hitler, Russians developed a contact culture reflecting the Russian soul. A contact culture is emotionally expressive and encourages people to communicate warmth, closeness, and availability for conversation. Intense eye contact, frequent touching, close physical distance, and smiling are emphasized (Andersen, 1994). And, given such a positive view of winter, it is little wonder that Russian art emphasizes winter scenes and activities. For example, many of the grand buildings in Saint Petersburg and Moscow were designed and colored to look their best when the pure white of fresh snow contrasts with their pastel exteriors.

The severe Russian climate is also responsible for both the resourcefulness and the strength of Russian people. For centuries, peasants have endured long winters of bitter cold temperatures, brutal winds, and frozen ground while longing for spring. Springtime inevitably brings the considerable work of quickly tilling soil and planting seeds so that crops may be harvested before the first frost less than 5 months later. Unpredictable weather and danger of crop failure are of great concern, yet Russians have proven able to endure hardship. Unable or in many cases unwilling to take risks with imported technologies, peasants rely on familiar if primitive tools and techniques. They are masters of patience and resolve, recognizing that they do not have control over everything in life. Yale Richmond (2003) explains, "Until recently, most Russians [unlike Americans] have lived much as their ancestors did before them—in small villages, distant and isolated, their freedom of movement restricted, and without the comforts and labor-saving tools provided by modern society" (pp. 9–10). In more recent years, there has been an increased acceptance of modern technology, but productivity still lags when compared to that of other developed nations.

The geography contributes to feelings of powerlessness; much of Russia's mountainous terrain and desolate barren spaces is under continual permafrost. Russia is one of the least densely populated nations in the world, with only eight inhabitants per square kilometer.

Intimacy appears to be more pronounced among Russian families than elsewhere in the world. Accommodations are typically crowded, with multigenerational families living in small spaces. Although this is changing, extended families have resided in cramped situations under relentless scrutiny for decades, usually within apartments. Beds serve as couches in sitting areas, and bathroom facilities are shared among many within the apartment. Privacy is an oddity; no Russian word exists to describe isolation in positive terms.

Throughout the arts, the Russian soul is the unmistakable power that compels the writer, actor, painter, or dancer to aspire to greatness. A potent force, the Russian soul shaped the insightful expression of Dostoyevsky's writings. His literature revealed the extent of responsibility that Russians feel for the afflictions and pain of the rest of the world. Company and conversations begin to matter as soon as one steps into a Russian's personal life. Among friends and family, Russians become the wonderful, flowing, emotional people of Leo Tolstoy novels, sharing humor and sorrows and confidences. They enter a simple intimacy in which individuals are less self-centered than in the West. Russians tend to pour out their hearts in total commitment to friendships and become easygoing, affectionate, and tender.

Furthermore, intellectuals look for a spiritual compensation to escape the boredom of everyday life, whether in ballet, novels, or poems. (There are, to be sure, exceptions to this generalization; for example, the night life of Saint Petersburg is lively.) Russian culture reveres poetry for its wit, courage, and creativity. Poets such as Alexander Pushkin are regarded as heroes for daring to use metaphor to conceal meanings from official censors.

Many Russians like to think that they have a monopoly on virtue, whether it refers to family loyalty, a sense of duty, or love of nature. Emotionality is considered a positive attribute, and some of the most convincing arguments appeal to the irrational element of human existence. Guilt is also a factor in emotionality. Similarly the presence of guilt helps the dancer to feel more deeply. Russians feel that they can communicate emotions through their eyes, conveying love, hate, or passion. Whether expressing unbounded joy or woeful melancholy, the Russian dancer performs with an inner dynamism that members of other cultures find difficult to duplicate.

Parenting and Education

Just as Russian workers in the city or country survive harsh winters and hot summers, children also learn to adapt to hardship. Parental indulgence is a national cult, and toys teach meaningful lessons. Russian-made toys tend to break easily, and when children experience the disappointment or anger of a new or favorite toy falling apart, they learn that they have little control over their world. Russian children learn to accept without too much bitterness the fact that their world is not perfect. Perhaps this is why Russian ballet students are able to adjust without bitterness to grueling schedules of dance instruction, traditional classroom subjects, and physical workouts that build strength and flexibility.

There is a collective responsibility for children, exhibited through overprotectiveness. By some accounts, Russian parents are even more overprotective of their children than American parents are. Part of the reason is the instability of life following the collapse of the Soviet Union, but another reason is wide media coverage (unlike in Soviet times) of crime, traffic accidents, terrorism, and kidnapping. Yet another reason is the declining birthrate and the small size of modern Russian families, which allows parents and grandparents to focus on one or two children. Parents generally accompany children to school at least until they are 12 years of age and monitor their social lives (Weir, 2008).

Without a doubt, Russian society has a pronounced collective emphasis. Szalay (1993) found that U.S. Americans make almost twice as many associations with the word *individual* compared to Russians, whereas Russians make almost three times as many associations with the word *people* compared to U.S. Americans. Young children are taught how to behave and relate to others at an early age. Respect and deference for authority figures is a norm in every classroom. Landon Pearson (1990) pointed out that "a respectful and, indeed, slightly fearful attitude to adult authority is inculcated into Soviet children from the moment they set foot into an educational establishment" (p. 111). Prime Minister Putin and his followers have reinforced this message in recent years, as exemplified in the adage that all should follow a strong leader without question, just as migratory birds follow one bird. From childhood on, Russians acquire an acute sense of place and propriety, of what is acceptable and what is not. They generally know what they can get away with and what should not be attempted. Student discussion is limited, and individual thought is not encouraged. Pupils learn that supplying "official" answers ensures good grades, which in turn can lead to admission to higher education and a good job after graduation.

Educational institutions are designed to shape young minds using structured discipline and group dynamics. Much learning is based on memory drills and the modeling of rigid prescriptions, although this is changing at some of the leading business schools. One of the downsides of this collectivistic culture is that it is hard for students to compete against one another as in Western educational environments, which are shaped by individualism. Enormous pressure is exerted on children to achieve stringent expectations. Russian children learn early the futility of challenging authority; teachers and other officials often chastise parents for the failure of offspring to meet social norms.

Formal ballet productions bring together dancing, music, design, and an audience. With the exception of solos by individual dancers, the ballet troupe dances together as one large body. Even solos are precisely staged by choreographers to balance the entire performance. All members of the company are mutually dependent on each other, and individual needs, rights, and desires are subordinated to the whole. It is the choreographer's job to integrate the dancer's body with the musical score, the possibilities of the stage, and the mood to be conveyed. Choreographers must "explore and expand the dancer's capabilities" while ensuring that the components of the ballet production, as well as the dancers, are all in sync (Clarke & Crisp, 1976, p. 38). As a result, Russian dancers think of themselves as members of a company and as "people's artists" rather than as individual dancers.

A Group Ethic

The group ethic can be traced to the *mir,* or the small village cooperative that made all farming decisions for the community, even through the early 1900s. Not only did the *mir* choose which crops to plant and when, but it also collected taxes and resolved conflicts. As Richmond (2003) notes, "The mir's authority, moreover, extended beyond land matters—it also disciplined members, intervened in family disputes, settled issues which affected the community as a whole, and otherwise regulated the affairs of its self-contained and isolated agricultural world" (p. 15). The *mir* consisted of household heads who discussed issues and reached consensus about courses of action. Decisions based on the "collective will" were binding on every household.

Even before the 1917 revolution, Russian tsars approved of this type of informal local government because such units were capable of controlling the vast populace. The *mir* enforced tax collection and military conscription as well as other programs.

In describing the *mir*, Richmond (2003) aptly concludes, "Because the mir affected so many people, and for such a long time, it played a major role in forming the Russian character" (p. 16). It is interesting to note that popular usage of the word *mir* references its other definition, that of "peace."

A few examples of collective behavior include communal seating in restaurants and group participation in attending cultural and sports events. Physical contact such as jostling or pushing among total strangers is typical in crowds, as is holding hands among friends of the same sex. Older Russians generally are more than happy to offer unsolicited advice, even to foreigners, and it is seldom considered impolite to drop in on friends unannounced (Richmond, 2003).

The GLOBE study (House et al., 2004) identified Russia as part of its Eastern European cluster, which scores high on gender egalitarianism, in-group collectiveness, and assertiveness but low on performance orientation, future orientation or deferring gratification to achieve long-term goals, and the acceptance of risk or uncertainty avoidance. These findings support using the Russian ballet as a metaphor for Russian culture.

In sum, like the ballet, Russian culture can be unpredictable and enigmatic. As Winston Churchill said in a 1939 radio broadcast, "I cannot forecast to you the action of Russia. It is a riddle wrapped in a mystery inside an enigma" (in Platt, 1989/2003, #1652). Russian culture today fuses the earnest elements of emotion, spirituality, and survival once found in Old Russia. Echelons within Russian society, drama and realism, and the Russian soul as expressed in Russian ballet are characteristics that have made the Russian people culturally unique. Although Russia may privatize its economy significantly and become more Western in its economic orientation—and the jury is still out on this matter—the characteristics of the Russian ballet described in this chapter should be of help in understanding its underlying culture for years to come.

PART VIII

The Base Culture and Its Diffusion Across Borders (Clusters of Nations)

The Example of China

I n the preceding chapters, the basic unit of analysis is each nation and its cultural metaphor. However, migration has played a critical role in cultural transmission. For example, the English culture has had a significant influence on the national cultures of Australia, New Zealand, Canada, and the United States.

In this part of the book, we focus on the base culture of the Chinese through a discussion of China's Great Wall and cross-cultural paradox. We then examine how this base culture influenced the overseas or expatriate Chinese living in various nations through an analysis of the Chinese family altar. Finally, we look at the creation of the Singaporean culture in a nation whose population is predominantly ethnically Chinese but also includes significant minorities of other ethnic and cultural groups. The Singaporean hawker centers, our cultural metaphor for Singapore, are a distinctive expression of this nation and its culture.

A useful discussion among readers of this book could center on other base cultures and their influence around the world. Several researchers have demonstrated cultural clusters of nations considered in such terms as shared religions, languages, and geography. In Chapter 1 we described one of the most prominent clustering studies, the GLOBE study (House et al., 2004). The reader may want to review these clusters.

It should be emphasized that the concept of country clusters is increasingly important in the modern world. Although we have a global economy, most nations tend to trade most heavily with their neighbors; for example, the North American Free Trade Agreement (NAFTA) facilitates trade among the United States, Canada, and Mexico. But bold experiments are taking place, such as the European Union's attempt to include a wide diversity of national cultures within its scope, not to mention the World Trade Organization whose membership includes over 150 of the world's 220 nations. Thus both regionalization as exemplified by NAFTA and globalization as exemplified by the World Trade Organization are simultaneously occurring, as are bilateral agreements between two nations. In such a complex world, understanding the cultural metaphors both for each nation and for the clusters in which they exist is not only helpful but necessary.

CHAPTER 25

China's Great Wall and Cross-Cultural Paradox

Donning a rough cotton white-and-red headdress, I took a place in the line of her descendants, trudging in her funeral procession and kowtowing to her casket as we wound our way through her lakeside township to a mountainside burial site. And as I did, I was struck by the enduring power of ancestors in the lives of the Chinese. Spirituality and authority emanate from a church or temple; they reside with the elderly and one's family tree. People don't disgrace themselves in the eyes of God; they do so in the eyes of their forebears.

—John Pomfret, a *Washington Post* writer married to a Chinese woman, describing the funeral of the wife's grandmother (2003)

China is undergoing massive changes that began in the late 1970s, at which time a new Communist government stressing a mixture of communism and free enterprise replaced the disastrous Mao Tse Tung government. Mao and his associates ridiculed and decimated the middle class and attempted to stamp out Confucianism with its emphasis on traditions, relationships, and education. Starting in the late 1970s, the government began sequentially to emphasize free enterprise and infrastructure development in various regions of the nation. As a result, the economy grew rapidly, and China's gross national product (GNP) is projected to surpass that of the United States by 2025. Ironically, the Chinese government now honors Confucian teachings once again and emphasizes their value in promoting free enterprise. A large statue of Confucius stands in Tiannamen Square, and he is the only person so honored other than Mao Tse Tung. The government promotes the spread of Confucius Institutes both in China and worldwide, and there are now 340 of them. There is even a Confucian Peace Prize whose supporters want it to rival the Nobel Peace Prize in terms of prestige and prize money.

While the standard of living rose, however, so did economic inequality. Regional governments own the land and began to move farmers off of it, with the result that China is now undergoing the largest transition from having a rural to an urban population in history. According to the World Bank, China's income inequality is now on a par with that of some Latin American and African nations. Agriculture still employs 41% of the working population, but it contributes only 11% of GNP. The population per square kilometer is 139.7, versus 32.9 for the United States, and the gross domestic product per head is US$3,270 versus $46,350 in the United States. On the 2011 Index of Economic Freedom, China ranks only 135th out of 179 nations (T. Miller, 2011). China and the United States lead the world as the greatest emitters of greenhouse gases. China leads all other nations in destroying the ozone layer, 70% of the country's lakes and rivers are polluted, and half of the population does not have access to clean drinking water.

China's demographics are very problematic as a result of the one-child-per-family rule. The number of children born to a Chinese woman stands at 1.8, below the replacement level of 2.1 for population stability. This is occurring as life expectancy has increased dramatically, from 35 in 1949 to 73 years. Thus the population is aging, and most citizens are not protected by either a government or a private pension system (see Pomfret, 2008). To complicate matters, parents favor male children over female children and act accordingly, with the result that in the future, many more males than females will be seeking marriage partners and be unsuccessful in their quest.

Still, visiting modern-day China is a shock for anyone who has not been there since 1978, when the major mode of transportation was the bicycle. People resided primarily in the countryside and were poor, even if there was paradoxically more equal income distribution. Mao's ideology emphasized the importance of the "iron rice bowl" from which all would eat, but unfortunately at least 50 million starved because of his ill-conceived policies, such as deliberately killing almost all of the birds in major cities by having the entire populace clang pots and pans, thus forcing the birds to stay aloft until they dropped dead. Reportedly the government viewed the birds as "dirty" and wanted to clean up the cities. An unforeseen consequence of this policy was that the dead birds could not eat parasites and other carriers of germs, and disease spread. Similarly, Mao wanted to create a modern steel industry and to that end confiscated the steel woks of the peasants, which were melted down for supposedly other, more modern uses. However, the peasants had only the woks, many centuries old, to cook food. As a result, many died. Ironically Mao's dream of a modern steel industry came to naught.

Today China is an automobile-clogged, fast-moving nation that is consuming vast amounts of resources such as steel and oil. China's population of 1.34 billion is the largest among the world's nations. There is a great emphasis on consumerism and satisfying one's own needs and desires, even at the expense of short-changing aging parents, long revered in the Chinese culture and its Confucian tradition. Public shaming of grown children who have abandoned their parents is common, and it is not unusual for them to be sent to jail for this violation of traditional Confucian practice.

Still, people value the past and tradition, as our introductory quotes suggest. Yu Dan, a relatively unknown professor of communications, has become famous as the author of a best-selling book on Confucius, and there are now schools for children stressing Confucian thought (Fan, 2007; Ni, 2007). Adults seeking to relate to Confucian tradition will devote a weekend or week to studying and practicing Confucianism.

Attempting to describe and explain any cultural group is a daunting task, and this is doubly true of the Chinese, who have been and continue to be stereotyped in various guises, such as the shifty-eyed Chinese, the unfathomable Chinese, and so forth. Ironically the Chinese have difficulty explaining themselves, in part because they tend to be high-context communicators; they also have faced exclusion and discrimination in various nations and tend to play things close to the vest. Almost all of the countless books and articles on the Chinese focus on "dos and taboos" or obvious facets of Chinese culture, such as that it is an authority-ranking and high-context culture and that the color red is a sign of good fortune. However, as we will see in Chapter 27, The Singapore Hawker Centers, even this generalization about high-context communication must be qualified.

In 1999 Tony Fang wrote a masterful book on the Chinese business negotiating style that provided the kind of insightful analysis that had been sorely missing from the literature. Fang, a native of China, was a business negotiator for Chinese firms for 20 years, after which he completed his doctorate at Linkoeping University in Sweden. These experiences provided him with a unique understanding of both Chinese and Western perspectives. His book revolves around a paradox, namely that Western negotiators have consistently described Chinese negotiators as both sincere and deceptive. How can this be?

To understand the Chinese, it is helpful to focus on both the paradox that Fang (1999) identifies and a cultural metaphor unique to China, its Great Wall. When we use the visible Great Wall as our cultural metaphor, we employ it to understand the invisible Great Wall of Chinese values, attitudes, and behaviors.

Paradox is central to Chinese thought. Essentially a paradox represents the concept of interdependent opposites or the existence of two opposite states of reality simultaneously. For example, *many* and *few* combine to mean *how much* in the Chinese language, and *inside* and *outside* together mean *everywhere*. Paradoxical thinking represents "both-and" rather than "either-or"; that is, it is a nuanced or gray perspective rather than a black-and-white perspective.

As in previous chapters, each subdivision of this chapter represents a dimension or aspect of the cultural metaphor. In this chapter, we use the three related explanations that Fang (1999) proposes to answer his paradox as the distinctive features of our cultural metaphor: China's long, tortuous, and complex history; the influence of

Confucian thought on Chinese behavior; and the Chinese perspective on war and the marketplace, particularly as enunciated in the writings of Sun Tzu and applied to the marketplace in terms of six principles of Sun Tzu (McNeilly, 2012).

The Great Wall: Long, Tortuous, and Complex History

Anyone who has ever visited the Great Wall of China tends to be overwhelmed by its scope, magnitude, and majesty. The Wall is 7,200 kilometers or 4,474 miles in length. It is frequently said that the first Emperor of China, Qin Shi Huang, began the construction project in 221 BCE by restoring the ruins of older walls and linking them with new construction; the result was a 3,000-mile wall. The intention underlying the construction was to ward off marauding warriors and tribes. Frequently marauders settled near the Wall after being repulsed, traded with the Chinese, and in many cases, intermarried with them and eventually were allowed to enter China. Unfortunately, however, the first emperor was repressive, harsh, and autocratic—even to the extent of outlawing Confucianism. As in the case of many such autocrats and individuals seeking to demonstrate that they are superior to others, Emperor Qin also constructed a Great Tomb for himself, on which 700,000 workers labored for 34 years. The well-known 7,000 terra-cotta warriors found in his tomb are a popular tourist attraction as well as a stark reminder of the futility of such efforts; the Qin Dynasty fell in a peasant revolt in 209 BCE, a year after the emperor's death.

In that same year, the Han dynasty arose. Today, about 85% of the Chinese are classified as Han, although China is home to about 400 ethnic groups (some as small as a few thousand in number) and 56 spoken languages. China is much more culturally integrated because of the Han association than most nations, as evidenced by the fact that there are only about 400 Chinese family names. It is easy for the Chinese to categorize one another because of such uniformity.

The Han conquered central Asia; extended the Wall for another 300 miles into the Gobi Desert; and provided protection for the legendary Silk Road, which linked traders from distant points. It was impossible for traders to reach their destination without passing through the Great Wall. The Han also added beacon towers to the Wall and used a sophisticated system of smoke signals to warn of impending invaders and their approximate numbers.

The Ming dynasty, which arose in 1368 CE, extended the Wall to its current length and is responsible for the structure we see today, although it is based on earlier work. Ming walls were bigger, more ornate, and more impressive. During this dynasty, China was at the height of its power, and the nation was increasingly referenced as "the Middle Kingdom," that is, the center of the Earth. Geographic maps were drawn to show that China was in the middle of everything. There was good reason for this perception, as China was far ahead of the West during this period, which lasted until the Industrial Revolution in the West.

As this discussion suggests, China has experienced a long, tortuous, and complex history extending over thousands of years. There have been periods of tranquility, sometimes lasting hundreds of years, but there have also been periods of extreme social unrest. Throughout these eras, the Wall has served the Chinese well and preserved their culture.

U.S. Americans who are at all familiar with Europeans quickly notice that they have a grasp of their respective nation's history that far exceeds the time perspective of many, if not most, U.S. Americans; Europeans talk easily about 10th-century kings and queens, for example, such as King John III or King John IX. In the case of the Chinese, the time horizon is much, much longer. It is frequently said that U.S. strategic planners think in terms of 3-year or 5-year plans, whereas Chinese strategic planners focus on plans extending 100 or more years into the future. This long-term perspective is associated with tradition and ancestors, as many firms are controlled by one family and frequently by the patriarch. In Asia, with its emphasis on the family and the past, approximately two thirds of publicly traded companies are controlled by a single shareholder, compared with just 3% in the United States, according to the World Bank (McBride, 2003). China follows this pattern.

Furthermore, China exemplifies a torn culture, having been ripped from its cultural roots several times. Since 1900 China has experienced a dizzying array of governmental arrangements, including the disastrous Mao Communist era starting in 1949, which effectively blocked China's entry into the global economic market. In the late 1970s, a newer group of more enlightened Chinese Communist rulers emerged who fostered China's integration with the global marketplace. As indicated previously, they introduced economic development in phases, developing specific areas of the nation before others to use scarce resources effectively. This approach, in sharp contrast to the approach used in Russia (see Chapter 24), has proved to be successful, and development economists uniformly praise it (see Stiglitz, 2002).

A visitor to Shanghai—which seems to combine the best of U.S., Asian, and European architecture—is immediately impressed by the skyline, and this positive impression is constantly reinforced when one talks with governmental officials and business executives, who exhibit a cultural uniformity of purpose. Shanghai is frequently called "the city of the future," and it and other Chinese cities are being built in the manner that guided the Great Wall's construction: with patience, hard work, a long time horizon, and a systematic approach integrating major cities and regions.

Confucianism and Taoism

It is impossible to understand China's culture without understanding Confucian thought. Confucius died in 479 BCE, frustrated that he was never able to become a major advisor to any of China's regional rulers. However, his ideas took hold in large part because of the vicious warfare that was occurring among these rulers, and his emphasis on forming, and permanently and deliberately maintaining, tradition in accordance with China's idealized past period of Great Harmony had wide appeal.

Confucian thought is encapsulated in five terms, the first of which is *Jen,* meaning human-heartedness or the simultaneous feeling of humanity toward others and respect for oneself (see H. Smith, 1991). Second, *Chuntzu,* "the Superior Man," is someone fully adequate and poised to accommodate others as much as possible rather than to acquire all he can selfishly. At all times he should be sincere with others, which accounts for the sincerity of Chinese negotiators that Fang (1999) highlights. Third is *Li* or propriety, which refers to the way things should be done. For example, the Five Relationships involve the appropriate conduct that should occur between father and son, older and younger siblings, husband and wife, older and younger friend, and ruler and subject. The Five Relationships are central in the Confucian system and clearly encourage the creation of an authority-ranking culture.

More specifically, *Li* reflects the importance that Confucius attached to the family. This idea evolved from the earlier era of ancestor worship to include the concepts of filial piety and veneration of age. From the Chinese perspective, a person exists only in relation to others, particularly but not exclusively members of the family. There is a second meaning of *Li,* ritual, which is envisioned as encompassing all of a person's activities during his or her whole life.

Te is the fourth term, and it refers to the power by which people should be ruled, not by force but by moral example. Finally, there is *Wen,* which accords a place of prominence to the arts as a means of achieving peace and as an instrument of moral education.

The device for developing tradition deliberately was extreme social sensitivity, and this is still reflected in the Chinese concept of face. As discussed in Chapter 3, The Japanese Garden, face is an unwritten set of rules by which people in society cooperate to avoid unduly damaging one another's prestige and self-respect. In bargaining, for example, the winner should allow the loser some minor tactical reward, especially when all the observers can ascertain the identity of the vanquished. If a father's business becomes bankrupt and he dies suddenly, frequently his sons will work for years to pay off the debt to maintain face for the family. When an individual loses face, he or she tends to adopt a stony or blank expression as if nothing has happened; generally face is forfeited through loss of self-control or a display of frustration and anger (Bonavia, 1989).

Of course, individuals in all cultures want to protect their face or honor. As a general rule, people do not enjoy losing, being humiliated, or experiencing any related outcome. However, the Chinese added a unique dimension to the concept of face, as it is incumbent on everyone in a transaction not only to preserve face but to give face, saving themselves and everyone else from embarrassment. This is how a Superior Man should behave.

Some experts have argued that Confucianism is not a traditional religion, as it has no concept of a personal god and only an amorphous concept of heaven or a shadowy netherworld in which ancestors live and help to guide the living. Thus the Chinese tend to focus on this world and not the next. David Bonavia (1989) aptly captures the essence of being Chinese in the following description, although he was primarily discussing modern China:

> The most determining feature of the Chinese people's attitude to the world around them is their total commitment to life as it is. . . . In this world view, all human activity—religion, sex, war—consists of functional acts aimed at achieving something. Only the arts are considered to have intrinsic value, and they are chiefly reflections of the real world or an imagined world, not abstract patterns. . . . Action must have a purpose, the Chinese feel; there is nothing enno-bling about pain, and death is an infernal nuisance. . . . Most Chinese, seeing a Hindu holy man stick a knife through his cheeks or walk on coals, would con-clude that he was either a fool or a fraud. . . . The central concept of Chinese society is functionality. (pp. 56–57)

Taoism is usually considered the primary religion among the Chinese, while Confucianism relates to the manner in which an individual is to behave in society. Taoism was supposedly created by Lao Tzu, who was born in 604 BCE, and its main tenets were outlined in one small book, *Tao Te Ching* or "The Way and the Power." *Tao*, or the way, has three overlapping meanings, the first of which is that it can be known only through mystical insight. In the second sense, *tao* refers to the ordering principle behind the universe or all life, and it represents the rhythm and driving force of nature. The third sense of *tao* is the way humans should order their lives to be in bal-ance with the universe.

The Nature of Power

Power, the second part of the title of this influential book, refers to the belief that a person gains power by leading a life that is in harmony with the dictates of the universe. This approach continues to shape the Chinese character and is manifested in the desire to achieve a state of serenity and grace. The basic approach to life that is consonant with the universe is *wu wei* or creative quietude. Paradoxically, *wu wei* is simultaneous action and relaxation and letting behavior flow spontaneously. Creative quietude is never forcing or straining but, rather, seeking the empty spaces in life and nature and moving quietly and without confrontation through the avenues of least resistance.

Taoists reject all forms of self-assertiveness and competition and seek union with nature and simplicity of life more than materialistic possessions. Their extreme aver-sion to violence verges on pacifism. Taoism also includes the traditional Chinese symbols of yin and yang, which connote that there are no clear dichotomies but rather all values and concepts are relative to the mind that entertains them; that is, values and concepts are by definition paradoxes representing nuanced "both-and" thinking.

Thinking in yin-yang terms means analyzing the universe in terms of pairs of interacting opposites, such as shadowed and bright, decaying and growing, moonlit and sunlit, earthly and heavenly, and feminine and masculine. Whether something is classified as yin or yang depends not on its intrinsic nature but on the roles it plays in relation to other things, which is consistent with the relation-based system of the Chinese. Clayre (1985) expands on these ideas as follows:

> In relation to Heaven man may be classified as yin, but when paired with Earth he would be seen as yang. Heaven itself is the supreme embodiment of the yang aspects of the cosmos: ethereal, bright, active, generative, initiatory and masculine. Earth is seen as deeply yin: solid, dark, cool, quiescent, growth-sustaining, responsive and feminine. (p. 201)

Men and women are not seen as exclusively yang or yin: Each has a predominance of one aspect or the other, and the balance within them and between them may change. The relation of the two elements is always changing, a continuous cycle where each may dominate in responsive sequence. This idea may have evolved from the annual cycle of growth and decay found in agricultural China and in the rotation of day and night and seasons of the year.

Taoists traditionally had little empathy for Confucians, whom they viewed as pompous and ritualistic. A more fundamental difference is summarized by the Chinese themselves, who say that "Confucius roams within society; Lao Tzu wanders beyond." However, in many ways Taoism, Confucianism, and Buddhism are complementary, and it is commonly said that they are "the Three Faiths in One." Thus many Chinese accept Confucianism as a guide to daily living, have recourse to Taoist practitioners for ritual purifications and exorcisms, and employ Buddhist priests for funerals.

We have sketched some of the major concepts and values that make up the Chinese value system. Note that there are wide divergences from it in many situations. Still, this value system has not been stamped out or radically changed for thousands of years, as Mao Tse Tung and others would have liked. Rather, it has evolved slowly over time. Ambrose King (as quoted in Kotkin, 1993) has pointed out that many of the approximately 60 million expatriate or overseas Chinese have developed a culture of "rationalistic traditionalism, a combination of traditional filial and group virtues with a pragmatism shaped by the conditions of a new competitive environment" (p. 177). Like the Italian Catholics who attend church only irregularly, these expatriate Chinese and even many living within the confines of China are more culturally than spiritually influenced by their Three Faiths.

Many Languages

In a similar manner, the Chinese culture is closely linked to language. People in China's various regions are of diverse ethnic origins who speak mutually unintelligible dialects.

Many inhabitants of southeastern China, where Cantonese is the primary dialect, find it difficult if not impossible to understand the dialect of northern China, which is Mandarin. Spoken Mandarin is very formal, whereas Cantonese includes many more slang words and is spoken more loudly, even to the extent that two people expressing love to one another can sound to outsiders as if they are quarrelling (Pierson, 2006). Remarkably, all dialects of spoken Chinese are written in the same way and can be understood by anyone, regardless of the pronunciation of words. Whereas the English language employs only 26 letters to represent all spoken sounds and written words, the Chinese language is a storehouse with more than 50,000 different symbols or logograms, each standing for a different word. Amazing feats of memory are required to master such a language, which tends to reinforce cultural values. This generalization is also valid for the Japanese language, which was derived from the Chinese (see De Mente, 1990).

As this discussion suggests, English is a low-context language that is direct and understandable, and this has facilitated the use of English worldwide, especially in business. However, both the Chinese language and the Japanese language are high context, and the writer must choose words carefully, as complex meanings may be inferred from the context in which words are spoken or written. Norman Fu, a well-known Chinese journalist with the *China Times,* once remarked that he much preferred to write in English than in Chinese because of this fact (see Chen, 2001).

When a visitor treks along part of the Great Wall, it is easy to imagine not only the repulsion of invaders but also the long and complex development of the Chinese perspective, thought systems, and language. Like the Wall, Confucianism and Taoism did not happen overnight, and although the Chinese have adopted other perspectives such as Buddhism, they retain the best of their own systems. Chinese thought is conservative, but it does allow for change, a topic to be explored in depth in the next chapter.

Sun Tzu, War, and the Marketplace

Around 400 BCE, one of the greatest, if not the greatest, treatises on war and the manner in which it should be conducted successfully was written by Sun Tzu, a Chinese general. It is impossible to do justice to this great work in a short summary, and readers should form their own judgment by reading the original, which is reprinted fully in McNeilly's 2012 *Sun Tzu and the Art of Business.* McNeilly derives six principles from Sun Tzu's work and applies them specifically to business and the marketplace. In this section, we describe these six principles and relate them to the paradox that Fang (1999) identifies, namely that Chinese negotiators are both sincere and deceptive simultaneously.

As both Fang (1999) and Chen (2001) point out, Sun Tzu's book should have really been called *The Art of Peace,* as the very first principle that Sun Tzu postulates is that war should be avoided if at all possible, as it necessarily results in the destruction of resources and people. McNeilly (2012) phrases this principle as follows: Win all without fighting; that is, capture the market without destroying it. In the airline industry, for example, about half of the strategic and tactical moves that companies make are price reductions, which tend to result in vicious price wars and frequently excessive losses for all companies involved (K. Smith, Grimm, & Gannon, 1992). Part of Cisco's success, by comparison, was based on acquiring competitors through stock swaps that greatly benefited all parties. To alleviate anxiety among employees in the newly purchased subsidiary, Cisco also established the principle that the CEO of Cisco and the CEO of the subsidiary would need to agree before a major downsizing of the subsidiary's workforce would occur.

The other five principles are avoiding strength and attacking weakness, or striking where competitors least expect it; deception and foreknowledge, or maximizing the power of market information; speed and preparation, or moving swiftly to overcome your competitors; shaping your opponent, or employing strategy to master the competition; and character-based leadership, or providing effective leadership in turbulent times. In addition to Sun Tzu, an anonymous writer penned 36 famous stratagems somewhere between 1368 and 1600—for example, clamor in the East but attack in the West—which tend to be consistent with Sun Tzu's principles.

Fang (1999) profiles the differences in Chinese and Western thought by comparing *The Art of War* to Karl von Clausewitz's (1832/1989) classic *On War*. Both generals agree that war should be used for political purposes. However, whereas Sun Tzu emphasizes winning without fighting and related principles, von Clausewitz promotes the use of maximum force to overwhelm the enemy. World Wars I and II and their extreme devastation of populations, land, and cities are examples of the use of von Clausewitz's principles.

Fang (1999) proposes that an invisible Great Wall separates Western and Chinese negotiators; he also points out that many other Asian negotiators have been heavily influenced by the Chinese and exhibit many of the same patterns of behavior, thought, and high-context communication. While Chinese negotiators are hospitable to Western negotiators and take them as a matter of courtesy to visit the Great Wall, they protect their invisible fortresses as much as possible.

Three Forces

For Fang (1999), three forces have molded the Chinese personality or negotiating style. The first is China's long history and particularly its recent history since 1949, when Mao came to power. The Chinese are acutely aware of the damage that Mao inflicted on the nation and want to avoid it in the future. Around 1990 two Carnegie Mellon professors completed a video on business in China, but many of the interviewed executives demanded that their faces be unidentifiable on the videotape because of fear that their interviews would come back to haunt them. Such fears are justified, as having worked for a Western company in China in the 1920s was grounds for arrest under Mao after 1949.

Capitalism and "capitalist roaders" or sympathizers were personified as intrinsically evil. Today the Chinese government monitors and controls the Internet closely and shuts down websites that are too anti-government in tone. Arrests and imprisonment of violators are not uncommon. Even Western companies such as Google and Yahoo! must abide by restrictions in China that are not imposed elsewhere. Thus Chinese negotiators in many ways tend to be conservative, although business executives in China typically do not mask their identities as they did in 1990.

Fang's (1999) second force is the Chinese perception of the marketplace. Chinese negotiators have been heavily influenced by Sun Tzu, and they view the marketplace as a place of war in which the goal is to win all without fighting. They employ all sorts of ruses, subterfuges, strategies, and stratagems (including the famous 36) in their interactions with Western negotiators, whom they frequently regard as marauders seeking to penetrate the invisible Great Wall. U.S. negotiators, for example, get down to business as soon as possible and quickly establish an opening position from which they bargain. Chinese negotiators, however, tend to focus on establishing a relationship, trying to understand the other party, and allowing a position to be established naturally over a long period of time. They are accustomed to extended haggling, which tends to bother many U.S. negotiators. These patterns represent the "both-and" perspective that is often associated with high-context communication.

Fang's (1999) third force is the Chinese personality or negotiating style, which has been molded in large part by Confucianism and its concept of the Superior Man who is sincere. Thus Western negotiators confront a conservative negotiator who is well prepared, kind, and sensitive to the needs of the other party but also deceptive because the marketplace is a place of ongoing war.

China is a large nation, about equal in geographic size to the United States, and its citizens constitute about one out of every five people in the world. As Western and Chinese negotiators learn more about one another, their perspectives will probably begin to overlap. Still, the long, convoluted, and complex history of China, plus its simultaneous emphasis on both deception and sincerity, will continue to support the invisible Great Wall that must be patiently addressed if it is to be scaled. It is not an impossible task, as Western companies have learned. After years of complaining that Western investment in China was not profitable, economic reports suggest that many Western companies are now beginning to make a return on their investments. Still, the message of this experience, and the tripartite model that Fang has developed to explain the Chinese perspective, suggest that the task will be long and involving—but ultimately rewarding both in personal relationships and market success.

CHAPTER 26

The Chinese Family Altar

One of the most famous sites on the campus of Tianjin University . . . is a stone engraved with a copy of the very first diploma. . . . Next to the date on the diploma, 1900, the graduate's name is printed, along with the names of his father, grandfather, and great-grandfather. . . . The diploma speaks volumes about the strength of family tradition in Chinese society. Like any individual in Chinese society, the graduate exists primarily in the context of his family. His achievements belong to them all.

—Ming-Jer Chen (2001, p. 19)

When Westerners visit a traditional Buddhist temple in Asia, they see different images of the Buddha, such as the Reclining Buddha, the Sitting Buddha, and so forth. However, in a Chinese Buddhist temple these images are supplemented by a formidable group of statues that seem to represent massive and formidable warriors. These fierce-looking figures frequently have rough-looking beards and mustaches, and they carry large swords. It is a surprise for many Westerners, then, to learn that these warriors are actually representations of important people within extended kinship and family groups and that they actually lived in Chinese villages 1,000 or 2,000 years ago. The position of honor that these warriors have in the temple is but one demonstration of the importance that the Chinese place on the family and kinship group, even to the extent of allowing them to be situated alongside the images of Buddha.

Throughout this book, we have given prominent attention to the nation as our unit of analysis. However, as many studies such as the GLOBE study (House et al., 2004; see Chapter 1) have demonstrated, it is possible to cluster countries into groups that are similar to one another in terms of language, religion, and geographical closeness. Nevertheless, we have found it difficult to identify metaphors that are appropriate for groups of nations.

The ethnic Chinese, however, represent one ethnic group for which one metaphor is appropriate, regardless of the nation in which they reside. This does not seem to be true for other ethnic groups. Joel Kotkin (1993) has described the major ethnic groups—the expatriate or overseas Chinese, the Japanese, the Jews, the English, and the Asian Indians—that have achieved remarkable economic success outside of their homelands. However, the metaphors for the non-Chinese groups as described in this book—the Japanese garden, the kibbutzim and moshavim, the traditional British house, and the dance of Shiva, respectively—do not apply fully when members of these groups become expatriates.

The Importance of Family

The importance of the family and kinship group cannot be overestimated for the expatriate Chinese, and the metaphor we have selected for them—the family altar—reflects this fact. One Taiwanese diplomat who lived in several countries had a family altar in Taiwan but, when traveling, carried drawings of his ancestors to whom he and his children prayed. Amy Tan's (1991) best-selling novel, *The Kitchen God's Wife,* includes the concept in its title. Many expatriate Chinese travel to their original homeland so that they can visit the burial places of their ancestors at least once in their lives, because in Confucianism the living relatives have the obligation to tend such places on a regular basis if at all possible or at least to visit them. The Chinese family name is traditionally given before the personal name, unlike the Western practice of mentioning the personal name first. Furthermore, many Chinese long to return to their native villages for burial alongside their ancestors. These examples—and countless others could be cited—indicate the prominent place that family and kinship groups hold in Chinese society, whether at home or abroad.

Of course, other ethnic groups are also family oriented. However, Chinese society is neither individualistic nor collectivistic as are other family-based ethnic groups; instead, it is based on relations (Bond, 1986). Confucians, for example, feel that individuals have roles they must fulfill but that, in doing so, their individualism can enlarge and enrich them for the greater good of the family and kinship group. From the Chinese perspective, people exist only in relationship to others (Chen, 2001). The relation-based system of the Chinese in which roles are differentiated is quite different from the more collectivistic and nondifferentiated system of the Japanese, which helps to explain why the Japanese seem to favor the development of corporations such as Sony whereas the Chinese seem to favor family-centered businesses. As indicated in the previous chapter, approximately 25% of the publicly traded companies in Asia are controlled by a single shareholder, very often the founder, but the comparable figure in the United States is just 3%. Of course, many of these are Chinese family businesses (S. McBride, 2003).

Chen (2001) indicates that the correct term is not *family businesses* but *business families*, for which the business unites generations. Similarly Fang (1999) points out that these business families operate like insurance companies, focusing on building and preserving family assets. Nakane (1973) has noted the following:

> In the Japanese system all members of the household are in one group under the head, with no specific rights according to the status of individuals within the family. The Japanese family system differs from that of the Chinese system, where family ethics are always based on relationships between particular individuals such as father and son, brothers and sisters, parents and child, husband and wife, while in Japan they are always based on the collective group, i.e., members of a household, not on the relationship between individuals. (p. 14)

Hence the Chinese tend to take seriously their relations with others, whether inside the kinship group or outside of it. They have separate words for older brother, younger sister, and each aunt or uncle from each side of the family, and they tend to make lifelong friends who are clearly demarcated from acquaintances. Still, like many other high-context ethnic groups, the Chinese usually spend a long time getting to know people before doing business with them. Other unique characteristics of the Chinese family system are described below.

Furthermore, like the Japanese and members of other group-oriented cultures, the Chinese tend to experience difficulty differentiating the individual from the group. As noted previously, there is no equivalent word for *privacy* in Chinese and some other languages that stress the importance of the group rather than the individual, such as Japanese and Arabic. In fact, the word *I* has negative connotations associated with it in the Chinese and Japanese languages, as do many of the other characters that are used in conjunction with it.

Chinese culture is closely associated with Confucianism, Taoism, and, to a lesser extent, Buddhism (see Chapter 25). We will describe the Chinese altar and its three dimensions and assume that readers are familiar with these three religions. The specific aspects of the altar are roundness, symbolizing the continuity and structural completeness of the family; representation of harmony within the family and the broader society; and fluidity or the capacity to change while maintaining solid traditions. We will then briefly describe the activities of the approximately 63 million expatriate Chinese and the countries in which they have been an important economic driving force.

The Expatriate Chinese

Many expatriate Chinese have been spectacularly successful in businesses throughout the world when compared to members of many other cultural groups. Initially these emigrants from China did not come from mainstream Chinese society, which was at times insular and suspicious of foreigners; it tended to view other cultures as generally inferior to that of the Chinese. Rather, expatriates originated from the peripheral and much poorer southern regions of China where the control of the emperor was less rigid.

In some of the countries in which these expatriate Chinese settled, such as Thailand and the United States, they have integrated themselves effectively and have even married non-Chinese in increasingly large numbers. In other countries, such as Malaysia and Indonesia, the Chinese experience discrimination and resentment, and they tend to be less effectively integrated with the other cultural groups. Since the 1960s, sporadic violent riots have been directed against the Chinese and their properties in Malaysia and Indonesia in which thousands of Chinese have been killed and injured and their property destroyed.

In the late 1990s, the Indonesian government assumed control of major Chinese companies, valued in the billions, after a violent period of Chinese-focused riots; at the time 5% of the population was Chinese, but they controlled 70% of the nation's resources. Ironically, most of this wealth was controlled by only a small percentage of Chinese families who partnered with the government to expand business. These Chinese families were well positioned through *guanxi* (relationships or connections) and knew how to take advantage of business opportunities.

In Malaysia a Chinese cannot be the chief executive officer of a company seeking government contracts. To get around this restriction, the Chinese put a native Malay into this position while retaining most actual power. In recent years, the Malaysian Chinese have begun to withdraw into protected communities and send their children to Chinese-only private schools. Some have even emigrated to other nations because of such issues.

Some of this discrimination seems to be religious in nature, for example, Muslims versus Confucians in Malaysia and Indonesia. Whatever its causes, it has divided such countries into Chinese and non-Chinese groups that experience difficulty in developing harmonious relations.

Taiwan, a country of 22.9 million people, is an interesting example of the success that the expatriate Chinese have wrought. Taiwan was established as a separate country after World War II when the Communists drove Chiang Kai-shek and his followers out of China. Its rulers realized that the most important resource of Taiwan was the Confucian dynamic of its people, so laws were established that fostered entrepreneurship. Taiwanese businesses are generally small and family dominated, and they have been so successful that the country is now one of the richest in the world.

Hong Kong, 95% of whose citizens are Chinese, has a population of 7.3 million. Although it occupies only 412 square miles, more than 120 million visitors were flying into Hong Kong each year prior to the takeover of Hong Kong by China, and today the same pattern continues; most visitors to Hong Kong are there either for business or shopping. Business became so successful that executives were forced to build "vertical factories" in tall buildings, each factory built on top of the other. In recent years, some of these factories have been shut down, as the work has been transferred to China. Similarly shopping experienced dramatic growth, with extreme shoppers from other nations flying to Hong Kong, going to the tax-free section of the airport to purchase as much as possible, and flying home without ever leaving the airport.

In Singapore, with its population of 4.5 million, there are three ethnic groups: Chinese (approximately 77%), Malays (about 15%), and Indians (approximately 6%). Like Taiwan and Hong Kong, this country has been resoundingly successful, in large part because of the herculean efforts of the Chinese, as the country was extremely poor until recent years. These three countries have been so successful that they, along with Korea and Thailand, are nicknamed the "five tigers" of Asia.

Thailand has a population of 64.3 million with two main ethnic groups: native Thai (approximately 75%) and Chinese (about 14%). These two groups are quite comfortable with one another, and as indicated previously, intermarriage is common. While the Chinese play their traditional role as businesspeople, particularly small entrepreneurs, the Thais tend to control the government, the military, and the banks. Ironically, the Thais are continually debating the merits of "Taiwanizing Thailand," as many of them prefer to keep their traditional ways of doing business and enjoying life, ways that are frequently incompatible with modern approaches.

The expatriate Chinese are influential in most if not all of the countries in which they reside. Unlike many expatriate Japanese, who tend to separate themselves from the societies in which they reside and eventually want to return to Japan, expatriate Chinese seek to integrate. However, they stay in contact with one another through their far-flung families and the activities of the Chinese "spacemen," who roam the world seeking business opportunities.

In short, expatriate Chinese are similar to traditional Chinese in the sense that the family is the basic social unit through which all are united in a relation-based system. Roundness is emphasized by these families, who form a complex but informal network throughout the world, as are harmony and fluidity. The Chinese, regardless of their country of residence, tend to exhibit conservative and high-context behavior. While some Chinese may have moved away from the practice of honoring ancestors at the family altar, they typically accept the importance that is attached to the need for roundness, harmony, and fluidity. In this sense, the family altar is not only an appropriate metaphor for the Chinese but also clearly illustrates the major values of this ethnic group, no matter where they settle permanently.

Roundness

The Chinese family altar is the cornerstone of family life for Chinese in many parts of the world. The altar is the "tie that binds" a dispersed family, and it serves as a focal point for viewing an extended family as including the living, the dead, and those as yet unborn. Although it may be thought of as a traditional and ancient aspect of Chinese society, and even as an anachronism in present-day mainland China, the Chinese altar is helpful in providing insight into the values, attitudes, and behaviors of the Chinese today, wherever they may live.

The physical presence of the altar represents the family as a well-knit integrated unit. A house with two altars contains two families; a household with no altar usually considers itself part of another family, and its members will go to the house in which the altar resides for important rituals. In many parts of the world, the Chinese tend to live in family or kinship compounds that have several houses, and frequently each of them contains a family altar. Typically the altar stands in the central room of the house, opposite the principal door. Such altars are meant to be publicly seen: Many are visible from the street, and guests usually sit in front of them. An incense pot normally rests on the left side of the altar, because this is the position of honor for any of the animistic gods that the Chinese revere; the ancestral tablets are placed on the right side alongside their incense pot. Most of the altars have a backdrop depicting some of the more popular deities. The newer, more prestigious backdrops are painted on glass in glittering, bright colors.

Varying numbers of religious odds and ends, including written charms and souvenirs of visits to temples, also decorate the altar, and frequently a Buddha image also stands on it. The ancestral tablets affirm the idealized picture of the Chinese family as a patrilineal kinship group and commemorate its immediate patrilineal forebears and their wives. The family may also have a larger ancestral hall housing the tablets of more distant forebears. In many Chinese restaurants around the world there is a Chinese altar, frequently by the cash register, which possibly symbolizes the functional and earth-focused perspective of the Chinese.

Many families worship at the family altar regularly, sometimes every day. A representative of the family, usually one of the older women, burns three sticks of incense. One stick goes into the ancestor's incense pot, another stick is positioned in the incense pot reserved for the gods that the family members revere, and a third stick is placed outside the door to welcome the gods and ancestors. As might be expected, older members of the family tend to worship more frequently than younger members.

Furthermore, the family tends to commemorate the death days of their closer ancestors or those whom they have personally known. On such occasions, the living members of the family serve its deceased members full meals complete with bowls and chopsticks, rice and noodles, and some of their favorite dishes; food is also provided for the animistic gods in many instances. In this context, people treat ancestors almost as if they were still living kin. Family members typically eat the food after the ancestors have supposedly eaten, that is, once the incense sticks have burned out. Ancestors also receive food offerings during major festivals for the gods; domestic worship of the gods tends to occur on the 1st and 15th of every lunar month.

Roundness, the first of the three characteristics of the family altar, stands for the continuity and structural completeness of the family; it symbolizes that the family is the basic, distinct, and enduring feature of the Chinese culture. The family altar as such represents the critical point of continuity between the natural world and the supernatural world. As indicated previously, Confucianism does not posit a Western conception of heaven, but it holds that the dead exist in a shadowy netherworld and can communicate with and directly influence living relatives. For the Chinese, there is no sharp demarcation between birth and death. Rather, all humankind is considered to be part of an organic system; in yin-yang fashion, individuals are continually being born into it and processed in it, but they do not experience final separation from it or death in the Western sense. To the Chinese, the system, life, and time itself are circular, and all are joined to one another because of this circularity. This perspective is consistent with both Buddhist and Taoist beliefs.

According to this rounded viewpoint, what is crucial is that the Chinese have descendants who can worship them and provide them with food and sacrifices; under such conditions they will lead contented lives in the netherworld. All of the efforts of the living are directed toward obtaining a rounded family in which the descent line is preserved. Thus roundness suggests a unity of the family circle that is related to the structural ideal of flawless Chinese patriarchy. Male children (especially the oldest son), who are obligated to perform ceremonial and ancestral rites, are preferred over female children. Hence roundness also suggests that men should have wives who can bear sons.

The Role of Women

There are some problems with this idealization of roundness. Some women cannot bear children or do not bear sons. Under classical Chinese law, failure to bear a son was grounds for divorce. Some children die before they are of an age to produce offspring, and historically it was common for them to be buried unceremoniously and without mourning. Sometimes the father does not live to an old age, and his family does not receive the honor accorded to those who have achieved such a distinction. However, the premature death of parents does not preclude their participation in the family, as they can be enshrined in ancestral tablets; the premature death of a husband does not weaken his wife's claim to a position in the descent line; and the failure to have children is correctable by adoption.

Such a patriarchal approach has led to inequality of the sexes. Daughters occupy an inferior position to sons in the family, as do wives to husbands, and the mother assumes a position of relative equality with her husband and authority over her adult sons only when she is old, at which point she is accorded a position of honor and prestige. In such a context, most activities are segregated by sex.

In previous eras polygamy was common among the Chinese, and it can still be found in isolated instances in rural areas. This practice complicated the familial structure, but the first wife was usually accorded the most honor and authority. In the modern world, it is typical for a Chinese man to marry only one woman, although the practice of having a "minor wife" or mistress is common. Because of the emphasis on the family, the Chinese businessman frequently works alongside his wife, or she will handle office matters while he is in charge of external relations. This pattern has limited the growth of many Chinese businesses, as only the wife and other family members are given positions of authority. Sometimes the husband and wife rarely see each other because of his external activities, but this is acceptable provided that the husband is working hard on behalf of the family.

One Chinese family living in Thailand is typical in that every Sunday the wife of the oldest son hosts all family members at her home, including the younger sons and their families. Even though some of the brothers are not very competent, the eldest son and chief executive officer of the family business allows them to keep their positions as vice presidents and heads of the family's factories, but non–family members actually are the key decision makers in their factories. However, these non–family members participate in the Sunday activities irregularly. Because they are excluded from becoming full members of the familial in-group and can never aspire to become owners of the factories, it is common for them to quit after a few years and establish their own businesses. Frequently the family provides the financial support to start new enterprises for such loyal employees, thus strengthening family-based networks of long-term contacts.

Looking at the Long Term

This rounded perspective leads the Chinese to take a long-term perspective on problems and issues that they face. Unlike U.S. Americans, most of whom feel that a long-term plan involves looking ahead 3 to 5 years, the Chinese tend to be comfortable with plans that are expressed in 10-, 20-, and even 100-year increments. Geert Hofstede (2001), whose 53-nation study of cultural values is highlighted in this book, has expanded his four-dimensional framework into five dimensions because of more recent research on the Chinese. He calls this dimension the Confucian dynamic, and it reflects a long-term rather than a short-term orientation; it also resembles in some ways the Protestant ethic in that deferred gratification of individual needs is accepted for the purpose of long-term success that helps the family.

Louis Kraar (1994), commenting on the causes of the success of the overseas or expatriate Chinese, begins his analysis by emphasizing this Confucian ethic:

Regardless of where they live or how rich they are, the Overseas Chinese share an abiding belief in hard work, strong family ties, frugality, and education. Yes, this same constellation of virtues defines much of what Westerners have labeled the Protestant Ethic, but for the Overseas Chinese these attributes are not musty relics from their culture's past but compelling rules to live by. (pp. 92–93)

This rounded conception of familial relationships is distinctively Chinese, and it encompasses members of the family over space and time. The family, rather than the individual, has been the basic unit of social organization among the Chinese since the time of the Duke of Chou in the 12th century BCE. He established the system of *bao-jia* or family/kinship rule and divided society into units of 10, 100, 1,000, and 10,000 families arranged by neighborhoods and districts. Each unit chose a leader from its ranks who was responsible for the behavior and welfare of all of the families in that jurisdiction, and this leader in turn reported directly to the leader of the next *bao-jia* unit. If a man committed a crime, the head of his own household would be held accountable, followed by the head of his 10-family unit, the 100-family unit, and so on. As a result, minor crimes were rarely reported beyond the smallest unit, which had the authority to settle such matters. In one way or another, modern Chinese follow this pattern of collective responsibility, although practices vary widely by the nations in which they reside.

Furthermore, the concept of roundness helps to explain the well-known Chinese practice of *guanxi*. As indicated in the previous chapter, from the Chinese perspective, a person exists only in relation to others. The lifeblood of a Chinese company is *guanxi*. Penetrating the layers of *guanxi* is like peeling an onion. First come connections between people and ancestors; then between people from the same village; then between members of the family; and finally between the family and close associates who can be trusted, such as the competent executives who are not family members but who actually run the factories. All of these relationships are considered to be continual in nature, and obligations go far beyond what can be put into a contract. For example, a Chinese businessman will help household servants establish their own small business after they have served the family faithfully for several years; he will also expect Western colleagues to help his son gain admission to a prestigious Western university after they have worked together on a joint venture for some years.

Historically, the Chinese, like people in many other high-context cultures, are less concerned with what is written in the contract than with the actions that people take to meet their obligations as they emphasize *guanxi*. For example, the U.S. Chamber of Thailand spent 2 years identifying a U.S. partner for a Chinese Thai businessman who was seeking to establish a joint venture. At long last all of the principal parties were to gather for dinner in Bangkok to finalize the arrangements. However, the Chinese Thai businessman angrily stormed out of the room when the U.S. businessman showed up with a lawyer and a written contract, thus putting an end to the potential joint venture. To the high-context Chinese, this was an affront of the highest order. In recent years, especially since China joined the World Trade Organization and must accept the sanctity of contracts, many Chinese firms now accept the inevitability of strict contracts. Still, *guanxi* is such an ingrained value that it continues to influence Chinese behavior.

The Chinese also tend to bypass the use of banks because of this system of *guanxi*. In fact, banks were unknown in China until the 20th century. Throughout the world the Chinese establish communal investment and credit associations. A group of friends, relatives, and colleagues pool their money to form a mutual fund from which each member may take turns borrowing, and the Chinese rely on the personal closeness of the group to inhibit fraud or default. Sometimes these associations will lend money to other Chinese who cannot afford to contribute to the association. Furthermore, the Chinese are well known for lending their personal funds to their relatives in other nations as, for example, in the case of Taiwanese investment in Malaysia, Thailand, and China. It was Taiwanese investment in China starting in the late 1970s that largely jump-started the Chinese economy.

The largest Chinese families even establish private social welfare agencies that are open to anyone from the family. For example, the Chinese Lee family—there is also a Korean Lee family—operates a social welfare agency in a large building in New York's Chinatown that helps any Lee of Chinese origin obtain employment or solve any crisis, such as dealing with immigration officials who may be trying to deport him and his family.

The Modern Businessman

The conception of the modern Chinese businessman is also related to the concept of roundness. Many Chinese businessmen fly around the world so frequently that they have been caricatured as "spacemen." They meet regularly with business associates in other nations who are united to one another through *guanxi*. If they are working with non-Chinese businessmen, they spend a great deal of time getting to know them so that the noncontractual nature of their relationships is given prominence.

Still, it must be stressed that *guanxi* has severe limitations. It develops slowly and excludes many individuals who might provide new business opportunities. *Guanxi* also is at odds with the strong movement toward contract-based business transactions that is championed by many nations and particularly the World Trade Organization. In the past, Chinese firms have found it difficult to become global in scope because of the use of *guanxi* at the expense of contractual relationships, and many firms are now emphasizing the importance of contracts and law.

Harmony

As described in Chapter 3, The Japanese Garden, the need for harmony and its development as a cultural ideal seem to have originated in the activities surrounding wet rice farming, and this generalization is also valid for China. Given the need to cooperate closely to provide subsistence for all, the Chinese accorded primacy to harmony rather than to other ideals, such as the Western conceptions of life, liberty, and the pursuit of individual happiness. When disharmony infects relationships in the family, supernatural explanations are frequently offered, and engaging the support of ancestors and gods is the natural way to reestablish harmony.

Roundness is a necessary but not sufficient condition for the second characteristic of the family altar, harmony. The ideally harmonious family is one in which there are few if any quarrels, financial problems, or illnesses. The most common prayer among many devout Chinese is for harmony, and it is frequently printed on door frames, charms, wedding cakes, and the walls of homes. It is a prayer that is directed to both ancestors and gods. And, as indicated above, the members of the living family offer food and rituals in return for the harmony that they are seeking.

People make all kinds of requests at the family altar, for example, to help a child pass an examination, to cure a sick spouse, and to obtain employment for oneself. Although the requests are not always met, devotees often feel renewed hope and comfort, in large part because of the rituals that unite deceased and living family members through the medium of the family altar. Even the skeptical carry out the rituals—just in case.

While the Chinese seek to achieve harmony, their worldview is not nearly as comforting as that of the Christian, who can aspire to a tranquil heaven that is under the supervision of a benign and personal God. The shadowy netherworld represents a degree of uncertainty that the Christian does not have to take into account. It may be for this reason that the Chinese tend to believe in luck and fate and that they have little if any control over events. In a Chinese Buddhist temple, for example, worshippers can purchase a set of fortune sticks, which they throw on the ground and then rearrange before consulting a book that predicts their future in terms of this rearrangement. Similarly many Chinese do not use car seatbelts because they believe that nature will take its normal course, no matter what they do.

Also, although other cultural groups like to gamble, many Chinese clearly are attracted to it, seemingly in part because of this sense of uncertainty, luck, and fate. The major sense of security and harmony comes from the rounded family and the all-encompassing family altar. Many times gambling and games of chance reinforce both harmony and roundness. For example, large Asian families, each of which may include 30 or more individuals and several generations, go to restaurants for several hours of convivial conversation and relaxation, during which time they leisurely play cards and other games of chance. Similarly it is not unusual for a Chinese family of 30 or more members, including several generations and close family servants, to go to the seashore for 4 or 5 days and spend most of the time inside an air-conditioned house talking to one another, drinking, eating sumptuous meals, and playing games of chance in which all participate. Sometimes no one ventures to the beach because of the enjoyment that family members experience interacting with one another.

Fluidity

The third characteristic of the family altar is fluidity or the capacity to change while maintaining solid traditions. It reflects the relation-oriented approach of the Chinese, which allows them to be individualistic as long as they meet their many obligations to various family members, including the deceased. Thus, although the Chinese tend to be conservative, they are frequently innovative and entrepreneurial. The number of Chinese inventions and scientific breakthroughs is startling. Joseph Needham and his associates have written a well-known multivolume series of books, *Science and Civilisation in China* (1954–), that describes these inventions and breakthroughs in detail. These include the first suspension bridge, fishing reels, rudders for ships, hang gliders, parachutes, fireworks, lacquer, wallpaper, paper, armor made from paper, wheelbarrows, and the first design for a steam engine. Similarly, as Kotkin (1993) and many others have described, the Chinese have been disproportionately successful in business and entrepreneurship compared to members of most if not all other ethnic groups. This balanced emphasis on conservatism and innovation clearly reflects the concept of fluidity.

In traditional Chinese religion, there is a huge pantheon of gods and goddesses, most of whom are the heroes of Chinese myths, legend, and history and deified either by imperial order or popular choice. Some communities have cult followings that have evolved around a particular historical figure who supposedly protects and guides the town or who may have worked a miracle in it. The reputed powers of the best-known deities have been affirmed by generations of the Chinese over the centuries. However, devotees believe that the power of a deity tends to decline with age and eventually loses its efficacy completely. The Chinese generally pray only to gods who have answered at least some of their petitions. When the decline in power occurs, the devotees begin to worship a new god. When Neil Armstrong walked on the moon in 1969, many elderly Chinese stopped praying to this heavenly body because of a supposed loss of efficacy. Thus there is fluidity, as change does occur but devotion at the family altar continues.

The history of China can be interpreted in terms of the three characteristics of the family altar. Han, the largest cultural group, includes about 85% of the population. However, given the 1.34 billion people in China, it is not surprising that there are about 400 ethnic groups ranging in size from millions of people to only a few thousand, and most of them have and have had harmonious relations with one another. Almost all of Chinese history can be divided into periods defined by dynasties. Families or rulers would occupy the throne until another would take the power away. History was viewed as endless cycles of renewal and decline, starting with the first dynasty in approximately 1953 BCE and not ending until the retirement of the last emperor in 1911 CE. Each ruler was considered to have a mandate bestowed on him by the gods to rule fairly and wisely. When an heir became corrupt or lazy, rebellions would break out, and a new emperor would surface. Typically he would introduce reforms that were consistent with the underlying cultural values of roundness, harmony, and fluidity.

The fact that China was the most developed civilization in the world for a significant portion of this long period may also be attributed to the emphasis on these three characteristics. As a broad generalization, the dynastic cycle helps to explain, through the mechanism of periodic renewal, how the Chinese were able to retain a consistent and continuous pattern of government for thousands of years (Major, 1989). Thus this cycle exemplifies all three characteristics of the family altar: roundness or continuity and structural completeness of the family and family-based nation; harmony over thousands of years marred only by periodic revolutions; and fluidity or maintaining the past while accepting change. An illustration of this linkage is the economic jump-start of the Chinese economy starting in 1978 when Premier Deng proclaimed that it is good to be rich, as opposed to Mao's decimation of the middle class and leveling of income. Taiwanese business owners were the first to invest in China, frequently establishing factories and businesses in the villages and cities in which their families had originated. Many of these businesspeople also desired to be buried in their traditional family funeral plots in these areas. Given this long historical tradition, we can expect to see the prominence of the Chinese family altar as a touchstone of the expatriate Chinese for many decades, if not millenia.

CHAPTER 27

The Singapore Hawker Centers

Some [hawkers] were such excellent cooks that they became great tourist attractions. A few became millionaires who drove to work in their Mercedes Benz and employed waiters. It was the enterprise, drive and talent of such people that made Singapore.

—Lee Kuan Yew (2000)

Hawker centres ... have helped to put the country on the world map. ... Hawker centres are one of Singapore's most unique and notable social icons, [an] important part of the Singaporean way of life.

—Lee Yuen Hee, CEO of Singapore's National
Environment Agency (NEA, 2007, 2008)

A Singaporean can be defined as someone who loves to eat Singaporean style hawker food. I have not met anyone who has grown up in this country who does not have an intimate relationship with the dishes that define our culture.

—Leslie Tay, from the food blog ieatishootipost.sg
reporting for CNN International (2010)

First impressions of Singapore among first-time visitors tend to be positive, and it is easy to understand why. The taxi from the airport to the hotel cruises along miles of flower-bedecked streets and buildings, some of which emphasize traditional Asian architecture while others are strikingly modern; the taxicab driver slows down when a bell automatically sounds, indicating that he is driving over the 50 mph speed limit; and everyone is courteous and efficient.

If the visitor arrives around noon at Raffles Place, the business center of Singapore, the sun is normally blazing. People begin to emerge from the skyscrapers one after another. Most of them are the businesspeople who work in Singapore's high-powered finance industry; they are going to take their lunch break. As in many cities of the world, the crowd includes a mixture of various cultural and ethnic groups. Asians might be Chinese, Japanese, or Thai; others may be Malay, Indian, or Indonesian. Caucasians could be U.S. American, European, or Australian. Everyone is headed for one of the most unique and emblematic eating places in Singapore, the hawker centers. Regardless of ethnic groupings or residential status—citizens, permanent residents, or expatriates—many people go to the hawker centers to find something they like during their limited lunch break.

The hawker centers are venues where one can try a wide variety of traditional ethnic foods, the latest fad in beverages, or even simple fruits. These centers are clean, and the personnel serving the food are, like the cabdriver, efficient and courteous. Each center is a collection of at least 20 food stalls at the same location and is casual or informal in motif, presentation of food, and seating arrangements. The hawker centers are such a unique aspect of Singapore's culture that the National Environment Agency commissioned a book entitled *Singapore Hawker Centers—People, Places, Food* in 2007 and followed up with a traveling exhibition in 2008 (Kong, 2007).

The hawker centers constitute a remarkable parallel to the features of modern Singapore—an integration of variety, efficiency, tremendous energy, safety, and a symbiosis of the old and new. This island nation of 4.5 million was poor 50 years ago, and some ethnic tensions existed among the Chinese (74.1% of the population), Malays (13.4%), Indians (9.2%), and citizens of other ethnic groups. Some of these issues related directly to a lack of education and infrastructure, and the crowded conditions only exacerbated them. Singapore's population density is 7,042.2 persons per square kilometer, whereas the U.S. density is 32.9. Nevertheless, today Singapore is a leading banking and finance center with robust bank secrecy laws, its workforce is highly educated, and government and business foster cutting-edge technologies and industries through the development of Science Parks. As a result, Singapore has a healthy gross domestic product per person of US$37,600. Life expectancy for men is 78.5 years and for women is 83.4 years. Adult literacy is 94.5%. The highly respected Global Competitiveness Report from the World Economic Forum ranks Singapore number 2 in the world (the highest rating for an Asian country) on global competitiveness for 2011–2012. The country's institutions continue to be ranked as the best in the world because of a lack of corruption and government efficiency. Singapore also places 1st for the efficiency of its goods and labor markets and 2nd for financial sophistication. It has become one of the world's most prosperous countries and is one of the world's busiest ports with a world-class infrastructure. *From Third World to First: The Singapore Story (1965–2000)* is the apt title of the memoir of Singapore's legendary leader, Lee Kuan Yew (2000), who helped bring about this remarkable change. The broad elements of the story are described below.

Origins of the Hawker Centers

Numerous hawker stalls were a familiar sight in Singapore's streets and alleys in the 1950s and 1960s. They were not much different from the hawker stalls that visitors to many developing nations see: colorful, arranged in a disorderly pattern, and inviting visitors to use them but unconsciously sending the message *caveat emptor*. While there's little argument that these hawkers brought a certain charm to the social and cultural landscape of Singapore, many stallholders operated under unhygienic conditions, contending with a lack of piped water and inadequate facilities to prepare and cook their food. To compound the problems, the authorities and wider population had to deal with the indiscriminate disposal of wastes into drains. Over time, these conditions caused considerable water pollution, endangering both public health and the environment.

As a result, the government developed a plan to build designated areas for hawkers. These areas, which we now know as hawker centers, were to have a complete infrastructure to support hawkers' day-to-day operations. An island-wide census in 1968 and 1969 was the first step in the systematic phasing out of old-style hawkers. The census registered a total of 18,000 street hawkers, who were then issued temporary hawking licenses. The exercise effectively curbed illegal hawking in Singapore, as all hawkers now needed to follow strict regulations or face financial penalties as well as the inability to operate their businesses.

In 1970 the government began to relocate street hawkers. The new hawker centers were equipped with proper facilities for food preparation and cooking and were supported by clean and efficient drainage systems as well as proper sanitation facilities. By February 1986, all street hawkers were completely relocated in hawker centers. The process, although long and difficult, was ultimately completed.

In 2000 there were 139 hawker centers owned by the Ministry of the Environment (ENV), the Housing and Development Board (HDB), and the Jurong Town Corporation (JTC). Collectively, these hawker centers held a total of 17,331 occupied stalls; 10,333 are market stalls, and 6,998 are stalls for preparing and serving cooked food. The environment and public health agencies have been largely responsible for transforming hawking from a public health disaster to a world-renowned icon that is uniquely Singaporean and celebrates this nation's ethnic diversity and foodie culture. The National Environment Agency's 2007 book referred to earlier reports 113 centers with more than 6,000 food stalls. These figures are smaller than those of 2000, probably because the government streamlined the hawker centers by imposing strict regulations, efficiency, and profitability. All stallholders in hawker centers are licensed by the ENV. They are required by law to ensure that food prepared in their stalls is safe for public consumption. Stallholders are expected to be vigilant in adhering to proper food and personal hygiene practices and to ensure that their stalls are free from pests and other infestation.

Launched by ENV in April 1994, the Stall Ownership Scheme enables stallholders to own their stalls. Under the program, stalls in ENV and HDB hawker centers are sold to incumbent stallholders on a 20-year lease at a discount. Those declining to buy their stalls can surrender them and opt for cash grants, or they can continue to rent their stalls at a revised rate. Stallholders who buy their stalls are allowed to sublet them. As a result, many of these stalls are open for many hours. These stallholders were also permitted to sell their stalls. Some have, and, consequently, more innovative and enterprising players have joined the trade.

ENV launched the Stall Assignment Scheme in February 1998 to allow stallholders to assign their stalls to operators who are willing to pay rent as assessed by the chief valuer. The assignees can sublet the stall or get someone to run the stall on their behalf. Legal restrictions apply in all cases, but there are more restrictions on stalls subsidized by the government.

As an extension to the Stall Assignment Scheme, stallholders currently paying subsidized rent may opt to assign the stall to themselves. This effectively means that they can opt to pay rental rates as assessed by the chief valuer and can operate the stall free of the more onerous restrictions imposed on subsidized stalls. The assignees are granted a 3-year tenancy agreement with an option for renewal if the hawker center is not affected by redevelopment. If the stalls in the hawker center are offered for sale under the Stall Ownership Scheme, the assignees may also buy the stalls at the assessed values. Whether subsidized or not, stalls must follow strict guidelines on food preparation, cleanliness, and polite treatment of customers.

Singapore's History

Just as the hawker centers faced many turbulent changes, Singapore has also experienced struggles to reach its current status as a prosperous cosmopolitan society. Modern Singapore began in 1819 when Sir Stamford Raffles claimed this Malay island, at the time nothing more than a large fishing village, as a regional base for the British East India Company; it flourished in large part because of its central location at the crossroads of Asia. In 1832 Singapore, along with Malacca and Penang (now part of Malaysia), were established as the Straits Settlements under the control of British India, and in 1867 the settlements became a separate British crown colony after Singapore merchants started agitating against British India rule.

During World War II, the Japanese occupied the nation after the largest surrender of British-led forces in history and renamed it Syonan-to or "Light of the Island." In 1946 Singapore (including Penang and Malacca) became a British crown colony with a civil administration headed by a governor. Then Penang and Malacca became a part of the Federation of Malaya in 1948. Communists attempted to take over both

Singapore and Malaya in 1948, resulting in a state of emergency for 12 years. After a few more tempestuous years, Singapore became a self-governing state. Lee Kuan Yew, a legendary figure in the nation's history, became prime minister.

At least in part because of the continuing Communist threat, Malaysia was formed in 1963; it included Singapore, Sarawak, and North Borneo. However, the merger was shaky from the beginning with continual race riots and allegations of unfair treatment. In 1965 Singapore became a sovereign, democratic, and independent nation, much to the anguish of Lee Kuan Yew, widely considered the father of modern Singapore, who had always believed in the merger of the territories.

Now on its own, Singapore initiated a massive industrialization project. After the shock of two oil crises, in 1979 the government initiated a program of economic restructuring, which emphasized technology and computer education and offered financial incentives to industrial enterprises.

Almost immediately, the Confucian ideals of the Chinese were employed as public policy. The Confucian philosophy argues that before an individual can be expected to perform as an ideal and sincere person (see Chapter 25: China's Great Wall), he or she must have the basic necessities such as clothes, food, and a place to live. Lee Kuan Yew, the first prime minister, endorsed a program of public housing because of his Confucian ideals. It proved to be enormously successful, and today the vast majority of Singaporeans live in such housing. To encourage home ownership, Singaporeans were allowed to use their Central Provident Funds savings (similar to a pension fund) to pay for the apartments. Singapore's civil servants are among the highest-paid civil servants in the world, and their salaries are pegged to those in the private sector. This was done in the early 1990s with the belief that it would eliminate corruption in political and civil service positions. Singapore's high rankings (signifying low corruption) on Transparency International's Corruption Perceptions Index seem to support the practice of paying government officials a high salary. However, cabinet ministers earned between 1.57 million and 3.04 million Singapore dollars (between US$1.28 million and US$2.47 million) in 2009, and against a backdrop of rising cost of living and income inequality, these salaries raised the ire of ordinary Singaporeans. Accordingly the government undertook a review of cabinet ministers' pay in 2011.

At least five features of the hawker centers help us to profile Singapore. These are ethnic diversity but unity, efficiency, the power of women, safety, and synthesizing traditional and modern values. We discuss each briefly.

Ethnic Diversity but Unity

As discussed above, customers can find any cuisine—Chinese, of course, but also Malay, Peranakan, Indian (both north and south), and international food (Japanese and Western)—in a typical hawker center. The stalls are close together, and their owners frequently sit and talk with one another. Singaporeans enjoy visiting their friends and neighbors from other ethnic communities and celebrating their food and festivals. Chinese noodles, Malay satay, and Indian curry are all part of the hawker center experience.

The Singapore population includes three major ethnic groups: Chinese, Indian, and Malay. The government encourages citizens to intermingle and understand one another in a variety of ways, for example, by ensuring that public housing includes all ethnic groups. Apartments are strictly allocated based on the proportion of each ethnic group in Singapore. In like manner, the government allocates hawker stalls according to the percentage of each ethnic group in the population. There is one section for each group in each hawker center, with the largest number of stalls naturally serving Chinese food.

Some of the older hawker centers share a communal water supply located in the center; hence they automatically learn how to behave as responsible shop owners and cooperate with others who have different skin colors, customs, or cultures. To survive in competition with other hawker centers, stallholders work together to maintain their hawker center, making it clean and efficient enough to attract more customers. This in miniature is exactly the Singaporean ethos: all ethnicities working hard and sharing values to survive in the face of international competition.

To shape the destiny of such a multiethnic country, the Singaporean government has embarked on a program called Shared Values to forestall conflicts among groups. First discussed in 1988, Shared Values was to be a blueprint for the development of a national ideology that Singaporeans of all ethnicities and faiths could comfortably accept. In addition, a pledge, written in 1966 during a time of great turmoil and uncertainty after independence, captures the idea that Singaporeans can overcome any difficulties if they come together as one.

The aim of this national ideology was to create a Singaporean identity by incorporating the relevant parts of citizens' various cultural heritages as well as the attitudes and values that have helped them survive as a nation. This formulation also included an anti-Western bias, because the government wanted to safeguard against "undesirable" values such as an excessive emphasis on individualism and self-centeredness at the expense of group obligations. Some of Singapore's neighbors had already developed this concept of a national ideology. For example, Indonesia had drawn up the *Pancasila* or five principles, a set of common beliefs to unite its peoples:

Nation before community and society before self.

Family as the basic unit of society.

Community support and respect for the individual.

Consensus, not conflict.

Racial and religious harmony.

In accordance with Singapore's Shared Values, citizens are actively encouraged to understand different points of view. In business discussions, Singaporeans try to avoid conflicts and strive to solve problems with compromise. They are genuine collectivists. In the GLOBE study (House et al., 2004), Singapore was ranked with the Confucian Asia cluster and ranked high in both institutional and in-group collectivism.

In many ways Singaporeans are competitive collectivists. Although this is a paradox, it is reality and is expressed in a local term, *Kiasu-ness*, which roughly translates into "scared to lose" and is uniquely Singaporean. Mr. Kiasu originated as a cartoon character and is roughly equivalent to "the ugly American"; he cuts into lines, heaps food on his plate at the expense of others in a cafeteria line, and loudly insists on fast and efficient service before others are helped. Singaporeans are aware of this paradox, which one would normally associate with individualism, and any long-term visitor will probably experience its manifestation. These days, it is often discussed on social media outlets such as Twitter. The norm, however, is to follow the rules, be efficient but courteous, and be sensitive to the needs of others.

In addition to *Kiasu-ness,* Singaporeans have other terms that reflect a peculiar brand of English called "Singlish," which mixes English with common phrases from Chinese dialects and Malay. Needless to say, as in other countries (e.g., Nigeria, India) with a colonial past, die-hard Anglophiles bemoan the loss of the Queen's English, but Singlish makes for efficient communication.

Military training also contributes to cooperation among different ethnicities. British forces remained in Singapore after independence but had withdrawn by 1971, and Singapore built up its own military. The Singaporean military includes an equal number of professional and conscripted soldiers because of the small population. This training is compulsory for men, and they serve periodically from the age of 16.5 years until they are in their 40s as per the requirements of the Enlistment Act. During hard training, their cohesion and friendship across ethnic boundaries becomes deeper.

Singapore's educational system also fosters cooperation among different ethnicities. The government encourages students to mingle to strengthen ties among ethnic groups. Because Singapore possesses no natural resources, no major industries, and a limited workforce, the united power of its citizens will be important to its survival and prosperity in international competition.

Efficiency

When customers order food in a hawker center, they must follow one well-known but unspoken rule: Be quick and efficient. At lunchtime each hawker center is teeming with prospective diners, and stall owners naturally like to take as many orders as possible. Likewise, other customers want to receive an order as soon as possible and enjoy their lunch. The first step is to *chope* or reserve a table. This is accomplished by placing a packet of tissues on the table or parking a friend at the table while the others order food at the stalls. When a stall owner's eyes meet yours, he or she slightly jerks the chin upward, signaling that it is your turn to order. You have to immediately say loudly: "One curry chicken packet," and announce your table number. This is the correct way to order food in the hawker centers in Singapore: Succinct orders are the rule. All meaningless conversation is left out; for instance, one does not say, "How are you doing today? I would like a curry chicken for takeout."

This tendency to make conversation short and efficient is typical of Singaporeans. They are not interested in niceties, and they prefer a quick yes or no answer so that their time is not wasted. Normally it is sufficient to say either yes or no on the telephone when a person asks if it possible to obtain a loan, to purchase a ticket to an event, or something similar. Singaporeans are paradoxically polite, but they become annoyed when interactions are not efficient.

This efficiency is also demonstrated by the cutting-edge technology found in Singapore, which employs numerous advanced technologies in its finance and transportation systems. We have already talked about the automatic bell in taxis indicating that the speed limit has been exceeded. We should also emphasize that these taxis are a convenient form of transportation because of their availability and reasonable price. A central satellite monitoring system links all taxies; when you book a taxi over the automated phone system, the system automatically hails the nearest taxi and dispatches it to your precise location. Public buses use the satellite system, too. When public buses approach traffic lights during morning and evening rush hours, the lights turn green immediately.

The downside to this excessive emphasis on work, efficiency, and productivity is that Singaporeans tend to deemphasize leisure. The birth rate is only 1.4 babies per woman, much lower than the 2.1 necessary to maintain a steady population, and by 2030 it is estimated that one third of Singapore's population will be over 60 years of age. Married couples routinely point out that they do not have sufficient time for leisure and do not even see their spouses on some days. Of course, U.S. Americans voice a similar complaint, expressed in the acronym DINS: double income, no sex. Unmarried Singaporeans frequently say that they have no time for dating. In true Singaporean fashion, the government created a department, the Social Development Unit (SDU, called facetiously "single, desperate, and ugly"), to encourage college graduates to marry. SDU sponsors events featuring speed dating (see Chapter 16: American Football) and zodiac dating. The number of college-educated men marrying college-educated women increased, but this did not have much effect on the fertility rate. The government is looking desperately at immigrants to the small, densely populated island to make up for small families among the native born.

The Power of Women

A distinctive feature of the hawker center is the ratio of men and women who work there. Almost the same number of men and women work in a hawker center, and they work in similar positions and equally long hours. Women can frequently be seen occupying the upper hierarchy of the power structure—many owner-operators of the hawker stalls are women who deal with issues such as accounting, food preparation, and sales.

Because human resources are comparatively scarce in Singapore, the government encourages equal opportunity in the workplace. In fact, women are among the most powerful influence brokers in Singapore. This is remarkable in view of the fact that in most other Asian countries, women rarely have high positions in politics and business. However, Singaporean women operate successfully in these areas. This is reflected in the high scores for Singapore on gender egalitarianism in the GLOBE study (House et al., 2004). Singapore's mean score (3.70) is closer to that of the high-scoring Eastern (3.84) and Nordic European (3.71) cluster nations than to that of its fellow Confucian Asia cluster nations (3.18).

Women have become CEOs of major companies, ambassadors, and leaders in all walks of life. However, this is not to say that Singaporean women do not face the challenges of earning less than men, hitting the glass ceiling (especially in the civil service), and achieving work-family balance. The government is very cognizant of these challenges and responds with public policy initiatives such as flex time, job retraining, and family-care leave.

Safety

As we have seen, first-time visitors to Singapore tend to have a positive reaction, but they also observe the many rules and regulations governing Singaporean life. The standing joke is that Singapore is a "fine" nation, for everything you do is fined, including the failure to flush public toilets. Some youth tend to feel stymied because of the large number of rules. Hence it was not surprising that some of them began urinating in elevators, a practice that was soon outlawed. They then began carrying water bottles with them and, when caught by inspectors, indicated that water had spilled. Soon the inspectors developed a test that could determine immediately whether the offending pool was indeed urine.

There are fines for littering; first-time offenders are fined 1,000 Singapore dollars, and second-time offenders may not only pay double that fine but have to clean up litter wearing bright jackets in front of an audience. The death penalty is standard for trafficking in drugs ranging from 15 g of heroin to 1.2 kg of opium. The import, sale, and possession of chewing gum are banned because of the high cost and difficulty of removing gum from public places.

Arguments can be made for and against the Singaporean system, which has tended to loosen somewhat in recent years. However, in accordance with the yin-yang tradition of looking at each situation before making a value judgment, we must take into account Singapore's tortuous history, its need to align the goals of individuals and the

470 PART VIII: THE BASE CULTURE AND ITS DIFFUSION ACROSS BORDERS (CLUSTERS OF NATIONS)

state closely if economic success for all is to be attained, and its crowded conditions. Unlike the situation in so many other modern nations, there are no homeless in Singapore, and the population is well-off in terms of education, standard of living, and the ability to withstand major difficulties.

The government makes use of Singapore's Internal Security Act (ISA), which lets officials detain people without trial, although extremely judicious use of this legislation has been the norm. Basically this nation is small enough to control tightly. This is a major reason Singaporeans are law abiding. Paradoxically, however, prostitution is openly countenanced in the better sections of the city, presenting a contrast to the power of women discussed above. Singapore is clearly an authority-ranking culture in which there is a high degree of collectivism but also a relatively high degree of power distance.

Furthermore, this strict control seems to have had the undesirable side effect that citizens have become more comfortable being followers than entrepreneurs. This may well be reflected in the low risk acceptance or tolerance (or high uncertainty avoidance) value score (5.31) that emerged in the GLOBE study (House et al., 2004). Compared to Hong Kong, another Chinese-dominant society, Singapore doesn't have many major local businesses. Citizens view a paternalistic government as an all-providing authority; they delegate decision making to the government and expect to be well cared for in exchange.

The hawker centers are open for long hours, and many of them remain open 24 hours a day, 7 days a week. This is reflected in the Singaporean work ethic: The average Singaporean has been taught from birth to be hardworking and diligent. The Singaporean government abhors safety violations and takes measures to assure the public that hawker centers are safe places. The ENV even started a 24-hour service to attend to complaints. Enforcement officers respond quickly to illegal-hawking complaints as well as environmental health complaints about issues such as noise pollution, illegal dumping, smoking in prohibited areas, and so on. As might be expected, Singapore has a low crime rate compared to neighboring nations.

Synthesizing Traditional and New Values

The hawker centers sell traditional fare from the Southeast Asian region as well as newer Western food. It is common in hawker centers throughout Singapore to see traditional Chinese herbal tea being sold next to fried chicken. Old and new are mixed without any sense of incongruity. Similarly Singapore is attempting to maintain its traditional values while pursuing efficiency and practicality. An example of this emphasis on traditions is the celebration of festivals. All three ethnic groups (Chinese, Malays, and Indians) celebrate their major festivals, thus reinforcing traditional values and heritages. The government has officially decreed that all such ethnic celebrations are national holidays. Family and close friends celebrate most festivals, and the traditions of the culture are passed to the young through such communal celebrations. Neighboring Malaysia does the same (see Chapter 18).

The city-state has also dropped a 45-year-old ban on gambling in an attempt to double tourism revenue by 2015. The Marina Bay Sands casino and the Resorts World Sentosa casino complex, which opened in 2010, were set to exceed the revenues from the entire Las Vegas strip and possibly add almost a full point of growth to GDP (Adam, 2010). Low taxes help make the casinos extremely profitable. The Marina Bay Sands with its iconic 57th-floor Skypod, which seems to balance precariously on three curving towers, and infinity Skypool adds a "gasp" factor to Singapore's skyline and is a very popular destination for the rich and famous and tourists alike. However, the government controls access to the casinos by allowing foreign tourists to enter free while insisting that locals pay a hefty entrance fee. The casinos were also designed as a part of larger entertainment complexes in an effort to mitigate the crime and social ills that they might breed ("Sin Galore," 2011).

Similarly, as Singapore prepares for the challenges of the 21st century, it is increasingly looking at blending the old and the new in its educational systems. Nothing is given more importance in Singapore than preparing the young to be the workforce of tomorrow. The main challenge has been keeping in touch with Singapore's cultural heritage (be it Chinese, Malay, or Indian) while adopting the cosmopolitan ways that a global marketplace demands. Also, Singapore is discarding the old-style educational tenets of rote learning and memorization, holdovers from the British colonial past, and a rigid emphasis on mathematics and the sciences. The curriculum is gradually broadening to inculcate the broad and creative thinking appropriate for a globalized world. Singapore's critical role as a trading center between East and West continues into the information age, and it has one of the world's busiest ports and one of the world's leading airports.

On an individual level, parents still motivate and pressure their children toward constant improvement, but a previous emphasis on strictly academic achievement has been broadened to include some new areas, for example, extra classes promoting computer skills, confidence building, and an appreciation for the arts.

This, then, is Singapore. It is a unique country, and some question whether its approach would work in other situations, such as large nations, countries with even more ethnic diversity than Singapore, and so on. Regardless, Singapore's achievements are significant, and all of us can benefit from studying this traditional but modern nation that is a major player in the global economy.

PART IX

India, Shiva, and Diversity

India is a fascinating nation in which one finds great ethnic, religious, and geographic diversity. While arguably India possesses more contrasts and diversity than any other nation, its people also feel a surprising degree of unity. English, one of 16 official languages, is used by many, if not most, Indians and is the language of business and trade. More than 80% of the population is Hindu, but other religions also have large memberships, some numbering in the millions.

Given both unity and diversity, we present two chapters on India. The first looks at the dominant culture, Hinduism, as manifested in our cultural metaphor, the dance of Shiva. The second chapter, "India: A Kaleidoscope of Diversity," describes the various differences and diversity found in this nation. This chapter serves as a model for understanding many nations, as fewer than 10% of the 220 nations in the world are monocultural.

CHAPTER 28

India

The Dance of Shiva

> *Sex may drive the soap operas in America. But in India, what really moves the dishwashing liquids are serials based on ancient myths of Indian gods.*
>
> —Jonathan Karp and Michael Williams (1998)

ndia is the second-largest country in the world with a population of more than 1.1 billion (after China, with 1.3 billion residents); it is about one third the size of the United States and is the seventh-largest country by area. India is the world's most populous democracy. It became independent in 1947 after the British ceded control. At the same time neighboring Pakistan was also created. India is a poor nation, but on many measures it has achieved substantial success since 1947. Since 2003 it has been identified as a member of the BRIC club (Brazil, Russia, India, and China), nations that are expected to become wealthier by 2050 than most of the leading economic powers of today. Life expectancy has increased from 32 to an average of 65 years (for men and women), and adult literacy is 62.8%. Although gross national product per person has increased in recent years, it is still only US$1,020, compared to $46,350 in the United States and $3,270 in China. This nation has the largest number of college-educated scientists and computer specialists in the world and a middle class that is estimated at over 250 million people, but 41.6% of the population lives on less than US$1.25 per day. Well-intentioned programs to benefit the rural poor, such as the US$9 billion Mahatma Gandhi National Rural Employment Guarantee Scheme, are riddled with corruption and inefficiency and present a sharp contrast to India's image as a global powerhouse with a surging economy (Wright & Gupta, 2011).

India has surpassed such nations as Pakistan on most measures of economic and social success, but its success is limited when compared to that of China. A major reason for India's limited success is a dramatic increase in population without corresponding growth in resources. Health and education spending each constitute 4.1% of gross domestic product (GDP). The comparative figures for the United States are 15.7% of GDP on health and 5.7% of GDP on education. India scores 61.2 on the Human Development Index as compared to 77.2 for China and 95.6 for the United States.

India, with its youthful population, growing middle class, and rising demand, could become the third-largest economy after China and the United States by 2030, according to a prediction by Standard Chartered (Timmons & Polgreen, 2011). In 1991 the *Economist* published an influential "Survey of India"; the cover featured a picture of a caged tiger with the title "Caged" (Crook, 1991). The basic message was that India was too bureaucratic and centralized. Manmohan Singh, India's finance minister at the time, and others were influenced by this negative depiction and began efforts to privatize the economy. These efforts are continuing but are retarded by infighting among political parties and interest groups. On the 2011 Index of Economic Freedom, India ranks only 124th of 179 nations, which means that it is difficult to do business in India, despite government efforts to decrease red tape and corruption (T. Miller, 2011). A dramatic illustration is provided by the government's decision in December 2011, spurred by public sentiment, to suspend plans to open up India's US$450 billion retail market to foreign supermarket chains such as Wal-Mart and Tesco. The decision does not make good economic sense in the context of low foreign investment, rising inflation, and the miserable performance of the Indian rupee against the dollar. As a minister in government put it, "Our democracy is so much that it destroys ourselves" (Lakshmi, 2011).

Religious diversity is a major feature of India, and it is fitting that our image of, and cultural metaphor for, this country should be based on religion. As Swami Vivekananda (1897/2011), one of India's foremost thinkers, stated,

> Each nation, like each individual, has one theme in this life, which is its centre, the principal note round which every other note comes to form the harmony.... In India, religious life forms the centre, the keynote of the whole music of national life.

For 2,000 years of its history, India was almost completely Hindu, but for the last millennium or more, Indian culture has been a synthesis of different racial, religious, and linguistic influences. Hinduism itself has undergone many changes owing to the impact of other faiths. It is, therefore, incorrect to contend that Indian culture is solely a Hindu culture, although Hindus constitute 81% of the population.

To begin to understand India, we must start with Hindu traditions. The overwhelming majority of Indians are still tradition oriented, and changes in their culture and society cannot be understood without reference to that tradition. In this chapter, we examine Hindu culture using the dance of Shiva as our organizing principle.

Shiva's Dance

Each of the numerous deities or gods in the Hindu religion is a different manifestation of one Supreme Being. The most important gods are Brahma (the Creator), Vishnu (the Preserver), and Shiva (the Destroyer). Among the various physical manifestations of Shiva is Nataraja, Lord of the Dancers, arguably the most apt and well-known depiction of what the dance of Shiva represents. The dance of Shiva has been described as the "clearest image of the activity of God which any art or religion can boast of" (Coomaraswamy, 1924/1969, p. 56), and it also reflects the cyclical nature of Hindu philosophy. Through this metaphor we will begin to explore Indian culture and society.

Among Hindus dancing is regarded as the most ancient and important of the arts. Legend even attributes the creation of the world to dance: Brahma's three steps created earth, space, and sky. Every aspect of nature—man, bird, beast, insect, trees, wind, waves, stars—displays a dance pattern, collectively called the Daily Dance (*dainic nrtya*). But nature is inert and cannot dance until Shiva wills it; he holds the sacred drum, the *damaru,* whose soundings set the rhythms that beat throughout the universe. Shiva is like a master conductor, and the Daily Dance is the response of all creation to his rhythmic force.

Shiva is seen as the first dancer, a deity who dances simply as an expression of his exuberant personality (Banerji, 1983). His dance cannot be performed by anyone else, as Shiva dances out the creation and existence of the world. However, just as the mortal dancer gets tired, Shiva too periodically lapses into inactivity. The cosmos then becomes chaos, and destruction follows the period of creation. This concept of the dance of Shiva is innate in Eastern ideas of movement and history; it is continuous and both constructive and destructive at the same time (Gopal & Dadachanji, 1951).

The dance of Shiva represents both the conception of world processes as a supreme being's pastime or amusement (*lila*) and the very nature of that blessed being, which is beyond the realm of purpose or understanding (Coomaraswamy, 1924/1969). The dance symbolizes the five main activities of the Supreme Being: creation and development (*srishti*); preservation and support (*sthiti*); change and destruction (*samhara*); shrouding, symbolism, illusion, and giving rest (*tirobhava*); and release, salvation, and grace (*anugraha*).

Considered separately, these are the activities of the deities Brahma, Vishnu, Rudra, Mahesvara, and Sadavisa, respectively. Taken together, the cycle of activity illustrated by the dance of Shiva encapsulates Hinduism as the main driving force of Indian society. The idea of cycles is a common thread in traditional Indian philosophy, and this is the theme that will run through our discussion of India's culture.

In January 2003, Martin Gannon and his wife took a car trip from New Delhi to Agra to see the wondrous Taj Mahal and Red Fort. Leaving at 6:30 AM, they saw incredible diversity along this main highway, with two lanes in each direction. The poor with their deeply lined faces were huddled by fires alongside the highway; there were no sidewalks, so people walked on the highway, as did animals of all types, including monkeys, water buffalos, cows, and so on. There was even a caravan of camels. Under these conditions travel was very slow, averaging 15 to 20 miles an hour, and many vans and cars bore the sign "Honk your horn when passing," which resulted in a constant din. All of these discomforts disappeared at the first sight of the magnificent Taj Mahal. This experience, repeated several times in other parts of India in one form or another, confirmed that the choice of the dance of Shiva was appropriate for understanding this nation.

Indian Culture: Early History

Two distinctive variants of basic Indian culture spring from the people's Dravidian and Aryan ethnic origins. The Dravidians probably came to India from the eastern Mediterranean coast, forming the highly developed Indus Valley civilization 3,000 years before Christ. About 1500 BCE this civilization fell into decline, and its people migrated to the southern part of the Indian subcontinent. At about the same time, Aryans arrived in India from Persia, settling almost all of the Indo-Gangetic Plain. Today 72% of the population is of Aryan origin, while Dravidians account for 25%. The remaining 3% is made up of a myriad of other groups including Mongoloids. India's most populous cities, all ranking among the 40 largest in the world, are Mumbai (20 million) to the west, Kolkata (15.6 million) to the east, Delhi (22.1 million) to the north, and Chennai (7.6 million) and Bangalore (5 million) to the south.

India's history reflects the cycles of chaos and harmony epitomized by the dance of Shiva. Time after time India has recovered from episodes that would have ended the existence of many other nations. In fact, Shiva's son, Ganesh, is the symbol of good arising from adversity. According to the legend, Parvati, the consort of Shiva, would spend hours bathing, dressing, and adorning herself. This often meant that Shiva was kept waiting, so Parvati set their son, Ganesh, on guard to prevent Shiva from bursting in on her unannounced and catching her in a state of unreadiness. One day Shiva was so frustrated by Ganesh's actions that he cut off the child's head. Distraught, Parvati completely withdrew from her lord, and Shiva realized he would have to restore the child to her if he was to win her back. He resolved to use the first available head he could find, which happened to be that of a baby elephant. The boy regained his life and now had the added advantage of the elephant's wisdom. Similarly, India's past and present contributions to art, science, and the spiritual world are immense, despite periods of turmoil and apparent anarchy.

The tension between north and south India, illustrated by an ongoing debate over language, has historical roots that reach far into the past. The south has enjoyed calm and relative tranquility throughout most of its history, whereas the north has been subjected to a series of foreign invasions, often on a grand scale. Consequently, the northern culture is more a product of a mixed heritage. Among the most significant modifying influences in the north were various Muslim invasions beginning about

1000 CE. As a result of these invasions, the administrative structure of northern India was repeatedly destroyed, society often deprived of leadership, and religious faith shaken.

Muslim Rule

Muslim rule of north India began early in the 13th century and lasted until the middle of the 19th century. Muslim rulers were harsh on Hindus with the notable exception of the great Mughal emperor Akbar, who married a Hindu princess and attempted to foster the development of a new faith, *Din-i-Ilahi*, which blended the best of the leading religions. He also fostered tolerance for all religions and routinely appointed Hindus to high positions and received Jesuit priests in his court. However, it is against Muslim beliefs to worship any idol or image of God, so most of the invaders destroyed many thousands of Hindu temples and replaced them with mosques. A discriminatory tax was imposed on non-Islamic subjects, and Hindus were given low-level positions if they were employed at all.

Forceful conversion of Hindus to the Islamic faith was widely carried out. Hindus were turned into second-class citizens and almost never shown the beautiful side of Islam. The confrontation between two virtually incompatible religious systems led to implacable mutual hatred between their respective followers. The echoes of this conflict resound even today. For instance, in 1992 more than 200,000 Hindus stormed and destroyed a 450-year-old Muslim mosque erected by the Mughals to replace a Hindu temple on the site that marks the birthplace of the Hindu god, Rama; hundreds of people were killed in the ensuing bedlam. Such instances are relatively common. In 2002 a group of Hindus were returning by train from a pilgrimage to the same trouble spot when they were reportedly attacked by a Muslim mob in Gujarat, a Western Indian state. This set off a full-scale massacre in retaliation, which left nearly 2,000 dead, mostly Muslims.

Unlike the north, southern India enjoyed a stable, almost uninterrupted regime of Hindu kingdoms until 1646, when the Mughal rulers succeeded in conquering and unifying all India. The Muslim Mughal empire began to disintegrate during the 18th century, with independent regional kingdoms springing up everywhere. The influence of the British East India Company rose as Britain ousted rival Western colonial powers in the south. During those days of weakness, plundering invaders came from Persia and Afghanistan. North India entered a state of anarchy from which it did not emerge until the British gradually extended their control, leading to the establishment of the British Raj (*raj* means "rule" in Hindi and Urdu) in the 19th century.

The British Raj

The British government instituted direct rule over India in 1858 following the Sepoy (Indian) mutiny. Many Indians think of this event as the first war of independence.

The Sepoys, Indian soldiers in British employ, mutinied over a rumor that animal fat was being used in the cartridges they had to bite to load their rifles. Hindus heard it was beef fat, while Muslims heard it was pig fat; both groups felt their taboos had been violated. British troops barely put down the insurrection; the British garrison at Kanpur, including women and children, was slaughtered, and Kanpur became a rallying cry for British vengeance (Arden, 1990).

Early expressions of nationalism first crystallized in the Indian National Congress in 1885 and the All-India Muslim League in 1906. Following the infamous massacre of more than 400 unarmed demonstrators at Amritsar by General Dyer's troops in 1919, Indian leaders put aside their previous faith and hope in the good intentions of the British Empire. Inspired by M. K. Gandhi, the Indian National Congress began a program of peaceful noncooperation (*satyagraha*) with British rule. Tragically, just months after India's independence was finally granted, Mahatma (Great Soul) Gandhi was killed by a Hindu extremist who had denounced him as an appeaser of the Muslims. However, Mahatma Gandhi's legacy lived on in the civil rights movement in the United States, Nelson Mandela's fight against apartheid in South Africa, and Lech Walesa's Solidarity movement in Poland. It continues to inspire all those who live under tyranny.

The British granted independence in 1947, but the Raj was partitioned into a largely Hindu India and a Muslim Pakistan. Overnight partition created great communal strife, and 12 million refugees moved across the new India-Pakistan border from 1946 to 1947, Hindus into India and Muslims into Pakistan. More than 200,000 people were killed in the accompanying riots, giving the world a lasting image of a modern India seemingly at war with itself. In fact, except for times of crisis, India has managed to accommodate and contain the destructive forces latent in group differences. But it is also true that today, the political and social compromises that have permitted the country to deal with its diversity are under extreme pressure.

As India's central authorities have faced threats of secession, caste warfare, and sectarian violence, they have sometimes adopted stern measures. The army has been called out more frequently in recent years to restore order to the country's troubled provinces than to defend the country from external threats.

Modern Leaders

Jawaharlal Nehru, the head of the Congress Party, became the first prime minister of India in 1947. He was unwaveringly loyal to the basic concepts of freedom, democracy, socialism, world peace, and international cooperation and emerged as an eloquent spokesperson for the world's nonaligned, less developed nations. Two years after Nehru's death in 1964, his daughter, Indira Gandhi (no relation to Mahatma Gandhi), succeeded her father. Indira Gandhi struggled to modernize India and make it an economic power, but she may have lacked her father's devotion to "the spirit of man." She invoked the emergency provisions of the constitution in 1975 and suspended civil liberties, citing the need to address some of the nation's persistent problems "on a war footing." When elections were called in 1977, the Indian people expressed their resentment against the methods of "the Emergency" and voted Gandhi out of office. After full democracy was restored, an apparently chastened Indira Gandhi returned to power in 1979, where she remained until she was assassinated 5 years later.

Rajiv Gandhi, Indira's son, became prime minister on her death, but amid claims of widespread corruption in the government, his Congress Party lost a general election. The succeeding government was short-lived, unable to sustain a parliamentary majority for its policies. During the next campaign, Rajiv Gandhi was also assassinated, and the Congress (I) Party was swept back to power on a huge sympathy vote.

It appears that the Nehru-Gandhi dynasty, which has dominated India's modern political system, is still a force to reckon with in Indian politics. Rajiv Gandhi's widow, the Italian-born Sonia Gandhi, is the president of the Congress Party and was identified by *Forbes* magazine as the sixth most powerful woman in the world in 2007. Although no longer in the top 10 on the Forbes list, Sonia Gandhi is still influential in Indian politics. Her son, Rahul Gandhi, is often portrayed as a prince in waiting and heir to the dynasty. However, he has been dogged by political gaffes and setbacks in recent years. The family's journey—its sequence of evolution, power, death, return, creation, destruction, and, perhaps, ultimate salvation—epitomizes the dance of Shiva and the cyclical nature of Hindu philosophy.

Sonia Gandhi's rise to her position of power followed the shocking 2004 defeat of the ruling Bhartiya Janata Party (BJP), a conservative Hindu-centric party, which had risen in stature and won major elections. The BJP party leadership had been responsible for building on the reforms that jump-started the Indian economy in the 1990s and led to India's emergence as an Asian superpower. However, people at the lower end of the socioeconomic ladder did not experience the benefits of the reforms and voted out the BJP in favor of the Congress Party and its allies. As the low GDP per head and the challenges facing the multibillion-dollar rural employment scheme indicate, India still has a long way to go in its quest to help those on the lower economic rungs of society.

Cyclical Hindu Philosophy

The Indian perspective on life tends to differ most sharply from that of Europeans and U.S. Americans in the value that it accords to the discipline of philosophy (Coomaraswamy, 1924/1969). In Europe and America the study of philosophy tends to be regarded as an end in itself—some kind of mental gymnastics—and as such it seems of little importance to the ordinary man or woman. In India philosophy tends to overlap with religion, and it is regarded as the key to life itself, clarifying its essential meaning and the way to attain spiritual goals. Outside of India, philosophy and religion pursued distinct and different paths, which may have crossed but never merged (Munshi, 1965). In India it is not always possible to differentiate between the two.

In Hindu philosophy, the world is considered illusory, like a dream, the result of God's *lila*. According to one interpretation, *Bharata Varsha,* the ancient name of India, literally means "land of the actors" (Lannoy, 1971, p. 286). In an illusory world, people cannot achieve true happiness through the mere transient physical enjoyment of wealth or material possessions. The only happiness worth seeking is permanent spiritual happiness. Absolute happiness can result only from liberation from worldly involvement through spiritual enlightenment. Life is a journey in search of *mukti* (salvation), and the seeker, if he or she withstands all the perils of the road, is rewarded by exultation beyond human experience or perception (*moksha*). In the same way that the dance of Shiva leads the cosmos through a journey, Hindu philosophy directs each individual along a path.

There are basically four paths or ways that lead to the ideal state: intense devotion to or love of God (*bhakti yoga*), selfless work or service (*karma yoga*), philosophy or knowledge of self (*jnana yoga*), and meditation or psychological exercise (*raja yoga*). The four ways are not exclusive, and people may choose among or combine them according to the dictates of temperament and circumstance. Whatever path is followed, every Hindu is aware of the difficulty of reaching the ideal state in a single lifetime. This is the point at which the concept of reincarnation, or the cycle of lives, becomes important. Individual souls (*jivas*) enter the world mysteriously; by God's power, certainly, but how and for what purpose is not fully explainable (Smith, 1991). *Jivas* begin as the souls of the simplest forms of life, but they do not vanish with the death of their original bodies. Rather, they simply move to a new body or form. The transmigration of souls takes an individual *jiva* through a series of increasingly complex bodies until a human one is achieved. At this point the ascent of physical forms ends, and the soul begins its path to *mukti*. This gives an abiding sense of purpose to the Hindu life, a goal to be actively sought and patiently awaited through the cycles of many lives.

The doctrine of reincarnation corresponds to a fact that everyone may have noticed: the varying age of the souls of people, irrespective of the age of the body. Some people remain irresponsible, narcissistic, uncontrolled, and inept to their last days; others are serious, friendly, self-controlled, and talented from their youth onward. According to Hindu philosophy, each person comes equipped with a highly personalized unconscious, characterized by a particular mix of three fundamental qualities: *sattva* (clarity, light), *rajas* (passion, desire), and *tamas* (dullness, darkness). Their relative strength differs from one person to another, but, in the Hindu idea of destiny, the unconscious has an innate tendency to strive toward clarity and light (Kakar, 1978).

The birth of a person into a particular niche in life and the relative mix of the three fundamental qualities in an individual are determined by the balance of the right and wrong actions of his or her soul through its previous cycles. The rate of progress of the soul through this endless cycle of birth, life, and death—the soul's karma—depends on the deeds and decisions made in each lifetime. One way of mapping the probable karma of an individual is to consult astrological charts at the time of his or her birth, and this is an important tradition in Indian society.

The dance of Shiva portrays the world's endless cycle of creation, existence, destruction, and re-creation, and Hindu philosophy depicts the endless cycle of the soul through birth, life, death, and reincarnation. We will now turn to examining the cycle of individual life within that greater series of lifetimes.

The Cycle of Life

According to Hindu philosophy, a person passes through four stages of life, the first of which is that of a student. The prime responsibility in life during this stage is to learn. Besides gaining knowledge, the student is supposed to develop a strong character and good habits and emerge equipped to live a good and effective life.

The second stage, beginning with marriage, is that of a householder. During this stage, human energy turns outward and is expressed on three fronts: family, vocation, and community. The needs of pleasure are satisfied through the family, needs of duty through exercising the social responsibilities of citizenship, and the needs of success through employment.

The third stage of life is retirement, signifying withdrawal from social obligations. This is the time for people to begin their true education: to discover who they are and what life is all about. It is a time to read, think, ponder life's meaning, and discover and live according to a philosophy. At this stage people need to transcend the senses and dwell in harmony with the timeless reality that underlies the dream of life in this natural world.

The Hindu concept of retirement is exemplified in a story told by a traveler in India (Arden, 1990). The traveler saw a white-bearded man seated on a blanket, writing in a notebook. The man looked up and smiled as the traveler walked past. "Are you a Buddhist?" the traveler asked, to which the man shook his head. "A Hindu? A Muslim?" Again, he shook his head and replied "Does it matter? I am a man." The traveler asked what the man was writing. "The truth," he said, "only the truth."

The final stage is one of *sannyasin*, defined by the Bhagavad-Gita as "one who neither hates nor loves anything." In this stage people achieve *mukti* (salvation) and are living only because the time to make the final ascent has not come. When they finally depart from this world, freedom from the cycle of life and death is attained.

People can pass through the four stages of life in a single lifetime or stay at each stage for many lifetimes. Even Buddha is reputed to have passed through several hundred lives. Progress is determined in the light of the activities and inclination of the person at each stage of life. For example, Indian religion is replete with rituals, the primary purpose of which is to receive the blessings of God. Each ceremony involves the singing of religious songs (*bhajans*) and discourses by priests and other religious persons (*satsang*). The sincerity with which people indulge in these activities and apply the tenets of the philosophy in their practical life determines their progress through the cycle of life and death. A person may expound philosophy at great length, go to the temple every day, and offer alms to saints and the poor yet indulge in all sorts of vices. These contradictions in life are resolved on death by karma, which dictates that on reincarnation, each person will receive rewards or punishment for their accumulated good and bad deeds.

The Hindu desire for positive outcomes of daily activities, resulting in positive karma, leads us to a brief discussion of the importance of astrology. With so much at stake, most Hindus in India consult the stars, if not on a daily basis, then at least on important occasions. Matching the horoscopes of a bride and groom is as much a part of planning a marriage as choosing the flower arrangements. It is routine for Indians to consult the stars about the best day to close on a house or sign an important contract. Indian astrology is one of the oldest systems in the world and differs from Western astrology in that it is based on the actual constellations as seen in the sky instead of divisions in the plane of the ecliptic. When it was revealed that an astrologer helped former president Ronald Reagan's wife, Nancy, set her schedule, U.S. Americans hooted with derision. In contrast, India leaders routinely consider the charts, local television channels devote airtime to discussing political and personal astrological predictions, and all major newspapers and magazines run daily predictions or articles based on astrology. It is reported that a New York–based financial astrologer, Ashok Motiani, predicted the 2008 subprime crisis in the United States. A common trend is for moms-to-be to consult their astrologers to request a cesarean section on the appropriate day and time. Astrologers believe that the right timing can ensure a more beautiful child or one that is quiet, is obedient, or can excel at a particular profession (Bellman, 2010). One Mumbai gynecologist agreed to perform a cesarean section at the unearthly but auspicious hour of 3:30 AM after powerful friends of the parents-to-be applied pressure (Bellman).

Like Hindu philosophy, the Indian concept of time is cyclical, characterized by origination, duration, and disappearance ad infinitum. This is reflected in the dramatic structure of traditional Sanskrit plays, which are typically based on the themes of separation and reunion and tend to end as they begin. Various devices are used— the dream, the trance, the premonition, and the flashback—to disrupt the linearity of time and make the action recoil on itself (Lannoy, 1971). Similarly, the dance of Shiva is a repetitive cycle of creation, existence, and destruction; constant change within a period of time, but ultimately time itself, is irrelevant.

In an attempt to neutralize the anguish of impermanence and change, the carved religious images in every village home are made of permanent materials, such as clay or metal. This also reveals the functional role of the image in a materially restricted environment. The practice of religion at home is one of the main reasons Hinduism was able to survive the invasion of foreign powers over the centuries. Just as religion is important to the family, so too the family plays a dominant role in Indian society.

The Family Cycle

Most Indians grow up in an extended family, a form of family organization in which brothers remain together after marriage and bring their wives into their parents' household or compound of homes. Recent migration to cities and towns in search of economic opportunities has contributed to the weakening of many traditions, including that of extended families. In this section we describe family traditions that exist most strongly among the 500 million Indians who continue to be only marginally affected by industrialization. While weakened in some parts of society, many aspects of the family cycle are still important to all.

The preference for sons is as old as Indian society. A son guarantees the continuation of the generations, and he will perform the last rites after his parents' deaths. This ensures a peaceful departure of their souls to their next existence in the ongoing cycle of life. The word *putra,* son, literally means "he who protects from going to hell." In contrast, a daughter has negligible ritual significance. She is normally an unmitigated expense, someone who will never contribute to the family income and who on marriage will take away a considerable part of her family's fortune as her dowry. Although formally abolished by the Dowry Prohibition Act of 1961, the institution of dowry is still widespread in India. It is becoming increasingly fashionable among educated Indians not to indulge in the practice. However, a number of embittered wives have misused the provisions of the act to seek revenge on their husbands and their husbands' families, causing women activists to be alarmed at the possibility that hard won antidowry laws could be brought into disrepute.

A striking reflection of gender preference is the continued masculinization of the Indian population, particularly pronounced in the north but also present elsewhere in the country. The census of 2011 shows that there are now 914 girls ages 0–6 years (down from 927 in the 2001 census) for every 1,000 boys in the same age group. The general decline in sex ratios occurred in 28 of the 35 states and territories in the country ("Sons and Daughters," 2011). The main reasons for this ratio are the higher mortality rate of female children and the tendency to limit family size once there are a sufficient number of sons. Also, the recent availability of sex-determination tests has allowed women to ensure that their first-born is a boy, as they can abort unwanted female children. It should be noted, however, that Indian legislation enacted in 1994 and amended in 2002 (Pre-Natal Diagnostics Techniques Regulation and Prevention of Misuse Act) bans sex-determination tests.

Nurturing Children

Just as the dance of Shiva represents preservation, caretaking, and support, parents tend to nurture their children with great care. A Hindu child grows up in the security of the extended family and has few contacts with other groups until it is time for school. Although the mother is chiefly responsible for the care of the child, there is also close contact with other females and mother-surrogates, and this continues for much longer than in many other cultures. The strong ties of home life do not conflict with the Hindu belief in the liberty of the soul removed from worldly concerns. Love of family is not merely a purpose in itself but a way to the final goal of life. Love will not yield the rewards of *mukti* (salvation) when it remains self-centered; that is why the Hindu try to diffuse their love over sons, daughters, guests, and neighbors (Munshi, 1965).

Children in India are considered sacred, a manifestation of God, but if the Hindu ideal is a high degree of infant indulgence, reality is somewhat different in the poorer areas of India. Here, many young children typically live under one roof, and 1 in 10 will die in infancy, so babies are not regarded as extraordinary creatures. Except for the first-born son, children tend to be taken for granted. This is reinforced by the belief in rebirth; as an individual is not born just once, he or she cannot be regarded as a unique event. The mother has probably witnessed the birth of several babies and may have seen some die, too. When her child cries, falls sick, or is accidentally hurt, she is not beset with feelings of intense guilt. A mother's work may be long and hard, both in the home and in the fields, so she is unable to give her child undivided attention.

Even as the dance of Shiva leads the world through the joys of existence, an element of chaos is inherent in the world's Daily Dance. Similarly, the environment in India has been full of threats to a child's safety: famine, disease, and chronic civil disorder. As a rule, until modern times more than half of all deaths befell children in their first year of life. As the nation got a grip on its affairs and as campaigns against diseases such as malaria and smallpox took hold, mortality rates fell. The cultural importance of children is derived from the need to carry on the cycle of life. This continued importance is reflected in statistics showing that while death rates since 1921 have fallen, birth rates have declined much more slowly. One of India's great assets is its population of children, which exceeds the total population of the United States.

Government attempts to regulate the birth rate have become synonymous with sterilization programs. Resentment against coerced sterilization in India helped to defeat Indira Gandhi's government in 1977. As a result of the political fallout, birth control was set back as a popular cause. Middle-class Indians, influenced by education and the desire for an improved standard of living, are increasingly adopting family-planning methods. However, when the formidable psychic barrier of traditional Hindu beliefs in the life cycle is considered, it seems clear that rapid population growth will continue in the poorer, rural areas.

An Indian father is frequently remote, aloof, and a much feared disciplinary figure, just as Shiva is distant from the world he nurtures, but there are also special bonds between father and son, and the relationship is one of mutual dependence. A son must obey his father unquestioningly, pay him respect, and offer complete support in every need, both in life and after death. The father owes his son support, a good education, the best possible marital arrangement, and inheritance of property. One Indian proverb reads, "A son should be treated as a prince for 5 years; as a slave for 10 years; but from his 16th birthday, as a friend."

The Status of Women

Very early in life, the son learns that women are lower in status than men. The position of women in this hierarchical society means that they must constantly be making demands and pleading with superiors for one thing or another. The son soon develops an attitude of superiority. A female's authority can seldom be absolute, except for the unchallengeable position that the senior grandmother may inherit. A son finds out that anger may be productive; violent outbursts of anger are often effective if directed against someone of uncertain status. Similarly the destructive powers of the dance of Shiva are effective in creating new opportunities and patterns. We underscore the point here that we are referring mainly to those millions of Indians who live in rural areas and are marginally affected by industrialization. We recognize that Indian society is undergoing some tremendous changes, especially in the urban areas, following the liberalization of the Indian economy in the early 1990s.

The relative position of men and women is clear in Indian society, and the question of competitive equality is not customarily considered. The Hindu marriage emphasizes identity, not equality. Generally, women are thought to have younger souls, and therefore they are nearer to the world than men and inferior to them. Girls are trained to be submissive and docile, to fulfill culturally designated feminine roles. The ideal of womanhood in Indian tradition is one of chastity, purity, gentle tenderness, self-effacement, self-sacrifice, and singular faithfulness. Throughout history, Indian women have had dual status: As a wife, a woman seduces her husband away from his work and spiritual duties, but as a mother, she is revered.

Among the crosses women have had to bear in Indian society are female infanticide, child marriage, *purdah* (feminine modesty and seclusion), marital mistreatment, and the low status of widows. According to UNICEF's *State of the World's Children* (UNICEF, 2008), 47% of India's women ages 20–24 were married before the legal age of 18, and this figure is 56% in rural areas. The report also documents that 40% of the world's child marriages occur in India. Until the mid-19th century, the voluntary immolation of the widow on her husband's funeral pyre (*sati*) was not uncommon; the widow believed her act would cleanse her family of the sins of three generations. Poor families are more likely to be fearful of not being able to scrape together enough money to find their daughters husbands and may resort to killing infant girls.

The dance of Shiva is not destined to lead to joy throughout the world, and if the corresponding experience of humanity includes some unhappiness for women, that is simply the way things are. However, many activists attribute the rise in sexual harassment against women to the influence of Western culture. Police often treat such crimes as minor incidents, and there is a tendency to suggest that women invite sexual harassment by the way that they dress. At the same time, India selected Pratibha Patil as the first woman president (a largely symbolic position in a parliamentary democracy) in 2007. Patil strongly advocated for the education and social development of women and urged the Society for Human Resources Management, India to focus its energies in this direction. The country has also produced many successful women entrepreneurs and political leaders. More women are enrolling in MBA programs and engaging in entrepreneurship activities.

Marriage and Family

A man's worth and identity are intimately bound up in the reputation of his family. Lifestyle and actions are rarely seen as the product of individual effort but are interpreted in light of family circumstance and reputation in the wider society. Individual identity and merit are enhanced if people have the good fortune to belong to a large, harmonious, and close-knit family, which helps to safeguard children's upbringing and to advance them in life. The family contributes to decisions that affect an individual's future, maximizes the number of connections necessary to secure a job or other favors, comes to aid in times of crisis, and generally mediates an individual's experience with the outside world. For these reasons, the character of the respective families weighs heavily in the consideration of marriage proposals.

Arranged marriage is still the norm in India. Advertisements regularly appear in European and U.S. newspapers and on the Internet for the purpose of identifying potential candidates. The Western concept of romantic love arises from the Western concept of personality and, ultimately, from the un-Indian concept of equality of the sexes. In addition, the concept of life as an illusion makes the idea of a loveless marriage easier to understand.

Marriages are traditionally for a lifetime, as divorce is considered socially disgraceful, although this is changing in the urban areas of the country. There is even a website, Secondshaadi.com, catering to the needs of the divorced, a phenomenon that would have been unthinkable a decade ago when such people were social outcasts and treated like misfits. One major reason for the rapid increase in divorce rates is the growing number of working women in urban areas who have independent incomes and are refusing to submit to their husbands' traditional views of the role of men and women within marriage.

In the case of child marriage, the girl lives at her parents' home until she is about 15 or 16 years of age, after which she moves to the home of her husband's family. A newly arrived daughter-in-law is sometimes subjected to varying forms of humiliation until she becomes pregnant. This treatment originated historically from the urgent need to ensure the early birth of a son in times of low life expectancy. Also, the size of the dowry that a girl brings with her can determine how she is treated or mistreated in her husband's home. The husband's family may keep demanding additional support from her family, and if it is not forthcoming, she may be tortured or even burned alive, although the outcry against such treatment seems to have diminished such illegal practices.

The restricted life of women in the conservative atmosphere of India does not prevent them from developing a strong sense of self-respect. Their ultimate role is to preserve unity and continuity in the chain of life, and there is pride and dignity in their sense of identity with the family and their roles as wife and mother. Indian society seems to have given women, rather than men, resilience and vitality under the difficult circumstances of life in that country. Ultimately, all respond to the dance of Shiva, and whether that brings great joy or unhappiness to the current life is irrelevant compared to the ongoing search for salvation, or *mukti*.

Since the beginning of time, dancing has been a rite performed by both men and women; Shiva and his wife, Parvati, are often depicted in ancient sculptures as one composite figure, half male and half female (*Ardhanarishwara*). Typical figurines of

Shiva are four armed, with broad masculine shoulders and curving, womanly hips. Similarly both genders contribute to Indian society today. In this century, Indian women have undergone a social revolution more far-reaching and radical than that of men and have attained positions of distinction in public and professional life.

In summary, it can be seen that the extended family unit is still a strong feature of Indian society. Just as the dance of Shiva wills all of nature to respond to its rhythm, so too each member of the family fulfills a role dictated by family tradition.

The Cycle of Social Interaction

A sense of duty (*dharma*) is the social cement in India; it holds the individual and society together. *Dharma* is a concept that is wider than the Western idea of duty, as it includes the totality of social, ethical, and spiritual harmony (Lannoy, 1971). *Dharma* consists of three categories: universal principles of harmony (*sanatana dharma*), relative ethical systems varying by social class (*varnashrama dharma*), and personal moral conduct (*svadharma*). Among the prime traditional virtues are generosity and selflessness, truthfulness, restraint from greed, and respect for elders. These principles are consistent with a virtual global idea of righteousness. Through India's moments of crisis, Hinduism has repeatedly raised the banner of the highest ideals. The image of the dance of Shiva is strongly evoked by the following passage from the Bhagavad-Gita:

> Whenever the *dharma* decays, and when that which is not *dharma* prevails, then I manifest myself. For the protection of the good, for the destruction of the evil, for the firm establishment of the national righteousness, I am born again and again.

The oldest source of ethical ideas is the *Mahabharata,* or Great Epic (of Bharata), the first version of which appeared between the 7th and 6th centuries BCE. This huge composite poem of 90,000 couplets in 18 books traces the rivalry between two families involved in an unrelenting war. The story is interrupted by numerous episodes, fables, moral tales, and long political and ethical discourses, all of which serve to illustrate the illusory nature of the world and encourage the reader to strive for God. This sacred book, a repository of Hindu beliefs and customs, is based on the assumption that *dharma* is paramount in the affairs of society. The epics took at least 1,000 years to compose and are still the most widely read and respected religious writings of the Hindus. The most popular and influential part of the epics is the Bhagavad-Gita (Song of the Blessed One), a book Gandhi (1946) once said "described the duel that perpetually went on in the hearts of mankind."

A recent European traveler in India gave the following illustration of the power of *dharma.* Sitting precariously among local people on top of a bus during a long journey, a traveler was astounded when a sudden shower of money fell into the dusty road behind them. An Indian alongside the traveler began shouting and pounding on the roof of the bus for the driver to stop. Some way down the road, the bus pulled over, and the man rushed away. All the passengers disembarked and waited for the Indian to return, laughing at his comic misfortune and manic disappearance. Eventually the man reappeared, clutching a big handful of notes, including Western money. It was then that the traveler realized his own wallet was gone from his back pocket; it had come loose and blown away from the top of the bus, scattering the equivalent of a year's income for the average native. The Indian, a total stranger, had run back and convinced the poverty-stricken locals to hand over the money they were ecstatically gathering from their fields. The traveler began to thank his new friend for his troubles, but with the comment, "It was my duty," the Indian declined to take any reward. This is a comment that many travelers hear when similar incidents occur.

Power and Purity

Hindus generally believe that social conflict, oppression, and unrest do not stem from social organizations but originate in the nonadherence to *dharma* by those in positions of power. Their actions have created the cycle of disharmony. Hindus see a quarrel as a drama with three actors—two contestants and a peacemaker—and it is not the protagonists but the peacemaker who is seen as the victor in the dispute, as it is he or she who has restored harmony (Lannoy, 1971).

Individuals who head institutions are believed to be the sole repositories of the virtues and vices of the institution. Traditionally social reform movements focused not so much on abolishing hierarchical organizations or rejecting the values on which they are based but on removing or changing the individuals holding positions of authority in them (Kakar, 1978). For example, during the declining years of both the Mughal and British Indian empires, the ruling classes enjoyed lives of luxury and extravagance in India. Conspicuous consumption by the aristocratic elites at the expense of the productive classes is with us still in the India of the early 21st century. The identity of the elites may have changed, but their attitude of entitlement remains. Establishing one's place in the pecking order is not only in line with a high–power distance culture but reflects a demand that built up over several decades prior to market liberalization. Some estimates indicate that the luxury-brand industry in India will increase by almost 10 times to $30 billion by 2015 (Dehejia, 2010).

The issues behind the social and political ferment in India today are not rooted primarily in economic deprivation and frustration, although these make the mix more volatile (Narayana & Kantner, 1992). Rather, there is a widespread feeling that the institutions on which the society was founded no longer work.

The tragic recourse to mob violence by religious followers at different times in the country's history is a contradiction that astounds casual observers of India. How can such terrible things happen in a country where everyone believes in harmony and awaits the ultimate consequences of good and bad deeds in reincarnation? Hindus believe that *sila*, character or behavior, has its roots in the depths of the mind rather than in the heat of the action (Lannoy, 1971). Because all worldly acts are transient or part of the illusion of life, they can have no decisive moral significance. Within the dance of Shiva, destruction exists as strongly as creation and preservation; so it is with India.

This is not to say that violence is condoned by Hindu faith; just the opposite is the case. However, Hindus avoid the theological use of the terms *good* and *evil* and prefer to speak of knowledge and ignorance, *vidya* and *avidya*. Destructive acts done by people who are ignorant are not regarded as sins, but those acts committed by people aware of their responsibilities are counted against them in their seeking of *mukti*.

Bathing in the holy water of the Ganges River is believed to wash away all of a person's sins and is required of all Hindus at least once in their lives. Indians tend to integrate with nature because they assume this is the natural relationship of human beings with the world, unlike others who may exploit the physical environment for their own purposes. But the belief in the spiritual purity of the Ganges is so strong that government attempts to clean up the badly polluted waters have little chance of being effective. Many people simply do not accept that anything can spoil the Ganges's perfection. As a consequence, rotting carcasses of both animals and partly cremated people are a common sight along the river banks. The image of death among life, decomposition next to creation, and pollution mixed with purity is evocative of the dance of Shiva.

Caste Tensions

Another pervasive social dimension in India is the caste system (*Varna*). Discrimination based on this system is now officially outlawed but is still a source of constant tension. Following the assumed natural law that an individual soul is born into its own appropriate environment, Hindus assume an individual belongs to a caste by birth. There are four main castes, each of which contributes to society in specific ways: *Brahmans* as priests, teachers, and intellectuals; *Kshatriyas* as warriors, police, and administrators; *Vaishyas* as skilled craftspeople and farmers; and *Shudras* as artisans and workers. Each of these natural classes has its appropriate honors and duties, but as privilege has entered the scale, with top castes profiting at the expense of those lower down, the whole system has begun to disintegrate.

Below the system is a group that has been termed the *panchama* (the fifth *varna*) or the Untouchables (now called *Dalits*), who lie outside of the major activities of society. *Dalit* is an ancient word from Marathi (a Western Indian language), which may be defined as "ground" or "broken in pieces." According to the Dalit Freedom Network, it refers to people who have deliberately been broken or ground down by those above them. Members of this group are engaged in work that is considered socially undesirable and unclean. Clay cups were historically used by restaurants and other establishments to serve Dalits, and these were supposed to be destroyed so that no upper-caste customer would ever use them and risk contamination by a Dalit's "uncleanness." Untouchability, as it exists today, is often described as a perversion of the original caste system.

Within each caste or group are numerous subcastes, or *jati,* which influence the immediacy of all daily social relations, including work. About 3,000 *jati* exist, and they are further divisible into about 30,000 sub-*jati,* with unwritten codes governing the relationships between *jatis.* Friendships with members of the same *jati* tend to be closer and more informal than those with members of other *jatis.* As a general rule, a person's name provides information not only about his or her *jati* but also about the region of the country from which the person's family originated. For example, *Gupta* is a family name from the trading class, although many have gone into the professions, especially teaching. Most Guptas come from the north Indian states of Haryana and Uttar Pradesh and from the eastern state of West Bengal.

The *jati*'s values, beliefs, and prejudices become part of each individual's psyche or conscience. The internalized *jati* norms define the right actions or *dharma* for an individual; he or she feels good or loved when living up to these rules and guilty when transgressing them.

When society was divided strictly by caste, there was no attempt to realize a competitive equality, and within each caste all interests were regarded as identical. But that also meant equality of opportunity for all within the caste: Every individual was allowed to develop the experience and skills that he or she needed to succeed at the caste's defined role. The castes were self-governing, which ensured that people were tried and judged by their peers. Central authorities punished crimes committed by upper caste members more severely than those committed by the lower caste. As it was simply not possible to move outside of the caste, all possibility of social ambition, with its accompanying tension, was avoided. This suits the Hindu belief in harmony. The comprehensiveness of the caste system, together with holistic *dharma,* contributed to the stability that prevailed among the vast mass of people for much of India's history. Preservation of order, interspaced with disorder, is a characteristic of the dance of Shiva.

The Untouchables

The worst fate of the caste system falls on the Untouchables. This caste, victims of a system that allows people to live in squalor, has come to be the symbol of India's own brand of human injustice. Of course, social hierarchy is universal, found not only among the Hindus but also among the Muslims, Christians, Sikhs, Jains, and Jews (Srinivas, 1969/1980). In addition, pollution taboos are prevalent in all civilizations, including the most advanced and modern, and eliminating dirt is an attempt to introduce order into the environment (Lannoy, 1971). But Hindu society pays exceptional attention to the idea of purity and pollution, and historically this has resulted in the virtual ostracism of the Untouchables from the rest of society.

By way of historical explanation, Hindus believed that proximity to the contaminating factor constitutes a permanent pollution, which is both collective and hereditary. Therefore, they had a dread of being polluted by members of society who were specialists in the elimination of impurity. Hindu society was more conscious of grading social groups according to their degree of purity than of dividing castes precisely into occupations. The Untouchables—traditionally society's cleaners, butchers, and the like—were at the bottom of the Hindu hierarchy because they were considered irrevocably "unclean." A similar caste system was developed in Japan, and it too has been outlawed, although its effects are still being felt.

While India's traditional social structure was based on institutionalized inequality, today the government, and supposedly the nation, is committed to social equality. Beginning with Mahatma Gandhi, public figures have tried to reform the attitudes of Indian society toward the Untouchables. Gandhi named them Harijan, literally "children of God," and this was a popular term until the 1980s. The entire caste system was declared illegal by the constitution, and today "scheduled castes" (which include the Untouchables) are guaranteed 15% of central government jobs and 15% of seats in universities as compensation for traditional disfavor. These policies have met with some success, but such deep-rooted prejudice cannot be eliminated by a mere stroke of the pen. As recently as 2010, terrible atrocities (including torture and murder) were reported against Dalits who dared fall in love with a member of the upper caste.

The ambiguity of caste in occupational terms is another wedge by which the lower castes push their way upward on the scale. However, ambiguity is not so great as to render the system inoperative. Violations of caste norms, such as intercaste marriage, still evoke responses of barbaric ferocity. Educated Indians look on such incidents as throwbacks to the inhumanity of feudal times and believe that the authorities should deal with them sternly. But efforts to create greater equality of opportunity for members of the traditionally disadvantaged castes meet stiff resistance (Narayana & Kantner, 1992). At times activists from the upper castes have immolated themselves outside government offices to protest against any kind of accommodation through "affirmative action."

Attempts at Reform

Additional reforms remain problematic, as recent history suggests. In 1990 the government introduced policies reserving 27% of jobs in federal and state jobs for lower castes and for some Christian and Muslim groups that many considered socially backward. In protest, dozens of upper-caste students burned themselves to death. The upper-caste Brahmins, a mere 5.5% of the population, have traditionally run government departments, but the struggle for jobs in India is so intense that the students saw themselves as victims of injustice, not as historical oppressors. The prime minister at the time, V. P. Singh, was forced to resign when the government's coalition partner withdrew its support, mainly over caste reform issues.

The Harijan quickly realized their ability to assert their democratic rights as equal citizens through organized political activity. The politicization of caste in modern times has made it clear that power is becoming ascendant over status. In 2008 Mayawati (who goes by one name), a Dalit leader, was elected as the chief minister of the state of Uttar Pradesh, which is India's most populous state and home to several former prime ministers. She is reported to be eyeing the biggest prize of all—the prime ministership of India. Her meteoric rise, achieved through an unlikely coalition of supporters from opposite ends of the caste spectrum (Brahmins and Dalits), has truly shaken up Indian politics (Chu, 2008). However, her future prospects outside the state of Uttar Pradesh depend upon extending her base of support to the rest of the country.

Modern education also acts as a solvent of caste barriers. The government has been playing its part by offering financial incentives to people who marry members of the lowest Hindu castes. These factors hold out the best hope for the disappearance of caste over the long term. Interestingly, Dalits in Britain have been leading the fight against caste discrimination even among second-generation Asian families settled in the United Kingdom. As Keith Porteous Wood of the National Secular Society observed, "The blight of caste discrimination, under which millions in India are regarded as 'untouchable,' has spread to this country virtually unnoticed" ("Caste Prejudice," 2010). In 2011 the U.K. government started evaluating evidence to determine whether to enact a legal ban on caste discrimination.

The hierarchical principle of social organization goes beyond caste, however, and has been central to the conservatism of Indian tradition. Among the criteria for ordering are age and gender. Elders, especially in traditional families, have more formal authority than younger people, and, as we have already related, men have greater authority than women. Many times women are not involved in social functions or conversations and are required to cover their heads in front of elders or mature guests. Most relationships are hierarchical in structure, characterized by almost maternal nurturing on the part of the superior and by filial respect and compliance on the part of the subordinate. The ordering of social behavior extends to every institution in Indian life, including the workplace, which we will examine shortly.

It is clear that the traditional social structure of India is undergoing change and reform. This is consistent with the evolutionary aspects of the dance of Shiva. But any change requires the destruction of old ways, and pressure is beginning to build within the old system. It may be that before change is complete, Shiva will rest, and chaos will rule for a time. Or perhaps a new rhythm is beginning for the dance of the 21st century, and the Daily Dance of Indian society will quietly adjust in response.

The Work and Recreation (Rejuvenation) Cycle

There are several perspectives on the importance of work: to earn a living; to satisfy the worldly interests of accomplishments, power, and status; and to fulfill the desire to create and care for the family. An aspect considered more important in India is that work enables, prepares, and progresses the individual through the cycle of life toward the ultimate aim of achieving *mukti*. The Indian approach to work is best defined by the Bhagavad-Gita:

> Both renunciation and practice of work lead to the highest bliss.
>
> Of these two, the practice of work is better than its renunciation.

Work was originally prescribed as duty (*dharma*) without any concern for material outcomes. Castes were occupational clusters, each discharging its role and, in turn, being maintained by the overall system. But meeting obligations to one's relatives, friends, and even strangers and maintaining relationships constituted the ethos of the system. Even with the rapid expansion of industrial activity in the 20th century, requiring large-scale importation of Western technology and work forms, Indians have only partially internalized Western work values. Today, with government-mandated affirmative action, it is not unlikely that someone from a higher caste may work for someone from a lower class. Many Indians have developed a state of mind that allows them to put aside caste prejudice in the workplace but, on returning home, to conduct all their social activities strictly according to caste norms.

We have already seen how family life develops an acute sense of dependence in people, which serves to fortify the participative and collective nature of society. Similarly most Indian organizations have numerous overlapping in-groups, with highly personalized relationships among the members of each group. Members cooperate, make sacrifices for the common good, and generally protect each other's interests. But in-groups often interfere with the functioning of formally designated sections, departments, and divisions, and their presence can lead to factionalism and intense power plays within an organization. Just as disorder within order is a characteristic of the dance of Shiva, so too incompetence is often overlooked because evaluation of work performance is more relationship oriented than contractual in nature. Competent people may be respected but not included in a group unless they possess the group characteristics.

Loyalty to Group

Family, relatives, caste members, and people who speak the same language or belong to the same religion may form in-groups. There are typically regionally oriented subgroups, formed on the basis of states, districts, towns, and villages from which people's families originated. Within the group, Indians are very informal and friendly.

Geert Hofstede's (1980a) attitudinal survey of the cultural differences among 53 countries is especially helpful in the case of India, which tends to cluster with those countries where there is a high degree of uncertainty avoidance. Indians tend to work with lifelong friends and colleagues and minimize risk-taking behavior, although this is changing in modern India. Interestingly, India and the United States are tied in the more recent GLOBE (House et al., 2004) rankings of uncertainty avoidance at 4.15 (Switzerland was highest at 5.37). This orientation is consistent with the Hindu philosophy of life as an illusion, Indians' preoccupation with astrology, and their resignation to karma. India also falls with those countries characterized by large power distances, and this is consistent across both Hofstede's study and the GLOBE study. However, India ranks 21st of the 53 nations on individualism and is fairly high on the GLOBE collectivism rankings, especially with regard to in-group collectivism, which reflects close ties with family members and respect for authority. Finally, India has a high score on masculinity, which is consistent with Hinduism's emphasis on male domination. This is also borne out by the low scores on gender egalitarianism in the GLOBE study. Generally the values described by Hofstede and the GLOBE studies reflect a historical continuity and resilience of the Indian social system, despite a series of foreign invasions, colonial rulers, and economic dislocations.

The hierarchical principle continues to be a source of stagnation in modern Indian institutions. Younger people have limited or no say in decision making. The persistent critical questioning or confrontation necessary to effect change simply does not occur. Gradually younger workers resign themselves to waiting until they become seniors in their own right, free to enjoy the delayed gratification that age brings with it in Indian society. The apparent lack of control and ambition displayed by most workers is similar to the resignation of the world to the will of Shiva. The world responds to Shiva's rhythm, captive of its pace, and is unable to influence it.

Bureaucracy and Corruption

The importance of honoring family and *jati* bonds leads to nepotism, dishonesty, and corruption in the commercial world. These are irrelevant, abstract concepts in India; guilt and anxiety are aroused only when individual actions go against the principle of primacy of relationships, not when foreign standards of ethics and efficiency are breached. This gives rise to legendary tales of corrupt officials, widely shared among travelers and businesspeople who have spent time in India. It is this corruption that is holding India back, and in 2011 a Gandhian activist, Anna ("elder brother") Hazare, captured the imagination of Indians all over the world when he launched a hunger strike to demand that the government take steps to end corruption. His key supporters, "Team Anna," ran a very disciplined campaign using social media to get the message out to millions of people. Twenty years after market liberalization and deregulation, there is a website, IPaidaBribe.com, where Indians can check the going rate for getting a son or daughter into college or winning job transfers, based on self-reported data from the site's users (Pearlstein, 2011). Despite a deep-rooted culture of corruption, there is also a strong awareness among the business and government elite that India's impressive growth cannot continue for long unless it reforms this culture (Pearlstein).

Indian organizations have been shaped by colonial experiences that have bureaucratized them and polarized the positions of the rulers (managers) and the ruled (workers). As a consequence, the role of the manager tends to be viewed as that of an order giver or autocrat. In contrast, American managers generally perceive their role to be that of problem solver or facilitator and attempt to involve subordinates in routine decisions (Adler, 2007). In a much-used cross-cultural training videotape, a U.S. manager attempts to use this style with an Indian subordinate, who wonders about his superior's competence and holds him in some contempt for not being autocratic. The clear implication is that U.S. managers must act more authoritatively in India than in the United States. Being overly familiar with junior colleagues is not encouraged. However, in India's Silicon Valley, Bangalore, where managers are trying very hard to recruit and retain talented engineers and information technology professionals, human resources is adopting some interesting practices that reverse the traditional hierarchical relationship between managers and employees. In one company, the best-performing employees of the month are treated to a special breakfast cooked by their bosses in appreciation of their efforts. Still, Western companies wishing to do business in India must leave their relatively egalitarian culture behind and respect the hierarchy, which is present almost everywhere in corporate India.

Religious Festivals

One source of rejuvenation and recreation for the Indian people is the many religious festivals held throughout the year. These festivals are usually associated with agricultural cycles or the rich mythology of India's past. In some regions, community festivals involve the active participation not only of Hindus but of members of other religions, too. Family bonds are recurrently emphasized and strengthened through the joint celebration of religious festivals. The Indian sense of fun and play is given free rein during the festivities, which often include riddles, contests of strength, role reversals, and rebellious acts. Just as the dance of Shiva is an expression of his joy and exuberance, festivals give Hindus an opportunity to express their feelings of devotion and happiness.

Gods and the God-like

Memorials to the grand line of India's "modern gods"—Mahatma Gandhi, Jawaharlal Nehru, and now Indira Gandhi—are as much the objects of pilgrimage as any temple or festival. Indira Gandhi was killed by her own trusted Sikh bodyguards just 5 months after she had ordered the storming of the Golden Temple at Amritsar by the Indian army to dislodge Sikh rebels. Her home in New Delhi is now a museum and shrine visited by thousands daily. The spot in her garden where she was gunned down is bracketed by two soldiers; her bullet-riddled sari is on display inside. Crowds gather before these, many weeping.

Another example is that of N. T. Rama Rao, a former movie star and chief minister of the state of Andhra Pradesh from 1983 to 1989. Rama Rao acted in leading roles in more than 320 films with mythical, historical, and folkloric themes. Among the masses, Rama Rao was associated with the qualities of the gods he played, and when he gave up his movie career to establish a new political party, he was immediately voted into office. This tradition has continued, with many members of both Bollywood and the regional film industries being voted into office almost as an extension of their "reel-life" roles. The fact that Rao's party's radical Hindu fundamentalist policies sometimes caused strife within society is not inconsistent with the concurrently constructive and destructive nature of the dance of Shiva.

The favorite pastime of Indians is watching movies, either at movie theaters or by renting videos from the shops that have sprung up all over the country, and today India's Bollywood is the largest producer of films in the world, releasing upward of 800 movies per year. Hollywood studios such as DreamWorks SKG and Paramount Pictures come calling on a regular basis for financing and distribution contracts. In 2011 UTV motion pictures announced a creative alliance with Disney to coproduce and distribute films targeted at the Indian audience. Movies that draw on images and symbols from traditional themes are dominant in popular Indian culture. They incorporate but go beyond the familiar repertoire of plots from traditional theater. Films appeal to an audience so diverse that they transcend social and regional categories.

The language and values from popular movies have begun to influence Indian ideas of the good life and the ideals of social, family, and romantic relationships. Robert Stoller's (1975) definition of fantasy, the "protector from reality, concealer of truth, restorer of tranquility, enemy of fear and sadness, and cleanser of the soul" (p. 55), includes terms that are equally attributable to the illusory nature of the dance of Shiva, and it is easy to understand why films play such a major role in Indian recreation and rejuvenation.

India is the heart of Asia, and Hinduism is a convenient name for the nexus of Indian thought. It has taken 1,000 to 1,500 years to describe a single rhythm of its great pulsation, as described by the *Mahabharata,* or Great Epic. By invoking the image and meaning of the dance of Shiva, and drawing parallels between this legendary act of a Hindu deity and many of the main influences of traditional Indian life, we have attempted to communicate the essence of India's society in this chapter.

It is not always possible to identify a nicely logical or easily understandable basis for many of the contradictions and paradoxes that exist in Indian society, just as it is difficult to explain the existence of racism, sexism, and other forms of intolerance and injustice in Western countries. In India the philosophy of life and the mental structure of the people come not from a study of books but from tradition (Munshi, 1965). However much foreign civilization and new aspirations might have affected the people of India, the spiritual basis of Hindu philosophy has not dried up or decayed (Munshi); within this tradition the role of the dance of Shiva is accepted by all Hindus (Coomaraswamy, 1924/1969):

Shiva rises from his rapture and, dancing, sends through inert matter pulsing waves of awakening sound. Suddenly, matter also dances, appearing as a brilliance around him. Dancing, Shiva sustains the world's diverse phenomena, its creation and existence. And, in the fullness of time, still dancing, he destroys all forms—everything disintegrates, apparently into nothingness, and is given new rest. Then, out of the thin vapor, matter and life are created again. Shiva's dance scatters the darkness of illusion (*lila*), burns the thread of causality (*karma*), stamps out evil (*avidya*), showers grace, and lovingly plunges the soul into the ocean of bliss (*ananda*). (p. 66)

India will continue to experience the range of good and bad, happiness and despair, creation and destruction. Through it all, its people will continue their journey toward *moksha,* salvation from the worldly concerns of mankind. Hindu philosophy is the key to understanding India and how a nation of such diversity manages to bear immense burdens while its people seem undeterred and filled with inner peace and religious devotion.

And through it all, Shiva dances on.

CHAPTER 29

India

A Kaleidoscope of Diversity

Studying India is like looking into a kaleidoscope which is turning constantly. India is complex. It is colorful. It offers multiple evolving patterns which are contained within one framework.

—From a 10-part radio documentary series
Passages to India (Cappello & Hollick, 1986–1989)

The diversity in the Indian cultural [sic] is not merely in its ethnic or racial composition. It is in every walk of its life. Starting with the geographical features, climatic conditions, and the vast regional and intra regional differences one can go on to religion, customs, attitudes, practices, language, food habits, dress, art, music, theatre and notice that no two regions are alike in these matters.

—Sreenivasarao Subanna, writing in online
history community Allempires.com (2007, sect. 6.2)

India is often described as one of the world's most culturally and geographically diverse nations. It is also a land of great contrasts where you can expect to see Mercedes Benzes and BMWs vying for road space with ox carts and motorcycles, especially in the major urban centers. High-rise residential complexes for the moneyed upper classes rise like so many lotuses from the swamps. Slums develop around these complexes to house the domestic servants who take care of the needs of the apartment dwellers. A 27-story structure, the world's first billion-dollar home in Mumbai, has been built for India's richest man, Mukesh Ambani, and his family. The parking garage alone fills six levels, and there are three helipads on the roof, terraces upon terraces, hanging gardens, and airborne swimming pools (Yardley, 2010). Oddly juxtaposed with this new tower is the fact that 62% of Mumbai's 20 million population lives in slums. The 2009 Oscar-winning movie *Slumdog Millionaire*, with British director Danny Boyle, was set in Mumbai in Asia's largest slum. Writing in a 2008 *Harvard Business Review* online post, world-renowned executive coach Marshall Goldsmith observes, "In the cities, I saw a longing for extreme opulence—countless ads with rich people living lavish lives—next to the reality of extreme poverty—countless shanties with poor people living harsh lives."

In 2006, 60,000 fans of an aging but iconic regional movie star, Rajkumar, went on a rampage in India's hi-tech hub, Bangalore, after he died of a sudden heart attack. They set fire to cars and buses and attacked Microsoft and other software firms, bringing India's fastest-growing city to a virtual standstill. The actor was seen as a defender of a regional cultural identity, which was perceived as being increasingly under siege. Some wondered whether the two Indias, representing prosperity and poverty, were drifting apart.

Once famous for holy men in sackcloth and ashes who renounced the world, and for its elephants and sacred cows, today India is equally as well known for having one of the largest pools of educated scientists and engineers in the world and as a base for research and development for leading multinationals. In this country millions of Hindus, Muslims, Sikhs, Christians, and Buddhists have lived in relative harmony for several decades. Thomas Friedman (2005), *New York Times* columnist, points out that the reason for this state of affairs is to be found in India's multiethnic, pluralistic, free-market democracy. In 2004 India experienced an election event unprecedented in human history: A nation of more than 1 billion people went to the polls in large numbers who were willing to elect a party headed by a foreign-born (Italian) Catholic political leader (Sonia Gandhi), who peacefully and firmly made way for a Sikh (Manmohan Singh) to be sworn in as prime minister by a Muslim (President Abdul Kalam). This took place in a country that is more than 80% Hindu.

The kaleidoscope is an appropriate metaphor for modern India. It presents an ever-changing set of colorful images not only to the foreigners who flock to do business there and the nonresident Indians who return every year for quick visits but also to the people living in the country. This is the result of India's unmatched diversity of cultures and its dramatic transformation from a third-world country to an Asian superpower in the 21st century. As Chhokar (2008) suggests, "What may be termed as the culture of India today is the outcome of, or merely the current stage in, a process of evolution of a continually living and changing culture" (p. 972). Thus, using the kaleidoscope metaphor, we will explore the diversity that lies within India. The kaleidoscopic areas we discuss include the variety of religious and culture celebrations; the distinctive festivals and feasts held throughout the year; modern India's call centers and cell phones; and the changing game of cricket, which has recently imported cheerleaders from the United States.

The Kaleidoscope of
Religions and Cultural Celebrations

Religion and language separate the people of India far more than ethnic background or geography. India is the birthplace of four major religions: Hinduism, Buddhism, Jainism, and Sikhism. Although 81% of the Indian population is Hindu, sizable numbers belong to other religious groups: Muslim (14%), Christian (3%), Sikh (1.86%), Buddhist, Jain, and aboriginal animist. Hindus live throughout India, with smaller concentrations at the southern, northeastern, and northwestern extremities. The minority populations (the term is relative, as Muslims alone number more than 140 million, the third-largest concentration of Muslims after Indonesia and Pakistan) actively resist being dissolved into a Hindu melting pot. Muslims are in the majority in Kashmir, and Sikhs are concentrated in Punjab.

Hinduism, Islam, Christianity, and Sikhism are all associated with the specific languages in which their original scripts were written: Sanskrit, Arabic, Latin, and Gurumukhi, respectively. The first three are not spoken languages in India, and the fourth in a modernized form is a state language of Punjab. In addition to speaking Arabic, Muslims in India evolved a language of their own, Urdu, and a number of other regional languages. There are at least 300 known languages in India, 24 of which have at least 1 million speakers each.

India has had a long tradition of embracing various religions throughout its history. Christianity came to India as early as the middle of the first century CE. Jewish people have lived in India for centuries. Islam came to India in the 13th century, and its influence lasted for several hundred years. Through extensive trading relationships over the centuries, India has absorbed characteristics of foreign cultures and shared the best of her culture with other nations in an early version of globalization. Thus, not only has India witnessed the birth of several world religions, but it has also absorbed and integrated other faiths. "India: The Dance of Shiva" (Chapter 28) presents the tenets of Hinduism in great detail, and in this chapter we highlight some of the other great religions that were born in India.

Buddhism

Buddhism began in India with the life of Siddhartha Gautama, a prince from a small kingdom in the foothills of the Himalayas who grew up in luxury but soon left home in search of the meaning of existence. He finally found enlightenment under a tree in the forests of Gaya (the modern state of Bihar in northern India) and achieved the knowledge that he later expressed as the Four Noble Truths: All of life is suffering; the cause of suffering is desire; the end of desire leads to the end of suffering; and the means to end desire is a path of discipline and meditation. Gautama was now the Buddha, or the Awakened One, and he spent the remainder of his life traveling about northeast India converting large numbers of disciples.

The great emperor Ashoka of the Maurya dynasty was largely responsible for spreading Buddhism outside of India's borders in the 3rd century BCE and dispatched his own son, a monk, to spread Buddhism to Sri Lanka. Ashoka is said to have converted to Buddhism after the battle of Kalinga, where his men killed more than 100,000 people. He was filled with great remorse and gave up war and other violence.

Buddhism today has about 350 million adherents all over the world, mainly in Asia, and is reputedly the fourth-largest religion in the world. The Dalai Lama, who is considered to be a reincarnation of a great Buddhist master, is exiled from Tibet and has been living in Dharamsala, India, since the Chinese takeover of Tibet in 1951.

Jainism

Jainism, another religion that was born in India, attained major status in the time of Mahavira, who was born into a princely family in 599 BCE and abandoned his aristocratic surroundings when he was 30 years of age in favor of a more ascetic life. Jainism, which has nearly 4 million followers today, teaches that the way to liberation is to live a life of nonviolence and renunciation. Jains believe that animals, plants, and human beings have living souls and that each of these souls has equal value and should be treated with respect. The three jewels or the guiding principles of Jainism are right belief, right knowledge, and right conduct.

Jains are strict vegetarians and believe that they have to live in a way that minimizes the use of the world's resources. This strict practice of vegetarianism has given rise to some interesting tensions with nonvegetarian tenants of high-rise apartment complexes in Mumbai. Some critics have attached the label of *apartheid* to the intolerance of nonvegetarian food in these upscale, Jain-dominated housing complexes, where prospective buyers have been grilled about their food habits, charged exorbitant prices, or banned outright from owning property.

Sikhism

Sikhism, yet another religion that was born in India, is considered to be the youngest of the world religions, having been founded about 500 years ago by Guru Nanak, who was born in 1469. Nanak believed that we are all one, created by one Creator of all creation. He taught his followers to align with no other religion but to respect all religions. Today, Sikhism's followers are in the millions (23 million at last count), and most of them live in the Indian State of Punjab, with several hundred thousand more living in North America, especially Canada.

They are highly visible because of their distinctive turbans, which caused some of them in the United States to be mistaken for members of the Taliban after the September 11, 2001, terrorist attacks in New York and Washington, D.C. In one incident in Mesa, Arizona, a peaceful Sikh gentleman, Balbir Singh Sodhi, was killed in a hate crime, prompting the Sikh community to explain their religion to their fellow Americans.

Sikhs form 1.86% of India's population but 8% of the Indian Army. By contrast, Muslims are 14% of the population and 2% of the army. The prime minister of

India is Manmohan Singh, a Sikh who is the first person in that highest of offices to hold a doctorate. He is widely respected for being the architect of the economic reforms of the early 1990s, which set India on the path to economic prosperity. The ethnic backgrounds of India's presidents and prime ministers over the years highlight not only the country's amazing diversity but also the secular nature of its constitution.

Zoroastrianism (Parsis)

It is also important to mention the small community of Parsis, whose numbers belie their extraordinary contribution to Indian industry. Members of the Parsi community, who originally migrated from Iran, are followers of one of the oldest religions in the world, Zoroastrianism. Many Parsis escaped persecution in Persia (Iran) and settled down in India between the 6th and 7th centuries. Their numbers (a little more than one hundred thousand) are dwindling because they guard their culture and customs zealously. Most of them live in Mumbai, which is one of the most cosmopolitan cities in the country.

The Parsis believe in the existence of one invisible god. They also believe that there is continuous war between the good forces (forces of light) and the evil forces (forces of darkness). The good forces will win if people do good deeds, think positively, and speak well. God is represented in their temples through fire, which symbolizes light. Parsis were favored by the British because of their knowledge of English, as well as their trading skills and facility with global trade.

The first steel plant in India was built by a Parsi, the industrialist J. R. D. Tata, over a hundred years ago in Jamshedpur as a model workplace. Tata's heirs are among the wealthiest industrialists in India today, and they manage the widely diversified Tata conglomerate, which rivals industrial dynasties in other parts of the world. In 2008 Tata Motors unveiled the world's cheapest car, the Nano, and took control of iconic brands like the Jaguar and Land Rover from Ford Motors. In 2011, after a widely followed and thorough search process, the first non-Tata heir apparent to the US$70 billion Tata empire was announced in the person of successful businessman and member of the Tata board, Cyrus P. Mistry, also a Parsi. He will understudy the current chairman, Ratan Tata, and take over when Tata retires at the end of 2012 ("Cyrus P. Mistry," 2011). Other famous Parsis include Zubin Mehta, the renowned conductor; Homi Jehangir Bhabha, the founder of India's nuclear program; Rohinton Mistry, the award-winning novelist who lives in Canada; and Adi Godrej of the Godrej family, which controls another of India's leading billion-dollar conglomerates.

Despite all this diversity, as M. C. Chagla, a renowned former Indian jurist, diplomat, and cabinet minister, observed, there is something to the idea of Indian-ness:

> There is an Indianness and an Indian ethos, which has been brought about by the commission and intercourse between the many races and the many communities that have lived in this land for centuries. There is a heritage which has

devolved on us from our Aryan forefathers. There is an Indian tradition which overrides all the minor differences which may superficially seem to contradict the unity. (quoted in Iyer, 2000)

Images of Festivals and Feasts

Every turn of the kaleidoscope reveals a different festival in all its myriad colors. These festivals are celebrated throughout this vast country. Sometimes it feels as if there is a festival every day of the year. Religious raptures, possessions, and trances are common during Indian seasonal festivals. This is a structured and, in some cases, highly formalized phenomenon that enriches the consciousness of the individual and the group. The attendant danger, however, is that the group's mood can degenerate into a hysterical mob psychology, which Indian history has witnessed many times. Festivals allow the discharge of intense emotion, which is otherwise submerged in a network of reciprocity and caste relations, but they also can be used to reestablish order.

Religious Festivals

The birthday of Lord Ganesh is one of the most popular festivals in India and often involves 10 days of feasting, fund-raising, and performances of music and dance, with music blaring from loud speakers on every street corner, especially in Mumbai. The festival gained currency during the independence movement in India as a way of uniting various castes and communities against British rule. Massive processions through the streets feature large and small clay idols of Lord Ganesh, and the final goal is to immerse these idols in the sea. Millions of citizens patiently tolerate the ensuing traffic jams for several days every year in August as the monsoon rains finally taper off and the festival season begins in earnest.

Another festival that is celebrated throughout India is Deepawali or Diwali. It celebrates the victory of Lord Rama over the 10-headed evil demon king, Ravana, and his return from exile with his devoted wife and brother. Diwali ushers in spring cleaning, and it includes decorating the home with lights ranging from beautiful earthen lamps to colorful lanterns swaying in the breeze. The celebration also involves setting off all kinds of firecrackers and visiting family and friends with plates of mouthwatering sweet treats and gifts.

A festival that aptly captures the kaleidoscope metaphor is the festival of Holi, which is celebrated all over India at the advent of spring. One of the most colorful festivals in India, Holi involves people spraying each other joyously with colored water or powder in all hues of the rainbow to celebrate the vibrant colors of spring. Markets are filled with vats of yellow, blue, pink, green, and red powders several days before the festival, and old and young get into the spirit of this colorful celebration.

Holi is also marked by India's own version of Guy Fawkes Day (see Chapter 17: The Traditional British House), when bonfires are lit across the country and effigies of

Holika are burned to commemorate one of the many legends associated with the festival. The legend holds that King Hiranyakashap was displeased with his son Prahalad, who worshipped Lord Visnu and thus was not his father's greatest admirer. The king ordered his sister, Holika, to sit in a blazing fire with Prahalad on her lap. Although Holika had been granted a boon that protected her from being burned, that blessing did not work when she entered the fire with her nephew in her lap, and she burned to death. Lord Vishnu, however, protected his young devotee, Prahalad, who survived.

Janamashtami or the birthday of Lord Krishna is celebrated with the popular Dahi-Handi ceremony, which is the most visible aspect of the festival and has become synonymous with it. In his childhood, a naughty Lord Krishna and his friends raided the houses of their neighbors and merrily helped themselves to caskets of milk and butter, which had been hung from the ceilings to prevent domestic animals from raiding the precious contents. They accomplished this by building human pyramids.

During the modern-day Dahi-Handi ceremony, a large earthenware pot is filled with milk, curds, butter, and honeyed fruits and is suspended from a height between 20 and 40 feet. In cities like Mumbai, these pots are sometimes suspended between tall buildings. Several young men work collaboratively to claim the prize. They build a human pyramid by standing on each other's shoulders until the pyramid is high enough to enable the person at the top to reach the pot, break it, and take the contents. Prize money, which is usually tied to the rope by which the pot is suspended, is shared among those who participate in the pyramid building.

Muslims in India celebrate the various Eids (celebrations or festivals) and are greeted by their non-Muslim fellow citizens in a display of religious unity that generally permeates festivals of all religions in this secular country. The main Eid is the Eid-ul-Fitr, which marks the end of a period of fasting during Ramadan. Eid is celebrated with feasts and the exchanging of food and gifts with neighbors and family. Many give food, clothing, blankets, and books to orphanages and the poor. This Eid is also a time when religious and political leaders throughout the nation stress the need to remain united across various religious beliefs.

Christians in India celebrate Easter and Christmas with their Christian counterparts all over the world. Many non-Christians get into the Christmas spirit and pay a visit to Santa Claus in the department stores in the shopping districts of major cities and decorate their homes with colorful lights. Some even attend midnight Mass with their Christian neighbors and friends.

Buddha Purnima or the birthday of Buddha is the most sacred day in the Buddhist calendar and is celebrated all over the world by the faithful. By a strange threefold coincidence, the day commemorates the birthday, the enlightenment, and the attainment of Nirvana by Lord Buddha. Buddha Purnima is a holiday in most Southeast Asian nations, especially India, Sri Lanka, Laos, Cambodia, Thailand, and Myanmar (Burma). The main Jain festival is Mahavir Jayanti, which is the birthday of Mahavira. It is marked more by quiet reflection and prayer than any demonstration of outward gaiety.

Sikhs widely celebrate Nanak Jayanti or Guru Nanak's birthday. His birth anniversary is marked by prayer readings and processions, especially in Amritsar in Punjab State and Patna in Bihar State. The Sikhs also celebrate Baisaki or Vaisaki with great gusto, for it marks the beginning of the new harvest season. Much feasting and dancing ensue after prayers are offered at the *gurudwaras* or Sikh temples.

Indian Cuisine and Wedding Feasts

No discussion of festivals and feasts is complete without a mention of the variety of Indian cuisines. India is widely considered to possess one of the most diverse cuisines in the world and has more regional variations than the countries of Europe. Food plays a very important role in Indian culture and is an integral part of weddings, festivals, and day-to-day living. Wedding feasts in India are unlike any others in the world, catering to hundreds of guests and influenced by regional tastes and practices. Frequently a wedding celebration unfolds over several days of feasting and rejoicing. A wedding feast in southern India (and other parts of the country) may be served on banana leaves with guests sitting cross-legged on the floor while a small army of servers doles out delicious items with the precision of an assembly line. The colorful arrangement of food on each guest's banana leaf changes with each pass of the rapidly moving servers through the line, resembling a food kaleidoscope.

A modern Indian wedding feast is often a marvelous integration of international and national cuisines. Thai, Mexican, Chinese, and Italian food stations are interspersed with various regional Indian cuisines. Multiple courses include appetizers, chutneys, dips, and desserts. Depending on the preferences and origins of the bride and groom, both vegetarian and nonvegetarian dishes may be served. The changing patterns on the plate remain a constant feature of these multicourse wedding feasts. If the traditional wedding feast menus from the different regions of the country were displayed on plates, they would look like a kaleidoscope of food, ever changing and forming fascinating combinations of rice, lentils, vegetables, yogurt, and sweets and sometimes meat, fish, and chicken. Excessive spending on splashy weddings with guest lists that resemble sporting events has caused the government to take notice, especially as poor families get mortgaged to the hilt to compete with wealthy families. Arriving by helicopter to the ceremony and hiring A-list Bollywood actors for entertainment is old news for the bridal couple and their families. According to Ashish Abrol, founder and CEO of BigIndianWedding .com, "People haven't seen wealth like this before, so in the initial stages, you have ostentatious displays of wealth. There is this absolute need for display" (Hannon, 2011). Many Indians in the United States and the United Kingdom also host elaborate wedding ceremonies that last several days and sometimes stop traffic (to allow the groom to arrive on a horse).

Cell Phones, Call Centers, and Curriculum

Cell Phones

Among the many images that emerge with each turn of the kaleidoscope of modern India is the cell phone, which has permeated every walk of life. Cell phones are simply everywhere you go. Shashi Tharoor (2007), a UN undersecretary general for communication and public information and author of the book, *The Elephant, the Tiger, and the Cell Phone,* observes, "One of my favorite photographs of India shows a *sadhu* right out of central casting—naked body, long matted hair and beard, ash-smeared forehead—chatting away on a mobile phone" (p. 377).

The mobile phone revolution in India is nothing short of remarkable in a country that had millions on waiting lists for landlines right up until the 1990s. In 2006 India overtook China in the number of new telephone subscribers per month, and it is now the fastest-growing cell phone market in the world, followed by China and the United States. In early 2011, the number of new telephone subscribers reached 791 million (China has almost 900 million), which represented a 15% jump over the previous 5 months. Low cell phone charges, competition in the telecommunications industry, and lifetime unlimited incoming calls for a low one-time fee have made the cell phone accessible to people of less means. It is quite common to see street vendors (vegetable sellers), launderers, and tea stall owners taking orders on the cell phone. In fact, observing his compatriots and their mobile phone craze, one Indian exclaimed half in exasperation, "They won't have food on the table but they will have their cell phone!"

In a December 2007 National Public Radio segment, Laura Sydell, who had spent time in India, was amazed to find that cell phones were ubiquitous there. Most Indians use their cell phones for double duty: communication and entertainment. They call and text each other (as is common in most parts of the world), and they also download Bollywood movies and MP3 files, a popular pastime in this movie- and music-mad culture. It was not uncommon, according to Sydell, for cell phone users to have huge flash memory cards to download movies; the idea that it was not routine for U.S. Americans to have FM radio on their cell phones was incomprehensible to most Indians. In recent years, a few film schools dedicated to teaching the art of making movies for the mobile phone have sprung up, and one even partnered with Nokia to hold a competition for such movies. Cell phone companies today are using incentives to make major inroads into rural India, where 70% of the more than 1.2 billion people still live. A startup company, EKO India Financial Services, created an innovative software program to enable migrant workers in New Delhi to use their cell phones and a proof of identity to open a bank account registered on the cell phone's text system. Mom-and-pop shops then act as neighborhood bankers and allow workers to remit money to their families in rural areas with few banks (Friedman, 2010).

Call Center Employment

Yet another image associated with modern India is the call center. After India's independence from Britain in 1947, Hindi, a north Indian language, was proclaimed the national language. Hindi was spoken at that time by about 25% of the people, but it was the single most prevalent language in the country. The south had virtually no Hindi speakers, and the southern people opposed learning an "alien" language. As a result of these objections, the original constitution recognized no fewer than 15 official languages (3 more were added in 1992), and English was designated an "additional official language" as a compromise. Today Hindi is the native tongue of about 30% of all Indians, but English is often the language of national communication and is spoken throughout the country.

This facility with spoken English has been partly responsible for the enormous growth of call centers in India. Today it is almost impossible to call the customer service number of a major U.S. corporation and not be struck by the fact that you are talking to someone from India. Call centers are part of business process outsourcing (BPO), which arose when Western companies discovered the large pool of English-speaking, educated workers in India who could handle customer service at a fraction of the cost in the United States or the United Kingdom. This workforce has given India a competitive edge among other Asian nations. To keep up with demand from the United States and the United Kingdom, accent training classes have mushroomed in the cities where most of the call centers are located. The call center experience recently inspired a short-lived prime-time sitcom in the United States appropriately titled *Outsourced*, which highlighted cross-cultural differences through the experiences of a naive but goodhearted American boss and his Indian call center staff in Mumbai.

In the beginning, many young Indians wanted to work in call centers because of the attractive salaries. Call center employees have tough schedules because they work at night in India when it is daytime in the United States. They usually party together, and their jobs motivate them to learn American pop culture and pronunciation. Many even adopt a dual identity (e.g., "Susan" or "John" by night and Savitri or Venkateshwar by day). However, the job is stressful, and employee turnover is high. One call center owner told Rajnandini Pillai that he had to constantly work at keeping the employees motivated by changing his BPO service offerings so that the work was interesting and challenging to them. To this end, although he had started out with a customer service call center operation a few years ago, he was now running a medical transcription services business, having outsourced the initial operation to other English-speaking countries such as the Philippines.

In 2005 Chetan Bhagat wrote a fictional account of call center life titled *One Night @ the Call Center: A Novel,* which chronicled the mundane lives of several call center workers. It became a best seller in India. The next area of growth in Indian BPO is legal process outsourcing. Thousands of English-speaking lawyers in India are employed by U.S. companies and law firms to do legal work at a small fraction of the cost of using U.S. legal assistance (Lakshmi, 2008). The legal process–outsourcing business is expected to grow from US$440 million in 2010 to over $1 billion in 2014 as Wall Street firms try to cut costs by moving these processes outside the United States (Timmons, 2010). However, a glut of domestic law school graduates and a narrowing wage gap between domestic and outsourced contract lawyers may squeeze profits out of this industry (J. Smith, 2011). Health care is another major area of opportunity.

Call center employment has changed the dynamics among members of different generations within the family. Young people are able to afford the same brand names as their counterparts in the West, can splurge on high-end restaurants and nightclubs, and can enjoy a lifestyle that was beyond the reach of their parents. They are able to move from job to job, motivated almost entirely by salary considerations, and it is quite common for some to hold four jobs in the space of 2 years. Often, the BPO workers are seen as avaricious and individualistic, an anomaly in a largely collectivistic society that espouses the philosophy of work as an end in itself. After all, the essence of the Bhagavad-Gita, which is the most famous text of ancient India and exerts considerable influence to this day, can be summed up as "Your business is with the deed, and not the result" (Chhokar, 2008, p. 978).

BPO jobs have often changed perceptions of the female child in the family. Instead of considering her a burden for whom a massive dowry has to be amassed, in some families parents rely on their daughters, smart upwardly mobile call center employees, to help finance the education of their younger brothers. The growth in demand for information technology (IT) services from India has provided bright young English-speaking, college-educated women some remarkable opportunities for career development. However, India faces a potential shortage of 500,000 professional employees in the IT sector in the next few years, according to the National Association of Software and Service Companies, a trade group (Sengupta, 2006). The highly competitive environment has forced the BPO companies to adopt many elements of U.S. business culture. Managers constantly monitor the performance of their employees, offering them rewards and perks for exceptional performance and keeping them motivated with company-paid dinners and contests. Although many of these employees became comfortable with credit card debt through their day-to-day interactions with American customers, the struggles of these customers to pay down massive credit card debt in the aftermath of the global recession have become a cautionary tale for these young employees. However, as India's economy continues to boom, upwardly mobile young people find it hard to resist the allure of cars, refrigerators, and vacations, which are paid off in equal monthly installments (EMIs) deducted from every paycheck for years to come. This creates another division between the older and younger generations because the former did not grow up in an India where financing for education, housing, and consumer goods was freely available. Most parents admonish their children to spend within their means and never get into debt, and they may get upset when this advice is ignored.

The Downside

Parents of call center employees also complain that young people no longer accompany them to religious functions and weddings and instead observe U.S. holidays such as Labor Day and Christmas (Kalita, 2005). In rapidly changing India, young people are making much more money than their parents, are less likely to follow traditional dating practices, and want the same things as their Western counterparts. In an interesting compromise, however, many IT professionals are finding a balance between the traditional arranged marriage and the Western idea of marrying for love. They go online to Indian matrimony websites, exchange emails and photographs, and if they find that they have a lot in common with each other, they introduce the two sets of parents, who seal the match.

As the kaleidoscope turns, so does the image of the call center employee. Today, the reputation of a call center job has taken a nosedive, and call center employees are often perceived by their peers to have limited educational opportunities. A traditional call center job with long hours, usually at night, poses widely reported health risks such as multiple personality and bipolar disorder and excessive stress. Often such jobs subject the employee to verbal abuse from unhappy overseas customers, and they involve tedious work.

However, the maturing Indian economy is no longer only about call centers handling back office operations for U.S. companies. It is more about research and development centers springing up with a view to turning India into a global hub for companies such as Microsoft, GE, and Motorola. In the thriving city of Gurgaon, which has easy access to New Delhi's international airport, 500,000 jobs were created in 2010, and over the last decade, Coca-Cola, PepsiCo, Motorola, Ericsson, Nestle India, and other foreign and Indian companies have opened offices there. Status symbols like Mercedes-Benzes and BMWs are parked outside luxury shops selling Chanel and Louis Vuitton. However, the city suffers from a lack of basic public utilities, and people use a number of private sector workarounds to deal with government inefficiency and corruption. Gurgaon represents the conundrum at the heart India's growth by managing to be a complete disaster and an economic powerhouse, a microcosm of Indian dynamism and dysfunction (Yardley, 2011).

Education Highs and Lows

India is becoming known as a country with a highly educated workforce and a very strong scientific community. Indeed, large pools of educated workers and professionals have been crucial to India's ascent in both manufacturing and services. As a legacy of the strategic vision of the first Indian prime minister, Jawaharlal Nehru, India has a vast pool of engineers and scientists. The Indian Institutes of Technology (IITs) have drawn high praise from Microsoft founder Bill Gates and other U.S. business leaders for the whiz kids that they produce. These aces then go on to contribute in a substantial way to companies such as Microsoft, Intel, and Cisco Systems.

"This is IIT Bombay. Put Harvard, MIT, and Princeton together, and you begin to get an idea of the status of this school in India," observed Lesley Stahl (2003), co-anchor on CBS's *60 Minutes,* when she profiled the Institutes. Competition for admission to the seven IITs is fierce, as only a few thousand students are admitted each year. Entrance is determined by rankings in a nationwide examination.

Japan has recently discovered that it can learn a lot from the Indian model because many Japanese see India as an ascendant education superpower. Japanese bookstores are filled with titles like *Extreme Indian Arithmetic Drills* and the *Unknown Secrets of the Indians.* At the Little Angels English Academy and Kindergarten in Tokyo, students are taught by South Asian teachers, and classroom posters depict animals out of Indian stories (Fackler, 2008a). This is not the first time that Asian powers have turned to the Indian education model. Several centuries ago, India was home to one of the world's first universities, the famous Nalanda University, which was founded by Buddhist monks in 427 CE and played host to more than 10,000 students of various religious traditions. It was destroyed three times by invaders but rebuilt only twice. Asian scholars who travelled to India to study at Nalanda wrote vivid descriptions of the university. In December 2006, India and a consortium of other nations announced plans to rebuild the university as a postgraduate research institution. The Chinese government gave the university a check for US$1 million in November 2011 to build a Chinese-type library in fulfillment of a promise made by Premier Wen Jiabao during his visit in 2010 ("China Donates," 2011).

Turn the kaleidoscope again, and a different picture of India's education system emerges. Underfunded schools, a massive bureaucracy, outdated teaching methods, poorly compensated teachers, and financial pressures contribute to a public education crisis of vast proportions. Business executives complain that schools are hampered by bureaucracy and rote learning rather than critical thinking and comprehension. A call center company, 24/7 Customer Pvt. Ltd., recently found itself so short of talent that in a country of 1.2 billion that had made offshoring a household word, it had to expand its search to the Philippines and Nicaragua (Anand, 2011). Private school education is often beyond the means of most families. Government statistics indicate that only about 25% of students make it past eighth grade, and 15% get to high school. About 200 million start high school, but only about 7% graduate. The adult literacy rate is 62.8% compared to 99% in the United States. Only one in five job seekers has had any vocational training, and about 14 million people are added every year to the labor market. India needs to invest in education and devise a strategy to find employment for these people. Otherwise, these challenges will greatly inhibit India's ability to compete as a global power. World-class companies like WIPRO and Tata Consultancy Services are trying to bridge the widening gap between job requirements and the skills of graduates by designing their own internal training programs (Anand).

With foreign investment and job opportunities exploding, India may have a shortage of trained professionals because of its poor educational infrastructure. India graduates about 900 engineering PhDs per year, which is simply not enough to meet the growing staff requirements at Indian universities. Efforts are underway to increase the number of private colleges and universities and ease rules for foreign universities that may want to establish branches in India. Furthermore, leading Indian companies, such as Infosys, have achieved nothing short of a miracle by relying not on India's education system but on their own resources to recruit, train, and develop their workforces.

The Changing Image of Cricket

When we discussed our metaphors for India with a focus group of Indian professionals, many suggested that an apt metaphor for India would be the game of cricket. The unofficial national sport of India is cricket (the official sport is field hockey). In simple terms, cricket is a team sport involving two teams of 11 players each. Although the game play and rules are very different, the basic concept of cricket is quite similar to that of baseball. Teams bat in successive innings and attempt to score runs, while the opposing team fields and attempts to bring an end to the batting team's inning. After each team has batted an equal number of innings (either one or two, depending on conditions chosen before the game), the team with the most runs wins. A formal game of cricket can last anywhere from an afternoon to several days.

Test matches last for 5 days in an extended version of the 1-day game. As in many other sporting events, such as World Cup football, test matches between rival cricketing nations such as India and Pakistan arouse a great deal of nationalistic fervor. When test matches are played, work in government offices almost comes to a standstill, as employees listen to the broadcasts. In the past, when the only means of obtaining the scores was through a radio broadcast, it was quite common to see people walking around with their ears practically glued to transistor radios, which looked like curious appendages attached to one side of the head. Today giant screens are set up at street corners, and text messages are sent via mobile phone. Work still comes to a standstill during crucial international test matches.

In 2007 India clinched the inaugural Twenty20 World Cup after a thrilling five-run victory over archrival Pakistan in the final in Johannesburg, South Africa. In 2011 India won the World Cup for the first time since 1983, and the country erupted in joyous celebration. To some people, the national cricket team is regarded as a metaphor for the country: young, increasingly confident, and slowly moving forward in fits and starts (Bajaj & Yardley, 2011). The team was given a parade through the streets of Mumbai, which practically shut down the city as thousands of fans lined the streets and the stadium to honor their cricket heroes. Team members were also showered with extravagant gifts.

Cricket was introduced to India by the British. Some accounts suggest that the first game was played in 1721 by British sailors on shore leave. The Parsis were the first Indians to play the game with the Europeans and participated in many tournaments. Soon the Hindus and Muslims fielded their own teams and played in the famous Bombay Quadrangular tournaments. The game took on many forms over time and is now the most popular sport in India. Cricketers are almost on par with movie stars in the degree of attention that their personal lives receive. Not surprisingly, many of them date and marry Bollywood stars, and some even graduate to starring in Bollywood blockbusters. In 2010 the annual *Sports Illustrated* Power List named Sachin Tendulkar, one of the country's most respected cricketers, as the most influential person in Indian sports ("Sachin Named," 2010).

The game can be seen as slow moving and dull, however, by people in countries that do not share the enthusiasm of the few cricketing nations. The Indian Premier League was formed with the goal of changing these perceptions abroad and attracting a new and youthful fan base at home with a mixture of sportsmanship and entertainment. The Premier League version of the sport evolved into a 3-hour match play with a shortened format in 2008, and teams chose colorful names—for example, the Bangalore Royal Challengers and the Kolkata Knight Riders. Entertainment came in the form of the Washington Redskin cheerleaders. Of course, there was a stir across conservative, Hindu-dominated India where traditional women usually wear saris or *salwar kameezes,* which cover most of their bodies. Some TV pundits argued, however, that the dance sequences in Bollywood films, featuring scantily clad gyrating women, were far worse than the spectacle of the foreign cheerleaders in their go-go boots, yellow shorts, and bikini tops. Cricket purists also criticized the shortened format of the hallowed game, but by all accounts, the new formats resulted in a financial success for the promoters. Sony reportedly signed a US$1 billion deal for exclusive rights to film and photograph Indian Premier League games over the next 10 years (Wax, 2008).

Images of the Future

The dictionary has a technical definition of the kaleidoscope as a tube-shaped optical instrument that is rotated to produce a succession of symmetrical designs by means of mirrors reflecting the constantly changing patterns made by bits of colored glass at one end of the tube. It also describes a constantly changing set of colors or a series of changing phases or events. We have used the kaleidoscope as a metaphor to describe the diversity that is integral to India and the dynamic elements of its modern culture. It seems as if with every turn, one sees a pattern that is different, and one is never sure whether one will see the same configuration again.

On the one hand, the current economic boom is unprecedented in the country's history. On the other, crumbling infrastructure threatens to derail India's economic agenda. On the key access road to the famous electronics city in Bangalore (dubbed India's Silicon Valley), cars, motorcycles, taxis, rickshaws, dogs, and cows compete for space and create a traffic jam that even seasoned Los Angeles commuters would balk at. The same goes for Mumbai, where negotiating the roads can seem like a Darwinian challenge where only the fittest survive. Horns blare constantly and evoke the same response as car alarms in New York City; they are routinely ignored. Highways, airports, the power grid, and major bridges need to be upgraded before they crumble. Spending on major infrastructure such as ports, power plants, and highways is expected to top US$60 billion annually over the next few years, but there is a tremendous shortage of skilled labor. Major delays and cost overruns are plaguing almost half the projects that are underway (Bellman & Range, 2008).

Asia's largest slum is on the route from Mumbai airport to downtown with its fine hotels and gleaming corporate headquarters. Some experts have argued that India should imitate China, which launched a major infrastructure upgrade over a decade ago that is paying dividends today. In India it is commonly known that growth occurs *despite* the government, whereas in China growth occurs *because* of the government. China's leaders have built a world-class infrastructure, while in India the infrastructure and the gargantuan bureaucracy are woefully outdated (Yardley, 2011). In the 1960s, India had a higher per capita gross domestic product (GDP) than China. Today, at US$1,020, India's GDP is less than half of China's (US$3,270). Growth in modern India has taken place in a chaotic, often unplanned, entrepreneurial, noisy, democratic way despite the bureaucratic obstacles presented by the government. Jim O'Neill, the Goldman Sachs banker who coined the acronym BRIC to represent the emerging economies of Brazil, Russia, India, and China, recently singled out India as the most disappointing of this group in terms of attracting foreign investment, productivity, and the pace of reform ("Retail Volte Face," 2011).

Another threat is the growing Naxalite movement (Maoist insurgents who despise the landowning and business classes and seek to overthrow the state), which is operating on the periphery of some major industrial states. Prime Minister Singh has acknowledged that the Naxal groups are targeting all aspects of economic activity and that India "cannot rest in peace until we have eliminated this virus" (Kripalani, 2008). The rebels have a presence in more than 223 of the 624 districts in India, and more than 6,000 people have been killed in the decades-long fight. The Maoists are active in the country's poor, rural areas, and widespread violence in mineral-rich eastern districts has worried investors and disrupted mining and rail transport. In recent years, they have won support from lower-caste farm laborers displaced by government-backed mining operations and new industrial plants. In 2010 alone, 713 civilians and 285 police officers were killed in Maoist-related violence, which prompted the government to launch decisive strikes against them. This is an ongoing challenge to India's security.

However, as Edward Luce (2008) contends in his book *In Spite of the Gods: The Rise of Modern India*, although India's challenges may be Herculean, it also has colossal advantages. He goes on to describe how the Indian economy will benefit from a demographic dividend in the coming years, with the proportion of dependents to workers falling from 60% of the population to 50%. India also has built-in institutional advantages such an independent judiciary and a free media, and it has accomplished "a high growth rate without the tools of an autocratic state" (Luce, p. 352). After independence, many predicted that India's linguistic, religious, and social divisions would cause it to fall apart. This has not happened because India has had a stable democracy that capitalizes on its plurality and diversity. No one is certain what India will look like in the coming decades, but we are sure that the next time we take a turn at the kaleidoscope, we will see a different set of images of this colorful, vibrant, emerging Asian power of the 21st century.

PART X

Same Metaphor, Different Meanings

Sometimes seemingly the same cultural metaphor is interpreted in a radically different manner in different nations. For example, the symbols connected with the Spanish bullfight are radically different from those related to the Portuguese bullfight. In the Spanish bullfight the bull is killed, whereas it is only harnessed or stopped physically in the Portuguese bullfight. Thus we need to be sure that the metaphor we choose to study is one for which there is no ambiguity or confusion. However, one small area in Portugal now permits the killing of bulls, and we examine the reactions of various Portuguese citizens to this practice. How and why these two cultures and their respective cultural metaphors differ is the subject of this part.

CHAPTER 30

The Spanish Bullfight

The killing of the bull is either loved or hated. There is no middle way.

—"Manolo Chopera" (2002, p. 82)

It is a cultural component that comes from times that we no longer even remember. . . . It is something that is ours, something intrinsic. It is a world that once you enter, you like it more and more, and you want to be more a part of it.

—Victoria Caceres, 24, who has been attending bullfights regularly since childhood (quoted in Wilkinson, 2007b)

Yesterday's vote confirms a rising wave of opposition that could lead to a more widespread prohibition of the spectacle known in Spain as la fiesta nacional.

—Mulligan (2010a, p. 6)

As the reader can see from the contradictory information provided above, there are many passionate fans of bullfighting in Spain and simultaneously many who hate it. The last quote is particularly important, as the large region of Catalonia, which has its own regional parliament independent of the Spanish Parliament because of the regional decentralization practiced in Spain, outlawed bullfighting in 2010. Only the Canary Islands, also a part of Spain, had done so earlier.

There are several reasons why the aversion to bullfighting has increased significantly in recent years, even while aficionados of the ritual watch bullfighting intensely and treat it as similar to a religious experience or religious ritual. Among these reasons, cruel treatment of animals is important. Today in Spain there is also more interest in football or soccer and other forms of sports and entertainment than in bullfighting. And, as in the case of Catalonia, opposition to bullfighting represents a political statement. Because Catalonia and a few other regions of Spain want their independence so that they can be autonomous states, they attack that which is considered to be most representative of Spain and the Spanish, namely bullfighting. However, Spain's constitutional court has ruled, somewhat paradoxically, that the decentralized regions such as Catalonia represent nationalities but only one nation, Spain.

Bullfighting was introduced by the Moors, who were of the Muslim faith, from West Africa in the 13th century when they ruled the southern part of Spain, although bullfighting has its origins in ancient societies. They emphasized the killing of the bull during a bullfight that was a quasi-religious ritual and a highlight of festivals, and Spaniards of all varieties responded enthusiastically for the reasons detailed in this chapter. For over 300 years, until the 1960s, the Spanish regarded the bullfight as quintessentially Spanish in terms of values and practices. Non-Spanish commentators such as Ernest Hemingway, whose gripping description of the death of a noted Spanish bullfighter in *Death in the Afternoon* is considered a classic work of literature, were no less enthralled. Only in recent decades has bullfighting been questioned in Spain and elsewhere.

As suggested above, one of the main reasons many Spaniards have unquestionably loved the bullfight for centuries is that it succinctly expresses Spanish values more clearly than any other potential cultural metaphor for Spain. The first characteristic expressive of Spanish values is a contagious vitality, a love of life. Therefore it may seem paradoxical that the metaphor used in this chapter to describe Spanish culture is the bullfight, a confrontation with death. Yet this feature touches on other, less obvious qualities pervasive among Spaniards: Underlying their outer joy, or *alegría*, Spaniards tend to host a deeply ingrained sensitivity to the tragic and an equally strong emotional pull toward the heroic. Perhaps these characteristics, more than their love of life, have made the bullfight *la fiesta nacional* for hundreds of years; in combination these characteristics are manifested in a unique form of individualism emphasizing self-reliance and pride. The bullfight combines a passionate celebration of life with an elaborate system of rituals—a grandiose and artistic spectacle with blood, violence, and an all-too-real danger to the valiant performers. It exemplifies Spanish pride, individualism, emotionalism, and many other characteristics of Spanish people and culture.

As might be expected, flamenco and the bullfight are closely intertwined, and both activities highlight the proud and self-sufficient flavor of individualism unique to Spain. Whatever Spaniards do, they want it to be a personal expression of individuality. For example, in Germany a symphony may advertise that its program will be the same on both Friday and Saturday night, and there will be few if any differences between the performances. This is not true in Spain, for each bullfight and each flamenco dance is or should be unique.

However, as already noted, many Spaniards are not enthusiastic about bullfighting and regard the killing of the bull as barbaric. The European Union (EU) formally requested that Spain abolish bullfighting, and it stopped subsidizing Spanish farms that raise bulls for this purpose. The state-run Spanish television broadcaster, which started live coverage of bullfighting in 1948, stopped in 2007 during prime time because of the alleged barbarism; it now shows only delayed coverage late at night. Still, regional state channels and pay TV do provide live coverage. Although attendance has been declining, over 60 million Spaniards still attend bullfights each year, many of them more than once. In addition, periodically a particularly brave bullfighter or matador who takes great risks and demonstrates unusual skills captivates the public, as in the case of both Jose Tomas (Wilkinson, 2007b) and Sebastian Castella (K. Johnson, 2006), and attendance and coverage markedly increase.

The ritual of the classic bullfight, too, seems to be losing some of its appeal in contemporary Spanish society because of the popularity of soccer matches and other forms of Sunday afternoon entertainment. In more than half of Spain, bullfighting barely exists. To stem this decline, some matadors have turned the bullfight into stunts. Jesulin de Ubrique, for example, has performed on television in front of live all-female crowds numbering in the thousands, and audience members often throw bras and other accessories into the ring. Traditionalists regard such displays as vulgar. Although bullfighting employs about 200,000 Spaniards or 1% of the labor force, financial rewards tend to flow disproportionately to a small number of matadors (about 170).

It is critical that these matadors are trained from childhood onward, as they face incredible danger when a bull weighing a few tons charges them in the ring. They must pierce a precise spot on the head of the bull for the crowd to recognize them as heroic. A few of the bravest matadors will develop special moves such as going down on one knee when the bull charges. The great 20th century matador, Manolite, actually placed the cape and small sword behind his back and moved only the upper part of his body when the bull charged. He died in the ring, as have countless other matadors. Even when they escape death, they typically experience major wounds during their careers.

Furthermore, of more than 300 bullrings in Spain, fewer than 10 are deemed first-class. The newer forms of bullfighting, including the use of female matadors, have helped to increase bullfighting's popularity in specific segments of the population. However, the traditional Spanish form of bullfighting is a serious ritual involving a high probability of injury to the matador. It is a ritual of death, and there is always the possibility that the death will be that of the matador, not the bull. About 20,000 bullfights take place annually in Spain.

It is important to stress that even soccer does not capture the essence of Spanish culture in the way that the bullfight does, probably because soccer is too universal a sport. Although soccer draws excited crowds, just as the bullfight does, soccer fans have no role in the game comparable to audience in the bullfight, which judges the matador. Further, whereas soccer players form highly cooperative teams, bullfighters' groups are much looser. The latter more accurately reflect Spanish collective behavior.

Finally, in contrast to the fact that the bullfight is an elaborate ritual, soccer is a sport, albeit a popular one. Therefore, there is little chance that soccer will ever completely replace the bullfight in Spanish culture.

The following discussion will relate different aspects of Spain's culture to the many facets of the bullfight. But first, the sequence of the event itself is provided to establish the language and imagery of the bullfight.

The Bullfight Begins

The bullfight, or *corrida de toros,* meaning "running of the bulls" (also, *la corrida* or *los toros* for short), takes place on Sunday afternoons or on holidays, timed precisely against the setting of the sun. The *corrida* begins with a white handkerchief signal by the officiating president and the sounding of a trumpet. The commencement of the bullfight is celebrated with the colorful opening *paseillo* or parade of participants, who march in hierarchical order to the upbeat tune of the *paso doble.* Once the parade is over, the president again uses his white handkerchief to signal the entrance of the first bull, as he does to signal the beginning of each stage of the event.

There are three separate groups (*cuadrillas*) of principal participants in the *corrida.* Each group is made up of a matador and his assistants. The *cuadrillas* fight and kill two bulls each, for a total of six bullfights during the event. When the first bull is released into the ring, it is confronted by three of the matador's assistants, the *banderilleros.* The *banderilleros* maneuver the bull with their magenta and gold capes, revealing to the matador the bull's peculiarities of movement; sometimes the matador participates in this stage as well.

A few minutes later, the matador enters the ring and demonstrates his bravery with his more artistic cape passes, including the classic *verónica.* The matador's valor or lack thereof often evokes emotional responses among the spectators. They applaud, cheer, and shout "*Olé!*" when impressed by the matador's bravery, or they boo and whistle when they are displeased. In this way the public interacts with the matador, prompting him to perform more and more dangerous and aesthetically beautiful moves. These in turn further arouse the audience.

After the initial demonstrations with the bull, the two *picadores* enter the ring on horseback. One stands by as a reserve, while the other provokes the bull into charging his own horse. This allows him to get close enough to the bull to jab it with his long, spiked pole. The *picador*'s task is to weaken the bull enough to decrease his speed, thus allowing the bullfighter to show his abilities.

Moving Toward the Kill

The second stage of the bullfight allows the bull to perk up from its difficult ordeal with the picador. In this more exciting part of the fight, the *banderilleros,* on foot, each place two *banderillas* (colorfully decorated wooden sticks with barbed tips) into the bull's neck, where they should remain. At this point the bull is rested and more ferocious than ever and is ready to challenge the matador in the final stage of the fight.

In the last phase, the matador has 15 minutes to display his skill and build up the drama of the "moment of truth," performing dangerous passes with the much smaller red cape (*muleta*), which is draped over his sword. Before beginning, he salutes the president and asks permission to kill the bull if it is his first bull of the afternoon, and he may dedicate the kill to a friend, a dignitary, or the public. Once the kill is complete, the response of members of the audience determines to a large extent the level of the reward the matador is to receive. Ultimately the president decides on the level of the reward. A brave bull, too, is applauded as it is dragged out of the arena.

The same three stages are repeated for each of the five remaining bulls in the *corrida,* alternating *cuadrillas* with each new bull. The bullfight officially ends when the president leaves his seat.

The bullfight has long been a popular feature of Spanish culture. Its appearance in Spain has been attributed to a number of possible sources, including festivities of the ancient Minoan culture on the island of Crete 2,000 years BCE, Roman circus combats, and the Moors. Whichever explanation may be true, the roots of the Spanish bullfight lay buried under layers of different peoples who invaded the Iberian Peninsula (now Spain and Portugal), bringing their respective cultures with them. As indicated previously, the Moors popularized the traditional Spanish bullfight as a ritual of death during festivals.

The same waves of invasion that somewhere along the way gave birth to the bullfight also bred the uniquely Spanish people. People have inhabited what is now Spain for more than 100,000 years. Traces of the peninsula's prehistoric inhabitants include the famous cave paintings of Altamira, which are at least 13,000 years old. Recorded history picks up with the migration of the Iberian people from northern Africa into the southern two thirds of the peninsula around 3000 BCE. A series of other peoples subsequently came to Spain to conquer, trade, or settle there. Phoenicians (a Semitic race) came first, followed by Celts (a Nordic race), Greeks, Carthaginians (from Carthage in northern Africa), Romans, Jews, Germanic tribes, and Moors. Romanies (Gypsies) are the most recent racial group to have taken their place in Spanish society, arriving from Egypt in the Middle Ages.

The bullfight has several features that clearly reflect what makes it, and metaphorically Spain, different from the cultures of other nations. These include *cuadrillas, sol y sombra,* the pompous entrance parade, audience involvement, and the ritual of the bullfight. Each feature is treated below.

Cuadrillas

The successive waves of invasion and immigration that came to the Spanish peninsula can be likened to the repeated attacks of the fighting bull and, even more appropriately, to the series of six bulls that are released into the ring during the course of the event. In terms of this metaphor, foreign invasions were so common throughout Spain's early history that it would take two consecutive *corridas* for the defending *toreros* to experience as many attacking bulls as there were invading peoples.

A Varied People

The physical characteristics resulting from the coming together of these various groups on the Iberian Peninsula are short, dark, Semitic types (predominant in the south) and taller, fair descendents of Celtic and Germanic ancestors (most common in the north). Combinations of these traits are also frequently seen, such as in the large number of people with dark hair and blue eyes. Another prevalent trait among Spaniards is the classic Roman nose. In sum, no single image would accurately portray a "typical" Spaniard, although certain combinations of features are notably Spanish, especially if one looks separately at the different regions of Spain.

In addition, certain personality traits cross tribal boundaries. Wheaton (1990) reports, "The Greek philosopher Stabo found common traits among all the isolated bands living on the peninsula: hospitality, grand manners, arrogance; indifference to privation, and hatred of outside interference in community affairs" (p. 21). These characteristics are still frequently used to describe the Spanish temperament.

The various invading peoples are also responsible for importing a number of prominent cultural attributes into Spain. The Romans (who ruled Spain for 400 years beginning around 200 BCE) brought their "vulgar Latin" language with them, which was to evolve into today's Castilian Spanish. The Spanish word for Spain, *España,* is a slightly modified version of the Latin name *Hispania,* which the Romans gave to the country (Spain had previously been called Iberia by its Iberian inhabitants and Hesperia by the Greeks). The Romans also constructed aqueducts, bridges, roads, and walls. The famous two-level aqueduct of Segovia stands as an impressive relic of the Roman rule. Finally, the Romans were responsible for the spread of Christianity into Spain.

Attributable to the more than 700-year presence of the Muslim Arabs, or Moors, are more than 4,000 words used in modern Spanish. Words for many agricultural products the Moors brought with them derive from this source, such as the Spanish word *arroz* from the Arabic *al ruzz* (rice), *aceite* from *al zait* (olive oil), and *naranja* from *naranj* (orange), foods now an integral part of the Spanish diet (Graham, 1984), as well as many words beginning with the letters *al.* The Arabic influence in Spain is also responsible for advances in the fields of irrigation, mathematics, medicine, and, most notably, architecture among others. The light, airy, and colorful *mezquita* or mosque in Córdoba and the impressive palaces, the Alhambra and the Generalife, in Granada are present-day monuments of Moorish architectural feats.

The *cuadrillas* in the bullfight clearly show Spaniards' attitude toward teams and collectivism. In a country with strong individualism but a shared need for defense, association with others is sometimes necessary. *Cuadrilla,* translated, does not mean "team"; the men in the *cuadrilla* do not work closely together. Rather, *cuadrilla* means "group, bank, or gang," reflecting the fact that there is safety in numbers and the toreros combine their distinct, individual efforts to achieve the death of the bull.

Spanish history is full of heroic events when strong and proud individuals gathered to achieve a common temporary and difficult goal. For example, the French under Napoleon lost as many soldiers to Spanish guerillas as during the infamous invasion of and retreat from Russia. Napoleon called these fighters the "Spanish cancer" that slowly ate away his army's determination. In fact, the term *guerrilla warfare* was first used to describe the seemingly unorganized but systematic attacks that the Spanish used to defeat Napoleon. Ironically, Napoleon's army easily defeated the regular Spanish army.

Repeated invasions of the Iberian Peninsula encouraged the inhabitants to cluster together for a sense of security. This effect, and a lack of abundant water, is reflected in the fact that Spanish peasants on the steppes of central Spain chose to build their houses near one another, forming many small hamlets, villages, and towns. Their fear of loneliness and desire for security were so strong that they were, and still are, willing to travel great distances to work their fields just so that they may live near others (Crow, 1985).

Honoring the Collective

The tendency for Spaniards to live close together has generalized to urban housing arrangements, which take the form of apartments rather than isolated homes. In Spain, as in much of Europe, it is desirable to live as close as possible to the center of the city, where the action is. Marvin (1988) writes, "It is felt that as one moves further from the centre, so the quality of life gradually diminishes, because at the far limits of the town there are few bars, shops and *plazas* [squares] where people gather" (p. 129). Compare this, for example, to housing patterns in the United States. The middle-class American's ideal house is in the suburbs and has a large yard, or for the wealthy, it is a mansion with many acres of land. In Spain, the wealthiest citizens make their urban apartments their permanent dwellings. They may, however, enjoy a country home as a secondary weekend getaway. Describing this logic, Marvin writes:

> Nowhere is this subordination and "culturizing" of nature, in Andalusian terms, more dramatically demonstrated than in the *corrida*. It is an urban event intimately linked with the country, which brings together, in the centre of human habitation, an uncontrolled wild bull, an item from the realm of nature, and a man who represents the epitome of culture in that, more than any ordinary man, he is able to exercise control over his "natural" fear (the fear felt by the human animal), an essential prerequisite if he is to control the wild animal. . . . The *corrida* is constructed in such a way that the imposition of human will is extremely uncertain because of the difficult circumstances; a situation which in turn generates tension, emotion, and dramatic interest. (pp. 130–131)

However, Spaniards' true loyalty does not extend to the larger collective; it is generally directed toward a smaller unit: family, friends, town, or region. Like the *cuadrilla,* the family is a large and affectionate clan whose members ferociously defend each other's honor, rights, jobs, and so on. The worst insult one can give a man is to derogate his mother, and the worst thing one can say to a woman is to insult her child (Wheaton, 1990). The protective spirit of the family also extends to the upbringing of children. Parents dress their children well and pamper them. They bring them along wherever they go and allow them to stay up until all hours of the night. This produces children who are good-natured and outgoing and who have a strong sense of self and of their own importance (Wheaton).

The backbone of the tribal system during Spain's history of warfare was the women. Tough and resourceful, they held the group together and catered to the needs of family members (Crow, 1985). However, historically the woman's role is more nurturing than authoritative. Thus, it is the husband, not the wife, whose role can be compared to that of the matador, as the person who has the last word. Like the matador who adoringly dedicates the kill to his wife or sweetheart, the Spanish husband accords his wife her due respect as the heart of the family; he thinks of her as if she were a saint. And he expects her to behave like one. Until recently, the laws supported this expectation. However, there have been many social changes in recent years, as discussed later in this chapter.

General Franco's 36-year dictatorship, from the Spanish Civil War until his death in 1975, led to more regressive policies for women than in any other European country. A wife had to have her husband's written permission to do many things outside the home, such as opening a bank account, obtaining a passport, or traveling abroad. Civil divorce was illegal until 1981. Abortion, homosexuality, and adultery, too, were punishable by law. Extramarital affairs were considered unconditionally criminal for women; men were at fault only if they tainted the family's honor by failing to keep their affairs clandestine (Wheaton, 1990). The macho Don Juanism is so ingrained in Spanish culture that it was considered perfectly acceptable for a husband to keep a mistress on the side. However, although the famous, nonfictional Don Juan conquered numerous women's hearts, he usually pursued them circumspectly to keep their reputations and status intact.

All this has been rapidly changing in the past 30 years. Now, several hundred thousand mothers are unmarried, and the use of contraceptives among married women is widespread. Kissing and embracing in public are common. University attendance is split equally between the sexes. However, few women in Spanish society attain high-level jobs, and Spanish heritage is, of course, still patrilineal. Children go by both their father's and mother's last names. In addition, when a woman gets married, she keeps her name but adds her husband's name to her own, linking the two by the possessive word *de* or "of." For example, if a woman named Maria Alberti married a man named Miguel Sanchez, her name would officially become Maria Alberti de Sanchez. If her husband then died, she would become Maria Alberti Viuda de Sanchez—literally, Maria Alberti Widow of Sanchez.

The family is only one place where the Spanish tend to cluster into loose groups like the *cuadrilla*. Historically, when the people of Spain started grouping together, they did not unite under a national flag; the geographical boundaries that sliced up the country topographically and climatically also kept invaders and inhabitants within isolated regions of the peninsula. Foreign influences and native loyalties were therefore determined by region, resulting in vastly differing cultures and distinct personal appearances. Four languages and many dialects are spoken in Spain: Castilian, known outside of Spain as Spanish, Catalonian, Galician, and Basque. Despite the similarities, the cultural differences between these regions remain significant.

The greatest geographical barriers in Spain are its mountain ranges. Although foreigners normally think of Spain's sunny beaches and flat, coastal plains, it is actually one of the most mountainous countries in Europe, second only to Switzerland. Also, Spain is a large nation and has a population of 44.6 million. Although urban Spaniards live close to one another, the population density is only 88.3 per kilometer; compare this to 230.5 for Germany. Therefore distance separates people and allows for great variation in culture and landscapes.

Sol y Sombra

Seating at the bullfight is divided into three sections: sun (*sol*), shade (*sombra*), and a combination of sun and shade (*sol y sombra*). Tickets for seats in the shade are the most expensive. They cost about double the price of seats in the sun, which are the cheapest. Because bullfight tickets are relatively expensive to begin with, the price differential in seating separates the members of the audience into wealthier and poorer groups.

With a few exceptions, Spain itself can be divided into the relatively cool, wet, more prosperous north and the hot, dry southern regions. Spain also has a large, central plateau area (the *meseta*, or tableland), which undergoes extremes of both heat and cold and poverty and wealth, making it comparable to the *sol y sombra* sections. A more detailed description of some of the better-known Spanish regions will illustrate the depth of regional differences in geography, climate, people, and culture.

There are 17 regional states in Spain, and in recent years there has been a devolution of power from the national government to them. As the *Economist* points out ("Spanish Centrifuge," 2007), this devolution of power has not yet resulted in the loose federation found in Belgium and elsewhere where the federal government is responsible for only a few functions such as national defense, but there is a definite movement in this direction. Catalonia's banning of the bullfight is an example of such loosening. Given their unique languages and cultures, the Basque provinces and Catalonia are of particular interest in the debate about devolution, as noted below.

In the northwestern corner of Spain just above Portugal lies Galicia. Its frequent rain and drizzle, lush vegetation, and wide *rías* (fjords) simulate the landscape of the natives' Nordic ancestors who settled in the region. The Gallegans also share the fair skin, light eyes, and bagpipe music of their Celtic cousins, the Scots. Working as fisher-men, shepherds, and farmers, the people in rural areas of Galicia speak their own language, a mixture of Portuguese and Castilian Spanish.

Moving eastward along the northern coast of Spain, one eventually encounters the Basque provinces. The region is one of Spain's most prosperous. Bilbao, the nation's industrial capital, is situated on the Basque coastline. The Basque countryside is adorned with beautiful Alpine vistas of rolling hills and Swiss-style farmhouses and is home to the hard-working, rugged descendants of the Iberian Peninsula's earliest settlers, the Iberians. The Basque language, Euskara, bears no demonstrable relation to any other known language. It is thought to date back to the prehistoric Bronze Age. The Basques have one of the strongest separatist movements of all the Spanish regions. Their notorious radical, separatist organization, the ETA (an acronym for Basque Nation and Liberty), is responsible for widespread terrorist activities against the Spanish Civil Guard, Spanish civilians, and the Basque Autonomous Police. However, there is only limited support for this activity, and in recent years the ETA's power has decreased significantly.

In Spain's northeastern corner, sandwiched between the Pyrenees Mountains and the Mediterranean Sea, is the other region that harbors resentment against the control of Madrid. Supported primarily by its large textile and tourist industries, Catalonia shares the prosperity of the Basque region. Its culture is more European than that of the rest of Spain. The Catalan language is highly related to the southern French Provençal and is taught in school and spoken by most Catalans. Barcelona, the capital of Catalonia, rivals Madrid in population and is playing an increasingly central role in European life and international affairs. Catalans, often characterized by their "canny common sense," or *seny*, also demonstrate an artistic streak. The region has produced a number of Spain's master artists, such as Salvador Dalí and Joan Miró, as well as architect Antoni Gaudí, and it contributed to the artistic development of Pablo Picasso, who was born in southern Spain. In recent years the movement to become a separate nation has accelerated in Catalonia, and the federal government has granted many of its institutions independence or great latitude; for example, classes in schools are taught in Catalan, not Spanish.

In the center of Spain, on its sparsely populated plateau or *meseta* at an altitude of 2,000 to 3,000 feet, lies Castile, which exerts a dominant influence on Spanish cul-ture. It is the birthplace of Spain's official national language, known outside of Spain as Spanish and within it as Castilian. Castile is politically dominant, too, and the federal government resides in Spain's capital, Madrid. The landscape of this region consists of vast expanses of arid steppes on which 10,000 castles were built during the battles of the Middle Ages (hence the name *Castilla*). The dryness of the Castilian air allows for extremes of temperature, making the region akin to the *sol y sombra* seating at the bullfight. A Spanish proverb says, *Nueve meses de invierno y tres de infierno* (Nine months of winter and three of hell), and it accurately describes the

Castilian climate. In Madrid, for example, even on the most treacherously hot days of August, the temperature can be deliciously cool in the shade, and one quite often needs a sweater in the evening.

Finally, Andalusia, in southern Spain, is home of the bullfight, the Romany, and stereotypically dark Spaniards. The climate is relentlessly hot and dry. The peasants' parched faces mirror the parched face of the land, which teaches the Andalusians how cruel yet beautiful life can be (Wheaton, 1990). Strongly influenced by the long Moorish presence in Andalusia, the natives express their intense feelings of joy and tragedy through flamenco dancing and the lamenting "deep song," the *cante jondo*. Andalusia's scattered towns of whitewashed houses and red-tiled roofs reveal its Mediterranean essence. The majority of Andalusian land, however, belongs to a small number of large estates where acres and acres of irrigated, rolling hills and valleys are used to cultivate olives and other agricultural products.

The above descriptions only hint at the variety of Spain's regions and at the harshness of life in the heat of the Spanish sun. Although Spain lies roughly between the same parallels as Cape Cod, Massachusetts, and Cape Hatteras, North Carolina, in the United States, and Madrid is at the same latitude as New York City, the mountains around Spain's periphery keep the Atlantic and Mediterranean moisture out. The central plateau bakes like an oven. The resulting austere living conditions throughout much of Spain are what engendered that underlying Spanish sense of sadness and tragedy, which seems to relate more closely to the Spanish love of the bullfight than does the Spaniards' outward gaiety. It is perhaps for this reason that Spaniards don't smile quietly and peacefully but laugh loudly and cry deeply in a land of extreme change and passion.

The Pompous Entrance Parade

A more joyful side of Spanish culture is represented by the *paseillo* at the beginning of the bullfight. The *corrida* opens with the proud march of all those individuals who appear in the arena during the course of the afternoon accompanied by the sound of the happy *paso doble* music. Lavishly costumed, everyone from the matador to the *areneros,* who tidy up the sand, struts into the ring in descending hierarchical order according to the importance of the participant's role. Every last one proudly shows himself off to the public eye. The aristocratic opening stems from the bullfight's aristocratic past; until the late 1600s, only noblemen (*hidalgos*) fought bulls to prove their manhood to their ladies, peers, and underlings (Crow, 1985).

The values permeating both the *paseillo* and Spanish culture are honor, dignity, and pride, as well as a contempt for manual labor. These aristocratic values seeped into Spanish culture during its centuries of battles and heroism. The swelling of the noble class in Spain at this time was so great that it has been estimated that about 50% of the Spanish population has some claim to a title (Wheaton, 1990). Together, these values make up the most important overriding Spanish characteristic—its unique type of individualism. Analogously, the pompous entrance parade highlights the individualistic, proud, and fun-loving aspects of Spanish culture. Crow (1985) eloquently describes this aspect of the Spanish mind-set:

> The Spaniard, thus, does not feel that he is born to realize any social end, but that he is born primarily to realize himself. His sense of personal dignity is admirable at times, exasperating at others; selfhood is the center of his gravity. His individual person has a value that is sacred and irreplaceable. In the universe he may be nothing, but to himself he is everything. (p. 11)

Proud Spanish individualism influences Spanish culture in a number of ways. It helps to explain the Spanish people's lack of effective collective efforts. In fact, the anarchist movement was particularly popular in Spain at the turn of the 19th century, as we might expect in a nation valuing proud and self-sufficient individualism so highly. Because Spaniards refuse to subordinate their personal beliefs to a collective goal, and because everyone has to have a say in everything, there is a tendency for nothing ever to get done. Many Spaniards who can afford it opt to hire a *gestor*, a person who will wait in the necessary lines and wade through the bureaucracy in their place (Wheaton, 1990). Crow (1985) observes:

> Spanish individualism is still anarchic and inorganic. The race is not cohesive except when it is unified "against someone or something." If Spaniards could only work as hard for as they do against things, their country would be one of the most dynamic and most progressive in Western Europe, perhaps in the world. (p. 361)

Since 1975, due to globalization and the greater legal freedoms afforded to Spaniards, this type of individualism has seemed to be changing. Still, Spain's proud and self-sufficient individualism is in marked contrast to U.S. competitive individualism, Danish interdependent individualism, and the other specific types of individualism and collectivism described in this book.

On top of their difficulties in cooperating, Spaniards have had trouble being productive because their culture does not teach them to view work in the same positive light in which U.S. Americans see it. Work is seen as a means to an end—survival—not an end in itself. For example, while U.S. teenagers are often encouraged or forced by their parents to take summer jobs or part-time jobs during the school year, even if the parents could easily support them, in Spain families prefer to give their children educational and cultural experiences, such as sending them to France or England for the summer. The independence gained through work experience is not considered as important. In fact, one Spanish king in the 18th century issued a royal document telling his people that work is indeed honorable.

Further complicating the situation, jobs in some parts of Spain are often difficult to obtain and not very lucrative. As a result, Spaniards may be extremely hardworking when necessary to make ends meet (moonlighting is common in Spain), but in many regions the economic constraints on getting ahead curb their ambition. The Spanish word for business reveals the culture's disdain for commercial and administrative activities. The term used is *negocio,* translated as "the negation of leisure" (Graham, 1984).

Many Spaniards do not mind if they accomplish little because they value self-expression more than material success. This is why the Spaniard has to be neither a Picasso nor a successful businessperson to be self-satisfied; recall that even participants in the mundane aspects of the bullfight parade proudly around the ring. Crow (1985) quotes an Englishman he met in Spain as having said, "In this country every blessed beggar acts like a king!" (p. 362). Rather than through material goods, Spanish individuals tend to be content to express their self-sufficiency through "wit, grandiloquent phrases, appearances, courtesy, generosity, and pride" (Wheaton, 1990, p. 68). Extremely articulate and enjoying the sound of their own voices, Spaniards will often spend hours conversing in the street cafes or bars where they meet. The odd result of this manifestation of Spanish individualism is that "often the most arrogant person in a group is the most charming" (Wheaton, p. 68).

However, globalization has influenced these patterns of behavior in many ways. For example, many businesspeople have stopped taking a long midday siesta, a practice originally motivated in large part by the heat of the day. Because workplaces are typically air-conditioned now, many managers and workers prefer a regular 9-to-5 workday rather than one ending at 8:00 PM or later so that they can spend more time at home (Woolls, 2005). Although Spain, along with other EU nations such as Greece and Ireland, is experiencing high unemployment and weak economic conditions, it still ranks relatively high on the Index of Economic Freedom (T. Miller, 2011): 31st out of 179 nations.

Like the bullfighters with their elaborate costumes, Spaniards tend to spend a large chunk of their monthly salary on fashionable clothes to enhance the effect of their performance. The expense is not wasted, however, because they spend much of their time under the scrutiny of the public eye. They tend to get together in public places rather than in their homes, partly because of cramped living spaces.

The proud marchers of the *paseillo* adhere to a rigid hierarchical order as they file around the ring. Spaniards readily accept a certain amount of inequality in the power structure of their society. But in Hofstede's (2001) study of 53 countries' cultural values, Spain actually clustered with those nations deemphasizing power distance, ranking 31st of 53. Similarly it ranked 20th out of 53 nations on individualism. These are predictable results, given the balance that Spaniards seek between hierarchical order and individualistic expression, and they support the idea that a proud but self-sufficient individualism is found in Spain.

Finally, the pride and acceptance Spaniards feel about everyday life have contributed to the realism portrayed in Spanish art. Wheaton (1990) writes, "An invitation to contemplation, careful observation of life as it is, and directness of expression are qualities that come to mind when one asks what it is that has remained consistently 'Spanish' about Spanish art" (p. 290). From ordinary scenes like a shepherd feeding his dog to images of Christ with streams of blood pouring from beneath his crown of thorns and Picasso's horrifying cubist depiction of the bombing of Guernica, Spanish artists concerned themselves with documenting the world around them as each artist would uniquely see it. The same tradition has allowed Spaniards over the years to face violence and death with dignity.

Audience Involvement

The excited cheers and shouts of "*Olé!*" as the bull's horns whisk past the matador's gracefully leaning body highlight the strong Spanish emotionalism. The shouts and cheers are a form of self-expression and of audience participation, affecting the matador's behavior and motivating his performance. Furthermore, once the matador makes his kill, the public displays its judgment of his performance. The audience's judgmental response in turn indicates the appropriate salute for the matador to make. If the members of the audience are displeased, they boo and whistle, and the matador does not reenter the ring. If they are pleased, they cheer, and the matador will step back into the ring to acknowledge the applause. If the positive public response is prolonged, the matador will take a lap of honor around the ring with his *banderilleros*. If the matador's performance was very good, the members of the public wave handkerchiefs to request that he be honored with an ear of the bull. The president must comply if most people in the audience wave their handkerchiefs. It is then up to the president to decide whether or not to award two ears for an exceptional performance or, in rare cases, even the tail. After any of these rewards, the matador takes a lap of honor around the ring, during which the audience throws objects (wineskins, hats, articles of clothing, and so on) to the matador, which are then thrown back, much in the way that other stars give autographs. Other objects, such as flowers and cigars, are meant as gifts to the matador.

Likewise, the emotional nature of Spanish expression is not only a one-sided outpouring but also an interactive form of communication. Therefore, while Spaniards' emotionalism might on the one hand reflect their proud individualism, on the other hand its participative and empathetic qualities transcend this notion. They convey the Spanish culture's emphasis on relationships, generosity, hospitality, and recognition of social needs.

These attributes relate to the social behavior introduced in the previous section. The Spaniards' gregarious and fun-loving nature is magnified by their uninhibited emotionalism. Spanish men are not too shy to compliment women, whether acquaintances or strangers. There is even a special name for these pleasant remarks—*piropos*. Spaniards are not afraid, either, to allow the conversation to move onto a personal level, which helps avoid the small talk of the U.S. cocktail party and shoptalk between business acquaintances. Thus Spaniards come across as genuine, interesting individuals rather than as superficial socialites or narrow-minded career people.

In allowing themselves to act on their emotions, Spaniards are generous and hospitable. Just as they enthusiastically wave their handkerchiefs in the air if they are moved by a matador's performance so that he may be rewarded with a trophy from the bull, the Spaniards are moved by their relationships with other people to give them whatever they can. This takes the form of sharing food, cigarettes, or general kindness, which contributes to an upbeat social atmosphere.

Spanish social life, for example, is often accompanied by the communal enjoyment of food and drink. Spanish bars serve a wide variety of appetizer-sized portions of food called *tapas,* which groups of friends order to share. Overall, the loud talking, odor of food, and joviality generated by beer and wine create a sense of vitality and life that intensify the emotional nature and gaiety of Spanish social interactions, much like the interactive involvement of an excited audience with a bullfighter.

Spaniards also share their day-to-day lives outside of social gatherings. If a Spaniard brings a package of food to eat on the train, the first thing he or she does after opening the packet is to offer its contents to everyone nearby. Travelers in Spain should not feel reluctant to accept a cookie or a piece of sausage (chorizo) in such a situation and should avoid hoarding their own food.

Spanish hospitality is primarily an outgrowth of the Arabic culture. Phrases and customs expressing courtesy, such as *esta es su casa* (this is your home) and *buen provecho* (enjoy your meal), are traces of Moorish influence (Wheaton, 1990). Spanish hospitality is not to be mistaken, however, for the U.S. custom of inviting virtual strangers into one's home. In Spain (as in other Latin countries), one can know people for years without being invited into their home for a meal; if a dinner invitation is issued, the meal is much more likely to take place in a restaurant.

In addition, like the Arabs, Spaniards are generally relationship oriented. So, as with their propensity toward sharing things, Spaniards' concept of time focuses on interpersonal interactions. Thus, for example, completing the natural cycle of a conversation or other human interaction is often more important to the Spaniards than punctuality. In Hall and Hall's (1990) terms, Spaniards have a polychronic orientation toward time, doing several activities simultaneously while being highly involved in interactions.

Spanish emotionalism and generosity are also related to Spain's national social policies. A strong social security program, almost totally subsidized universities, and a mandatory month's paid vacation for all workers reflect Spaniards' responsiveness to people's needs. As noted previously, however, Spain is currently experiencing a high level of unemployment (about 20%) and a weakening of its financial system, and these developments have put a heavy strain on the social security program. Still, Spain is less materialistic and aggressive than many other nations, such as Japan and the United States: In Hofstede's study (2001) of 53 nations, Spain clustered with those nations that were more feminine, as we would expect.

The Ritual of the Bullfight

The logical outcome of all the overarching features of Spanish culture described above—regionalism, a sense of tragedy, proud individualism, and emotional interaction—is an attraction to the ritual, which provides an arena for all of these characteristics. The ultimate ritual in Spanish society is the bullfight. From its ritualistic handkerchief signals to its precisely regulated sequence and strictly defined roles of the matador, *banderilleros,* and *picadores,* and from the official role of the president to the sacrifice of the wild bull in the moment of truth, the *corrida* is permeated with rituals. Rituals define the bullfight; they make it what it is. Foreigners who mistake it for some sort of cruel sport often miss this point. It is not a sport. The ritual is a way of combining festivity with solemnity and life with death. These are some of the features that draw Spaniards to the bullfight, and these are the same features that draw Spaniards to a more encompassing ritual in Spanish society: religion.

Christianity entered Spain during Roman rule in the first century CE. Although the Romans resisted it, Spaniards took up Christianity with an unparalleled fervor. The tales of torture, martyrdom, and sainthood of the early Spanish Christians appealed highly to their sense of tragedy; the Spaniards' many hardships made them appreciate ascetic Catholic values. At certain times in history the Spanish zeal for Christianity ran to excess, to the detriment (and death) of many. In particular, at the end of the 15th century under the reign of the Catholic monarchs Ferdinand and Isabella, religion sowed the seeds for the persecution and expulsion of hundreds of thousands of Jews under the auspices of the Holy Inquisition. At the same time, a large missionary effort was launched to convert the "heathen" native peoples of the recently discovered New World. Whole cultures were consequently disrupted.

In addition to its fervor, Spanish Catholicism differed from that of other Catholic countries in that Spanish people preserved their pagan traditions right alongside their new Christian beliefs. Therefore, to the Spaniard, God is not an intangible, elusive concept but instead an almost human, concrete presence. The Spaniard's relationship with God is thus a personal one. Spaniards see God as patient and forgiving of human weaknesses and are not afraid to have conversations with him, asking for personal favors.

The personal aspect of Spanish religion was enhanced by the Moors as well as by Spain's pagan past. The Moors, too, enjoyed an all-encompassing relationship with God (Allah) and left evidence of this fact in the Spanish language. The expression *si Dios quiere* (if God wills it) is widely used, as is the phrase *ojalá,* meaning "I hope so," derived from the Arabic *wa shá' allah* (may God will it; Wheaton, 1990).

However, Spanish people do not always deal directly with God. Because they like religion to have a personal flavor, it is at least as common for Spaniards to pray to the Virgin Mary and the saints. Thus one often finds small candles lit in front of images of these icons in churches, with a charitable contribution box nearby to compensate for the requested favor. However, favors are not asked randomly of any saint. When you lose something, you pray to Saint Anthony; when you travel, you may wear a protective medallion with the image of Saint Christopher. Many Spaniards also make pilgrimages to places where the Holy Virgin is said to have appeared. Finally, these religious references surface in everyday life, such as the common female name Maria del Pilar, usually Pilar for short, after the Virgin of the Pillar in Zaragoza, and the equally common name Conchita, a nickname for Maria de la Conceptión (Mary of the Immaculate Conception).

A wilder aspect of paganism that is wound into Spanish religion is the popular celebration, or fiesta. The fiesta is a ritual like the bullfight (the bullfight is actually part of many fiestas, exemplifying their pagan nature). Each region of Spain has its most famous fiesta, like the fiesta of San Fermín in Pamplona, Las Fallas in Valencia, El Roco in Andalusia, and Holy Week celebrations throughout the country. These celebrations involve extravagant costuming, floats, processions, and drinking, elements that would seem to stray far from piety. As a case in point, does the scene of dozens of men running in front of rushing bulls sound more Christian or more pagan? The answer is obvious, yet this ritual is observed as part of the celebration of a Christian saint in Pamplona. To the Spaniard, religion simply does not occupy a separate compartment in life; it can be incorporated into life's most mundane and most dramatic moments. The Spanish fiesta shares many similarities with the Mexican fiesta (see Chapter 23), but there are also many points of difference.

The pervasiveness of religion in Spanish day-to-day life would seem to work in favor of the church, but Franco's death in 1975 was followed by an anticlerical period and a negative reaction to conservative Catholicism. Still, almost half of the population attends church regularly, and 90% of the population define themselves as Catholic, suggesting that Catholicism as a cultural influence is strong. In recent years there has been a renewed interest in Catholicism, as manifested in popular recordings and films. For many years movie directors had difficulty persuading actors to play priests and nuns in films, but this is no longer true.

A U.S. American's experience as an exchange student living with a Spanish family illustrates the importance of bullfighting in Spanish culture. One Sunday the father turned on the televised bullfight and said to his houseguest: "I hate bullfighting, but if you want to understand the Spanish, you had better learn about it."

As already indicated, however, Spain is undergoing rapid change, particularly since Franco's death. It is now a member of the EU. After a long period of conservative Catholicism, a strong movement toward freedom and creativity has attracted worldwide attention. The *movida* (cultural movement) has been propelled by the activities of such artists as Barcelo (painting), Almodovar (cinema), Dominguez (fashion design), and Mecano (pop music). Social customs have relaxed, and some argue that Spain is being too influenced by the United States. Although such change is real, it is difficult to imagine Spain without the traditional rituals of the bullfight and the underlying Spanish culture that the bullfight expresses.

In summary, a passage by Crow (1985) concisely recapitulates some of the points made in this chapter:

> Spain today is a composite of all that has gone before. Her taproot reaches into the bottomless past. On several successive occasions in history she has flowered in beauty, shedding her glory over the civilization of Europe. On many other occasions she has grimly closed her door on the outside world, and retired into the gloom of fixed memories. In spite of her perennially poor government, her vitality is ever present, and appears inexhaustible. The Spanish people are among the most generous, the most noble human beings on earth. Their spontaneous art places them in a unique category among the nations of Europe, both for its quantity and for its incomparable beauty. With one foot in the present and the other in the past, Spain today stands straddling the unfathomable abyss. (p. 356)

As the people of Spain pursue an accelerated course of modernization, they are evolving into the more cosmopolitan embodiment as envisioned by the founders of the EU—but without, we hope, losing the special love of life that makes Spain so unique and wonderful. Whatever the eventual outcome, the bullfight will remain an important metaphor for understanding deep-seated cultural values and attitudes among the Spanish people.

CHAPTER 31

The Portuguese Bullfight

Bullfighting is like a ballet in which the bullfighter and the bull dance a perfect pas de deux.

—Pedrito de Portugal, the most famous matador
in Portugal (quoted in Bilefsky, 2007b)

S uperficially Spain and Portugal are similar in many ways. As inhabitants of the Iberian Peninsula, they have experienced hundreds of years of successive invasions. Both were seafaring nations that became world powers during the era of the conquistadores. In the GLOBE study (House et al., 2004) of cross-cultural differences, both Spain and Portugal score in the high collectivism group and are placed in the Latin Europe cluster. Portugal scored higher than Spain on gender egalitarianism in practice, and both had similarly high scores on power distance.

Comparing Portugal and Spain on the indices in *Pocket World in Figures* (2011) yields many more similarities than differences. Spain, of course, has a land area more than 5 times larger than Portugal's. It is also wealthier (US$35,220 gross domestic product [GDP] per person versus US$22,920), and purchasing power parity (the United States equals 100) is 68.3 for Spain versus 50.2 for Portugal. Portugal's population is about 10.7 million while Spain's is 44.6 million, and the languages are different. Today, Portugal is one of the poorest countries in Western Europe, and its recent history has been marred by corruption scandals, a far cry from the days of the great 15th-century explorer Vasco da Gama, who along with other explorers helped build a vast empire that included the country of Brazil and parts of Africa and Asia. In March 2011, Portugal became the third euro zone country after Greece and Ireland to require a bailout from the European Union (EU) and the International Monetary Fund (IMF). Portuguese debt was high, at 90% of GDP, and the economy had been sputtering along. Its problems were further exacerbated by the global financial crisis of 2008. Spain is not far behind with a 20% unemployment rate, the highest in Europe, and an annual GDP growth of just 0.6%. Portugal, however, ranks fourth in Europe in using renewable resources to produce energy and expects to have 20% of its energy come from renewable resources by the year 2020. Despite its economic problems, the country recently inaugurated the 240 MW Alto Mino Wind Park, powered by 120 turbines and billed as continental Europe's largest wind farm. The Portuguese are very proud of their achievements in this sector, which is normally dominated in Europe by the Scandinavian countries and Germany. Government and industry are setting good examples of energy efficiency for the broader population by placing renewable technologies at the heart of energy policy and industrial reconversion plans (Mulligan, 2010b).

For 60 years, Portugal was a part of Spain; a revolt in the 17th century established Portuguese independence, which is celebrated annually. It is instructive to compare the cultural metaphors for these two nations: the bullfight. In both Spain and Portugal, the bullfight celebrates emotionalism, love of life, and heroism. But the Spanish bullfight emphasizes tragedy and is a ritual of death, and there are more expressions of individualism in the Spanish version than in the Portuguese version, although such expressions are present in Portugal. Studying these two types of bullfights sensitizes us to subtle cultural differences that may otherwise be overlooked.

As we will see, substantive cultural differences do indeed exist between Spain and Portugal. These differences are also reflected in the countries' treatment of their colonies: The Spanish conquistadores usually conquered and destroyed in South America. In Brazil, by contrast, the Portuguese took the natives, and even later their black slaves from Africa, as concubines, thus legitimizing the resulting children.

As in Spain, bullfighting in Portugal was once the sport of noblemen. In the 18th century, Marquees de Pombal, the Portuguese prime minister, prohibited the killing of bulls after the son of the Duke of Arcos was killed in a bullfight. This prohibition profoundly changed the nature of Portuguese bullfighting and over time led to expressions of cultural values that are, to an outsider, startling and unique. In 2007 the celebrated Portuguese bullfighter Pedrito de Portugal was fined 100,000 euros for the crime of killing a bull, and this gave rise to a national debate between supporters and critics (Bilefsky, 2007b). Supporters felt that a death-free struggle was sacrilegious, whereas critics wanted Portugal to continue its traditions of civility and humanity toward animals. In this chapter, we describe the Portuguese bullfight in terms of four cultural characteristics: pride in traditions, stratification amid unity or collectivism, artistry and human gore, and profitless bravery.

Pride in Traditions

There are six separate rounds in the Portuguese bullfight, each with a specific *cavaleiro* (mounted horseman) and *forcados* (footmen). The bullfight spectacle begins with the grand entrance into the bullring by all the participants. The *cavaleiros* enter the ring first, wearing the traditional costumes of the 17th century. Their embroidered vests and feathered hats clearly emphasize the cultural heritage of the Portuguese. The *forcados,* or footmen, are attired in more humble yet traditional brown pants and small vests. The *toreiros,* or cape men, stand out because of their embroidered pants and vests, which are similar to those worn by the Spanish matadors. Metaphorically the *cavaleiros* stand for the noble class with its elegance and style, while the *forcados* represent the common laborer of Portugal. These *forcados,* much like their ancestors, are not flashy and don't mind getting dirty while performing their task. They understand and accept their role in society and are proud to contribute in any way possible.

The Bullfight Proceeds

The bullfight begins by pitting a fast bull against a graceful horse and rider. The *cavaleiro* must first demonstrate his control of the horse and his ability to avoid the charging bull, after which he faces the bull from across the ring and rides furiously toward him. At the last split second the *cavaleiro* swerves to avoid the bull but simultaneously drives a wooden spear into his neck. The *cavaleiro* repeats this activity six or seven times, and each encounter is more dangerous than the previous one. Then he exits the ring, and the *forcados* enter.

Metaphorically the *cavaleiro* is the authority figure in the bullfight. The *toreiros,* men with the capes, are used only to support him by distracting the bull long enough so that the *cavaleiro* can transition to another horse or grab another spear. (Of course, the *torero* is the most important person in the ring in Spain.)

The *forcados,* an eight-man team, line up as if playing leapfrog. The leader hollers "*O toro!*" continuously until the bull charges. Fortunately the horns of the bull are covered in a leather sheath. When the bull plows into the leader, the man doesn't get gored. Instead, the bull easily picks up the entire eight-man team, and the action becomes furious. Finally the group brings the bull to a standstill, and one man takes hold of the tail. The intended outcome is a successful *pega*; that is, the seven descend from the bull while the eighth man hangs onto the tail and stays upright behind the speeding beast until the bull comes to a halt.

The entire process is repeated with five additional bulls. After each of the six rounds, the *cavaleiros* and *forcados* meet in the center of the ring and take a victory lap around it while the crowd shows its appreciation by throwing flowers, hats, and other accessories. Then the *cavaleiros* and *forcados* throw these items back to the crowd as a sign of respect and appreciation for the crowd's support.

This description is a poor substitute for actually seeing a Portuguese bullfight. When the bull picks up one *forcado* or several *forcados* and hurls them into the air, the sensation is stunning. It is even more stunning to see a seemingly foolhardy *forcado* break loose of the eight-person team in an attempt to stop the bull all by himself.

Sometimes he is actually successful, but it is more likely that he will sail high into the air over the bull's back when the bull rushes into him, picks him up, and treats him with disdain. But is the *forcado* really being foolhardy? Only an understanding of Portuguese culture will help us to answer this question.

Community and Church

The soul of Portugal is reflected in the warmth of the people, who are spiritually connected to the land. As noted, the *forcados* represent the typical Portuguese laborers: simple and honest people who work all day and then come home at dusk to a warm supper and a carafe of homemade wine. After dinner they often go to the local cafe to drink an espresso and talk to their friends about the local soccer team. These people are repeating the pattern of simple lifestyles that their ancestors established. They realize that they are separate from the upper class (represented by the *cavaleiros*), but they are proud of their role in the bullfight and in society.

It is not surprising that religion is important in the culture; Portugal is 97% Catholic. Similarly the *cavaleiros* bless themselves, asking God for protection while in the ring with the bull. Metaphorically each of the participants in the bullfight seeks truth. For example, the *cavaleiros* test their control of horse and bull, each time being more daring and trying riskier moves. The *forcados* also search for truth and test their courage by facing the bull head on. For the most part, the Portuguese seek inner truth and strength, and they believe that actions speak louder than words.

Portugal is still a Catholic nation heavily influenced by the clergy, and it did not suffer from the anticlericalism unleashed in Spain after Franco's death in 1975. As we might expect in a culture that values the search for truth, regular church attendance is widespread. As Catholics, the Portuguese believe all of us are sinners in some way, for which we must atone. Hence many people go to confession on a weekly basis and find this activity as important as attending Sunday Mass.

Clergymen are considered experts, and their opinions are highly regarded. Many Portuguese use the clergy in the same way that Americans use psychologists. The Catholic Church and its teachings are an important source of stability for its members.

People's role in the social structure of both the family and extended family gives them a sense of security. Ordinary citizens respect anyone who is a symbol of authority, whether a clergyman, doctor, or manager. Authority is rarely challenged in this hierarchical culture, although the value system is in transition from the old authoritarian approach to a more democratic style in both the political and economic arenas. Portugal was governed for almost half of the 20th century by a dictator, Antonio de Oliveira Salazar, who hated modernity and treated his people like children; nevertheless, he established a degree of stability and kept Portugal out of World War II. In 2007 there was quite an uproar when Salazar was voted the "greatest Portuguese that ever lived," beating out the great Portuguese explorer, Vasco da Gama. Some people argued that the vote reflected disillusionment with the present state of affairs and a longing for the past (Bilefsky, 2007c). Portugal describes itself as a country of *bran-dos costumes,* a term that loosely translates into "mild ways" and alludes to an understanding tolerance and also to the kind of acquiescence that accepted the repressive rule of Salazar. There is therefore an aversion to the kind of social unrest that swept Greece after the economic bailout in 2010 (Wise, 2010). The Portuguese will most likely try to soldier on through the current economic crisis with the help of tough love from the euro zone.

Roles for Men and Women

Gender roles are clearly defined. While the *toreiros,* the cape men who help distract the bull for the *cavaleiro,* are men, they play a supportive role similar to that of women in Portuguese society. The man is seen as the conqueror and hunter who provides for the family, while the woman is the supporter who does all the cooking and cleaning. Even though more and more women are entering the workforce, they are normally not considered the breadwinners of the household. Working women are still expected to come home and take care of responsibilities such as cooking, cleaning, and taking care of the children. Based on this pattern, one would expect that Portugal is a masculine country, but actually it ranks 45 of 53 nations on the masculine-feminine dimension (Hofstede, 1991) and high on gender egalitarianism in the GLOBE (House et al., 2004) study, presumably because the Portuguese place great value on the land, the environment, and relationships. Hence it is acceptable for a man to be nurturing.

Just as the *cavaleiros* and *toreiros* are loyal and demonstrate mutual respect for each other, so too do men and women. Divorce is uncommon in Portugal and considered a disgrace. Actually, when a husband cheats on a wife, or vice versa, the cuckolded partner is said to *meter os cornos,* which literally means to be "gored by the bull." When a man is gored, as with the *pega,* he is expected to try to remarry. If he is unsuccessful, family members may well experience a sense of shame and derisively call him a quitter.

Given the significance of tradition, long-term trust is important in business. Metaphorically the bull represents an outsider trying to conduct business; the Portuguese are suspicious and afraid of getting "gored by the bull." Paradoxically, then, Portuguese people are friendly but simultaneously suspicious. Relationship building, especially outside of work, is important in gaining the trust needed to do business, and establishing a strong rapport through personal contact is key to negotiating effectively in Portugal.

Although there are few women in management roles, the Portuguese will conduct business with women if they feel that they are figures of authority. Although gender is important, authority outweighs it. Moreover, more women now graduate from university than men, and a majority of new judges are women (Wise, 2010).

Timeliness is important, and a person who arrives late is viewed as disrespectful. It is uncommon to be late for work or a meeting. Unlike the Spanish, who are known for being tardy, the Portuguese see being on time as reflective of character and inner strength and thus extremely important.

Finally, in light of the emphasis on tradition and following rules, it is easy to understand why change is slow and innovation deemphasized. Deviating from the norm is rarely accepted. In a recent bullfight, for example, one of the *forcados* decided to do a 360-degree spin while the bull was charging, but this act was not viewed favorably by the public. While it was innovative and more exciting due to the increased risk, the traditional *pega* is still preferred by a majority of the crowd. This lack of innovation has retarded Portugal's development. However, one surprising innovation emerged from the great Lisbon earthquake of 1755: Military engineers under the leadership of the Marquis de Pombal, one of Portugal's great modernizers, invented Europe's first earthquake-proof buildings (Schrady, 2008).

Stratification Amid Unity

One interesting feature of Portugal is that it is a collectivist society. Although it is important to define rules clearly, the most critical outcome is for the group to be successful. This is clearly demonstrated in the bullfight: When a *cavaleiro* enters the ring, for example, the other five *cavaleiros* shake his hand and wish him luck in the bullfight, thus signifying that it is more important to be part of the group than to win. Likewise, before the *pega* it is customary that the lead *cavaleiro* dedicates his efforts to a spouse, teacher, or even the entire crowd. In many instances, he will give his hat to the individual to whom he is dedicating the event and collect it once his "job" has been completed. This tradition dates back to the time when soldiers would go out to battle, leaving behind a token for their loved ones to remember them by. What the *cavaleiro* asks for in return is permission to proceed, which is usually signaled by a wave, hug, or applause.

After each bullfight, *cavaleiros* and *forcados* meet at the center of the ring and shake hands, which symbolizes the coming together of social classes. They explicitly recognize that it is not the nobleman or the common citizen who achieves success independently but rather all parties working together.

While Spain and Portugal are similar on objective measures, as noted previously, the Portuguese have developed a decidedly different character from that of the people of Spain. International travelers who mingle with the Portuguese usually return home filled with special warmth for the people. The Portuguese are easily approachable and helpful. Nonetheless, the family is perhaps the single most important institution in society, and many people have no close friendships outside the family unit. Although city dwellers have become increasingly sophisticated, families in the more rural areas still manifest this pattern of behavior. As a result, it is common for people to marry their neighbors, and newlyweds tend to live close to their parents, friends, and place of birth.

Similarly it is common for the entire family to gather for lunch at home. Lunch is by far the most important meal of the day, and everything in the country shuts down between noon and two in the afternoon so that people can eat. At lunchtime people do not discuss work, as there is a clear separation between work and family life that is rarely crossed. Food is important to the Portuguese, and they usually make elaborate meals at lunchtime, while dinner is much lighter and less formal. Beer and wine are consumed during lunch and constitute an important part of the culture. Many families grow their own grapes and make enough wine to last an entire year.

After dinner everyone usually gathers at a local cafe to have an espresso and to socialize. The family will go as a group, but on arrival each member will join natural subgroups. Men will sit with their friends and play cards, women will discuss the events of the day for an hour or two and return home to start preparing the next day's meals, and the children will play a game of *fusebol* or watch television with their friends. This is really the only time that people socialize outside the family, spending time with their friends.

It is important to understand the stratified collectivist norms of Portuguese society. To conduct business in Portugal, it is critical that a relationship be developed. One of the best ways to establish such relationships is over lunch. One frequently repeated aphorism is that the Portuguese need 2 hours for lunch owing to the fact that 1 hour is for eating while the other hour is for talking. Many business deals are finalized during lunch, and presumably the better the lunch, the better the deal. Bribery is commonly used to get things accomplished and is an accepted way of life. If a businessperson is trying to get paperwork signed or to close a deal, he or she may want to host lunch at the most expensive restaurant in town, and by the time the dessert is served, the issue will probably have reached a successful resolution.

Artistry and Human Gore

The beauty of the Lusitano horse, the elaborate costumes worn by the *cavaleiros,* and the elegance of the opening ceremony demonstrate the artistry that is seen throughout the country. In Portugal the performance of the horse in the bullring is perhaps one of the most important factors in the breeding and selection process of the Lusitano horse. The horses are trained by their riders and learn many things, including prancing, moving sideways, and standing on their hind legs. These skills are shown off during the bullfight and are needed to avoid the bull. The movements of the horse are admired by all, and the *cavaleiro* is applauded for his efforts in training the animal. It is extremely important that the *cavaleiro* demonstrate control of the bull and horse by repeatedly spearing the bull.

This artistry is also seen in music, arts and crafts, and architecture. In *fado* houses throughout Portugal, the female *fadista,* clutching a traditional black shawl, sings the nation's traditional sad and romantic songs. A rough translation of *fado* is "fate," from the Latin *fatuum,* meaning "prophecy." *Fado* usually tells of unrequited love, jealousy, and a longing for days gone by. *Fado* became famous in the 19th century when Maria Severa, the beautiful daughter of a Romany (Gypsy), took Portugal by storm, singing her way into the hearts of the people, especially the Count of Vimioso, the most renowned bullfighter of his day.

Hand-painted ceramics called *azuleijos* constitute an important craft in Portugal. Because of their decorative design, these tiles have been adopted by builders and are seen in almost every house. Other hand-painted pottery is also seen throughout the country, especially in the northern region. The architecture of Portugal is visible in cathedrals, churches, and castles across the country. For the most part, Portuguese architecture imitates Italian and Spanish designs. There is little if any uniqueness to the architecture, but its beauty is undeniable.

What we see at the bullfight is not only artistry but also human gore. The *forcados* are often injured while trying to wrestle the bull, and it is common to see blood on their faces and clothing. In the Spanish bullfight, the gore usually comes from killing the bull, but the Portuguese bullfight is said to be the "revenge of the bull." The first time that people watch the *pega*, they are amazed at the violence and pain that the bull inflicts on the *forcados*. In an attempt to stop the charging bull, the *forcados* are often trampled, thrown, and injured. The gore, however, is experienced only by the working class (*forcados*) and not the upper class (*cavaleiros*), which is symbolic of what has occurred during wartime. The *forcados* are similar to the front line of the army, while the *cavaleiros* are the generals. Still, a *forcado* is rarely killed (less than one every 10 years or so). The Portuguese see the bullfight as an art form and not as an exhibition of bloody violence, although international visitors frequently focus on the latter.

In business, much as in the bullfight, the Portuguese are perfectionists. If something goes wrong, they will do it over and over again until they get it right. The *cavaleiro,* for example, will sometimes change horses three or four times to find the one that will help him put on the best show. The Portuguese are also detail oriented. If the bull clips the horse or the *cavaleiro* drops one of his spears, he will go back and do it again. This level of detail is seen in business negotiations involving contracts. Unlike the Spanish, who finalize many business transactions orally, the Portuguese require that everything be in writing.

The Portuguese believe in the status quo and are suspicious of those who try to do things differently. Their belief is that if they have done it a certain way successfully many times in the past, what need is there to change? This thinking is different from the individualistic approaches that we see in the United States, where creativity or "thinking outside the box" is rewarded. In Portugal this type of thinking is seen as breaking tradition, so it is probably wise for foreigners to follow the maxim "When in Portugal, do as the Portuguese."

Profitless Bravery

When U.S. Americans attend the Portuguese bullfight, they tend to focus on the *pega,* probably because they see only the violence, human triumph, and misfortune (see Chapter 16: American Football). But whereas U.S. Americans may equate the physical violence of the *pega* to that of football, the Portuguese see the *pega* as a symbol of bravery.

In U.S. football, stars are role models for children because of their athletic ability and the money they earn. A major criticism of today's football players is that they lack the love for the game that previous generations had; some think the players are more interested in the money than in the game itself. The average salary for a professional football player is more than $1 million a year, and many players make far more than the average. On sports talk shows and in letters to the editors, fans continually complain that players have no loyalty to their teams and cities, especially since the advent of free agency. Many fans have difficulty identifying with the football players who supposedly represent their teams and cities.

Conversely, the *forcados* are amateurs and don't make any money at all, whereas the *cavaleiros* are paid. How can this be? In many cases the *forcados* are battered and bruised by the bull, and no one in his right mind would do this without getting paid, one might think. But the Portuguese bullfight is not about making money or being a hero. Rather, it is a joyous celebration of tradition and bravery. These *forcados* do it for the love of the ritual and the lessons that it has taught them. The bullfight forces a man to look deep within himself for a sense of pride, and it is a reminder of the hardships faced by previous generations.

Often during the *pega*, a *forcado* acting as team captain is not successful in holding the bull the first time. As opposed to quitting or giving way to another *forcado,* he will go out again. Sometimes three and four attempts must be made to grab the bull, but it is always the same brave lead *forcado* who is involved in the *pega.* Broken ribs and legs are common in the sport but are ignored until the bull is captured.

Saving face is important to the Portuguese. Regardless of how badly the *forcado* is injured, nothing can be worse than injury to the ego. The shame that a person would bring to the family by quitting an important task before completion is unthinkable. Playing with pain is a part of the game with which U.S. Americans are familiar, but most have never witnessed it to the extent that is visible in the bullfight. Portuguese are extremely proud of the fact that the *pega* is performed only in Portugal and believe that it symbolizes the courage of the people.

One business implication of this pattern of behavior is that the Portuguese are stubborn but persistent. The *forcado* can be knocked down repeatedly but will get back up again, no matter how battered he is. Although persistence is an excellent characteristic, some people see this stubbornness as illogical when carried beyond a reasonable point. Whether in a bullring or business environment, it is important to prepare for dealing with this extreme level of persistence.

Persistence typically leads to completing tasks. Hence a contract made with the Portuguese is generally ironclad. However, they are hard negotiators. Because they are so persistent and stubborn, negotiation is typically difficult. The U.S. saying when something is going to take a long time is "You better bring your lunch." In Portugal it should be "You better go out for lunch," because unless a relationship can be built outside a business setting, negotiations will not be successful. Portuguese do not consider themselves to be slaves to the clock. The process tends to be long and drawn out and will normally require many lunches.

As this chapter has demonstrated, the Portuguese and Spanish bullfights are as different as the people themselves are. The people of Portugal are less aggressive than those of Spain, and killing the bull is repulsive to them. As discussed earlier, the characters of the two peoples are reflected in the way that they administered their colonies in their glory days as colonial empires: The Spanish pillaged, while the Portuguese intermarried. Sociologists argue that bullfighting in Portugal is less of a blood sport than in Spain because the Portuguese are "soft machos" (Bilefsky, 2007b).

One of the main characteristics of the bullfight is audience involvement. The Spanish will applaud an excellent performance by the matador or *torero* but will not hesitate to whistle and boo if displeased with the performance. If they boo, the *torero* will not reenter the ring. However, prolonged applause and the waving of handkerchiefs are a great honor, and the *torero* is rewarded with an ear and in some cases the tail of the bull; he is also well paid. In the Portuguese bullfight, on the other hand, rarely does the audience boo a performance. Regardless of how the *cavaleiro* and *forcado* performed, they are treated with respect. This pattern reflects the origin of the Portuguese bullfight, which is a celebration of bravery and life, not death.

Furthermore, the bullfight is symbolic of the battles that Portugal and its people faced during invasion by the Moors. If people were to boo and whistle, then metaphorically it would be a sign of disrespect for the soldiers who served the country. Thus it is important that, at the end of each of the six stages or rounds, the participants gather at the center of the ring so that the audience can acknowledge and applaud their efforts.

There is also a great deal of difference in the role of hierarchy in both nations. In Spain the participants enter the ring in descending order of importance, while in Portugal all the participants are viewed as being of equal importance, even though the *cavaleiros* represent the noble class while the *forcados* represent the working class. In Spain the president determines the award given to the matador, but in Portugal the people decide on the reward by applauding. In the bullfight and throughout Spain, people like to show off by dressing nicely, whether rich or poor. This is clearly not the case in Portugal as evidenced by the humble clothing worn by the *forcados*.

The biggest difference between the two bullfights, however, is deeply rooted in the meaning of the spectacle for each country. In Spain the bullfight is about control and conquest through death. The matadors are expected to control the bull, and, once this control is demonstrated, they kill it. In the Portuguese version of the bullfight, death is not a part of the ritual. The true meaning for all Portuguese is the celebration of bravery demonstrated by the *cavaleiro* and *forcado*. According to a full-length documentary film, *Taking the Face: The Portuguese Bullfight* (Bishop & Kossakowski, 2008), Barrancos, a border town near Spain, is the only place in Portugal where the bull is killed in defiance of Portuguese law.

Today Portugal is trying to position itself as the "West Coast of Europe," drawing tourists as well as investors with its natural beauty, history, and strength as an environmentally friendly energy producer (Pfanner, 2007). Portugal is also reaping dividends by diversifying into markets in Africa and Brazil where Portuguese is spoken. This allows the country not only to take advantage of the opportunities in emerging economies but also to leverage technological innovation by adapting products and packaging to the needs of these markets (Wise, 2010).

Still, similar to other nations facing globalization, Portugal is understandably concerned that its culture not be significantly altered. Some Portuguese are even concerned about the symbolism found on the new euro coins in which Portugal looks as if it were a part of Spain (see Trueheart, 1998). And in 2003, 40 prominent Portuguese economists and business leaders published an open letter in which they warned against the rising danger of Portugal's corporations being purchased and controlled by other nations, particularly Spain ("Those Big Boys," 2003). However, cultural patterns that have taken hundreds of years to develop are difficult to destroy, and we can expect that the Portuguese bullfight will continue to reflect the underlying values that the Portuguese hold dear, even if changes are introduced into this beloved activity.

PART XI

Popular Music as Cultural Metaphors

I t is a widely accepted truism that music, classical painting, sculpture, and other art forms are expressive of culture. In this book, we have employed the arts to describe some national cultures through distinctive if not unique cultural metaphors (e.g., the German symphony, the Italian opera, and the Russian ballet). However, these art forms represent what is generally considered to be high art that many of us, unfortunately, do not experience firsthand at a live performance and some of us do not even experience through television, recordings, or YouTube.

However, almost all of us have listened to the popular music that originates in our own culture, such as rock and roll and jazz. In this part of the book, we examine in depth two popular musical forms, the Brazilian samba and the Argentine tango, that have very successfully represented the cultures of Brazil and Argentina both within their countries of origin and worldwide. In fact, both musical forms have been awarded the UNESCO status of Intangible Cultural Heritage of Humanity. Because of the symbolism of these two musical forms and the manner in which they express and demonstrate the distinctive cultures of their nations, we have chosen to highlight them as cultural metaphors in this part of the book.

CHAPTER 32

The Brazilian Samba

It is probably unwise to draw too many conclusions about Brazilian perceptions on the grandeur of the country and of the grand endeavors of its people, but it would not be excessive to assume that they naturally regard Brazil as an extraordinary place, which would imply that other countries are somewhat less so. In a country with so many monumental things, both natural and man-made, any comparisons with its immediate neighbors make the neighbors look pretty puny.

—Jon Vincent (2003, p. 15)

Getting close to a samba school drum section is, literally a moving experience. The bass drums set your body vibrating and the high-pitched tambours assault the ears and leave them ringing. Before you know it, you're swaying along to the rhythm.

—Wheatley (2010, p. 12)

B razil, with a population of 186 million, is extremely diverse and encompasses several distinct regions and 26 states. In land area, Brazil is almost equal to the entire United States: 8,511,965 square kilometers versus 9,372,610. It lays claim to many aspects of bigness and grandeur, including the Amazon, the world's most voluminous river; the Amazon forest, the largest oxygenating forest; the world's largest wetland; the world largest soccer stadium; and the world's largest samba dance stadium. Twelve Brazilian cities have populations of more than a million each, and São Paulo with its population of 18.3 million is tied with Mumbai, India, for being the fourth-largest city in the world. (Tokyo has 35.3 million, followed by Mexico City at 19.3 million.) Goldman Sachs, the investment bank, has designated Brazil as one of the BRIC countries, along with China, Russia, and India. Its research suggests that these four developing nations will be the dominant world economies by 2050 (Wilson & Purushothaman, 2003).

Brazil is also a land of contrasts. The industrialized south with São Paulo as its center is far wealthier than the north. The northeastern part of the country has been particularly poor, but in the past 10 years its gross domestic product rose by 4.2% a year compared to the 3.6% for the nation as a whole. The government introduced an antipoverty program in this region that has been very successful. About three quarters of the growth, however, has come from a boom in improvements in infrastructure, while the major problem seems to be a poor educational system. The northeast has seen such growth previously, but a lack of trained workers undermined it ("Catching Up in a Hurry," 2011). In 2007, as Brooke Unger emphasizes in his 2007 review of Brazil, many issues required attention, particularly a high rate of taxation, excessive government bureaucracy, and the destruction of the Amazon forest, of which about 18% has disappeared since the 1960s. However, the future looks bright, and efforts to address these issues have been ongoing, especially in the last decade.

A striking illustration of this increasing prosperity is the increased demand for nannies, who historically have had very low wages. Because many women are returning to the workforce after childbirth and there is limited access to day care, well-trained and educated nannies are in high demand. Some nannies are making so much money that they hire other nannies to take care of their own children. For example, one nanny earns US$4,300 a month and hires her own nanny for US$900 (Barrionuevo, 2011). Still, the gross domestic product per person is only US$6,860 in comparison to that in the United States of $45,492.

Brazilians have tremendous spirit in the face of adversity. The well of this spirit is continually replenished by the Brazilian's passion for life. Metaphorically the samba encapsulates this passion for life and serves to replenish the well in both good times and bad.

The samba has truly become a national symbol. For example, at a beauty pageant for Italian-Brazilian young women, held in Brazil, all contestants were asked what they first thought of when hearing the word *Brazil.* Immediately all of the young women began to samba. The samba's technical definition is "a binary, percussive rhythm in which the first beat is never sounded, causing a continual, hesitant urgency" (Krich, 1993, p. 73). This idea parallels the Brazilian's polychronic nature and seemingly constant movement, although the business-centered south tends to be more monochronic. For example, participants are expected to arrive on time to a business meeting in the south, and doing otherwise is viewed negatively. Brazilians are naturally uncertain about their future when the first indication of the direction in which they are going cannot be seen nor heard. One long-standing joke that is now outdated, as evidenced by Brazil's designation as a BRIC nation, is that Brazil is the country of the future and always will be. Since 1988 the nation has undergone significant changes. Inflation is now manageable at less than 10% and frequently less than 5% per year, and both the government and private businesses are capitalizing on Brazil's vast resources to strengthen the political system, the economic system, and institutions such as the educational system and legal system.

There is some truth that Brazil's potential far outstripped its achievements until recent years. It is not that Brazil is the country of the future and always will be. Rather, Brazil did not emphasize the future until recently, as the three founding groups—the conquering and rapacious Portuguese, the indigenous Brazilians, and the slaves—had limited reasons for doing so. Today, this generalization is no longer valid (Unger, 2007).

Evolution of the Samba

The very existence of the samba is owed to the musical talent of the plantation workers. It was on the plantations that the first whispers of what is now known as the samba were heard. Decades later the samba's predecessors appeared in civil society in the form of elegant tangos, as Blacks rose in social status in Brazil's bigger cities. The initial characterization of this dance as the samba occurred at free slaves' dance parties in Bahia in the 1870s. Bahia was and is a center of Black culture in Brazil. As the story goes, a woman from Bahia named Tia Amelia took the samba further south to the slums of Rio de Janeiro. Her son, Donga, composed the first recorded samba in 1916. As early as 1923, samba schools were born. These schools flourish today and symbolize the spirit of the samba to most of the outside world, especially during Carnival, the annual pre-Lenten celebration. Although part of the spirit of the samba is captured in the glorious dancers and floats in the samba school parades during Carnival, the samba is much more complex. Its physical characteristics and musical qualities weave an intricate web around Brazilians and influence many facets of life.

The samba takes on many forms, including "samba *pagode*, samba *raiado*, samba *de partido alto*, samba *do morro*, samba *de terreiro*, samba *canção*, samba *enredo*, samba *choro*, samba *do breque*, *sambalero*, *sambalanço*, and *sambā*" (Krich, 1993, p. 73). Various sambas are appropriate for specific situations and social levels. For instance, the samba *enredo* is composed and used in the samba schools. The samba *de terreiro* is less sophisticated and likely to be danced in more rural areas. Other sambas are simply musical innovations. For instance, the samba *do breque* incorporates a rhythmic spoken part, much like rap, in the middle of the traditional samba music.

The lyrics of the various types of sambas are varied as well, although all have a common theme, for the words center around people's trials and tribulations across history and in daily life. Popular subjects include corruption, poverty, historical events, and local heroes. The number of samba songs that have been composed is enormous: On average samba schools produce 2,000 new songs a year for Carnival.

Five characteristics of the samba, when explored in detail, delineate the culture of this country with respect to its people, their behavior, and their manner of conducting business. We have chosen to discuss primarily the physical attributes of this dance as opposed to the musical and lyrical aspects for the sake of brevity, although there is an obvious overlap. These characteristics are small-step circularity, physical touch, undulation, spontaneous escape, and the paradox of dancers.

Small-Step Circularity

When dancing the samba, people move in small, somewhat controlled steps in a circular pattern, while holding the upper torso still. This notion of small steps and circularity has been present in Brazil since its discovery by Europeans in 1500. Pedro Alvares Cabral, a Portuguese trying to find an oceanic passage to Asia, accidentally and literally ran into what would be Brazil. Columbus had run into land along the same parallel, and Cabral was presumably hoping to do the same. But earlier, in 1494, Spain and Portugal had divided the New World in the Treaty of Tordesilhas, and Brazil was given to Portugal, even though Europeans were not yet aware of its vast size. In other words, this land became part of the Portuguese empire largely through default and not through competition or war.

Historical Evolution

In general, "Brazil's development as a nation has been essentially evolutionary with few sharp breaks or drastic discontinuities" (Schneider, 1996, p. 35). Brazil grew amid small steps that were often circular, for example, from military to civilian rule and back. In the early 1800s the Portuguese emperor, Dom João VI, moved to Brazil because he feared Napoleon's power in Europe. Under his rule growth truly began. After the situation in Europe stabilized, Dom João returned to Portugal and left his son, Dom Pedro I, to rule Brazil. The latter realized Brazil's need to separate itself from Portugal officially; on September 7, 1822, he declared Brazil's independence.

Several years later, he, too, returned to Portugal, but he left his son, Dom Pedro II, in charge of Brazil. While Dom Pedro II was away on business, his daughter signed a document freeing the slaves. Soon thereafter two army generals took the initiative to oust Dom Pedro II from Brazil. Hence, in 1889 the monarchy was dead, and the Republic of Brazil was formed. This transition from monarchy to a republic demonstrates how Brazilians move in small steps. It took them 67 years after their country became independent to remove the Portuguese monarchy from power.

The existence of several different forms of government over time, as well as the vacillation between these forms, also reflects the metaphor of small steps and their circularity. It is significant that the republic was proclaimed by two generals, as military dictatorship has been prevalent in Brazil for most of the nation's history.

Many presidents have been military officers, thus further confounding military and democratic rule. In 1985 civilian rule and elections supplanted military rule, although the generals are still key players.

There are currently more than 20 political parties, in part because of the system of proportional representation in the legislature based on the total percentage that each party receives in national elections. In comparison to the U.S. practice of having two major parties and one or two independent parties in any election, the Brazilian system creates the conditions for a complex, multiparty system of government. This frequently results in weak governments ruled by coalitions of political parties which make deals with one another. It also results in excessive and inefficient bureaucracy; recently Brazil was ranked 121st out of 125 nations in terms of ease of doing business. In the 2011 Index of Economic Freedom ranking of 179 nations, Brazil ranked only 113 (for a description of this Index, see T. Miller, 2011). There are attempts to change such inefficient practices, but they contribute to the probability of small-step circularity.

Admittedly there is much circularity, overlay, and repetitiveness in the ideologies and activities of these various parties. But at the same time, people have significant freedom to express their beliefs and form organized groups representing these beliefs. Again, this notion dates back to Brazil's founding, when different groups were not forced to fully assimilate into Portuguese culture. This liberal attitude extended to the practice of interracial unions, resulting in many mixed marriages and mixed children. All types of Brazilians integrated themselves into a unified society through the small steps of increased racial integration. In fact, Krich (1993) believes that "a new generation of blacks is finding the samba one of the handier means of advancement" in Brazilian society (p. 82). Although practiced more devoutly in particular regions, the samba has been pervasive throughout the country, and knowing how to samba is part of being Brazilian. Hence this dance is a vehicle through which all of the diverse peoples and regions of this vast country can experience some degree of unity.

Economy and Education

The monetary and educational systems also demonstrate evolution and small-step circularity. Since 1940 Brazil has used five different currencies, including the *mil reis,* the *cruzeiro,* the *cruzado,* the new *cruzeiro,* and currently the *real.* Hesitant to bring about sweeping change, the Brazilians attempted to keep the *cruzeiro* by devaluing it many times. As indicated previously, the yearly rate of inflation reached a mind-boggling 2,500% in the early 1990s, but it has since leveled off to less than 10%, and it is frequently lower than 5%. When it was finally apparent that the situation was hopeless, a move was made to introduce the *cruzado.* However, when this did not work, the *cruzeiro* was brought back, and the currency was declared to be the new *cruzeiro;* again, the notion of circularity is evident.

The educational system in Brazil is quite interesting, as it is both lax and controlled. As with most educational systems, there are levels such as grade school, high school, and college. To enter a university, people must take an exam called the *vestibular.* Entrance to the university is based solely on performance on this exam; high school grades and extracurricular activities are not important. Thus some students in the early high school years tend to have a more relaxed attitude toward schoolwork. However, the high school curriculum is very structured and demanding; for example, everyone must take 3 years of mathematics, physics, chemistry, biology, and so on. It is impossible to go through high school without taking consecutive years of physics and chemistry, and failing one of them requires staying in the same grade for another year.

As the *vestibular* approaches, students push hard to pass this exam. Of significant interest is the fact that students take this exam in a particular subject area, such as history or physical education. Hence, at the age of 18, they must already commit to a field of study in college. Once they are accepted into a university for this field, they study only subjects related to it. This system is more similar to the German system than to the U.S. system, although grades in precollege classes are given more weight in the German system than in Brazil.

A typical university campus has separate buildings for each subject; for example, those studying history spend all of their time in the history building. Students are allowed to take only a few electives. If they decide that they do not want to continue studying history, they may not simply transfer into another department; they must take the *vestibular* again in a new subject. Hence students lose valuable time. In this manner the educational system is rigid, as symbolized in the tight control of the torso and movement found in the samba. However, it is also clear that many steps must be taken to reach a degree in the person's preferred field, thus confirming the notion of small-step circularity.

Education is an area in which the conflicts and contradictions in Brazilian culture become apparent. In recent years Brazil has improved significantly, achieving near-universal primary schooling and large increases in secondary and college enrollments. Still, Brazil came in last in mathematics and 4th from the bottom in reading in one study of standardized performance among students in 40 nations; half of 10-year-olds are functionally illiterate (see Unger, 2007, p. 13). Many of the schools are decrepit and underfunded, thus putting Brazil at a disadvantage in a globalized economy in which an educated workforce is critical. Sometimes the contradictions are startling.

For example, the Bulhões family in the northeast in the early 1990s exerted incredible power and influence over all aspects of life in the state of Alagoas, where the people suffered from the highest infant mortality rate in the region, the lowest child vaccination rate, the lowest rate of prenatal care, and one of the lowest rates of schooling (1.8 years per adult). Yet, by contrast, the local elite looked forward to the inauguration of cellular telephone service in January 1994. Wearing designer clothes, Mrs. Bulhões, the governor's wife, roamed among the shantytown dwellers and peasants proclaiming: "Poor people have just the same right to see me pretty as people in society" (quoted in Brooke, 1993).

About that time, she chartered an executive jet three times to fly to São Paulo and back, with the state treasury picking up the $24,000 tab. Meanwhile the state's public schools were closed for 7 months because teachers were protesting salaries of $80 a month. The person taking the hard line with the teachers was the secretary of education, also the governor's brother. This family is a prime example of the political oligarchy existing in some of the poorer states, which blurs lines between public and private consumption and responsibilities. Fortunately this is an extreme example from one of the most corrupt and poor states in the northeast of Brazil. As indicated above, even the northeast is going through an economic boom, and many other regions can offer contrasting examples.

Personal Lives

Small steps and circularity are found in the personal lives of Brazilians as well. Although it is quite easy to make acquaintances or *colegas* in Brazil, it takes some time to cultivate deep and lasting friendships. A typical pattern for foreign students is to establish a network of *colegas* and to socialize outside of school, where they develop friendships with a few individuals who become more than *colegas*. Later, such students may be invited to the homes of their friends and eventually may be treated as members of the family. Similarly business is typically conducted in restaurants, and it is a sign of honor and trust to be invited to a business colleague's home.

The transition of Brazilians from their parents' home to their own home also consists of many small steps. Family is the most important institution and, hence, greatly influences the individual. For instance, the dating process is regulated by the family, although much less so than in previous generations and not as much in urban areas as in rural areas. Even though times are changing, many young adults leave their parents' home only when they marry.

As in many cultures, relationships between men and women at work are complex, and what would be considered offensive behavior, even as the basis for a lawsuit in the United States, takes on a different meaning in Brazil and other Latin and non-Latin cultures. It is still common for a man to compliment a woman in a way that would be problematic in the United States, and it is common—but much less so—for men to make remarks to and about women that only they consider humorous. Frequently, however, the tables are turned, and the man's worst fear is to have a woman make an effective retort, particularly in a group setting. Still, while these patterns of communication are prevalent, they are counterbalanced by the conservative Brazilian perspective on marriage and family relationships, as noted previously.

The notion of extended courtship is found in business relationships as well. When conducting business in Brazil, people usually first establish a solid friendship. Only after a committed relationship is in place can a deal be struck. A typical piece of advice is "Be prepared to commit long-term resources (both in time and money) toward establishing strong relationships in Brazil. Without such commitments, there is no point in attempting to do business there at all" (Morrison & Conaway, 2006, p. 67). Hence, it is clear that patience and a willingness to cultivate solid personal ties through small steps are crucial to the success of business negotiations in this country.

Brazil is generally a patriarchal society where the father of the family is the final decision maker for many important matters. As they age, older members of the family also are accorded respect and are well taken care of by younger family members. Hence it is not surprising that in Geert Hofstede's study (2001) of 53 countries, Brazil ranks 14th in power distance. However, the more recent GLOBE study of 62 national societies (House et al., 2004) ranked Brazil low on the value placed on power distance (54th), even though it ranked 24th on its practice. In terms of business dealings, there are many layers of authority, and foreigners often must take many steps to find the person who can make things happen.

Also, compared to U.S. Americans and Japanese, Brazilians are much more likely to use commands and say no in negotiations (Adler, 2007). The use of commands can be traced back to Brazil's extensive history of military rule. This behavior is, thus, a small step away from the historical political system. The excessive tendency to say no is also a way to keep negotiations from forging ahead too quickly, behavior that again demonstrates the need to proceed in small steps.

Physical Touch

Due to on-again, off-again military rule and its declining but continued influence, the elite are widely seen as exercising power over the general population. In fact, modern society contains strong vestiges of colonial times, when the elite controlled nearly all of the wealth. Brazil has one of the widest disparities of wealth worldwide: The richest 10% control more than 50% of all wealth and the poorest 10% less than 1%. But, as indicated previously, poverty has declined significantly since 1992, and there are vast regional differences. Also, for the past few decades, the rate of income inequality has increased far more in developed nations such as the United States and Great Britain than in Brazil.

Generalizations about national cultures must take into account regional differences, and Brazil is no exception. Many of the behaviors such as small steps and circularity apply less well to some areas, such as São Paulo, where business is conducted in typically Western fashion and people are so organized that they will even line up to get onto buses. Still, São Paulo suffers from wide differences in wealth, even to the extent that wealthy businesspeople use helicopters to travel between their places of business and their gated communities to minimize the chances of becoming crime victims. They also hire armed guards at work and at home. As might be expected, armored cars are very popular.

The uncertainty about the future brought about by the small steps and circularity of this country's history also places stress on Brazilians. Brazil has been termed a big emerging market for quite some time and now is known, as indicated above, as a BRIC nation. The long wait for the awakening of this sleeping giant has instilled a sense of tension in the population, and people deal with this daily oppression and uncertainty in a variety of ways. One main way is a reliance on personal relationships and human warmth. We explore this idea further by analyzing the samba with regard to its characteristic of physical touch.

The samba is normally danced in close proximity to other people, and the movement is strenuous and continuous to keep up with the samba beat. The very history of the samba is indicative of the importance of physical touch. Reputedly the samba is the descendant of an Angolan fertility rite that features the "violent bouncing together of belly buttons" (Krich, 1993, p. 73). The *umbigada* ritual is thought by some to be another influence on the modern samba. This ritual is conducted in a circle, with people given the chance to dance by a thrust of the pelvic region. The word *umbigada* is derived from the word *umbigo,* meaning belly button. Hence the connection between this ritual and the former is clear. Also, in Ngangela, a Bantu language spoken in Angola, the word *kusamba* can be defined as "to skip, to gambol, to express uninhibited joy" (Krich, p. 73). Thus the importance of physical touch and human warmth is well captured in the metaphor of the samba.

Family Ties

This need for human contact is best exemplified through the Brazilian family. As noted earlier, family ties are of paramount importance in this country. Because children often do not leave their parents' home until they are married and then frequently establish their new homes close by, family members are usually found within a defined geographic area. This living arrangement allows family members to communicate with each other in person on a regular basis. The most common way to reaffirm family ties is by attending the Sunday meal. Normally the head of the clan hosts this meal, and all of his children and grandchildren congregate at his house to share conversation and good food. This idea is conveyed through the following quote, "We can't forget that with the Portuguese cooking we inherited the taste for a plentiful table, for varied foods, and the pleasure of eating with company, friends and family—the basis of Brazilian hospitality" (Buarque de Holanda, 1971, p. 121).

A natural progression of strong family unity is extensive nepotism in the business world. Family members take special care to make sure that all relatives are provided for. Unfortunately many employment opportunities are given to family members regardless of their ability to perform the job correctly.

If their family structure is weak or nonexistent, Brazilians are at a great disadvantage, given the importance of social networks based largely on family ties. An extreme example of how being outside of such social networks can leave individuals bereft of protection is the killing of orphans and sale of their body parts, fortunately a relatively rare occurrence. Similarly, the police sometimes act in a corrupt fashion, even to the point of killing civilians with little or no justification. A few years ago, the public responded with outrage when a judge did not punish two upper-class young men who had poured kerosene over a lower-class Indian who was demonstrating on behalf of his people. The judge argued that the young men were sensitive to others, as shown by the treatment of their dogs.

Still, there are some mechanisms, and increasing support for them, to increase social mobility. These include the *vestibular,* although children of wealthy parents can afford tutors and better schools, thus enhancing their chances of getting into college. Brazil recently passed its first equal employment opportunity legislation, similar to the law in the United States. Currently, 53% classify themselves as White, 6.2% as Black, 38% as "mixed," and 2.8% as either indigenous or no designation.

The Self and Collectivism

Still, it is important to remember that individual Brazilians value equality and the freedom to pursue their dreams. Throughout history people from different races were allowed some degree of religious freedom and had the right to procreate with whomever they chose. In business negotiations, for example, Brazilians are much less likely than Japanese or U.S. Americans to use a normative appeal, that is, one that uses societal norms to prove a point (Adler, 2007). Hence, Brazilians have a definite sense of self within the close-knit group. This notion of simultaneous collectivism and individual general freedom is well represented by Hofstede's (2001) rating of Brazil along this dimension. Because Brazil is precisely in the middle of the individualism-collectivism continuum among the 53 nations, it is not surprising to see such a contrast in ideals. Similarly research has demonstrated that Brazilians express much more concern for the outcomes of others than did U.S. Americans (V. Pearson & Stephens, 1998). While the GLOBE study of 62 national societies (House et al., 2004) ranked Brazil 52nd on practice of institutional collectivism, it also ranked Brazil as 2nd on the value placed on it. By contrast, the United States ranked 32nd and 54th, respectively.

When conducting business, it is important for U.S. Americans to remember that although their Brazilian contacts may seem to be similarly individualistic, they are linked to many groups and often place the needs of those groups, particularly their family, ahead of their personal goals. It is not uncommon for businesspeople to cancel a meeting or arrive late to a meeting because they needed to take care of a family issue.

Similarly, when negotiating with Brazilians, simply forging ahead to discuss the business at hand is not appropriate. Getting to know one another is very important to Brazilians. Because personal relationships are so valued, asking after the well-being of family members is generally a good place to start. Like any other relationship where personal time and care are important, a carefully cultivated business relationship with a Brazilian can yield long-term benefits to both parties.

This notion of physical contact, closeness, and human warmth is also evident in more specific negotiating behaviors. Brazilians have a much greater tendency than U.S. Americans and Japanese to engage in facial gazing and touching (Adler, 2007). Facial gazing is probably due to the desire of Brazilians to read the expressions of their business partners and gain knowledge about their personality, and the use of physical touch is often simply a reaffirmation of the relationship and a transfer of concern for the other person. "A normal conversation between two Brazilians generally takes place somewhere between 6 inches and 12 inches apart" (Morrison, Conaway, & Douress, 1995, p. 34). In the United States the typical space between two people is 2 feet or more.

Undulation

The characteristic of the samba described as undulation, a distinctive moving of the hips, also provides insight into the Brazilian culture. Undulation is an extension of the idea of circularity described earlier. Where circularity may result in either traveling a lengthy path to a solution or reaching a dead end, undulation most often results in taking a shortcut to a solution.

In Brazil it is common to get things done by circumventing rules and obstacles. Accomplishing a task in the face of the cumbersome bureaucracy found in this country is literally done through the art of dancing around things, as the metaphor of the samba suggests. This art can be dated back to the founding of the country. As Krich (1993) points out, many of the original Portuguese were underdogs or bandits who were suddenly given land and titles. The behavior of these people, now in high places, remained entrenched in what they knew best, how to survive on the streets. More often than not, their survival depended on making personal connections and navigating around societal norms.

It is particularly interesting to note a popular myth in Brazilian culture that exemplifies this ideal of ignoring rules. The protagonist of this myth is the Saci, a short Black man with one leg who smokes a pipe and dons a red cap. There are many stories about this Saci, all with the same central theme of mischief. This character generally plays pranks on people and gets away with it. For example, in one story, he goes to a farm, and because of his presence the milk sours. According to Solomon (1996), a myth is "a story containing symbolic elements that expresses the shared emotions and ideals of a culture. In this way, a myth reduces anxiety because it provides consumers with guidelines about their world" (p. 543). Hence it is not surprising that in many social circles in Brazil, an individual who succeeds through mischief is seen as a hero or as a worthy successor to Saci.

The Brazilian penchant for breaking rules and reaching goals outside of proper procedures is evident at traffic lights, which are frequently disregarded. In fact, stopping at a red light can be dangerous, especially at night, for drivers are frequently accosted.

The Impact of Status

Another way to find a way around the rules is through using status. Because Brazil has a hierarchical structure, respect must be paid to those of a higher status, as evidenced by a standard response, "Do you know to whom you are speaking?" This response is intended to point out the status the individual wishes to invoke as justification for contending that the law was not intended for such a special person (Schneider, 1996, p. 193). Again, the speaker demonstrates the importance of personal relationships and whom you know. An effective personal network can frequently get people much farther than following the law. Even the 1988 constitution, which restored democracy after two decades of military rule, did not abolish the culture of *cordialidade,* that is, the primacy of personal bonds over rules (Unger, 2007).

This type of personal bonding, when not invoked by rank, is called a *jeitinho.* To give a *jeitinho* is loosely translated as enlisting a fellow human being to help one circumvent the rules due to one's personal circumstance. In general, this notion is closely connected to the Brazilian belief in the equality of individuals and in preserving human relationships in the face of extensive bureaucracy. "From this perspective, the *jeitinho* is a flexible way of dealing with the surprises of daily life, a way of humanizing the rules that takes into account the moral equality and social inequalities of persons in the society" (Hess, 1995, p. 40). Pulling rank when asking for a *jeitinho* will surely backfire on the individual asking for a special exception.

For instance, in dealing with the Brazilian embassy, travelers might ask the clerk if they could make a *jeitinho* and process the paperwork sooner. Travelers might say that they need to return to Brazil as soon as possible to be with a relative who is seriously ill. This appeal to the clerk's compassion and strong family values will tend to facilitate the process. But to accompany this appeal with any display of superiority will likely result in the denial of the request. Engaging in the *jeitinho* ritual allows Brazilians both to bypass impersonal rules and to exert a certain amount of control over their daily lives.

Navigating the Bureaucracy

In purely business transactions, asking for a *jeitinho* may not be enough. In this case businesspersons might hire a *despachante* or agent to aid in the navigation of Brazil's numerous and complicated bureaucratic rules. Twenty-five years ago, the extensive bureaucracy inherited from the Portuguese was simplified to a certain extent, and the need for such a service has diminished somewhat. Nonetheless, there are whole offices composed of *despachantes* whose work is devoted to wading through regulations for their clients. Furthermore, Brazilians have such little faith in the written word, in particular in personal signatures, that every conceivable document has to be notarized. Thus the usefulness of the *despachante* becomes evident. Ironically, it is easy to file income taxes; Brazil had a Web-based electronic system in place by 1995, far ahead of many nations.

The structure of the *despachante* business is somewhat complex. Often a head *despachante* takes leadership over a person's individual request. However, the head *despachante* has several layers of subordinates who perform the more tedious tasks. One such task is waiting in line for hours to get a particular document signed by the appropriate person. Hence the very system that has evolved to aid an ordinary citizen in navigating the Brazilian bureaucracy has become cumbersome in its organization as well. However, wealthy U.S. Americans and business firms hire temporary workers for the same purpose within the United States.

The notion of circumventing rules can also be found in issues that affect international relationships. In the arena of intellectual property rights (IPR), Brazil has a very poor record, even though it is a signatory to the Paris, Berne, and Universal Copyright conventions on IPR and is in agreement with the GATT Trade-Related Aspects of Intellectual Property accord. In fact, in terms of software piracy, for every legal copy sold in Brazil, about four illegal copies are made. This is typical of a developing nation with an inefficient bureaucracy. Here again, the degree of collectivism in the Brazilian culture, coupled with the importance of personal relationships, encourages this behavior. Many commentators have argued that Brazil must alter its behavior so that it can be seen as a legitimate business partner in the global environment. Dancing around the obstacles that numerous and complex regulations create has become so ingrained in this culture that seemingly only the need to conduct international business will result in Brazilians conforming to more universal norms.

Spontaneous Escape

Spontaneous escape represents the fifth characteristic of the Brazilian samba. As might be expected, Brazilians tend to get lost in this notion of escape and lose track of time. Frequently they do not strive to avoid the uncertainty of their lives, but too much uncertainty motivates them to escape tension through the music and dance of the samba. For Brazilians the samba represents this notion of a spontaneous escape from the everyday reality of unemployment, low standard of living, and poverty that affects many Brazilians.

Yet, on a closer look, the country is still smiling. Why? Perhaps it's because Brazilians can dance the samba and, for a brief moment, be the center of attention in a world full of freedom. In a country that was under military rule for many years and is plagued with a distrust of government and widespread bribery and corruption, escape is something many Brazilians crave. The samba is an escape because its music and dance sweep people away, and they lose track of time and their troubles. It is no wonder that Brazilians are described as being polychronic. Again, however, in such a land of diversity and contrasts, this generalization must be tempered. In the business-like south, for example, businesspeople are expected to arrive on time and even early for meetings, and southern Brazilians generally frown on not completing a work assignment on time. Such expectations represent monochronic behavior.

As noted earlier, the samba came to be seen as synonymous with carnivals, the most well-known of which occurs in Rio. Throughout the world most carnivals last 1 day, but in Rio, Carnival extends over 4 days. Each of the 16 samba schools works steadily over the year preparing its float for various parades and competitions, and the final parade occurs in the Sambodromo, a one-of-a-kind parade stadium that can hold 60,000 people. Various theories are used to explain the uniqueness and popularity of Brazilian Carnival. One prominent explanation emphasizes the escape this celebration allows from daily drudgery, as well as the spontaneous and unexpected activities, the parties and parades, which let members of different social classes mingle easily with one another.

The spontaneity of Brazilian culture can be seen at times within its institutions. One Brazilian recounted her college years in Brazil by describing situations when students would just spontaneously take whatever was in reach and start tapping out the samba beat. For example, a pencil may be tapped on a desk or a ruler slapped on a chair. Many Brazilians can describe their school days with similar stories. For this reason, samba is even more clearly a cultural representation of Brazil. How to achieve spontaneity and escape reality through the dance and motions of samba are taught to all Brazilians from their early years of education through university graduation.

Soccer, or what most of the world calls football, is yet another cultural aspect of Brazil that reflects the spontaneity of the samba. In fact, the Brazilian style of play is called "samba soccer" and is characterized by flashy, complicated, and high-risk offensive maneuvers. Brazil has won more world championships than any other nation, and arguably the greatest soccer player of all time is the Brazilian Pelè. Brazil will host the soccer World Cup in 2014 and the Olympic Games in 2016.

Rich and Poor

The people of Brazil also feel a need to escape the day-to-day realities of the economy. Despite significant displays of prosperity, Brazil's largest cities are overcrowded and home to some of the poorest people in the world. In fact, Brazil is the country with the most *favelas* or ghettos in Latin America, and escape for these Brazilians is essential to their endurance and survival.

The idea of escape is very much a part of the Brazilian culture and language. One of the most famous phrases that Brazilians use, which best sums up the Brazilian civilization, is *tudo bom*—everything about life turns out to be good in some way or another. This phrase is illustrative of the Brazilians' attitude toward life and the negative twists and turns of daily life. Brazilians have endured much political and economic hardship, but they have frequently emerged from difficult situations dancing … the samba. One Brazilian demonstrated this phenomenon daily at the office when she would use the phrase *tudo bom* even when she was having a bad day.

It was her belief, as with most Brazilians, that disappointment is a fact of life; only by maintaining a positive attitude will everything eventually work out.

In terms of business practices, U.S. managers trying to do business in Brazil should realize that meetings will not always start or finish on time, that agendas may not be followed, and that requests may not be granted right away. As mentioned earlier, time is less important to Brazilians than to Americans, and schedules are frequently viewed simply as a formality. Again, however, this is much less true in the south than in the north.

Conventional U.S. rules of behavior in business situations, such as negotiations, are virtually nonexistent. One of the most significant differences between communication behavior in Brazil and in the United States is in the number of silent periods and conversational overlaps (Adler, 2007). The number of silent periods is somewhat larger in the United States, while conversational overlaps occur more often in Brazil. Brazil tends to be a more polychronic than monochronic society, and Brazilians tend to be a spontaneous people. For example, Brazilians typically feel that their opinions are most important, and they speak when they feel like doing so, even to the point of interrupting others abruptly. Brazilians tend to interrupt each other constantly, perhaps reflecting the need for individual expression for the good of the whole, consistent with this culture's relative rankings with respect to collectivism/individualism. Brazilians are very open to negotiations, and nothing is considered absolute. This approach to bargaining reflects the need of Brazilians to be individualistic and not to conform.

Mixing Business and Social Life

In addition, given the collectivist orientation of Brazilian society, it is not uncommon to see a high correlation between people's personal and work lives. For example, major firms in Brazil help their employees out with their financial problems and are very accommodating to family illnesses and other personal needs.

Another aspect of conducting business in Brazil that relates to the spontaneous escape of the samba is the need Brazilians have to socialize at lunch with potential business partners. Specifically, as in most Latin cultures, Brazilians do not feel life is all work and no play. The lunch setting is the typical Brazilian businessperson's escape from an often frustrating work environment. So when attending a business lunch with a Brazilian, one should accept small talk and non-business-related conversations and adapt. Managers should also be open to questions about their hobbies and families. The business lunch in Brazil is an opportunity for potential business partners to get to know each other and not necessarily to talk about the bottom line. Brazilians take their meal times very seriously and cherish the chance to get away from business issues. Typical business lunches in Brazil can last anywhere from 1½ to 3 hours. For U.S. Americans hoping to form alliances in Brazil, it is helpful to recognize and respect this need to escape as part of the Brazilian culture.

Moreover, people hoping to conduct business in Brazil might be most comfortable if they realize and appreciate that Brazil is a country with few clear-cut rules.

For example, in Brazil, behavior such as reneging on a contract is treated as ethical when the person is seeking to protect long-term relationships not covered by the contract. For many Westerners, this type of behavior would be considered unethical and reprehensible. When doing business with Brazilians, it is useful to understand their way of going around things instead of confronting them . . . dancing around things. Thus, for most Brazilians, the samba represents a stable factor over time, amid changing currencies, inflation, and political parties.

Paradox of Dancers

It is not unusual for Brazilian factory workers to spend a month's salary on the costumes they will wear at the Carnival parade. With friends from their samba school, with whom they have been rehearsing the entire year, they will dance on top of a gigantic dragon during the parade and experience a short but heavenly sense of existence. Such experiences portray very well the influence and impact of samba in Brazil. Samba schools in Brazil started more than 70 years ago and are as much a part of regional identity as soccer teams. Such behaviors, however, best illustrate the paradox of the dancers of the samba.

As the story demonstrates, in Brazil the dancers of the samba are full of contrasts. When preparing to compete with other samba schools or to dance samba in Carnival, Brazilians escape to another world where they can be anything they want. For that one moment, the samba is their ticket to paradise. For example, samba costumes can cost up to US$4,000 (a year's income for slum dwellers). This figure is probably at the high end; most slum dwellers, while spending a good amount of money, do not spend their entire year's salary on a costume. For some, however, "their investment pays off by bringing to life a daydream appropriate to the ancestors of slaves. . . . They for a day become a friend of the king" (Krich, 1993, p. 69). This paradoxical way of living is seen in many aspects of the Brazilian culture.

As Krich (1993) points out, whole samba parades are constructed as a tribute to an obscure, bygone composer; a forgotten slave revolt; the history of rice cultivation; or even the glory of the banana. This contrast between pleasure and pain can be seen throughout the Brazilian countryside. Eugene Robinson (1997) identifies the city of Salvador da Bahia as the pulse of Brazilian music. In this city, the contrasting images that Brazilians carry within them become most evident through activities in the central plaza. The plaza is a tourist mecca where travelers pose for pictures and dreadlocked entrepreneurs sell local crafts; years ago, this same plaza was the site of the public torture of slaves.

Contrast and Paradox

Historically Brazil has been a country of contrasts and paradoxes. As noted earlier, Brazilian people come from various social and economic backgrounds and races, and few nations can match this nation's diversity. Although many experts believe people of European descent have made the greatest contribution to the physical appearance of Brazilians, they also believe that extensive interracial marriage throughout history has created a population so genetically complex that Brazilians constitute a new and distinct people.

The people of Brazil can easily confuse outsiders. Although most Brazilians look "black," at least to North American eyes, only about 6% tell census takers they consider themselves Black. Furthermore, Brazilians have many terms describing *mestiços,* or mixed races. Brazilians use numerous and creative metaphorical names for describing the various skin types found in Brazil. For example, they refer to very dark African types as *cor do carvão* (color of coal) and to dark-skinned people occupying important positions in society as *branco da terra* (white of the earth). One household survey indicated that respondents employed an astounding 136 terms to describe individuals along the black-white continuum ("No Black and White," 2006). These results may seem surprising because Brazilian society has been successful in combining many racial and ethnic elements in its art, food, and music. Although differences in social status exist, there are times, such as when dancing the samba, that the overall feeling of the people is "We are all Brazilian." This slogan identifies the overarching feeling of Brazil as a culture and perhaps even an ethnic unit.

Still, the issue of race is extremely complicated in Brazil. There is a good amount of income inequality, and much poverty is concentrated among those with darker skin pigmentation, even though Brazilians of all types tend to interact more easily in daily life than their U.S. counterparts. Eugene Robinson (1995, 1999), an African American journalist, attributes the difference between Brazil and the United States to the "one-drop" theory prevalent in the United States; that is, one drop of African blood leads to a classification as Black. As a result, there is a wide "Black versus White" gap in the United States, supported by demographic classifications.

In Brazil the opposite theory was prevalent, that is, one drop of white blood makes the person White. Hence it is popular to use the term "Brazilian rainbow" but not "American rainbow," even though gradation of skin color is a point of discussion among African Americans. Because of this indeterminacy of skin color, some observers argue that social class is much more important than race in Brazil, and even more important in Brazil than in class-conscious England (P. B. Smith & Bond, 1998). Ironically, scientists now argue that race is a useless and superficial classification, an artifact of archaic pseudoscience informed by colonialist biases. To complicate matters, it should be noted that there are large numbers of other ethnic groups in Brazil. In fact, few nations have a population more diverse than Brazil, which includes people of Native American, European, African, and East Asian origin of both pure and mixed blood. Brazil has not only the largest concentration of Blacks and their descendants outside of Africa but also the largest concentration of Japanese and their descendants outside of Japan. All or almost all of them identify primarily with Brazil. For example, 100,000-plus Japanese Brazilians work in low-level jobs in

Japan because of the lack of jobs in Brazil, but virtually none speak the Japanese language, and they are shunned by the Japanese. Similarly, German Brazilians, almost all of whom use Portuguese as their primary language, celebrate Oktoberfest in the traditional German manner until midnight, when Brazilian music like the samba transforms the event. Commenting on such phenomena, the *Economist* ("Eine Kleine Samba," 1995) argues that "the Brazilian rainbow," even with its defects, should be studied in depth: "Brazilians are remarkable more for what brings them together than for what keeps them apart" (p. 49).

This ironic unity is also reflected in the Brazilian cuisine. Many traditional dishes, such as seafood stews, replete with palm oil and coconut milk, have been heavily influenced by African cuisine. The arts and crafts, particularly wood carvings, look as though they could have been produced in Senegal or Ghana. These examples are part of the everyday surroundings of Brazil.

The contrast between rich and poor appears in almost every aspect of Brazilian culture. For example, many cities in Brazil are a paradox of modern-day skyscrapers and industry and colonial churches and villages. It is not uncommon to see luxury apartments and houses at the foot of slum hills, or *favelas*. The government also reflects the paradox of the tango in that its business is half privatized and half government run, again placing Brazil in the middle of the individualism/collectivism continuum.

The Role of Religion

In addition, religion illustrates the contrasts of the Brazilian people. The pervasive religion in some parts of Brazil is a syncretism of Roman Catholicism and African cult worship, featuring a pantheon whose origins can be traced directly back to Africa. The many religions of Brazil also reflect contrasts in that numerous witch-craft and cult religions have borrowed symbols, such as the crucifix and various saints, from Catholicism. Hence religious components are intermingled such that conservative Catholic traditions are adapted to practice of witchcraft and belief in supernatural powers. In the census, 73% of Brazilians identify as Catholics, 15% as evangelicals, 5% as other religions, and 7% as of no religion. In Brazil there is great tolerance for contradiction.

In Latin America the estimated number of evangelical Protestants increased from 5 million in 1960 to 60 million in 1997, and there is no indication that this trend will reverse. To counter this movement, Brazilian Catholic priests now use rap music, sambas, and related music as a means of attracting Catholics back to the fold (Faiola, 1997).

As a final statement on the paradox of Brazil and its people, we can look to the Brazilian flag, which has a large yellow diamond on a green background. The color green stands for the lush fields and forests of Brazil. The color yellow represents its wealth in gold, which is found in many areas of the country. In the center of the yellow diamond is a blue sphere that symbolizes the usual navy blue sky that one finds in the Earth's tropical areas. In that sky are stars that represent the capital of the country and its federal states. In the middle of the sphere is a white banner with a legend *Ordem e Progresso,* which means "Order and Progress." This description of Brazil by the Brazilian people is a paradox in itself. Although Brazilians take pride in their abundant national resources, current business practices are actually eroding these resources, such as the Amazon forest. Furthermore, the notion of "Order and Progress" is quite contrary to how the country has largely been governed in its colorful history.

The paradox of the dancers of the samba has important implications for business-people wanting to work with Brazilians. As we have illustrated above, Brazilians are a melting pot of people with characteristics that are not easily categorized or, for that matter, understood. When trying to work with Brazilians, it is helpful to remember their rich history and cultural triumphs. Patience is the key virtue in forming business partnerships in this country, although Brazilians are very hospitable to visitors, going out of their way to ensure that they are comfortable. Still, sensitivity to class differences and various special-interest groups is necessary when forging political alliances and strategic advantages. Brazil is a country of many differences, yet it can be united through dancing the samba for a common cause. For this reason, it is important to understand the various elements in the Brazilian population to become comfortable with its economy, society, and culture (people).

In sum, Brazil is a vast nation comprised of great diversity and contrasts. Still, as the opening quote for this chapter suggests, most if not all Brazilians regard the nation and its culture as special and extraordinary. Despite the significant changes that Brazil has made and must continue to make to its infrastructure and regulatory environment, it will continue to be diverse, complex, and mysterious, and the samba will continue to express these cultural themes in new and exciting ways.

CHAPTER 33

The Argentine Tango

Tango . . . that infinite possibility.

—poet Leopoldo Marecal, quoted in
Nielsen and Mariotto (2006, p. 20)

*Now that I am well-seasoned and can move with the best of them, some-
times I love to simply sit and watch this dance that is more than a hundred
years old. I notice that many tangueras, like me, close their eyes as they give
themselves over to what is summarily called a "three-minute love affair
with a stranger."... Those of us who want the whole world to dance the
dance that elevates the common hug to a lyrical art form feel validated: In
2009, the United Nations gave Argentine tango protected cultural status,
designating it "part of the world's Intangible Cultural Heritage of Humanity."*

—Camille Cusumano, a U.S. American who
is so entranced by the tango that she lived in
Buenos Aires for 4 years just to dance and
study it (Cusumano, 2010, pp. 36–37)

Argentina is Latin America's second-largest country in terms of geography,
spanning 2.8 million square kilometers, and with a population of over 40
million, it is the fourth-largest in terms of population, following Brazil,
Mexico, and Colombia (U.S. Department of State, 2011). It is a country of dramatic
contrasts, extending from the subtropical beauty of the north, to the large panoramas
of the Pampas, to the wine country of Mendoza and the Andes, to the vast lands of
Patagonia, and finally to the sub-Antarctic, encompassing the farthest southern point
in the Western Hemisphere. Unlike Brazil, Argentina is not a melting pot of indigenous
and European populations. The vast majority is Caucasian (97%), mostly derived

from Spanish and Italian roots, with only 3% of the population representing mestizo, Amerindian, and other non-White groups. Argentina's minority population is found primarily in the far north, northwest, and south of the country (U.S. Department of State, 2011). The majority of Argentines live in cities and towns, with the largest concentration (one third) residing in greater Buenos Aires, the country's capital.

In contrast to Argentina's more homogenous population, Brazil's diversity is reflected in the languages used. Morrison and Conaway (2006) point out that 26 languages are in use in Argentina, while in Brazil the number is 192. Spanish is the dominant language of Argentina, while in Brazil it is Portuguese. Italian has had a major influence on Argentine Spanish. Many Italian words have been incorporated in the Argentine language, and an estimated 1.5 million citizens speak Italian, reflecting a linguistic influence that is unique in Latin America. As noted in Chapter 32, Brazil has the largest community of Japanese outside of Japan, although most speak only Brazilian Portuguese, and a large community of Germans, many of whom speak both Portuguese and German.

There are other significant differences. Brazil is much larger geographically at 8.5 million square kilometers, and Brazil's population of 194.2 million is also much larger. Argentina has only 14.4 individuals per square kilometer, while Brazil has 22.8. Still, in comparison with many other nations, such as Singapore and Taiwan, neither figure is large. In Singapore's case, the comparable figure is 7,042.2. There are also significant differences in the structure of employment: In Argentina 1% of the workforce is employed in agriculture, 23% in industry, and 76% in services, while the comparable Brazilian percentages are 21%, 19%, and 60%, respectively. Argentina is particularly well-known for raising beef cattle and growing wine.

Argentines have a high level of literacy at 97.7%, with compulsory education to 18 years of age. Argentina ranks 61st among nations in public expenditure on education, at 4.9% of gross domestic product; by contrast Brazil ranks 55th and the United States 43rd based on 2007 statistics. The gross domestic product (GDP) per individual in Argentina is US$8,240, while that of Brazil is US$8,210; in the United States the comparable figure is $46,350.

Brazil and Argentina share more than geographic borders. Argentina was colonized by the Spanish while the Portuguese colonized Brazil, but Spain and Portugal are both located on the Iberian Peninsula and are close neighbors. Less than 200 years ago, Spain ruled Portugal for a brief period. However, citizens of Brazil and Argentina do not speak the other's language as a general rule. In large part for this reason, English has become the most commonly used language, as it bridges cultural and ethnic linguistic differences. Today both countries are democratic republics featuring bicameral houses of representation, a supreme court, and a presidential system based on popular elections.

Argentina and Brazil belong to the Latin American cultural cluster and share a number of cultural values, based on rigorous analysis in the GLOBE study (Gupta & Hanges, 2004). Nielsen and Mariotto (2006) co-authored a major scholarly article on the Argentine tango based on the approach to cultural metaphors used in this book. Among the factors identified as cultural characteristics of Argentina, they, too, found a number that are identical or similar to those found in Brazil. These include a polychronic rather than monochronic orientation, high-context communication in many situations, hierarchical and group orientation, and an emphasis on the belief that humans are capable of both good and evil (see Table 32.1 at the end of this chapter).

However, immersion in these two countries reveals that the national characteristics of these neighbors diverge in significant ways. Understanding of the Argentine tango and the Brazilian samba provide an excellent basis for cross-cultural comparison. They offer significant insights into each country's evolution and national characteristics that persist today. Through the Argentine tango and the Brazilian samba we can delve more deeply into these two cultures, enabling us to understand their similarities and the significant differences that are not revealed through cultural dimension frameworks. It is noteworthy that both of these music traditions have received UNESCO status as Intangible Cultural Heritage of Humanity (UNESCO, 2010). The tango was nominated by the cities of Buenos Aires, Argentina, and Montevideo, Uruguay; and the nominated samba was a traditional version from the Brazilian state of Bahia.

The tango is a vital part of the cosmopolitan life of Buenos Aires, generating substantial economic activity through tango shows, clubs, and many other venues throughout the city. The tango adds US$135 million annually as direct income to the city and triple that amount indirectly (UNCTAD & UNDP, 2010).

The Tango's Evolution

Over 400 years of Argentina's development, the tango has grown to a place of preeminence, a symbol of the Argentine national character. Its roots lie in the *habernera* (dances) of Black slaves and the *milongas* (folk songs) of the gauchos. It was first established as a unique dance form in the *arrabales* (lower-class neighborhoods) of Buenos Aires and gradually engaged the participation of the complete array of Argentina's socioeconomic classes and political persuasions.

Hierarchical Groups and Collectivism

At the turn of the 20th century, the lower classes of Buenos Aires lived and worked under difficult, hazardous conditions. Racial and economic groups lived in segregated areas of the city. The unskilled worked at the port, in slaughterhouses, in meatpacking plants, in construction, at railroad stations, in wholesale and retail trade, in public services, and as migrant workers during harvesting seasons in the interior. Women and children worked in manufacturing in crowded, unhealthy conditions.

Skilled and semiskilled workers also worked long hours in such trades as carpentry, butchery, and shoemaking (Rock, 1987). The lives of the poor and working class of Buenos Aires were dramatically different from those of the elites, who built mansions and chalets on the north side of the city, and the middle class, who settled on the west side. By 1910, the city's centennial, Buenos Aires claimed the title of "Paris of South America" (Scobie, 1910/2002).

Economic booms in the 1880s and again from the late 1890s to 1912 were driven by high levels of trade and foreign investment and dramatic increases in immigration. During these periods, immigrants and creoles (native born) from the lower classes received high wages (relatively speaking) for hard work. There was great optimism regarding future growth and prosperity. By 1898 Argentina ranked as 1 of the top 10 wealthiest countries in the world based on GDP per capita (Molteni, 2003), a distinction it held through 1913 (The Long Road Back: A Survey of Argentina, 2004). During the 1890s, 850,000 immigrants arrived in Buenos Aires, and during the period 1900–1913, the net balance of immigrants over emigrants was nearly 1.7 million (*Economic Development of Argentina*, 1919). Yet this rosy picture masked a darker side. A pattern of boom and bust cycles became common, coincident with great economic inequality and periods of intense unrest and civil strife.

The immigrants were predominantly male; they came to make their fortunes and then return home to Europe. For most, traditional family life was elusive in Argentina. Prostitution proliferated, with 300 legal brothels registered by 1913 and many more illegal *clandestinos* operating in the outer districts of Buenos Aires. Brothels and dance halls (where the tango was the "star") were frequently the same thing.

Due to the strongly hierarchical structure of society, the tango's association with the disadvantaged and the poor created an initial barrier to its acceptance by the country's elite. However, by 1910 the tango had made its way to France; by 1913 "tangomania" was spreading in Europe, despite the outrage expressed by some, and the majority of tango enthusiasts on the Continent were members of the elite classes. Ricardo Guiraldes, a handsome young writer and a member of the Argentine elite, is given considerable credit for the positive reception that the tango received in France. Frequently spending "the season" in Paris, he literally swept his admirers off their feet with his expressive, passionate tango dance (Cooper, 1995). Although he had learned the dance in "disreputable" nightspots in Buenos Aires, he carried the dance to Europe with the imprimatur of the elite. Once accepted on the Continent, the tango was embraced by the wealthy classes at home.

The reality of rigid hierarchical groups and the desire for upward mobility are constant themes upon which the tango rests. According to the GLOBE study, the practice of collectivism is pronounced in Argentina, which ranked 58th highest out of 62 countries on the practice of institutional collectivism and 8th highest in terms of the value placed upon it (Gupta & Hanges, 2004). This result contrasts to a degree with Hofstede's (1991) earlier work, which classified Argentina as a moderately collectivist country.

Tango Music and Composers

The cultures of Argentina and Brazil can be effectively described by cultural metaphors emphasizing specific types of dance that originated in the slums or barrios of these two nations. However, the interpretation of the major features of these two cultural metaphors is markedly different. As indicated in the previous chapter, the samba tends to be a noisy dance during which it is difficult to hold any conversation, whether one is dancing or just sitting in the room where dancing takes place. Similarly, the earliest tango music was based on important but light-hearted aspects of lower-class life, such as the search for love and amorous conquests. The earliest records of tango musicians indicate that many were Black or mulatto, and early tangos were sung and danced in brothels and dance halls.

However, the tango evolved into a far more sophisticated and complex dance with growing popularity throughout the world. There are now tango festivals from Europe to Asia, and tango musicians, dancers, and singers can be found in many nations. The tango takes place with musical accompaniment, but not when a tango vocalist is singing. When the singer is performing, the focus is on the lyrics and on the human and social themes conveyed by the interaction between the musicians and singer. It is this ability to convey themes and emotions that many devotees of tango find irresistible. Some Argentine dance companies, like Tango Argentina, are famous internationally and tour around the world.

Melancholy and Pessimism

To understand the tango, we need to explore the instruments in a tango orchestra or band. A key instrument is the bandoneon, a small German accordion that produces a sound of deep sadness and melancholy. In fact, the Argentines changed the structure of the bandoneon in order to produce this unique sound. When it is joined with other tango instruments, the integrated sound can be expressive of a range of moods, including great passion, struggle, and perseverance. Tango orchestras place significant emphasis on this sound. A traditional group would include four bandoneons and four violins in addition to piano and bass guitar.

The appearance of the bandoneon underlines the foundation of tango as an original musical genre. The symbolism of the sound emanating from the bandoneon runs deep and demonstrates a close relationship between tango music and the spirit of lower classes at the end of the first decade of the 1900s. By this time, the working class had found that the economic prosperity of the country was concentrated in the upper classes. While immigration had been seen as central to the nation's growth and prosperity in the mid-1800s, by 1910 Argentine elites and native-born lower classes were feeling threatened by the hoards of newcomers.

The mind-set of the new nation was splitting along class lines: elites against the lower classes and Porteños (Buenos Aires residents) against the landowners of the interior and rural poor (Shumway, 1991). The irony was that the shared bond of the "outsider" and "outcast" among these poor and working-class groups served as a unifying force and the beginning of a new, shared identity. Lacking any formal or political power, these alienated citizens found their political voice in the tango. Tango was proving to be more than simply a musical genre; it had enveloped cultural traits related to loyalty and dedication to values such as pride and courage. These have been decisive factors in national political processes, including mass movements and popular proactive engagement in seizing power.

Perseverance and Defiance

This recurring struggle among socialism, capitalism, and sometimes communism, in which the military has periodically played a key role, is another characteristic that Argentina shares with Brazil and other Latin American nations. We described this struggle in Brazil in Chapter 32. Perhaps the leading example of the Argentine military's role in this cyclical struggle is the Army's 1943 coup, which succeeded due to a coalition of nationalist hardliners and moderates. Other than for brief periods under Yrigoyen (1916–1922 and 1928–1930), this was the first time in over 350 years that working-class living standards and conditions were raised to paramount importance.

Colonel Juan Perón emerged as leader, securing his power through a coalition of various social sectors, and he created a middle class with solid purchasing power and better economic and working conditions for the lower classes. As head of the Secretariat for Labor and Social Welfare, Perón emerged as the leader of the working class, settling strikes and in general improving their plight (D. K. Lewis, 2001). Labor unions and their leaders became his conduit to the popular power base. Perón's wife, Evita, became the subject of Andrew Lloyd Webber's international stage hit and musical, which was subsequently turned into an international best-selling movie. It is well worth seeing this film and interpreting it within the framework of this chapter.

During this Golden Age of tango (1920–1955), before the military took over the government (1955–1983), tango composers emphasized the struggles that the working poor faced, the loves that were lost, and similar themes. When Perón became president in 1946, there was an upsurge in confidence, and one well-known composer, Hugo del Carril, was so committed to Perón's socialistic policies that he composed "The Perónist March," a happy and well-known song that became the anthem of the Perónists.

Other well-known composers during this period included Osvaldo Pugliese, a staunch Communist and bandleader, who was arrested even while performing and imprisoned several times. He prepared for this inevitable imprisonment by wearing his pajamas under his suit when leading his band.

Anébal Troilo, a composer whose long career began in the 1930s and ended in the 1970s, is generally considered the patriarchal defender of the tango and related cultural values because of his stubborn insistence that he would compose tango music and lead his own band in playing it, even when the military government put severe restrictions upon the venues in which tango dancing was permitted.

As this discussion suggests, the military was well aware of the potential of the tango's power to be used in the service of revolution and for that reason restricted what could occur in the tango night clubs and dance halls. It did not want potential revolutionaries meeting to plot the government's overthrow. Hence the popularity of the tango declined during the 1950s, and younger Argentines began to frequent U.S. American–style nightclubs featuring rock and roll. Even though the military also put restrictions on these nightclubs, enforcement was lax except in the case of the tango. It was only the tango dancing halls and nightclubs that were feared. Since 1983 the popularity of the tango has increased significantly, not only in Argentina but worldwide.

Uncertainty Avoidance Versus Risk Taking

A remarkable composer whose fame is now worldwide, Astor Piazzolla revolutionized tango music by introducing such features as new rhythms, new instruments, complexity, and dissonance. Founder of tango's Advant-Garde School in 1955, he offended many tango traditionalists who were appalled by his innovations. They frequently confronted and jeered him in concerts and went so far in some cases as to send him death threats. At one performance of his newest tango, some members of the audience were so offended by his innovative music that they threw coins at him. Today his music is performed by professional tango dance companies and symphonic orchestras throughout the world. The integration of tango instruments, music, and moods into the symphonic setting has given tango music new dimensions, speaking to the strength and perseverance of the Argentine people.

If Troilo is the exaltation of the tango's roots, Piazzolla represents its growth and its quest for change. While Argentines had adjusted to gradual, evolutionary developments, many were hostile toward any abrupt departure from tango's roots. Piazzolla's innovations evoked strong emotions, including outright hatred from many traditionalists who believed he was destroying the tango by changing it.

Power Struggle

Traditional frameworks of Argentina's culture describe the country as one of high power distance, with power distributed unequally among society's members and within the family structure, the workplace, social institutions, and the political sphere. On Hofstede's power dimension, Argentina ranked 18/19 out of 50 countries, assigning Argentina to a high–power distance cluster (Hofstede, 1991). (Hofstede's second edition of *Culture's Consequences*, 2001, includes 53 nations—49 nations plus 4 territories that he treats as nations.) This measure of Argentina's hierarchical nature is consistent with its ranking in the more recent GLOBE study (Gupta & Hanges, 2004), in which Argentina was 5th out of 61 countries in terms of society's practice of greater power distance. As with Brazil, this high–power distance ranking for practice contrasts with beliefs in both countries that less power distance is to be valued; Argentina ranked 56th out of 61 in valuing high power distance. However, the tango metaphor reveals a more dynamic understanding of Argentine's true values. The tango is emblematic of a power struggle and the desire to overthrow unjust political structures.

Closely linked to power hierarchy is a desire for security and equilibrium, elusive qualities in Argentina's experience. Yet the tango, in all its aspects, speaks not only of power but also of submission, with utmost respect for the delicate balance that holds society in check. The predominant desire for stability is consistent with the characterization of Argentina as a society with high uncertainty avoidance. Historically Argentina ranks high in risk avoidance. According to Hofstede (1991), the country ranked a high 36/41 out of 50 countries in desire to avoid uncertainty. According to Hofstede, in such societies pressure builds toward a "trigger point" by which time inequalities have grown into abuses so severe that the subjugated can no longer tolerate them, and a revolution ensues. As the culture builds toward this trigger point, sadness turns to bitterness and anger; submission moves to subversive actions, violence, and rebellion. Political activism grows as courageous individuals and groups organize for collective action. Risk taking supplants risk aversion. Despite such sacrifices, once the old regime is overthrown, the new regime is just as likely as its predecessor to hold substantially unequal power as long as the organizing principle of society remains one of vertical hierarchy.

Hofstede's results contrast somewhat with the more recent GLOBE results in which Argentina scored 48th highest in the practice of uncertainty avoidance, while scoring 37th in valuing risk avoidance (Gupta & Hanges, 2004). This shift toward moderation between risk aversion and risk taking is consistent with Argentina's national profile today.

The Dynamics of the Dance

Another key feature of the tango is its kinetics, or the manner in which the motions and actions in the dance create a unique sense of energy and dynamism. In this regard the Brazilian samba is fundamentally different from the tango. As indicated in the previous chapter, the samba emphasizes the use of the hips to achieve undulation, small step circularity, and physical touch. The noise level associated with the samba is also much louder and can be ear splitting. Unlike the samba, the tango relies on the use of the legs and feet to create complex dance movements. Tightening the legs before beginning to dance and throughout results in tension and uncertainty. The samba and tango are similar in that the samba music skips the first beat, thus also resulting in a feeling of uncertainty and tension. However, in most other ways, tango dance movements are fundamentally different from those of the samba, just as Argentina is significantly different from Brazil.

High Context

When one observes the tango for the first time, one may notice that the dancers tend to be formal and that they perform quickly and efficiently a large number and variety of complicated steps and moves in which they share the space between them. Historically, the early tangos featured close embraces by the dancers that conveyed clearly the passion of the dancers for one another. However, the evolution of the tango led to the creation of many rules in which the dancers must adroitly cooperate to use a defined space between them, called the *sphere of contention,* for each move or step. The dancers do not look at each other; rather each stares out into space, a gaze known as the tango *visteo.* This blank stare originates from the earliest tangos, enacted by men who were mimicking their knife-fighting positions. By not looking at his opponent, the fighter was able to conceal his next moves and keep his intentions hidden. Cooperation is essential to dance the tango, but the air of tension within the dancers' shared space is palpable.

Typically, the dance begins with a pair of tango dancers standing in a fixed embrace but motionless on the dance floor, waiting to begin a few moments after the orchestra has started to play in order to absorb the context of music and mood. Then they begin to engage in their complex moves. However, the upper part of their bodies remains stable while the legs and feet are constantly in motion.

Polychronic Dimension

Unlike most popular dances, the tango is performed in a circular rather than a forward and backward pattern. A distinctive element of the tango's design is the angle of movement:

> Dancers use foot and leg rotations to change direction. Because the angle variations are limitless, so are the directions the dance can take. . . . Unlike more mechanical dances that are choreographed along well-defined patterns, the tango is biological and organic design. (Nielsen & Mariotto, 2006, p. 20)

Needless to say, to become an expert tango dancer takes times and practice. Still, one can learn some basic tango steps within the space of 30 to 60 minutes, and frequently lessons for beginners are offered before the official dancing period begins. Being in good physical condition is helpful, as constant motion and dramatic steps and kicks are part and parcel of the tango. Ordinarily an orchestra will play continuously and highlight several pieces over 15 minutes. While it is not necessary to dance every tango, experienced dancers and tango orchestras prefer the inclusion of several pieces of music over this period rather than dancing to just one 3-minute piece at a time. Moods may change as each 3-minute tango begins. At times, each 3-minute tango is integrated into one mood over the 15-minute dancing period.

Tango Singers and Their Lyrics

As the tango developed, the lyricist became a fundamental actor in the process. This poetic aspect of the tango took root and became deeply valued by the public. The cultural construction initiated with tango music is completed by the lyrics, because they reveal fundamental characteristics of Argentine identity, linked to emotions and behaviors. There is no contradiction between tango dance and tango song: Lyrics and music come together in a complementary manner to deliver the full impact of the tango message.

Particularist Society

While the earliest tango lyrics were light and frequently bawdy, the struggles of the lower classes came to dominate the lyrics and tone of the tango. One of the frequent tango themes over the decades focuses on the Argentine sociopolitical environment in which powerful leaders cared nothing about the disadvantaged. In the first half of the twentieth century, the government even restricted the use of some words and themes, such as grinding poverty and a stratified society, found in some tango songs. It outlawed the use of words and phrases in *lunfardo,* a working-class invention of a language that those speaking only Spanish could not understand.

As our discussion of the ideological conflicts that have occurred and are occurring in Argentina and Brazil suggests, we would expect that their respective rankings on the 2011 Index of Economic Freedom would be similar. This is generally confirmed, with Brazil ranking 113th and Argentina 138th out of 189 nations. This Index incorporates 10 measures of economic freedom such as degree of corruption, fiscal soundness and openness to trade and investment, government size, business and labor regulation, property rights, monetary stability, and financial competition (T. Miller, 2011). There are still many impediments to economic progress in both nations.

Throughout much of Argentina's history, powerful and wealthy families tended to dominate both political and economic spheres and frequently changed the rules and laws to preserve and foster their own well-being. Transparency International publishes an annual Corruption Perceptions Index (CPI) focusing on public sector corruption worldwide. In the most recent report, Argentina ranked 100th of 178 countries, indicating a high level of corruption that impedes economic development. Brazil scored better at 73rd, while the United States was 24th (Transparency International, 2011).

Generally societies that do not value the rule of law and do not enforce equal rights independent of social and economic standing are referred to as particularist societies, as opposed to universalist societies in which people believe that everyone should be equally accountable under the law. In particularist countries, people believe that protecting friends and families from the official judicial structure is more important than following the law because the legal system has a track record of being unfair. While this way of viewing the world becomes a self-fulfilling prophecy over the long run, the experiences of the majority of Argentines during much of the twentieth century reinforced this perspective.

A leading example is provided by the horrific aftermath of Perón's departure. Despite many positive outcomes for the working class during Perón's leadership (1946–1955), his charismatic hold on the country did not last. Miscalculation of fiscal and monetary policies, combined with an international trade regime stacked against Argentina's full participation, led to deteriorating economic and political conditions (D. K. Lewis, 2001). However, these did not justify the violence of the opposition. In September 1955, after some military factions bombed Plaza de Mayo (Mayo Square) to demand Perón's resignation, leaving several hundred civilians dead, he stepped down and went into exile for 18 years (Rock, 1987). During the period between Perón's overthrow and the fall of the last military junta in 1983, government changed 16 times in a sequence of military and civilian, non-Perónist and Perónist administrations, all of which failed to achieve a balance between economic growth and political stability. This became known as tango's Dark Age (1955–1983).

Forces of change on the left grew out of social action groups within the Catholic Church, a major force in Argentina's history. To this day, 92% of Argentines are nominally Catholic, although fewer than 20% are practicing. Growing numbers among the middle and upper-middle classes, including university professors and other professionals, joined in support of the resistance. By 1970 the country had deteriorated into a state of armed struggle. When the military grasped power in 1976, General Jorge Rafael Videla attacked rebels and members of the civilian population with a vengeance and without any pretense of upholding the rule of law. Videla's police forces and military units tortured tens of thousands and murdered 30,000 (National Commission on the Disappearance of Persons, 2002). Thousands more fled Argentina.

The tango song "Bronca" (1962), authored by Mario Battistella, expresses the grief and bewilderment of the middle class in the face of the inexplicable political decisions of the governments that came one after the other:

These are the modern times

when crooks are winning,

and those who want to be decent

date back to the time of Columbus ...

What is going on in this country,

what is going on, my God,

that we had come so low?

Year sixty-two

has made its point!

What is going on,

what is this evil sign

that not even brothers understand each other

in this atrocious confusion?

Is it lack of bucks,

is it that there is no more loyalty . . .

isn't our conscience worth much more?

Shoot, this unfair mankind

makes me so angry!

The horrors of this regime and its puppet generals finally became widespread knowledge by the early 1980s, due largely to the persistence and courage of the Mothers of the Disappeared, women who publicly commemorate the many casualties of the junta whose fates were never disclosed. With the army's failure in its execution of the Malvinas Islands invasion, the last vestiges of support for military rule evaporated.

This period marked one of the major "trigger points" in Argentine history. The Argentine people could no longer bear the corrupt power of the political system, and the military was ousted from power. Since 1983 the country has followed civilian rule, with transitions from one president to the next through democratic elections, ushering in what is referred to as tango's Contemporary Period. However, by 2001 the inflation rate reached 5,000%, and the country erupted with general strikes, looting, protests, and some violence. Unemployment soared, reaching 25% or more, akin to the U.S. unemployment rate during the Great Depression. Control returned to the Justicialist Party (Perón's Party) under the leadership of President Nestor Kirchner, former governor of a rural province in Patagonia and son of Croatian and Swiss immigrants. Kirchner's election demonstrated Argentina's willingness to elect a political "outsider" and symbolized the country's embrace of the heroic tango "outsider" ("Becoming a Serious Country," 2004). He took a tough stand against Argentina's foreign bondholders and creditors, including the International Monetary Fund (IMF). This made him unpopular internationally but enhanced his standing at home ("Grinding Them Down," 2005). Argentina defaulted on its international loans, effectively meaning it would not get additional loans without making major changes. In 2005 conditions began to improve markedly. Today the government's socialist policies are still popular and are being implemented side by side with capitalist policies, but the future is uncertain in terms of whether changes in government will emphasize the power of socialistic or capitalistic orientations.

Political oligarchy continues in Argentina. The current president, Christina Fernández de Kirchner, is the wife of the past president. She has continued the economic policies of her husband, who died suddenly in 2010, lessening the direct impact of an economic downturn in 2009 through continued government spending. However, a major disadvantage of this approach is increasing inflation, which is unofficially far more than the official rate of 11% ("Happy-go-lucky Cristina," 2010). Feelings about tango as a symbol of national identity continue to intensify—so much so that a significant group of Argentine tango lovers is taking action to bar immigrants from competing in national and international dance contests representing Argentina (Moffett, 2011). However, the liberal Justicialist Party stands for the "outsider"; hopefully its traditional support for the tango will hold sway. It would be ironic if the national dance born of Argentina's immigrant class would come to exclude them.

Task/Achievement Orientation
Versus Humane Orientation

Hofstede (1991) concluded that Argentina is a moderately masculine (task-oriented) society, ranking 30/31 out of 50 countries. This national profile of valuing achievement over human relations appears consistent with the results of the GLOBE study. Although the latter did not have a "masculinity-femininity dimension" per se, findings indicate that its Humane Orientation is a similar construct, akin to Hofstede's femininity classification on the masculinity-femininity continuum. Argentina fell close to the mean score, ranking 33rd out of 62 in society practices of a human orientation and 21st out of 62 in valuing a humane orientation.

It is true that Argentina is an achievement-oriented society. Despite the odds, people from the lower classes may rise to achieve social and economic standing. For this reason, working hard and playing hard are valued highly. Among the working class characters who populate the tango song are individuals, mythical and real, who possessed the traits, capabilities, and motivation to overcome class barriers. The most famous of these may be tango singer Carlos Gardel, who arrived in Argentina at the age of 2, the illegitimate son of a French woman who took in ironing to support them. He rose from poverty to become the most famous tango singer of all times, a superstar to millions in Argentina and abroad. He began his career in popular music, such as *canciones camperas* (folk music), but Gardel turned to the tango by the mid-1910s and became its most virtuosic interpreter and the most genuine representative of this genre. Prolific in his production, the singer left more than 900 recordings, and he starred in a number of remarkable films for Paramount Studios. In his poem "Gardel," Humberto Constantini captured the people's aspirations to believe in role models who could achieve success and excel despite the odds against them.

"Let us make up a name, a smile,

a voice that lasts for centuries,

a nice and easy posture in the world,

like sending aces to destiny."

And of course we wanted it

and it came.

And he came out dark haired, glorious, with grease in his hair,

eternal like a God or like a record.

The skies opened on the side

and his voice was singing to us:

My dear Buenos Aires . . .

Gardel is still revered in Buenos Aires, in Argentina and throughout Latin America. Because his life and work symbolized the ability of ordinary people to rise above desperate circumstances, gain acceptance, and succeed in Argentine society, he rose to mythical stature.

Gender Relations

In this section, we explore the complex and dynamic elements of gender relations, always a topic of interest to those interested in culture. The tango expresses this complexity and dynamism well and perhaps better than any other form of dance and/or music.

Hierarchical Groups

The earliest tangos were free-flowing, allowing freedom of movement of both female and male dancers. The first female tango dancers—European, *Chinas* (of Amerindian blood), and *Pardas* (Black or mulatto)—were found in the brothels and dance halls of Buenos Aires (Collier, 1995). During tango's Golden Age, lower-class women associated with upper-class men in the cabarets. They weren't referred to as prostitutes but as *alternadoras,* women who could entertain, talk, and dance with all classes of customers. They were viewed as "independent" to an extent that they sometimes appeared dangerous to the existing social structure. A growing number of women became recognized as composers and singers and were accepted into the tango culture (Savigliano, 1995). A leading example is soprano Libertad Lamarque, whose songs appealed to women, as her lyrics focused on the abuses and inequalities shared by many, including those in the middle and upper classes (Susmano, 2000).

In terms of dance dynamics, male dominance came to the fore over time. As the tango is most commonly danced today, the male has the responsibility to lead and direct the action. He indicates through gestures and other unspoken directions how the female dancer is to proceed. Among certain groups of tango dancers, this is an inviolate rule (J. Taylor, 1998). But there is also movement toward shared leadership today (Dinzel & Dinzel, 2000).

Group Orientation

Cooperation between male and female dance partners is essential, and the dance is emblematic of true partnership. The male and female dancers engage in the famous tango embrace. Both must constrain their movements within the sphere of contention, a limited space within which to complete complex kicks and side movements. Thus the female dancer demonstrates her skills simultaneously with the male. The tango today represents this shared experience. The dancers' moves echo society's evolution through periods of domination and dependence to "trigger points" in which power is transferred from one element to another.

Applying What We've Learned

Knowledge of the tango metaphor deepens our understanding of Argentina, its cultural dimensions, and complexities. Comparing cultural characteristics as portrayed in country clusters, one observes fundamental differences in prevailing attitudes, behaviors, and underlying values between Argentina and Brazil, classified within the Latin American cultural cluster, and countries lying within other clusters, such as those representing the Anglos (e.g., the United States, Canada, and Britain), and the clusters of Germanic Europe, Confucian Asia, the Middle East, and others (Gupta & Hanges, 2004). Such differences reinforce the need for cross-cultural understanding if cross-border relationships are to be built with individuals and groups in Argentina and if joint initiatives in business and society are to succeed. For example, the United States is described as operating within a low–power distance environment, valuing individualism and risk taking. On the other hand, Argentina is generally characterized as a high–power distance environment, valuing groups, human relations, and security. Regional differences are observed also in communication styles, many diverse behaviors, and gender relations. Understanding how these differences might impact successful cross-cultural interactions and long-term business success is extremely important. A number of these major differences are highlighted below.

Navigating Bureaucracy. The World Bank and the International Finance Corporation publish a global study that ranks countries based on the relative ease of setting up a business and doing business within their institutional and regulatory environments.

This comprehensive review includes the relative ease of starting a business, dealing with construction permits, registering property, getting credit, protecting investors, paying taxes, enforcing contracts, and closing a business. In its most recent report, Argentina ranked 115th out of 183 countries. Its neighbor, Brazil, received a dire ranking of 127th. By contrast the United States ranked 5th worldwide (World Bank & International Finance Corporation, 2010).

Midsize to large organizations in Argentina tend to be hierarchical structures, with formal authority and decision making flowing from the top down. In general, Argentine Business Groups (ABGs) are structured in this way. Thirty-seven of these represent 10% of Argentina's private sector activity in terms of annual revenues (Carrera, Mesquita, Perkins, & Vassolo, 2003). In lieu of instituting market and labor efficiencies, these firms tend to operate as related and unrelated diversified conglomerates in order to internalize and control necessary activities both central and peripheral. Group strength is beneficial, given the historical relationship between power politics and success. ABGs recognize the strategic advantage of extending their portfolios internationally to balance the persistent risk of operations in Argentina.

The majority of businesses in Argentina are small-scale operations. In these one would expect less hierarchy and formality. It is understood that those in power will benefit from privileges and special advantages. Hiring of family and friends is viewed positively in this environment, and once hired, it is expected that their employment will be protected. Loyalty is expected in exchange for such protections. Patriarchal structures are common. As an outsider, one should not expect to exercise formal authority without building relationships first.

Because the rule of law is often not respected in Argentina, one should not be surprised to learn that the underground economy is large, estimated at 25.4% of gross national income according to a 2004 World Bank report. In comparison, Brazil's is even larger at 39.8%.

Security. Argentines value security and are motivated to maintain stability even under difficult conditions. However, as at the macro level, dissatisfaction may brew under the surface and erupt in a heated debate or argument. In business dealings, Argentines do not appreciate surprises and expect major themes and details to be conveyed early so that they do not appear to be thrown in carelessly or to create an unfair advantage.

Emotions. Sense of security is a strong motivator, and the ability to offer permanent employment with fringe benefits is viewed positively. Mental health benefits are valued, and more industries and unions are offering these services as part of an employee benefits package. Sadness, melancholy, and depression are understandable reactions given the severe hardships endured in recent years (Whittle et al., 1998).

Behaviors. In an authority-ranking culture such as Argentina's, groups hold unequal power, and certain groups are viewed as being at the pinnacle of the power structure.

In this environment, one would expect reciprocity between those in command and those dependent on the system. Given this orientation, not only the powerful but also those at the bottom of the hierarchical pyramid accept such inequality as reality—up to a point. High power distance translates into relationships of dependency, with the underlying assumption that the superior has a responsibility to take care of the subordinate. As long as this responsibility is realized, high–power distance societies tolerate substantial levels of inequality along with concomitant differences in economic and political rights. However, beyond a certain trigger point, one can expect assertive or aggressive action. Ethical behavior is judged in terms of human relations, group loyalty, and status. This is consistent with Argentina's experience, not only domestically but also within the geopolitical power structures in which it is challenged to operate.

Relationships. Building relationships provides a means of establishing trust between parties, an essential ingredient in business dealings. Face-to-face meetings are essential. The process of getting to know one another begins with an exchange of general information and progresses to more specific business details. One should expect to share information about many areas of personal, family, and professional life. Communication is high context, meaning that Argentines read your nonverbal cues within the context of the exchange, and they will expect you to do the same. Direct answers may not be forthcoming, and confrontation will be avoided.

Task Orientation and Competitiveness. Argentines are willing to work hard to achieve their goals, but they are also committed to enjoying life. This translates into long hours at the office being followed by late-night dinners and social activities that last well into the night. A focus on human relations should not be construed as a lack of competitiveness. In fact, Argentines are skilled negotiators and can turn high-context communications to their advantage. Strategies may range from subtle and disguised to bold and matter-of-fact.

Innovation. Companies that have survived the past decade of economic turmoil have had to operate in efficient and innovative ways. Many companies have survived by modernizing plants and equipment. Commercial innovations are prevalent even in some traditional industries, such as agriculture. For example, productivity per hectare has risen 17% over the past decade, and Argentine crops remain competitive in world markets despite hefty export taxes and government subsidies of foreign growers ("The Long Road Back," 2004). Entrepreneurs are springing up, creating business opportunities in a wide variety of industries.

Time Dimension. Argentines do not rigidly hold to schedules. Giving time to others in personal and business settings is valued. Impatience is considered uncultured and rude.

Gender Relations. Women have made significant strides in business settings, and many now hold professional and management positions. However, such achievements require high levels of competence, perseverance, and patience. Many Argentine women with professional education and skills are underemployed. One should not underestimate their intelligence, their capabilities, or their motivational levels.

Summary

As indicated earlier, one of the key features of the tango is its ability to convey an amazing number of emotions and moods. While the tango originated in the barrios, Spanish and Italian patterns of thought and action have been integrated into the dance. Other influences include those of African slaves, Amerindians, and the working classes. Members of the upper classes also began to frequent the dance hall and influenced the tango. Indeed they championed the tango, which made it popular with all social classes. All of these influences helped the tango evolve into what it is today.

We have provided only a brief summary of the major characteristics of the tango. Nielsen and Mariotto (2006) classify these characteristics into four broad categories—music, kinetics, lyrics, and gender relations—all of which we have discussed above. As one becomes adept at dancing the tango, one appreciates it with deeper levels of understanding that only repeated practice can illuminate. Camille Cusumano, as noted at the beginning of the chapter, became so entranced by the tango that she devoted 4 years to living in Buenos Aires in order to study it in depth and participate regularly in tango dancing. She is not alone in making such a move because of the fascination that the tango holds on people's imaginations (see Mooney, 2001). Tango aficionados around the world are uniformly enthusiastic, and many, if not all, equate the many moods and complex movements of tangos with the complexity and universality of living, even to the extent of saying that "tango is life," just as many U.S. Americans feel that "football is life" (see Chapter 16). This expression shows the clear relationship between the tango and values associated with it, especially in Argentina. It is little wonder that Argentina is succinctly described as the land of the tango.

As indicated in Chapter 1, we have combined two approaches to the study of each national culture: the *etic* or culture-general approach that applies to all national cultures and the *emic* or culture-specific approach. The work of Hall and Hall (1990), Hofstede (1991, 2001), and Kluckhohn and Strodtbeck (1961) represent the *etic* perspective; cultural metaphors illustrate the *emic* perspective. In their scholarly article on the tango, Nielsen and Mariotto (2006) also combine these two approaches; Table 33.1 presents their conclusions about the manner in which the tango expresses the values of Argentina.

The only factor not emphasized in this book is that derived from a large questionnaire survey of many nations completed by Trompenaars and Hampden-Turner (1998). This factor refers to whether a rule is applied universally and objectively or subjectively based on relationships. For example, an owner of a company might hire the best-qualified candidate, or he or she might opt to hire a nephew who is much less qualified. Based on the discussion in this chapter, the reader should be able to read Table 33.1 and see the clear relationship between the tango and the cultural values of Argentina. The reader should also note the difference between the *etic* and *emic* factors. Both are important, and they complement one another.

This, then, is the culture of Argentina, still evolving and still being reflected in the tango. Undoubtedly Argentina will experience change over time, and, if history serves as a guide, we can expect that the changes in the tango will parallel changes in the national culture. As the quote at the beginning of the chapter states, tango emphasizes infinite possibility, which implies evolution over time, a variety of moods and themes, and a unique approach to dance that relies upon complexity. While life is different from its expression in the moods and steps of the tango dancers, the close relationship between life and tango will continue. As such, tango is not only a suitable cultural metaphor for this nation but even a barometer of what is currently happening in Argentina and what may well happen in the future.

Table 33.1 Argentina's Cultural Characteristics

Research Framework	Argentina's Value System Revealed Through Traditional Frameworks	Argentina's Value System Revealed Through the Tango Metaphor
Hall and Hall (1990)	(a) High context	(a) Kinetics
	(b) Polychronic	(b) Kinetics
Hofstede (1980a)	(a) Large power distance	(a) Partial support through music, kinetics, lyrics, and gender relations
	(b) High uncertainty avoidance	(b) Partial support through music, kinetics, lyrics, and gender relations
	(c) Group orientation	(c) Music, gender relations, partial support through kinetics
	(d) Task/achievement orientation	(d) Kinetics, lyrics, partial support through gender relations
Kluckhohn and Strodtbeck (1961)	(a) Humans capable of good and evil	(a) Kinetics, lyrics
	(b) Dominant over nature	(b) NO SUPPORT
	(c) Hierarchical groups	(c) Music, lyrics, gender relations
	(d) Task/achievement orientation	(d) Kinetics, lyrics, partial support through gender relations
	(e) Private space	(e) Partial support through kinetics
	(f) Time orientation in the present	(f) NO SUPPORT

(Continued)

Table 33.1 (Continued)

Research Framework	Argentina's Value System Revealed Through Traditional Frameworks	Argentina's Value System Revealed Through the Tango Metaphor
Trompenaars and Hampden-Turner (1998)	(a) Rules applied subjectively, based on relationships	(a) Lyrics
Characteristics of Argentina's Value System Not Covered by Traditional Frameworks		
Tango Metaphor	*Values:*	
	(a) Power struggle	(a) Music, kinetics, lyrics, gender relations
	(b) Risk-taking/innovation	(b) Music, kinetics, lyrics, gender relations
	Attitudes and Emotions:	
	(a) Melancholy	(a) Music, lyrics
	(b) Fear of isolation/abandonment	(b) Lyrics
	(c) Pessimism and despair	(c) Music/lyrics
	(d) Perseverance and defiance	(d) Music/lyrics
	(e) Passion	(e) Music, kinetics
	(f) Existence and temporal orientation disassociated	(f) Kinetics

Source: Reprinted with permission: Nielsen, C. S., & Mariotto, J. G. (2006). The tango metaphor: The essence of Argentina's national identity. *International Studies of Management and Organization, 35*(4), Table 2, pp. 29–30.

PART XII

Perspectives on Continents

A s one moves from the ethnic group to the nation to a group of nations to a continent, it is still possible but increasingly difficult to employ cultural metaphors as effective devices for profiling underlying cultural values and assumptions. This is true even for the one nation, Australia, that is also a continent. But it is even more true for other continents. Europe, for example, has numerous cultural and ethnic groupings. However, the globalized economy requires that we at least attempt to profile the underlying values and assumptions of continents if at all possible. Some citizens of various nations on the European continent, for example, now identify with the European Union (EU) as much as, or more than, their respective nations. However, surveys indicate that only 1 in 10 people think of themselves as European. The vast majority of respondents still identify themselves as citizens of specific nations. Of course, the complexity of this issue increases in the World Trade Organization, which includes a far larger number of nations.

In this part of the book, we profile two continents, Australia and Africa, although the cultural metaphor for Africa—the bush taxi—relates primarily to sub-Saharan Africa. We focus on Africa because almost all of the cross-cultural research to date, particularly among management and cross-cultural researchers, has disregarded this continent. We can only speculate on the reasons for such disregard, as we do in the chapter itself, but we maintain that it is essential for Africa to become better integrated into the world economy, and such integration is facilitated by an enriched cross-cultural comprehension of its strengths and problems.

CHAPTER 34

Australian Outdoor Recreational Activities

"Australians believe in mateship and a 'fair go' and have a strong affection for the underdog or 'battler.' These values stem from convicts and early colonialists who struggled against a harsh and unfamiliar land and often unjust authority."

—About Australia (www.australia.com/about/culture.aspx)

Australians and U.S. Americans tend to get along well with one another. Both tend to be highly informal in interactions and to downplay pomposity. Speaking the same language also facilitates comfortable communications. The two nationalities share historical experiences, as the British sent prisoners to populate the U.S. colonies until the American Revolution, after which the British shipped their prisoners to the "godforsaken" continent of Australia. Both nations are large, and Australia is about equal in size to the 48 contiguous states in the United States. The global economic upheaval that began in 2008 did not affect Australia as much as it did most of the Western world. The country benefited from growth in the Asian economies and one of the biggest resource booms in its history, which kept its mines, farms, and pipelines humming with activity (Curran, 2011). According to the *Economist,* unemployment was at 4.9% in 2011 and is expected to keep falling through 2012. In 2010, with unemployment in the United States close to 10%, American citizens headed to Australia in small but growing numbers to seek their fortunes (Rogow, 2010).

But there are vast differences between these two friendly nations. In this chapter, we discuss how and why Australia is so captivating to the imagination, not only of Americans but also of people throughout the world; we examine new realities that go beyond stereotypes; and we look at the phenomenon of equality matching "among the tall poppies"—cutting down to size those who manifest superior ability or high levels of motivation—especially if they are seen as pompous and self-aggrandizing.

In fact, there are so many fascinating aspects of Australian culture that it is difficult to select one of them as a cultural metaphor, and the changes in the past 50 years have been profound, thus compounding this difficulty. What seems to unify Australians, regardless of ethnic background, is outdoor recreational activities, including playing sports of all types and frequenting outdoor restaurants and coffeehouses. According to the Australian government, the 10 most popular physical activities are walking, aerobics/fitness, swimming, cycling, tennis, golf, running, bushwalking, football (often referred to as soccer in Australia), and netball. Other popular sporting activities include Australian football, rugby, hockey, basketball, baseball, car racing, horse racing, sailing, and snow skiing. We employ such recreational activities as our cultural metaphor.

Capturing the Imagination

Few, if any, nations capture the imagination of visitors as effectively as Australia. Quite a distance separates Australia from the United States and Europe, and even from Asia, although less so. Nonetheless, many people around the world want to visit Australia. In recent years Australia's relationship with Asia has been strengthened, as noted below. Australia is simultaneously an island, a nation, and the driest and most fragile of the seven continents. About a third of Australia is desert, but there are also mountains and rain forests.

Australia is an urbanized country, with more than half of its population settled in just five cities and almost 85% living in towns, most of which are close to the coasts. Nevertheless, the sparsely populated outback fascinates in a manner similar to America's Old West. For instance, Ned Kelly of outback fame is a real bandit whose death by hanging made him mythic, somewhat like Billy the Kid in the United States, and Australians know that he looked the judge straight in the eye before being hanged and said, "I will see you there where I go."

Even archetypal films from these two nations are similar. For example, arguably the greatest Western of all is *High Noon,* starring Gary Cooper as the marshal and Grace Kelly as his newly married wife who opposes violence because of her Quaker beliefs; the townspeople fail to support him when a gang of outlaws whom he sent to prison returns to exact revenge, and even his wife is initially noncommittal and even negative about his involvement in the coming fight. Still, he fights the gang against long odds and ultimately emerges as the winner, with some critical help from his wife at the last moment. The Australian counterpart film is *Mad Max,* in which Mel Gibson plays a lawman in the outback seeking justice because his wife and young child are brutally murdered. This film was so popular in the United States that it led to two sequels. Both films idealize the individual standing up against the unjust group and the environment surrounding him.

Robert Basham, CEO and one of three founders of the very successful Outback Steakhouse restaurant chain in the United States, is among the many U.S. business executives capitalizing on the fascination surrounding Australia. After many years in the industry, he and his two partners came to believe that successful restaurants frequently fail because the most competent cooks and waiters quit due to overwork from having to serve both lunch and dinner. Hence a good part of their initial business strategy revolved around serving only dinner. Just as important, however, was branding the image of the new restaurant in the minds of potential customers. They did so by naming the chain "Outback Steakhouse" and marketing and advertising extensively with this theme, even though they had never visited Australia. (They did visit the country some time after founding the restaurant chain.) Later they expanded the simple menu to include a taste of New Orleans cuisine, thus differentiating Outback Steakhouse from competitors, but they have successfully continued to emphasize the Australian theme. In keeping with the Australian love of sports, the restaurant chain also has a long history of supporting sports from national football to Little League games to golf and NASCAR in the United States.

Australia is fascinating for many other reasons, including the fact that it is home to a host of unusual creatures and animals, including wombats, koala bears, and kangaroos. It is also host to some dangerous snakes against which it is difficult to protect. In the outback, campers routinely construct fences around their sleeping areas to ensure that wandering crocodiles do not enter. The late Steve Irwin, nicknamed the "crocodile hunter," drew attention to Australia's rich wildlife through his television shows and his work with conservation. His family continues his work today.

Widely known landmarks include the 1,200-mile Great Barrier Reef, the groundbreaking architecture of the Sydney Opera House, and the monumental Ayers Rock in the interior. Australians are keenly aware that this cornucopia of unusual and attractive features sparks the imagination of long-term and short-term visitors and joke among themselves about promoting "the Rock, the Reef, and Ropera." It is not surprising that tourism generates more than 10% of Australia's export revenues, with tourists coming from more places every year, especially from the Chinese mainland.

Australian English is also a great source of fascination, as it is a mixture of British English, aboriginal sayings, and locally derived terms that the settlers used in everyday life. The Australian Tourist Commission publishes a quaintly titled short pamphlet, "A Fair Dinkum Aussie Dictionary," which is useful for the visitor seeking to understand the Australian mind-set. For example, a *hoon* is a lout, *hard yakka* is hard work, and a *dill* is a simpleton. The two different but overlapping types of English used in the United States and Australia help to facilitate a common bond, as both are replete with colorful words and slang that enrich conversations and experiences, sometimes humorously. Addressing the Australian Parliament in 2003 and referring to Prime

Minister Howard, U.S. President Bush famously said, "I called him a 'man of steel.' That's Texan for 'fair dinkum'" ("Australian Slang," 2007). However, the slang term got an Aussie passenger intro trouble on a Delta Airlines flight in 2007 when the flight attendant thought that the passenger was using some choice curse words and called the authorities. All was well after it was explained that "fair dinkum" was common Aussie slang. When used as a question, it can mean "For real?" ("Australian Slang"). In some ways Australians are much more colorful and direct than their U.S. counterparts when it comes to language and insults. Former prime ministers are on record in Parliament as calling their political opponents scumbags, "perfumed gigolos," and "brain-damaged looney crims." This tendency to debate publicly and intermittently to spice up the debate with creative language is clearly traceable to Australia's British heritage. Still, what is acceptable speech in Australia might well constitute a basis for legal action in the United States.

Given the climate, which in some parts of the nation is warm 12 months of the year, and the large number of enjoyable activities that the outdoors offers, it is little wonder that Australians love outdoor recreational activities. Australians are sports mad—this is perhaps the most sports-mad nation in the world, although this is difficult to believe if one is a U.S. American—and they engage in and watch a large variety of sports, including those with English origins (cricket, tennis, rugby, and lawn tennis), soccer or football, sailing, and horse racing. Australian football is unique and difficult to describe, other than by saying that it is both a cross between soccer and rugby and simultaneously a version of U.S. football without protective outfits. New South Wales and Queensland are characterized as rugby states. Victoria, South Australia, Tasmania, Western Australia, and the Northern Territory are considered the strongholds of Australian rules football ("The Evolving Platypus," 2011). Hiking and camping are also popular. Each year in January, this tennis-mad nation hosts the first Grand Slam event of the year, the Australian Open, in Melbourne. More than half the population claims to have tried one sport or the other.

Still, many and perhaps most Australians do not exercise regularly or engage in outdoor sports. They do, however, watch them intensively and at great length. In 2007 BBC News reported that 80% of the adult population of Australia gambles, making it first among nations in gambling, and it is a safe bet that a large portion of the gambling involves sports (Bryant, 2007). This country has the 53rd-largest population but the most gambling machines. According to the report, one gambler joked that Australians would gamble on two flies climbing a wall. Sydney, Brisbane, and Melbourne have some of the largest gambling casinos in Australia. The one in Sydney is reported to be the size of seven football fields, and the Crown Entertainment Complex in Melbourne attracts more than 12 million visitors per year. In 2011 Australians were still on top of the charts of the world's biggest gamblers, measured as net spending in the country's legal forms of betting divided by the number of residents over age 16, with Singapore coming in a close second ("The Biggest Losers," 2011).

New Realities: Beyond Stereotypes

Because Australia is so vast and varied, there are major differences among various parts of the nation. Still, given its urban flavor, it is difficult to reconcile the stereotypes about Australia with modern realities. For example, Australians tend to be amused by the popularity of the *Crocodile Dundee* films, whose theme is that someone expert in living in the bush experiences all sorts of difficulties and adventures when visiting cities such as New York and Los Angeles. Most Australians are far removed from such bush experiences.

A majority of Australians still claim British-derived heritage, but Australia has become the most immigrant-influenced nation in the world. About 25% of the estimated population of over 21 million people was born in another nation, and about an equal percentage of citizens come from families in which at least one parent was born elsewhere. Australians now trace their heritage to 165 nationalities.

The relationship with Britain, in many ways, has weakened considerably, perhaps irretrievably. It was strong until World War I, during which Britain, at the urging of Winston Churchill, pursued a controversial and ultimately senseless attack on Turkey at Gallipoli; thousands of soldiers died, and a large percentage of these were Australians. During World War II, Churchill decided not to use English troops to protect Australia against the invading Japanese; this role was assumed by U.S. troops, which helps to account for the good feelings between the two nations. Gradually Australians realized that they would be economically vulnerable if they continued to bolster their relationship with Britain at the expense of other relationships. Former prime minister Paul Keating in the early 1990s publicly proclaimed that Australia had to cease being a "branch office of empire," to become a republic, and to aim for "enmeshment" in Asia (quoted in Huntington, 1996, p. 151). In a national election in 1999, voters narrowly defeated a proposal to replace the monarchy with a republic; had the proposal passed, the queen of England would have been removed as the titular head of state. An opinion poll in April 2011 showed that 41% of Australians were in favor of the country becoming a republic, down 11 points from a decade earlier. However, the debate flared up briefly after a last-minute ban on an irreverent "alternative" commentary of the royal wedding (of Prince William and Catherine) proposed by a satirical television team ("We Are Not Amused," 2011).

As in the United States, there has been organized opposition to immigrants. This was legally incorporated into the "White Australia" policy from 1901 until 1973 and specifically directed against Asians. The aborigines, the original settlers in Australia who currently comprise 2% of the population, also suffered greatly for decades, and white Australians treated them in about the same inhumane manner as settlers in the United States treated Native Americans; for example, they suffered deliberate massacres and the involuntary removal of children from their families (the Stolen Generations). This is portrayed movingly in the award-winning 2002 film *Rabbit-Proof Fence,* which tells the true story of Molly Craig, who escaped with her younger sister and cousin from a government camp where they were kept after being forcibly removed from their mother. Molly led the other girls on a journey of 1,500 miles in search of the rabbit-proof fence that bisects the continent and would take them home.

Following the abolition of the White Australia policy in 1973, several initiatives were launched to build racial harmony based on a policy of multiculturalism. Australia is still coming to terms with its past as it welcomes waves of immigrants every year. In 2008 former prime minister Rudd led a parliamentary apology to members of the Stolen Generations of aborigines. The apology came 11 years after a report found that during the period 1910 to 1970, between 1 in 3 and 1 in 10 aboriginal children were taken from their families. Some aboriginal groups now have significant income from mining royalties, and mining companies do make considerable efforts to hire aborigines ("The Evolving Platypus," 2011).

Asian immigration from several nations has increased significantly since 1990. Australia has been particularly attractive to Indian students, who came in large numbers and supported Australia's multibillion-dollar education industry. Since June 2009, however, there have been more than 100 attacks on Indian students, raising tensions between India and Australia. One of India's iconic movie stars, Amitabh Bachchan, who is enormously popular the world over, even turned down an honorary doctorate from the Queensland University of Technology, Brisbane, in protest against the violence. Australia has now launched a multimillion-dollar advertising campaign to attract Indians. As a vibrant country with a population of only around 22.5 million, Australia needs hard-working immigrants from around the world. Immigrants to Australia have enhanced the sporting tradition by fostering new sports such as "baseball, basketball, callisthenics, gymnastics, snow sports and softball and have made sports, such as soccer and weightlifting, more popular" (Walla Walla Press, 1997).

The wisdom of expanding Australia's international relationships beyond Britain has generally been confirmed. The gross domestic product (GDP) per person is $47,370. In a May 2011 Organization for Economic Cooperation and Development (OECD) survey, Australia emerged as the world's happiest industrialized nation among the 34 members. The index found that 75% of Australians were satisfied with their life, a figure well above the OECD's average of 59% (Curran, 2011).

The fragile environment may only be able to sustain successfully approximately 20 million, but a government report in 2010 predicted that the population will increase to 36 million in the next 40 years. Also, a decade of droughts has left the water supply depleted; the drought recently ended, and thousands of acres of farmland were flooded in 2011. At the same time, the population is aging, and to provide social services Australia must either keep emphasizing immigration to ensure there are enough workers to sustain the tax base or increase productivity dramatically. Wise government action will be needed to steer the nation into the future ("Hot, Dry and Crowded," 2010).

Barbecue

Perhaps the best way to capture the relationship between these profound changes and our cultural metaphor, outdoor recreational activities, is to explore the evolution of the barbecue, which supposedly originated in Australia and is common in many nations today. Originally, a family held a barbecue at home on Sunday after church and invited only family members and perhaps a few close friends. Over time, however, the barbecue grew into a larger affair, with many families and friends participating at someone's home. Everyone would prepare and bring food, and there was generally a clear separation of sexes, with the men hanging out by the barbecue pit, playing sports or cards or talking and eating.

Conversations at barbecues tend to be casual, involving sports, children, and the weather. Most Australians do not attend church regularly, and religion is seldom discussed at barbecues. The subject of sex is not completely taboo, but it is handled gingerly, if at all, in mixed or polite company. Political discussions tend to focus on "poli bashing" or the awful behavior and low intelligence of politicians. The barbecue has also been brought to the beach, where it includes even more people, who play organized sports such as beach volleyball and race sailboats.

Because of the diversity of Australia's current population, the barbecue is not important among some ethnic groups. They have replaced it by eating out at ethnic restaurants or popular coffeehouses, especially in the eight largest cities, each with more than a million inhabitants. There has never been a cuisine regarded as typically Australian. Instead, each new culture has contributed its own unique flavor to Australian food. However, Australians who are away from their home country do hanker for the delights of vegemite, a spread made from yeast products.

Equality Matching Among the Tall Poppies

Until recently, Australia was ashamed of its criminal origins. This embarrassment found expression in such phrases as "the cultural cringe," meaning that Australia looked to its supposed superior, Britain, for guidance and help; and "down under," signifying that Australia was far away from the centers of power in Britain and the United States. Even the most important national holiday, ANZAC Day, celebrates the defeat of the Australian army at Gallipoli, whereas national holidays elsewhere usually celebrate victories. Unlike U.S. Americans, who love winners and ignore losers, Australians hold the "Aussie battler" in high esteem, especially if he tries valiantly but loses. Perhaps the most famous Australian song of all time, "Waltzing Matilda," connotes a despairing outlook on life.

Such historical experiences led to the well-known phenomenon of "cutting down the tall poppies." Australia is an equality-matching or egalitarian nation, as its scores on the Hofstede (2001) dimensions and the more recent GLOBE (House et al., 2004) study dimensions confirm: It is both highly individualistic and low on power distance.

But it is unlike other nations that fit into this generic category such as Sweden and Norway, which tend to emphasize individual development or related personal characteristics. Australia historically reinforced a negative approach, being neutral or negative about achievement and cutting down anyone striving to be "better than others," regardless of motivation, effort, or reason for doing so. Australians especially disdain pomposity in any form. Richard Brislin (1993), a prominent cross-cultural psychologist, advised colleagues on lecture tours in Australia to be aware that at least a third of any Australian audience would openly question their credentials.

Similarly another cross-cultural psychologist, N. T. Feather (1994), developed a scale to measure the tendency to cut down tall poppies and compared Japanese and Australian respondents using it. He confirmed that Australians have a significant tendency to cut down the tall poppies, but he also discovered that this tendency was higher among his Japanese respondents, a result he attributed to their collectivistic orientation. Also, Feather found that Australian respondents did not begrudge others their success as long as it was earned; they were simply initially suspicious of the validity of such success, especially if it was self-promoted as is commonly done in the United States. In recent times, however, the tall poppy syndrome is beginning to be viewed as an obstacle to success, wealth creation, and excellence, with former prime minister John Howard arguing that "if there's one thing that we need to get rid of in this country it is our tall poppy syndrome" (Bowring, 2007).

Given modern Australia's international prominence in many areas such as sports, films, and theater, it seems clear that the "cultural cringe" is losing its potency and appeal. Still, there is ambivalence about the type of success most commonly associated with market-pricing cultures such as the United States and Britain. For several years, Martin Gannon lectured to and interacted with about 45 Australian students a year, during which time they completed a 34-item scale, each of whose items require that the respondent select only one of four responses tailored to the four generic cultures highlighted in this book: community sharing, authority ranking, equality matching, and market pricing (see the discussion of these four types in Chapter 1). Overwhelmingly the results indicate that these Australian students, regardless of ethnic background, are equality matching in orientation.

However, when Gannon presented a scenario requiring the person either (a) to go immediately to a business meeting at which a contract will be signed resulting in a million-dollar bonus or (b) to assist a long-term friend who needs immediate help (no other responses were allowed), most but not all of the students opted for the million dollars (Gannon, 2003). One student even opined that a million dollars would buy a lot of friends, which evoked an immediate roar of disapproval. The student papers also revealed this ambivalence, as they tended to classify Australia as an equality-matching culture that was quickly taking on many of the characteristics of a market-pricing culture.

Government policy favors equality matching, and Australia does not confront some of the social problems found in other industrialized countries such as the United States. The Australian concept of equality matching seems to have evolved from the concept of "mate," that is, helping out one another in the bush when the environment is harsh and dangerous and resources are scarce. Australians historically have been individualistic, and this characteristic is reflected in more recent studies, such as the GLOBE study (House et al., 2004), in a remarkably consistent manner. Once mates, however, Australians are close to one another emotionally and psychologically. There is a clear distinction between members of the in-group and out-group, and becoming a member of the in-group requires time, patience, and appropriate behavior. Most probably this tendency is even stronger among newer immigrants, the majority of whom come from authority-ranking cultures. In fact, some have wondered whether the concept of "mateship" is the key ingredient for success in Australian sports (e.g., sailing teams) as well as in business (M. Burns, 2001). The famously egalitarian culture even influences the management structure of Aussie football and has proven to be very effective in promoting the sport and keeping elite player salary aspirations under control. This is supported by Australians' legendary devotion to their "footy" clubs ("Raking It In," 2011).

The ambivalence that Australians have about the conflict between different outcomes associated with market pricing and equality matching tends to manifest in various ways. Australians strongly support the welfare system as long as individuals make a "fair go"—make a genuine effort to find a job. It is not necessary to be outstanding to receive help, support, and even respect. However, Australians expect individuals to be "Aussie battlers" and speak disparagingly about "dole bludgers," people who are unfairly taking advantage of the welfare system. In one instance, a public debate centered on a young man who refused to take work if he had to cut his long hair. Fortunately a hairdresser saved the day by offering him a position without this requirement, which satisfied most people that he was not really a "dole bludger." David Alexander, who worked for former Prime Minister Howard, suggests that by being neither small-government and inequality tolerant, as America is, nor high taxing and egalitarian, as the Scandinavian countries are, Australia has a "platypus model" with fewer chances for populism and great opportunities for reforms and real competition ("The Evolving Platypus," 2011).

In 1999 there was public outcry and debate over adding the concept of "mate" to the constitution. The proposed passage originally read:

> Australians are free to be proud of their country and heritage, free to realize themselves as individuals, and free to pursue their hopes and ideals. We value excellence as well as fairness, independence as dearly as mateship. (Murray, quoted in Birns & McNeer, 2007, p. 1)

Given the multicultural diversity in modern Australia and the country's ineluctable movement toward becoming a key player in the World Trade Organization and a globalized economy, such an outcry is understandable. Australian culture is changing, and so is its economy; their interlocked nature will lead to more major changes in the future.

One of the most significant changes taking place in Australia, especially in Western Australian cities such as Perth, is the growth of Chinese economic and social influence. China has become Australia's number one trading partner. According to Chen Jie, a senior lecturer in international relations at the University of Western Australia, "China is remaking the social and political fabric of this country" (Pomfret, 2010). For instance, Chinese diplomats demanded that a film about a Chinese dissident be pulled from the Melbourne Film Festival. (It was not.) On the other hand, the average income of Western Australia jumped from $10,000 to more than $70,000 in 5 years in 2010 thanks to Chinese investment (Pomfret). Australians are understandably alarmed and excited by these changes.

Another significant challenge facing Australia in the future is its inability (thanks to a poor ecology) to sustain large population growth. Some experts suggest that the country cannot maintain the same quality of life and rank high on the Human Development Index if the population increases much beyond 24 million, which it is expected to reach by the middle of the 21st century. Overseas migration plays an important role in replenishing an aging population with young people, with the majority of immigrants coming from the United Kingdom and New Zealand and, increasingly, from China and India. A real estate boom is fueled by migration from China and India. A recent summit on Australia's future highlighted the challenges facing the country from crime involving narcotics, terrorism, weapons proliferation, and people smuggling (*Australia 2020,* 2008). The country also experienced several years of drought in recent years, and it is feared that climate change will pose the biggest threat to Australian agriculture in the future. In December 2010 and continuing into early 2011, the state of Queensland experienced devastating floods, which affected at least 70 towns and more than 200,000 people. The floods dealt a blow to the Australian economy, although Aussie mateship and neighborliness were very much in evidence as people tried to recover.

The government is cognizant of the policy choices that it will have to make to sustain the GDP growth of the last several years in the face of demographic and climate challenges. A recent survey of Australia by the *Economist* suggested that Australia, with textbook economic policies and sound management strategies, is poised to become the next Golden State, an even more successful version of the California of 30 years ago ("Australia's Promise," 2011).

The fascination that the world has with Australia will continue to be strong. Australia has one of the most dynamic economies in the world, with strong ties to both Europe and the Americas and to Asia, and is a country where mateship coexists with individualism. As a native put it, "It has all that the U.S. has to offer with very few of its negatives." Similarly it is difficult to imagine Australia without an amazing array of outdoor recreational activities. And, while tall poppies will stand, we can also expect that equality matching will not disappear, as it is fundamental to the Australian mind-set and culture.

CHAPTER 35

The Sub-Saharan African Bush Taxi

Early in my tenure as Country Director in Niger, I became convinced that the greatest threat to the safety and security of our Peace Corps Volunteers is not terrorism (as one might be led to conclude from the amount of attention and resources devoted to it) but bush taxis.

—J. R. Bullington (2004)

A share taxi is a vehicle which travels around a fixed route and either departs when it's totally full, or allows customers to hop on and off wherever they want. In Rwanda, they are also a zeitgeist of what's hip now; an opportunity to unabashedly tell the world that you have the "Bieber Fever" or that you are a die-hard Eminem fan.

—Adam Cohn, Kiva.org (2011)

Many of the natural resource-rich states in sub-Saharan Africa suffer from the resource curse—the failure of resource-abundant countries to benefit from their natural endowments.

—Donald Sparks (2011)

Before discussing the African bush taxi as a cultural metaphor for the whole of sub-Saharan Africa, it is necessary to offer an opening explanation. How can one apply a single metaphor to most of a continent, especially a continent of such diversity? After all, five of the world's six major divisions of humanity can be found in Africa (Diamond, 1999)—Blacks, Whites (in South Africa), Asians (in Madagascar), Khosians (the Bushmen of Southern Africa), and Pygmies (in Central Africa)—and three of those originated as natives in Africa (Blacks, Khosians, and Pygmies). One quarter of the world's languages are spoken only in Africa (Diamond). By contrast, applying a single metaphor to the European subcontinent would be difficult, if not impossible, and it has only a fraction of the diversity of Africa.

Africa is not a monolithic entity, but notwithstanding its cultural diversity, writers such as Edoho (2001) and Choudhury (1986) have recognized that "certain indige-nous trends of thought, cultural influence, and value orientation are commonly shared by the majority of people in Africa" (Edoho, p. 79). The danger is that these similarities will blind us to the underlying differences and the richness of cultures and attitudes found across this continent.

We must also add a second explanation. Our metaphor applies only to sub-Saharan Africa. The Sahara has always been a huge physical and hence cultural barrier in Africa. Of course, there has always been trade and exchange of ideas and peoples across the Sahara, but for the most part, the regions north and south of the Sahara are more dissimilar than alike. The peoples and cultures of North Africa are probably closer to those of the European Mediterranean and the Middle East than to those in sub-Saharan Africa. Hence, for convenience, when we refer to "Africa," we mean Africa south of the Sahara and not the entire geographical continent.

This area has a population of more than 840 million and includes 47 countries, the largest being Nigeria with more than 151 million and the smallest being Seychelles with fewer than 0.1 million. The United Nations forecasts a population level of 1.5 billion by 2050. According to the World Bank, South Africa has the largest gross domestic product (GDP; $364 billion), and Sao Tome and Principe has the smallest GDP ($197 million). South Africa's and Nigeria's GDP comprise over 50% of sub-Saharan Africa's GDP, and the total GDP per capita of the richest 10 nations in this region is 25.2 times that of the poorest 10. Nevertheless, according to a recent special report in the *Economist,* Africa's economies are consistently growing faster than those of almost any other region. Considerable progress is being made toward the Millennium Development Goals (a series of poverty-reduction milestones set by the UN), a genu-ine middle class is emerging, labor productivity is showing gains of an average of 2.7% per year, foreign debt is generally declining, and trade with the rest of the world is increasing ("The Sun Shines Bright," 2011). A recent entrant is South Sudan, which gained independence from Sudan on July 9, 2011, and stands to benefit from its oil wealth. In recent years, the region's public stock markets have been attracting inves-tors, and it may well be that the economic progress that billions in aid have failed to achieve will be brought about by investors interested in generating good returns from some of these resource-rich nations. Countries such as China and India have also come courting with partnership opportunities. On the one hand, demand is growing in Africa for manufactured goods from these Asian giants. On the other hand, China and India continue to have an unprecedented demand for African natural resources. However, many African countries suffer from what is popularly called "the resource curse" or "the paradox of plenty" (Sparks, 2011).

In most parts of Africa, ownership of private vehicles is limited due to economic conditions. Travel is difficult, there are few paved roads, and paved and dirt roads alike are poorly maintained. Few buses travel African roads, and the old colonial railroads are, for the most part, in poor repair. The main form of transport in many parts of Africa is the bush taxi. These vehicles go by many different names: bush taxi in Anglophone countries, *taxi brousse* in most Francophone countries, and *matatus* in Kenya. Bush taxis take many forms. They may be cars (usually station wagons) or vans. In many of the former French colonies, they are often Peugeot station wagons, called *sept places* (seven seaters), although they seldom conform to their name. In some cases, they are converted pickup trucks with bench seating installed, and in other cases large trucks fill the role. Nowadays, they increasingly take the form of colorfully painted minibuses. In Kigali, Rwanda, students wait for a bus that suits their particular cultural preferences of the moment (Cohn, 2011).

Whatever they are called, they share many similarities: They are always privately owned; they seldom, if ever, operate on a fixed schedule; they are usually overcrowded; and they are almost always in poor condition. Riszard Kapuscinski (2001), a Polish journalist and author, describes a bush taxi trip he took from Dakar in Senegal to Abdallah Wallo, a small village on the Senegalese side of the Senegal River, marking the frontier of that country and Mauritania:

> Finally a small Toyota van pulled up. These vehicles are built to seat twelve, but here they accommodate more than thirty passengers. It is difficult to describe the number and nature of all the additions, the welded-on extensions, the little benches inside such a bus. When it is full, for one passenger to either get out or get in, all the others must do so as well; the intricate calibration of the internal arrangements is as tight and precise as the workings of a Swiss watch, and whoever occupies a place must take into account the fact that for the next several hours, for all intents and purposes, he will not be able to move so much as a toe. (p. 214)

Kapuscinski's description of the bush taxi captures many of the paradoxes of Africa to an outside observer. Behind the seeming chaos of Africa there is an ordered structure, and the workings of an African village, or an African business, may be as tight and precise as the workings of a Swiss watch. As we will see, African culture is bound by conventions and rules, many not immediately obvious to an outsider.

Basic Operations

Bush taxis are usually owned by an individual who has managed to save the money to invest in a vehicle. If all goes well, this local entrepreneur may acquire several such vehicles, hiring drivers to operate them. They fill an important role in a community, often serving as the only regular link (apart from walking or cycling) between a village and the outside world. Often the driver will carry letters or verbal messages from one village to another. The bush taxis transport both people and goods. Africans seldom travel light, and people returning to their villages by bush taxi may bring pots, pans, sacks of produce or grain, chickens or goats, bags of cement, and furniture—all competing for space with the other passengers.

The importance of bush taxis varies from one country to another depending on economic conditions. In Benin, a small country in West Africa, bush taxis are the predominant form of transport, even between the main towns. By contrast, in neighboring Burkina Faso, efficient private bus companies service the main towns, but bush taxis are the main transport in rural areas (where 80% of Burkinabé live). In Nigeria large buses ply the crumbling freeway system mainly at night (with armed guards on board to deter bandits), while by day the Peugeot seven-seaters take over, dodging giant potholes and oncoming traffic at speeds usually reserved for German autobahns.

Safety is not a concern of most bush taxi drivers. For instance, two tourists in Nigeria, having seen cars driving the wrong way on Nigerian freeways, were concerned about safety in taking a night bus. They were reassured by the owner of the bus that "at night the cars stay off the road—the buses are so big and powerful they crush any cars in their path." Author Paul Theroux describes a bush taxi trip to Nairobi, the Kenyan capital:

Our overstuffed Peugeot was doing eighty. I said to Kamali, "Mind asking the driver to slow down?" "Pole-pole, bwana" [slow-slow boss], Kamali said, leaning forward. Insulted by this suggestion, the driver went faster and more recklessly. Because so many of the roads were better than before, people drove faster and there were more fatal accidents. (p. 174)

A Short History of Africa

Mankind was born in Africa, with human history beginning there about 7 million years ago, when a population of African apes gave rise to the ancestor of modern humans (Diamond, 1999). These early hominids developed the ability to walk upright. About 2.5 million years ago, a more modern precursor, *Homo habilis,* the toolmaker, arose in the African river valley (present-day Ethiopia, Kenya, and Tanzania). An even closer ancestor, *Homo erectus,* arose 1.5 million years ago and is believed to have spread from Africa to populate the rest of the globe (BBC World Service, 2003). *Homo erectus* looked a lot like modern humans with a larger brain than the earlier hominids. *Homo erectus* gradually evolved into modern humans: *Homo sapiens.*

The first African civilization was that of Egypt. The Sahara desert was fertile 8,000 years ago. As the climate changed and the deserts advanced, the Nile river valley gained importance, and the people living there assumed great power and influence.

These people gave rise to the great Egyptian civilization, which from about 3,000 BCE to the birth of Christ was the most powerful the world had ever seen.

Until 2,000 or 3,000 years ago, Africa south of the Sahara was populated by scattered groups of hunter-gatherers. Then the face of the continent changed when the Bantu peoples left the rain forests of West Africa (present-day Cameroon) and gradually dispersed south and east to cover most of equatorial and subequatorial Africa (Davidson, 1984). These peoples possessed metallurgy and agriculture (based on yams), which was enough of a technological advantage to allow them to displace the original non-Bantu inhabitants.

Agriculture and metallurgy allowed the creation of kingdoms. The non-Bantu peoples of West Africa, with a millet- and sorghum-based agriculture, created several powerful kingdoms from about 200 BCE. The ancient kingdom of Ghana (centered around present-day Mali) was renowned in the Arab world for its power and learning, beginning in the 5th century. Meanwhile ancient kingdoms also flourished in Zimbabwe (Davidson, 1984), and in East Africa the Swahili civilization was founded by seafaring traders about 700 CE. The Swahili civilization and many of the West African empires were predominantly Muslim.

The Impact of Slavery

As in most parts of the world, slavery was always practiced in Africa. However, the arrival of Europeans about 1500 led to an explosion in the practice. Slaves, mainly from West Africa, were transported from the Gold and Slave Coasts to the plantations of the Americas. (These areas correspond approximately to the Gulf of Guinea from Côte D'Ivoire to Cameroon, although the slave trade extended as far south as Angola.) By the late 19th century, when slavery was finally abolished legally in the Western world, an estimated 15 million Africans had been sold into slavery, most of them the strongest and the most productive members of society. A smaller trade to Arab countries was centered in the Swahili regions of East Africa.

The European slave trade in Africa slowly transitioned into a colonial invasion, preceded by Christian missionaries. Davidson (1984) quotes an African saying: "First they had the Bible and we had the land. After a while we found things had changed round. Now they have the land and we have the Bible" (p. 167). While Europeans had always maintained trading posts along the African coasts, the "scramble for Africa" did not begin in earnest until around 1880. Within 30 years five countries—Britain, France, Germany, Portugal, and Italy—and one individual, King Leopold of Belgium, controlled virtually the whole of Africa, apart from Ethiopia and Liberia (Pakenham, 1997). The case of King Leopold is interesting: The Belgian Congo (present-day Democratic Republic of Congo or Congo-Kinshasa) was originally his personal fiefdom. Eventually he had so mismanaged the colony that he was forced, in 1908, to hand it over to the Belgian state (Pakenham).

The end of World War II gave rise to decolonization, and between 1959 (Ghana was the first African nation to achieve independence) and 1973 (when the Portuguese were finally driven out of Angola, Mozambique, and Guinea Bissau), 47 independent nations were born. Many would see the final death knell of colonization in the end of the apartheid regime in South Africa in 1991.

Modern Africa is best known in the West for its problems rather than its successes, although this perception is slowly but surely changing. Famine, civil wars, military coups, poverty, AIDS, Ebola, and genocide seemed to be the only headlines to come from Africa. Few African countries have been able to overcome the colonial legacy of artificial frontiers, absence of infrastructure, lack of civil institutions, and the scarcity of economic and educational opportunities for their people. According to the World Bank, before the global financial crisis that began in 2008, Africa's poverty rate was falling slowly but steadily, child mortality rates were declining, HIV/AIDS was stabilizing, and several countries that previously experienced conflict—such as Mozambique, Rwanda, and Uganda—were at 4% or higher growth. Between them, the International Monetary Fund and the World Bank expect growth in sub-Saharan Africa to average about 5.3% in 2011 and increase in 2012 to about 6% if all goes well.

Foreign direct investment (FDI) in Africa is increasing, especially from the emerging Asian superpowers China and India, who are competing for resources and influence in sub-Saharan Africa. African economies are dependent on the export of raw commodities, such as oil, diamonds, gold, cotton, cocoa, and coffee. Increasingly, however, FDI is being directed toward the telecommunications and retail sectors. Natural resources and energy sector continue to attract the majority of FDI, but mobile phones and shopping malls are changing the lives of African consumers all over the continent. The World Bank contends that the private sector is creating an emerging African middle class of hundreds of millions of consumers. Returns on investment in Africa are among the highest in the world. According to studies by the London Business School, the World Bank, and consultants at Deloitte, every 10 additional mobile phones per 100 Africans raises the GDP 0.6% to 1.2%, and this is mirrored by high-speed Internet connection growth, with Internet traffic in Africa being among the fastest growing in the world (Perry, 2011). Crude oil comprises more than half of Africa's exports, and in two thirds of sub-Saharan Africa, one or two products account for more than 60% of exports.

According to the Doing Business website ("Economy Rankings," 2011), Mauritius (23), South Africa (35), Rwanda (45), and Botswana (54) are ranked among the top third of 183 countries on ease of doing business. Within the region, Ghana (63) rounds out the top five countries on this indicator. Most of the other countries in this region unfortunately rank at the bottom of the list. Botswana is a success story as the world's largest producer of diamonds and one of Africa's most stable countries. It ranks number 40 out of 179 countries on the 2011 Index of Economic Freedom (T. Miller, 2011). Mauritius ranks an enviable number 12 and Namibia, South Africa, and Rwanda come in at numbers 73, 74, and 75, respectively.

Despite all the problems, there is an optimism and a vitality about Africa and Africans that is unmatched on any other continent. Anybody who has visited the continent will readily attest to the energy and warmth found there. African culture is unique, and intrinsic African values such as communalism and respect for elders should eventually allow Africa to solve its own social and economic problems in its own way and to fully exploit its natural resources for the benefit of its people. For example, Kenyan mobile phone operator Safaricom became the first-ever telecom company to create a mobile banking system, which is setting industry standards for the world, and Kenya's love of information technology has earned it the nickname "Silicon Savanna" (Perry, 2011).

African Time Orientation and Fatalism

African bush taxis do not operate on any fixed schedule. It is normal for people to arrive early in the morning for a departure and then to spend the entire day waiting for their transport to leave. Africans like to joke with U.S. Americans that in the United States, "time is money." Well, in Africa, time most certainly is not money. Gas is money, leaving with unoccupied space for one more fare is money, but waiting all day just to fill the vehicle is not money. To Westerners, time is a commodity to be bought and sold, but not to Africans. People will wait patiently, mostly unconcerned about any schedule they might have, because they know they will eventually get to where they want to go. Impatient expatriates or even "modern" Africans, with more money than sense, will be allowed to purchase extra seats to fill the bush taxi, but otherwise all will wait patiently for the last passenger to be crammed in. Once that happens, the scene will suddenly change, the calm will be shattered, and people will scramble for their seats in frantic haste as the taxi pulls away, often with several passengers running after it.

The Sense of Fatalism

Closely related to the African attitude about time is the sense of fatalism that many Africans possess. There is a sense that what will be will be, and there is little an individual can do about it. This sense of fatalism helps people to wait patiently or react calmly when their tire blows out (with no spare) in the middle of nowhere. However, bush taxi riders in West Africa are known to protect themselves against the "demons of the road" by obtaining talismans, because they are never sure if they will arrive safely at their destinations without these. In some ways, the sense of fatalism could be considered an aspect of Islam, in which believers put their trust in God and everything that happens depends on God's willingness to let it happen.

Islam is the predominant religion in West Africa and in parts of East Africa, and Africans have readily adapted to the Muslim idea of *Inshallah* or God willing. So, if a desire to meet a friend for a drink the next day elicits only an *Inshallah*, it does not mean that your friend is reluctant to meet but only that the decision to meet is out of his hands; it literally rests with God. However, African fatalism goes deeper than Islam, which is a relatively recent arrival to Africa. African fatalism has its roots in ancient African culture and the African environment. Dorothy Pennington (1985) discusses the African concept of time in terms of the extent to which people feel in control of their destiny or feel subject to the control of external forces: "To what extent does a group rationalize its fate by postulating mysterious forces and beings in nature and mysterious powers among their fellows or higher forces?" (p. 123).

U.S. Americans feel that they can, to a large extent, control their destiny. Witness the difficulty people have in accepting an incurable illness or a death; there is a sense of being cheated or being let down by medical science. Africans, on the other hand, find it easier to accept the hand fate has dealt them. Although the expatriate will become upset at sitting around all day waiting for the bush taxi to leave, for the African, it's not such a big deal. Where does this fatalism come from?

It is common in Burkina Faso, when drinking a beverage (especially an alcoholic one), to pour a small amount onto the ground as an offering to the ancestors. This is done in an unselfconscious manner, even by Western-educated Africans, Christians, or Muslims, as if it were a perfectly normal thing to do. Expatriates have adopted this custom (although, truth be told, probably more because it doubles as an opportunity to rinse their glass before drinking). Davidson (1984) notes the same practice throughout West Africa.

For an African, including a Christian or Muslim, the ancestors are an everyday presence. In African religious ontology, five divisions are ranked in order of importance (Mbiti, 1970): God, spirits (ancestors), humans, animals and plants, and inanimate objects. God is the Supreme Being, but the ancestors and the past define humanity. Humans are at the center of the universe and have responsibilities to maintain balance and order in the universe. Living in harmony with nature and fulfilling obligations are important concepts. When people die, time does not come to an end; they live on as spirits. In Ghana there is a colorful tradition of organizing a grand funeral for the departed and burying them in coffins that reflect their personality, occupation, and status in life. Some common examples are an airplane for a businessperson who is a frequent flyer, a banana-shaped coffin for a poor banana seller, and even a cigarette-shaped coffin for someone who probably died as a result of this smoking addiction! Coffin design, intended to ease the deceased person's journey into the afterlife, has developed into a fine art limited only by the imagination.

A story illustrates this concept. Ouidah, in present-day Benin, was one of the main Portuguese slaving ports in the 18th and 19th centuries. On the route the slaves took from the town to the beach where the slave ships waited, there was a sacred tree. It was believed that if the slaves rounded the tree a certain number of times, their souls would return to Africa as spirits when they died. Deeply upsetting as a life of slavery was, even more upsetting to the slaves was the idea of their spirits being lost in a foreign land, far from their native place and their descendants. The slavers used this to control their charges because denial of this ritual was truly a fate worse than death.

Ideas About Time

Africans also have little concept of future time, as Mbiti (1970) argues:

> The linear concept of time in Western thought, with an indefinite past, present and infinite future is practically foreign to African thinking. The future is virtually absent because events which lie in it have not taken place, they have not been realized, and cannot, therefore, constitute time. (p. 20)

Future events are simply potential events, but actual events are what has already taken place and are more important. People tend to look backward rather than forward, and thus there is not the same belief in progress and improvement that characterizes Western thought. A living past is going on all around, and the African sense of time is more circular or cyclical than linear (Lessem & Palsule, 1997). People who see time as a linear progression are likely to be more time conscious than those who see time as a repeating cycle. Africans do not perceive time in terms of a clock but rather in terms of events, or how time is used. Sitting around talking all day with friends is not a waste of time; rather it is an event, making a connection with people, and worthwhile (Upkabi, 1990). Thus for an African, social relations in the workplace are important. Time spent chatting is, again, not a waste of time but part of relationship building and essential for group harmony.

To an African, fate lies in the hands of a living and omnipotent God. This is regardless of whether the person is nominally Christian or Muslim or a follower of traditional religion. Most Africans are tolerant of religious freedom but cannot understand atheism. An educated Catholic African recounted how he met a European tourist who professed to be an atheist. To the African this was just absurd. He could understand somebody being Muslim, Christian, Hindu, or Buddhist, but to be an atheist, this European must have been crazy, he thought. While the idea of atheism may be deeply upsetting to many Africans, it is not uncommon for Africans to change religions, and they tend to be quite flexible in their beliefs.

A Peace Corps volunteer teacher in Burkina Faso noticed one of his students, a Muslim, wearing a crucifix one day. When questioned, the student said that she had decided to become a Catholic and her parents didn't care what religion she held. A voodoo fetish priest in Lome, the capital of Togo, reported that some of his best clients were Catholic (although he said some of the new Protestant converts were deeply hostile to his practice). The living omnipresent God intervenes regularly in human affairs, as do the spirits, according to this way of thinking. Because humans are not the ultimate arbiters of their fate, there is little point in planning for the future. People who believe in an all-powerful God are more likely to be less time conscious than people who believe in their own power to influence events.

That is not to say that Africans listlessly drift through life, passively awaiting the hand of God and their ancestors to decide events. First, we are speaking of tendencies, not strict causal relationships. Second, as argued by Pennington (1985) and Albert

(1970), fatalism is not a belief in the complete futility of action; rather, it means dignity in the face of adversity and humility in the event of prosperity. The distinction between fatalists and doing-oriented people is one of the degree to which people control their lives: "No matter how conscientiously a man may perform his duties, he may fail or suffer, whereas some men who are worthless or evil may prosper" (Albert, p. 106).

Also, as Africa becomes more and more Westernized with urbanization, modern education, and exposure to Western media, Africans subscribe more and more to Western concepts of time and doing. When events are believed to be unpredictable, planning and regularity become less important. Thus the bush taxis only leave when they are full; however, many buses now operate on regular schedules.

Of course, religion is only one contributor to an African sense of time and fatalism. A second interpretation depends on the nature of the activities in which a society is engaged. In a technological, commercial society, time is a valuable commodity to be bought and sold, whereas in an agrarian society, time is controlled by the cycle of nature. In traditional African society, life is unhurried, travel and the pace of life are slow, and so strict timekeeping is not important. In a business setting, this attitude cuts both ways. Africans may sit around talking for several hours during the workday and then work late (without overtime) to complete their daily tasks. An expatriate manager, accustomed to doing a day's work and then leaving work to socialize, would consider this bizarre, but to an African this behavior is perfectly normal. And agrarian societies are not indolent. For instance, African farmers, when the rains come, will work feverishly to plant their crops because that is what is needed. Then, when the planting is done, an unhurried pace will reassert itself.

Africans then have a more relaxed view of time than U.S. Americans or Europeans. Time is a complex affair, and Africans tend to be polychronic, often working on several tasks at the same time. There are many consequences of this sense of time (Edoho, 2001). For instance, arranging a deal may take many meetings, and patiently taking the time to get to know partners is important. Deadlines may be flexible, and no offense should be taken if people arrive late for meetings. Important people are expected to arrive late for meetings or events; the more important the personage, the later he or she turns up.

Communalism and Community Sharing

Riding on an African bush taxi is an intimate experience. Westerners who are used to having a fairly broad personal space sometimes find the intimacy upsetting. People are crammed into the bush taxi, and in the mainly tropical regions of Africa, maintaining personal hygiene is difficult. As a bush taxi passes through a town, there are frequent stops—for traffic, police checkpoints, breakdowns, and so on. Each stop is an opportunity for an army of vendors—women selling peanuts or fruit, men selling grilled chicken, boys selling plastic bags filled with water or juice, young men selling the latest in women's fashions—to mob a bush taxi or bus. Business is conducted through the open windows, with the vendors often forced to run to obtain payment from passengers as the bush taxi suddenly speeds off.

Passengers readily share their food and drink with each other; it is impolite not to offer to share your meal with your fellow passengers and only slightly less impolite to refuse an offer. Not only food and drink are shared. For example, a U.S. Peace Corps volunteer in Senegal ended up holding a stranger's baby for the duration of a trip; it is normal for friends and neighbors or acquaintances to care for others' children, and this extends to the communal bush taxi.

The bush taxi is an important community service, serving as a link between a community and the outside world. Although all passengers are expected to pay a fare, exceptions may be made. Normally, seated passengers pay a regular fare, whereas those who lack the means are allowed to cling to the outside of the bush taxi or ride on the roof. Departure of the bush taxi is accompanied by a scramble of young men who jump on the fender or climb on the roof to make a precarious and dangerous journey. This is more common in remote rural areas where transport options are limited and the driver/owner is more likely to know the people concerned.

Sometimes a seat may be given to a non-fare-paying passenger, although he may be asked to vacate the place if a paying passenger is picked up. These casual passengers are always male; a woman's movements are more restricted, and a woman would never travel (or be allowed to travel) without the means of paying.

The Trait of Communalism

Communalism is a strong trait in African culture. Land is often held in common with relatives or an extended family. Communalism starts with the family and extends outward. The African family includes several degrees of relations and several generations:

[The African family] extends outwards to a great distance and backward to many generations, and may even include unborn children. So, whereas Westerners generally have little family awareness beyond, say, first cousins, and to map out a family tree would be no more than amusing diversion, to an African such a mental map of his family is the focus and center of his identity. (S. McCarthy, 1994, p. 14)

Again we see the importance of ancestors (see Chapter 26: The Chinese Family Altar). The strength of the African family was seen in Ghana in 1983 when 1.3 million Ghanaians (10% of the total population of Ghana) were deported suddenly from Nigeria. The expected refugee crisis never materialized, however, for the deportees were quickly reassimilated by their families (Siegel, 1992). Some have seen the tradition of sharing among family members as an impediment to entrepreneurship and enterprise. Many educated Africans, living in cities, bemoan the fact that they are expected to take care of several distant relatives. Educated, salaried Africans, in addition to their immediate families, may have several nieces, nephews, and cousins living with them, for whom they are paying school and living expenses. In addition, those who are relatively well off may send money home to their villages for medical expenses or a tin roof on a house. The more successful the person is, the more he or she is expected to give back. Often, one son will be selected from a family to go to school and be educated, at the expense of the rest of the extended family, in the hope that he will obtain a salaried position that will allow him to provide for the family in the future. However, claims on excess earnings may serve as a disincentive to educated Africans to improve their position.

The African sense of community extends beyond the family to the village, which is seen almost as an extended family. When Africans are asked where they are from, they will typically give the name of their village. Even if they were born in a city, and even if their parents before them were born in a city, they will still name their parents' or grandparents' village. For example, an urban-educated Burkinabé took a detour from a business trip to visit his village. He himself had been born in a city several hundred kilometers to the south but still identified with the village. He was deeply embarrassed and upset when he got lost in the bush looking for the village, finding it only after seeking directions. In urban settings Africans will form village committees to plan social events, to network for jobs, to help recent arrivals, and in general to retain their village identity. While this network weakens over time, it is still a very real presence in urban Africa.

Associated with communalism is a different sense of personal space than that of U.S. Americans. The people crammed together in the bush taxi have little problem with the intimacy this imposes. By contrast, a local politician in Fairfax, Virginia, opposing the proposed installation of bench-style seating in the Washington, DC, Metro, was aghast that people might be forced to establish eye contact with their fellow passengers. Africans are comfortable with physical contact (although between the sexes certain public contact is inappropriate). Handshakes are long, often maintained for minutes on end, and accompanied by backslapping. As in many Muslim countries, it is common for men in many parts of Africa to hold hands in public to signify a close friendship. Privacy is not well understood, doors are left open, and friends and neighbors often arrive uninvited to pass an evening. Expatriates are often uncomfortable with this and often pretend to be out to avoid unwelcome guests. Kapuscinski (2001) describes this sense of space and openness as he walked with his host in a Senegalese village greeting his neighbors:

> As we walked the village it became clear that in the tradition of its inhabitants, and even in their imagination, the concept of divided, differentiated, segmented space does not exist. There are no fences, boards, or wires, no hedges, nets, ditches or demarcation lines anywhere. The space is single, communal, open— transparent even; there are no screens in it, no erected barriers, dams and walls; it puts up no limits, offers no resistance. (p. 216)

Communalism or collectivism, in contrast to individualism, is one of the dimensions Hofstede (2001) uses to differentiate national cultures. Individualism implies a loose social structure with people taking care of themselves and their immediate families only. Collectivism means people belong to tightly woven in-groups. African cultures, while varying from country to country (or among ethnic groups), are collectivistic. The Individualism Index values of Hofstede were low for East and West Africa and high for the United States (Nnadozie, 2001): West Africa scored a 20 on individualism, and East Africa scored a 27; by contrast, the United States scored a 91.

In writing about the sub-Saharan cluster in the more recent GLOBE study, Gupta and Hanges (2004) suggest that a distinctive philosophical concept in sub-Saharan Africa is *Ubuntu* or the humaneness that individuals and groups display for one another, a concept that is summed up in the phrase *umntu ngumntu ngabanye* (a person is a person through others). *Ubuntu* encourages individuals to express themselves through the group and focuses on concern for people, cooperation, and sharing. Expatriate managers are likely to achieve more success if they understand sub-Saharan Africa's culture and tap into the *Ubuntu* philosophy. The countries included in sub-Saharan Africa in the GLOBE study are Namibia, Zambia, Zimbabwe, Nigeria, and South Africa (Black sample).

Business Consequences

There are many important consequences of communalism for managers in Africa (Blunt & Jones, 1992). Because people often owe their first loyalty to their extended family, village, or clan, communalism may complicate managerial and supervisory relationships. Personal relationships between individuals may be more important than the business context. Rules and regulations may be circumvented due to reciprocal relationships that exist between people. Loyalty to family and financial demands on employees by the family may lead to corrupt practices. It is not surprising that sub-Saharan Africa scores high on humane orientation in the GLOBE study (House et al., 2004).

Often the sense of communalism extends to the corporation. Managers are expected to take care of their employees. Layoffs are serious in any society but perhaps more so in Africa, where there is little paid employment and an individual may be supporting a large number of people. Managers must remember this when layoffs or downsizing are impending. Blunt and Jones (1992) have applied the low individualistic orientation of African society and research on corresponding cultural orientations (unemotionality and subordination) to suggest that African organizations will have associated outcomes of excessive caution and lack of decisiveness and creativity in problem solving. However, communalism can have benefits if managers can extend the communalistic orientation to the organization.

Hierarchy in African Society: Seating Arrangements in the Bush Taxi

Although bush taxis are uncomfortable and impossibly crowded, there is a method to the seating arrangements. Given the speed at which bush taxis drive and the absence of seat belts, non-Africans might not think of the front seat as the prime seat. But it is the seat of honor and is normally reserved for elders of status or expatriate visitors. This illustrates the African concept of hospitality. A visitor is a guest to a country and will be treated as such. Visitors to Africa rarely need maps or timetables, for often all that is needed is to ask directions of a passerby. Invariably visitors will be swept away and brought to the point of departure of the bush taxi they seek, installed in a good seat with a negotiated fare, and given advice as to whom to trust and whom not to trust, the name of a relative at their destination who will take care of them, and perhaps a gift of peanuts or a drink. Because it is normal to reciprocate, and those that have wealth are expected to share with the less well off (and expatriates are invariably better off than Africans), a gift from visitors, whether monetary or not, will not give offense, even if it is not expected.

African culture can be characterized by a high power distance. As defined by Hofstede (2001), power distance is the willingness of people to accept unequal power distributions. East Africa and West Africa scored 64 and 77, respectively, for power distance, higher than the U.S. score of 40. In Africa, however, power does not necessarily equate to material wealth; age is also respected. It is common in a bush taxi for a passenger to be demoted to a less desirable seat when a more important passenger gets on. Similarly, a U.S. American visiting his daughter, a Peace Corps volunteer in Mali, told of how a bush taxi he was riding in broke down. A young boy passed on his bicycle. The driver commandeered the boy's bicycle to ride into town in search of a mechanic. The boy was clearly upset but could do nothing about it, for he was expected to obey the instructions of any adult or elder.

This tendency is reflected in many aspects of organizational culture. Promotion is often based on seniority, not ability. Teachers, for instance, are held to be infallible sources of knowledge, and students do not appreciate teachers who profess ignorance or uncertainty. Managers and supervisors are expected to direct and command, and organizations are characterized by strong centralization and little initiative taking. This can lead to many problems, with junior staff being unwilling to make any decision without first clearing it with their supervisors and even constructive criticism of managers being frowned on (Blunt & Jones, 1992). African managers may tend not to delegate, engage in participatory forms of management, or share information with their subordinates.

Expatriates, as outsiders, are in some ways removed from the African hierarchy. So a young expatriate manager may not have the same status problems as an African manager of the same age. Nevertheless, an awareness of status and the role it plays is vital. Formality is important. An expatriate manager in Ouagadougou (the capital of Burkina Faso) complained that even though he lived only a 5-minute walk from his office, he was expected to be driven to work by his chauffeur in the morning. If he walked, his standing would have dropped among his staff. Leaders are expected to act, dress, and behave in a manner befitting their position. This can give rise to the "big man" syndrome, a preference for powerful autocratic rule.

For example, an expatriate watched the film *Mobuto: Roi de Zaire,* a documentary about the late dictator Mobuto Sese Seko of Zaire (Democratic Republic of Congo), in a movie theater in Burkina Faso. As the film displayed the opulent, lavish, and decadent lifestyle of the dictator, there were gasps of both awe and admiration from the audience. Although all were shocked by the atrocities he committed, there was also a sense of admiration for the absolute power he wielded and the lifestyle he enjoyed. Again, this is only a tendency. In the same country, the most revered political leader is Thomas Sankara, president from 1983 to 1987, when he was overthrown and murdered in a coup. Sankara was a man of the common people who rejected the trappings of power, selling the government Mercedes in exchange for Renaults and hitching rides on the airplanes of other African leaders. Similarly Nelson Mandela is revered throughout Africa for the simplicity of his lifestyle.

Politeness and Respect

A great deal of politeness is expected in daily interactions. In learning Mooré, the language spoken by the Mossi, the major ethnic group of Burkina Faso, the first thing one learns is the ritual greetings that seem to go on and on endlessly (Hello, how are you, and your family, and your health, and your sleep, and your wife?—and so on). To a Westerner, accustomed to a passing nod to acquaintances, this endless repetition may seem amusing and childish, but for Africans this is an important ritual, establishing status and position and reinforcing communal ties. Although in a business setting the greetings are certainly shortened, it is vital to greet coworkers verbally and shake hands. To pass a colleague without a greeting can cause offense and lead the offended party to wonder what he did to receive such rude treatment.

Along with long formal greetings, it is also important to use titles. A secondary school teacher in Francophone Africa is expected to greet his school principal with Monsieur Le Proviseur, never the principal's first name or even family name. It is invariably better to use a person's title (doctor, chairman, chief, and so on) rather than his or her name. Note that we are again speaking about tendencies, and the notion of hierarchy varies among different ethnic groups.

As an example, Burkina Faso, a landlocked Sahelian country in West Africa, is comprised of more than 60 different ethnic groups. The main ethnic group, the Mossi, constitutes more than 40% of the population and had a highly evolved, rigid hierarchical system before colonization by the French in the 1890s. The Mossi had an overall king (Naba) with absolute power. The Naba had a standing army and exacted tribute from regional kings and chiefs, and so the system continued down to the village level. The French retained this feudal system as a means of control, and today Mossi villages typically have a powerful chief. By contrast, in the southwest of the country near the border with Ghana, the Lobi people live in separate extended family compounds loosely joined to form a village, with a titular chief, but real power resides in a group of elders. Lobi family compounds resemble small fortresses and were built out of arrow range of their neighbors, such was the suspicion they held about their out-group clan members. Today, Lobi villages are characterized by a more democratic if sometimes chaotic approach to decision making.

The Role of Women

There is some ambiguity about how Africa measures on Hofstede's (2001) concepts of masculinity and uncertainty avoidance. Hofstede measures both East and West Africa as moderately masculine, with scores lower than the United States. Yet in Africa, gender roles are well defined, and males have far more opportunities than females. Gender imbalances are far greater than in the United States. Polygamy is common in some parts of Africa and is tolerated under both Islam and many traditional religions. Female excision is also widely practiced. Certainly one would never meet a female bush taxi driver.

A great deal of variation exists within sub-Saharan Africa. For instance, the World Economic Forum's Global Gender Gap Index for 2010, which measures women's participation and opportunity in the labor force, education, and politics, shows Lesotho as 8th out of 134 countries and South Africa as 12th. Mali and Chad, on the other hand, are at the bottom of the list at 131 and 133, respectively. Lesotho and Botswana (number 62 overall) are two countries in the region that have achieved gender parity in education. Although Ghana (70) and Burkina Faso (111) are lower in the hierarchy, what is notable is that Ghana moved up 10 places over the previous year and Burkina Faso moved up 9 places in the same period. Overall, the sub-Saharan Africa region performed well on economic participation and opportunity for women, overtaking Latin America, the Caribbean, Asia and the Pacific, the Middle East and North Africa. In the GLOBE study (House et al., 2004), the sub-Saharan Africa cluster had a mean score of 3.29 in gender egalitarianism, very similar to the Southern Asian cluster (3.28), lower than the Eastern Europe cluster, which scored 3.84, and higher than the Middle Eastern cluster (2.95).

One would expect African cultural groups to score high on uncertainty avoidance or risk acceptance. As a traditional society, without a strong belief in modernization and continuous improvement but rather tending to look toward the past for inspiration, Africans might be less willing to accommodate change and uncertainty. This is borne out by the findings of the GLOBE study (House et al., 2004) in which the sub-Saharan Africa cluster was among the highest in uncertainty avoidance, similar to Southern Asia, the Middle East, Eastern Europe, and Latin America.

Triandis (1984) has produced a useful summary of African cultural values compared to those of developed Western nations. As we have already discussed, Africans tend to believe in external causation and in their limited potential to change events. They are past oriented, more focused on being than doing, and more passive than active. Success in endeavors is judged more on the process or on the well-being of the group, rather than guided by absolute principles and measured by results. The influence of contextual factors may negate Western principles of management (Gray, 2001).

Summing up, we can say that the African bush taxi captures much of the essence of Africa and its culture. These beat-up and bedraggled cars and vans that dash furiously across the savannahs, jungles, deserts, and cityscapes of Africa personify the energy and ingenuity of Africans. They have been repaired and added to so many times that they scarcely resemble the original vehicle. They are held together with rope, twine, rubber bands, nails, and pieces of clothing. People wait patiently for the eventual departure of their bush taxi, rarely complaining, for what is the point of complaining? People keep their good spirits, even when 30 are crammed into a vehicle built for 12. They share both their food and their jokes with their neighbors, and they watch out for each other's children, for this is the way in the African community. They give up their seats for an elder for age is to be respected. They give up their seats for foreigners because they are guests and should be treated with courtesy.

The bush taxi is Africa, in the creativity and ingenuity involved in getting it to go at all and in the cheerfulness and vitality of the people who ride it. Too often African values of family, communalism, hierarchy, and respect for age are cited as obstacles to good management and organization in Africa. Yet cultures with many similar values, such as South Korea, Taiwan, and Japan, have shown that individualism and a doing orientation are not prerequisites to economic development and good management (Ugwuegbu, 2001). Good managers, whether African or expatriate, should be able to exploit rather than overcome African cultural values to build strong organizations.

When Africa does fully "develop," when it finally can offer its people decent health care, decent education, and economic opportunities, these successes will be based on African cultural values such as communalism, teamwork, concern for others, respect for age, and a strong sense of place and tradition. As noted above, Africa's political and technological progress has attracted investors from around the world, and Africans have more opportunities for making life more rewarding for themselves ("The Sun Shines Bright," 2011). All indications point to a successful journey for the African bush taxi.

References

Please note that, when an author is anonymous, the article or book is referenced by the title.

Accents: We want to talk proper. (2002, December 5). *The Economist*, 55. Retrieved from http://www .economist.com/node/1477669

Achebe, C. (2011, January 15). Nigeria's promise, Africa's hope. *The New York Times*. Retrieved from http:// www.nytimes.com/2011/01/16/opinion/16achebe.html

Adam, S. (2010, July 19). A new growth champ? It might be Singapore. *Bloomberg Businessweek*, 15.

Adler, N. (with Gundersen, A.). (2007). *International dimensions of organizational behavior* (4th ed.). Cincinnati, OH: South-Western.

Africa rising. (2011, December 3). *The Economist*. Retrieved from http://www.economist.com/ node/21541015

Albert, E. (1970). Conceptual systems in Africa. In J. N. Paden & E. Soja (Eds.), *The African experience* (Vol. 1, pp. 99–107). Chicago, IL: Northwestern University Press.

Al-Zahrani, S. S. A., & Kaplowitz, S. (1993). Attributional biases in individualistic and collectivist cultures: A comparison of Americans with Saudis. *Social Psychology Quarterly*, 56(3), 223–233.

American football: The search for supermen. (2006, September 28). *The Economist*, 95. Retrieved from http://www.economist.com/node/7963514

Anand, G. (2011, April 5). India graduates millions, but too few are fit to hire. *The Wall Street Journal*. Retrieved from http://online.wsj.com/article/SB10001424052748703515504576142092863219826.html

Andersen, P. A. (1994). Explaining intercultural differences in nonverbal communication. In L. A. Samovar & R. E. Porter (Eds.), *Intercultural communication: A reader* (7th ed., pp. 4–24). Belmont, CA: Wadsworth.

Andrews, J. (1999, July 22). A survey of Canada: Holding its own. *The Economist*. Retrieved from http:// www.economist.com/node/224910

Angelos, J. (2010, July 3). Many Germans would rather waive the flag: Immigrant's banner raises a ruckus with Berlin leftists. *The Wall Street Journal*. Retrieved from http://online.wsj.com/article/SB100014 24052748704699604575343004038839936.html

A party animal. (2011, January 20). *The Economist*, 63–64. Retrieved from http://www.economist.com/ node/17965515

Arana, M. (2002, February 24). Edna O'Brien: Doyenne of Irish letters. *The Washington Post*. Retrieved from http://www.washingtonpost.com/ac2/wp-dyn/A49394-2002Feb21

Arden, H. (1990, May). Searching for India: Along the Grand Trunk Road. *National Geographic*, 177–185.

Aronson, D. R. (1978). *The city is our farm: Seven migrant Ijebu Yoruba families*. Cambridge, MA: Schenkman.

The ascent of British man. (2002, December 5). *The Economist*, 53. Retrieved from http://www.economist .com/node/1477687

Ashkanasy, N., Gupta, V., Mayfield, M. S., & Trevor-Roberts, E. (2004). Future orientation. In R. J. House, P. J. Hanges, M. Javidan, P. W. Dorfman, & V. Gupta (Eds.), *Culture, leadership, and organizations: The GLOBE study of 62 societies* (pp. 282–342). Thousand Oaks, CA: Sage.

Atkins, R. (2010, August 22). The consensus in favour of Swedish thinking. *Financial Times.* Retrieved from http://www.ft.com/intl/cms/s/0/8fa7eca8-ae08-11df-bb55-00144feabdc0.html

Australia 2020 summit: Final report. (2008). Retrieved from http://www.australia2020.gov.au/final_report/index.cfm

Australian slang "fair dinkum" gets airline passenger into trouble. (2007, August 10). *FoxNews.* Retrieved from http://www.foxnews.com/story/0,2933,292920,00.html

Australia's promise: The next Golden State. (2011, May 26). *The Economist,* 12. Retrieved from http://www.economist.com/node/18744197

Azuma, H. (2011, March 16). For a change, proud to be Japanese (S. Kono & J. E. Abel, Trans.). *The New York Times.* Retrieved from http://www.nytimes.com/2011/03/17/opinion/17azuma.html

Bac to school. (2007, September 6). *The Economist,* 55. Retrieved from http://www.economist.com/node/9769433

Badawi, A. (2008, March 2). Badawi: "Malaysia is one nation" [Press release]. Retrieved from http://www.reuters.com/article/2008/03/02/idUS37298+02-Mar-2008+PRN20080302/

Bajaj, V., & Yardley, J. (2011, April 3). Cricket victory brings relief from scandal in India. *The New York Times.* Retrieved from http://www.nytimes.com/2011/04/04/world/asia/04mumbai.html

Banerji, P. (1983). *Erotica in Indian dance.* Atlantic Highlands, NJ: Humanities Press.

Barnlund, D. (1989). *Public and private self in Japan and the United States: Communicative styles of two cultures.* Yarmouth, ME: Intercultural Press.

Barrionuevo, A. (2011, May 19). Upwardly mobile nannies move into the Brazilian middle class. *The New York Times.* Retrieved from http://www.nytimes.com/2011/05/20/world/americas/20brazil.html

Barzini, L. G. (1964). *The Italians* (1st Touchstone ed.). New York: Simon & Schuster.

Barzini, L. G. (1983). *The Europeans.* New York: Simon & Schuster.

BBC World Service. (2003). Early history: Origins of the human race. In *The story of Africa: African history from the dawn of time* . . . Retrieved from http://www.bbc.co.uk/worldservice/specials/1624_story_of_africa/index.shtml

Beckett, J. C. (1986). *A short history of Ireland.* London, UK: Cresset Library.

Becoming a serious country. (2004, June 3). *The Economist.* Retrieved from http://www.economist.com/node/2704457

Beech, H. (2011, June). Sumo wrestles with globalization. *McKinsey Quarterly.* Retrieved from http://www.mckinseyquarterly.com/Sumo_wrestles_with_globalization_2829

Bellman, E. (2010, October 5). When the stars align, Indians say, it's a good time to have a C-section. *The Wall Street Journal.* Retrieved from http://online.wsj.com/article/SB10001424052748704394704575495413840008880.html

Bellman, E., & Range, J. (2008, May 1). Shortage of laborers plagues India. *The Wall Street Journal.*

Belluck, P. (2010, November 26). Children ease Alzheimer's in land of aging. *The New York Times.* Retrieved from http://www.nytimes.com/2010/11/26/health/26alzheimers.html

Bempechat, J., & Omori, M. C. (1990). *Meeting the educational needs of Southeast Asian children* (ERIC/CUE Digest No. 68). New York: Urban Education. Retrieved from ERIC Document Reproduction Service: http://www.ericdigests.org/pre-9218/asian.htm

ben-Aaron, D. (2010, December 2). After Nokia, can angry birds propel Finland? *Bloomberg Businessweek.* Retrieved from http://www.businessweek.com/magazine/content/10_50/b4207048626069.htm

Benet, S. (1951). *Song, dance, and customs of peasant Poland.* London, UK: Dennis Dobson.

Benton, W. (Ed.). (1970). *Encyclopedia Britannica* (Vol. 13, p. 85). Chicago, IL: Encyclopedia Britannica.

Berg, S. (2011, July 8). Five schools "send more to Oxbridge than 2000 others." *BBC Today.* Retrieved from http://www.bbc.co.uk/news/education-14069516

Berry, M. (1990). The limits of community: Finland as a symbol of frontier-infused liberalism. In M. Berry, G. Maude, & J. Schuchalter (Eds.), *Frontiers of American political experience* (pp. 31–86). Turku, Finland: Turku University Press.

Berry, M. (1994). If you run away from a bear you will run into a wolf: Finnish responses to Joanna Kramer's identity crisis. In J. Knuf (Ed.), *Texts and identities: Proceedings of the Third Kentucky Conference on Narratives, 1994* (pp. 32–48). Lexington: University of Kentucky.

Berry, M. (2009a). Epilogue. In M. Berry, D. Carbaugh, C. Innreiter-Moser, M. Nurimikari-Berry, & W. Oetsch, *"That's not me": Learning to cope with sensitive cultural issues* (2nd ed.). Finland: Authors.

Berry, M. (2009b). Finnish intercultural business overlaps with student experience. In M. Berry, D. Carbaugh, C. Innreiter-Moser, M. Nurimikari-Berry, & W. Oetsch, *"That's not me": Learning to cope with sensitive cultural issues* (2nd ed.). Finland: Authors.

Berry, M., Carbaugh, D., & Nurimikari-Berry, M. (2004). Communicating Finnish quietude: A pedagogical process for discovering implicit cultural meanings in languages. *Language and Intercultural Communication, 4*(4), 261–280.

Berry, M., Carbaugh, D., & Nurimikari-Berry, M. (2009). "Discomfort with silence" in a culture "comfortable with quietness." In M. Berry, D. Carbaugh, C. Innreiter-Moser, M. Nurimikari-Berry, & W. Oetsch, *"That's not me": Learning to cope with sensitive cultural issues* (2nd ed.). Finland: Authors.

Bettelheim, B. (1969). *The children of the dream.* New York: Macmillan.

Beyond the start-up nation. (2010, December 29). *The Economist,* 60. Retrieved from http://www.economist.com/node/17796932

Bhagat, C. (2005). *One night @ the call center: A novel.* New Delhi, India: Rupa.

The biggest losers. (2011, May 16). *Graphic Detail* [blog]. *The Economist.* Retrieved from http://www.economist.com/blogs/dailychart/2011/05/gambling/

Bilefsky, D. (2007a, April 9). Belgians hail the Middle Ages (well, not the plague part). *The New York Times.* Retrieved from http://www.nytimes.com/2007/04/09/world/europe/09medieval.html

Bilefsky, D. (2007b, August 12). Matador wins. Bull dies. The end? Not in Portugal. *The New York Times.* Retrieved from http://www.nytimes.com/2007/08/12/world/europe/12portugal.html

Bilefsky, D. (2007c, July 25). A TV contest sets off a furor over Portugal's ex-dictator. *The New York Times.* Retrieved from http://www.nytimes.com/2007/07/25/world/europe/25portugal.html

Birns, N., & McNeer, R. (Eds.). (2007). *A companion to Australian literature since 1900.* Rochester, NY: Camden House.

Bisbee, S. (1951). *The new Turks: Pioneers of the republic, 1920–1950.* Philadelphia: University of Pennsylvania Press.

Bishop, M., & Kossakowski, J. (Directors). (2008). *Taking the face: The Portuguese bullfight* [documentary film]. Wind Fish Motion Pictures.

Blow, C. M. (2011, February 18). Empire at the end of decadence. *The New York Times.* Retrieved from http://www.nytimes.com/2011/02/19/opinion/19blow.html

Blunt, P., & Jones, M. (1992). *Managing organizations in Africa.* Berlin, Germany: de Gruyter.

Boerner, S., & Freiherr von Streit, C. (2005). Transformational leadership and group climate: Empirical results from symphony orchestras. *Journal of Leadership and Organizational Studies, 12*(2), 31–41.

Bonavia, D. (1989). *The Chinese.* London, UK: Penguin.

Bond, M. H. (1986). *The psychology of the Chinese people.* New York: Oxford University Press.

Boorstin, D. J. (1965). *The Americans: The national experience.* New York: Random House.

Borton, L. (2004). Working in a Vietnamese voice. In S. M. Puffer (Ed.), *International management: Insights from fiction and practice* (pp. 203–213). Armonk, NY: M. E. Sharpe.

Borton, L., & Ryder, P. R. (2000). Working in a Vietnamese voice. *Academy of Management Executives, 14*(4), 20–31.

Boswell, R. (2011, June 13). 'Celine Dion phenomenon' could boost patriotism: Poll (updated August 25, 2011). *National Post.* Retrieved August 26, 2011, from http://news.nationalpost.com/tag/association-for-canadian-studies/

Boudreaux, R. (2007, December 27). Struggle rooted in land. *Los Angeles Times.* Retrieved from http://www.latimes.com/news/nationworld/world/la-fg-hilltop27dec27,0,1247857.story

Bowring, P. (2007, February 26). Tall poppies flourish Down Under. *The New York Times.* Retrieved from http://www.nytimes.com/2007/02/26/opinion/26iht-edbowring.html

Braganti, N. L., & Devine, E. (1992). *European customs and manners* (2nd ed.). Minneapolis, MN: Meadowbrook.

Brett, J. M. (2001). *Negotiating globally: How to negotiate deals, resolve disputes, and make decisions across cultures.* San Francisco, CA: Jossey-Bass.

Brint, S. (1989). Italy observed. *Society, 26*(5), 71–76.

Brislin, R. (1993). *Understanding culture's influence on behavior.* New York: Harcourt Brace.

British stiff-upper lip "prevents heart attack patients getting help." (2006, November 20). *Daily Mail* (UK). Retrieved from http://www.dailymail.co.uk/news/article-417510/British-stiff-upper-lip-prevents-heart-attack-patients-getting-help.html

Brooke, J. (1993, November 12). Even Brazil is shocked: State is one family's fief. *The New York Times.* Retrieved from http://www.nytimes.com/1993/11/12/world/even-brazil-is-shocked-state-is-one-family-s-fief.html

Brown, D. L. (2001, July 5). The boundaries of ignorance: Canadian TV show satirizes Americans. *The Washington Post.* Retrieved from http://www.washingtonpost.com/ac2/wp-dyn?pagename=article&node=&contentId=A20075-2001Jul4

Bryant, N. (2007, January 30). Australia in thrall of gambling mania. BBC News. Retrieved from http://news.bbc.co.uk/2/hi/asia-pacific/6313083.stm

Brzezinski, Z. (2000, January 7). War and football. *The Washington Post.*

Buarque de Holanda, S. (1974). *História do Brasil: Curso moderno.* São Paulo, Brazil: Companhia Editora Nacional.

Bullington, J. R. (2004, November 16). *Letter from Niger.* Retrieved from http://www.unc.edu/depts/diplomat/archives_roll/2004_10-12/bullington_0411/bullington_0411.html

Burns, A. C. (1963). *History of Nigeria.* London, UK: Allen & Unwin.

Burns, M. (2001). Australian mateship: An ingredient of successful teams? *Australian Business Foundation.* Retrieved from http://www.abfoundation.com.au/research_knowledge/opinions/153/

Burr, A. (1917). *Russell H. Connell and his work.* Philadelphia, PA: Winston.

But did they buy their own furniture? (2006, August 10). *The Economist,* 46. Retrieved from http://www.economist.com/node/7289005

By hook or by crook. (2007, May 31). *The Economist,* 49–50. Retrieved from http://www.economist.com/node/9259081

Cahill, T. (1995). *How the Irish saved civilization: The untold story of Ireland's heroic role from the fall of Rome to the rise of medieval Europe.* New York: Doubleday.

Campbell, J. (1962). *The masks of god: Oriental mythology.* New York: Penguin Books.

Cannadine, D. (1999). *The rise and fall of class in Britain.* New York: Columbia University Press.

Can the doves take off again? (2011, January 20). *The Economist,* 55–56. Retrieved from http://www.economist.com/node/17963325

Cappello, D. (Writer and producer), & Hollick, J. C. (Creator and producer). (1986–1989). Kaleidoscope of cultures: Part 1 of *Passages to India* [Radio broadcast]. Littleton, MA: Independent Broadcasting Associates. Retrieved from http://www.ibaradio.org/India/passages/passages.htm

Carême, A. (1833). L'art de la cuisine français au dix-neuvième siècle. Paris, France.

Carrera, A., Mesquita, L., Perkins, G., & Vassolo, R. (2003). Business groups and their corporate strategies on the Argentine roller coaster of competitive and anti-competitive shocks. *Academy of Management Executives, 17*(3), 32–43.

Carroll, R. (1987). *Cultural misunderstandings: The French American experience.* Chicago, IL: University of Chicago Press.

Carroll, S. J., & Gannon, M. J. (1997). *Ethical dimensions of international management.* Thousand Oaks, CA: Sage.

Casciato, P. (2011, June 8). Americans rated most hilarious in global poll. Reuters. Retrieved from http://www.reuters.com/article/2011/06/08/us-humour-nationalities-idUSTRE7563XB20110608/

Caste prejudice "may exist" in British workplaces. (2010, March 3). BBC News. Retrieved from http://news.bbc.co.uk/2/hi/uk_news/politics/8546661.stm

Castle, S. (2011, February 17). In Belgium, beer and frites honor political failure. *The New York Times.* Retrieved from http://www.nytimes.com/2011/02/18/world/europe/18belgium.html

Catching up in a hurry. (2011, May 19). *The Economist,* 37–38. Retrieved from http://www.economist.com/node/18712379

Chambers, K. (1997). *Succeed in business: Vietnam; The essential guide for business and investment.* Portland, OR: Graphic Arts Center.

Chazan, G., & Thomson, A. (2011, January 21). Tough Irish economy turns migration influx to exodus. *The Wall Street Journal.* Retrieved from http://online.wsj.com/article/SB10001424052748703921504576094201825868600.html

Chen, M.-J. (2001). *Inside Chinese business: A guide for managers worldwide.* Boston, MA: Harvard Business School Press.

Chhokar, J. S. (2008). India: Diversity and complexity in action. In J. S. Chhokar, F. C. Brodbeck, & R. J. House (Eds.), *Culture and leadership around the world: The GLOBE book of in-depth studies of 25 societies* (pp. 971–1011). Thousand Oaks, CA: Sage.

China donates one million $ for Nalanda University revival. (2011, November 15). *The Economic Times* (India). Retrieved from http://articles.economictimes.indiatimes.com/2011-11-15/news/30401527_1_nalanda-university-revival-project-chinese-premier/

Chinese Culture Connection. (1987). Chinese values and the search for culture-free dimensions of culture. *Journal of Cross-Cultural Psychology, 18*(2), 143–164.

Choi, H. S. (n.d.). *Hee Seop Choi quotations.* Retrieved from http://www.baseball-almanac.com/quotes/hee_seop_choi_quotes.shtml

Choi, H. W. (2001, June 26). After massive layoff, Daewoo's CEO begs a thousand pardons. *The Wall Street Journal.*

Choi, H. W. (2002, January 9). Korean club scene: How guys and gals use cupid for hire. *The Wall Street Journal.*

Choudhury, A. (1986). The community concept of business: A critique. *International Studies of Management and Organization, 16*(2), 79–95.

Chu, H. (2008, March 30). From low caste to high office in India. *Los Angeles Times.* Retrieved from http://articles.latimes.com/2008/mar/30/world/fg-mayawati30/

Chua, A. (2003). *World on fire: How exporting free market democracy breeds ethnic hatred and global instability.* New York: Doubleday.

Clarke, M., & Crisp, M. (1976). *Understanding ballet.* New York: Harmony.

Clausewitz, C. von. (1989). *On war* (M. Howard & P. Paret, Trans.). Princeton, NJ: Princeton University Press. (Original work published 1832)

Clayre, A. (1985). *The heart of the dragon.* Boston, MA: Houghton Mifflin.

Cohen, R. (2011, June 9). When fear breaks. *The New York Times.* Retrieved from http://www.nytimes.com/2011/06/10/opinion/10iht-edcohen10.html

Cohn, A. (2011, April 26). Share taxis around the world: The how, why, & design. *Kiva Stories from the Field* [blog]. Retrieved July 8, 2011, from http://fellowsblog.kiva.org/2011/04/26/share-taxis-around-the-world-the-how-why-design/

Collier, S. (1995). The tango is born: 1880s–1920s. In S. Collier, A. Cooper, M. S. Azzi, & R. Martin (Eds.), *Tango! The dance, the song, the story* (pp. 18–65). London, UK: Thames and Hudson.

Colvin, G. (2002, July 22). Sick of scandal? Blame football! *Fortune,* 44. Retrieved from http://money.cnn.com/magazines/fortune/fortune_archive/2002/07/22/326310/

Colvin, G. (2003, February 17). For touchdown, see rule 3, sec. 38. *Fortune,* 17, 34. Retrieved from http://money.cnn.com/magazines/fortune/fortune_archive/2003/02/17/337324/

Coming apart? It is time to start worrying about Turkey—and looking for ways to revive its European hopes. (2006, May 4). *The Economist.* Retrieved from http://www.economist.com/node/6882629

Connors, W. (2011, June 28). In Nigeria, "lace" market reflects rising middle class. *The Wall Street Journal.* Retrieved from http://online.wsj.com/article/SB10001424052702304665904576383833455318532.html

Controversial Turkish television: Magnificent no more. (2011, January 27). *The Economist.* Retrieved from http://www.economist.com/node/18013830

Conty, M. (1999, Fall). Belle of the ball. *Hermes* [Columbia Business School], 42–44.

Coomaraswamy, A. (1969). *The dance of Shiva.* New York: Sunwise Turn. (Original work published 1924)

Cooper, A. (1995). Tangomania in Europe and North America: 1913–1914. In S. Collier, A. Cooper, M. S. Azzi, & R. Martin (Eds.), *Tango! The dance, the song, the story* (pp. 66–113). London, UK: Thames and Hudson.

Copland, A. (1957). *What to listen for in music.* New York: McGraw-Hill. (Original work published 1939)

Cottrell, J. (1986). *Library of nations: Germany.* Alexandria, VA: Time-Life Books.

Could Flanders be reinvented? (1997, September 18). *The Economist,* 54. Retrieved from http://www .economist.com/node/157189

Coy, P. (2011, March 7–13). Why Saudi hope still floats. *Bloomberg Businessweek,* 7.

Craig, J. (1979). *Culture shock: What not to do in Malaysia and Singapore; How and why not to do it.* Singapore: Times Book International.

Crook, C. (1991, May 4). A survey of India. *The Economist,* 1–18.

Crow, J. (1985). *Spain: The root and the flower* (3rd ed.). Berkeley: University of California Press.

Crozier, M. (1964). *The bureaucratic phenomenon.* Chicago, IL: University of Chicago Press.

Crystal, D. (2011). *Evolving English: One language, many voices.* London, UK: British Library.

Curran, E. (2011, May 25). Australians among the happiest, OECD lifestyle index shows. *The Wall Street Journal.* Retrieved from http://online.wsj.com/article/SB10001424052702304520804576344131765 917532.html

Cusumano, C. (2010, July–August). For the love of tango. *Westways,* 35–38. Retrieved from http://www .camillecusumano.com/uncategorized/for-the-love-of-tango-2010-2/

Cyrus P. Mistry is Ratan Tata's heir apparent. (2011, November 23). *The Hindu* (India). Retrieved from http://www.thehindu.com/business/companies/article2653420.ece

Daniszewski, J. (2005a, April 17). Catholicism losing ground in Ireland. *Los Angeles Times.* Retrieved from http://articles.latimes.com/2005/apr/17/world/fg-ireland17/

Daniszewski, J. (2005b, April 24). A twist for an ancient tongue trying to survive. *Los Angeles Times.* Retrieved from http://articles.latimes.com/2005/apr/24/world/fg-gaelic24/

Daun, Å. (1991). Individualism and collectivity among Swedes. *Ethnos, 56*(3–4), 165–172.

Davidson, B. (1984). *The story of Africa.* London, UK: Mitchell Beazley.

de Gramont, S. (1969). *The French: Portrait of a people.* New York: G. P. Putnam's Sons.

Dehejia, R. S. (2010, April 30). India journal: Conspicuous under-consumption. *The Wall Street Journal.* Retrieved from http://blogs.wsj.com/indiarealtime/2010/04/30/india-journal-conspicuous-under-consumption/

de Jorio, A. (2000). *Gesture in Naples and gesture in classical antiquity* [*La mimica degli antichi investigata nel gestire napoletano*] (A. Kendon, Trans.). Bloomington: Indiana University Press.

Delaney, M. M. (1974). *Of Irish ways.* Minneapolis, MN: Dillon.

De Mente, B. (1990). *Japan's secret weapon: The kata factor; The cultural programming that made the Japanese a superior people.* Phoenix, AZ: Phoenix Books.

Demick, B. (2006, May 21). Koreans' kimchi adulation, with a side of skepticism. *Los Angeles Times.* Retrieved from http://articles.latimes.com/2006/may/21/world/fg-kimchi21/

de Soto, H. (2000). *The mystery of capital: Why capitalism triumphs in the West and fails everywhere else.* New York: Basic Books.

de Mooij, M. (2011). *Consumer behavior and culture: Consequences for global marketing and advertising* (2nd ed.). Thousand Oaks, CA: Sage.

Diamond, J. (1999). *Guns, germs, and steel: The fates of human societies.* New York: W. W. Norton.

di Lampedusa, G. T. (2007). *The leopard [Il gattopardo].* (A. Colquhuon, Trans.). New York: Random House. (Original work published 1958)

Dindi, H., Gazur, J., Gazur, W. M., & Kirkkorpru-Dindi, A. (1989). *Turkish culture for Americans.* Boulder, CO: International Concepts.

Dinzel, R., & Dinzel, G. (2000). *Tango: An anxious quest for freedom.* Stuttgart, Germany: Editorial Abrazos.

The Dominion Institute. (2007). *Annual Canada Day survey.* Retrieved from http://www.dominion.ca/ Canada_Day_Survey_2007.pdf

The Dominion Institute. (2008). *Canadians choose the people, places, events, accomplishments and symbols that define Canada.* Retrieved from http://www.dominion.ca/polling.htm

Dougherty, C. (2007, December 26). Denmark feels the pinch as young workers flee to lands of lower taxes. *The New York Times.* Retrieved from http://www.nytimes.com/2007/12/26/business/ worldbusiness/26labor.html

Echikson, W. (2008, April 7). The Scandinavian secret: Why does Sweden churn out so many great golfers? *The Wall Street Journal.* Retrieved from http://online.wsj.com/article/SB120718283035984931.html

The economic development of the Argentine Republic in the last fifty years. (1919). Buenos Aires, Argentina: Ernesto Tornquist.

Pocket world in figures (2012 ed.). (2011). London, UK: The Economist with Profile Books.

Economy rankings. (2011, June). *Doing Business.* Retrieved December 22, 2011, from http://www.doing business.org/rankings/

Edoho, F. M. (2001). Management in Africa: The quest for a philosophical framework. In F. M. Edoho (Ed.), *Management challenges for Africa in the twenty-first century: Theoretical and applied perspectives* (pp. 73–90). Westport, CT: Praeger.

Eine kleine samba. (1995, November 4). *The Economist,* p. 49.

Elon, A. (1971). *The Israelis.* New York: Penguin.

Emsden, C. (2008, January 26). Euro-Zone growth may rest with Germany. *The Wall Street Journal.*

England's shame. (1998, June 18). *The Economist,* 49. Retrieved from http://www.economist.com/ node/136016

Erez, M. (1986). The congruence of goal-setting strategies with socio-cultural values and its effect on performance. *Journal of Management, 12*(4), 585–592.

Ever higher society, ever harder to ascend. (2004, December 29). *The Economist,* 22–24. Retrieved from http://www.economist.com/node/3518560

The evolving platypus. (2011, May 26). *The Economist,* 10–12. Retrieved from http://www.economist .com/node/18719578

Fackler, M. (2007, August 5). Career women in Japan find a blocked path. *The New York Times.* Retrieved from http://www.nytimes.com/2007/08/06/world/asia/06iht-06equal.6995284.html

Fackler, M. (2008a, January 2). Japan's new education model: India. *The New York Times.* Retrieved from http://www.nytimes.com/2008/01/02/business/worldbusiness/02iht-yen.1.8984635.html

Fackler, M. (2008b, February 24). Michelin gives stars, but Tokyo turns up nose. *The New York Times.* Retrieved from http://www.nytimes.com/2008/02/24/business/worldbusiness/24guide.html

Faiola, A. (1997, October 2). Priest tries to rap Brazilians back into fold. *The Washington Post.*

Faiola, A. (2010, December 19). Kate Middleton's "commoner" status stirs up Britons' old class divide. *The Washington Post.* Retrieved from http://www.washingtonpost.com/wp-dyn/content/article/2010/12/18/ AR2010121803829.html

Fan, M. (2007, December 26). Children of China's elite get lessons in family values. *The San Diego Union-Tribune.* Retrieved from http://www.signonsandiego.com/uniontrib/20071226/news_1n26china.html

Fang, T. (1999). *Chinese business negotiating style.* Thousand Oaks, CA: Sage.

Feather, N. T. (1994). Attitudes toward high achievers and reactions to their fall: Theory and research concerning tall poppies. *Advances in Experimental Social Psychology, 21,* 697–715.

Ferguson, N. (2002). *Empire: The rise and demise of the British world order and the lessons for global power.* New York: Basic Books.

Ferguson, N. (2006, February 27). The crash of civilizations. *Los Angeles Times.*

Ferguson, W. S. (2007). *Why I hate Canadians* (10th anniversary ed.). Vancouver, Canada: Douglas & McIntyre.

Fieg, J., & Mortlock, E. (1989). *A common core: Thais and Americans* (Rev. ed.). Yarmouth, ME: Intercultural Press. (Original work published 1976; author J. Fieg)

Fine, J. (1985). *Your guide to coping with back pain.* Toronto, Canada: McClelland & Stewart.

Fine, J. (1987). *Conquering back pain.* New York: Prentice Hall Press.

First things first. (1998, August 27). *The Economist.* Retrieved from http://www.economist.com/node/162741

Fisher, G. (1988). *Mindsets: The role of culture and perception in international relations.* Yarmouth, ME: Intercultural Press.

Fiske, A. P. (1991a). The four elementary forms of sociality: Framework for a unified theory of social relations. *Psychological Review, 99*(4), 689–723. Retrieved from http://www.sscnet.ucla.edu/anthro/faculty/fiske/pubs/Fiske_Four_Elementary_Forms_Sociality_1992.pdf

Fiske, A. P. (1991b). *Structures of social life: The four elementary forms of human relations; Communal sharing, authority ranking, equality matching, market pricing.* New York: Free Press.

Fitzgerald, M. (2007, March 25). How to improve it? Ask those who use it. *The New York Times.* Retrieved from http://www.nytimes.com/2007/03/25/business/yourmoney/25Proto.html

Fleckenstein, B. (2000). Germany: Forerunner of a post-national military? In C. C. Moskos, J. A. Williams, & D. R. Segal (Eds.), *The postmodern military: Armed forces after the Cold War* (pp. 31–53). New York: Oxford University Press.

Fleming, C., & Lavin, D. (1997, November 5). How many protests can the French take? About 10,000 a year. *The Wall Street Journal Europe.*

Foroohar, R. (2011, June 27). Prime Minister Erdogan: Turkey's man of the people. *Time.* Retrieved from http://www.time.com/time/magazine/article/0,9171,2078021,00.html

Freeland, C. (2010, January 29). What Toronto can teach New York and London. *Financial Times.* Retrieved from http://www.ft.com/intl/cms/s/2/db2b340a-0a1b-11df-8b23-00144feabdc0.html

Friberg, E. (Trans.). (1988). *The Kalevala: Epic of the Finnish people* (4th ed.). Helsinki, Finland: Otava.

Friedman, T. L. (1995). *From Beirut to Jerusalem.* New York: Random House. (Original work published 1989)

Friedman, T. L. (2005). *The world is flat: A brief history of the twenty-first century.* New York: Farrar, Straus, and Giroux.

Friedman, T. L. (2010, November 2). Do believe the hype. *The New York Times.* Retrieved from http://www.nytimes.com/2010/11/03/opinion/03friedman.html

Frost, E. (1987). *For richer, for poorer: The new U.S.-Japan relationship.* New York: Council on Foreign Relations.

Fuller, T. (2011a, May 12). The fallout for chiding the royals in Thailand. *The New York Times.* Retrieved from http://www.nytimes.com/2011/05/12/world/asia/12thai.html

Fuller, T. (2011b, January 1). When the spirits talk, as they frequently do, Thais are eager to listen. *The New York Times.* Retrieved from http://query.nytimes.com/gst/fullpage.html?res=9501EFDC1139F932A35752C0A9679D8B63

Furniss, N., & Tilton, T. A. (1977). *The case for the welfare state: From Social Security to social equality.* Bloomington: Indiana University Press.

Gabrielidis, C., Stephan, W., Ybarra, O., Dos Santos-Pearson, V., & Villareal, L. (1997). Preferred styles of conflict resolution. *Journal of Cross-Cultural Psychology, 6*(28), 661–677.

Galbraith, J. (1958). *The affluent society.* Boston, MA: Houghton Mifflin.

Gamerman, E. (2008, February 29). What makes Finnish kids so smart? *The Wall Street Journal.* Retrieved from http://online.wsj.com/article/SB120425355065601997.html

Gannon, M. J. (2008). *Paradoxes of culture and globalization.* Thousand Oaks, CA: Sage.

Gannon, M. J. (2011). Cultural metaphors: Their use in management practice and as a method for understanding cultures. In W. J. Lonner, D. L. Dinnel, S. A. Hayes, & D. N. Satler (Eds.), *OnLine readings in psychology and culture: Unit 7.* Retrieved from http://scholarworks.gvsu.edu/orpc/vol7/iss1/4/

Gannon, M. J., Locke, E. A., Gupta, A., Audia, P., & Kristof-Brown, A. L. (2005). Cultural metaphors as frames of reference for nations: A six-country study. *International Studies of Management & Organization, 35*(4), 37–47.

Gardner, A. (2003). The new calculus of Bedouin pastoralism in the Kingdom of Saudi Arabia. *Human Organization, 62*(3), 267–276.

Garret FitzGerald [obituary]. (2011, May 26). *The Economist,* 91. Retrieved from http://www.economist.com/node/18740946

Gaskell, E. (1995). *North and south.* New York: Penguin Putnam (Original work published 1855)

Geertz, C. (1973). *The interpretation of cultures: Selected essays.* New York: Basic Books.

Gelfand, M. J., & Holcombe, K. M. (1998). Behavioral patterns of horizontal and vertical individualism and collectivism. In T. Singelis (Ed.), *Teaching about culture, ethnicity, & diversity* (pp. 121–132). Thousand Oaks, CA: Sage.

George, P. (1987). *University teaching across cultures: Lessons from U.S. Fulbrighters in Southeast Asia and their colleagues in Thailand.* Bangkok, Thailand: U.S. Information Service.

Gandhi, M. (1946). *Anasakti yoga, or the gospel of selfless action; An extract from Ghandi's commentary on the Bhagvad Gita* (M. Desai, Ed.). Retrieved from http://www.mkgandhi.org/swmgandhi/chap01.htm

Ghemawat, P. (2011). *World 3.0: Global prosperity and how to achieve it.* Boston, MA: Harvard Business Review Press.

Gladwell, M. (2008). *Outliers: The story of success.* New York: Little, Brown.

Gledhill, R. (2007, February 15). Catholics set to pass Anglicans as leading UK church. *Times Online* (UK). Reprinted at http://www.freerepublic.com/focus/f-religion/1785394/posts/

Glyn, A. (1970). *The British: Portrait of a people.* New York: Putnam.

Gochenour, T. (1977). The albatross. In D. Batchelder & E. Warner (Eds.), *Beyond experience: The experiential approach to cross-cultural education* (pp. 131–136). Brattleboro, VT: Experiment Press.

Goldin, I., & Reinert, K. (2006). *Globalization for development.* New York: Palgrave Macmillan.

Goldstein, P. (2004, September 12). The game of life. *Los Angeles Times.* Retrieved from http://articles.latimes.com/2004/sep/12/entertainment/ca-goldstein12/

Gopal, R., & Dadachanji, S. (1951). *Indian dancing.* London, UK: Phoenix House.

Gorman, J. (2011). *Don't think you're anything special: The presence of the law of Jante in Norwegian cinema.* Paper submitted in fulfillment of the requirements of CMC 350L: Topics in Media and Culture, Rollins College, Winter Park, FL. Retrieved from http://www.akastatistic.org/mediawiki/images/c/c7/Gorman_Julie_Paper2_JanteLaw.doc

Graham, R. (1984). *Spain: Change of a nation.* London, UK: Michael Joseph.

Gray, K. R. (2001). Small business management in Africa: Prospects for future development. In F. M. Edoho (Ed.), *Management challenges for Africa in the twenty-first century: Theoretical and applied perspectives* (pp. 259–275). Westport, CT: Praeger.

Green, R. E. (1996). *Ho Chi Minh biography.* Retrieved from http://www.tactileint.com/seasia/saigon/hochiminh.html

Grinding them down. (2005, January 13). *The Economist,* 35. Retrieved from http://www.economist.com/node/3564904

Guiliano, M. (2005). *French women don't get fat: The secret of eating for pleasure.* New York: Knopf.

Gupta, V., & Hanges, P. J. (2004). Regional and climate clustering of societal cultures. In R. J. House, P. J., Hanges, M. Javidan, P. W. Dorfman, & V. Gupta (Eds.), *Culture, leadership, and organizations: The GLOBE study of 62 societies* (pp. 178–215). Thousand Oaks, CA: Sage.

Habermas, J. (2010, October 28). Leadership and *Leitkultur*. *The New York Times*. Retrieved from http://www.nytimes.com/2010/10/29/opinion/29Habermas.html

Haire, M., Ghiselli, E. E., & Porter, L. W. (1966). *Managerial thinking: An international study*. New York: John Wiley.

Haley, E. (1996, March 22). How French advertising professionals develop creative strategy. *Journal of Advertising*. Retrieved from http://www.allbusiness.com/marketing-advertising/advertising/554562-1.html

Hall, E. T. (1966). *The hidden dimension*. Garden City, NY: Doubleday.

Hall, E. T. (1983). *The dance of life: The other dimension of time*. Garden City, NY: Doubleday.

Hall, E. T., & Hall, M. R. (1990). *Understanding cultural differences*. Yarmouth, ME: Intercultural Press.

Halonen, T. (2007, February 16). *Opening address by president of the Republic of Finland, Tarja Halonen, at the Innovation Seminar in Sydney, Australia*. Retrieved from http://www.finland.com.au/news_innovation_seminar.html

Hamzah-Sendut, T. S. D., Madsen, J., & Thong, G. T. S. (1989). *Managing in a plural society*. Singapore: Longman.

Handley, P. M. (2006). *The king never smiles: A biography of Thailand's Bhumibol Adulyadej*. New Haven, CT: Yale University Press.

Hand of God, hand of Italian man. (1998, May 14). *The Economist*, 56. Retrieved from http://www.economist.com/node/129193

Hann, C. M. (1985). *A village without solidarity: Polish peasants in years of crisis*. New Haven, CT: Yale University Press.

Hannon, E. (2011, May 21). India's government aims to curb excessive weddings. *Time*. Retrieved from http://www.time.com/time/world/article/0,8599,2068450,00.html

Happy-go-lucky Cristina. (2010, August 19). *The Economist*. Retrieved from http://www.economist.com/node/16846418

Happy-ish birthday. (2011, March 17). *The Economist*, 61. Retrieved from http://www.economist.com/node/18400574

Harden, B. (2008, May 6). Japan steadily becoming a land of few children. *The Washington Post*. Retrieved from http://www.washingtonpost.com/wp-dyn/content/article/2008/05/05/AR2008050502224.html

Harris, E. (2008, March 2). Nigerians' English goes its own way. Associated Press. Retrieved from *USA Today* website: http://www.usatoday.com/news/world/2008-03-02-2756073788_x.htm

Haskell, A. L. (1963). *The Russian genius in ballet*. Elmsford, NY: Pergamon Press.

Haskell, A. L. (1968). *Balletomania*. New York: AMS Press.

Hausmann, R., Tyson, L. D., & Zahidi, S. (2011). *The global gender gap report: 2011*. Geneva, Switzerland: World Economic Forum. Retrieved from http://www3.weforum.org/docs/WEF_GenderGap_Report_2011.pdf

Haycraft, J. (1987). *Italian labyrinth: Italy in the 1980s*. New York: Viking Penguin. (Original work published 1985 in the UK)

Heclo, H., & Madsen, H. (1987). *Policy and politics in Sweden: Principled pragmatism*. Philadelphia, PA: Temple University Press.

Heinrich, B. (1990). A matter of degrees. In F. R. Thomas (Ed.), *Americans in Denmark* (pp. 35–53). Carbondale: University of Southern Illinois Press.

Henderson, A. (2010, Winter). A Danish Christmas carol. *Copenhagen Exclusive*, 13–15. Retrieved from http://www.copenhagenexclusive.dk/Copenhagen_exclusive_17.pdf

Hess, D. (1995). *The Brazilian puzzle: Culture on the borderlands of the Western world*. New York: Columbia University Press.

Hofstadter, R. (1955). *Social Darwinism in American thought*. Boston, MA: Beacon.

Hofstede, G. H. (1980a). *Culture's consequences*. Beverly Hills, CA: Sage.

Hofstede, G. H. (1980b). Motivation, leadership, and organization: Do American theories apply abroad? *Organizational Dynamics, 9*(1), 42–63.

Hofstede, G. H. (1991). *Cultures and organizations: Software of the mind.* New York: McGraw-Hill.

Hofstede. G. H. (2001). *Culture's consequences: Comparing values, behaviors, institutions, and organizations across nations* (2nd ed.). Thousand Oaks, CA: Sage.

Hogg, C. (2006, January 11). Japan bows to code of respect. BBC News. Retrieved from http://news.bbc .co.uk/2/hi/asia-pacific/4594782.stm

Hollinger, C. (1977). Mai pen rai *means never mind* (1st Far East reprint ed.). Tokyo, Japan: John Weatherhill. (Original work published 1967)

Hookway, J. (2010, June 24). "Young Imam" is the reality show creating all the buzz in Malaysia. *The Wall Street Journal.* Retrieved from http://online.wsj.com/article/SB10001424052748704911704575326623895421154.html

Hot, dry and crowded. (2010, February 4). *The Economist.* Retrieved from http://www.economist.com/ node/15469287

House, R. J., Hanges, P. J., Javidan, M., Dorfman, P. W., & Gupta, V. (2004). *Culture, leadership, and organizations: The GLOBE study of 62 societies.* Thousand Oaks, CA: Sage.

How Britain's elite has changed. (2002, December 5). *The Economist,* 15. Retrieved from http://www .economist.com/node/1477598

Huntington, S. P. (1996). *The clash of civilizations and the remaking of world order.* New York: Simon & Schuster.

Huxley, A. (1951). *Antic hay.* New York: Modern Library.

Illarionov, A. (2009). *The* siloviki *in charge. Journal of Democracy, 20*(2), 69–72. Retrieved from http:// www.journalofdemocracy.org/articles/gratis/Illarionov-20-2.pdf

The importance of sex. (2006, April 12). *The Economist.* Retrieved from http://www.economist.com/ node/6800723

In a league of its own. (2006, April 27). *The Economist,* 63–64. Retrieved from http://www.economist .com/node/6859210

Inyang, A. (2010, September 29). [Comment in response to M. Dan-Ali, *Viewpoint: What it means to be Nigerian.*] Retrieved from http://www.bbc.co.uk/news/mobile/world-africa-11406730

Iwao, S. (1990). Recent changes in Japanese attitudes. In A. D. Romberg & T. Yamamoto (Eds.), *Same bed, different dreams: America and Japan—Societies in transition* (pp. 41–66). New York: Council on Foreign Relations.

Iwatani, N., Orr, G., & Salsberg, B. (2011, June). Japan's globalization imperative. *McKinsey Quarterly.* Retrieved from http://www.mckinseyquarterly.com/Japans_globalization_imperative_2824/

Iyer, V. R. K. (2000, October 22). Personality par excellence. *The Hindu* (India). Retrieved from http://www .hinduonnet.com//2000/10/22/stories/1322078e.htm

Jago, A. G., Mączyński, J., Reber, G., & Böhnisch, W. (1996). Evolving leadership styles? A comparison of Polish managers before and after market economy reforms. *Polish Psychological Bulletin, 27*(2), 107–115.

Jago, A. G., Reber, G., Böhnisch, W., Mączyński, J., Zavrel, J., & Dudorkin, J. (1993). Culture's consequences? A seven-nation study of participation. In D. F. Rogers & A. S. Raturi (Eds.), *Proceedings of the 24th Annual Meeting of the Decision Sciences Institute* (pp. 451–454). Washington, DC: Decision Sciences Institute.

Jakobson, M. (1987). *Finland: Myth or reality?* Helsinki, Finland: Otava.

Jarvenpaa, S. L., Knoll, K., & Leidner, D. E. (1998). Is anybody out there? Antecedents of trust in global virtual teams. *Journal of Management Information Systems, 14*(4), 29–64.

Jenkins, D. (1968). *Sweden and the price of progress.* New York: Coward, McCann & Geohegan.

JETRO (Japan External Trade Organization). (2006). *Japan is the world's most concentrated source of revenue for luxury brands.* Retrieved from http://www.jetro.org/content/361/

Jobless pay around the globe. (2010, May 16). *Bloomberg Businessweek,* 14. Retrieved from http://www .businessweek.com/magazine/content/10_20/b4178014086188.htm

Johnson, H. (1985). *How to enjoy wine.* New York: Simon & Schuster.

Johnson, K. (2006, July 24). Bullfighting, besieged in Spain, has found young French savior. *The Wall Street Journal.*

Jones, H. (2010, December 10). Why British students are rioting in London. *Time.* Retrieved from http://www.time.com/time/world/article/0,8599,2036392,00.html

Joyce, J. (1964). *Portrait of the artist as a young man.* New York: Viking. (Original work published 1914–15)

Kâgitçibâşi, Ç. (1990). Family and home-based intervention. In R. W. Brislin (Ed.), *Applied cross-cultural psychology* (pp. 121–141). Newbury Park, CA: Sage.

Kahin, G. M., & Lewis, J. W. (1967). *The United States in Vietnam.* New York: Dial Press.

Kahn, G., & Di Leo, L. (2007, June 28). In Italian crackdown, tax cheats get the boot. *The Wall Street Journal.*

Kahn, M. E., & Lostys, F. (2007, October). Living green. *Reader's Digest.* Retrieved from http://www.rd.com/travel/greenest-locations-on-the-globe/

Kaiser, R., & Perkins, L. (2005, June 3). Finland diary: The Finnish sauna. *The Washington Post.* Retrieved from http://blog.washingtonpost.com/finlanddiary/2005/06/the_finnish_sau.html

Kakar, S. (1978). *The inner world: A psycho-analytic study of childhood and society in India.* New York: Oxford University Press.

Kalaycıoğlu, E. (2011). *Turkey's views on the European Union in 2011.* Retrieved from the German Marshall Fund of the United States website: http://www.gmfus.org/galleries/ct_publication_attachments/Kalaycioglu_TT2011Results_Sept11.pdf

Kalita, S. M. (2005, December 27). Hope and toil at India's call centers. *The Washington Post.* Retrieved from http://www.washingtonpost.com/wp-dyn/content/article/2005/12/26/AR2005122600852.html

Kang, K. C. (2008, February 26). Americans loosening their church loyalties. *Los Angeles Times.* Retrieved from http://articles.latimes.com/2008/feb/26/nation/na-religion26

Kanter, R. M. (1979). Power failures in management circuits. *Harvard Business Review, 57*(4), 65–75.

Kaplan, R. (2010, September 20). The trouble after empire [Review of Peter Cunliffe-Jones's book, *My Nigeria: Five decades of independence*]. *The Wall Street Journal.* Retrieved from http://online.wsj.com/article/SB10001424052748703376504575492382253507788.html

Kapuscinski, R. (2001). *The shadow of the sun.* New York: Knopf.

Karp, H. (2008, February 1). What game? *The Wall Street Journal.* Retrieved from http://online.wsj.com/article/SB120182489659533665.html

Karp, J., & Williams, M. (1998, April 22). Leave it to Vishnu: Gods of Indian TV are Hindu deities. *The Wall Street Journal.*

Kaufman, J. (1999, October 22). Why doesn't business, like baseball, create improbable heroes? *The Wall Street Journal.*

Keefe, E. K. (1977). *Area handbook for Italy.* Washington, DC: American University.

Keirsey, D. (1998). *Please understand me II: Temperament, character, intelligence.* Del Mar, CA: Prometheus Nemesis Book.

Kershner, I. (2010, December 28). Some Israelis question benefits for ultra-religious. *The New York Times.* Retrieved from http://www.nytimes.com/2010/12/29/world/middleeast/29israel.html

Kesselman, M., Krieger, J., Allen, C., DeBardeleben, J., Hellman, S., Pontrisson, J., & Ost, D. (1987). *European politics in transition.* Lexington, MA: D. C. Heath.

Kettenacker, L. (1997). *Germany since 1945.* Oxford, UK: Oxford University Press.

Keyes, R. (2006). *The quote verifier: Who said what, where, and when.* New York: St. Martin's Press.

Khalid, M. (1979). The sociocultural determinants of Arab diplomacy. In G. Atiyeh (Ed.), *Arab and American cultures* (pp. 123–142). Washington, DC: American Enterprise Institute for Public Policy Research.

Khalil, A. (2007, December 7). In Israel, it's temple vs. state over farming. *Los Angeles Times.* Retrieved from http://articles.latimes.com/2007/dec/07/world/fg-shmita7/

Khoi, P. V. (2008, June). Vietnamese agriculture: One year entering the WTO (East Asia Economic Research Group Discussion Paper No. 15). Brisbane, Australia: School of Economics, The University of Queensland. Retrieved from http://www.uq.edu.au/economics/eaerg/dp/EAERG_DP15.pdf

Kightly, C. (1986). *The customs and ceremonies of Britain.* London, UK: Thames & Hudson.

Kimmelman, M. (2010, December 10). In Italy, a political opera about opera. *The New York Times.* Retrieved from http://www.nytimes.com/2010/12/11/arts/music/11scala.html

King, L. (2011, March 13). Japan's massive earthquake has little effect on culture's impeccable manners. *Los Angeles Times.* Retrieved from http://articles.latimes.com/2011/mar/13/world/la-fg-japan-quake-polite-20110313/

Kluckholn, F. R., & Strodtbeck, F. L. (1961). *Variations in value orientations.* Evanston, IL: Row, Peterson.

Knight, C. (2007, July 25). The grandstand erected by Italy. *Los Angeles Times.* Retrieved from http://articles.latimes.com/2007/jul/25/entertainment/et-getty25/

Kohl K. S. (2007, Fall). *Americans doing business in Vietnam: Communication differences.* Paper submitted in fulfillment of the requirements of COM 9656: International Business Communication, Baruch College, New York, NY.

Kong, L. (2007). *Singapore hawker centres: People, places, food.* Singapore: National Environment Agency. Retrieved from http://app.nea.gov.sg/ (no longer available online)

Kotkin, J. (1993). *Tribes: How race, religion and identity determine success in the new global economy.* New York: Random House.

Kraar, L. (1994, October 31). The overseas Chinese. *Fortune, 91*–114.

Kras, E. S. (1989). *Management in two cultures.* Yarmouth, ME: Intercultural Press.

Kresge, N. (2008, February 17). Aging guest workers are fresh poser for Germany. Reuters. Retrieved December 20, 2008, from http://www.reuters.com/article/worldNews/idUSL0521752720080218/

Krich, J. (1993). *Why is this country dancing?* New York: Simon & Schuster.

Kripalani, M. (2008, May 7). In India, death to global business. *Bloomberg Businessweek.* Retrieved from http://www.businessweek.com/magazine/content/08_20/b4084044908374.htm

Kristof, N. D. (2010, July 7). In Israel, the noble versus the ugly. *The New York Times.* Retrieved from http://www.nytimes.com/2010/07/08/opinion/08kristof.html

Kristof, N. D. (2011, March 11). Sympathy for Japan, and admiration. *The New York Times.* Retrieved from http://kristof.blogs.nytimes.com/2011/03/11/sympathy-for-japan-and-admiration/

Kuttner, R. (2008). The Copenhagen consensus: Reading Adam Smith in Denmark. *Foreign Affairs, 87*(2), 78–94.

Laaksonen, P. (1999). Sauna. In O. Alho, H. Hawkins, & P. Vallisaari (Eds.), *Finland: A cultural encyclopedia* (pp. 278–279). Helsinki, Finland: Finnish Literature Society.

Lakoff, G., & Johnson, M. (1980). *Metaphors we live by.* Chicago, IL: University of Chicago Press.

Lakshmi, R. (2008, May 11). U.S. legal work booms in India. *The Washington Post.* Retrieved from http://www.washingtonpost.com/wp-dyn/content/article/2008/05/10/AR2008051002355.html

Lakshmi, R. (2011, December 7). India suspends plan to open up retail market to foreign chains. *The Washington Post.* Retrieved from http://www.washingtonpost.com/world/asia_pacific/india-suspends-plan-to-open-up-retail-market-to-foreign-chains/2011/12/07/gIQA74wqbO_story.html

Lannoy, R. (1971). *The speaking tree: A study of Indian culture and society.* New York: Oxford University Press.

Laporte, N. (2011, May 6). The Korean dads' 12-step program. *The New York Times Sunday Magazine.* Retrieved from http://www.nytimes.com/2011/05/08/magazine/mag-08Here-t.html

Laurent, A. (1983). The cultural diversity of Western concepts of management. *International Studies of Management and Organization, 13*(1–2), 75–96.

Leggett, K. (2005, May 26). Pay-as-you go kibbutzim. *The Wall Street Journal.*

Lessem, R. (1987). *The global business.* London, UK: Prentice-Hall International.

Lessem, R., & Palsule, S. (1997). *Managing in four worlds: From competition to co-creation.* London, UK: Blackwell Business.

Levine, I. R. (1963). *Main Street, Italy.* Garden City, NY: Doubleday.

Lewis, B. (1995). *The Middle East: A brief history of the last 2,000 years.* New York: Simon & Schuster.

Lewis, D. K. (2001). *The history of Argentina.* New York: Palgrave Macmillan.

Lewis, M. (2006). *The blind side: Evolution of a game.* New York: Norton.

Lights, camera, Africa: Movies are uniting a disparate continent, and dividing it too (2010, December 16). *The Economist,* 85–88. Retrieved from http://www.economist.com/node/17723124

Liker, J. K., & Ogden, T. N. (2011). *Toyota under fire: Lessons for turning crisis into opportunity.* New York: McGraw-Hill.

Lintner, B. (2009). The battle for Thailand: Can democracy survive? *Foreign Affairs, 88*(4), 108–118.

Lipsyte, R. (2007, January 30). The church of football. *The Nation.* Retrieved from http://www.thenation.com/article/church-football/

The long life of *Homo sovieticus.* (2011, December 10). *The Economist,* 27. Retrieved from http://www.economist.com/node/21541444

Lucas, E. (2006, May 13). Cheer up: A survey of Poland. *The Economist,* 1–12. Retrieved from http://www.economist.com/node/6875791

Lucas, E. (2010, September 17). State security post-Soviet style [Review of Andrei Soldatov and Irina Borogan's book, *The new nobility: The restoration of Russia's security state and the enduring legacy of the KGB*]. *The Wall Street Journal.* Retrieved from http://online.wsj.com/article/SB10001424052748703466704575489774021664514.html

Luce, E. (2008). *In spite of the gods: The rise of modern India.* New York: Anchor Books.

MacFarquhar, N. (2011, May 24). Saudis arrest woman leading right-to-drive campaign. *The New York Times.* Retrieved from http://www.nytimes.com/2011/05/24/world/middleeast/24saudi.html

Mackey, S. (2002). *The Saudis: Inside the desert kingdom* (Rev. ed.). New York: W. W. Norton.

Major, J. S. (1989). *The land and the people of China.* New York: J. B. Lippincott.

Malarney, S. K. (2002). *Culture, ritual and revolution in Vietnam.* Honolulu: University of Hawaii Press.

Mango, A. (2010, June 26). Ottoman past shadows Turkish present. *The Wall Street Journal.* Retrieved from http://online.wsj.com/article/SB10001424052748703615104575328622438027714.html

Manolo Chopera. (2002, September 12). *The Economist,* 82. Retrieved from http://www.economist.com/node/1325151

Marvin, G. (1988). *Bullfight.* New York: Basil Blackwell.

Mayes, F. (1996). *Under the Tuscan sun: At home in Italy.* San Francisco, CA: Chronicle Books.

Mazen, M. (2011, June 28). Nigeria's economy could overtake South Africa by 2025, Morgan Stanley says. *Bloomberg.* Retrieved from http://www.bloomberg.com/news/2011-06-28/nigeria-s-economy-may-overtake-south-africa-by-2025-morgan-stanley-says.html

Mbiti, J. (1970). *African religions and philosophy.* New York: Doubleday.

McBride, E. (2002, February 28). A new order: A survey of Thailand. *The Economist.* Retrieved from http://www.economist.com/node/998338

McBride, S. (2003, August 7). Gray area: In corporate Asia, a looming crisis over succession. *The Wall Street Journal.*

McCarthy, D. J., Puffer, S. M., & Darda, S. V. (2010). *Convergence in entrepreneurial leadership style: Evidence from Russia* (Harvard Business School Case # CMR464-PDF- ENG). Available from http://hbr.org/store/

McCarthy, S. (1994). *Africa: The challenge of transformation.* London, UK: Tauris.

McClave, D. E. (1996). The society and its environment. In E. Solsten (Ed.), *Germany: A country study* (3rd ed., pp. 131–192). Washington, DC: Library of Congress.

McCourt, F. (1996). *Angela's ashes: A memoir.* New York: Scribner.

McDating. (2002, January 31). *The Economist,* 30. Retrieved from http://www.economist.com/node/966859

McDermid, C. (2010, September 13). Turkey unites over basketball, if not a constitution. *Time.* Retrieved from http://www.time.com/time/world/article/0,8599,2017792,00.html

McDonald, M. (2011, May 22). Elite South Korean university rattled by suicides. *The New York Times.* Retrieved from http://www.nytimes.com/2011/05/23/world/asia/23southkorea.html

McFaul, M., & Stoner-Weiss, K. (2008). The myth of the authoritarian model: How Putin's crackdown holds Russia back. *Foreign Affairs, 87*(1), 68–84. Retrieved from http://iis-db.stanford.edu/pubs/22072/Myth_of_the_Authoritarian_Model.pdf

McKinsey & Company. (2008). *Germany 2020: Future perspectives for the German economy; Summary of findings.* Frankfurt, Germany: McKinsey & Company. Retrieved from http://www.mckinsey.de/downloads/profil/initiativen/d2020/D2020_Exec_Summary_englisch.pdf

McNeilly, M. (2012, Revised Ed.). *Sun Tzu and the art of business: Six strategic principles for managers.* New York: Oxford University Press.

McPherson, M., Smith-Lovin, L., & Brashears, M. E. (2006). Social isolation in America: Changes in core discussion networks over two decades. *American Sociological Review, 71*(3), 353–375.

Md. Zabid, A. R., Anantharaman, R. N., & Raveendran, J. (1997). Corporate cultures and work values in dominant ethnic organizations in Malaysia. *Journal of Transnational Management Development, 2*(4), 51–65.

Mead, W. R. (1989). Perceptions of Finland. In M. Engman & D. Kirby (Eds.), *Finland: People, nation, and state* (pp. 1–15). London, UK: C. Hurst.

Meichtry, S. (2011, March 31). Italian mammas put meals on wheels, say "Mangia!" to faraway offspring. *The Wall Street Journal.* Retrieved from http://online.wsj.com/article/SB10001424052748704520504576162382890059622.html

Mexico, haunted by new ghosts. (1999, November 4). *The Economist, 36.* Retrieved from http://www.economist.com/node/256028

Meyer, L. (1982). *Israel now: Portrait of a troubled land.* New York: Delacorte.

Michon, J. (1992, December 5). Crown & crisis: Profiles of 20th-century British nobility [Television series episode]. In *Time machine with Jack Perkins.* New York: Arts & Entertainment.

Milbank, D. (1993, March 17). We make a bit more of St. Patrick's Day than the Irish do. *The Wall Street Journal.*

Miller, L. C., & Hustedde, R. J. (1987). Group approaches. In D. E. Johnson, L. R. Meiller, L. C. Miller, & G. F. Summers (Eds.), *Needs assessment: Theory and methods* (pp. 91–125). Ames: Iowa State University Press.

Miller, T. (2011, January 12). The U.S. loses ground on economic freedom. *The Wall Street Journal.* Retrieved from http://online.wsj.com/article/SB10001424052748703779704576074193214999486.html

Milner, H. (1989). *Sweden: Social democracy in practice.* New York: Oxford University Press.

Milton Friedman goes on tour. (2011, January 27). *The Economist, 63.* Retrieved from http://www.economist.com/node/18010553

Moffett, M. (2011, July 20). It takes two to tango, so long as they're both Argentines. *The Wall Street Journal.* Retrieved from http://online.wsj.com/article/SB10001424052702303661904576456210544473444.html

Molson Canadian Beer (Producer). (2000). *I am Canadian* [Television advertisement]. Retrieved from http://www.youtube.com/watch?v=BRI-A3vakVg

Molteni, G. R. (2003). Structural change in Argentina: Economic ideas, economic policy and institutional constraints during the interwar period; The case of Alejandro E. Bunge. *Cuestiones Sociales y Economicas, 1*(2), 21–30.

Montignac, M. (1987). *Je mange, donc je maigris!* Paris, France: Artulen.

Mooney, C. J. (2001, March 2). Deconstructing tango: The passion and power of a great dance. *The Chronicle of Higher Education,* A56.

Moore, M. (Producer and Director), & O'Hara, M. (Producer). (2007). *Sicko* [Motion picture]. United States: Dog Eat Dog Films.

Moore, T. (1841). *The poetical works of Thomas Moore collected by himself* (Vol. 3). London, UK: Longman, Orme, Brown, Green, & Longmans.

Moriguchi, C., & Ono, H. (2006). Japanese lifetime employment: A century's perspective. In M. Blomström & S. La Croix (Eds.), *Institutional change in Japan* (pp. 152–176). New York: Routledge.

Morin, R. (1998, September 6). Shy nations. *The Washington Post*.

Morrison, T., & Conaway, W. A. (2006). *Kiss, bow, or shake hands* (2nd ed.). Avon, MA: Adams Media.

Morrison, T., & Conaway, W. A. (2007). *Kiss, bow or shake hands: Asia; How to do business in 12 Asian countries*. Avon, MA: Adams Media.

Morrison, T., Conaway, W. A., & Douress, J. (1995). *Dun & Bradstreet's guide to doing business around the world*. Englewood Cliffs, NJ: Prentice Hall.

Mouawad, J. (2008, January 20). The construction site called Saudi Arabia. *The New York Times*. Retrieved from http://www.nytimes.com/2008/01/20/business/ worldbusiness/20saudi.html

Mulligan, M. (2010a, July 28). Catalonia votes to ban bullfighting. *Financial Times, 6*. Retrieved from http://www.ft.com/intl/cms/s/0/d47aded4-9a4a-11df-8346-00144feab49a.html#axzz1hBGwFS5J

Mulligan, M. (2010b, July 14). Green technology at heart of state policy. *Financial Times, 5*.

Munshi, K. (1965). *Indian inheritance* (Vol. 1). Bombay, India: Bharatiya Vidya Bhavan.

Musashi, M. (1974). *A book of five rings* (V. Harris, Trans.). Woodstock, NY: The Overlook Press.

Nakane, C. (1973). *Japanese society*. London, UK: Penguin.

Narayana, G., & Kantner, J. F. (1992). *Doing the needful: The dilemma of India's population policy*. Boulder, CO: Westview Press.

National Commission on the Disappearance of Persons. (2002). Never again. In G. Nouzeilles & G. Montaldo (Eds.), *The Argentina reader: History, culture, politics* (pp. 440–447). Durham, NC: Duke University Press.

National Environment Agency. (2007, December 1). "Singapore Hawker Centres—People, Places, Food": *The first definitive book on the social history of a uniquely Singapore icon* [Press release]. Retrieved from http://app2.nea.gov.sg/news_release.aspx?year=2007

National Environment Agency. (2008, January 27). *Roving exhibition for the book* "Singapore Hawker Centres—People, Places, Food" *kicks off at East Coast Lagoon Food Village* [Press release]. Retrieved from http://app2.nea.gov.sg/news_release.aspx?year=2008

Needham, J. (1954–). *Science and civilisation in China*. Cambridge, UK: Cambridge University Press.

Newman, P. C. (1987, December 7). A national contempt for the law. *MacLean's, 40*.

Ni, C.-C. (2007, May 7). She makes Confucius cool again. *Los Angeles Times*. Retrieved from http://articles .latimes.com/2007/may/07/world/fg-confucius7/

Nielsen, C. S., & Mariotto, J. G. (2006). The tango metaphor: The essence of Argentina's national identity. *International Studies of Management and Organization, 35*(4), 8–36.

The Nielsen Company. (2009). *HCMC v Hanoi: Understanding consumer differences*, Retrieved from http:www.slideshare.net/ngvdung/researchmarket-research1

Nnadozie, E. (2001). Managing African business culture. In F. M. Edoho (Ed.), *Management challenges for Africa in the twenty-first century: Theoretical and applied perspectives* (pp. 51–62). New York: Praeger.

No black and white matter. (2006, July 13). *The Economist, 38*. Retrieved from http://www.economist .com/node/7176779

Northern Nigeria: Sounding like the Middle East. (2011, August 27). *The Economist, 40*. Retrieved from http://www.economist.com/node/21526939

Nossiter, A. (2011, February 8). Riches flow into Nigeria, but are lost after arrival. *The New York Times*. Retrieved from http://www.nytimes.com/2011/02/09/world/africa/09nigeria.html

Nydell, M. K. (1987). *Understanding Arabs: A guide for Westerners*. Yarmouth, ME: Intercultural Press.

O'Brien, F. (1961). At Swim-Two-Birds. In U. Mercier & D. Greene (Eds.), *1000 years of Irish prose*. New York: Gross & Dunlap. (Original work published 1939)

O'Brien, F. (1974). *The poor mouth: A bad story about the hard life*. New York: Seaver. (Original work published 1940)

OECD (Organisation for Economic Co-operation and Development). (2008). *Growing unequal? Income distribution and poverty in OECD countries.* Paris, France: OECD. Available at http://www.oecd.org/els/social/inequality/GU/

Olson, M. (1982). *The rise and decline of nations: Economic growth, stagflation, and social rigidities.* New Haven, CT: Yale University Press.

Onishi, N. (2008, June 13). Japan, seeking trim waists, measures millions. *The New York Times.* Retrieved from http://www.nytimes.com/2008/06/13/world/asia/13fat.html

Ortony, A. (1975). Why metaphors are necessary and not just nice. *Educational Theory, 25*(1), 45–53.

Osawa, M., & Kingston, J. (2010, July 1). Japan has to address the 'precariat.' *Financial Times.* Retrieved from http://www.ft.com/intl/cms/s/0/359fa9a8-8545-11df-9c2f-00144feabdc0.html

Ottoman dreaming: The Turks have new ambitions for trade and influence in Africa (2010, March 25). *The Economist.* Retrieved from http://www.economist.com/node/15772860

Ouchi, W. G. (1981). *Theory Z: How American business can meet the Japanese challenge.* Reading, MA: Addison-Wesley.

Ouroussoff, N. (2010, December 30). Reshaping of Mecca turns to gargantuan glitz. *The New York Times.*

Paglia, C. (1997, September 17). Gridiron feminism: Why women should love football. *The Wall Street Journal.*

Pakenham, T. (1997). *The scramble for Africa: White man's conquest of the Dark Continent from 1876–1912.* London, UK: Abacus.

Parker, J. (2003, November 8). A nation apart. *The Economist,* 1–20. Retrieved from http://www.economist.com/node/2172066

Parker, T. (Producer and Director), & Stone, M. (Producer). (1999). *South Park: Bigger, Longer & Uncut* [Motion picture]. United States: Comedy Central & Braniff Productions.

Paul, A. (2007, January 19). The year of the pigskin. *The Wall Street Journal.*

Paz, O. (1961). *The labyrinth of solitude: Life and thought in Mexico.* New York: Grove.

Pearlstein, S. (2011, April 3). India's costly culture of corruption. *The Washington Post.* Retrieved from http://www.washingtonpost.com/business/economy/indias-costly-culture-of-corruption/2011/03/28/AFXoUMPC_story.html

Pearson, L. (1990). *Children of glasnost: Growing up soviet.* Seattle: University of Washington Press.

Pearson, V., & Stephens, W. (1998). Preferences for styles of negotiation: A comparison of Brazil and the U.S. *International Journal of Intercultural Relations, 22,* 80–99.

Peet, J. (2004, October 14). The luck of the Irish. *The Economist,* pp. 1–12. Retrieved from http://www.economist.com/node/3261071

Peet, J. (2005, November 24). Addio, dolce vita: A survey of Italy. *The Economist,* 1–16. Retrieved from http://www.economist.com/node/5164061

Peet, J. (2010). The trouble with Ottomania. *The Economist.* Retrieved from http://www.economist.com/node/17493321

Pennington, D. L. (1985). Time in African culture. In M. K. Asante & K. Welsh-Asante (Eds.), *African culture: The rhythms of unity* (pp. 123–139). Westport, CT: Greenwood.

Perry, A. (2011, June 30). Silicon Savanna: Mobile phones transform Africa. *Time.* Retrieved from http://www.time.com/time/magazine/article/0,9171,2080702,00.html

Peters, S. (1980). *Bedouin.* Morristown, NJ: Silver Burdett.

Pfanner, E. (2007, December 20). Portugal polishes its image as the "West Coast of Europe." *The New York Times.* Retrieved from http://www.nytimes.com/2007/12/20/business/media/20adco.html

Pierson, D. (2006, January 3). Cantonese is losing its voice. *Los Angeles Times.* Retrieved from http://articles.latimes.com/2006/jan/03/local/me-cantonese3/

Platt, S. (Ed.). (1989/2003). *Respectfully quoted: A dictionary of quotations requested from the Congressional Research Service.* New York: Bartleby.com. Retrieved from http://www.bartleby.com/73/1652.html (Original work published 1989)

Pomfret, J. (2003, April 27). My place in the procession of tradition. *The Washington Post.*

Pomfret, J. (2008, July 27). A long wait at the gate to greatness. *The Washington Post.* Retrieved from http://www.washingtonpost.com/wp-dyn/content/article/2008/07/25/AR2008072502255.html

Pomfret, J. (2010, February 14). Australia welcomes China's investment, if not its influence. *The Washington Post.* Retrieved from http://www.washingtonpost.com/wp-dyn/content/article/2010/02/13/AR2010021303651.html

The potential heirs to Buffett's throne. (2011, April 1). *Dealbook.* Retrieved from http://dealbook.nytimes.com/2011/04/01/the-potential-heirs-to-buffetts-throne/

Punctured football. (1993, January 9). *The Economist,* 83.

Putnam, R. D. (with Leonardi, R., & Nonetti, R. Y.). (1993). *Making democracy work: Civic traditions in modern Italy.* Princeton, NJ: Princeton University Press.

Quang, T., & Vuong, N. T. (2002). Management styles and organisational effectiveness in Vietnam. *Research and Practice in Human Resource Management, 10*(2), 36–55.

Rachman, G. (1999, December 16). A survey of wine: The globe in a glass. *The Economist,* 91–105. Available at http://www.economist.com/node/268095

Radzinsky, E. (2006, July 10). What is Russian civilization? (A. W. Bouis, Trans.). *The Wall Street Journal.* Retrieved from http://www.fbird.com/assets/What%20is%20Russian%20Civilization__7112006153129.pdf

Raking it in. (2011, November 11). *The Economist.* Retrieved from http://www.economist.com/blogs/gametheory/2011/11/labour-relations-australian-football/

Ralston D. A., Terpstra-Tong, J., Maignan, I., Napier, N. K., & Nguyen, V. T. (2006). Vietnam: A cross-cultural comparison of upward influence ethics. *Journal of International Management, 12*(1), 85–105. Available at http://ufirc.ou.edu/publications/Vietnam.pdf

Ralston D. A., Thang, N. V., & Napier, N. (1999). A comparative study of the work values of North and South Vietnamese managers. *Journal of International Business Studies, 30*(4), 655–672.

Ramstad, E. (2007a, December 26). Korean equality starts early. *The Wall Street Journal.* Retrieved from http://online.wsj.com/article/SB119863284477950065.html

Ramstad, E. (2007b, April 25). Why Korea makes the world's best women golfers. *The Wall Street Journal.*

Reforming gloomy France. (2011, April 20). *The Economist,* 27–29. Retrieved from http://www.economist.com/node/18584584

Ray, N., Balasingamchow, Y.-M., & Stewart, I. (2009). *Lonely planet Vietnam* (10th ed.). Melbourne, Australia: Lonely Planet.

Reid, M. (2004, June 5). The long road back: A survey of Argentina. *The Economist,* 1–12.

Reid, M. (2006, November 18). Time to wake up: A survey of Mexico. *The Economist,* 1–16.

Reid, T. R. (2000, January 14). The Yanks have landed. *The Washington Post.*

Reischauer, E. O. (1988). *The Japanese today: Change and continuity.* Cambridge, MA: Belknap Press.

Rentoul, J. (2011, June 26). Threatened, isolated, under siege: The UK's working class today. *The Independent* (UK). Retrieved from http://www.independent.co.uk/news/uk/home-news/threatened-isolated-under-siege-the-uks-working-class-today-2302850.html

Retail volte face confirms India as BRIC that disappoints. (2011, December 6). *Global Investing* [blog]. Reuters. Retrieved from http://blogs.reuters.com/globalinvesting/2011/12/06/retail-volte-face-confirms-india-as-bric-that-disappoints/

A reverse brain drain. (2011, May 5). *The Economist,* 45. Retrieved from http://www.economist.com/node/18652195

Reversing inequality: For he that hath. (2010, January 28). *The Economist,* 66–67. Retrieved from http://www.economist.com/node/15407957

Richmond, Y. (2003). *From* nyet *to* da: *Understanding the Russians* (3rd ed.). Yarmouth, ME: Intercultural Press.

Ricks, D. A. (2006). *Blunders in international business* (4th ed.). Malden, MA: Blackwell.

Ries, N. (1994). Mystical poverty and the rewards of less: Russian culture and conversation during *perestroika*. *Dissertation Abstracts International, 54*(09A), University Microfilms AA (No. 9406121).

Robinson, E. (1995, December 10). Over the Brazilian rainbow. *The Washington Post*.

Robinson, E. (1997, September 28). Sound treks, musical adventures in India, Brazil and Italy. *The Washington Post*.

Robinson, E. (1999). *Coal to cream*. New York: Free Press.

Robinson, M. (2011, June 8). Hate crimes on rise in Canada, but not B.C. *The Vancouver Sun*. Retrieved from http://www.canada.com/vancouversun/news/westcoastnews/story.html?id=91ea9e92-98de-4511-a44a-d663a4d5bc36

Rock, D. (1987). *Argentina 1515–1987*. Berkeley: University of California Press.

Rodriguez, G. (2007, March 11). Is success killing South Koreans? *Los Angeles Times*. Retrieved from http://articles.latimes.com/2007/mar/11/opinion/op-rodriguez11/

Rogow, G. (2010, December 27). More U.S. job-hunters try Australia. *The Wall Street Journal*. Retrieved from http://online.wsj.com/article/SB10001424052748704118504576034130441492962.html

Rose, D. (2006, June 29). Britain is running more than a day late. *The Times* (UK). Retrieved from http://www.thetimes.co.uk/

Ross, A. S. C. (1954). Linguistic class indicators in present-day English. *Neuphilologische Mitteilungen, 55*, 113–149. Retrieved from http://www.scribd.com/doc/39396431/Ross-Alan-1954-Linguistic-Class-Indicators-in-Present-Day-English/

Ross, A. S. C. (1956). U and non-U. In N. Mitford (Ed.), *Noblesse oblige: An enquiry into the identifiable characteristics of the English aristocracy*. London, UK: Hamish Hamilton.

Ross, A. S. C. (1969). *What are U?* London, UK: Andre Deutch.

Ross, H. C. (1979). The beauty of Bedouin jewelry. *Saudi Aramco World, 30*(2), 4–9. Retrieved from http://www.saudiaramcoworld.com/issue/197902/the.beauty.of.bedouin.jewelry.htm

Rugman, A. M. (2005). *The regional multinationals: MNEs and "global" strategic management*. Cambridge, UK: Cambridge University Press.

Russian exceptionalism: Is Russia different? (1996, June 15). *The Economist*, 19–21.

Ruth, A. (1984). The second new nation: The mythology of modern Sweden. *Daedalus, 113*(2), 53–96.

Sachin named most influential person in Indian sports. (2010, March 9). *The Times of India*. Retrieved from http://articles.timesofindia.indiatimes.com/2010-03-09/sachin-tendulkar-s-half-century-of-centuries/28136263_1_indian-sports-double-hundred-history-of-one-day-cricket/

Sachs, J. D. (2011, May 30). Nigeria's historic opportunity. *The New York Times*. Retrieved from http://www.nytimes.com/2011/05/31/opinion/31iht-edsachs31.html

Sajavaara, K., & Lehtonon, J. (1997). The silent Finn revisited. In A. Jaworski (Ed.), *Silence: Interdisciplinary perspectives* (pp. 263–283). Berlin, Germany: Mouton de Gruyter.

Samovar, L. A., & Porter, R. E. (1994). *International communication: A reader* (7th ed.). Belmont, CA: Wadsworth.

Sanchanta, M. (2010, July 13). Japan's women advance—but slowly. *MarketWatch*. Retrieved from http://www.marketwatch.com/story/japans-workplace-gender-gap-2010-07-13-22600/

Sanford, C. L. (1961). *The quest for paradise: Europe and the American moral imagination*. Urbana: University of Illinois Press.

Sani, A. H. A. (2011, April 28). Social injustice main cause of country's brain drain, says World Bank. *Malaysian Insider*. Retrieved from http://www.themalaysianinsider.com/malaysia/article/social-injustice-main-cause-of-countrys-brain-drain-says-world-bank/

Savigliano, M. E. (1995). *Tango and the political economy of passion*. Boulder, CO: Westview Press.

Schaap, J. (2008, February 3). We will catch excellence. *Parade*, 8–9.

Schein, E. H. (2010). *Organizational culture and leadership* (4th ed.). San Francisco, CA: Jossey-Bass.

Schneider, R. (1996). *Brazil, culture and politics in a new industrial powerhouse*. Boulder, CO: Westview.

Schrady, N. (2008). *The last day: Wrath, ruin and reason in the great Lisbon earthquake of 1755*. New York: Viking Press.

Schrank, D. (2008, January 30). Belgians limp along, hobbled by old language barriers. *The Washington Post*. Retrieved from http://www.washingtonpost.com/wp-dyn/content/article/2008/01/29/AR2008012903286.html

Schrotenboer, B. (2006, April 26). Legal in state since December, mixed martial arts sells out arenas. *The San Diego Union-Tribune*. Retrieved from http://www.signonsandiego.com/uniontrib/20060426/news_1n26fight.html

Schulze, H. (1998). *Germany: A new history* (D. L. Schneider, Trans). Cambridge, MA: Harvard University Press.

Schwartz, H. W. (1938). *The story of musical instruments: From shepherd's pipe to symphony*. Elkhart, IN: Pan-American Band Instruments.

Schwartz, S. H. (1994). Beyond individualism/collectivism: New cultural dimensions of values. In U. Kim, H. C. Triandis, C. Kâgitçibâşi, S. Choi, & G. Yoon (Eds.), *Individualism and collectivism: Theory, method, and applications* (pp. 19–40). Thousand Oaks, CA: Sage.

Sciolino, E. (2007, September 21). Calls for breakup grow ever louder in Belgium. *The New York Times*. Retrieved from http://www.nytimes.com/2007/09/21/world/europe/21belgium.html

Scobie, J. (2002). The Paris of South America. In G. Nouzeilles & G. Montaldo (Eds.), *The Argentine Reader* (pp. 170–181). Durham, NC: Duke University Press. (Original work published 1910)

Segon, M., & Booth, C. (2010). Managerial perspectives of bribery and corruption in Vietnam. *International Review of Business Research Papers, 6*(1), 574–589.

Sengupta, S. (2006, October 17). Skills gap hurts technology boom in India. *The New York Times*. Retrieved from http://www.nytimes.com/2006/10/17/world/asia/17india.html

Shadid, A. (2011a, January 4). Resurgent Turkey flexes its muscles across Iraq. *The New York Times*. Retrieved from http://www.nytimes.com/2011/01/05/world/middleeast/05turkey.html

Shadid, A. (2011b, May 28). Can Turkey unify the Arabs? *The New York Times*. Retrieved from http://www.nytimes.com/2011/05/29/weekinreview/29ottoman.html

Shamberg, M. (Producer), & Crichton, C. (Director). (1988). *A fish called Wanda* [Motion picture]. United States: Metro-Goldwyn-Mayer Pictures.

Shaw, G. B. S. (1916). *Pygmalion: A romance in five acts*. Retrieved from http://www.bartleby.com/138/ (Original work published 1912)

Shorto, R. (2011, February 9). The Irish affliction. *The New York Times Magazine*, 41–51. Retrieved from http://www.nytimes.com/2011/02/13/magazine/13Irish-t.html

Shiflett, D. (2000, September 1). Praise the lord and pass the football. *The Wall Street Journal*.

Shumway, N. (1991). *The invention of Argentina*. Berkeley: University of California Press.

Siegel, B. (1992). Family and kinship. In A. A. Gordon (Ed.), *Understanding contemporary Africa* (pp. 175–200). Boulder, CO: Rienner.

Siegele, L. (2006, February 9). Waiting for a wunder: A survey of Germany. *The Economist*. Retrieved from http://www.economist.com/node/5465017

Simon, S. (Host). (2011, April 9). 300 days without government no worry for Belgium [Radio broadcast episode]. *Weekend Edition Saturday*. Washington, DC: National Public Radio. Retrieved from http://www.npr.org/2011/04/09/135266035/-300-days-without-government-no-worry-for-belgium/

Singalore. (2011, February 24). *The Economist*, 72. Retrieved from http://www.economist.com/node/18231454

Slackman, M. (2010a, October 1). For some Germans, unity is still a work in progress. *The New York Times*. Retrieved from http://www.nytimes.com/2010/10/01/world/europe/01germany.html

Slackman, M. (2010b, December 11). Poland, bastion of religion, sees rise in secularism. *The New York Times*. Retrieved from http://www.nytimes.com/2010/12/12/world/europe/12poland.html

Smith, E. D., Jr., & Pham, C. (1996, May–June). Doing business in Vietnam: A cultural guide. *Business Horizons*, 10–16.

Smith, H. (1991). *The world's religions* (Rev. & updated ed.). San Francisco, CA: HarperCollins.

Smith, J. (2011, December 9). Legal outsourcing: Is the bloom already off the rose? *Law Blog. The Wall Street Journal*. Retrieved December 23, 2011, from http://blogs.wsj.com/law/2011/12/09/legal-outsourcing-is-the-bloom-already-off-the-rose/

Smith, K. G., Grimm, C. M., & Gannon, M. J. (1992). *Dynamics of competitive strategy.* Newbury Park, CA: Sage.

Smith, L. (1990, February 26). Fear and loathing of Japan. *Fortune,* 50–60.

Smith, P. B., & Bond, M. H. (1998). *Social psychology across cultures* (2nd ed.). Boston, MA: Allyn & Bacon.

Smith-Spark, L. (2006, June 1). Finland's trailblazing path for women. BBC News. Retrieved from http://news.bbc.co.uk/2/hi/europe/5036602.stm

Solomon, J. (2001, August 17). Stinky national dish seeks smell of success and a global market. *The Wall Street Journal.*

Solomon, M. (1996). *Consumer behavior.* Englewood Cliffs, NJ: Prentice Hall.

Solsten, E. (1996). Introduction. In E. Solsten (Ed.), *Germany: A country study* (pp. xxxvii–l). Washington, DC: Library of Congress.

Some Friday afternoon polls. (2011, September 30). *Open Europe Blog.* Retrieved from http://openeuropeblog.blogspot.com/2011/09/some-friday-afternoon-polls.html

Sons and daughters. (2011, April 4). *Graphic detail* [blog]. *The Economist.* Retrieved December 23, 2011, from http://www.economist.com/blogs/dailychart/2011/04/indias_sex_ratio/

The Spanish centrifuge. (2007, March 1). *The Economist,* 56–57. Retrieved from http://www.economist.com/node/8786353

Sparks, D. L. (2011). India and China's growing economic involvement in sub-Saharan Africa. *Journal of African Studies and Development, 3*(4), 65–75.

Srinivas, M. N. (1980). *India: Social structure.* Delhi, India: Hindustan. (Original work published 1969)

Stahl, L. (Co-host) (2003, January 12). *60 Minutes* [Television series episode, IIT segment]. United States: CBS. Broadcast transcript retrieved from http://www.csee.wvu.edu/~juggy/60minutes_iit_TRANSCRIPT.htm

Stalling by calling. (2006, July 23). Deutsche Press-Agentur. *Sunday Nation* (Thailand). Retrieved from http://news.google.com/ (no longer online)

Starr, J. R. (1991). *Kissing through glass: The invisible shield between Americans and Israelis.* Chicago, IL: McGraw-Hill Contemporary.

Statistics Canada. (2008). *Canadian demographics at a glance* (91-003-X). Ottawa, Canada: Statistics Canada. Retrieved from http://www.statcan.gc.ca/pub/91-003-x/91-003-x2007001-eng.pdf

Statistics Canada. (2011, June 7). *Police-reported hate crimes: 2009.* Retrieved from http://www.statcan.gc.ca/daily-quotidien/110607/dq110607a-eng.htm

Stecklow, L. (2001, January 20). Helsinki on wheels: Fast Finns find fines fit their finances. *The Wall Street Journal.*

Stephens, P. (2010, June 18). The West must offer Turkey a proper seat. *Financial Times.* Retrieved from http://www.ft.com/intl/cms/s/0/90750c70-7a45-11df-aa69-00144feabdc0.html

Stewart, E., & Bennett, M. (1991). *American cultural patterns: A cross cultural perspective* (2nd ed.). Yarmouth, ME: Intercultural Press.

Stiglitz, J. E. (2002). *Globalization and its discontents.* New York: W. W. Norton.

St. John, A. (2009). *The billion dollar game: Behind the scenes of the greatest day in American sport—Super Bowl Sunday.* New York: Doubleday, 2009.

Stoller, R. (1975). *Perversion: The erotic form of hatred.* New York: Pantheon.

Subanna, S. (2007, April 5). The cultural diversity of the Indian subcontinent. *Allempires.com.* Retrieved from http://www.allempires.com/article/index.php?q=The_Cultural_Diversity_of_the_Indian_Subconti

Sugawara, S. (1998, August 21). From debt to desperation in Japan. *The Washington Post.*

Sullivan, K. (2002, December 26). The union boss is the only man to see. *The Washington Post.*

Sundberg, G. (1910). *Det Svenska folklynnet.* Stockholm, Sweden: Norstedt & Soners.

The sun shines bright. (2011, December 3). *The Economist,* 82–84. Retrieved from http://www.economist.com/node/21541008

Sun Tsu. (1963 ed.). *Sun Tzu and the art of war* (S. B. Griffith, Trans.). London, UK: Oxford University Press.

Susmano, A. (2000). *Two 2 tango.* Chicago, IL: The Chicago Literary Club.

Swardson, A. (1996, November 30). Surly Parisians taught to grin and bare their friendly side. *The Washington Post.*

Sydell, L. (Correspondent). (2007, December 24). Cell phones do double duty in India [News report]. In *All Things Considered.* Washington, DC: National Public Radio. Retrieved from http://www.npr.org/templates/story/story.php?storyId=17587238

Szalay, L. (1993). *The subjective worlds of Russians and Americans: A guide for mutual understanding.* Chevy Chase, MD: Institute of Comparative Social and Cultural Studies.

Tabuchi, H. (2011, January 3). Japan keeps a high wall for foreign labor. *The New York Times.* Retrieved from http://www.nytimes.com/2011/01/03/world/asia/03japan.html

Tagliabue, J. (2011, January 31). A Swede by any other name. In fact, many Swedes. *The New York Times International.* Retrieved from http://www.nytimes.com/2011/02/01/world/europe/01stockholm.html

Tan, A. (1991). *The kitchen god's wife.* New York: Ballantine.

Tasker, P. (1987). *The Japanese: Portrait of a nation.* New York: New American Library.

Tavernise, S. (2008, February 9). Turkey's parliament votes to lift head scarf ban. *The New York Times.* Retrieved from http://www.nytimes.com/2008/02/09/world/europe/09cnd-turkey.html

Tay, L. (2010, August 12). The best hawker food stalls in Singapore. *CNNGO.com.* Retrieved from http://www.cnngo.com/singapore/eat/hawker-food-singapore-636748/

Taylor, J. (1998). *Paper tangos.* Durham, NC: Duke University Press.

Taylor, S. A. (1990). *Culture shock! France.* Portland, OR: Graphic Arts Center.

Thais tickled pink by unlikely fashion trendsetter: King. (2007, December 1). *The San Diego Union Tribune.* Retrieved from http://www.signonsandiego.com/uniontrib/20071201/news_lz1n1nowread.html

Thang, L. C., Rowley, C., Quang, T., & Warner, M. (2007). To what extent can management practices be transferred between countries? The case of human resource management in Vietnam. *Journal of World Business, 42*(1), 113–127. Retrieved from http://www.vnep.org.vn/Upload/Human%20resource.pdf

Tharoor, S. (2007). *The elephant, the tiger, and the cell phone: Reflections on India, the emerging 21st-century power.* New York: Arcade.

Theroux, P. (2003). *Dark star safari: Overland from Cairo to Capetown.* New York: Houghton Mifflin.

Thomas, F. R. (Ed.). (1990). *Americans in Denmark: Comparisons of the two cultures by writers, artists, and teachers.* Carbondale: Southern Illinois University Press.

Thomson, A. (2010a, September 14). Mexico finds itself with little to celebrate. *Financial Times,* 8. Retrieved from http://www.ft.com/intl/cms/s/0/9ba52bbe-c01a-11df-b77d-00144feab49a.html

Thomson, A. (2010b, November 4). Progressive Prince Alwaleed Bin Talal Bin Abdul Aziz using wealth to heal wounds of 9/11. *The Australian.* Retrieved from http://www.theaustralian.com.au/news/executive-lifestyle/progressive-prince-alwaleed-bin-talal-bin-abdul-aziz-using-wealth-to-heal-wounds-of-911/story-e6frg9zo-1225947710969

Those big boys next door. (2003, January 23). *The Economist.* Retrieved from http://www.economist.com/node/1552536

Tierney, J. (2011, May 16). A new gauge to see what's beyond happiness. *The New York Times.* Retrieved from http://www.nytimes.com/2011/05/17/science/17tierney.html

Timmons, H. (2010, August 4). Outsourcing to India draws Western lawyers. *The New York Times.* Retrieved from http://www.nytimes.com/2010/08/05/business/global/05legal.html

Timmons, H., & Polgreen, L. (2011, June 14). As India's growth slows, leaders face political headwinds. *The New York Times.* Retrieved from http://www.nytimes.com/2011/06/15/business/global/15rupee.html

Tolan, S. (2006, May 21). The incredible shrinking Palestine. *Los Angeles Times.* Retrieved from http://articles.latimes.com/2006/may/21/opinion/op-tolan21/

Too many laws, too many prisoners. (2010, July 22). *The Economist,* 25–29. Retrieved from http://www.economist.com/node/16636027

Törnblom, K. Y., Jonsson, D. R., & Foa, U. G. (1985). Nationality, resource class, and preferences among three allocation rules: Sweden vs. USA. *International Journal of Intercultural Relations, 9*(1), 51–77.

Tough love, or plain tough? (2011, May 12). *The Economist.* Retrieved from http://www.economist.com/node/18682532

Transparency International. (2010). *Corruption Perceptions Index.* Retrieved from http://www.transparency.org/policy_research/surveys_indices/cpi

Triandis, H. C., (1984). Toward a psychological theory of economic growth. *International Journal of Psychology, 19,* 79–95.

Triandis, H. C. (2002). Generic individualism and collectivism. In M. Gannon & K. Newman (Eds.), *Handbook of cross-cultural management* (pp. 16–46). London, UK: Blackwell.

Triandis, H. C., Brislin, R., & Hui, C. H. (1988). Cross-cultural training across the individualism-collectivism divide. *International Journal of Intercultural Relations, 12*(3), 269–289.

Triandis, H. C., & Gelfand, M. J. (1998). Converging measurement of horizontal and vertical individualism and collectivism. *Journal of Personality and Social Psychology, 74*(1), 118–128.

Trompenaars, F., & Hampden-Turner, C. (1998). *Riding the waves of culture: Understanding cultural diversity in global business* (2nd ed.). New York: McGraw-Hill.

Trueheart, C. (1998, January 30). Can Portugal survive the euro? *The Washington Post.* Retrieved from http://www.washingtonpost.com/wp-srv/inatl/longterm/euro/stories/portugal013098.htm

Tsunoda, T. (1985). *The Japanese brain: Uniqueness and universality.* Tokyo, Japan: Taishukan.

Tuchman, B. (1962). *The guns of August.* New York: Macmillan.

Twitchin, J. (1991). Training notes. *Crosstalk at work: Cross cultural communication in the workplace.* London: BBC Training Videos. Available at http://ftvdb.bfi.org.uk/sift/title/486435

Two pints of lager and a decaf latte. (2010, September 16). *The Economist,* 71. Retrieved from http://www.economist.com/node/17043860

Ugwuegbu, D. (2001). *The psychology of management in African organizations.* New York: Quorum.

UKIP (UK Independence Party). (2010). *UKIP manifesto: Empowering the people.* Retrieved from http://www.ukip.org/media/pdf/UKIPManifesto2010.pdf

The uncivil partnership. (2011, May 12). *The Economist,* 71. Retrieved from http://www.economist.com/node/18681847

UNCTAD & UNDP (United Nations Conference on Trade and Development & United Nations Development Programme). (2010). *Creative economy: A feasible development option.* Retrieved from http://www.unctad.org/en/docs/ditctab20103_en.pdf

UNESCO (United Nations Educational, Scientific and Cultural Organization). (2010). UNESCO: Culture: Intangible heritage: Intangible heritage lists: The tango. Retrieved December 24, 2011, from http://www.unesco.org/culture/ich/index.php?RL=00258

Unger, B. (2007, April 14). Dreaming of glory: A special report on Brazil. *The Economist,* 1–16.

UNICEF. (2008). *State of the world's children 2009: Maternal and newborn health.* New York: United Nations Children's Fund. Retrieved from http://www.unicef.org/sowc09/

Upkabi, C. (1990). *Doing business in Africa.* Amsterdam, The Netherlands: Royal Tropical Institute.

U.S. Department of State. (2011, July 22). *Background note: Argentina.* Retrieved July 12, 2011, from http://www.state.gov/r/pa/ei/bgn/26516.htm

Vedel, A. (Ed.). (1986). *The Hachette guide to French wines.* New York: Knopf.

Venezia, E. (1997). *Cross-cultural management: UN solo management nella differenziata realta Italiana?* (Unpublished doctoral dissertation). Universita Boccon, Milan, Italy.

Verleyen, F. (1987). *Flanders today.* Tielt, Belgium: Lannoo Editions.

Vincent, J. (2003). *Culture and customs in Brazil.* Westport, CT: Greenwood Press.

Vivekanada. (2011). Lectures from Colombo to Almora: My plan of campaign. In *The complete works of Swami Vivekananda* (Vol. 3). Retrieved from http://www.ramakrishnavivekananda.info/vivekananda/

volume_3/lectures_from_colombo_to_almora/my_plan_of_campaign.htm (Originally presented as a lecture, February 9, 1897, in Madras [Chennai], India)

Vogel, E. F. (1979). *Japan as number one: Lessons for America.* Cambridge, MA: Harvard University Press.

Wainer, D. (2010, June 24). Israel's kibbutzim shift from red to green. *Bloomberg Businessweek,* 41–42. Retrieved from http://www.businessweek.com/smallbiz/content/jun2010/sb20100623_004082 .htm

Wakin, D. J. (2006, May 5). An organ recital for the very, very patient. *The New York Times.* Retrieved from http://www.nytimes.com/2006/05/05/arts/music/05cage.html

Waldman, P. (2007, June 26). As Israel prospers, some fear its defenses may grow soft. *The Wall Street Journal.* Retrieved from http://online.wsj.com/article_email/SB118278573665647174-lMyQjAxMDE3O DIyNjcyODY1Wj.html

Wallace, P. M. (1999). *The psychology of the Internet.* Cambridge, UK: Cambridge University Press.

Walla Walla Press. (1997). *Sporting Immigrants: Sport and ethnicity in Australia* [Abstract]. Retrieved from http://www.wallawallapress.com/sports-immigration.php

Wang, G. (1962). *Latar belakang kebudayaan cina: Basis of Chinese culture.* Kuala Lumpur, Malaysia: Dewan Bahasa dan Pustaka.

Ward, A. (2010, August 18). Sweden loses patience with refugee champion role. *Financial Times.* Retrieved from http://www.ft.com/intl/cms/s/0/7536ee44-aadb-11df-9e6b-00144feabdc0.html

Waters, M. (1984). *The comic Irishman.* Albany: State University of New York Press.

Wax, E. (2008, April 19). Redskins cheerleaders shake up cricket in modest India. *The Washington Post.* Retrieved from http://www.washingtonpost.com/wp-dyn/content/article/2008/04/18/AR200804180 3577.html

Waxman, S. (1993, June 9). Brussels, capital of confusion. *The Washington Post.*

We are not amused. (2011, April 29). *Banyan* [blog]. *The Economist.* Retrieved from http://www.economist .com/blogs/banyan/2011/04/australia_under_monarchy/

Weber, M. (1947). *Theory of social and economic organization* (A. Henderson & T. Parsons, Trans.). New York: Free Press.

Weiner, E. (Correspondent). (2001, September 4). Life as an "outside person" (Essay). In *Morning Edition.* Washington, DC: National Public Radio. Retrieved from http://www.npr.org/programs/specials/ racism/010904.weiner.essay.html

Weir, F. (2008, May 22). Russian parents make no apologies for being "hyperprotective." *The Christian Science Monitor.* Retrieved from http://www.csmonitor.com/The-Culture/The-Home-Forum/2008/0522/ p18s01-hfgn.html

Weisbart, M. (2010, November 8). So fast, so dynamic—yet so hierarchical. *The Wall Street Journal.* Retrieved from http://online.wsj.com/article/SB10001424052702303496104575559931746274998 .html

Wheatley, J. (2010, February 11). The dance professionals: The Brazilian samba schools behind carnival are discovering the art of management. *Financial Times,* 12.

Wheaton, K. (Ed.). (1990). *Insight guide: Spain.* Singapore: APA.

Whitlock, C. (2008, February 2). Germany rebuffs U.S. on troops in Afghanistan. *The Washington Post.* Retrieved from http://www.washingtonpost.com/wp-dyn/content/article/2008/02/01/AR2008020103141.html

Whitlock, C., & Smiley, S. (2008, March 14). Non-European PhDs in Germany find use of 'Doktor' verbo-ten. *The Washington Post.* Retrieved from http://www.washingtonpost.com/wp-dyn/content/arti cle/2008/03/13/AR2008031304353.html

Whittle, J., Woznick, A., Shippey, K., Nolan, J. L., Hinkelman, E. G., & Reif, J. (1998). *Argentina business: The portable encyclopedia for doing business with Argentina* (2nd ed.). San Rafael, CA: World Trade Press.

Wilkinson, T. (2005, August 24). Wiretaps unfold Italian tycoons' dirty laundry. *Los Angeles Times.* Retrieved from http://articles.latimes.com/2005/aug/24/world/fg-wiretaps24/

Wilkinson, T. (2007a, February 18). Italy's rich pay to look richer. *Los Angeles Times*. Retrieved from http://articles.latimes.com/2007/feb/18/world/fg-bella18/

Wilkinson, T. (2007b, October 16). Rebirth in the arena. *Los Angeles Times*. Retrieved from http://articles.latimes.com/2007/oct/16/world/fg-bulls16/

Wilkinson, T. (2007c, January 9). Taking the "honor" out of killing women. *Los Angeles Times*. Retrieved from http://articles.latimes.com/2007/jan/09/world/fg-honor9/

Will, G. F. (2006, November 12). The next big thing [Review of Michael Lewis's *The Blind Side: Evolution of a Game*]. *The New York Times*. Retrieved from http://www.nytimes.com/2006/11/12/books/review/Will.t.html

Willey, D. (1984). *Italians.* London, UK: British Broadcasting Corporation.

Wilson, D., & Purushothaman, R. (2003). *Dreaming with BRICs: The path to 2050* (Global Economics Paper No. 99). New York: Goldman Sachs. Retrieved from http://www2.goldmansachs.com/our-thinking/brics/brics-reports-pdfs/brics-dream.pdf

Wilson, J. Q. (2007, April 20). In defense of guns. *Los Angeles Times*. Retrieved from http://articles.latimes.com/2007/apr/20/opinion/oe-wilson20/

Wines, M. (2011, March 23). As tsunami robbed life, it also robs rite of death. *The New York Times*. Retrieved from http://www.nytimes.com/2011/03/24/world/asia/24burial.html

Wise, P. (2010, July 13). New markets: Effort to exploit ties with former colonies pays dividends. *Financial Times*, 3. Retrieved from http://www.ft.com/intl/cms/s/0/09c1829e-8e0e-11df-b06f-00144feab49a.html#axzz1hBGwFS5J

Woolls, D. (2005, December 29). Spaniards' long lunch losing its allure. *The San Diego Union Tribune*. Retrieved from http://www.signonsandiego.com/uniontrib/20051229/news_1b29siesta.html

World Bank & International Finance Corporation. (2010). *Doing business 2011: Making a difference for entrepreneurs*. Washington, DC: World Bank, International Finance Corporation. Retrieved from http://www.doingbusiness.org/reports/global-reports/doing-business-2011/

The world in figures: Nigeria. (2010, November 22). *The Economist*. Retrieved from http://www.economist.com/node/17510444

World Trade Organization. (2011). *Accessions: Viet Nam.* Retrieved November 20, 2011, from http://www.wto.org/english/thewto_e/acc_e/a1_vietnam_e.htm

Wright, T., & Gupta, H. (2011, April 29). India's boom bypasses rural poor. *The Wall Street Journal*. Retrieved from http://online.wsj.com/article/SB10001424052748704081604576143671902043578.html

Yardley, J. (2010, October 28). Soaring above India's poverty, a 27-story home. *The New York Times*. Retrieved from http://www.nytimes.com/2010/10/29/world/asia/29mumbai.html

Yardley, J. (2011, June 8). In India, dynamism wrestles with dysfunction. *The New York Times*. Retrieved from http://www.nytimes.com/2011/06/09/world/asia/09gurgaon.html

Yeung, I. Y. M., & Tung, R. L. (1996). Achieving business success in Confucian societies: The importance of *Guanxi* (connections). *Organizational Dynamics, 25*(2), 54–65.

Yew, L. K. (2000). *From third world to first: The Singapore story: 1965–2000.* New York: HarperCollins.

Zaman, A. (1999, December 2). Spreading faith through fashion: Turkish chain promotes Islamic clothing. *The Washington Post*. Retrieved from http://www.washingtonpost.com/wp-srv/WPcap/1999-12/02/096r-120299-idx.html

Zetterberg, H. L. (1997). The rational humanitarians. In R. Swedberg & E. Uddhammar (Eds.), *Sociological endeavor* (pp. 320–335). New Brunswick, NJ: Transaction.

Photo Credits

Index

About the Authors

Martin J. Gannon (PhD, Columbia University) is Professor of International Management and Strategy, College of Business Administration, California State University San Marcos. He is also Professor Emeritus, Smith School of Business, University of Maryland at College Park. At Maryland he held several administrative positions, including the Associate Deanship for Academic Affairs and the Founding Directorship of the Center for Global Business, and he received the University's International Landmark Award. Professor Gannon has authored, co-authored, or co-edited 90 articles and 17 books, including *Paradoxes of Culture and Globalization* (2008), *Handbook of Cross-Cultural Management* (2001), *Dynamics of Competitive Strategy* (1992), *Managing Without Traditional Methods: International Innovations in Human Resource Management* (1996), and *Ethical Dimensions of International Management* (1997). Professor Gannon has been the Senior Research Fulbright Professor at the Center for the Study of Work and Higher Education in Germany and the John F. Kennedy/Fulbright Professor at Thammasat University in Bangkok, Thailand, and he has served as a visiting professor at several Asian and European universities. He has also been a consultant to many companies and government agencies. Professor Gannon has lived and worked in more than 30 nations for various periods of time as a visiting professor, consultant, and trainer. For additional information on Professor Gannon, please visit his home page at California State University San Marcos: http://faculty.csusm.edu/mgannon/.

Rajnandini Pillai (PhD, State University of New York at Buffalo, 1994) is a Professor of Management at the College of Business, California State University San Marcos (CSUSM). She is also Executive Director and founding member of the Center for Leadership Innovation and Mentorship Building (CLIMB) at the university. Her areas of research interest are leadership and cross-cultural management. She has published her work on charismatic and transformational leadership, leadership and voting behavior, and cross-cultural differences in organizational justice in some of the leading journals in her field such as the *Leadership Quarterly, Journal of Management*, and *Journal of International Business Studies*. She has also co-edited two books, *Teaching Leadership: Innovative Approaches for the 21st Century* (2003) and *Follower Perspectives* *on Leadership* (2007) and is co-author of the 4th edition of *Understanding Global Cultures* with Martin J. Gannon. She serves on the editorial board of the *Leadership Quarterly*. Rajnandini Pillai has held midlevel management positions in the banking industry in India, consulted with organizations in the United States on leadership effectiveness, and conducted workshops on leadership and global issues. She has received awards for excellence in teaching and research, including the College of Business Outstanding Professor Award, the Western Academy of Management Ascendant Scholar Award, the CSUSM President's Award for Scholarship and Creative Activity, and the Harry E. Brakebill Distinguished Professor Award.

⑤SAGE research**methods**
The Essential Online Tool for Researchers

The essential tool for researchers . . .

. . . from the world's leading research methods publisher

Discover SRMO Lists—methods readings suggested by other SRMO users

"I have never really seen anything like this product before, and I think it is really valuable."

John Creswell, University of Nebraska–Lincoln

Find exactly what you are looking for, from basic explanations to advanced discussion

Explore the Methods Map to discover links between methods

Watch video interviews with leading methodologists

Search on a newly designed taxonomy with more than 1,400 qualitative, quantitative, and mixed methods terms

Uncover more than 100,000 pages of book, journal, and reference content to support your learning

find out more at
srmo.sagepub.com